The Handbook of
INTERNATIONAL
SCHOOL
PSYCHOLOGY

*This handbook is dedicated to the professionals around
the world who work to enhance the education and mental health of children and
families. It is also dedicated to those who have been instrumental in helping to develop
school psychology internationally, including those providing leadership within the
International School Psychology Association, in particular, Cal Catteral and
Anders Poulsen, and those providing leadership nationally. We hope that this handbook
contributes to the development and understanding of school psychology internationally.*

The Handbook of
INTERNATIONAL
SCHOOL
PSYCHOLOGY

EDITORS
Shane R. Jimerson
University of California, Santa Barbara

Thomas D. Oakland
University of Florida

Peter T. Farrell
University of Manchester, UK

SAGE Publications
Thousand Oaks ■ London ■ New Delhi

For information:

 Sage Publications, Inc.
2455 Teller Road
Thousand Oaks, California 91320
E-mail: order@sagepub.com

Sage Publications Ltd.
1 Oliver's Yard
55 City Road
London EC1Y 1SP
United Kingdom

Sage Publications India Pvt. Ltd.
B-42, Panchsheel Enclave
Post Box 4109
New Delhi 110 017 India

Printed in the United States of America on acid-free paper

Library of Congress Cataloging-in-Publication Data

The handbook of international school psychology / edited by
Shane R. Jimerson, Thomas D. Oakland, Peter T. Farrell.
    p. cm.
Includes bibliographical references and index.
ISBN 1-4129-2669-6 (cloth)
   1. School psychology—Handbooks, manuals, etc. 2. School psychology—Cross-cultural studies.
I. Jimerson, Shane R. II. Oakland, Thomas D. III. Farrell, Peter.
LB1027.55.H357 2007
371.4—dc22

                2006008360

06 07 08 09 10 10 9 8 7 6 5 4 3 2 1

Acquiring Editor:	Cheri Dellelo
Editorial Assisant:	Karen Ehrmann
Production Editor:	Sanford Robinson
Typesetter:	C&M Digitals (P) Ltd.
Copy Editor:	Colleen Brennan
Indexer:	Molly Hall
Cover Designer:	Michelle Kenny

Contents

Acknowledgments

The editors would like to acknowledge the outstanding efforts of colleagues around the world who contributed to this handbook as authors, and also to the individuals at Sage Publications who were instrumental in bringing this handbook to print: Jim Brace-Thompson, Cheri Dellelo, Karen Ehrmann, Sanford Robinson, and Colleen Brennan. The collective efforts of all those involved have resulted in the timely publication of this tremendously informative handbook.

Dr. Jimerson—I would also like to acknowledge my wife, Kathryn O'Brien, son, Gavin O'Brien Jimerson, and parents, Avona Navarro and Rik Jimerson, who contributed by enriching my life and reminding me of the importance of my personal and professional activities. In addition, I would like to acknowledge my international colleagues who inspired me to learn more about school psychology around the world. I also express my sincere gratitude to Drs. Oakland and Farrell for their extraordinary efforts in this collaborative endeavor; I am truly fortunate to have such talented and special colleagues.

Dr. Oakland—My life, both personally and professionally, has been blessed by the hundreds of friends and colleagues who have contributed to my understanding of school psychology internationally through their scholarship, discussions, and visits. I am especially appreciative of my colleagues with whom I have conducted research and published, including Drs. Jimerson and Farrell.

Dr. Farrell—I would also like to acknowledge all of the school psychologists from around the world who have willingly given their time to share their views about developments in school psychology in their countries. These comments have been influential in shaping my thinking about the key contributions that school psychologists can make toward promoting the mental health and well-being of all children and young people. And, of course, my colleagues, Drs. Jimerson and Oakland, have been a great support to me in the process of compiling this volume.

1

Introduction to
The Handbook of International School Psychology

Shane R. Jimerson

Thomas D. Oakland

Peter T. Farrell

The primary purpose of *The Handbook of International School Psychology* is to provide a description of the specialty of psychology devoted to the provision of services to children and youth, their teachers, and parents. The descriptions found in the handbook's 49 chapters characterize this specialty as one whose practitioners collectively provide individual assessment of children who may display cognitive, emotional, social, or behavioral difficulties; develop and implement primary and secondary intervention programs; consult with teachers, parents, and other relevant professionals; engage in program development and evaluation; conduct research; and help prepare and supervise others. We have used the term *school psychology* to refer to this specialty.

There are a number of striking similarities and differences among those who provide these services. First, the titles used to describe these professionals are many, including counselor, educational psychologist, professional educational psychologist, psychopedagogue, psychologist, psychologist in education, psychologist in the schools, or school psychologist. The term *school psychologist* is used throughout this chapter and is most frequently used in others. Furthermore, those who provide these services may work in schools, clinics, hospitals, private practice, universities, or other settings, and this, in part, reflects the differences in the nature of services offered around the world. Services within each country often reflect important historical, social, political, language, religious, and geographic qualities. The strength of school psychology is found in its diversity, its ability to adjust to local conditions in ways that provide services to children and youth together with their teachers and parents. This introductory chapter is intended to enable readers, and those interested in subsequent research on school psychology internationally, to understand the context of this handbook.

Collaboration Through Scholarship

The development of *The Handbook of International School Psychology* resulted from a confluence of collaborative scholarly activities and was motivated, in part, by a desire to update information on school psychology internationally. This is not the first effort to discuss school psychology. In 1948, following World War II, ministries of education in 43 countries provided brief summaries of information on the work of school psychologists, their professional preparation, and salaries (United Nations Educational, Scientific and Cultural Organization, International Bureau of Education, 1948). In 1956, Wall reported on efforts to provide educational and mental health services to children in Europe and recommended basic requirements for the preparation of school psychologists (Wall, 1956).

Catterall's three edited volumes (1976, 1977, 1979) constitute the first attempt to provide an international perspective on school psychology. Other scholarship followed, including *International Perspectives on Psychology in the Schools* (Saigh & Oakland, 1989) and other works (e.g., Jimerson et al., 2004; Jimerson et al., 2006; Oakland & Cunningham, 1992). Oakland and Cunningham's (1992) study of school psychology in 54 countries constitutes the most comprehensive single survey of this specialty. Recent international efforts to systematically gather data from practicing school psychologists in countries around the world led to the development of the International School Psychology Survey (Jimerson & International

School Psychology Association Research Committee, 2002), which has been administered in multiple countries (e.g., Albania, Cyprus, Estonia, Greece, Northern England, Australia, China, Germany, Italy, Russia, and the United States).

Two of the three handbook editors, Shane Jimerson and Thomas Oakland, first recognized the need for a book on school psychology that acknowledged and attempted to build on these prior efforts while providing an updated discussion of school psychology internationally. This interest led to a review of existing literature on school psychology around the world and the development of guidelines to assist potential authors in writing chapters that contain similar and relevant information.

We are fortunate to have contributions from 95 colleagues in 45 countries who have an instrumental understanding of, and appreciation for, school psychology practices in their respective countries. Those contributing to this handbook were identified through our knowledge of their scholarly abilities, professional relationships (e.g., as members of the International School Psychology Association), or long-standing friendships. We are fortunate to have been able to collaborate with this excellent and committed group of scholars. A brief description of each contributor is provided in the section titled About the Contributors.

Timing and Purpose

The contributors were asked to describe school psychology in their countries in ways that would enable readers to understand the context for its practices and then to discuss professional preparation and services. Thus, most chapters include information on the country's history and current status; infrastructures that impact education, psychology, and school psychology; preparation, roles, functions, and responsibilities of school psychologists; and current issues and seminal references. Thus, this handbook is intended to provide fundamental and comprehensive information that may be of interest to students, practitioners, and scholars.

Colleagues who agreed to contribute a chapter were provided drafts of chapters addressing school psychology in Albania, Estonia, and the United States to serve as models, along with a set of questions each chapter should address. Authors of each country chapter were responsible for gathering needed information. Information gathering involved a review of published and unpublished documents and reports as well as communication with colleagues. Given a lack of existing scholarship and documents, some authors established a research network that provided needed information. As anticipated, chapters differ in the extent to which all topics are addressed. The intent of this design was to develop a common structure for reporting information from each country so as to allow for easy comparison and accessibility.

Chapter Content

Authors were asked information in each of the following areas: (1) the context of school psychology; (2) the origin, history, and current status of school psychology; (3) the infrastructure of school psychology; (4) the preparation of school psychologists; (5) the roles, functions, and responsibilities of school psychologists; (6) current issues impacting school psychology; and (7) references. The following information was provided to authors to assist them in their work.

Context of School Psychology

Authors were asked to describe the country's prevailing geographic, demographic, and economic characteristics; the number of school-age children and number of students; the country's educational system(s), including types of schools, percentage of students who graduate, average age of high school graduates, average class sizes in elementary and secondary schools, and percentage of students with special needs; and the age of compulsory education and the degree to which compulsory education is enforced.

Origin, History, and Current Status of School Psychology

Authors were asked to discuss the origins of school psychology, including the conditions that gave rise to this specialty; major events that helped shape school psychology since its introduction; titles used to describe those who practice this specialty; number and gender of practitioners and their average salaries in comparison with those of other professionals who work in schools or in private practice. Authors also were asked to discuss the settings in which school psychologists work; their distribution in urban and rural areas; typical student-to-school psychologist ratios; job stability, attrition rates, and satisfaction; and opportunities for professional development.

Infrastructure of School Psychology

Authors were asked to provide names of national and regional professional organizations serving the interests of school psychology; laws or other regulations regarding licensure of psychologists and school psychologists; others who may be allowed to provide similar work in schools; laws or other regulations governing the general practice of psychology and school psychology; laws or other regulations governing special educational services that have implications for school psychologists; and titles of professional journals and newsletters relied on by school psychologists.

Preparation of School Psychologists

Authors were asked to provide information on the number of programs that prepare school psychologists, the average numbers of students entering the programs and graduating annually, the number of years of postsecondary education required to become a school psychologist, the specific degree(s) and/or professional credentials required to become a school psychologist, and their academic (e.g., course work) and professional (e.g., practicum and internship experiences) preparation.

Roles, Functions, and Responsibilities of School Psychologists

Authors were asked to provide information on school psychologists' typical activities, roles, and responsibilities, including work involving interventions, consultation, program development, testing and assessment models and methods, supervision, and other activities.

Current Issues Impacting School Psychology

Authors were asked to describe major problems or challenges impacting school psychology, initiatives being attempted in an effort to address these problems or challenges, and the country's most urgent research needs.

References

Authors were asked to provide names of key scholarly publications that address issues important to education and school psychology services.

In addition to the country chapters, the handbook includes a section consisting of chapters that review the key considerations of school psychology internationally and trends influencing school psychology's international development. This section includes chapters that discuss the past, present, and future of the International School Psychology Association, findings from the International School Psychology Survey that examine characteristics and responsibilities of school psychologists, and a summary and synthesis of the information in the handbook.

References

Catterall, C. D. (Ed.). (1976). *Psychology in the schools in international perspective,* Vol. 1. Columbus, OH: International School Psychology Steering Committee.

Catterall, C. D. (Ed.). (1977). *Psychology in the schools in international perspective,* Vol. 2. Columbus, OH: International School Psychology Steering Committee.

Catterall, C. D. (Ed.). (1979). *Psychology in the schools in international perspective,* Vol. 3. Columbus, OH: International School Psychology Steering Committee.

Jimerson, S. R., Graydon, K., Farrell, P., Kikas, E., Hatzichristou, C., Boce, E., Bashi, G., & International School Psychology Association Research Committee. (2004). The International School Psychology Survey: Development and data from Albania, Cyprus, Estonia, Greece and Northern England. *School Psychology International, 25*(3), 259–286.

Jimerson, S. R., Graydon, K., Yuen, M., Lam, S.-F., Thurm, J.-M., Klueva, N., Coyne, J., Loprete, L. J., Phillips, J., & International School Psychology Association Research Committee. (2006). The International School Psychology Survey: Data from Australia, China, Germany, Italy and Russia. *School Psychology International, 27*(1), 5–32.

Jimerson, S. R., & International School Psychology Association Research Committee. (2002). *The International School Psychology Survey.* (Available from the author at the University of California, Santa Barbara; e-mail: Jimerson@education.ucsb.edu)

Oakland, T. D., & Cunningham, J. L. (1992). A survey of school psychology in developed and developing countries. *School Psychology International, 13,* 99–129.

Saigh, P. A., & Oakland, T. D. (1989). *International perspectives on psychology in the schools.* Hillsdale, NJ: Lawrence Erlbaum.

United Nations Educational, Scientific and Cultural Organization, International Bureau of Education. (1948). *School psychologists* (Publication No. 105). Paris: Author.

Wall, W. D. (Ed.). (1956). *Psychological services for schools.* New York: New York University Press for UNESCO Institute for Education.

SECTION I

Country Chapters

2

School Psychology in Albania

Gladiola Musabelliu

Context of School Psychology

Albania is located in Southern Europe and is one of more than 10 Balkan nations. Albania is an old Mediterranean country, with a history dating from the 4th century BC. It is bordered by Montenegro in the north, Kosovo in the northeast, the Republic of Macedonia in the east, and Greece in the south. The Adriatic and Ionian Seas lie to the west of Albania and provide beautiful views with mountains, hills, and beaches. Its area is 28,748 square kilometers. It has six main rivers, four natural lakes, four artificial lakes, and mountains. Albania, an emerging democracy, was formally named the Republic of Albania. According to a 1989 estimate, 95% of Albania's population are Albanians (Shqiptare), descendents from the ancient Illyrians, 3% are Greek, and 2% are other (Vlach, Roma [Gypsy], Serb, Macedonian, Bulgarian). Languages that are spoken in the territory of Albania are Albanian (the official language, derived from the Tosk dialect), Greek, Vlach, Romani, and Slavic dialects.

Albania was a closed country for 47 years (1944–1991), due to a dictatorship regime and a communist ideology. But in the 1990s, political and economic changes drastically altered Albanians' lives. Under communism, most Albanian households shared similar standards, conditions, and lifestyles, but the changes fostered differences among Albanian households. Changes within the political system and the introduction of a market economy caused radical economic reforms. In 2004, the gross domestic product was about US$17.64 billion, US$4,900 per capita (Institute of Statistics, 2005). Albanians are generally impoverished, with a monthly average income per capita of 37 euros. Almost half of the economically active population is still engaged in agriculture, and a fifth still works abroad. The country has a high unemployment rate (15%–30%), there are almost no exports, and it imports many goods from Greece and Italy. Income is obtained mainly from employment in private and agricultural sectors, self-employment, or from unemployment benefits.

Since 1990, migration has had a significant influence on the country's structure and growth. The movement of people has increased, with a 10% growth rate between 1990 and 2000, with many moving to urban areas. Within its population of 3,563,112 (July 2005), 25.6% are age 14

7

years or younger (476,989 males, 434,298 females), 65.8% are ages 15 to 64 years (1,199,964 males, 1,144,886 females), and 8.6% are 65 years and older (141,559 males, 165,416 females). The Albanian population is young, with an average age of 31 years. The free and uncontrolled movement of people has affected the change of ratio of rural and urban populations. By the end of 2003, the urban population had grown to 44.5%, with 22% of the population living in the capital of Albania, Tirana. The new administrative division of Albania does not allow for the calculation of population growth per district, as this is a continuous process. Today, due to these demographic and political changes, Albania is divided into 12 prefectures, 36 districts, and 374 communes and municipalities (Institute of Statistics, 2005).

Although the Albanian education system relies primarily on its public schools, many private schools have opened, mostly in larger cities. The basic characteristics of current Albanian education are (a) an increase in the number of pupils registered in professional and technical high schools and the profiling of public high schools in two directions (natural and social sciences) after some years of a successful pilot program, (b) an increase of new arrivals to universities in response to the numerous requests from students finishing high school, (c) an improvement in the curriculum and the physical conditions of schools, and (d) the opening of private universities (Albanian Ministry of Education and Science, 2005). The foundation of education in Albania is the National Education Program, whose aim is to meet the educational needs of all Albanians. It encompasses all activities of the system and offers a variety of programs and types of education based on the national tradition. The National Education Program addresses class-based learning, and teachers should follow the strict plan it prescribes. Due to the lack of laboratories and materials, this plan is very theoretical and involves almost no practical work. The National Education Program also includes a system of statistical indices that can provide information on

the educational process, direction and management of schools, and the state administration.

Since 1997, following UNESCO (United Nations Educational, Scientific and Cultural Organization) recommendations on the classification of schools and fields of study defined by the International Standard Classification of Education 1997 (UNESCO, 1997) and directions of the Ministry of Education and Science, the education system was divided into the following levels: Level 0: pre-elementary education (with 79,905 students ages 6 and younger); Level 1: lower level of 9-year education (ages 6–10); Level 2: higher level of 9-year education (ages 10–15; total of 505,141 students at Levels 1 and 2); Level 3: high school education (with 142,402 students ages 15–19); Level 4: Post–high school education but not university (with few students); Level 5: university education (with 40,125 students); and Level 6: post-university education (leading to advanced research qualification).

The university education includes 11 public universities: Ten are universities and one is the High School of Nurses in Tirana and its branches in district universities. Fields of study and training are divided in nine broad areas, 25 limited fields, and 80 detailed ones. High school and university education is mainly organized to offer full-time education and less so for part-time education. Since 2004, two private universities have opened: the University of New York with 245 students and the Law University with 160 students (Albanian Ministry of Education and Science, 2005).

Before September 2004, compulsory education was based on an 8-year education system (Levels 1 and 2). After a decision made by the Ministry of Education and Science, this system has been extended to a 9-year system of compulsory education. According to the Institute of Statistics (2005), a total of 776,627 students in Levels 0 through 3 were enrolled in public and private schools (not including special education), including students who repeated the academic year because they failed in the previous one. During the 2003–2004 school year, in

Levels 0 through 3, there were a total of 701,998 students and 35,884 teachers in 3,773 public schools and 25,450 students and 2,010 teachers in 225 private schools.

Ninety-five percent of students graduate from Levels 1 and 2, and 90% graduate from Level 3. The average age of students graduating from Level 3 is 18. Sixty-six percent of students graduate from Level 5. Although statistics about the average class size nationally are not available because of the continuing and uncontrolled migration, the capital of Albania, Tirana, has classes that range from 40 to 50 students at Level 3 and from 30 to 40 students at Levels 1 and 2. Other Albanian cities and rural areas have an estimated 20 to 30 students per class. Studies by the Albanian Ministry of Education and Science (2005) compared the ratio of students to teachers during the academic year 2003–2004 (21.4:1, Level 0; 18.8:1 Levels 1 and 2; 19.3:1 Level 3) to the Organization for Economic Cooperation and Development guidelines (15.5:1, Level 0; 16.3:1, Levels 1 and 2; 13.9:1, Level 3). The variation in class size results from the shortage of schools and the concentration of population in the urban areas.

The field of special education has two national institutions, six special schools, and four daily centers of special education. These 12 institutions offer 77 classes with 10 to 12 students per class and 184 teachers. Eight hundred students attend these institutions, and 36% of the students are female. Special education students constitute 0.12% of the students in Albania (Levels 1–3). The number of children with special needs is much higher, but the infrastructure and the mentality of parents hinder delivery of special education. Some parents prefer not to send children with moderate retardation to special schools, because they do not want to admit that their child is "sick," or they are not aware of how their children can benefit. At the same time, children with retardation are not welcomed in the public schools, because of the lack of qualified teachers to help them.

Origin, History, and Current Status of School Psychology

In 1996, a department of psychology was created at Tirana University with 42 students. At that time, the professors who taught at the University had no diploma/degree in psychology. They had diplomas as teachers and had attended universities abroad to acquire an introduction to general psychology and its specializations. In 1999, school psychology began as a division of the Psychology Department. After 3 years of general education in psychology, students choose whether to pursue school psychology or clinical psychology. In 2000, students graduated as school or clinical psychologists, according to the direction they chose. Ten selected school psychology; 32 selected clinical psychology. The term *school psychologist* is used in Albania. The first 10 school psychologists graduated in 2000. Since then, 63 school psychologists, six males and 57 females, have graduated (2004).

Since 2004, school psychologists have worked in public schools with different programs funded by different organizations. They also work in centers and for associations, which implement different programs related to categories of people in need. None work in private practice or in schools in rural areas. The majority of school psychologists work in Tirana. A few work in other cities in other professions.

In September 2004, the Ministry of Education and Science decided to expand the psychological service to Levels 0, 1, 2, and 3 of the education system for 2 years (2004–2006). The aim was to increase the number of professionals who could offer psychological services to schools. In Tirana, 20 psychologists (school and clinical psychologists) work in Levels 1, 2, and 3, 5 work in the 40 public kindergartens, and 5 in the 29 nurseries (Level 0). The salaries of psychologists who work in different levels of education are different. The average annual salary of school psychologists in Albania is estimated to be between 1,600 and 2,000 euros annually, depending on the levels of education in which they work. Salaries of school psychologists and teachers are comparable.

In 2003, using the International School Psychology Survey (Jimerson & International School Psychology Association Research Committee, 2002), Boce and Bashi (Musabelliu) gathered information regarding the roles, responsibilities, and activities of school psychologists in Albania (Jimerson et al., 2004). Using the phone list of the Albanian Association of School Psychologists, Boce and Bashi (Musabelliu) contacted every school psychologist living in Albania ($N = 11$) at the time. Most of the respondents (9) were living in the capital area. All distributed questionnaires were completed and returned. The results of this survey revealed that all school psychologists were female, between ages 23 and 25, held a bachelor's degree in school psychology, and were at least bilingual (Albanian, English, French, and Italian were the most common languages). The ratio of school psychologists to students in the schools where school psychologists were employed was 1 to 580 on average (ranging from 1:200 to 1:1,500). All 11 were members of the national school psychology association. External challenges jeopardizing service delivery in Albania most often referred to were the low status of school psychology, the lack of money to properly fund services, and the lack of public support for education. Since the changes of 2004, the ratio of school psychologists to students is 1:2,000 to 1:2,500 students in Levels 1 and 2; 1:1,800 to 1:2,000 students in Level 3; 1:1,200 students in Level 0 (kindergarten); and 1:300 students in Level 0 (nurseries).

Opportunities for professional development are few. Although some organizations offer training, not all school psychologists are able to attend, and the majority of courses on offer have no connection to school psychology. In 2000, the first postgraduate school psychology program was launched. This program lasts three semesters (12 months), and students who complete the program receive master's degrees in counseling. Although the Ministry of Education and Science currently offers employment opportunities for school psychologists, there are no guarantees that this will continue (because it is experimental for 2 years), and the job satisfaction is not high because of the very low salary and poor work environment. The majority of schools have no counseling office at all, and one psychologist is responsible for two or three schools, depending on the number of students they have.

Infrastructure of School Psychology

There are no professional organizations to offer support to school psychologists, except for the Albanian Association of School Psychologists, which has no funding for its projects. In addition, no standards exist for credentialing and licensing school and other psychologists in Albania. With the employment of psychologists in schools, Ministry of Education and Science specialists, with the help of other professionals, compiled some regulations to direct the work of school psychologists in the education system, but no psychologists are involved with this process. In 1995, the Ministry of Education and Science proposed the law "For the Pre-university Education System," in which normative provisions about special education were included. This law was enacted by the Council of Ministers that same year.

Since 2004, the employment of school psychologists has been restricted to very few schools, for brief periods, through different nongovernmental organizations' programs or centers. Various foreign organizations have specific programs that attempt to improve students' academic lives or help them to cope with establishing new relationships with other students from different areas of Albania. School psychologists or social workers are employed by these organizations to fulfill their projects. Psychologists, sociologists, teachers with courses in psychology, and any other professional related to the field of psychology are eligible to offer psychological services in schools.

There are no professional journals for school psychologists. The problems of school psychologists or the problems of education are discussed in periodicals, such as *Nentori*, a publication of the Institute of Pedagogic Research, which deals with education issues, and *Arsimi Sot*, a publication of the Tirana Regional Department of Education.

Preparation of School Psychologists

Only one school psychology program within the psychology department at the University of Tirana prepares school psychologists. The average number of school psychologists admitted into and graduating from the program annually is 12. To become a school psychologist, one must have concluded 3 years of general education in psychology and complete a year-long program in school psychology. The program requires the following courses: psychology of environment (one semester, 4 months); organizational psychology (one semester); test theory (one semester); psychological evaluation (annual, 8 months); scientific research (annual, 8 months); psychology of people with special needs (one semester); speaking disorders (one semester); school psychology (one semester); psychotherapy, cognitive-behavioral approach (two semesters); and practice (annual, 8 months).

Students must pass all exams in these courses. There is no credentialing system. The performance of students is determined by their marks. After earning a bachelor's degree, a student may enter the master's program for counseling in psychology at the University of Tirana. This program takes three semesters (12 months) to complete and requires the following courses: developmental psychology (one semester, 4 months); psychological evaluation (one semester); gestalt psychotherapy (one semester); social psychology (one semester); therapeutic groups (two semesters); cognitive-behavioral psychotherapy (one semester); ethics of counseling (one semester); scientific research (one semester).

In general, these programs provide school psychologists with (a) theoretical knowledge of psychology related to development, learning, cognition, personality, human biology, social aspects, and evaluation; (b) a focus on children and youth related to the psychological services in schools and communities and relationships between teachers and students; (c) interpersonal skills related to listening and communication and attitudes toward clients; and (d) knowledge of statistical and basic research methods.

Roles, Functions, and Responsibilities of School Psychologists

The major roles assumed by school psychologists depend on the professional environment in which they work. Common roles include counseling, consultation, and intervention. Consultations with teachers and parents address developmental problems of children and help monitor their progress in school. The common goal of intervention is to minimize students' learning difficulties, improve their temperaments, help solve family and community problems related to the child, and engage children in community programs to increase collaboration (establishing and maintaining relationships) between peers from different cultures and educational backgrounds. Through migration, many people with differing cultural backgrounds have come to Tirana from other cities and villages. This poses a significant problem in Albania because this movement has highlighted individual differences between children.

Psychologists who work in Level 0 perform these duties: (a) assess physical, social, emotional, cognitive, and linguistic development of children; (b) develop program services or education programs for individual children; and (c) train education staff about psychological services. In 2004, the Ministry of Education and Science enacted a bylaw in which the duties of psychologists who work in Levels 1 through 3 are described. The most common duties are to (a) counsel members of education staff and parents about students' needs and collaborate with different services in communities; (b) provide individual psychological counseling to students; (c) provide group counseling to two or more students to solve different problems; (d) assess each child's behavior and progress in school; and (e) develop specific and general programs related to education in school and children's behavior.

The information from the 2003 survey revealed that school psychologists in Albania reported that, on average, approximately 50% of their time was spent counseling students, 20% consulting with teachers and staff, 15% conducting staff training and in-service programs, 12% consulting with parents and families, 10% in administrative responsibilities, 9% providing direct services, 8% completing psychoeducational evaluations, and 6% providing primary prevention programs (Jimerson et al., 2004). School psychologists in Albania ranked psychoeducational evaluations as the ideal role and counseling students as the second most ideal, with administrative responsibilities ranked last.

Current Issues Impacting School Psychology

School psychology is still young in Albania; thus, it suffers from the problems and challenges of a new field. One is professional development: School psychologists acquire their specialization in only 1 year plus the master's program in counseling. Thus, their professional development is minimal, especially in practical experience, including the use of tests to measure achievement and intelligence. The field of school psychology has yet to develop tests, and thus school psychologists have no tests to use in their work. Knowledge of tests and their use comes from the Internet or from a limited

number of psychology texts. This is a great barrier to the psychologists who work in the education system because they cannot perform the duties they should.

Some internal challenges also jeopardize service delivery in Albania. Along with the fact that more able professionals are leaving the field, the profession lacks leadership, research and evaluation, professional standards governing professional services, and adequate supervision (Jimerson et al., 2004). Almost all issues important to school psychology need to be researched. School psychologists have little practical experience conducting research and receive no funds from the University or other foundations to support research. Some do not understand the need for research in this field. Most urgently, research should focus on the need for school psychologists and their roles and functions, as well as on how school psychologists can best meet the needs of public schools. Research on students' satisfaction with schools, including teaching and peer, student, and teacher relationships, is also needed. Professional development and the inclusion of school psychologists within the educational system infrastructure were noted as important areas for future emphasis in the 2003 International School Psychology Survey (Jimerson et al., 2004).

The Albanian Association of School Psychologists, the only organization attempting to address professional issues and problems of school psychologists, is collaborating with the International School Psychology Association Research Committee to compare the status of school psychology in Albania with that of other countries. It is also working with other associations to promote psychologists and psychology and to have psychologists licensed by the government of Albania.

References

Albanian Ministry of Education and Science. (2005). *Statistical information 2004–2005.* (Partial statistics are available at www.mash.gov.al/struktura/Ars.Larte%2004-05%20web-i.xls)

Albanian Ministry of Science and Education. (1995, June 21). *About the pre-university education system, Chap. XIII: Education of students with special needs* (Law No. 7592).

Albanian Ministry of Science and Education. (2004, October 11). *About putting into practice Executive Order No. 321 of the Ministry of Education and Science for the experimentation of the psychological service in the pre-university education system for the academic years 2004–2005 and 2005–2006* (Bylaw No. 30). (Partial statistics related to the Albanian education system are available at www.mash.gov.al)

Institute of Statistics. (2005). *Statistical yearbook.* (Partial statistics are available at www.instat .gov.al/repoba/default.htm)

Jimerson, S. R., Graydon, K., Farrell, P., Kikas, E., Hatzichristou, C., Boce, E., Bashi (Musabelliu), G., & International School Psychology Association Research Committee. (2004). The International School Psychology Survey: Development and data from Albania, Cyprus, Estonia, Greece and Northern England. *School Psychology International, 25*(3), 259–286.

Jimerson, S. R., & International School Psychology Association Research Committee. (2002). *The International School Psychology Survey.* (Available from the author at the University of California, Santa Barbara; e-mail: Jimerson@education .ucsb.edu)

United Nations Educational, Scientific and Cultural Organization. (1997, November). *International standard classification of education 1997.* Retrieved March 17, 2006, from http://www.unesco.org/ education/information/nfsunesco/doc/isced_ 1997.htm

3

School Psychology in Australia

Michael Faulkner

Context of School Psychology

In 2001, Australia, a federation of six states and two territories, celebrated its centenary as a nation. Before 1901, Australia was a dispersed collection of British colonies, the earliest settlement (Sydney) dating from 1788. Located between the Indian Ocean and the South Pacific Ocean, Australia is an island of 7,686,850 square kilometres and nearly the size of the contiguous 48 United States. According to the Australian Bureau of Statistics, the nation's population in June 2005 was 20.3 million. Demographically and culturally, Australia is a highly urbanised nation, with 64% of its population residing in six state capital cities and 85% of Australians living in, or close to, an urban centre. Major cities are separated by vast distances: Perth and Sydney by 4,000 kilometres, Hobart and Darwin by 4,700 kilometres. Regional and rural Australians (36%) locate mainly along the narrow fertile coastline in smaller population centres, which verge to the nation's vast, sparsely populated inland area.

In 2005, Australia had a high percentage of foreign-born citizens, 24%, an outcome of the sustained immigration policies for 60 years. Immigrants from many nations and cultures contribute to an Australian cosmopolitanism, particularly in Sydney (31% of 4.1 million) and Melbourne (28% of 3.4 million). In demographic and cultural contrast to its major cities, generally, regional Australia reflects the predominantly Anglo-Irish settlement patterns of the 19th and early 20th century. Most people of Aboriginal indigenous background (2.4% of the population in 2004) live in regional and remote areas. Rising exports of raw materials and agriculture have fueled the economy. In 2004, the gross domestic product was estimated at US$611.7 billion, US$30,700 per capita. These historical, geographical, and demographic characteristics strongly influence Australian national life, its education systems, and, too, the development of Australian school psychology.

School Systems and Governance

School governance in Australia has long been the responsibility of state governments. Throughout the 20th century, large state bureaucracies developed, within which education power became strongly invested. Though increased governance powers have been devolved to local school communities in the past decade (i.e., 1995–2005), this is stronger in some states than in others. The states maintain their financial and policy purview of public school education; however, since the early 1970s, national governments of different political persuasions have been strategic and proactive stakeholders in educational politics and, from time to time, pursue alternative policies from those prevailing at the state level. The present Commonwealth government (1996–2006) continues this tradition (Nelson, 2004). Religious organisations have long assumed a role in Australian schooling and continue to educate many young Australians.

The organisation of Australian schooling varies from state to state, but its dominant form for students is 1 preschool year, 7 years at primary school, and 6 years at secondary. Student retention rates to a final year of school vary across the government and nongovernmental sectors, and across urban and regional communities. The compulsory school-age band is 6 to 15 years, with school entry age typically being 5 years. In 2004, participation rates of full-time school students were 93% at 15 years, 82% at 16 years, and 64% for 17-year-olds. The rate of continuous enrolment from Year 7 to Year 12 (for full-time students) was 76%, but a significant gender difference exists, with female enrolment (81%) higher than male enrolment (70%). There are 38 universities and dozens of technical and further education colleges across Australia, offering diverse postschool options.

In 2004, there were 9,615 schools in Australia, with 6,938 (72%) government schools and 2,677 (28%) in the nongovernmental sector. Of the nation's 3.3 million students, 67% were attending government schools in 2004. From 1995 to 2004, the number of students attending nongovernmental schools has increased by 22%, compared with a 2% increase in government schools. Enrolments in the nongovernmental sector are higher in the cities and in the secondary years of schooling. In most state capitals, nongovernmental secondary school enrolments exceeded 40% of students, spread between Catholic and independent schools. Nationwide over the past two decades, there has also been a steady growth in the number of independent schools, rising from 6% in 1983 to 13% in 2003. This shift is a function of a steadily widening wealth gap across Australia and a response to the present Commonwealth government's increasing financial support to the nongovernmental schools sector.

Average class sizes do not vary significantly across the Australian states but can vary between urban and some rural school communities. Generally, average teacher-to-student ratios are 1 to 20, with class sizes averaging around 25. In Australia's declining number of rural schools, ratios can be lower. Overall, between 10% and 15% of students have special needs. This cohort comprises two subgroups: (1) students with significant learning disabilities (2%–3%), requiring additional funding for ancillary teacher support or specialised equipment; and (2) those with less challenging problems, defined as "learning difficulties" (10%–12%). Foreman (2005) estimates that 7% of students have "moderate learning or behavioural difficulties."

In 2002, the Australian government commissioned a Senate inquiry to investigate the educational circumstances of school-age students with disabilities. *The Education of Students With Disabilities* (Commonwealth of Australia, 2002) summarised findings drawn from extensive expert sources, invited submissions, and held a nationwide community consultation process. A key finding was that from state to state, considerable diversity exists in the definitions about student disabilities in schooling, particularly relating to special educational needs funding eligibility criteria.

Origins, History, and Current Status of School Psychology

Though Australian school psychology emerged as an educational specialty following World War II, its origins are decades earlier. From the 1870s, colonial governments enacted compulsory education laws, seeking to address child welfare issues through the combined effects of education and welfare legislation (Bessant & Spaull, 1976). The emerging professions of law, medicine, education, and social welfare aided this process, assuming services as intermediate agents for developing state governance (Davidson, 1991). Following the achievement of universal education by 1910 in most regions, Australian public education began developing differentiated curricula through the establishment of segregated special schools and special classes in mainstream schools (Ashman & Elkins, 2005). The first Australian government special school was established in 1913 in Melbourne. Stanley Porteus, its inaugural head teacher, provided a gatekeeper role for this school. Using an adaptation of the Binet-Goddard instrument, Porteus identified children with suspected mental retardation; in so doing, he became Australia's first school psychologist (Porteus, 1969). At the Melbourne Teachers College in 1923, a "psychological laboratory" was established, where a small number of specially trained educators were employed as mental testers and educational advisers to both special and regular schools.

Similar developments occurred elsewhere. In 1922, a psychologist was appointed to the fledgling special education system in Tasmania (Hall, 1977), and, in 1924, Constance Davey, a doctoral student of Charles Spearman, began employment as a psychologist in the Medical Branch of the South Australian Education Department (Shute, 1995). In 1925, psychologist Ethel Stoneman commenced with the Western Australian Education Department to establish a psychological clinic to support the education of children with intellectual retardation (Turtle & Orr, 1990). Through the 1930s and 1940s across Australia, child guidance clinics were established (Hughes, 2002), a response to growing government and community expectations that suitable educational arrangements were needed for *all* children in an age of universal compulsory schooling.

By 1920, Australian public school systems had begun providing services for students with learning and intellectual disabilities in regular schools and were beginning to establish special schools for children with intellectual retardation. The administrative and educational uses to which the newly developed intelligence tests were put drove these developments, aiding conditions for the emergence of a school psychology. Between 1920 and 1945, and particularly following the establishment of the Australian Council for Educational Research, psychometrically oriented services emerged. From the mid 1920s, Australian teachers were encouraged to study the characteristics of their pupils and to divide their large classes into groups on the basis of students' intelligence test scores (McCallum, 1990).

Sixty years ago, there were few school-focused psychologists in Australia. A 1948 United Nations Educational, Scientific and Cultural Organization (UNESCO) survey of educational psychology services in 41 nations estimated just 20 school psychologists in Australia, mostly located in the state of New South Wales (Korniszewski & Mallet, 1948). This same survey noted an emerging specialisation of applied educational psychology, summarising its directions within three broad areas: the detection of "backward" children, educational guidance involving the testing and adaptation of educational methods, and the use of prevocational guidance.

The establishment of the Australian Council for Educational Research, in 1930, occurred within a context of reduced educational funding. The 1930s economic depression delayed the attainment of the goals for universal secondary schooling until the early 1950s, and by 1936, all 45,000 Year 6 students in New South Wales were administered intelligence tests to aid secondary school selection (Hughes, 2002). The growth of the Australian Council for Educational Research through the 1930s provided considerable impetus to psychometric testing in schools. The expansion of special "opportunity classes" in regular schools for the educationally retarded, based on intelligence and scholastic achievement data, and the establishment of specialist child guidance clinics in New South Wales in 1934 fuelled the growth of a psychological assessment tradition in Australian education (Shute, 1995).

An optimistic postwar climate emphasised the virtues of preparing youth for a better world. Educators and psychologists, drawing on the insights of social psychology (Oeser, 1955), emphasised the importance of contributing to a wider national mission in which the education of youth figured importantly in promoting Australian citizenship and stability (Faye, 1999). Unprecedented levels of immigration through the 1950s and 1960s contributed to the expansion of state secondary school systems. The 1950s saw an emerging discourse and expectations for schooling relating to student pastoral care, anticipating specialist psychological services in education around which the postwar Australian school guidance and counselling movement in Australia gradually formed (Faulkner, 2000).

During the 1950s and 1960s, state-supported school psychology and guidance services developed with social psychology research applications being adapted to schooling. In Victoria, school guidance services were developing based on the belief that school psychological services needed to be provided in homes and neighbourhoods as well as in schools (Faulkner, 2000). However, the demand for psychologists to utilise psychometric techniques for educational selection and placement as well as vocational counselling in secondary schools took precedence to other forms of service. State differences existed in the extent of use of group testing to classify students for selection purposes (Hall, 1977).

Although at the beginning of the 21st century, the general patterns in the nature of Australian school psychological services across all school systems are broadly similar, school psychological services have developed differently across the six states, reflecting differences in climate, history, demography, and state government educational priorities. As Taylor and Taft (1977) observed in their review of Australian psychology three decades ago, Australians essentially live their lives

within the framework of their own city and, to a lesser extent, of their own state. This historically based and cultural regionality of Australian life has led to distinctive differences in professional designation.

Thus, in 2006, there is still no single national occupational designation for what constitutes the roles and functions of Australian "school psychology" (Armstrong et al., 2000). However, since the mid 1970s, the certification and registration of psychologists by state authorities, the powerful influence of the Australian Psychological Society, and the emergence of the Australian Guidance and Counselling Association have all contributed to a more nationally oriented school psychology.

There are approximately 2,000 school psychologists working in Australian schools, double the number of the mid 1970s (Nixon, 1977). Estimates of psychologist numbers in the public schooling sector are between 1,400 and 1,500 (Armstrong et al., 2000). The growth of school psychology in Australia has been broadly consistent with developments in other Western nations (Oakland & Saigh, 1992). As elsewhere, the profession's origins and development relate intrinsically to the changing character of public education. Whereas the nature of Australian school psychology services has evolved, changed, and diversified over the decades (Faulkner, 1993; Hall, 1977), the educational and psychological rationale still remains closely associated with special needs educational provision.

Most Australian school psychologists (80%–90%) are employed by the state governments or in the nongovernmental school sector. The profession is slowly becoming a predominantly female one (75%–80% female), mirroring historical developments in the teaching profession. On a state-by-state basis, school psychologists are employed differently: either (1) in multidisciplinary school and student support centres servicing district schools or (2) working individually or in small teams in a host school and providing services to a cluster of schools (Armstrong et al., 2000). Few work in just one school; those who do tend to work in wealthier private schools. In several states, school systems contract private psychologists to undertake particular forms of educational psychology work in schools (Faulkner, 1999b).

Salaries are commensurate with those of teachers in the middle salary ranges within the government school sector. In 2006, this range is US$40,000 to US$65,000 and is generally higher than remuneration for other human services professionals in education, social workers, school nurses, and speech pathologists. In some states, such as Western Australia and New South Wales, there is an open professional career structure and provision for advancement within the special services. In other states, career structures are more limited. The past decade has seen some psychologist services contracted out to specialist "boutique" psychologist organisations, as part of an evolving management ethos in the Australian public sector (Faulkner, 1994).

In Australia in the early 1990s, school psychologist–student ratios for New South Wales, Queensland, Tasmania, and Western Australia were less than 1 to 2,000. In South Australia and Victoria, they were considerably higher (Whitla, Walker, & Drent, 1992), and nationwide, ratios are generally higher in regional and rural areas. In 2006, the situation remains much the same, though urban-rural differences have improved a little. For many school psychologists, entry to the profession occurs in midcareer, following some years of teaching; for these people, there is a strong likelihood of career stability. A study of school psychologists in regional and rural locations found this to generally be the case, with many practitioners having long served their district communities (Faulkner, 1999a).

Infrastructure of School Psychology

The national organisation most closely serving the interests of Australian school psychology is the Australian Guidance and Counselling Association (www.agca.com.au). Established in 1985 (Prescott, 1995), it originated from state-based professional organisations. The organisation grew slowly through the 1990s, stabilising its membership base between 1,100 and 1,250. The association publishes two issues of a refereed journal each year, the *Australian Journal of Guidance and Counselling,* and two issues of the national *Australian Guidance and Counselling Association Newsletter,* which provides information about developments for the profession across all states and short articles of current professional relevance.

The Australian Guidance and Counselling Association affiliated with the International School Psychology Association in 1995, provides biannual national conferences for its members, and co-hosted the 20th International School Psychology Association School Psychology Colloquium in 1997 in Melbourne. Since 1997, Australian Guidance and Counselling Association policies and practice have assumed a more international orientation in three ways: (1) by encouraging association delegates to attend the annual International School Psychology Association Colloquium; (2) by sponsoring international, high-profile leaders in school psychology to share their ideas, research, and work with Australians; and (3) in the sponsorship and the financial support offered to overseas delegates to attend the national association conferences, from nations where school psychology is less developed than it is in Australia. The Australian Guidance and Counselling Association state branches provide regular professional development programs for their members, including annual conferences in some states.

Australian school psychologists can belong to the Australian Psychological Society (www.psychology.org.au). Established in 1965 (having been a branch of the British Psychological Society since 1945), the society now has 14,000 members and offers an elaborate professional support structure of nine colleges, 39 regional groups, and 21 specialist interest groups to cater to the diverse interests of its members. Through its colleges, the

Australian Psychological Society provides members with advanced membership status, based on their qualifications, training, and professional experience.

In 2005, membership of the College for Educational and Developmental Psychologists was 317, 50% of whom live in Victoria. Similarly, of the 700 College of Counselling members, 61% reside in Victoria. Although not all of these society college members are school psychologists, Victorian membership contrasts with the low Victorian school psychologist membership to the Australian Guidance and Counselling Association, further testimony to the regional character of Australian school psychology. The Australian Psychological Society College publishes a refereed journal twice annually, the *Australian Educational and Development Psychologist,* but its content is less school education focused than that of the Australian Guidance and Counselling Association publication. In 2005, the society established a working party on school psychology. Some school psychologists hold concurrent membership in both organisations.

Certification and Regulation of School Psychologists

Australian psychologists must meet their respective state Psychologists Registration Board guidelines. Each state licenses psychologists, with registration being generic. State licensure is influenced by, but remains independent of, the society accreditation processes. At present, there is no national accreditation body for psychologist practitioners, other than the society, the membership of which includes many academic psychologists and researchers. On the other hand, for several decades now, the society has been the principal advising agent to all state psychologist registration authorities. The most recent guidelines (updated in 2005), generated by a state regulatory authority for probationary psychologists and their supervisors, come from the Psychologists' Registration Board of Victoria (www.psychreg.vic.gov.au). These are generalist

guidelines for the professional supervision of all probationary psychologists and are very comprehensive in their coverage of all matters relating to professional psychology competencies.

Since 1965, the Australian Psychological Society has strongly influenced the professional training, accreditation, and development of professionally oriented psychology. Psychologist registration eligibility is framed by the Australian Psychological Society's accreditation requirements. All undergraduate and postgraduate university psychology programs are evaluated for possible accreditation. Australian Psychological Society membership eligibility requires 6 years: 4 years of sequential study in psychology in an approved university undergraduate program, a master's qualification in psychology, and a 2-year approved individually supervised professional experience that may be part of a postgraduate studies program. The historical absence of a national government mandate for education ensures continuity in the diversity of state education structures and programs. In the first decade of the 21st century, the ways in which school psychology has developed reflects the nation's regional history and diversity. Such diversity is most obviously manifest in the different professional designations used.

Only one state, Western Australia, uses the title "school psychologist." New South Wales uses "school counsellor," although their staff are state-registered psychologists. Elsewhere, "guidance officer" is the most commonly used professional designation, which typically means a psychologist with teacher qualifications and teacher experience. In the sparsely populated Northern Territory, and in the Australian Capital Territory (Canberra), "educational psychologist" is currently the official designation. Generally, most school psychologists come from the teaching force. Typically, guidance officers possess double professional certification: as teachers and as psychologists. In Queensland, until recently, the title "guidance officer" did not necessarily denote the status of a "registered psychologist" as in other states.

School psychology everywhere has a long-standing symbiotic relationship with educational bureaucracy, and Australia is no exception. For the evolving school psychology profession, as a low-incidence profession in public sector organisations shaped by administrators and teachers, its relationship with schools, teachers, and parents has been continually influenced by the periodic transformations in educational philosophy, organisational restructuring, and the funding shifts following new policy initiatives (Faulkner, 1993). For example, in Victoria, during the 1960s and 1970s, prevailing government policies saw a rapid expansion of segregated special schools for students with an intellectual disability, thus intensifying demands for psychological assessment, developments that increased school psychologist numbers. The significant mid 1980s policy shift pursued by subsequent Victorian governments, toward a rights model for students with disabilities to attend mainstream schools, impacted significantly on the retention of school psychologists, reducing numbers from 330 in 1982 to about half that number by 1997 (Faulkner, 1999b). In 2006, state-based differences exist in public school systems with respect to school psychologist's work locations, their employment conditions, and the nature of support services they provide (Armstrong et al., 2000). Locations vary from multidisciplinary group community centres to lone placement or location with several others in a host school.

In New South Wales, 63% of 6.7 million people (31% born overseas) live in Sydney. School counsellors (registered psychologists, all with teaching qualifications and experience) are based in host schools, serving both primary and secondary schools, and report to district-based senior school counsellors. Through the 1990s, successive governments financially supported the graduate training of selected teachers to become school counsellors, making the service in 2006 both numerically and professionally robust, and with a viable career structure.

In Western Australia, where the title "school psychologist" is used, staff are based in off–school site service centres together with curriculum consultants and special education advisers under educational administrators. For Western Australia school psychologists, less emphasis is now placed on teacher experience than in other states. Given the state's geographical vastness, the maintenance of professional support to school psychologists working in rural and remote areas remains an ongoing agenda. Western Australia also has the highest percentage of Aboriginal Australians, many living in small communities in the vast north of the state. Providing culturally appropriate psychological services to these regions includes many pressing challenges.

Queensland's population is highly dispersed, with many regional towns and remote rural communities. Guidance officers are not necessarily required to be registered psychologists and may possess postgraduate counselling qualifications. In contrast to guidance officers in other states, those in Queensland specialise either in primary (including preschool) education or in secondary education (Rice & Bramston, 1999). Some work in one high school; others work with clusters of preschools and primary schools, adopting a family and community focus. The guidance services of the Catholic school system, which educates 20% of the nation's students, have grown rapidly in recent years, particularly in Brisbane (Quinn & Reynolds, 2001).

Of the 5 million people in the state of Victoria, 72% reside in its capital, Melbourne. The ratio between school psychologists and government school students is the poorest in the nation, the result of the macroeducational policies of successive governments through the late 1980s and 1990s. During the 1980s, Victoria led the nation with the development of multidisciplinary school support centres, which were disbanded by 1995. In 1998, the assessment of children considered eligible for additional special education funding was contracted to private psychology organisations (Faulkner, 1999a). School psychologists in Victoria now work in pairs or trios from host schools servicing school districts.

Like Victoria and Western Australia, South Australia is primarily a city-state, with one major city, Adelaide (population 1 million), several small regional cities, and widely dispersed rural and isolated regions. The state's population is 1.5 million. Unlike school psychologists elsewhere, those in South Australia are employed to work in both primary and secondary schools and in early childhood services within the Department of Education and Children's Services. School psychologists are located in multidisciplinary professional support teams across 18 districts. One district encompasses the sparsely populated remote area of the indigenous Pitinjinjara people.

Tasmania has a predominantly rural population, with half its population (200,000) situated in its capital, Hobart. School psychology services are divided into six districts covering the island, servicing many isolated small school communities. The sparsely populated Northern Territory, with its many remote indigenous community settlements, contrasts with the compact Australian Capital Territory, which surrounds the national political capital, Canberra. School psychology in these two regions necessarily assumes different forms.

Preparation of School Psychologists

From the late 19th century, psychology was taught in departments of philosophy (Turtle & Orr, 1990). By the early 20th century, an era when academic researchers and social reformers were beginning to turn their attention to schools and other societal institutions, the study of psychology had moved from its philosophical roots to an emphasis on new empirical and applied foci (Taft & Day, 1988). From 1913, teachers in Victoria were able to take educationally focused in-service psychology courses, an initiative reflecting the growing interest in psychology among members of the teaching profession at the Melbourne Teachers College. Departments

of psychology were established at the University of Sydney and the University of Western Australia in the 1920s, at the University of Melbourne in the 1940s, and at the University of Adelaide and Canberra's Australian National University in the 1950s (O'Neill, 1977). The 1930s and the 1940s saw rapid advances in the teaching of psychology with the establishment of psychology departments in most universities and the expansion of psychology-trained graduates through the 1950s and 1960s, from whom the second generation of school psychologists came. By the mid 1970s, master's degree programs in educational or school-related psychology began proliferating in the expanding universities sector, overwhelmingly within education faculties. Such developments fostered Australian psychologists' strong identification with the teaching profession, providing the postgraduate professional education market with a new generation of school psychologists. From the 1980s (Ritchie, 1985) and into the 1990s, course offerings expanded, allowing for greater specialisation options, particularly in psychoeducational assessment, counselling psychology, and school counselling.

Australian school psychology maintains its traditionally strong links with the teaching profession. In some states, school psychologists are still employed as part of the teaching force salary structures. Traditionally, school psychologists enter the profession from a teaching career, having completed an undergraduate degree in psychology, having qualified as teachers, and then having taught in schools for some years. Then, they take postgraduate studies in educational psychology. For these individuals, school psychology becomes a second career.

Several years of school teaching experience, in addition to academic and professional training requirements, were considered minimal as an experiential entry requirement to school psychology in most states. In recent years, some states have relaxed this prerequisite for school psychologist employment. In the past decade, a change within the profession has been occurring in Western Australia, with many younger psychologists entering the profession. This shift is a function of the University of Western Australia's academic pathways, combining with the public school system's relaxation of teaching experience criteria as an entry to school psychology. Though a 1-year teaching qualification is required to work in government schools, increasingly for Western Australian psychologists, their first professional allegiance is to school psychology.

Undergraduate and Postgraduate Professional Preparation

There are diverse academic pathways into school psychology. Most of Australia's 38 universities provide Australian Psychological Society–accredited, undergraduate, 3- and 4-year degrees in sequential psychology studies. Of the many postgraduate degree programs in psychology in 2006, there are 13 universities offering almost 50 society-accredited, advanced coursework studies in areas of direct relevance to school psychologists. These programs can be studied at the master's or doctoral level. These postgraduate studies include the Australian Catholic University's programs in child and family psychology and postgraduate programs in educational (and/or developmental) psychology, separately offered by the University of Queensland, the University of Melbourne, and the University of Tasmania. Victoria's La Trobe University is one of several universities offering doctoral studies in neuropsychology that may be tailored to the school-age demographic.

Many universities now offer accredited master's or doctoral programs in counselling for those with undergraduate psychology qualifications. The University of Sydney offers a 5-year double-degree program specifically oriented to training school counsellors. A degree in arts or science specialising in psychology studies is combined with a bachelor's of education. This enables students to meet the separate

registration requirements of both New South Wales Psychology and Teaching Registration Boards. Graduates are encouraged to take positions in regional New South Wales. The Charles Sturt University offers a double degree in social science (psychology) and teaching (primary level), and the New South Wales Department of Education releases a number of qualified teachers each year to undertake postgraduate counsellor training at either Charles Sturt University or the University of Western Sydney. The University of Western Australia offers something similar for psychology graduates, a master's of psychology and a 1-year diploma of education qualification. The University of South Australia offers a 6-year sequence in specialist areas of psychology culminating in a bachelor's of psychology and a master's of psychology. Flinders University in South Australia offers comparable postgraduate qualifications and professional accreditation packages.

Roles, Functions, and Responsibilities of School Psychologists

Australian psychologists provide a range of direct and indirect services to the school population and are guided by the Australian Psychological Society professional competencies and the codes of ethics of either the Australian Psychological Society or the Australian Guidance and Counsellor Association. The roles, functions, and responsibilities of school psychologists vary both within and across states. The most recent comparative review of Australian public-sector school psychology (Armstrong et al., 2000) compared the major professional responsibilities and the forms of professional support state by state. The primary professional responsibilities lie in the following areas: (a) individual and group counselling of students; (b) psychoeducational student assessments and report writing; (c) the provision of consultancy advice on effective behaviour management programs; (d) consultancy regarding psychological service to schools and communities; (e) liaison with other government or nongovernmental welfare agencies or medical specialists; (f) parent counselling, undertaken individually, or in small groups; and (g) response teams for critical incidents management and support in schools.

Armstrong et al. (2000) also found differing emphases across school systems, depending on a school system's charter for school psychology and guidance work. These included (a) student advocacy; (b) assisting schools to develop more effective policies and practices of a whole school nature (e.g., antibullying practices, encouraging proactive student behaviours, or improving school safety net practices for students at risk); (c) training and development activities with teacher groups; (d) close in-house teamwork with other professionals such as speech pathologists, social workers, or early childhood educators; and (e) participation in specially funded innovative "lighthouse" projects with a small number of schools.

School psychologists use a variety of psychological assessment tools, and usage varies according to state and region. Psychological assessment instruments are restricted to use by registered psychologists, and these include the various Wechsler Intelligence Scales, the Stanford-Binet Test of Intelligence, the Vineland Adaptive Behaviour Scales, the Achenbach System of Empirically based Assessment, and the British Ability Scales. The Australian Council for Educational Research (www.acer.edu.au) offers a wide range of intellectual, school achievement, behavioural, and social and emotional functioning assessment measures for school-age students, and in recent years, American and British publishing houses have augmented this range, offering a sometimes bewildering choice for school psychologists. The Australian Council for Educational Research has available a number of Australian norm-referenced and recently developed diagnostic assessment batteries for reading and

numeracy skills, and there are a number of locally developed instruments such as the Adolescent Coping Scale (1997) and the Children's Depression Scale (2004).

A study of the work of guidance officers in Queensland (Rice & Bramston, 1999) found that 20% of their time was allocated to consultation with teachers, principals, parents, and allied professionals, 13% to administration and travel, and 3% to reading and research. Differences exist among those who work in primary and secondary schools. Primary guidance staff spend 22% of their time on assessment and reporting and 8% on student counselling. Secondary guidance officers limited their assessment and reporting (7%) and devoted more time to student counselling (31%). Although Queensland is unique in its specialisation of school guidance work according to level of schooling, similar differences in work patterns among elementary and secondary school service provision are found in other states.

A national study of school guidance and counselling staff located in regional and rural Australia (Faulkner, 1999b) found that student assessment work accounted for at least 25% of their time, individual student counselling and leadership work with student groups accounted for more than 25% of their professional time, and about 10% was allocated to teacher consultancy and intervention work with schools. Counselling and related work with parents amounted to just 5%, and organisational workplace commitments and travel were estimated as involving about 10% of their time. This sample of guidance and counselling staff rated their time to their own professional development as low—less than 5% of their total time commitment.

Current Issues Impacting School Psychology

There are a number of themes that are likely to continue to impact the profession of Australian school psychology in the coming decade. These include the ageing of the teaching force, now undergoing a youth revitalisation, a shift that is slowly occurring in school psychology. We can also expect an increase in the number of younger, early-entry, "first-career" psychologists employed within school systems. There is an emerging need to professionally equip these people with the consultancy skills to work with, and within, the structurally and pedagogically restless organisations that epitomise contemporary schooling. Related to this evolving demographic change is a need to encourage participation and ownership in the professional associations to which school psychologists belong.

There is emerging through school system priorities, a focus on optimising children's futures through early intervention work with families or in the early childhood years. In 2004, the Victorian government school system began employing school-based "well-being officers," who liaise within schools, with parents, and who run proactive programs with students. Australian school psychologists now have greater intersectorial liaison with professions from health care and human services, as well as from education and psychology.

School systems are likely to increasingly demand specialised as well as generalist school psychology competencies. Whether they use contracted specialists or their own psychologist employees, the demands for "just-in-time" project work, such as professional development for teachers or postintervention work relating to traumatic events, debriefing, and grief counselling, can be expected to increase. Professional organisations such as the Australian Psychological Society and Australian Guidance and Counsellor Association also demand of their members an ability to maintain current knowledge relating to professional issues and practices and to be "ahead of the game" in some ways. This will place school psychologists under increasing pressure to upgrade their professional knowledge, one likelihood being an increased demand for more professional doctorates.

Contemporary school administration— whether at the state, district, or school level—is about the promotion and management of change. With school systems increasingly focused on advancing and promoting educational changes, grounded knowledge from evidence-based research and best practices is now strongly valued. In their quest to be politically responsive and innovative, school systems are increasingly likely to value and provide some top-down support for promising grassroots initiatives. This is a promising area for school psychology skills development.

School Psychology's Relationship Within and With Educational Bureaucracy

School psychology's development in the 20th century is intrinsically related to mass schooling, and, as such, its relationship with educational bureaucracy remains deep and complex. Since a managerial ethos swept through public-sector organisations (Faulkner, 1994), there has been an increase in comments by Australian school psychologists in the Australian Guidance and Counselling Association *Newsletter* on their shifting organisational structures and supervision arrangements or on the new ethical issues arising from mixed accountabilities to administrative line managers, senior professional staff, and the students, parents, and teachers with whom they work on a regular basis. Twenty years ago, most school psychologists were solely responsible to a senior psychologist or guidance and counselling specialist. Now they may be directly responsible to an individual or small team of school principals or to a district student services manager.

Following the deregulation of the Australian dollar in 1983, Australian governments have become more subject to the dynamics of economic globalisation, resulting in increased volatility in public-sector administration (Marginson, 1997). This has impacted government-employed professionals, supporting those with low-incidence disabilities. These developments have also influenced public school systems and the school psychologists who work within them (Faulkner, 1999b). The pervasive restructuring and down-sizing of Australian public-sector organisations, beginning in the late 1980s, was followed by the outsourcing of some long-established, government-based professional services in the helping professions.

At the same time, most contemporary governments experience intensely the pressures of accountability and are more open to incorporating external ideas or new initiatives into their quest for electoral appeal. Within this framework, increased opportunities exist for school psychologists to form new networks, undertake collaborative research, and influence new practices, as in the national project to facilitate strategies aimed at developing prosocial behaviours in students (Griffiths, 2002; Prescott, 1996). In recent years, the Australian Guidance and Counselling Association has taken a lead role in a national student mental health outcomes initiative in schools, Mindmatters Plus (Herbert, 2004). In addition, school psychologists have become more engaged in crisis intervention, critical incident debriefing and post-trauma counselling with students and staff, following the occurrence of atypical and distressing circumstances (Whitla, 1994, 2003).

Changing Demographics in Australian Society and the Urban-Rural Divide

Since 1945, Australia has received immigrants in large numbers, and its cities are now home to many people who differ by ethnicity, language, and culture. School psychologists in urban Australia have long attempted to address social and educational issues arising from multicultural communities. In Victoria in the early 1970s, school psychologists and school social workers lobbied successfully for the Department of Education to employ language interpreters to assist them in their work with children from non-English speaking backgrounds (Faulkner, 1992). However, each wave of immigrants brings new

language and cultural populations into the Australian community, and school psychologists are faced with the ongoing challenges of advising schools to assist children who inhabit two worlds.

Almost 90% of Australians live within an hour of the coast; a steadily shifting population distribution is slowly depopulating rural and inland Australia. Few professionals, including school psychologists, seek to work in rural areas (Harvey, 1997). Publicity on issues of professional services in rural areas features the scarcity. However, the provision of school psychology services to remote areas is part of this wider national concern. Professionals providing services to people with disabilities report working under difficult conditions and not obtaining sufficient employer support or recognition (Gething, 1997). Rural psychologists, including school psychologists, experience similar difficulties (Mair, 1996), that is, context-specific ethical challenges in small communities. However, new technologies permit innovative professional supervision arrangements (McMahon, 2002).

Evolving Professional Forms and Professional Practices

The traditional pathway to professional school psychology in Australia has been through teaching, and, in most states, that remains so (Burnett, 1997). School psychologists generally commence their professional postgraduate preparation in school psychology as qualified and registered teachers with minimally several years' classroom teaching experience, following their undergraduate psychology and education qualifications. Through the 1960s and 1970s, state education departments and universities provided professional education courses. Now, universities assume greater responsibility for professional preparation through graduate level courses.

In 2006, government-employed school psychologists typically provide services to a cluster of primary and/or secondary schools; some provide preschool services. Larger private schools are able to employ a psychologist full-time.

Although patterns vary across states, Australian school psychologists continue to provide a blend of services: individual psychoeducational assessment, student and parent counselling, teacher consultation and teacher in-service programs, committee work on behalf of schools and districts, and liaison with other government or private organisation professionals. Most states mandate the reporting of suspected child abuse that may involve psychologists liaising with government social workers and child care workers in addition to their usual school-focused work.

Themes emphasising school effectiveness, school improvement, school renewal, and effective leadership gained stronger political traction internationally during the 1990s. In Australia, these developments have given expression to increased school district or principal autonomy and greater systemic valuing of principals' educational leadership skills. Through charter school arrangements, schools are increasingly encouraged to aspire to become better learning organisations.

Contemporary Australian school psychologists now experience an increased engagement with the systematic and ecological maintenance of school communities, a greater emphasis on providing assistance in relation to schoolwide approaches to curriculum development, student welfare, and discipline, and greater opportunities to participate in proactive student well-being programs. At the same time, the traditional functions of psychoeducational assessment and counselling assistance continue to be common activities.

References

Armstrong, S., Kelly, P., Phillips, J., Royle, B., White, J., & Yates, K. (2000). The status of school counselling and guidance in Australia: A summary report. *Australian Guidance and Counselling Newsletter, 2,* 20–25.

Ashman, A., & Elkins, J. (2005). *Educating children with diverse abilities* (2nd ed.). Sydney: Pearson Education Australia.

Bessant, B., & Spaull, A. (1976). *Politics of schooling.* Melbourne: Pitman.

Burnett, P. (1997). The face of guidance and counselling, what will it look like in 25 years? *Australian Journal of Guidance and Counselling, 7*(1), 23–34.

Commonwealth of Australia. (2002, December 10). *Education of students with disabilities* (Report of the Senate Employment, Workplace Relations and Education References Committee). Canberra: Senate Printing Unit.

Davidson, A. (1991). *The invisible state: The formation of the Australian State 1988–1901.* Melbourne: Cambridge University Press.

Faulkner, M. (1992). *Vision and rationalisation: A study of the development of the school psychology profession within the Victorian Education Department.* Unpublished doctoral dissertation, Deakin University, Geelong, Australia.

Faulkner, M. (1993, September). *Paradigm and contestation in school psychology within the Victorian Education Department.* Paper presented at the Fourth National Conference of the Australian Guidance and Counselling Association, Adelaide.

Faulkner, M. (1994). Managerialism and the professions: The case of school psychology in the 1990s. *Australian Journal of Guidance and Counselling, 4*(1), 19–38.

Faulkner, M. (1999a). Inside the vortex: The transformation of the public service sector: Implications for the school psychology profession. *Australian Journal of Guidance and Counselling, 9*(2), 93–117.

Faulkner, M. (1999b, September). *School psychology in the bush: A report of the 1998 survey of AGCA guidance and counselling members working in rural and remote areas of Australia.* Paper presented at the Seventh National Conference of the Australian Guidance and Counselling Association, Perth.

Faulkner, M. (2000). J. R. McLeod, an innovating school psychologist in Victorian government schools. *Melbourne Studies in Education, 41*(1), 115–136.

Faye, E. (1999). The school as a miniature society: Libidinising Australian citizenship in the 1950s. *History of Education Review, 28*(1), 20–38.

Foreman, P. (2005). *Inclusion in action.* Melbourne: Thomson.

Gething, L. (1997). Providing services in remote and rural Australian communities. *Journal of Community Psychology, 25*(2), 209–226.

Griffiths, C. (2002). *Countering bullying in schools training package.* Perth: Western Australia Department of Education.

Hall, J. (1977). Educational psychology in public service. In M. Nixon & R. Taft (Eds.), *Psychology in Australia: Achievements and prospects.* Sydney: Pergamon Press.

Harvey, D. (1997). *Report on survey of members of the Australian Psychological Society's Interest Group in Rural and Remote Psychology.* Unpublished report. Melbourne: Australian Psychological Society.

Herbert, R. (2004, December). The challenge of suicide prevention: Where to with Mindmatters Plus. *Australian Guidance and Counselling Association Newsletter,* pp. 18–21.

Hughes, J. (2002). Harold Wyndham and educational reform in Australia, 1925–1968. *Educational Research and Perspectives, 29*(1), 1–65.

Korniszewski, P., & Mallet, J. (1948). *A survey of educational psychology services in 41 countries.* Paris: United Nations Educational, Scientific and Cultural Organization.

Mair, P. (1996). Psychology in the Australian outback: Rural health services. In P. Martin & J. S. Birnbrauer (Eds.), *Clinical psychology: Profession and practice in Australia* (pp. 480–507). Melbourne: Macmillan Education.

Marginson, S. (1997). *Educating Australia: Government, economy, and citizen since 1960.* Melbourne: Cambridge University Press.

McCallum, D. (1990). *The social production of merit: Education, psychology and politics in Australia.* London: Falmer Press.

McMahon, M. (2002). Structured peer group supervision by e-mail. *Australian Guidance and Counselling Association Newletter, 1,* 19–24.

Nelson, B. (2004, August 26–27). *Making schools better.* Speech presented at the Making Schools Better Conference, University of Melbourne, VIC, Australia. Available at http://www.dest .gov.au/Ministers/Media/Nelson/2004/08/n9012 60804.asp

Nixon, M. (1977). Educational psychology in Australia. In C. Catterall (Ed.), *Psychology in the schools in international perspective* (Vol. 2, pp. 15–23). Columbus, OH: International School Psychology Steering Committee.

Oakland, T., & Saigh, P. (1992). A survey of school psychology in developed and developing countries. *School Psychology International, 13*(2), 99–129.

Oeser, O. (1955). *Teacher, pupil, and task: Elements of social psychology applied to education.* London: Tavistock.

O'Neill, W. (1977). Teaching and practice in psychology in Australia in the first phase. In M. Nixon & R. Taft (Eds.), *Psychology in Australia: Achievements and prospects.* Sydney: Pergamon Press.

Porteus, S. (1969). *A psychologist of sorts.* Palo Alto, CA: Pacific Books.

Prescott, K. (1995). History of the Australian Guidance and Counselling Association. *Australian Guidance and Counselling Association Newsletter, 3,* 9–12.

Prescott, K. (1996). *The teaching prosocial skills to adolescents project.* Canberra: Commonwealth of Australia, Department of Employment Education and Training, Quality Schooling Program.

Quinn, M., & Reynolds, R. (2001, November). Guidance and counselling services to Brisbane: Catholic schools on the move. *Australian Guidance and Counselling Association Newsletter,* pp. 19–20.

Rice, D., & Bramston, P. (1999). The guidance role in Queensland. *Australian Journal of Guidance and Counselling, 9*(2), 25–37.

Ritchie, M. (1985). School psychology in Australia. *Journal of School Psychology, 23*(1), 13–18.

Shute, R. (1995). The Inaugural Constance Davey Inaugural Lecture. *Australian Journal of Guidance and Counselling, 5*(1), 49–58.

Taft, R., & Day, R. (1988). Psychology in Australia. *Annual Review of Psychology, 39,* 375–400.

Taylor, K., & Taft, R. (1977). Psychology and the Australian Zeitgeist. In M. Nixon & R. Taft (Eds.), *Psychology in Australia: Achievements and prospects.* Sydney: Pergamon Press.

Turtle, A., & Orr, M. (1990). *The psyching of OZ.* Melbourne: Australian Psychological Society.

Whitla, M. (1994). *Coping with crises in schools: Preparation, response and recovery.* Melbourne: Collins Dove.

Whitla, M. (2003). *Crises management and the school community.* Melbourne: Australian Council for Educational Research Press.

Whitla, M., Walker, G., & Drent, A. (1992). School psychological and guidance services in Australia: Critical issues and implications for future guidance. *Australian Journal of Guidance and Counselling, 2*(1), 1–20.

4

School Psychology in Brazil

Raquel S. L. Guzzo

Albertina Mitjáns Martínez

Herculano Ricardo Campos

Context of School Psychology

Following three centuries under Portugal's rule, Brazil became an independent nation in 1822. Brazil is 8,511,965 square kilometers and is the fifth largest country in the world. It is bordered by the Atlantic Ocean to the east, and numerous countries in South America to the north (Guyana, Suriname, Venezuela), west (Colombia, Peru, Bolivia, Paraguay, Chile), and south (Uruguay). The climate is tropical. The terrain is diverse, including mountains, forests, arid regions, and over 7,500 kilometers of coastline. Brazil has a population of 183 million, and its gross domestic product in 2004 was US$1.492 trillion, US$8,100 per capita. The minimum wage is the equivalent of US$100 a month. There are tremendous disparities between the richest and the poorest, and a large proportion of the population in Brazil lives below the poverty line. The labor force is mostly in services (66%), agriculture (20%), and industry (14%), and the unemployment rate is estimated at 11%. Brazil is rich in minerals and produces 80% of the oil it needs for its own consumption. Only 5% of the land is used for agriculture. Brazil presently includes 27 states and one federal district grouped in five regions.

With about 92 million children and young people 19 years of age or younger, a large portion of the Brazilian population is between the ages of 14 and 19 years old. According to the recent major educational law (Brasil, 2002), the educational system includes five levels: preschool (not mandatory) for children from 2 months to 5 years old; elementary school (mandatory) from 6 to 14 years old; high school from 15 to 17 years old; and college after this age. There is also a compensatory level that includes students who failed at the regular system and adults who want to continue their education. Preschool, elementary, and high school take place during the day; compensatory education is at night. The school day is 5 hours long for private and public schools, according to the last government determination (Ministry of Education, 2005).

Although 95% of 7-year-old children attend elementary school and 36% graduate from high school, only 11% of the youth attend universities. The Brazilian Institute of Geography and Statistics (Instituto Brasileiro de Geografia e Estatística, 2000) reported high rates of students who were employed, usually full-time, at ages 15 and 16 years old. On average, classes in Brazilian schools have a ratio of 1 teacher per 36 students. No classroom assistants are available to help teachers. Children with special needs can attend special private schools or public regular schools, according to the recent law. When teachers at the regular schools have difficulties in dealing with children thought to have special needs, they receive no support from specialists. This situation, despite the inclusion public policy, is actually another form of exclusion. It only gives the child and his or her family the illusion of full inclusion. Several studies on special education in regular schools (Damião, 2000; Jesus, 2004) raised concerns that children with special needs were not receiving appropriate support to facilitate their learning.

According to the last educational census, Brazil has 210,000 elementary schools (Ministry of Education, 2005), of which 174,894 are private and only 35,200 are public. Among the public schools, only 15,837 offer special education to children with special needs, and only 784 do so in the private schools. This indicates that the majority of children with special needs attend schools in the public system. According to the Ministry of Education report, 51% of those students referred to special services (i.e., referred to a specialist such as a physician or psychologist) in the public and private systems are referred for cognitive or intellectual problems.

Each year, the Ministry of Education conducts an official, countrywide census to create a database of educational information. In 2005, for the first time, information about ethnic differences was included (descendents of Afro-Americans and whites). The preliminary results of this last official educational census (Instituto Nacional de Estudos e Pesquisa Educacionais Anísio Teixeira [National Institute of Educational Studies and Research Anísio Teixeira], 2005) reveals that Brazil has more than 55 million students attending the Basic Educational Level (i.e., preschool and elementary school). There was an increase of 4.35% in the number of students attending preschool, a reduction of 1.4% attending elementary school, and no variation at the high school level. This can be analyzed as a function of different factors, but the dropout rate is still a phenomenon that requires political and professional interventions. The results indicated that 46% considered themselves as *pardo* (descended from Africans and Whites), 41% indicated as White, 10% as African, and 1% from an indigenous background.

Origin, History, and Current Status of School Psychology

The history of school psychology in Brazil has been influenced by the education infrastructure and policies. The profession of psychology appeared in the country in 1962. Nevertheless, psychological knowledge in Brazil was evident prior to this, mostly contained within medical courses at the university. However, at the beginning of the 1960s, some psychological interventions and research were disseminated through preparation programs for elementary teachers, and it became a subject in the curricula of the educational institutions for the preparation of high school teachers.

Due to the medical/clinical model of providing interventions in a clinic setting, services for children were located in private clinical psychology practices, instead of through the school psychologist. This was the result of educational reforms that enhanced the private system and diminished the quality of the public system (Pfromm Netto, 1996; Yazle, 1997). Thus, although psychology is considered a profession in Brazil, school psychology does not have an established position in the educational system.

At the last census of the Federal Council of Psychology (Conselho Federal de Psicologia, 2004), 2,000 psychologists were consulted about their activities. The responses indicated that 55% reported their main activity as individual or group clinical services, 11% were mainly involved in educational activities, and the rest were distributed among other services, such as organizational, consultative, public, and forensic. Among those, 11% worked in educational activities, 41% worked in private offices, and only 10% worked directly in schools. The others were distributed in minor percentages in public organizations, health offices, and universities.

In relation to training, 42% of Brazilian psychologists complete their preparation at the undergraduate level, 49% continue in specialization programs after receiving a professional license (which may be obtained once undergraduate work is completed), 7% have a master's degree, and 2% a doctoral degree. Among those who continue their training and preparation, most are in the clinical area (45%); only 9% are in school psychology. The others are distributed in education, philosophy, organizational studies, and administration.

Infrastructure of School Psychology

The Brazilian Association of School and Educational Psychology, founded in 1990, integrates professionals, researchers, and students interested in school psychology in order to attain recognition of this profession in educational institutions, as well as to stimulate and spread the practice of school psychology

(Associação Brasileira de Psicologia Escolar e Educacional, 2005). According to this association, school psychologists are those professionals who work to improve the learning process in a global perspective (cognitive, emotional, social, and motor) through services offered to persons, groups, families, and organizations. The practice of school psychologists is more directly related to schools, whereas that of educational psychologists is related to teaching and research in this area.

On January 21, 1964, legislation (Law 53.464) defined the professional areas of psychologists as teaching psychology, clinical psychology, school psychology, and organizational or business psychology. School psychology, according to the work of Mello (1980, p. 17), includes "all activities of psychologists that were developed in schools or other related institutions, and which had the major goal of using psychological techniques for promoting the efficiency of teaching in all its dimensions." According to Article 14 of Law 53.464, "it is a privative function of the psychologist to utilize psychological methods and techniques with the following objectives: (a) psychological assessment, (b) professional orientation and selection, (c) psychopedagogic orientation, [and] (d) adjustment problem solution" (quoted in Mello, 1980, p. 121). The Federal Council of Psychology specifies the competencies, actions, and related professional attributes of psychologists. These include conducting research, assessment, and prevention as their school and educational professional responsibilities (Conselho Federal de Psicologia, 1988, 1992a, 1992b, 2000, 2001). Beyond this, psychology professionals are expected to manage organizations, teach psychology at the university, supervise professionals and students, advise different sections and organizations, and provide reports. Two conditions are necessary to practice as a school psychologist in Brazil: completion of a 5-year undergraduate psychology program authorized by the Ministry of Education and (after the implementation of Law 5.766 in 1977) registration in the Federal Council of Psychology (Brasil, 1977).

The Brazilian Association of School and Educational Psychology is also responsible for the country's only journal dedicated to this field. This journal is accredited by the National Commission of Scientific Journals and is available in all the libraries of universities with psychology programs. The National Association of Research and Graduate Psychology Programs has an internal group that is designated to discuss school psychology research and publish books about it (Almeida, 2003; Del Prette, 2003; Guzzo, 1999, 2003; Mitjáns Martínez, 2005; Wechsler, 1996).

Preparation of School Psychologists

There are 195 undergraduate psychology programs in different universities across the country (Associação Brasileira de Ensino em Psicologia, 2005). Because the training guidelines in psychology are directed to a generalist professional and prepare students to work in different fields in psychology, there are no programs responsible for training school psychologists specifically.

The Federal Council of Psychology (Conselho Federal de Psicologia, 2000, 2001) created the professional title of "specialist in psychology" for several areas, including school psychology. This resolution normalizes the title of specialist according to the criteria of a minimum of 500 hours concentration in the area of specialization (80% of the hours from the total amount of general hours of the course) and a minimum of 30% of the hours spent on practical experiences. The title is also conditional on the student's presentation of a monograph related to the area of specialization at the end of the course.

At the master's and doctoral levels, the periods of study are 24 and 48 months, respectively. In addition, students must, at the end of these periods, conclude their master's or doctoral research within a research group led by a research supervisor. The training programs rely primarily on translated literature from other countries. Despite the increasing number of publications, and the Brazilian psychological journals, school psychologists and researchers in the development and learning areas have had difficulties in disseminating knowledge, because only one journal, the *Brazilian Journal of School Psychology* (published by the National Association of School Psychology) is dedicated to this area.

The field of school psychology in Brazil has evolved significantly during the past two decades (Campos & Jucá, 2003; Cruces, 2003, 2005; Gomes, 1999; Guzzo, 1999; Maluf, 1994; Meira & Antunes, 2003a, 2003b; Neves, Almeida, Chaperman, & Batista, 2002; Senna & Almeida, 2005). For instance, school psychology has moved from a clinical model, oriented to individualized attention in relation to learning disabilities and behavioral problems, to a profession that involves diverse work that now includes other forms of interventions that are more preventive and communitarian, as well as group interventions. This does not mean that the traditional and mainstream forms of work have disappeared but that they coexist with new forms. School psychologists work in diverse segments of the school system (e.g., preschools, elementary schools, high schools, and universities) and also in centers for young and special children, and they give assistance in diverse institutions of popular education.

Roles, Functions, and Responsibilities of School Psychologists

School psychologists perform the basic roles and carry out the functions expected of psychology professionals (Mitjáns Martínez, 2003), according to the demands of their varied positions. Most positions require the following activities.

Assessment and diagnosis. One of the mainstream functions of the school psychologist is the assessment of students with learning disabilities, emotional problems, or behavioral problems; these students are generally referred to the school psychologist by teachers, families, or the school. The main goal of this service is to decide how to address the needs of students, who are mainly referred to other specialists or services outside the school, and also to recommend to teachers how they might deal with such students. Generally, this work is provided by psychologists who are members of psychopedagogic services from private clinics or from sections or divisions of the government. They use psychological instruments (Custódio, 1996) or qualitative procedures such as interviews (Machado, 2000, 2003; Neves, 2001; Neves & Machado, 2005). The use of psychological instruments for assessment in different contexts has, recently, been restricted to those instruments and procedures recommended by the National Council of Psychologists. Since 2003, official recommendations have been made about which psychological instruments and procedures can be used for assessment in Brazil (Conselho Federal de Psicologia, Resolution No. 002/2003). The Federal Council has authorized 64 tests for use in Brazil: 14 for intelligence and creativity, 12 for personality, 9 for emotional dimensions and stress, and 30 for different dimensions and uses, such as attention, self-concept, parental and family, driving skills, learning skills, development scales, and so on (Sistema de Avaliação de Testes Psicológicos [Assessment System for Psychological Tests], 2005). This situation shows the diverse uses of research in the assessment area. There is still no policy requiring the formal authorization of tests, despite the great advances in this area after the national movement for psychological assessment. There is no research examining the tests commonly used to assess different dimensions in school contexts. Noronha (1999) conducted a study with 214 psychologists from the São Paulo region to identify the most used test in the professional practice and the context of assessment. The participants indicated, without naming them, that personality tests were the most commonly used instruments and the context was a private office in a clinical setting.

Orientation or counseling. Most psychologists in schools use orientation or counseling, a procedure that refers to an individual or group discussion on a specific theme. There are directive and nondirective discussions. Topics commonly addressed include sexual orientation, discipline or school rules, interpersonal relationships, and various others according to the needs identified by teachers or parents. This is an intervention model that also can be used to collect information about the student's and the family's needs.

Interventions. The school psychologist collaborates with the elaboration, coordination, and implementation of several educational programs, especially those related to the prevention of drug abuse, violence, and early pregnancy. The service of the school psychologist as a member of the school team is in the process of consolidation, but great efforts are needed to regularly include the presence of this professional in the school system.

Professional education. School psychologists participate in workshops, courses, or other activities to inform teachers and parents, especially about the relationship of psychology and education and developmental psychology. Others work as professors in universities, preparing students to be psychologists.

Consulting. Some professionals are assessors for specific problems in educational settings and are also involved with public policy assessment or formulation.

Research. Developing research is rarely emphasized among school psychologists. Nevertheless, some school psychologists carry out important studies targeted to obtain information to assess the effects of an intervention. Most research is conducted by school psychologists at university centers. The school psychology group in the National Association of Research and Graduate Programs in Psychology has, in the past decade, published books that emphasize intervention and preparation among school psychologists (Almeida, 2003; Del Prette, 2003; Guzzo, 1999; Mitjáns Martínez, 2005; Novaes & Brito, 1996; Weschler, 1996).

Current Issues Impacting School Psychology

School psychologists and the field of school psychology face multiple challenges in Brazil. One challenge for school psychologists is to promote social equality in the education of children in Brazil. Given numerous social and political influences, this is a daunting task. Another challenge is to have the profession of school psychology more fully recognized in the educational context.

The following is a set of actions, some already initiated, that are needed to face the challenges and difficulties related to the field of school psychology: (a) provide university programs that prepare psychologists with national guidelines that include a description of school psychology; (b) improve research in school psychology by encouraging further discussions and exchange with national and international colleagues; (c) disseminate information about the field of school psychology within general associations, such as the federal and regional councils of psychology, scientific associations, such as the Brazilian Association of School Psychology and the National Association of Research and Graduate Programs of Psychology, and governmental sections, such as the Educational Secretary and Ministry; and (d) use professional organizations to emphasize the importance of the profession of school psychology.

Many challenges face the development of school psychology in Brazil, especially because many challenges concerning the organization of the educational system face Brazilian society. Despite the enormous difficulties in dealing with the consequences of actions by this political system, there is an optimistic perspective inside some universities regarding the future of school psychology.

Nevertheless, the future of school psychology will be determined by the training model constructed inside the universities, under the new guidelines for the basic preparation of psychologists in this context. Besides this, as soon as psychologists assume the role of improving social comprehension in schools and communities, school psychologists will be empowered to take responsibility in ensuring children's rights and to implement preventive models of intervention. Only then will some of the big challenges—consolidating the profession and transforming reality—be met.

References

Almeida, S. F. C. de. (Ed.). (2003). *Psicologia escolar: Ética e competências na formação e atuação profissional* [School psychology: Ethics and competencies in formation and professional practice]. Campinas: Alínea.

Associação Brasileira de Ensino em Psicologia. (2005). *Cursos de graduação em psicologia no Brasil* [Undergraduate psychology courses in Brazil]. Available: http://www.abepsi.org.br/abepsi/Curso Graduacao.aspx

Associação Brasileira de Psicologia Escolar e Educacional. (2005). *Associação Brasileira de Psicologia Escolar e Educacional* [Brazilian Association of School and Educational Psychology (Home page)]. Available: http://www.abrapee .psc.br

Brasil. (1977). *Decreto n°79.822 de 17 de junho de 1977* [Decree number 79.822, June 17, 1977]. Available: http://www.abepsi.org.br/abepsi/CursoGrad uacao.aspx

Brasil. (2002). Lei 9.394 de 20 de dezembro de 1996 [Law 9.394, December 20, 1996]. In R. S. L. Guzzo (Ed.), *Psicologia escolar: LDB e educação hoje* (2nd ed., pp. 131–189). Campinas: Alínea.

Campos, H. R., & Jucá, M. R. B. (2003). O psicólogo na escola: Avaliação da formação à luz das demandas do mercado [The psychologist at school: Evaluation of training in light of the market's needs]. In S. F. C. de Almeida (Ed.), *Ética e competências na formação e atuação profissional* (pp. 37–56). Campinas: Alínea.

Conselho Federal de Psicologia. (Ed.). (1988). *Quem é o psicólogo brasileiro?* [Who is the Brazilian psychologist?]. São Paulo: Edicon.

Conselho Federal de Psicologia. (1992a). *Atribuições profissionais do psicólogo no Brasil* [Professional attributions for the psychologist in Brazil]. Available: http://www.pol.org.br/legislacao/pdf/atr_prof_psicologo.pdf

Conselho Federal de Psicologia. (Ed.). (1992b). *Psicólogo brasileiro: Construção de novos espaços* [Brazilian psychologist: Building new spaces]. Campinas: Átomo.

Conselho Federal de Psicologia. (Ed.). (1994). *Psicólogo brasileiro: Práticas emergentes e desafios para a formação* (2ª ed.) [Brazilian psychologist: Emerging practices and challenges for formation (2nd ed.)]. São Paulo: Casa do Psicólogo.

Conselho Federal de Psicologia. (2000). *Resolução CFP N° 014/00* [CFP Resolution No. 014/00]. Available: http://www.pol.org.br/legislacao/pdf/resolucao2000_14.pdf

Conselho Federal de Psicologia. (2001). *Resolução CFP N° 02/01* [CFP Resolution No. 02/01]. Available: http://www.pol.org.br/legislacao/pdf/resolucao2001_2.pdf

Conselho Federal de Psicologia. (2004). *Pesquisa de opinião com psicólogos inscritos no Conselho Federal de Psicologia* [Survey of psychologists registered with the Federal Council of Psychology]. Available: http://www.pol.org.br/publicacoes/pdf/Pesquisa_IBOPE.pdf

Cruces, A. V. V. (2003). Psicologia e educação: Nossa história e nossa realidade [Psychology and education: Our history and our reality]. In S. F. C. de Almeida (Ed.), *Ética e competências na formação e atuação profissional* (pp. 17–36). Campinas: Alínea.

Cruces, A. V. V. (2005). Práticas emergentes em psicologia escolar [Emerging practices in school psychology]. In A. Mitjáns Martínez (Ed.), *Psicologia escolar e compromisso social: Novos discursos, novas práticas* (pp. 47–66). Campinas: Alínea.

Custódio, E. M. (1996). Avaliação das dificuldades de aprendizagem: Novas perspectivas para a avaliação educacional [Learning disabilities assessment: New perspectives for educational evaluation].

In S. M. Weschler (Ed.), *Psicologia escolar: Pesquisa, formação e prática* (pp. 157–176). Campinas: Alínea.

Damião, C. R. T. (2000). *Educação especial: Visão de professores e psicólogos* [Special education: Teachers' and psychologists' vision]. Unpublished master's dissertation, Pontifícia Universidade Católica de Campinas, Campinas, Brazil.

Del Prette, Z. A. P. (Ed.). (2003). *Psicologia escolar e educacional: Saúde e qualidade de vida* (2ª ed.) [School and educational psychology: Health and quality of life (2nd ed.)]. Campinas: Alínea.

Gomes, V. L. T. (1999). A formação do psicólogo e os impasses entre a teoria e a prática [The psychologist formation and the impasses between theory and practice]. In R. S. L. Guzzo (Ed.), *Psicologia escolar: Lei de Diretrizes e Bases e educação hoje* (pp. 49–76). Campinas: Alínea.

Guzzo, R. S. L. (Ed.). (1999). *Psicologia escolar:* Lei de Diretrizes e Bases *e educação hoje* [School psychology: *Law of Guidelines and Bases* and education today]. Campinas: Alínea.

Guzzo, R. S. L. (2003). Saúde psicológica, sucesso escolar e eficácia da escola: Desafios do novo milênio para a psicologia escolar [Psychological health, school success and school efficacy: Challenges of the new millennium to school psychology]. In Z. A. P. Del Prette (Ed.), *Psicologia escolar e educacional, saúde e qualidade de vida* (pp. 25–42). Campinas: Alínea.

Instituto Brasileiro de Geografia e Estatística. (2000). *Censo Demográfico 2000* [Demographic Census 2000]. Rio de Janeiro: Author.

Instituto Brasileiro de Geografia e Estatística. (2005). *Brasil em síntese* [Brazil in synthesis]. Available: http://www.ibge.gov.br/brasil_em_sintese/default.htm

Instituto Nacional de Estudos e Pesquisa Educacionais Anísio Teixeira. (2005). *Resultados preliminares do Censo Educacional de 2005* [Preliminary results from the Educational Census of 2005]. Available: http://www.inep.gov.br/basica/censo/default.asp

Jesus, D. M. (2004). Atuando em contexto: O processo de avaliação em uma perspectiva inclusiva [Acting in context: The assessment process in an inclusion perspective]. *Psicologia & Sociedade, 16*(1), 37–49.

Machado, A. M. (2000). Avaliação psicológica na educação: Mudanças necessárias [Psychological assessment in education: Needed changes]. In E. Tanimachi, M. Proença, & M. Rocha (Eds.), *Psicologia e educação: Desafios teórico-práticos* (pp. 143–166). São Paulo: Casa do Psicólogo.

Machado, A. M. (2003). O psicólogo trabalhando com a escola: Intervenção ao serviço de quê? [The psychologist working with the school: Intervention in service of what?]. In M. E. M. Meira & M. A. M. Antunes (Eds.), *Psicologia escolar: Práticas críticas* (pp. 63–85). São Paulo: Casa do Psicólogo.

Maluf, M. R. (1994). Formação e atuação do psicólogo na educação: Dinâmica de transformação [Formation and practice of psychology in education: Transformation dynamic]. In Conselho Federal de Psicologia (Ed.), *Psicólogo brasileiro: Práticas emergentes e desafios para a formação* (pp. 157–200). São Paulo: Casa do Psicólogo.

Meira, M. E. M., & Antunes, M. A. M. (Eds.). (2003a). *Psicologia escolar: Práticas críticas* [School psychology: Critical practices]. São Paulo: Casa do Psicólogo.

Meira, M. E. M., & Antunes, M. A. M. (Eds.). (2003b). *Psicologia escolar: Teorias críticas* [School psychology: Critical theories]. São Paulo: Casa do Psicólogo.

Mello, S. L. De. (1980). *Psicologia e profissão em São Paulo* (4ª ed.) [Psychology and profession in São Paulo (4th ed.)]. São Paulo: Ática.

Ministry of Education. (2005). *Números da educação especial no Brasil* [Special education numbers in Brazil]. Available: http://portal.mec.gov.br/seesp/index.php?option=content&task=view&id=62&Itemid=191

Mitjáns Martínez, A. (2003). O psicólogo na construção da proposta pedagógica da escola: Áreas de atuação e desafios para a formação [The psychologist in the building of a school pedagogical plan: Areas of practice and challenges to formation]. In S. F. C. de Almeida (Ed.), *Psicologia escolar: Ética e competências na formação e atuação profissional* (pp. 105–124). Campinas: Alínea.

Mitjáns Martínez, A. (Ed.). (2005). *Psicologia escolar e compromisso social: Novos discursos, novas práticas* [School psychology and social commitment: New discourses and new practices]. Campinas: Alínea.

Neves, M. B., Almeida, S. F., Chaperman, M., & Batista, B. P. (2002). Formação e atuação em psicologia escolar: Análise das modalidades de comunicação nos Congressos Nacionais de Psicologia Escolar e Educacional [Formation and practice in school psychology: Analysis of papers at the National Conferences of Educational and School Psychology]. *Psicologia: Ciência e Profissão, 22*(2), 2–11.

Neves, M. M. B., & Machado, A. C. A. (2005). Psicologia escolar e educação inclusiva: Novas práticas de atendimento às queixas escolares [School psychology and inclusive education: New practices in attending to school complaints]. In A. Mitjáns Martínez (Ed.), *Psicologia escolar e compromisso social: Novos discursos, novas práticas.* Campinas: Alínea.

Neves, M. M. B. da J. (2001). *A atuação da psicologia nas equipes de atendimento psicopedagógico da rede pública de ensino do Distrito Federal* [The practice of psychology in psychopedagogical intervention teams of the Federal District's public education system]. Unpublished doctoral thesis, Universidade de Brasília, Brazil.

Noronha, A. P. (1999). *Avaliação psicológica segundo psicólogos: Usos e problemas com ênfase nos testes* [Psychological assessment by psychologists: Uses and problems referring to the tests]. Unpublished doctoral thesis, Pontifical Catholic University of Campinas.

Novaes, M. H., & Brito, M. R. F. (Eds.). (1996). *Psicologia na educação: Integração entre a graduação e a pós e subsídios à prática pedagógica* [Psychology in education: Integration between undergraduation and graduation, and subsidies to pedagogical practice]. Rio de Janeiro: Associação Nacional de Pesquisa e Pós-graduação em Psicologia.

Pfromm Netto, S. (1996). As origens e o desenvolvimento da psicologia escolar [The origins and the development of school psychology]. In S. M. Wechsler (Ed.), *Psicologia escolar: Pesquisa, formação e prática.* Campinas: Alínea.

Senna, S. R. M., & Almeida, S. F. C. (2005). Formação e atuação do psicólogo na rede pública de ensino do Distrito Federal [Formation and practice of the psychologist in the Distrito Federal's public education system]. In A. Mitjáns Martínez (Ed.), *Psicologia escolar e compromisso social: Novos discursos, novas práticas* (pp. 199–230). Campinas: Alínea.

Sistema de Avaliação de Testes Psicológicos. (2005). *Relação de testes aprovados pelo Conselho Federal de Psicologia* [Tests approved by the Federal Council of Psychology]. Available: http://www .pol.org.br/satepsi/sistema/pagina/lista1pb.cfm

Wechsler, S. M. (Ed.). (1996). *Psicologia escolar: Pesquisa, formação e prática* [School psychology: Research, formation, and practice]. Campinas: Alínea.

Yazle, E. G. (1997). Atuação do psicólogo escolar: Alguns dados históricos [School psychologist practice: Some historical data]. In B. B. Cunha (Ed.), *Psicologia na escola: Um pouco de história e algumas histórias*. São Paulo: Arte e Ciência.

5

School Psychology in Canada

Donald H. Saklofske

Vicki L. Schwean

Gina L. Harrison

Juanita Mureika

Context of School Psychology

Canada is a country with almost 33 million people, occupying the world's third largest landmass (9,984,670 square kilometres), with the United States along its entire southern border and the Atlantic, Pacific, and Arctic Oceans to the east, west, and north, respectively. The landscape of Canada is varied and composed of mountains, prairies, desert, arctic tundra, glaciers, valleys, foothills, rivers, and lakes. It contains 10 provinces and 3 territories. Canada became a self-governing dominion in 1867, while retaining ties to the British crown. Canada maintains a system of government based on English common law except in

Quebec, where the civil law system is based on French law. Economically and technologically, Canada has developed in parallel with the United States. Health care, education, and language issues dominate the current political and social challenges. Most Canadians trace their lineage to British (28%), French (23%), other European (15%), and Aboriginal or Indigenous (2%) descent (Canadian Tourism Commission, 2004). The official languages of Canada are English and French, with 59% of the population speaking English and 23% speaking French. A number of native (aboriginal) languages are spoken throughout the country (Central Intelligence Agency, n.d.; Statistics Canada, 2001).

AUTHORS' NOTE: The authors would like to thank Caitlin McCleave, graduate student intern from Mt. St. Vincent's University school psychology program, for her assistance in researching material for this chapter.

Annual economic growth is projected at 3%. The gross domestic product is US$774 billion dollars. The primary sectors are service (74%), manufacturing (15%), construction (5%), and agricultural (3%). The major products and industries consist of processed and unprocessed minerals, food products, wood and paper products, transportation equipment, chemicals, fish products, petroleum, and natural gas (Canadian Tourism Commission, 2004). According to the Organisation for Economic Cooperation and Development, in 1999, Canada ranked first among G-7 countries (i.e., Britain, Canada, France, Germany, Italy, Japan, and the United States) with respect to the percentage of funding allocated to education. In 2001, Canada spent 15% of its total expenditure on education (Canadian Education Statistics Council, 2003).

Approximately 5 million children currently attend public schools in Canada (Communications Canada, Public Works & Government Services Canada, 2002). Due to a recent decline in birth rates, the population of children ages 5 to 13 is expected to drop by 14% between 2001 and 2011. A corresponding drop is expected in the population ages 14 to 18 years between 2006 and 2016. As a result, all jurisdictions will likely face some periods of decline in school-age children between 2001 and 2026, although the magnitude and timing of decline will vary considerably, due to a higher birth rate among aboriginal communities and national and international migration patterns. Some areas of Canada (e.g., British Columbia and Ontario) could stabilise their school-age population to reflect the enrolment rates in 1991. Other Canadian provinces (e.g., the Atlantic provinces) could have lower school-age populations than the enrolment rates during 1991 (Canadian Education Statistics Council, 2003). The home environment for children in the Canadian school system is also changing. In 2001, children were less likely to live in two-parent homes than children in 1991. Similarly, in 2001, there were higher proportions of children living in homes where one or both parents worked outside of the home than in 1991 (Canadian Education Statistics Council, 2003).

Since 1990, there has been an influx of immigrants to Canada that has profoundly impacted the ethnic, linguistic, and cultural climate of Canadian schools. Canada now boasts more than 200 different ethnic origins, as reflected in the 2001 census, with visible minorities comprising more than 13% of the population. This is particularly evident in major metropolitan areas such as Toronto, Calgary, and Vancouver (Canadian Education Statistics Council, 2003).

Canada does not have a federal education system. The Constitution granted the responsibility for education to each province and territory. Thus, each system represents the particular cultural, regional, and historical climate. An elected minister in each province is responsible to set standards, determine curricula, and designate educational grants (Canadian Education Statistics Council, 2003). By law, children are required to attend school from the age of 6 or 7 years until the age of 15 or 16. In most jurisdictions, 95% of 5-year-olds were attending school in 2000–2001 (Canadian Education Statistics Council, 2003). Private or separate schools are available as alternatives to the public school system. In 1995, Roman Catholic separate schools attracted approximately one fourth of the public school system enrolment. Independent schools offer a variety of religious, language, and academic curriculum options and service a quarter of a million students (Communications Canada, Public Works & Government Services Canada, 2002).

From 1995 to 2000, the secondary school graduation rates rose from 76% to 78%. Graduation rates for females (83%) are higher than graduation rates for males (73%). The number of students who withdrew from school prior to graduating fell from 18% in 1991 to 12% in 1999. The higher the parental education level, the more likely a student will graduate from high school (Canadian Education Statistics Council, 2003).

Origin, History, and Current Status of School Psychology

It has been suggested that school psychology is a broad form of child psychology, because it encompasses areas of family, education, development, and behaviour as they appear in all aspects of a child's life. However, having roots in two disciplines, education and psychology, as well as the variability of resources and needs among the provinces and territories, has posed challenges to the development of school psychology as an autonomous discipline. School psychology in Canada traces its roots to the first decade of the 20th century. Initially, psychologists working with school-age children performed many of the tasks now associated with school psychologists, although they were not employed in the schools. For example, in the 1920s, specialists in Manitoba were employed to test and conduct educational measurements. In the 1940s, mental health professionals affiliated with Winnipeg, Manitoba's Health Department, the school board, and child guidance centres worked in collaboration to address the needs of students (Oakland, Faulkner, & Annan, 2002).

From the 1950s to the 1970s, psychologists were found more frequently working in the schools, although often from a mental health or clinical perspective. In Alberta, psychologists were based in central offices and viewed as itinerant resources to the school system (Janzen & Carter, 2001). Often, roles were shared with guidance counsellors, teachers, or others within the educational system, because school psychology training programs were not yet formalised (Saklofske et al., 2000). During the 1970s, school psychology became more widely recognised as a specialised area of psychology. Graduate training programs were established in Canadian universities, at the doctoral level at the Ontario

Institute for Studies in Education, and at the master's level in the educational psychology departments at Memorial University, the University of Manitoba, the Universities of Alberta in Edmonton and Calgary, and McGill University. The passage of Public Law 94-142 in the United States in 1976 indirectly influenced educational practices in Canada. Hence, with wider training opportunities available and increasing demand for identification of students with exceptional learning needs, school psychologists became more visible within school systems, particularly in metropolitan regions, primarily filling a role of testing students to determine eligibility for placement and services in special classes.

It was not until the 1980s, however, that Canadian school psychologists began to firmly establish their role at the provincial and national levels, both professionally and in the education system (Oakland et al., 2002). The passage of the Canadian Human Rights Act in 1977 and the Canadian Charter of Rights and Freedoms in 1982 led to more inclusive practices in schools, more special classes and services for students, and, as a result, more need to determine eligibility for services and special class placement. There was also a need for teacher support in teaching students with behavioural, emotional, and learning differences, who were now being included in the regular school system.

At a professional level, some provincial regulatory organisations outlined the registration requirements for school psychologists within the respective provinces (e.g., Alberta, Nova Scotia). Similarly, school psychology interest groups began to be formed as adjuncts to some provincial psychological associations (e.g., British Columbia, Alberta, Saskatchewan, Manitoba, and New Brunswick). The Canadian Association of School Psychologists was formed in the early 1980s to address the needs, concerns, and interests of Canadian school psychologists and advocate for the goals of school psychologists on both national and international levels.

These goals continue to be achieved through the publication of the *Canadian Journal of School Psychology* and a joint newsletter in collaboration with the Psychologists in Education section of the Canadian Psychological Association; the sponsoring of workshops, conferences, and continuing education activities; and maintaining a working relationship with both provincial and national psychology organisations.

In recent years, the Canadian Psychological Association has actively promoted school psychology as a unique and important form of psychological practice though the development of documents, position papers, and policy documents supporting the role of psychologists in Canadian schools (e.g., Canadian Psychological Association, 2004; French & Mureika, 2002). In 2004, the Canadian Psychological Association approved specific procedures for accrediting programs in school psychology and currently is revising a document adopted from New Brunswick defining professional practice guidelines to reflect national practice (New Brunswick Department of Education, 2001).

Although there is no school psychology specialty designation described by regulatory bodies in Canada, the term *school psychologist* is most often used to describe those working in the profession. In Newfoundland and Labrador, perhaps as a result of strong ties to the United Kingdom, authorities continue to use the title "educational psychologist" (Martin, 2001). In some provinces, for example, Nova Scotia and Newfoundland, school psychologists are also licenced teachers; however, this requirement is not the norm in Canada. As well, in some provinces, school psychologists must be licenced with their regulatory body as psychologists (e.g., New Brunswick, Saskatchewan, Alberta), while in other provinces, government employees, including school psychologists, are exempted under the provincial licencing acts (e.g., Manitoba). There is wide variability in the credentialing of psychologists across the provinces and territories of Canada. Current and specific information related to the practice of psychology in each of the provinces and territories

can be found on the Web site of the Canadian Psychological Association (www.cpa.ca).

The ratio of students to school psychologists varies widely across the country and within individual provinces. For example, in some areas of Ontario, the ratio of psychologists to students is as low as 1 to 1,700 and as high as 1 to 12,000 (Carney, 2001). In several provinces, including Newfoundland, Nova Scotia, New Brunswick, and Saskatchewan, it is not uncommon for one school psychologist to service between 3,000 and 5,000 students (Hann, 2001; Martin, 2001; Mureika, 2001; Saklofske & Grainger, 2001). The smallest ratio of school psychologists to students (1:1,600) was reported in Manitoba (Bartell, 2001).

Both the urban and rural environments in which school psychologists work present certain advantages and disadvantages. Saklofske and Grainger (2001) explained that within Saskatchewan, cities offer more comprehensive programs for students with special needs and offer greater access to special services; however, the psychologists serve a greater number of students. In some smaller cities and towns, there are fewer students per school psychologist; however, commuting distances among schools in these more rural areas are much greater.

In some rural areas of Canada, there are significant shortages of school psychologists (Bartell, 2001; Blakely & Wells, 2001). In addition, some aboriginal communities are reported to be underserved. Within the next 10 years, the demand for school psychology services can be expected to continue to exceed the supply in some provinces (Bartell, 2001). As well, it can be challenging to recruit and retain psychologists in some provinces, due to extensive travel requirements, high union and professional fees, heavy caseloads, and scarce professional development opportunities.

Salaries for school psychologists vary across the provinces; however, most public service positions are competitive with other professionals at the same education and experience levels (e.g., teachers, speech/language pathologists) in the same province. The average hourly wage for public service psychologists in Canada is estimated at $27.12 Canadian dollars (Can$), in contrast to the average hourly rate over all professions of Can$16.91 (Government of Canada, 2003). By way of comparison, in British Columbia, the pay scale for school psychologists, with a minimum master's degree, is on par with teachers and ranges from about Can$42,000 to Can$68,000 per year after 10 years experience. On the east coast, New Brunswick school psychologists with a master's or doctoral degree working under supervision for licencing requirements (Psychometrist III) may start at about Can$40,000, whereas a Psychologist II (supervisory position) currently earns up to Can$62,000 per year. Much higher salaries are paid in larger urban centres such as Toronto, where psychologists with a master's degree may earn between Can$46,000 and Can$77,000 and psychologists with a doctoral degree and 10 or more years experience may earn more than Can$80,000.

At present, the role of the school psychologist in Canada is slowly evolving from one of primarily testing and placement of students with special needs to a broader role of consultant to teachers to support the needs of all students in school (Mureika, Falconer, & Howard, 2004). Although this role change for school psychologists was suggested more than a decade ago (Janzen, Paterson, & Paterson, 1993), it remains a point of contention and struggle among school psychologists, their employers, and stakeholder groups, such as parents, physicians, and disability groups, and so the progression has been slow but gradual. It will be interesting to watch how the profession develops in the next decade, given the challenges it is sure to face.

Infrastructure of School Psychology

The numerous organisations at both the national and provincial levels serving the interests of school psychology attest to the presence of a strong professional identity in Canada. At the national level, the Canadian Association of School Psychologists, founded just over 20 years ago, represents the national "voice" of school psychologists. The Canadian Association of School Psychologists' aims include facilitating communication between associations at the provincial and territorial levels, advocacy and advancement of the profession of school psychology, and serving as a source of information on the delivery of psychology in the schools to members and the general public. Members are employed or trained as school psychologists, university faculty, and students training to become school psychologists. Likewise, the Canadian Psychological Association has a section for psychologists in education, and many hold dual membership with the Canadian Association of School Psychologists.

There are strong provincial organisations that are aimed at connecting professionals, advancing the practice of psychology in the schools, and serving as a united voice in the advancement of the profession by communicating with provincial psychology regulatory bodies and departments of education. Most of the organisations have annual conferences or meetings affording participants opportunities for professional development and collegiality. A difference between regions is the presence of organisations specific to school psychology in some cases, special sections within the broader provincial psychological association in other regions, or affiliation with the general provincial psychological association alone in others. The varying degrees of specificity, however, do not reflect professional interest or commitment; rather, these differences reflect more the vast physical geography of Canada, the heterogeneity of instructional contexts (e.g., from small, multiage remote schools in the north, to large, multiracial urban classrooms in Canadian cities), and the diversity in the population of students and, thus, school psychologists represented therein. Moreover, because the general practice of psychology, and school psychology in particular, is governed from the provincial levels by ministries of health or education, there is considerable variability in the requirements for licensure impacting professional affiliation. Indeed, the activities within the organisations and the services afforded to members and the general public can be quite diverse.

For example, the British Columbia Association of School Psychologists is the only provincial organisation that provides certification for school psychologists. British Columbia Association of School Psychologists members are "certified" school psychologists and must pass stringent professional training criteria that parallel the standards set forth by the National Association of School Psychologists in the United States, including an acceptable score on the school psychology exam and required practicum hours working under the supervision of a school psychologist (Benson, 2001). Certification, however, reflects a standard of practice in school psychology, and the association does not have regulatory control over its members. Other provincial organisations specific to school psychology are the Saskatchewan Educational Psychology Association (the title "educational psychologist" is used for "school psychologist" in Saskatchewan, as it also is in Newfoundland), the Manitoba Association of School Psychologists, the Quebec Association of School Psychologists, and the New Brunswick Association of Psychologists and Psychometrists in the Schools.

In other provinces, school psychologists may be affiliated with special sections within broader provincial psychological associations. For example, Ontario school psychologists are represented by the Section of Psychologists in Education of the Ontario Psychological Association, as well as the Association of Chief Psychologists with Ontario School Boards (Carney, 2001). Similarly, the Association of Psychologists of Nova Scotia has a school psychology committee serving the interests of school psychologists in that province. Finally, the Psychologists' Association of Alberta, the Psychological Association of Prince Edward Island, and the Association of Newfoundland Psychologists provide school psychologists in those provinces with professional affiliation with psychology generally.

Within the past 10 years, an evolution has occurred in the training and standards associated with the practice of psychology in provincial and territorial schools. As a result, in many regions of Canada (i.e., Alberta, Saskatchewan, Ontario, Quebec, New Brunswick, Northwest Territories, Prince Edward Island, and Newfoundland), school psychological services are provided by "psychologists" or "psychological associates," registered at either the master's or doctoral level with the provincial college of psychologists charged with regulating the practice and licencing of psychological professionals. These regulations are set forth under the mandates of the different provincial ministries of health. A driving force behind the regulation of the profession involves the school psychologists' critical practices of assessment, identification, and diagnosis of disorders affecting learning and instruction. The recognition of school psychologists as "psychological" professionals serves to regulate who can provide such diagnostic services and who is qualified to communicate a diagnosis. For example, in Ontario, the act of reporting a diagnosis, including that of a learning disability, is a "controlled act" undertaken only by those professionals licenced by the Ontario Psychological Association (Carney, 2001). Saskatchewan also recognises "Authorised Practice," where only persons meeting the standards set forth by the Saskatchewan College of Psychologists may interpret assessment information and communicate a diagnosis (Saklofske & Grainger, 2001). In fact, in most cases, the use of the title "psychologist" is restricted only to professionals registered with the provincial psychological licencing boards.

In other provinces, school psychologists are exempt from registration with the provincial psychological licencing boards, but they must meet criteria set forth by their respective ministries of education. For example, in British

Columbia, school psychologists are exempt from registering with the British Columbia College of Psychologists as long as they are employed by a school district. The ministry of education sets its own standards for what qualifications school psychologists must possess, but they do not certify school psychologists. As previously mentioned, the British Columbia Association of School Psychologists provides certification; however, whether certification is a requirement of employment is left to the discretion of individual school districts across the province. Nevertheless, the British Columbia College of Psychologists recommends that school psychologists meet the standards for registration either as psychological associates (master's-level preparation) or psychologists (doctoral level). This is a requirement if school psychologists are contracting out their services or are working in private practice; namely, if they are not employed by a school district. Alternatively, Manitoba has a unique position in Canada. It is the only province where the certification of school psychologists occurs at the provincial ministry of education level (the Manitoba Education and Training Department). According to Bartell (2001), the standards for certification are high in that province, with provisional certification being awarded first, followed by full certification after a period of supervised practice within the schools.

The regulation of the "psychological" practice of assessment, identification, and diagnosis in the schools has limited who can conduct school psychological work and recognises the unique contribution of school psychologists beyond educational practitioners such as the classroom or special education teachers. However, Blakely and Wells (2001) recently described how such regulation in the Northwest Territories has served to significantly restrict the delivery of school psychological services in that region. These restrictions are mainly due to the fact that all psychologists registered in that region are trained according to standards for clinical psychology. There are no declared competencies or specialty

titles. As a result, psychologists may not have the specialised skills of a school psychologist, and schools do not hire their own school psychologists. As a result, school psychology activities may be undertaken by other school professionals such as classroom teachers and special education teachers. This is one reason why the professional organisations within the provinces serve an integral role in communicating to regulatory bodies about the special training and skills school psychologists, as opposed to clinical psychologists, possess.

Across the country, all Canadian provinces have adopted a policy of inclusion in the education of students with special educational needs (Hutchinson, 2002). Central to this policy is the social notion of inclusion in every aspect of life (including education) for all persons. The inclusion philosophy parallels similar movements in the United States and reflects the notions of equality and social justice as described in Canada's Charter of Rights and Freedoms. As a result, all children and youth in Canadian schools are, for the most part, educated in the general classroom with varying degrees of supports, special services, and specialised contexts for students with exceptionalities, depending on provincial educational mandates and individual students' needs.

Access to specialised educational resources within schools across the country, however, is invariably tied to provincial educational funding allocations. The onus rests, for the most part, on schools to gain access to these resources through the identification (i.e., diagnosis) of students with exceptional needs. The role of the school psychologist as diagnostician has therefore increased in many provinces. However, Mureika (2001) has noted the situation in New Brunswick, where there is increased demand for school psychological services, but the number of school psychologists has not increased. Ironically, it has been the greater emphasis on identification and assessment of students with special educational needs within an inclusive context that has prompted many school psychologists across the country to advocate for the expanded role of the school psychologist from mere assessor to collaborative consultant within a problem identification framework. Central to this expanded role is the early screening for learning and behaviour difficulties, prereferral intervention, and collaborative consultation through multidisciplinary teams. All of these activities are endorsed by the National Association of School Psychologists in the United States and similarly endorsed by the national and provincial school psychology organisations across Canada. As such, Canadian school psychologists are more likely today than in the past to assist, in varying degrees, in the development, implementation, and monitoring of individualised educational programs for students with exceptional needs. Indeed, as school psychologists continue to exercise their professional expertise in psychological assessment and diagnosis and students' educational outcomes within inclusive settings are inextricably linked to the efficacy of these diagnostic activities, there are greater opportunities today for situating assessment within collaborative, solution-focused, strength-based, multidisciplinary models of service delivery.

In spite of its small population relative to the United States, Canada is fortunate to have some outstanding national journals of interest to school psychologists. In particular, the peer-reviewed *Canadian Journal of School Psychology* publishes current research of interest to school psychologists as well as articles reflecting current best practices in the profession. *Exceptionality Education Canada* also provides peer-reviewed research and current educational practices within the context of Canadian special education. Other professional journals that may publish articles of interest and relevance to school psychologists include the *Canadian Journal of Behavioural Science,* the *McGill Journal of Education,* and the *Canadian Journal of Education.* As previously mentioned, the various provincial school psychology organisations disseminate their own newsletters to their members, and the Canadian Association of School Psychologists and the Canadian Psychological Association publish a joint newsletter on a more casual basis.

Preparation of School Psychologists

There are relatively few programs in Canada that prepare school psychologists (Saklofske, 1996). Currently, there are only five programs granting a Ph.D. in school psychology (McGill University, Ontario Institute for Studies in Education, University of Alberta, University of Calgary, University of British Columbia), and only the first two of these programs are accredited with the American Psychological Association. The Canadian Psychological Association passed accreditation standards for Ph.D. programs in school psychology in June 2004, and it is expected that the future accreditation applications by Canadian programs will be directed to the Canadian Psychological Association. In addition to these five programs (which also grant master's degrees), three additional programs offer programs that lead to a master's degree in school psychology (Mount Saint Vincent University, University of Manitoba, University of Saskatchewan). We encourage readers to visit the Canadian Psychological Association Web site to read further on the accreditation criteria for school psychology programs as well as descriptions relating to the core competencies required of all psychologists.

It is difficult to report on the number of school psychology students who are admitted into, or graduate from, existing Canadian school psychology programs on an annual basis, as virtually all existing Canadian school psychology programs vary their admittance rates annually. Further, it is important to note that the specific degrees and professional credentials required to become a school psychologist in Canada vary from province to province. For example, the requirement for certification as a psychologist in several provinces is master's-level preparation (e.g., in Alberta, Saskatchewan, Manitoba). In other provinces, doctoral-level preparation is required (e.g., British Columbia). Further, in some provinces, a degree in education is either preferred, or alternatively, considered necessary to work in schools.

Roles, Functions, and Responsibilities of School Psychologists

School psychologists work in schools and educational institutions (e.g., technical institutions, universities), but it is increasingly more common to see them employed in other settings (e.g., private practice, hospitals, industry) in Canada (Saklofske & Janzen, 1993). The past decade has witnessed slow but obvious changes to the traditional roles and practices of school psychologists. Fagan (1996) suggests that present-day roles and functions of Canadian school psychologists have been shaped by many different forces, including provincial and national education and psychology standards, school district demands, consumer response to the services provided, and the availability of training programs. Further, Canada is a geographically, culturally, and linguistically diverse country, which creates pressures for contextually sensitive and relevant school psychology services that focus on the promotion of wellness as well as addressing the problems of children, educators, and parents, and the larger community. Undoubtedly, the diversified training of school psychologists will benefit the profession of psychology as a whole, as well as promote the specialty of school psychology.

Studies of the practices of Canadian school psychologists (e.g., Dumont, 1989; Kaufman & Smith, 1998; Neudorf, 1989) suggest relative commonality. More traditional roles reflecting psychological and psychoeducational assessments, direct student service delivery models, and the development and implementation of clinical and educational prescriptive programs are still widely adhered to in Canada. However, the alternative roles of consultation, program prevention and intervention, and parent and teacher training are increasing.

Canadian school psychologists recognise that this expanded role is more effective and appropriate in meeting the needs of students, parents, and teachers (Bartell, 1995). Depositions prepared by school psychologists when a large reduction of school psychologists was suggested in one province showed this variability in school psychology services. The role of diagnostician as a primary function was mentioned in all of the presentations to the board. Carney (1995) stressed the proactive, early intervention and prevention programming functions carried out by school psychologists. Beal and Service (1995) reinforced the role of school psychologists in assessment and diagnosis but also described the provision of therapy to students presenting with personal problems. Hamovich (1995) added that school psychologists provide crisis intervention as well as consultation to both teachers and parents. All depositions argued that school psychologists play an important role in the life of a school system by offering a wide range of services that include, but are not limited to, assessment, treatment, counselling, consultation, and program development (Beal & Service, 1995, p. 92). Cole and Siegel (1990) have described both current and projected roles of Canadian school psychologists using a two-dimensional grid system outlining the goals of service delivery (primary, secondary, tertiary) and the various recipients of school psychological services (e.g., school system, teachers, parents, students). This model is clearly relevant to the practice of school psychology in Canada today.

Psychological and psychoeducational assessments. Psychological and psychoeducational assessments conducted by Canadian school psychologists will vary depending on the presenting problem and the reason for the referral (e.g., to develop a program for a particular child). These assessments will often include standardised instruments, some of which have been developed in Canada and others which have been standardised and normed in Canada (e.g., Wechsler Intelligence Scale for Children, fourth edition) to assess intellectual, educational, social, emotional, personality, and/ or neuropsychological development. Other types of assessment procedures that are commonly employed include curriculum-based instructional assessments, dynamic assessment, functional behavioural assessment, and continuous performance appraisals. Psychological assessments not only include standardised tests but also interviews with parents and teachers and observations of classroom behaviour. The most often used individually administered standardised intelligence tests are the Wechsler Intelligence Scale for Children–IV, Wechsler Preschool and Primary Scale of Intelligence–III, and Wechsler Adult Intelligence Scale–III. Achievement is frequently assessed with the Wechsler Individual Achievement Test–II or the Woodcock-Johnson Test of Achievement. The Behavioral Assessment System for Children and the Conners Rating Scales, along with the Achenbach System of Empirically Based Assessment, are the more commonly used measures to assess behaviour. Many school psychologists also employ short questionnaires and rating scales that may be completed by the student, teacher, and/or parent as well as shorter instruments to assess adaptive behaviour and giftedness.

Direct and indirect services. Direct services to students are common for Canadian school psychologists. However, district policies and caseloads sometimes limit the amount of time a school psychologist can devote to direct services. Most often, outside of the assessment role, school psychologists work more directly with teachers, administrators, and other agencies. Indirect services, such as the development of individualised educational programs and teacher in-service workshops on trauma or on implementing classroom observation strategies,

are a major part of the school psychologist's role in today's schools.

Referrals and consultations. School psychologists serve as referral agents to other community services (Carney, 1995). Multidisciplinary service delivery systems have resulted in consultation becoming a significant model for providing school psychology services to children and adolescents (Sladeczek & Heath, 1997). Consultation represents a cost-effective service and affords several additional benefits that are not usually associated with more traditional school psychology roles (e.g., assessment). Consultation allows for greater collaboration between the student's home and school. Increasingly, schools, families, and communities are addressing systemwide problems, such as violence (e.g., bullying), which call for a broader service model and consideration of the well-being of all school-children.

Crisis intervention and crisis team management. Canadian school psychologists have become much more visible in crisis intervention and crisis team management. School violence, catastrophic accidents, and natural disasters require swift, immediate action and intervention. Estimates indicate that approximately 31% of Canadian immigrant children have previously lived in some form of unstable and poor conditions (Cole, 1998). Another role of the school psychologist in crisis situations is to support school staff and assist in the overall coordination of the crisis response. Using aggression as an example, primary intervention programs can target all students in a school and encourage prosocial behaviours and antiviolence beliefs. Secondary programs target at-risk students who are experiencing academic, social, and emotional difficulties that could lead to violence. Tertiary prevention programs focus on students who have a history of difficulty and may require specialised programs, such as anger management (Cole, 1998). Canadian school psychologists engage in program development and/or the evaluation of existing school-based programs ranging from substance abuse to bullying prevention. Another area of needed involvement is in the provision of services to preschool children as well as adult education.

Thus, although school psychologists will always be required for psychological and psychoeducational assessment, there is a strong movement toward these other roles. Above all, school psychologists must assume a leadership role in raising social policy issues and promoting effective educational and psychological programs, which will positively contribute to each student's educational, social, and emotional development (Saklofske et al., 2000).

Current Issues Impacting School Psychology

Current school psychology definition and practice in Canada are shaped by our history but also by external societal and consumer forces whose influences, in many ways, serve to promote the broadening of the scope of school psychology practice and the recruitment of school psychologists into the mainstream of schools and schooling (Saklofske et al., 2000). The roles and functions of school psychologists in Canada continue to evolve and change for many reasons (Bartell, 1996; Cole, 1996). The Canadian mosaic has been rapidly changing during the past several decades, and Canadian society is now even more ethnically and culturally diverse. The influx of new Canadians is in addition to the large number of children of Aboriginal and First Nations ancestry; as well, English and French language and culture, which are so much a part of Canada's past, are a defining force in the present and future. Furthermore, school psychological services tend to be uneven across Canada's provinces and territories, influenced by unique contextual circumstances, such as a relatively small population spread over a vast territorial expanse and differences in socioeconomic and political factors. These

factors require a dynamic school psychology that is contextually sensitive and relevant and that continues to evolve within the discipline and practice of psychology.

The diversity of psychological services and service providers has contributed to a diffuse sense of professional identity that continues to be a critical issue for school psychologists. Previously, Saklofske et al. (2000) argued that the fundamental challenge and opportunity for the profession in general, and in Canada in particular, is to articulate a proactive and comprehensive conceptual framework to guide psychological service delivery models and practice in an ever-changing world. Closely related to the need to change limited models of practice (e.g., intelligence examiner) is also the need to regulate the profession by establishing national standards for the training, practice, and credentialing of school psychologists (Holmes, 1993; McKee, 1996). The lack of standards for the credentialing and practice of school psychologists in Canada inhibits the coming of age of the profession. As Pryzwansky (1993) observed, "Nothing defines a profession like its regulatory practices" (p. 220). The challenge of establishing common ground for the training and practice of school psychology in Canada is attainable in the foreseeable future. The initiative has already been taken by the Canadian Psychological Association and the Canadian Association of School Psychologists, respectively, in establishing the framework for the accreditation of preservice graduate programs and the proposal for the credentialing of practicing school psychologists in Canada.

References

Bartell, R. (1995). Historical perspective on the role and practice of school psychology. *Canadian Journal of School Psychology, 11*(2), 133–137.

Bartell, R. (1996). The argument for a paradigm shift or what's in a name? *Canadian Journal of School Psychology, 12*(2), 86–90.

Bartell, R. K. (2001). School psychology in Manitoba: 10 years later. *Canadian Journal of School Psychology, 16*(2), 59–66.

Beal, A. L., & Service, J. (1995). Submission to an Ontario Board of Education concerning proposed reduction in psychological services. *Canadian Journal of School Psychology, 11*(2), 90–92.

Benson, W. (2001). School psychology in British Columbia. *Canadian Journal of School Psychology, 16*(2), 85–86.

Blakely, D., & Wells, N. (2001). School psychology in the Northwest Territories. *Canadian Journal of School Psychology, 16*(2), 87–88.

Canadian Education Statistics Council. (2003, November). *Education Indicators Program 2003* (ISBN No. 0-660-19172-5). Retrieved August 24, 2005, from http:www.cecs-csce.ca/pceip/PCEIP 2003en.pdf

Canadian Psychological Association. (2004). *Policy 2004–2: Ethical use and reporting of psychological assessment results for student placement.* Retrieved March 30, 2006, from http://www.cpa.ca/documents/policy.html

Canadian Tourism Commission. (2004). *About Canada.* Retrieved June 7, 2005, from http://www.travelcanada.ca/tc_redesign/app/en/ca/aboutcanada.do

Carney, P. (1995). Submission to an Ontario Board of Education from the Canadian Association of School Psychologists. *Canadian Journal of School Psychology, 11*(2), 89.

Carney, P. (2001). The practice of psychology in Ontario schools. *Canadian Journal of School Psychology, 16*(2), 47–57.

Central Intelligence Agency. (n.d.). *World factbook—Canada.* Retrieved August 17, 2005, from www.cia.gov/cia/publications/factbook/geos/ca.html

Cole, E. (1996). An integrative perspective on school psychology. *Canadian Journal of School Psychology, 6*(2), 115–121.

Cole, E. (1998). Immigrant and refugee children: Challenges for education and mental health services. *Canadian Journal of School Psychology, 14*(1), 36–50.

Cole, E., & Siegel, J. A. (Eds.). (1990). *Effective consultation in school psychology.* Toronto, Ontario: Hogrefe & Huber.

Communications Canada, Public Works & Government Services Canada. (2002). *Education in Canada.* Retrieved June 8, 2005, from www.dfait.maeci.gc.ca/ics-cki/stu_ces-en.asp

Dumont, F. (1989). School psychology in Canada: Views on its status. In P. Saigh & T. Oakland (Eds.), *International perspectives on psychology in the schools* (pp. 211–222). Hillsdale, NJ: Erlbaum.

Fagan, T. K. (1996). Historical perspectives on the role and practice of school psychology. *Canadian Journal of School Psychology, 6*(1), 83–85.

French, F., & Mureika, J. (2002). *Enhancing the experience of children and youth in today's schools: The role of psychology in Canadian schools* (Position paper). Ottawa, Ontario: Canadian Psychological Association.

Government of Canada. (1982). *The Charter of Rights and Freedoms: A guide for Canadians.* Ottawa, Ontario: Minister of Supply Services. Retrieved July 30, 2005, from http://laws.justice.gc.ca/en/charter/index.html

Government of Canada, Service Canada. (2003). Psychologists—At a glance. *Job Futures, National Edition.* Hull, Quebec: Author. Retrieved August 17, 2005, from http://jobfutures.ca/noc/4151.shtml

Hamovich, G. (1995). Submission to the chair and members of the education and finance committee of an Ontario board of education. *Canadian Journal of School Psychology, 11*(2), 96–98.

Hann, G. S. (2001). School psychology in Nova Scotia. *Canadian Journal of School Psychology, 16*(2), 19–24.

Holmes, B. (1993). Issues in training and credentialing in school psychology. In K. S. Dobson & D. J. G. Dobson (Eds.), *Professional psychology in Canada* (pp. 123–146). Toronto, Ontario: Hogrefe & Huber.

Hutchinson, N. L. (2002). *Inclusion of exceptional learners in Canadian schools: A practical guide for teachers.* Toronto, Ontario: Prentice Hall.

Janzen, H. L., & Carter, S. (2001). State of the art of school psychology in Alberta. *Canadian Journal of School Psychology, 16*(2), 79–84.

Janzen, H. L., Paterson, J. G., & Paterson, D. W. (1993). Future of psychology in the schools. *Canadian Journal of School Psychology, 9*(2), 174–180.

Kaufman, F., & Smith, T. (1998, June). *The roles and function of Canadian psychological service providers.* Poster presented at the Canadian Psychological Association annual meeting, Edmonton, Alberta.

Martin, G. (2001). Educational psychology in Newfoundland and Labrador: A thirty-year history. *Canadian Journal of School Psychology, 16*(2), 5–17.

McKee, W. T. (1996). Legislation, certification, and licensing of school psychologists. *Canadian Journal of School Psychology, 12*(2), 103–114.

Mureika, J. (2001). New Brunswick school psychology. *Canadian Journal of School Psychology, 17*(1), 25–26.

Mureika, J. M. K., Falconer, R. D., & Howard, B. M. (2004, Spring). The changing role of the school psychologist: From tester to collaborator. *Trainers of School Psychologist Forum* (Canadian Association of School Psychologists/Canadian Psychological Association Joint Newsletter).

Neudorf, J. (1989). *The role and tasks of educational psychologists in Saskatchewan.* Unpublished master's thesis, University of Regina, Saskatchewan.

New Brunswick Department of Education. (2001). *Guidelines for professional practice for school psychologists.* Fredericton, New Brunswick: Author. Retrieved March 30, 2006, from http://www.cpa.ca/documents/Guidelines_School_Psychologists.pdf

Oakland, T., Faulkner, M., & Annan, J. (2002). School psychology in four English-speaking countries: Australia, Canada, New Zealand, and the United States. In C. L. Frisby & C. Reynolds (Eds.), *Comprehensive handbook of multicultural school psychology.* Hoboken, NJ: Wiley.

Pryzwansky, W. (1993). The regulation of school psychology: A historical perspective on certification, licensure, and accreditation. *Journal of School Psychology, 31,* 219–235.

Saklofske, D. H. (1996). Moving toward a core curriculum for training school psychologists. *Canadian Journal of School Psychology, 12,* 91–96.

Saklofske, D. H., Bartell, R., Derevensky, J., Hann, S. G., Holmes, B., & Janzen, H. L. (2000). In T. K. Fagan & P. S. Wise (Eds.), *School psychology: Past, present, and future* (2nd ed.). National Association of School Psychologists.

Saklofske, D. H., & Grainger, J. (2001). School psychology in Saskatchewan: The end of a decade, the start of a century. *Canadian Journal of School Psychology, 16*(2), 69–80.

Saklofske, D. H., & Janzen, H. L. (1993). Contemporary issues in school psychology. In K. S. Dobson & D. J. G. Dobson (Eds.), *Professional psychology in Canada* (pp. 313–350). Toronto, Ontario: Hogrefe & Huber.

Sladeczek, I., & Heath, N. (1997). Consultation in Canada. *Canadian Journal of School Psychology, 13*(2), 1–14.

Statistics Canada. (2001). *Visible minority population, by provinces and territories: 2001 Census.* Retrieved June 1, 2005, from www40.statcan.ca/101/cst01/dem052a.htm

6

School Psychology in China

Hongwu Zhou

Context of School Psychology

With a civilized history of 5,000 years, the People's Republic of China is located on the Asian continent bordering the East China Sea, Yellow Sea, and South China Sea and covers 9,596,960 square kilometers (about the same size as the United States) with a population of approximately 1,300,000,000. Among its population are 279.47 million children age 14 years or younger and about 358 million under age 18. In 2004, there were 15.93 million births in China, resulting in a birth rate of 12.29 per 1,000, and 8.32 million deaths, resulting in a death rate of 6.42 per 1,000. In 2004, the net growth of population was 7.61 million.

In 2004, the gross domestic product was 13,651.5 billion Yuan RMB (about US$7.262 trillion). The per-capita annual net income of rural households was 2,936 Yuan RMB (about US$358). In 2004, China registered the highest economic growth since 1997, with a real increase of 6.8% after price factors were deducted. The per-capita disposable income of urban households was 9,422 Yuan RMB (about US$1,149), a

real increase of 7.7%. The population in absolute poverty in rural areas with an annual per-capita net income of less than 668 Yuan RMB (equal to approximately US$81) was 26.1 million at the end of 2004, a decline of 2.9 million over the previous year. The low-income population in rural areas (with an annual per-capita net income between 669 and 924 Yuan RMB [between US$81 and US$112]) was 49.77 million, a decline of 6.4 million.

China's education system is divided into three parts: basic education, higher education, and adult and vocational education. In 2004, kindergartens accommodated 20,844,000 children, 112,462,000 students were in regular primary schools, 372,000 students were in special education schools, 64,750,000 students were enrolled in junior secondary schools, 22,204,000 students attended regular senior secondary schools, 13,679,000 students were in vocational secondary schools, 13,335,000 were regular undergraduates, and 820,000 were postgraduate students.

Basic education in China includes preschool education, primary education, and regular secondary education. Primary and secondary education extends 12 years and is divided into primary, junior secondary, and senior secondary stages. Primary education extends either 5 or 6 years, with the former accounting for 35% of the total enrollment and the latter 65% of the total enrollment. Junior secondary education is generally 3 years. Compulsory education lasts 9 years and includes primary and junior secondary schooling. General senior secondary education lasts 3 years.

In 1999, the Ministry of Education began to redesign the basic education system. All children age 6 are required to enter primary school, but in places where this level of education is not available, children begin school at age 7. In areas where junior secondary education is readily available, all primary school graduates should enter nearby junior secondary schools without sitting for entrance examinations. However, graduates from junior secondary schools seeking to continue their education in senior secondary schools must pass locally organized entrance examinations before admission.

Higher education is developing rapidly. In 2004, there were 2,236 higher education institutions, among which 1,736 were regular higher education institutions and the others were higher education institutions for adults. In the regular higher education institutions, there were 1,047 institutes of higher vocational education. Regular higher education institutions averaged 7,740 students in 2004, among which 4-year regular higher education institutions averaged 13,651 students and 3-year regular higher education institutions averaged 3,209 students.

Vocational education is provided at three levels: junior secondary, senior secondary, and tertiary. Vocational education is offered primarily in secondary schools with the goal of providing basic professional knowledge and skills to workers, peasants, and employees in various sectors. Junior vocational education refers to vocational and technical education after primary school education and is a part of the 9-year compulsory education. Secondary vocational school students should be primary school graduates or young

people with equivalent cultural knowledge; this schooling extends 3 to 4 years. Junior vocational schools are located mainly in rural areas where the economy is less developed and the need to develop the labor force is greatest.

The secondary level refers primarily to vocational education in the senior secondary school stage. Composed of specialized secondary schools, technical schools, and vocational high schools, secondary vocational education trains the workforce with various practical skills at primary and secondary levels. From 1980 and 2001, the proportion of regular senior high school students among all the students in senior secondary education decreased from 81% to 55%, whereas the proportion of secondary vocational school students increased from 19% to 45%. From 1980 to 2001, secondary vocational education schools produced 50 million graduates, fostering millions of secondary- and primary-level technical workers, managers, skilled workers, and other workers with vocational and technical education.

In recent years, the government has paid increasing attention to the education of children with special needs. Among the country's 358 million children, about 10 million demonstrate special needs. In 2004, 1,560 special schools served 371,800 students, and regular education served 242,790 students (Ministry of Education, 2005). Those special schools include schools for children with mental, visual, hearing, and/or speaking handicaps.

Origin, History, and Current Status of School Psychology

Nearly three millennia ago, in the ancient books of Chinese traditional medicine, Chinese ancestors had paid attention to persons' mental changes and the relationship between mental health and physical health. From the 1930s to the 1960s, psychology in China grew rapidly. However, beginning in the late 1960s, during the period referred to as the Chinese Cultural Revolution, psychology was widely considered to be a pseudoscience, and most psychologists were sent to the rural areas, together with other academics. Since the early 1980s and China's subsequent political and economic reforms, psychology in China, along with other fields of science, has become a fast-growing, well-respected field.

Until somewhat recently, China's government and higher education system have not considered school psychology a high priority. Many departments of psychology and education offer courses consistent with the interests and work of school psychology. Efforts have focused on the development of mental health education programs, the graduates of which may work in primary and secondary education. Their work often resembles that of school or educational psychologists in Western countries.

School psychology as a psychology specialty shows signs of development. For example, the country's first school psychology programs are being developed at Beijing Normal University and Southwest Normal University. Because school psychology within China is still emerging, it is impossible to describe the field in detail. Moreover, given the country's large size and population, regional differences can be expected. Readers are referred to Chapter 15 in this volume, which discusses the nature of educational/school psychology in Hong Kong.

The early 1980s marked a turning point for psychology in China, coinciding with reforms in the country's economy. As the living conditions gradually changed, Chinese parents, especially those in large cities, had increasingly higher academic expectations for their children. Ideology and Chinese traditions place a high priority on education and encourage parents to push their children to excel in obtaining knowledge. Parental high expectations seemed to be a form of compensation for their lost opportunities to receive a proper education. China had a small number of colleges and universities in the 1980s. Thus, the parents stressed to their children the importance of their doing better than their peers to gain acceptance into a college or university. This resulted in students feeling considerable

competitive pressure to do well on the yearly administered national entrance examination. Thus, children were often overloaded with homework and had no time to devote to their own interests or to develop their potential nonacademic talents.

Education reforms beginning in the early 1980s stressed two themes: Providing a good education is imperative, and it should occur in conjunction with efforts to fully develop children's various talents. Changes in educators' thinking opened new roles for psychologists. For example, some regular secondary education teachers came to understand that, in addition to improving teaching methods, eliminating unnecessary homework, and revising curricula, they had to acquire psychological expertise to better understand children's social and moral education and how to prevent mental health problems. Given these urgent needs, various theories and skills related to psychology, including school psychology, counseling, and mental health services, were introduced into China at that time. In some schools and some areas, especially in southeast China where the economy was comparatively well developed, counseling or mental health education centers were established with the main objective of helping children with learning disabilities, anxiety, and interpersonal relationship problems. This effort marked the starting point for school psychology practice in China.

In 1999, the government published *Decisions to Deepen Education Reform and Push Forward Qualification Education,* in which the directive was to strengthen mental health education for students and to improve their ability to live in society. In 1999, the China Ministry of Education published *Some Suggestions to Strengthen Mental Health Education in Primary and Secondary Schools,* in which the Ministry demanded that, from the autumn of 2002, all primary and secondary schools in China should include mental health education for students. In 2002, the China Ministry of Education published *Outline of Instructions to Mental Health Education in Primary and Secondary Schools,* which outlined the contents, methods, and the principles of mental health education. These suggestions and decisions stress the importance of mental health education and reflect the government's commitment to prevent mental health problems in children. These documents could be regarded as the milestone that provided the impetus for the development of school psychology in China.

Although the specialty of school psychology is not strong, the profession of mental health education can be thought of as providing a psychological presence in schools. In most large cities and in some comparatively developed provinces, schools have established a center or office of mental health education management and employ specialists in mental health education to provide mental health services, often at least one mental health education teacher in each school. Teachers become certified to teach mental health education after receiving special training in psychology or after graduating with a bachelor's degree from a department of psychology or department of education. Mental health education teachers usually receive a salary similar to that of other teachers with the same background and years of teaching.

In most provinces, university personnel cooperate with local departments of education management and local schools to train teachers of mental health education. The training programs are usually divided into different levels, from general knowledge to a postgraduate degree. The basic theories and skills of mental health education have been incorporated into teacher education programs. Within psychology, students obtaining a specialization in mental health education usually are enrolled in some subfield of psychology (e.g., applied, developmental, child, or educational psychology). Some universities offer master's and doctoral degrees in mental health education. Training programs often include the following subjects: theories and skills of psychological counseling, group counseling, developmental psychology, child psychology, psychological assessment, and theories and skills of organizing mental health education class activities.

Mental health education teachers generally are female (75%). Approximately 7,300 teachers of mental health education in Zhejiang Province have obtained the certification from the Zhejiang Province Mental Health Education Center (Zhou, 2005).

Support for the work of mental health education is found in the production and use of textbooks, handbooks, and guidebooks (including translated materials), as well as in research on child psychology and mental health education. Different models of mental health education have been developed, some of which include dimensions of school psychology, such as assessment of students, school-based psychological counseling, individual and group activities to promote mental health education, family mental health education, and the functions and roles of school counseling centers and offices.

The current service delivery model in primary and secondary schools generally has the following features: one or two full-time mental health education teachers and several part-time mental health education teachers in one school with 1,000 to 3,000 students; one office for individual counseling; the provision of several prevention and early intervention class activities consistent with students' developmental and mental health problems; and presentations to, or consultations with, parents, students, and teachers (in some schools, a counseling hotline). These components are becoming accepted practices and have set a strong base for the development of school psychology.

Infrastructure of School Psychology

The following national and provincial professional organizations and their subcommittees serve the interests of mental health, mental health education, crisis intervention, and school psychology. The Chinese Society of Psychology established a subcommittee on school psychology in 1993 under the name School-Management Psychology Subcommittee of the Chinese Society of Psychology. The Chinese Society of Education has a special education subcommittee and a children's educational psychology subcommittee. The Chinese Society of Education has provincial committees in all provinces. The China Association for Mental Health has special committees on adolescence, college students, and children.

No national laws regulate the licensure of mental health education teachers or school psychologists. In some provinces, such as Zhejiang and Guangdong, some regulations developed by the provincial mental health education centers affect the certification of mental health education teachers and psychology graduates. To be certified in mental health education, teachers should be licensed as teachers from the China Ministry of Education, should work as teachers for at least 2 years, and should receive systematic training in the specializations of school psychology and mental health education. Students graduating from departments of psychology or education can become certificated after they have worked in schools for 2 years.

There is no professional journal in China addressing issues related to mental health education or school psychology. However, some journals in psychology address issues important to these two specializations, including *Academic Journal of Psychology, Psychological Science, Chinese Mental Health Journal, Applied Psychology, Psychological Development and Education, Development of Psychology, Popular Psychology,* and *Mental Health Education in Schools.*

Preparation of School Psychologists

School psychology has not been established widely as a specialized preparation at either the undergraduate or graduate level. Two universities, Beijing Normal University and Southwest Normal University, recently established a master's degree in school psychology. Given their recent development, little can be stated about these programs. Students interested in a career as a school psychologist usually are prepared more broadly in psychology, in applied, developmental, educational, or basic psychology. Their preparation programs usually include courses common to majors of school psychology and mental health education.

Although universities differ in their curricula, required basic courses during the first and the second academic years generally include basic psychology, learning and cognitive psychology, developmental psychology, educational psychology, personality psychology, social psychology, experimental psychology, psychological assessment and statistics, and psychological research methodology. The alternative basic courses during the third and fourth academic years usually include psychological counseling, physiology and anatomy, mental health education, management psychology, child behavior psychology, advanced statistics, psychological statistics and software, history of psychology, and reading professional English. During the third and the fourth academic years, the students have a practicum on mental health education in schools for at least 3 months and receive additional practical experiences while studying psychological counseling and psychological research methods.

Roles, Functions, and Responsibilities of School Psychologists

School psychology does not exist widely in China. Mental health education provides some services similar to those typically provided by school psychologists. Thus, the roles, functions, and responsibilities of mental health education teachers will be described.

The primary responsibilities and roles of mental health education teachers are to investigate mental health problems displayed by students (e.g., through testing, interviewing, and observation, and by exploring environmental features that may influence students' behavior and attitudes) and to provide suggestions to teachers, headmasters, principals, and departments of education regarding how to deal with those mental health problems at school; to organize class activities designed to help students acquire greater self-awareness and self-development; to provide group counseling and other interventions for students who display mental health problems; to do individual counseling and guidance for students experiencing problems in their daily life and studies; to consult with teachers and parents; to help parents acquire effective ways to help and communicate with their children; to form and prepare a school crisis response team; to provide proposals for school crisis intervention when a violent or traumatic event occurs on the school campus; and to collaborate with other staff in publicizing mental health issues.

Current Issues Impacting School Psychology

The Chinese government and several national professional organizations have made efforts to advocate for mental health education. Local departments of education management have different perspectives regarding mental health education and thus deliver services differently in the various provinces and cities. These differences pose challenges to attempts to scientifically investigate the impact of these services as well as to attempts to establish a uniform national policy on mental health education, including certification and licensing standards.

A second challenge is to establish the specialty of school psychology by implementing strong university preparation programs, including undergraduate, master's, and doctoral degrees. A nationally approved training program in school psychology should be established for teachers seeking training in mental health education. Even if a standard were set for a ratio of 6,000 to 7,000 students per school psychologist in Chinese schools, the implementation of this standard would require the training and employment of 20,000 to 30,000 school psychologists in the coming years. This is a great challenge facing the field of school psychology in China. The School Psychology Subcommittee of the Chinese Society of Psychology discussed this issue recently at its executive committee meeting and plans to outline a curricula and training program for school psychologists and mental health education teachers at the undergraduate, master's, and doctoral levels, and to submit it to departments of psychology for reference.

A third challenge lies in developing research programs in school psychology that address issues important to training and practice and how to transfer different kinds of research results and models effectively into mental health education in primary and secondary schools. Many assessment models, psychological theories, and psychological research methods and skills are being used. However, most of these are translated from abroad with few adjustments made to national and local conditions. The need to establish different kinds of school-psychological models that are appropriate for use within the Chinese culture and society is urgent in order to make an impact on the development of school psychology in China.

References

Central Committee of Chinese Communist Party and China State Council. (1999, June 13). *Decisions to deepen education reform and push forward qualification education.*

Congde, L., & Yunhua, W. (2001). On future tendencies of school psychology. *Educational Research, 7,* 30–34.

Fagan, T. K., & Wise, P. S. (1994). *School psychology: Past, present and future.* New York: Longman.

Guoliang, Y. (2005). Research on mental health education for adolescents. *Academic Journal of Beijing Normal University, 1,* 64–70.

Gutkin, T. B. (1990). *The handbook of school psychology.* New York: Wiley.

Hongfei, Y. (2003). A study of the development of mental health in primary and secondary schools in Zhejiang Province. *Education Research, 24,* 88–92.

Martin, S., & Monitor Staff. (1998, October). China increasingly accepts psychology. *APA Monitor Online, 29*(10). Available online at http://www.apa.org/monitor/oct98/china.html

Ministry of Education. (2005, March 1). *Basic situation of education development in China, 2004.* Available online at http://202.205.177.9/edoas/website18/info8842.htm

Ministry of Education Press Office. (1994). *Communiqué about national educational development in the year of 1994.* Available online at http://www.moe.edu.cn

National Bureau of Statistics of China. (2005, February 28). *Statistical communiqué of the People's Republic of China on the 2004 national economic and social development.* Available online at http://www.stats.gov.cn and at http://www.stats.gov.cn/english/newsandcomingevents/t20050228_402231939.htm

Oakland, T., & Cunningham, J. (1997). International School Psychology Association definition of school psychology. *School Psychology International, 18,* 195–200.

Zheng Zhou, M. A. (2001). The status of school psychology in China at the millennium. *School Psychology International, 22,* 22–28.

Zhiliang, Q. (2002). *Report about the educational status of Chinese children with special needs.* Available online at http://www.edu.cn/2001 1112/3009417.shtml

Zhou, H. (2005, March). Investigation about the development of mental health education in Zhejiang Province. *Zhejiang Educational Research.*

7

School Psychology in Cyprus

Ernestina A. Papacosta

Context of School Psychology

Cyprus is an island situated in the eastern Mediterranean about 386 kilometers north of Egypt, 97 kilometers west of Syria, and 64 kilometers south of Turkey. The island is at the crossroads of Africa, Asia, and Europe. Its area is 9,251 square kilometers, of which 1,733 square kilometers is forested. It is the third largest island in the Mediterranean, after Sicily and Sardinia. Coastal lowlands, varying in width, surround the island. The Troodos Mountains cover most of the southern and western portions of the island and account for roughly half of its area. The Pentadaktylos Mountains extend along the northern coastline. Cypriot culture is among the oldest in the Mediterranean. A former British colony, Cyprus gained its independence in 1960, following years of resistance to British rule. Shortly after the founding of the republic, serious differences arose between Greek-Cypriots and Turkish-Cypriots about the implementation and interpretation of the constitution. In 1963, when Makarios, the first president of Cyprus, advanced proposals to amend the constitution in order to facilitate the functioning of government, the Turkish side strongly rejected them. The ensuing constitutional deadlock gave rise to intercommunal clashes and tensions. On July 15, 1974, the ruling military junta of Greece staged a coup to overthrow the democratically elected government of Cyprus. On July 20, 1974, Turkey, using the coup as a pretext, invaded Cyprus purportedly to restore constitutional order. It seized 35% of the territory of Cyprus in the north, an act universally condemned as a gross infringement of international law and the United Nations Charter.

AUTHOR'S NOTE: Special thanks to colleagues in the Educational Psychology Service (Ministry of Education and Culture) for their valuable contribution to this article: Michalis Ioannou, Head of the Department; Dr. Charalambos Tziogouros, Senior Educational Psychologist; and Dr. Michalis Papadopoulos, Senior Educational Psychologist. The author is grateful for their useful information and discussions and for their practical help in preparing this manuscript.

In November 1983, the Turkish-occupied area was unilaterally declared an "independent state." The international community, through United Nations Security Council resolutions 541 of 1983 and 550 of 1984, condemned this unilateral declaration by the Turkish Cypriot regime, declared it both illegal and invalid, and called for its immediate revocation. To this day, no country in the world except Turkey has recognized this entity. The Republic of Cyprus became a member of the European Union on May 1, 2004.

Cyprus has a population of 0.7878 million (Ministry of Labor, 2004). Ethnic diversity is reported as 77% Greek, 18% Turk, and 5% other. The population distribution by age is 14 years or younger, 21% (79,701 females, 83,256 males); 15 to 64 years, 68% (260,846 females, 267,446 males); 65 years and over, 11% (50,118 females, 38,766 males). Economic affairs are dominated by the division of the country as a result of the 1974 Turkish invasion. Cyprus has an open free, market, service-based economy with some manufacturing. Cyprus's accession as a full member of the European Union as of May 1, 2004, has been an important milestone in its recent economic development. The gross domestic product in 2004 was US$15.71 billion for the Republic of Cyprus, US$4.5 billion for North Cyprus, and US$20,300 and US$7,135 per capita, respectively. The service sector, including tourism, contributes 76% to the gross domestic product and employs 72% of the labor force. Industry and construction contribute 19% and employ 23% of the labor force.

During the 2003–2004 school year, 174,062 students were enrolled in schools: 25,674 were in pre-primary schools; 61,731 were in primary Greek community schools (Grades 1–6); 65,480 in secondary education (gymnasium Grades 1–3; lykeio Grades 3–6); 20,849 in public or private universities in Cyprus; and 17,631 were university students studying abroad (Statistical Service, 2004). There are three categories of nursery schools: public, community, and private.

Public nursery schools are established by the government and are supported partly by government and partly by the communities or parents' associations. Community nursery schools are nonprofit private schools supported by government subsidies or by parents' associations. Private nursery schools are established and supported by the owners of the schools, on a profit basis. Both private and community nursery schools are registered and supervised by the Ministry of Education and Culture and also by the Department of Welfare Services.

The integration policy to serve students with special needs is a relatively recent innovation, introduced in 1992. Most students with special needs are served within the regular stream of education. During school year 2003–2004, 11 special education schools with 328 students operated in Cyprus. However, a total of 4,000 students receive special education services (Ministry of Education and Culture, 2004). Three hundred and ninety-six primary education teachers with various specialties (special education teachers, teachers for the deaf and the blind) work to support and meet the needs of children with disabilities. In secondary education (gymnasium and lyceum), 137 teachers offer services to children with special needs. Special services such as music therapy, work therapy, speech therapy, physiotherapy, and psychological support are also available to these students.

In Cyprus, education is provided through pre-primary, primary, secondary general, and secondary technical/vocational schools, special schools, the University of Cyprus, and tertiary non-university public and private educational institutions. Public schools are mainly financed by public funds; private schools are primarily funded from tuition. At the secondary level of education, private schools receive a small state subsidy, and in a few cases, foreign aid is provided through various organizations. Education at the primary level has been free and compulsory since 1962. Compulsory education begins at age 4 years 8 months and lasts until age 15.

Formal school education is organized into three levels: pre-primary (ages 4 years 8 months–5 years 8 months); primary (ages 5 years 8 months–12 years); gymnasium (ages 12–15 years); and lyceum (ages 15–18 years). Schooling in the secondary level consists of two stages. Stage 1 (gymnasium) comprises the first three grades; Stage 2 (lyceum) comprises the last three grades leading toward a certificate (apolitirion). There are also evening gymnasia that enable young people and adults to complete their secondary education. Technical and vocational schools accept students at the second stage only, and each school has two departments, technical and vocational. Technical schools place an emphasis on theory and practice in science and technical skills, and vocational schools provide training for craftsmen and service trades.

The public education system in Cyprus is highly centralized. Head teachers and teachers are appointed, transferred, and promoted by the Educational Service Commission, an independent five-member body, appointed for a 6-year period by the president of the Republic. The preparation and enforcement of educational laws and legislation is the responsibility of the Ministry of Education and Culture. Syllabi, curricula, and textbooks are also the responsibility of the Ministry of Education. During the 2003–2004 school year, 1,233 full-time schools, at all levels of education, were operating in the government-controlled areas with 174,062 students and 14,290 teachers, thus giving a student-to-teacher ratio of 12.2 to 1 (Statistical Service, 2004). The average class size for public primary education is 24.7; for public secondary education, it is 25. The law specifies that all primary education grades have a minimum of 25 and a maximum of 30 students per class. In secondary education, the maximum number of students per class is also 30 (with the exception of the third grade in the lyceum, where the maximum number of students per class is 25). The Ministry of Education and Culture is now making initiatives to decrease the number of students per class in primary as well as in

secondary schools. In small schools at the primary level, several classes can be grouped together. According to law (Public Law for the Education and Training of Children With Special Needs, 1999), when a student with special needs is in a classroom, the average number of students can be lower.

The number of pre-primary schools increased from 638 (with 25,298 children) in 2002–2003 to 657 (with 25,674 children) in 2003–2004. Primary school enrollments decreased from 62,868 in 2002–2003 to 61,731 in 2003–2004. Of the total primary school population, 69% attended schools in towns and suburbs, and the remaining 31% attended rural schools (Statistical Service, 2004). During the school year 2003–2004, enrollments in secondary education increased to 65,480 from 64,711 in the previous year. Of the secondary school population, 87% were enrolled in public schools and the remaining 13% in private schools (Statistical Service, 2004). More than 50% of Cypriot high school graduates sought university education in other countries, with Greece, the United Kingdom, and the United States being the most popular destinations. During the academic year 2003–2004, 17,631 Cypriot university students were studying abroad. Since 1992, the newly established University of Cyprus has added to the total student population by about 2,500.

The University of Cyprus currently offers bachelor's, master's, and doctoral programs in most major disciplines. A number of private colleges offer mostly technical diplomas but also bachelor's programs, mostly in association with British universities.

Origin, History, and Current Status of School Psychology

Immediately after the establishment of the Cyprus Republic in 1960, psychology positions were included in two Ministries: the Ministry of

Education and the Ministry of Health. Two educational psychologists (Stelios Georgiades and Antonis Papaioannou) were appointed to develop a plan of action. The history of school psychology in Cyprus is closely related to that of vocational counseling. From 1974 until 1989, educational psychologists offered their services through the Counseling and Career Education Service in the Ministry of Education (Tziogouros, 1999). Within a few years, four more educational psychologists were appointed to join the service, and in 1989, the personnel numbered six. In 1995, the Educational Psychology Services Section was established in the Ministry of Education and Culture, and it has functioned as an independent body with a distinct identity ever since, now counting 35 full-time members who share the responsibility for all public schools in Cyprus (Papadopoulos, 2002).

The origins of the educational psychology practices in Cyprus can be traced to the foundation of the Cyprus Psychological Association (1980), as well as to the first professional efforts made by psychologists teaching in the Department of Educational Studies at the newly founded (1992) University of Cyprus (Papadopoulos, 2002). When the Cyprus Psychological Association was established in 1980, its membership counted 21, because young graduates started returning from their studies abroad at that time. In 2005, the Association had 185 members, an indication that psychology as a field and as a profession has enjoyed a remarkable increase in popularity in recent years (Georgiou, 1996).

Most school psychologists in Cyprus are employed by the government and work in public schools. The Educational Psychology Service is an interdepartmental service answerable to the Permanent Secretary of the Ministry of Education and Culture. Few psychologists work in private schools or in special schools. The aim of the service is the application of psychology and basic psychological principles to the educational system (pre-primary, primary, secondary, and technical education). The goal is to provide an environment within the school system that will promote mental health and academic enrichment and facilitate learning for all students according to their individual needs and abilities. The Educational Psychology Service has three district offices in the towns of Larnaca, Limassol, and Nicosia. Every school in Cyprus can consult the Educational Psychological Service for support and assistance.

The terms used in job descriptions and qualification standards are *educational psychologist* and *educational psychology services*. Most educational psychologists in Cyprus are female, between the ages of 25 and 58 (Jimerson et al., 2004). Educational psychologists must be qualified at the master's-degree level (clinical, school, or educational psychology). Before 1992, in the absence of a local university, Cypriots traveled abroad to obtain higher education degrees. Thus, all educational psychologists in the Educational Psychological Service have a degree from abroad. The great majority of them were trained in Europe and the United States. All of the educational psychologists are fluent in two or more languages (Jimerson et al., 2004). The ratio of school psychologists to students is 1 to 5,000 on average (Jimerson et al., 2004). Salaries are influenced by years of experience. On average, a school psychologist earns about 1,745 euros monthly (20,940 euros annually). Most school psychologists receive pay equal to that of teachers and other professionals who work in the schools.

Educational psychologists in Cyprus perform a variety of activities. Responses from educational psychologists on the International School Psychology Survey (Jimerson et al., 2004) indicate that the greatest amount of time is split between administrative responsibilities and psychoeducational evaluations. Although recent developments with regard to school psychology practices in the unified educational system look promising, there is still a lot to be done. A unified educational system will address the needs of a diverse student population. A fundamental principle of the system should be that all children can learn, and it will therefore provide students with opportunities to succeed academically as well as emotionally. In a unified educational system, educational psychologists will have a primary role in the decision-making process, by designing and implementing preventive programs and interventions in the schools and by developing and influencing educational policy and practice, especially regarding services for students with disabilities.

Decentralization of services in the Ministry of Education and Culture needs to take place, in an attempt to make Educational Psychology Service more flexible and available to those in the school system. There is still a great demand for human resources and expertise within the field of school psychology. In-service training courses are provided in several circumstances and by various trainers. However, there is still more to be done in the area of continuing education and training. Opportunities for advancement in Educational Psychology Services are minimal, but job stability is quite high.

Infrastructure of School Psychology

The Cyprus Psychological Association (i.e., the Union) does much to enhance the interests of psychology and all its branches, including school psychology. The Union was established in 1980 with 21 members. Currently, about 185 psychologists are members. Many local psychologists are members of professional associations in the country in which they studied and participate in conferences overseas. Most of the school psychologists are also members of international associations. Before 1995, in the absence of a law consolidating the psychology profession, the Cyprus Psychological Association played the role of the "gatekeeper" in the field of professional psychology. Its membership was restricted to graduates of psychology programs (Georgiou, 1996). According to the Association's constitution, the following qualifications were necessary for membership in the Association: (a) a university degree with psychology as the major subject (the competent authorities of the country where the student obtained the

degree must accredit the degree) and (b) a postgraduate degree in psychology obtained from a university or another institution considered equivalent to a university by the competent authorities of the country where the student studied. The aims of the Cyprus Psychological Association are to support and promote the practice of psychology as a profession and as a field and to serve the interests of its members. Furthermore, the Association aims to improve and enhance mental health. Since its establishment, the Association invests in the training and continuing education of its members through seminars, colloquia, and international events.

The practice of psychologists also follows the standards established by many European countries. In 1995, the Public Law for the Consolidation of Professional Psychology was passed. It requires the following qualifications of professional psychologists: (a) a degree in psychology and (b) 3 years of postgraduate studies in an area of professional psychology, including at least 1,500 hours of supervised training. The activities of the Cyprus Psychological Association, the University of Cyprus, and the Educational Psychology Service of the Ministry of Education promote the formulation of the roles and functions of educational psychologists and enhance the quality of services being provided today. The establishment of educational psychology training programs at the University of Cyprus in 1999–2000 is an attempt to improve the quality of services offered by educational psychologists.

The 1999 enactment of the Public Law for the Education and Training of Children With Special Needs could be considered one of the most significant events influencing the work of educational psychologists. The law, which extended and revised the Education Act of 1979, directs the state to develop and implement educational psychology programs in a unified educational system that refers to the needs of all students with and without disabilities. Inclusion became a policy of the state, and the law makes it mandatory for all children with handicaps in Cyprus to receive a free and appropriate education in the least restrictive environment. Educational psychologists then became instrumental in assessing the needs of students with disabilities, recommending the most appropriate school setting and evaluating individualized educational programs. The educational psychologist assumes a central role and responsibility in both assessment and diagnosis as well as in the decision-making process.

According to the job descriptions and qualification standards, educational psychologists' main activities include individual consultation and assessment of students, consultation and counseling with teachers or parents, design and implementation of intervention programs within the school system, and development and design of pedagogical research studies. Professional standards for educational psychologists are described in the law that governs credentialing and licensing of psychologists (Public Law for the Consolidation of Professional Psychology, 2004). Thus, no one can practice professional psychology (including educational psychology) without fulfilling the criteria required by the law. School psychologists report belonging to a variety of different professional organizations. Therefore, they follow the guidelines and principles of organizations or associations in which they are members. The Cyprus Psychological Association has also developed ethical issues and standards (1982) that exemplify the profession's values and principles.

Preparation of School Psychologists

Psychology is taught at the University of Cyprus (undergraduate and graduate levels) and at several private institutions of higher education. In January 2000, the Cyprus Council for the Recognition of Higher Education Qualifications started offering its services by examining applications for degree recognition. The Council operates under the jurisdiction of the Ministry of Education and Culture. In 2004, the educational evaluation-accreditation process was continued

by the Council of Educational Evaluation-Accreditation, which evaluates programs of study at the undergraduate and postgraduate levels. The University of Cyprus offers the only accredited program of study in psychology. The newly established Department of Psychology at the University of Cyprus has approximately 100 undergraduate psychology majors and 25 graduate students. The program offers degrees in social/clinical psychology and educational/developmental psychology at the undergraduate level; educational psychology at the master's level; and cognitive, developmental, and educational psychology at the doctoral level. The aim of the program in educational psychology is to provide students with a strong theoretical background in the areas of cognitive, developmental, and school psychology.

The first degree in psychology requires the completion of 134 credit hours. The study level consists of 33 compulsory courses of introduction to psychology. Then, a student can choose from three components: cognitive, social-clinical, or educational-developmental psychology (57 elective credit hours and 18 credit hours). Additionally, 14 credit hours of subculture and 12 credit hours of education courses are required. The program of psychology at the graduate level requires the completion of 120 credit hours, including 40 credit hours of supervised training. Nominal duration of the curriculum is 2 years. The master of educational psychology curriculum is designed to provide students with a strong theoretical background, and at the same time, prepare them for the practice of professional educational psychology. About five openings for postgraduate students are announced each year. The Ph.D. program is based on the general framework of postgraduate programs in the Department of Psychology. The program leading to a Ph.D. for students who already possess a master's diploma requires the completion of 15 credit hours of specialization courses. Additionally, students are required to perform successfully on a comprehensive examination, submit and successfully defend a research proposal, and complete a doctoral dissertation. Through addressing the training standards described in the previous section, programs at the University of Cyprus emphasize core academic knowledge of psychology, assessment procedures, and intervention strategies. Interpersonal skills (e.g., establishing trust and rapport, listening and communication skills) are emphasized throughout the program. Statistical design and research methods are also important aspects of the program. The ethical parameters, ethics codes, rules, and regulations governing the practice of psychology are another significant part of the program.

The graduate program in educational psychology offered by the University of Cyprus, the only accredited program of study in Cyprus, is a newly developed program. As a result, there are no educational psychologists currently trained in Cyprus. In 2005, 25 educational psychology students were in the program in Cyprus; these students will graduate in 2006.

Roles, Functions, and Responsibilities of School Psychologists

School psychology services are designed to support school personnel and parents to enhance academic adaptive and social skills for students. The work of the Educational Psychology Service at the Ministry of Education and Culture consists mainly of two broad sectors: individual referrals and program development and implementation within the school system. The school psychologist plays a primary role in the identification, assessment, diagnosis, and evaluation process. Referrals to the service can be made by schools or by parents. Students are referred for evaluation and assessment, for various problems, educational difficulties, emotional or physical problems, and special needs. Consultation with educators and parents follows an assessment and diagnostic procedure. In recent years, there has been a noticeable shift toward

the development and implementation of programs that are preventive, as well as therapeutic, within the schools. These programs last at least one academic year, and activities involve the educational psychologist, educators, and school administrators as well as the parents. Through these programs, a greater number of students can be served and mental health can be promoted for the school population in general.

In addition to the two sectors discussed previously, educational psychologists are constantly involved in research programs in the field of educational psychology. They cooperate with social groups and institutions within the community to enhance learning through seminars, discussions, and studies. The work of school psychologists can be briefly described by the following:

Individual referrals. A child can be referred to the service by the school, the parent, or other professionals. The educational psychologist needs informed consent from a parent or legal guardian to assess a child and give a written report. Diagnosis and recommendations for the school or the parents are included in the report. Individual or group counseling and consultation are provided by the service. Consultation takes many forms (with educators, school personnel, other professionals, family members, and the community).

Testing and assessment. A child needs to be assessed before he or she can be eligible for special education services within the school system. An educational psychologist has a major role in the assessment process. A significant time load is devoted to assessment techniques (interviewing, observation, testing). A multiprofessional team evaluates a child and various techniques are used for assessment. The Educational Psychology Service most often uses the Wechsler Intelligence Scale for Children–III (Greek version) to assess the intellectual abilities of students. Additionally, clinical observation and interviewing, as well as informal curriculum-based assessment and checklists, are used to assess achievement, behavioral, or personality difficulties. A list of other tests to assess personality, social adjustment, and skills are also used but those are not yet standardized to the population of Cyprus. Some attempts are now being made by the Service in cooperation with the University of Cyprus to standardize more tests to the Cypriot population and develop a library of tests to be used by educational psychologists. There are no standardized attainment tests for use by educational psychologists, and thus most of the educational psychologists rely on informal assessment and clinical interviews and observations.

Organizational and program development services. The Service is investing a lot of time in the development and implementation of preventive, as well as intervention, programs in the schools. These programs are developed for both primary and secondary schools and usually focus on dependency problems, school violence, self-esteem, and crisis intervention.

Supervision. There is a great need for supervision services, because no formal supervision is currently offered to the educational psychology service.

Other activities. The service is involved in a number of research programs (e.g., drug abuse, early reading difficulties). Also, educational psychologists assist school staff by providing training for teachers and other professional staff and participating or assisting in program evaluation and research activities. Educational psychologists work in conjunction with the schools in communicating with parents, so they arrange parent conferences or workshops to discuss important issues regarding students.

Individual educational psychologists provide these services in varying degrees. In Cyprus, the educational psychologist is seen to be the primary professional, in collaboration with families and regular classroom teachers, to help children achieve their full learning potential. Coordination, planning, and administration of educational programs are also applied in the

schools, with the educational psychologist having the primary role in this implementation and evaluation. Few school psychologists in Cyprus, employed by the government, are based in special schools. These individuals devote all of their time to students with special needs (behavior and emotional problems, mental retardation, physical problems).

A recent study provides data on the roles and functions of psychologists working with children and families in various settings. Commissioned by the International School Psychology Association's Research Committee, researchers compared the training, roles, and responsibilities of school psychologists in different countries (Jimerson et al., 2004). The sample in Cyprus included 50 psychologists employed in educational settings. According to the psychologists' report, they devoted 34% of their time to administrative responsibilities, 23% to psychoeducational evaluations, 15% to consultation with parents/families, 14% to counseling students, 14% to consultation with teachers and staff, 8% to providing direct interventions, 8% to conducting staff training and in-service programs, and 6% to providing primary prevention programs. In addition, the International School Psychology Survey also revealed that, ideally, the specific sample of psychologists working in educational settings would prefer the following roles/responsibilities/activities (cited in rank order): (1) providing primary prevention programs, (2) consulting with teachers and staff, (3) conducting staff training and in-service/education programs, (4) consulting with parents/families, (5) counseling students, (6) performing psychoeducational evaluations, (7) providing direct interventions, and (8) completing administrative responsibilities (Jimerson et al., 2004).

Current Issues Impacting School Psychology

Although recent developments with regard to educational psychology practices in the educational system of Cyprus look promising, there is an increased demand for human resources and funding. Financial constraints affect decisions made entirely by government bodies, and the centralization of the delivery of services in the school system make the whole process very slow. Lack of money to properly fund services is an external threat to service delivery and is an obstacle to proper intervention, program development, and implementation in the school system. There is a public demand for more educational psychologists to be employed by the government. The ratio of 1 psychologist to 5,000 students is substantially higher than most of the European countries, making the work of an educational psychologist extremely difficult, considering the complexity of the job and the many diverse responsibilities. The role of an educational psychologist is still perceived as that of "support" personnel in Cyprus. The emphasis on the supportive nature of an educational psychologist's role diminishes the importance and value placed on the rest of the work provided by the service. Educational psychologists are perceived as providers of ancillary services to the instruction offered by teachers and the administration of principals (Papadopoulos, 2002). This emphasis on support services tends to shift attention from the other more diverse roles of educational psychologists, who should have an essential role in the educational system. They can contribute toward change and become facilitators of learning for all children. Through ongoing assessment of the needs of children and guiding school personnel and parents, educational psychologists can promote mental health within the school system. Educational psychologists can assist school personnel and administrators in their efforts to provide quality services to all students.

The lack of research and evaluation has important implications in the delivery of psychological services. Research is perceived by educational psychologists to be very relevant to professional practice. There is a need for theory-driven research specifically deriving from local experiences. The cooperation of the Educational Psychology Service with the Department of Psychology of the University of Cyprus can provide a solid starting point for more research

studies to be designed. Test development and standardization of testing materials on the population of Cyprus is also an aspect that needs to be further studied.

There is also a need for more theory-based interventions that address the needs of the local population of students. Seventy-three percent of educational psychologists indicated that the lack of research and evaluation was a challenge that jeopardizes the quality of service delivery (Jimerson et al., 2004). In an attempt to develop interventions based on a theoretical background, the Department of Psychology in the University of Cyprus cooperates with the Educational Psychology Service on a regular basis. Focusing on early intervention and prevention, Papadopoulos, Das, Parrila, and Kirby (2002) have aimed to develop and test the short- and long-term efficacy of a cognitive intervention program for the remediation of early reading difficulties. The overall findings of these studies suggest that theory-based early remediation may positively influence reading performance. The long-term efficacy of these cognitive interventions is evaluated and studied by the Educational Psychology Service and the University of Cyprus. It is imperative that more studies and research programs be developed and thus more effective interventions be designed and applied within the school system.

Educational psychologists are responsible for many tasks and various assignments. Supervision services need to be made available to educational psychologists due to the difficult, complex, and emotional nature of their job. In addition, lack of professional supervision is an aspect that increases stress among educational psychologists and does not promote professional advancement. Educational psychologists in Cyprus report professional burnout (82%) due to the nature of their work and the lack of supervision (64%) as challenges that jeopardize the quality of service delivery (Jimerson et al., 2004).

Important areas for future research include multicultural schools, evaluation of the unified educational system, school violence, school failure and dropout, early interventions, and learning difficulties. There is a need for further education and in-service training in the field of educational psychology. Additional financial resources need to be invested by the government to provide continuing professional development and expertise. The profession of school psychology is constantly developing, so that new techniques of psychological assessment and interventions are evolving. There is a growing need for educational psychologists to undertake further training and update their professional knowledge.

References

Georgiou, S. (1996). Parental involvement: Definition and outcomes. *Social Psychology of Education, 1*(3), 189–209.

Jimerson, S., Graydon, K., Farrell, P., Kikas, E., Hatzichristou, S., Bashi, G., Boce, E., & International School Psychology Association Research Committee. (2004). The International School Psychology Survey: Development and data from Albania, Cyprus, Estonia, Greece, and Northern England. *School Psychology International, 25*(3), 259–286.

Ministry of Education and Culture. (2004). *Annual report 2004*. Nicosia: Author.

Ministry of Labor. (2004). *Annual report 2004.* Nicosia: Ministry of Labor and Social Security.

Papadopoulos, T. (2002). The impact of inclusion policy on educational psychology practices: The Cypriot reality. *Educational and Child Psychology, 19*(2), 33–45.

Papadopoulos, T. C., Das, J. P., Parrila, R. K., & Kirby, J. R. (2002). Children at risk for developing reading difficulties: A remediation study. *School Psychology International, 24*(3), 340–366.

Public Law for the Consolidation of Professional Psychology 234(1) 1995. *Official Cyprus Government Gazette.* Nicosia: Cyprus Government Printing Office.

Public Law for the Education and Training of Children With Special Needs 113(1) 1999. *Official Cyprus Government Gazette* (No. 3340/1567, pp. 338–350). Nicosia: Cyprus Government Printing Office.

Statistical Service. (2004). *Statistics of education 2003–2004.* Nicosia: Cyprus Government Printing Office.

Tziogouros, C. (1999). *Psychology in education.* Paper presented at the conference of the Greek Psychological Association, Athens, Greece.

8

School Psychology in Denmark

Anders Poulsen

Context of School Psychology

Denmark is located in Northern Europe, between the North Sea and Baltic Sea, with Germany to the south and the Scandinavian Peninsula to the north. Denmark is a small country, with an area of 44,000 square kilometres (approximately 16,600 square miles) and a population of 5.5 million. In addition to Denmark's landmass on the Jutland Peninsula, it has 406 islands, connected with numerous bridges and ferry services, resulting in a total coastline of 7,300 kilometres. Denmark also includes the world's largest island, Greenland, and the Faeroe Islands, both of which are located in the North Atlantic Ocean and have home rule. Data about those areas are not included here, although their educational systems, including provision for pupils with special needs, are similar to those found in Denmark.

Denmark's population growth is flat, with an annual increase of 0.34%. Its median age is 39 for males and 40 for females. Approximately 19% are between birth and age 14, 66% between 15 and 64, and 15% are 65 years and older.

Denmark is largely farmland (65%), along with woodlands (12%). The remaining 23% consists of towns, roads, and lakes. Thus, historically, agriculture provided a significant economic base. As of 2002, only 4% of the population was working directly with farming, with 17% working in industry and the remaining 79% in services (Denmark, 2005). Although a small percentage of its population works directly with farming, Denmark is the world's fifth largest exporter of food products, most of which are secondary agricultural products. Denmark is poorly endowed with raw materials, having only chalk and, in the North Sea, oil and gas. Denmark's other important resources are less tangible yet important: education, ideas, and commerce. Its most rapidly expanding industrial sectors focus on technology, including biotechnology, information technology and software, and technology for environmental protection and energy conservation. The country's important exports include windmills, pharmaceutical products, and hearing aids. Denmark has a market economy featuring high-tech agriculture, contemporary small and corporate industry, extensive government welfare measures, comfortable living standards, a stable currency, and a large amount of foreign trade. In 2005, the gross domestic product was estimated at US$188 billion, US$34,718 per capita (Denmark, 2005).

The Folkeskole, Denmark's public primary and lower secondary school system, was founded in 1814 to provide 7 years of education for all children. Several major changes have been made in the education system since then. Today, education, not schooling, is compulsory for those between ages 7 and 16. Parents may decide to educate their children in publicly supported municipal schools, private schools, or at home, provided certain standards are met and an adequate range of subjects is provided. Most children (88%) attend public schools. Education is free, from preschool class (kindergarten level) through university levels.

Preschool classes for children age 6 must be offered by the municipalities. Although attendance is voluntary, almost all children attend. Primary and lower secondary schools provide a basic education of 9 years. The pupils progress automatically from one grade to the next irrespective of their yearly attainment and may elect to attend school an additional 10th year. The number of pupils in a Folkeskole class may not exceed 28. However, classes normally are smaller, often considerably smaller. The average number of students per class is approximately 19. The pupil-to-teacher ratio is 11 to 1. Approximately 48,200 teachers are employed, of which 64% are women. The net operational annual expenditure per pupil averages DKK 47,850 (about 6,425 euros).

Approximately 13% of the pupils in the primary and lower secondary education levels receive special education services for some time during each school year. Most attend normal mainstream classes and may receive additional support either in their class or through group lessons each week outside the class. About 2% attend special classes in their local municipal school system or, in some very large municipalities, in special schools. Some of the most severely disabled attend special schools established at the county level. The Danish education system services approximately 55,000 bilingual pupils from 40 countries (a figure that constitutes 9% of the total number of pupils), of whom 20% are of Turkish origin and nearly the same percentage from other Middle Eastern countries, and with about 5% each from Iraq and Somalia. A few municipalities have almost 50% bilingual pupils.

On completing the compulsory 9 years of education, about 35% elect to continue in the general upper secondary education programme; more girls than boys elect to continue. About 13% discontinue their education after completing the lower secondary compulsory school. Some leave the educational system, at least for the time being. Most elect to receive a vocational education. Among teenagers ages 15 though 17, only 8% are not in education. Pupils from non-Danish ethnic groups are less likely to engage in education after completing lower secondary compulsory school.

The Folkeskole is regulated by the education acts that establish the framework for school activities. Individual municipalities decide how their schools are to implement practices within this framework. Children remain with their peers in the same class and often with the same teacher from the 1st to the 9th (or 10th) grades, sharing the same experiences in all subjects with peers from various backgrounds who display a range of abilities. The Folkeskole has three important and broad goals. The first is, in cooperation with the parents, to further the pupils' acquisition of knowledge, skills, working methods, and ways of expressing themselves so as to attain well-rounded personal development. The second goal is to create opportunities for experience, industry, and absorption that enable pupils to develop awareness, imagination, and an urge to learn, leading to self-confidence and the ability to express independent judgements and take personal action. The third goal is to familiarise pupils with Danish culture and contribute to their understanding of other cultures and of human interaction with nature. The school shall prepare the pupils for active participation, joint responsibility, and the rights and duties of citizens in a society based on freedom and democracy. Therefore, teaching both within the school and in daily life must promote intellectual freedom, equality, and democracy.

The Folkeskole is financed by grants from the government to municipalities. The school system always has been decentralised, with decisions on the content of the learning made at the municipal level. During the past 20 years, this autonomy has been further highlighted by allowing administrative decisions to be made at the local school level rather than by municipalities or the Ministry of Education. These efforts are intended to strengthen the influence of parents and pupils in the day-to-day running of their schools. Each school has its own school board, elected for a 4-year period, normally consisting of five to seven parents of pupils attending the school, two teachers, two pupils elected by their peers, and the head teacher. Administrative reform, to be introduced in 2007, will reduce Denmark's municipalities from its current figure of 275 to 98 and its 14 counties to 5 regions. These reforms are to impact both regular and special education services. The new and larger municipalities will assume total responsibility for all education, including pupils with severe disabilities, through the secondary level. An exception is for children with the most severe disabilities, such as deaf-blind children, where the five regions will assume collective responsibility. The effectiveness of the Folkeskole is under review, triggered, in part, by results of an international study by the Organization for Economic Co-operation and Development (2003), which ranks Denmark's achievement low in reading and science.

The availability of private school education constitutes an important feature within Danish education and reflects the country's democratic structure. Parents who believe the primary and lower secondary school programmes offered their children are unsuitable can elect to send their children to one of approximately 450 private schools attended by approximately 75,000 pupils. The cost of private school education is assumed largely by the State (80% to 85%), with parents assuming the additional 15% to 20%. About 12% of all pupils attend private schools. Although private school attendance has increased since the early 1980s, this trend now seemingly has stabilised. The decision by parents to send their children to private schools generally is prompted by one of three concerns: their religious denomination preferences, the pedagogical theories of the competing schools, or a family's political and social preferences. Most private school enrolments typically are small, usually with no more than 100 to 200 pupils. Private school attendance generally is not considered to be elitist. Pupils who attend them derive no added status or advantage that affords them a smoother passage through upper secondary and tertiary education and beyond (Ministry of Education, 2000).

Special education and other special educational assistance is given to children (also before school age) if their development requires special consideration or support. A teacher, head teacher, or parent may refer children who are thought to need special education assistance for a pedagogical-psychological assessment. After consulting the parents, the head teacher sends the referral to the Pedagogical Psychological Counselling Office (Pædagogisk Psykologisk Rådgivning). The staff at this municipal institution then evaluates the child and, in consultation with the parent(s) and the school, determines whether the child needs special education or other special pedagogical services. A parent can refuse to accept this recommendation.

Staff from the Pedagogical Psychological Counselling Office monitors the development of pupils who receive special education services. Various administrative options are available. Pupils may remain in a mainstream school class and either receive special education in one or more subjects as a supplement to the general education or receive special education services that substitute for their participation in regular education classes in one or more subjects. If these options are not viable, a pupil's participation in a mainstream school class stops in favor of having the child receive his or her entire education in a special class, either within a mainstream school or within a special school. As a third option, a pupil may receive education in both mainstream school classes and special classes.

Origin, History, and Current Status of School Psychology

The term *school psychology* first appeared in print in Denmark in 1880 (Merregaard, 1880), and the foundation for school psychology was laid during the first two decades of the 20th century. A major breakthrough came with the formation, in 1924, of *The Committee for School Psychological Examination,* in part, because it assumed responsibility for developing achievement tests in reading and arithmetic and, in 1930, for publishing a Danish version of the Binet intelligence test. The same year (1930), a wealthy municipal school system in the suburbs of Copenhagen asked one of its teachers, who had a master of arts degree in psychology, to examine 15 children to determine whether they needed services provided by special education classes to "protect" backward children. This event marked the beginning of school psychology in Denmark. In 1934, this teacher was appointed as the first school psychologist in the country. This appointment established a long-lasting tradition for school psychologists: All were former teachers with additional university degrees in psychology.

The connection between school psychology and the development of a modern Folkeskole is very close. Thus, a brief description of some major legislative changes concerning special education and school psychology services is provided to promote an understanding of the evolution of school psychology in Denmark. Originally, the Danish municipal Folkeskole was

not obligated to educate children with special needs. The Denmark Ministry of Social Affairs initially assumed this responsibility, with services provided in day schools and boarding schools. Although the Education Act of 1937 did not obligate the Folkeskole to provide special education, the Act, for the first time, acknowledged this issue and stated, "For children who cannot follow ordinary teaching, special education must be provided if conditions allow it" (Ministry of Education, 1937). Many municipalities introduced special education services following this recommendation, resulting in the initial growth of school psychology. Its further growth occurred at two other periods: after 1957, when the provision of special education services by municipalities became compulsory (Ministry of Education, 1958), and in 1975, when the Ministry of Education required that special education services be provided only on the recommendation of a school psychologist, based on an assessment of the child (Ministry of Education, 1975).

During the 1960s and 1970s, a large number of major and far-reaching reforms were introduced that impacted both the education and the social welfare systems. Those that had the most impact on school psychology are discussed here. In 1969, the Parliament passed a 9-point programme to reform the elementary and lower secondary education system (Ministry of Education, 1969). Parts of this programme were directed toward promoting educational facilities for children with disabilities with the goal of allowing them to remain, as long as possible, in their normal school environment. Soon thereafter, large social reforms occurred that were to impact the Folkeskole and school psychology in important ways. All authority for administering schools and institutions for the "handicapped" was transferred from the State to counties and the municipalities, including responsibility for providing educational services to those served in these institutions. In 1980, this programme was implemented nationwide.

From 1980, the Ministry of Education had a unified responsibility for all basic education. These changes led to numerous changes for children with disabilities and those who served them. Municipal educational authorities now were responsible for identifying special needs children and serving them, including providing support services, regardless of the nature and severity of the disability. If needed help and support could not be provided within local schools, local authorities were required to locate where needed help could be provided, usually by referring the child to an institution, school, or agency in the county in which the municipality was located. Reform also required municipal educational systems to introduce preschool stimulation programmes, thus providing other opportunities for school psychologists to work with special needs children. School psychologists strongly supported these reforms, given their belief that the reforms would have an enormously positive impact on children and allow school psychologists to better serve them.

The services provided by school psychologists expanded greatly following these and other reforms. As a result, no one school psychologist could be expected to provide the wide range of needed services. Thus, activities that involved examination, evaluation, counselling, and decision making had to be based on teamwork, which necessitated a staff with differentiated knowledge and experience. Thus, in the early 1970s, a Ministry of Education Commission recommended a staffing pattern for the Pedagogical Psychological Counselling Office to better address their functions, including the designation of catchment areas with a minimum of 5,000 pupils.

Staffing levels for the Pedagogical Psychological Counselling Office were recommended to consist of a chief school psychologist, two assistant school psychologists (who also would teach part-time), two clinical psychologists, a social worker, and part-time specialists in speech, hearing, mental retardation, and other areas as needed. These recommendations were not implemented uniformly in Denmark, and, for a number of years, services developed rather unevenly. Nevertheless, since the 1960s, teachers and parents throughout the country have been able to consult, at no charge to them, with qualified professionals with considerable experience with children who display varied educational problems.

School psychology services have been an integral part of the local educational system. Their central offices were either in a school, an independent building, or the town hall. Schools often had an office specifically for psychology services. Staffing patterns generally included various professions serving on one team. A school psychologist always served as the leader of this team. Clinical psychologists (i.e., persons with a Candidate in Psychology degree and an additional 2 years of supervised work experience) were added to this team to assume responsibility for pupils' school-related social and emotional problems. In addition to serving as team leaders, the chief school psychologists often had important roles as advisers to school principals and the director of the local school system.

Although school psychology flourished during the 1970s and most of the 1980s, the legislative and administrative decisions outlined earlier contained the seed for a fundamental restructuring of administrative and service delivery systems, including the roles and functions of school psychologists. Many municipal politicians and their administrative staff became motivated to use their local authority, one decentralised from the State, to serve their constituents, including children, in new ways. Various needs seemingly were not well served through locally provided and publicly funded professional services. For example, many children posed challenges to the local social welfare department as well as to schools, thus warranting close cooperation between the two service agencies.

As a result, most school psychologists, previously serving only the local educational system, now became responsible for providing various counselling services needs within the community.

Unfortunately, schools, which had formerly been the main area of their work, now often feel neglected. Further erosions occurred in the primary roles of school psychologists. For example, the leader of the municipal counselling services for children and young people is no longer always a school psychologist and instead may be a clinical psychologist, social worker, or from some other professional background. Due to these developments, nationwide statistics on psychological services provided in educational systems or on the number of pedagogical psychologists (school psychologists) are not available.

The salary system is rather complicated. Danish school psychology has its origin in Folkeskolen. Thus, for historical reasons, the teachers union negotiates salaries for psychologists holding a teacher's certificate (currently called "pedagogical psychologists" instead of "school psychologists"). Salaries for assistant pedagogical psychologists are similar to those of an assistant principal at a large school, and salaries for the leaders of the service, if they are pedagogical psychologists, are similar to those of a principal of a large school. Some of the psychologists employed by the Pedagogical Psychological Counselling Office may not hold a teacher's qualification, and their salaries are negotiated by the Union of Danish Psychologists. In 2005, the average annual salaries were estimated to be approximately DKK 270,000 to DKK 335,000 (equivalent to approximately 36,240 to 44,965 euros) and are a little lower than those with the teacher's certificate. Generally, psychologists, whether working for private or public employers, have the same salary level as all other university graduates with the same length of training. For instance, candidates of law, economy, and science receive similar salaries. The unemployment rate of psychologists generally is high, about 7%, and is somewhat lower for psychologists holding a teacher's certificate. Job security for psychologists at the Pedagogical Psychological Counselling Office is high. A recent survey by the Union of Danish Psychologists (Dansk Psykolog Forening, 2003) indicated that some employees of the Pedagogical Psychological Counselling Office experienced difficulty prioritising the services they perform and that they were unable to comply with the expectations of those they were serving. Nevertheless, they reported high rates of satisfaction in reference to their independence and freedom in planning their own work.

Infrastructure of School Psychology

The Union of Danish Psychologists (Dansk Psykologforening) serves as the professional association for Danish psychologists. Founded in 1947, it has about 7,400 members, among whom 73% are women. The Association of Pedagogic Psychologists, founded in 1956, has 882 members, among whom 70% are women. Psychologists holding a teacher's certificate and working in the Pedagogical Psychological Counselling Office generally are members of both the Union of Danish Psychologists and the Association of Pedagogic Psychologists. Among those eligible for membership in the Association of Pedagogic Psychologists, close to 100% are members. Almost all members of this association also are members of the Danish Teachers Union—given its important role in negotiating salaries. All three organisations function efficiently and effectively and are influential when negotiating with the central government on practice issues that impact the Danish municipalities and the general public. The Union of Danish Psychologists and the Association of Pedagogic Psychologists offer a large number of continuing education courses and other continuing education programmes.

Both professional associations publish journals. The Union of Danish Psychologists journal, *Psykolog Nyt* (Psychology News), is as old as the union itself. The Association of Pedagogic Psychologists journal, *Pædagogisk Psykologisk Rådgivning* (Pedagogical Psychological Counselling), publishes six issues annually; articles include English abstracts and are devoted to various educational and psychological subjects.

The journal *Pædagogisk Psykologisk Rådgivning* is highly respected for its professional quality, reflected, in part, by its wide distribution among not only psychologists but also other professionals. Its circulation of 1,900 is more than twice the number of association members. The Association of Pedagogic Psychologists also publishes a newsletter. The Association of Pedagogic Psychologists and the Union of Danish Psychologists established a publishing company many years ago, the Danish Psychological Publishing Company (Dansk Psykologisk Forlag), which develops national testing materials and also translates and adapts foreign tests. Its goal is to maintain high ethical and other professional standards in the development, distribution, and use of tests in Denmark. Today, it publishes many textbooks and journals.

Preparation of School Psychologists

In 1944, the University of Copenhagen established a 3-year programme to prepare school psychologists who held a teacher-training certificate. The programme awarded the degree of Candidate in Psychology, a title still used for graduates in psychology from three Danish universities. The contents of this programme have been changed at various times, most recently because of European Union efforts to bring consistency to academic and professional programmes in member countries. The current programme consists of a 3-year bachelor programme plus an additional 2 years of graduate preparation. This programme emphasises important theoretical as well as applied features of psychology. Those who complete this programme continue to hold the title Candidate in Psychology. The programme offers candidates various opportunities to specialise, including supervised training and workshop experiences, thus preparing them to provide a wide range of psychological services. However, if they are employed at a Pedagogical Psychological Counselling Office, they cannot be appointed to a job

with functions in traditional school psychology, as this requires a teaching certificate or a similar recognition of expertise and experience in education, a requirement the very strong teachers union has been able to maintain.

In 1963, the Royal Danish School of Educational Studies (currently the Danish University of Education) established a programme parallel to the Candidate in Psychology programme that built on the 4-year training required for a teacher's certification. This new 3- to 4-year programme was designed specifically for psychologists intending to work mainly with educational issues in the Folkeskole. The graduates of this programme received the Candidate in Pedagogical Psychology degree and enjoyed the same professional rights as those who received the Candidate in Psychology degree. Unfortunately, this programme recently was dropped as a result of efforts to bring greater unity to programmes in Danish universities. Current plans call for offering a 2-year programme, building on the 4-year training for a teacher's certificate, to prepare candidates to provide specialised services in educational systems. As this is not sufficient to train a candidate in psychology, strong efforts are being made to add additional training to this programme so as to preserve proper preparation programmes for school psychologists to work in the Pedagogical Psychological Counselling Office. This is not yet approved, for which reason Denmark currently does not offer any university programmes that prepare professionals to function in the role of traditional school psychologists in the Pedagogical Psychological Counselling Office. Thus, data on the number of candidates admitted to school psychology preparation programmes are unavailable. Professionals who hold a Candidate in Psychology or a Candidate in Pedagogical Psychology degree may elect to pursue a 3-year Ph.D. programme. Few have elected this programme because it is geared toward those who plan to teach at the university level and conduct research. Applied psychology is not emphasised.

Programmes that prepare students to take the degrees of Candidate in Psychology and Candidate in Pedagogical Psychology have high professional and academic standards. They typically offer the following courses: psychology of personality, cognition and learning, social psychology, developmental psychology, human biology, psychiatry, quantitative methods of research, the science theory of psychology and methodology, clinical psychology, psychology of labour, educational psychology, intervention techniques, history of psychology, and test theory. In 1993, the Act of Psychologists was passed, in part, to protect the title "psychologist" by using it to refer exclusively to persons holding the degree Candidate in Psychology or Candidate in Pedagogical Psychology. Furthermore, this Act introduced the title "authorised psychologist" to be used by those who, following their university degrees in psychology, work under supervision for 2 or more years, full-time, providing various services. Almost all psychologists work to obtain the designation authorised psychologist, in part, because it will add almost 10% to their annual salary.

On obtaining this title, many will further upgrade, often at their own expense, to specialise in one or more of 10 areas, among which 3 focus on providing services to children. Specialisation requirements are stringent and include at least 3 years of work experience within the specialisation area, 200 hours of personal supervision, 300 hours of theory, and the completion of a dissertation. The Union of Danish Psychologists and the Association of Pedagogic Psychologists support this upgrading programme by arranging courses and internships and through other ways. Universities also are supporting this effort by offering courses that emphasise theory. In addition to obtaining the teaching credential, a large proportion of Pedagogical Psychological Counselling Office psychologists will obtain their authorisation status, and about 20% will pursue the specialisation in pedagogic psychology.

Roles, Functions, and Responsibilities of School Psychologists

The roles, functions, and responsibilities of psychologists employed by the Pedagogical Psychological Counselling Office are broadly defined, not detailed: (1) They support and influence schools, administrators, and staff and foster instructional activities with the goal of serving all children, especially those with special needs, so that as few as possible are segregated from their classmates. (2) They evaluate pupils referred in light of their possible special needs. (3) They are committed to the implementation of preschool programmes that help prevent later academic and other school-related difficulties. These three statements provide some headlines for the multiplicity of activities and responsibilities in which a well-functioning and well-respected Pedagogical Psychological Counselling Office will be involved.

Some of the most important working methods include the parent meetings in kindergartens and in schools and group or individual consultation or counselling. In addition, the counselling service is represented in local committees consisting of leading representatives from the local police, social services, and schools, who collaborate to prevent drug problems, youth crime, and so on. Here, functions relating to consultation and systemic work are seen as important. In relation to the individual class or child, Danish school psychology has always stressed the importance of class observation; teacher, parent, and child counselling; and working within the total social and emotional context in which the child lives. Testing is a natural part of these functions but rarely the major or most important part. All the best-known international tests, from the United States and elsewhere, are used, to some extent, in Denmark but with the greatest degree of care and reservation if professional Danish adaptations and standardised instruments are not available.

A large number of achievement tests developed in Denmark are used (some reading tests have been translated and adapted in other countries, such as Greenland, Iceland, Norway, Sweden, and some of the Baltic States). Assessment tests available in Denmark include the Wechsler Preschool and Primary Scale of Intelligence–Revised and the Wechsler Intelligence Scale for Children–III (both adapted for use in Denmark) and a Danish version of the Differential Abilities Scales supplemented with elements from the original British Ability Scales. Numerous foreign tests, known all over the world, are also used in Denmark: for example, the Thematic Apperception Test, the Bender Visual-Motor Gestalt Test, and the Leiter International Performance Scale.

Current Issues Impacting School Psychology

Denmark is engaged in countrywide administrative evaluations that will lead to reforms to be implemented in 2007. These reforms will influence almost all aspects of government, including those relating to education. As can be expected, reforms lead to changes and thus foster insecurity. The Pedagogical Psychological Counselling Office views this transition period with concern as well as a time to assume additional responsibilities. Denmark generally is proud of its school system. For more than 30 years, professionals and politicians have been able to work together with the goal of fashioning a Folkeskole that serves all children in an institution that is inclusive and democratic and minimises labelling and segregating pupils. These efforts have not been fully

achieved, and these goals remain important. Thus, politicians, educationalists (including psychologists), and others are engaged in discussions to find areas of agreement about the reasons for problems and methods to solve them.

Some are concerned that the Danish school system is too expensive, especially special needs education and care, and that academic attainment is low. However, others focus on information that indicates that the Folkeskole is exceptional in its efforts to promote creativity and a cooperative spirit among children and adults and in its ability to prepare its citizens to compete favourably in a global world. Amendments to the General School Act are expected to be voted on by the Parliament during the first half of 2006. The goal is to improve learning in the basic subjects, and computerised national tests will be introduced, which are seen by some as a pedagogic tool. Details are not yet decided, but eventually they will be available at the Ministry's Web site. The functions and roles of the Pedagogical Psychological Counselling Office are being reviewed within the context described earlier in this chapter and are likely to change significantly. The Pedagogical Psychological Counselling Office anticipates its assessment work will further decrease and be replaced by an emphasis on its role as process consultant, given the goal to change the inner life of schools in the direction of being even more inclusive while improving achievement in the major school subjects. Political systems, including those in Denmark, often have the unrealistic expectation that significant social and education change can occur just by upgrading the qualifications of those employed. One may take solace in the following belief, expressed in 1899: "Well started as the school psychology now is, it will for sure have a bright future in our country" (Hansen, 1899). In the coming years, Denmark surely will experience various problems that require the continued services of school psychology.

References

Dansk Psykolog Forening. (2003). *Psykologers arbejdsmiljø.* [Psychologists' work environment]. (Available from Dansk Psykolog Forening [Association of Danish Psychologists] at http://www.danskpsykologforening.dk)

Dansk Psykolog Forening. (2006). *Løn, takster og honorarer, 2006* [Salary, tariffs and fees, 2006]. Retrieved from http://www.danskpsykolog forening.dk

Denmark. (2005). Retrieved April 4, 2006, from http://en.wikipedia.org/wiki/Denmark

Hansen, O. (1899). Skolepsykologi [School psychology]. *Vor Ungdom,* 20(4), 510–517.

Merregaard, J. (1880). Skolepsykologi i omrids [An outline of school psychology]. *Vor Ungdom, 1*(1), 94–109.

Ministry of Education. (1937). Lov om Folkeskolen af 18.5.1937 [Public School Act of 1937].

Ministry of Education. (1958). Lov om Folkeskolen af 7.6.1958 [Public School Act of 1958].

Ministry of Education. (1969). Folketingsbeslutning af 30.6.1969 om reform af de grundlæggende skoleuddannelser [Parliament decision about future changes in basic education].

Ministry of Education. (1975). Lov om Folkeskolen af 26.6.1975 [Education Act of June 26, 1975].

Ministry of Education. (2000). Private schools in Denmark. Retrieved April 4, 2006, from http://eng.uvm.dk//publications/factsheets/fact9.htm

Organization for Economic Co-operation and Development. (2003). Education at a glance—Denmark. http://www.oecd.org/

9

Educational Psychology in England and Wales

Garry Squires

Peter T. Farrell

In England and Wales, the term *educational psychologist* is used to denote psychologists who are predominantly employed by local education authorities. Therefore, in this chapter, the term *educational psychologist* will be used. Furthermore, only trivial differences exist between educational psychologist services in England and Wales. Thus, unless otherwise indicated, this chapter does not distinguish between them. Finally, some figures refer to all countries that compose the United Kingdom, including Scotland. This is because separate figures for England and Wales were not available. Figures from the United Kingdom are quoted when there is no reason to believe that they are different from those of England and Wales.

Context of Educational Psychology

Located in the North Atlantic Ocean and North Sea, with Ireland to the west and France to the south and east, England and Wales cover an area of 58,382 square miles (Gardner, 1992) and, in 2003, had a population of 52,794,000 (National Statistics Online, 2005a, 2005b). The older population is increasing, and the proportion of children is declining. A decrease in the number of students has led some local authorities to close some schools and merge others to reduce financial costs (Department for Education and Skills, 2005a). A mixture of high-density populations is centred on a few major cities and lightly populated rural areas. Unemployment in the United Kingdom is falling, as the economy is strong, with a gross domestic product of US$1.782 trillion, US$29,600 per capita. The average salary is £27,016 (i.e., $48,000, €37,539). The average house price in April 2005 was £154,107 (i.e., $278,363, €214,132; Nationwide Building Society, 2005). While there is a general increase in living standards and quality of life, some people remain in relative poverty. Government policy to address this has focused on social inclusion, and this attention to inclusion permeates all aspects of politics, including education.

Immigration to the United Kingdom is becoming an important factor in population change (National Statistics Online, 2005a) and contributes to the multicultural nature of the United Kingdom. In England in 2004, pupils belonging to ethnic minority groups represented 18% of the primary school population and 15% of the secondary school population; 10% of children speak English as their second language (Department for Education and Skills, 2005e). The immigrant population has increased by 20% since 1997. The ethnic population in some local education authorities is low (e.g., East Riding in Yorkshire has 1.5%), whereas in others it is much higher (e.g., Hackney has 84%). This means that educational psychologists working in different parts of the country may have very different experiences in working with people from different cultural and linguistic backgrounds.

Educational policy is determined at the national level through the Department for Education and Skills and implemented through 153 local education authorities, who are responsible for schools within their districts. Compulsory education is from age 5 through 16. However, most pupils start in nursery classes at age 4. Private nursery education may precede this. Local education authorities are required to provide special education services for children as young as 2 years old who have severe special educational needs. Many pupils remain at school past age 16. In 2003, just over 4 million primary school pupils (ages 5–11) and 3.3 million secondary pupils (ages 11–16) attended maintained schools (in England and Wales, schools that are supported by public money are referred to as maintained schools, and those that are paid for by parents are referred to as independent schools). Of these, 17% of primary pupils and 15% of secondary pupils were eligible for free school meals (Department for Education and Skills, 2005a), a proxy indicator of social and financial deprivation.

All maintained schools are required to adhere to a centrally devised national curriculum. The curriculum states which subjects should be taught and what areas of study should be covered at each grade level. Core subjects include mathematics, English, and science. There is emphasis on basic attainments, with pupils sitting examinations (Standard Attainment Tasks) in each of these subjects at ages 7, 11, 14, and 16. Individual pupil performance is reported to parents. In England, results published in performance tables, commonly referred to as league tables, compare the schools' ability to meet the expected standards. This sets an achievement agenda for schools and places pressure on teachers to focus on those pupils who are most likely to achieve the desired levels of attainment on standard attainment tasks. This policy can create tension when a school is asked to accept special needs children whose lower achievement may lower the school's academic average.

In addition to mainstream schools, others specialise in catering to students with low-incidence, high-severity needs. In some areas, units (e.g., a classroom attached to a mainstream school, a resource room, or a building on the same site as a mainstream school) are attached to mainstream schools. This type of provision is growing. A large number of private special schools and units are funded from public money allocated by local education authorities. The government encourages the placement of children with special educational needs in mainstream education, and parents have the right to have their child educated in mainstream schools if they desire. Less than 1% of all children attend special schools or other segregated settings. From 1994 to 2004, the average number of pupils per class has decreased slightly in primary (26.9–26.2) and increased slightly in secondary (21.4–21.8) schools. Class sizes are smaller in special schools and units, depending on the children's needs.

The proportion of pupils with special educational needs is difficult to quantify. There are no objective criteria for defining what constitutes a special educational need. Some definitions are circular: for example, "Children have special educational needs if they have a learning difficulty which calls for special educational provision to be made for them" (Department for Education and Skills, 2001, p. 6). The 1944 Education Act (Department for Education and Skills, 2001) and subsequent acts also define a learning difficulty in relativistic terms: (a) a "significantly greater difficulty in learning than the majority of children of the same age" or (b) "have a disability which prevents or hinders them from making use of educational facilities of a kind generally provided for children of the same age in schools within the area of the local education authority," "are under compulsory school age and will fall under [either of the above] definition[s] or would do so if special educational provision was not made for them."

> Special educational provision means for children of two or over, educational provision which is additional to, or otherwise different from, the educational provision made generally for children of their age in schools maintained by the Local Education Authority, other than special schools, in the area for children under two, educational provision of any kind. (Department for Education and Skills, 2001, p. 6)

In practice, schools define special educational needs on the basis of the population they serve. Local education authorities draw up criteria that define which children will be entitled to additional resources. A graduated response requires teachers to provide different levels of support depending on the needs of the child. This will move from simple differentiation to more intensive support and on to asking outside specialists to provide advice. Pupils with more extreme special educational needs are provided with a statement of special educational need (hereafter called Statement) following procedures established in the 1993 Education Act (and subsequent acts) and with guidance set out in the Code of Practice for Special Educational Needs (Department for Education and Skills, 2001). The lack of an objective definition of special educational need means that there will be individual cases for which the entitlement to additional support becomes a matter of dispute. The government has established an independent body, Special Educational Needs and Discrimination Act Tribunal, to which parents can appeal decisions and thus attempt to resolve disputes.

The numbers of pupils with Statements rose slightly in both England and Wales during the 1990s and reached a plateau in 2005 (Department for Education and Skills, 2005c; National Assembly in Wales, 2004). In England, the percentage of pupils with Statements rose from 1994 (2.5%) to 2004 (3.0%). There is a move to reduce the need for Statements and to provide funding to meet the additional needs of pupils through other means. Approximately 75% of all new Statements in England are for pupils placed in mainstream schools (Department for Education and Skills, 2005c). This does not necessarily mean that they will be placed in a mainstream class, as there has been a growth in the number of special classes or units attached to mainstream schools, particularly in Wales. In England, among students with Statements, 148,550 are in mainstream, 92,620 are in special schools and units, and 7,800 are in independent schools. In Wales, among students with Statements, 8,914 students are placed in mainstream (3,745 in special classes or units), 3,779 are placed in special schools and units, and 260 are enrolled in independent schools. For example, about 75% of Welsh pupils with Statements are educated in mainstream schools, and 52.6% are in mainstream classes (National Assembly in Wales, 2004).

Origin, History, and Current Status of Educational Psychology

Wooldridge (1994) provides a detailed account of the development of educational psychology in England and Wales between 1860 and 1990.

The 1870 Education Act marked the start of compulsory education. Thus, teachers had to teach children who displayed the full range of mental abilities. This created a culture shock for some teachers and was compounded with a system of "payment by results." Academically weaker children who failed to pass the yearly test earned the school less money. This led to a major concern that children with subnormal abilities were hindering the progress of other children in large, overcrowded classes. Hence, a number of local authorities started to experiment with the development of special schools.

A medical officer was responsible for deciding if children were suitable for mainstream school, if they could go to special school, or if they were uneducable and thus could not attend school. This system had major imperfections. Many medical officers did not have sufficient psychological knowledge to place children appropriately. There also were continuing concerns from teachers about maladjusted children who displayed social, emotional, or behavioural difficulties that prevented them from achieving their academic potential. The 1902 Education Act provided local education authorities additional authority and autonomy that allowed them to develop local solutions and policies while following the lead of the Board of Education. The Board of Education was established by the government to control education in England and Wales. In subsequent years, its title was changed to the Department for Education, and several name changes have followed.

The London County Council employed Cyril Burt as a psychologist on a part-time basis to try to help solve the problem of classifying children's suitability for schooling. By the 1920s, several other local education authorities also employed psychologists. Toward the end of the 1920s the child guidance movement reached the United Kingdom from the United States. Multiprofessional clinic-based teams consisting of a psychiatrist, psychologist, physician, and social worker were established to try to understand and possibly prevent juvenile misbehaviour. The London County Council relied on Burt's expertise to help them address organisational issues. He helped develop guidelines for the development of educational psychology services and for the continued development of child guidance clinics.

The duties of psychologists varied and depended on whether they were employed by educational or medical services. Those employed by education tended to go from school to school and advise teachers about individual pupils or teaching programmes. Those employed by medical services were involved in child guidance clinics. The 1944 Education Act required local education authorities to provide suitable education for children who were subnormal, maladjusted, or physically handicapped. This required further employment of psychologists who were trained to understand the needs of children with low academic ability.

The Underwood Committee emphasized the need for improved recruitment and deployment of psychologists in school services and child guidance clinics (Department for Education and Science, 1955). In 1965, the Department for Education and Science established a committee to examine the work and training of educational psychologists. The Summerfield Report (Department for Education and Science, 1968) indicates that, by the late 1960s, the number of full-time educational psychologists was 326, and 100 positions were unfilled. This extremely influential report also recommended that there should be one educational psychologist for every 10,000 pupils.

The 1981 Education Act heralded a major restructuring of all services for children with special educational needs and suggested educational psychologists should be involved in the assessment of pupils who might have special educational needs. This led to an expansion of the numbers of educational psychologists being employed by local education authorities who were responsible for administering the new act. The 1993 Education act and 1994 *Code of Practice for Special Educational Needs* emphasised the need for a staged approach to assessment and to strengthened moves toward inclusion. Further refinements came with the revision of the *Code of Practice* in 2001, which emphasises the role of teachers in identifying children's difficulties and adjusting their teaching accordingly in order to make a graduated response to learning difficulties. This places the child at the centre of support, with the class teacher responsible for meeting the child's needs. The class teacher is supported in turn by the school staff, especially the special needs coordinator. Further support and advice can be sought for school staff, including teachers. Educational psychologists frequently provide this service.

Most educational psychologists work for local education authorities. A few work privately or in independent schools. Educational psychologists are based in offices and offer services to the local education authority. They also work with nurseries and parents at home. Educational psychologists typically visit a number of schools on a regular basis to consult with teachers and parents and to work directly with pupils. Educational psychologists also are involved with school development work, including running projects; helping schools formally evaluate their programs, skills, or behaviour; acting as a critical friend (a familiar outsider who challenges a school to reflect on its work while remaining supportive and encouraging); and helping schools develop policies.

The number employed as educational psychologists has increased steadily, from 1,545 in 1990 to 2,647 in 2004 (Employers' Organisation, 2004), with 112 unfilled vacancies. Slightly less than 30% of these posts are filled on a part-time basis, and there remains a national shortage of qualified educational psychologists. As noted previously, the Summerfield Report recommended one educational psychologist for every 10,000 pupils. In 2004, the ratio of educational psychologists to students was approximately 1 to 2,757. Although these figures appear to be promising, they disguise the real ratio. If one eliminates those employed in management positions and employed parts time, the ratio is less favourable. Educational psychologists are paid on a national pay scale. As of April 2005, the salaries were assistant educational psychologist, £24,477–£27,471 (i.e., S$44,213–$49,621; €34,011–€38,171); main grade educational psychologist (Grade A) £29,670–£44,895 (i.e., US$53,593–$81,094; €41,226–€62,382); senior and principal educational psychologist (Grade B) £38,865–£57,027 (i.e., US$70,202–$103,008; €54,003–€79,239; National Union of Teachers, 2005a). By comparison, the following salaries are for other professionals who work in schools: Youth and Community Service Officers £30,651–£48,102 (i.e., US$55,365–$86,887; €42,590–€66,838); main scale teachers (not including management points or other responsibilities) £30,651–£48,102 (i.e., US$34,611–$58,936; €26,624–€45,337); head teachers £37,617–£93,297 (i.e., $67,948–$168,522; €52,269–€129,636; National Union of Teachers, 2005a, 2005b).

Entrance into the speciality of educational psychology has required teacher training and at least 2 years teaching experience. If salary comparisons are made, teachers may not consider educational psychology to be financially worthwhile. The development of teaching competencies and progress to advanced skills teacher status or assumption of management responsibilities may be more lucrative. Similar comparisons can be made with other professional psychologists. Educational psychologists on Grade A have comparable salaries to those in branches of psychology: for example, Clinical Scale A, £18,000–£39,000 (i.e., US$32,513–$70,446; €25,011–€54,191); Clinical Scale B, £39,000–£60,000 (i.e., US$70,446–$108,378+; €54,191–€83,370+); and Counselling, £26,000–£69,260 (i.e., US$46,964–$125,104; €36,127–€96,237). The Employers' Organisation for Local Government conducts a yearly workforce survey. The 2004 data show that, among educational psychologists, the average age is 45 or older, and 75% are female. Approximately 10% of educational psychologists changed positions; about a third of these moved to another post in another local education authority. The number of educational psychologists leaving the profession exceeds the number being trained. The shortage of educational psychologists is not due to a lack of people wanting to enter the profession. Approximately 400 people apply to undertake training each year in one of the 13 universities that offer training programmes (British Psychological Society Division of Educational and Child Psychology, 2003b). Between 110 and 130 educational psychologists are trained each year. Thus, approximately one third of the applicants are accepted and complete the program. Not surprisingly, a third of all local education authorities report difficulty recruiting main grade or senior educational psychologists (Employers' Organisation, 2004).

Infrastructure of Educational Psychology

Educational psychologists may but are not obligated to join the British Psychological Society. The Division of Educational and Child Psychology represents the interests of the profession within the British Psychological Society. Educational psychologists who join the Division of Educational and Child Psychology can become Chartered Educational Psychologists. The professional trade union for educational psychologists is the Association of Educational Psychologists. This body negotiates pay and conditions of service with employers.

The conditions of employment for educational psychologists state required qualifications and experience, though this is currently under review with changes in training expected to start in September 2006 (for further discussion, see the section titled "Preparation of Educational Psychologists"). Possession of a driving licence and freedom from any criminal convictions that would prevent working with children are additional requirements. There has been a move toward compulsory registrations (i.e., by law,

must be registered to practice); however, this is still being developed. The use of titles to describe psychologists is to be restricted. All educational psychologists are likely to be required to register with the Health Professions Council (British Psychological Society, 2005b), thus establishing requirements for minimum initial training and minimum levels of continuing professional development to establish and maintain professional competence to practice as an educational psychologist.

The Association of Educational Psychologists produces a peer-reviewed journal, *Educational Psychology in Practice*. The British Psychological Society circulates the monthly magazine *The Psychologist,* and the Division of Educational and Child Psychology publishes the journal *Educational and Child Psychology* and the newsletter *Debate.* Many educational psychologists also share views and ideas more informally through the e-mail newsgroup *EPNET.* Other journals and magazines relevant to the profession include *Educational Psychology, British Journal of Educational Psychology, British Journal of Psychology, British Journal of Developmental Psychology,* and *Special Children.*

Preparation of Educational Psychologists

Requirements for training educational psychologists are being reviewed. As of September 2005, training takes a minimum of 8 years: an honours degree or equivalent in psychology recognised by the British Psychological Society (3 years), qualified teacher status (1 year), at least 2 years teaching experience as a qualified teacher of children age 19 years or younger, and a postgraduate training course in educational psychology recognised by the British Psychological Society (1 year). This training includes a mixture of university-based training and supervised experience with an educational psychologist working in a local education authority.

Most educational psychology services provide ongoing professional supervision for all psychologists. All psychologists are expected to continue their professional development and update their skills and knowledge. Some psychologists elect to obtain a professional doctorate in educational psychology; this program can take at least 4 years. The need to reduce training time while strengthening educational psychology is apparent. Several alternative training models are being considered. One proposed model requires 6 years of training and is likely to require a Good honours degree, or its equivalent, in psychology recognised by the British Psychological Society for conditional registration. A 3-year training program as an educational psychologist at the doctoral level would also be required. Responsibility for this training is likely to be divided between a university and a local education authority. Twelve doctorate programmes in educational psychology have been accredited by the British Psychological Society (British Psychological Society, 2005a).

The government is reviewing the roles and functions of educational psychologists. This review, expected to be completed by the end of 2006, is to consider that the work performed by educational psychologists has widened considerably during the past few years (Department for Education and Skills, 2005d). The British Psychological Society has developed a curriculum in preparation for the revised training model (British Psychological Society, 2003). The curriculum assumes that all who are preparing to become educational psychologists will have an undergraduate psychology degree or equivalent. Academic courses at this level generally include core subjects, such as child development, cognitive psychology, social psychology, and research methods. The 3-year professional training focuses on how to apply psychology and is divided into learning outcome groups. The following are provided as a sample of learning outcome groups: core professional skills (e.g., reflective and critical thought and applications of psychological knowledge leading to assessment and intervention strategies); core professional practice skills (e.g., adherence to ethics and legal frameworks; using psychological

paradigms, theories, and frameworks; working competently and independently; engaging in supervision); practice of applied educational psychologists; application of evaluation, research, and enquiry; effective communication; and service delivery.

Roles, Functions, and Responsibilities of Educational Psychologists

Educational psychologists are applied psychologists who usually deliver services in a cluster of schools as well as provide services to preschool children and their parents. They collaborate with colleagues from the Health and Social Services departments and other education employees. The work is diverse and based on applications of psychological knowledge, skills, and principles to promote the inclusion of children with special educational needs, raise school standards, and carry out statutory duties. The roles of educational psychologists have changed significantly in response to educational legislation in recent years (British Psychological Society Division of Education and Child Psychology, 2003b; Department for Education and Employment, 2000). Educational psychologists focus on assessment and intervention for children age 19 years or younger who may have cognitive, linguistic, physical, sensory, social, or emotional difficulties. They work directly with pupils as well as with parents, teachers, and other professionals.

Educational psychologists generally work with children age 2 and older and occasionally will work with younger children. The District Health Authority generally refers very young children to the local education authority. In the past, the main role of educational psychologists with this age-group was to contribute to special educational needs assessments. However, their role recently has widened. Following the publication of *Removing Barriers to Achievement* (Department for Education and Skills, 2004), there has been a move toward working more closely with health professionals, social service department employees, and educational professionals. One example of this closer cooperation is seen in the creation of professional positions, such as Early Years Special Educational Needs Coordinators in local education authorities who work in nursery and preschool settings. Arrangements for health and educational professionals to work together in multidisciplinary teams to assess and support preschool children are being considered. If approved, educational psychologists will work with and may lead these teams.

The goal of assessment performed by educational psychologists is to help teachers meet the child's educational needs more effectively and to include the child more fully in the learning experience. Typically this includes a search for strengths as well as weaknesses and provides adults with information to guide understanding and to help them decide what to do next. Educational psychologists use a problem-solving framework when approaching assessments, and this will be informed by psychological theory. This tends to start with a clarification of the problem through discussion with teachers, parents, and children. This, in turn, raises assessment questions or hypotheses for further investigation. A wide variety of approaches are used in this investigation, with techniques and tools selected on their appropriateness to the question or hypothesis being explored. This may include classroom observations, further discussion with key adults or others who have been involved in working with the child, the use of personal construct psychology, solution-focussed approaches (based on the work of de Shazer, 1988, 1991), the use of rating scales and self-report questionnaires, dynamic assessment, and assessment through teaching or the use of tests. There are no legal requirements to carry out assessments in any particular way or to use particular instruments. Thus, some educational psychologists will not use any standardised tools, and others will draw heavily on them. A noncomprehensive list of examples of instruments used by educational psychologists includes

tests of cognitive ability (British Ability Scales–II; Wechsler Intelligence Scale for Children–IV; Bender-Gestalt); tests of attainment (British Ability Scales–II subtests for reading, spelling, and number skills; Neale Analysis of Reading Ability; Wechsler Individual Achievement Test for reading, spelling, math, and the Phonological Assessment Battery); measures of self-esteem (e.g., Culture Free Self-Esteem Index); and self-rating scales for behaviour or personality (e.g., Beck Youth Inventory). A small number of educational psychologists also use projective tests (e.g., Bene-Anthony Family Relations Test).

Educational psychologists offer support and advice when a teacher, parent, or health worker expresses concerns that a child may have learning, social, emotional, or behavioural difficulties. The work usually takes place in schools, colleges, and separate units. Educational psychologists initially will consult with the adults to clarify the concerns and to determine which interventions have been tried and their effectiveness. The goal of this involvement is to help develop a better understanding of the child and his or her circumstances to help teachers develop effective ways of overcoming the difficulties. Further work may involve joint problem solving, developing intervention programmes, assessing cognitive abilities or attainments, providing interventions including but not limited to therapeutic work with individuals or small groups, classroom or playground observations, gathering information from others, and helping others monitor the effectiveness of interventions.

Other personnel usually provide interventions. Teachers and teaching assistants are responsible for teaching children, and the educational psychologist is responsible for assisting school personnel. On occasion, educational psychologists will intervene (e.g., using cognitive behavioural therapy to help a young person make a more acceptable response or to manage his or her anger more effectively), running Quality Circle Time sessions (Mosley, 2005), or conducting other small group work.

Educational psychologists work directly with pupils being assessed in accordance with the 2001 Education Act. This work, although limited in time, obtains information from parents, teachers, and the pupil. Educational psychologists consider the child's special educational needs by assessing various areas of functioning, including cognition and learning, social and emotional development, language and other forms of communication, physical and sensory development, and independent living skills. It may be necessary to liaise with other professionals who have worked with the child. Following his or her assessment, educational psychologists report their findings and recommendations to the local education authority as part of the statutory assessment procedures.

Educational psychologists may work at the school level in various ways. They may help schools develop or review policies, help teachers review the effectiveness of school policies (e.g., those that address behaviour, special educational needs, inclusion, risk assessment for children with challenging behaviour, equal opportunities), interact with adults at many levels, assist others in the use of techniques to help manage pupils with behavioural difficulties, help schools implement legislative changes, help teachers engage in action research within their 'school, and act as a *critical friend* (as described earlier) to help teachers reflect on their practice and help schools carry out an evaluation of what they do and how well they do it.

Educational psychologists help local education authorities meet requirements of many central government initiatives to promote social and educational equality. Hence, they may become members of working groups and offer advice on a range of issues and legislative changes concerned with organisation and policy development. They may help local education authorities initiate action research, surveys, or evaluation of new initiatives or interventions. They may train colleagues in other services provided by the local education authority.

Current Issues Impacting Educational Psychology

While changing roles may mean a widening of tasks to produce a more diverse profession and a more interesting job, responsibilities also may be more demanding. Requests for involvement and demands from many quarters will lead to increased workloads. Educational psychologists ultimately must decide how to respond and to triage the work—what to do and what to leave for others. These changes may materially alter the nature of educational psychologist services, leading to more uniform services rather than allowing professionals to develop their own style, focus of work, and areas of expertise. Recruitment and retention remain important in determining the speciality's capacity to meet widening demands. Widening demands are not likely to be met, given the limited number of educational psychologists trained each year. Some services are responding to educational psychologist shortages by employing assistant educational psychologists who undertake more limited roles. Feelings of optimism generally prevail as the specialty is given opportunities to demonstrate what highly trained applied psychologists can do, what psychology has to offer, and what flexibility educational psychologists can bring to their interaction with others. This optimism is tinged with the worry that the ability to deliver these promises is limited by the lack of trained educational psychologists to engage in this work.

References

British Psychological Society Division of Educational and Child Psychology Training Committee. (2003a). *Criteria for the accreditation of three-year training programmes in educational psychology in England, Northern Ireland and Wales.* Leicester: Author. Retrieved February 20, 2005, from www.bps.org.uk

British Psychological Society Division of Educational and Child Psychology. (2003b). *New entry training route for educational psychologists (England): Report of an implementation study carried out on behalf of the educational psychology training and development subgroup.* Leicester: Author.

British Psychological Society. (2005a, February 28). *Educational psychology statement* [Position statement]. Leicester: Author.

British Psychological Society. (2005b, March 10). *Statutory regulation—Public consultation document* [Letter to members]. Leicester: Author.

Department for Education and Employment. (2000). *Educational psychology services (England): Current role, good practice and future directions. Report of the working group.* London: Author.

Department for Education and Science. (1955). *Report of the Committee on Maladjusted Children* (Underwood Report). London: Author.

Department for Education and Science. (1968). *Psychologists in the education services* (Summerfield Report). London: Author.

Department for Education and Skills. (2001). *Special educational needs code of practice.* London: Author.

Department for Education and Skills. (2004). *Removing barriers to achievement: The government's strategy for SEN (Special Education Needs).* London: Author.

Department for Education and Skills. (2005a). *School class sizes spreadsheets.* Retrieved March 30, 2005, from www.dfes.gov.uk/trends

Department for Education and Skills. (2005b). *Overview and schools inspections (OFSTED) spreadsheets.* Retrieved March 30, 2005, from www.dfes.gov.uk/trends

Department for Education and Skills. (2005c). *Special Educational Needs spreadsheets.* Retrieved March 30, 2005, from www.dfes.gov.uk/trends

Department for Education and Skills. (2005d, February 2). Statement released by Margaret Hodge (Minister for Education) about the role and training of educational psychologists in England. London: Author.

Department for Education and Skills. (2005e). *Ethnicity and education: The evidence on minority ethnic pupils* (Research Topic Paper RTP01-05). London: Author.

de Shazer, S. (1988). *Clues: Investigating solutions in brief therapy.* New York: Norton.

de Shazer, S. (1991). *Putting difference to work.* New York: Norton.

Employers' Organisation. (2004). *Employers' Organisation for Local Government: Soulbury Workforce Survey 2004.* Retrieved April 14, 2005, from www .lg-employers.gov.uk/conditions/education/ soulbury

Gardner, J. L. (Ed.). (1992). *Atlas of the world.* London: Readers Digest.

Mosley, J. (2005). *The basics of Circle Time.* Retrieved October 20, 2005, from http://www.circle-time .co.uk/site/what_is_qct/

National Assembly in Wales. (2004). *Schools in Wales: General statistics 2004* (chap. 8). Cardiff: Statistical Directorate for the National Assembly in Wales. Retrieved March 31, 2005, from http:// www.wales.gov.uk/keypubstatisticsforwales/ content/publication/schools-teach/2005/siwgs 2004/siwgs2004-ch8.pdf

National Statistics Online. (2005a, August 25). *Population estimates.* Retrieved April 6, 2005, from http:// www.statistics.gov.uk/CCI/nugget.asp?ID=6

National Statistics Online. (2005b). *Population spreadsheet.* Retrieved April 6, 2005, from http:// www.statistics.gov.uk/statbase/Product.asp?vlnk =601&More=N

National Union of Teachers. (2005a, April 18). *Soulbury pay agreement 2004–2006.* Retrieved April 6, 2005, from http://www.teachers.org.uk/ story.php?/id=3360

National Union of Teachers. (2005b, December 7). *Teachers pay agreement 2004–2006.* Retrieved April 6, 2005, from http://www.teachers.org.uk/story.php?id=

Nationwide Building Society. (2005). *Nationwide house price index.* Retrieved March 31, 2005, from http:// www.nationwide.co.uk/hpi/review.htm

Wooldridge, A. (1994). *Measuring the mind: Education and psychology in England c1860–c1990.* Cambridge: Cambridge University Press.

10

School Psychology in Estonia

Eve Kikas

Context of School Psychology

Estonia is located in northern Europe, on the eastern coast of the Baltic Sea. Estonia stretches 350 kilometers from east to west and 240 kilometers from north to south; its area is 45,226 square kilometers. Estonia shares borders with Russia to the east and Latvia to the south. Sweden is to the west across the Baltic Sea, and Finland is to the north, across the Gulf of Finland. Estonia's population ranks among the smallest in the world: As of 2005, an estimated 1,347,510 people live in Estonia (a density of only 29.80 people per square kilometer). Fifteen percent of the population are between birth and 14 years of age, 67% are 15 to 64 years old, and 17% are 65 years and older (Statistical Office of Estonia, 2006).

After centuries of Danish, Swedish, German, and Russian rule, Estonia attained independence in 1918, and a parliamentary republic was formed. After the conclusion of the supplementary secret protocol of the German-Soviet Non-aggression Pact on August 23, 1939, the Baltic countries were assigned to the Soviet sphere of influence and remained in isolation. In 1991, the Republic of Estonia was restored on the basis of continuity with the constitution prior to 1938. Estonia became a member of the European Union on May 1, 2004, and its main economic partners are the member states of the European Union. In 2004, the gross domestic product was US$19.23 billion, US$14,300 per capita. The labor force is 11% agriculture, 20% industry, and 69% services. Unemployment is estimated at 10%. The economy in Estonia benefits from strong electronics and telecommunications sectors and is influenced by developments in its three major trading partners: Finland, Sweden, and Germany.

In the 2004–2005 school year, there were 288,600 students, including 18,800 in basic schools, 42,100 in secondary schools, 29,900 in vocational institutions, and 67,800 in universities or applied higher educational institutions. The number of children in preschool institutions was 52,900 (Statistical Office of Estonia, 2006). The number of school-age children is decreasing yearly, whereas the number of children with special education needs is increasing. In the school year 2003–2004, there were 5,065 children in special schools, 1,859 children studying in special classes in mainstream schools, and 20,252 children in regular mainstream classes (in 1998–1999, these numbers were 5,185, 1,315, and 14,966, respectively). There has been a general decline in the percentage of children attending special schools and a rise in the percentage of children with special needs attending mainstream classes (Information Database on Education Systems in Europe, n.d.).

Educational System and Regulations

Education in the Republic of Estonia can be described as follows. Preschool education until the age of 7 is voluntary. Preschool child care institutions include crèches (lastesõim) until the age of 3 and nursery schools (lasteaed) for children ages 3 through 7, which are maintained either publicly or privately. There are also special nursery schools for children with special needs up to 7 years of age and adaptation groups. Nursery schools are divided into municipal and private child care institutions. Because preschool educational establishments get their funding from different sources, the cost to parents varies. Preschool education is followed by 9 years in school (põhikool); the first six years are referred to as primary school (algkool). After primary school, there are two pathways: the 3-year upper secondary school (gümnaasium) or the (at minimum) 3-year vocational school (kutsekool). The Estonian higher education system consists of universities (ülikool) and applied higher education institutions (rakenduskõrgkool). There are also some vocational higher educational (kutsekõrgharidus) programs at postsecondary vocational institutions. The higher education institutions can be state, public, or private institutions.

Schooling is compulsory between the ages of 7 and 17 and is free for all who study in state-financed or municipal schools. There are also private schools and private vocational schools,

which are fee-paying. Persons who have passed the minimum permitted school-leaving age and have not acquired basic education may study in the form of evening courses or distance learning and graduate from school as external students. In 2004, there were 603 diurnal (96 primary, 227 basic, 234 upper secondary) schools; 26 were private schools, and 46 (2 primary, 40 basic, 4 upper secondary) schools were for children with special needs (Statistical Office of Estonia, 2006). There were 46 higher educational institutions: 6 public universities, 6 licensed private universities, 7 state-owned applied higher education institutions, 17 private applied higher education institutions, and 10 vocational higher education institutions (Statistical Office of Estonia, 2006).

Starting from the 2004–2005 school year, the upper limits of class sizes are 24 for basic school and 36 for upper secondary school. The actual average number of students per class in basic school has been lower (e.g., in 2002–2003, it was 21.7), which, in essence, means that there have been big differences among class sizes. In some cases, composite classes are formed if the number of students in two or more classes together is small. In classes for children with special needs, the upper limit of the size of a class is smaller. Requirements of education are determined by the national curriculum for basic schools and upper secondary schools. The simplified national curriculum for basic schools and the national curriculum for students with moderate and severe learning disabilities determine the requirements of basic education for children with special needs. Each school develops its curriculum on the basis of the national curriculum.

Origin, History, and Current Status of School Psychology

The opportunities for the evolution of school psychology emerged after the department of psychology was established in the University of Tartu in

1968. Starting from this year, psychology as a discipline was taught, whereas earlier, only a few courses in psychology had been given (Allik, 1992). Two periods may be differentiated in the history of Estonian school psychology: the Soviet period (1970s to 1991) and the independent republican period (from 1991 through the present). The primary difference between these periods is in the emphasis of theory and practice. In the Soviet Union, applied psychology was not well accepted and developed. For example, tests were forbidden for a long time, and there were few possibilities to train in psychotherapy (Allik, 1992; Kikas, 1999). The education of psychologists was very theoretical, which caused problems in daily work. Presently, whereas the bachelor's-level education in universities emphasizes theory, practical courses are emphasized at the master's level and in in-service training courses.

The Soviet Period

The idea of school psychology began in Estonia in the beginning of the 1970s. The leaders, who introduced the ideas and worked out the first models of school psychological services, were Kalju Toim from the University of Tartu and Heino Liimets and Juhan Sõerd from the Pedagogical Institute of Tallinn. The first school psychologist, Lia Hanso, started to work in a special school for children with mental diseases in 1975. The history of school psychology in Soviet Estonia developed hand in hand with that of vocational counseling. In the Soviet Union, from time to time, the emphasis was on career planning. Through vocational orientation, different occupations were introduced to children from the very first grades onward. Together with helping children to discover their needs, interests, and abilities, another purpose of career orientation was made evident, namely to introduce children to working-class occupations that were not very popular.

The first vocational counseling centers were founded in the 1970s; psychologists worked in these centers alongside other specialists. Their task was to assess personality and abilities in order to help students find occupations most suitable for them. However, in 1988, the vocational guidance centers were closed down but for two big centers in Tallinn and Tartu. Several psychologists who had worked in these centers went to work for schools where they also carried out vocational guidance. Before 1991, there were 66 school psychologists in Estonia, the majority of them working in schools and the minority in counseling centers; all were officially referred to as "psychologists."

The Current Status

The terms *school psychology* (koolipsühholoogia) and *school psychologist* (koolipsühholoog) are used in Estonia today, but in some centers and schools, the official name for the job may be simply *psychologist*. Additionally, *counselors* (nõustaja) or *social pedagogues* (sotsiaalpedagoog) work in schools. These are professionals who do not have degrees in psychology even though some are involved in the activities generally carried out by school psychologists.

Most of the school psychologists work in public schools, and several of them additionally work in private practice or give lectures in the universities or schooling centers. One school psychologist serves either one school (mainly in towns) or two schools (mainly in the countryside or in smaller schools). A small number of psychologists work in private schools or in special schools. The number of psychologists working in special schools is increasing; thus far, these schools have been poorly supplied with psychologists. As a rule, psychologists do not work in preschool institutions. A few are employed by vocational institutions and universities.

The exact number of practicing school psychologists is not available, although it is known that more than 150 persons are currently employed, with few male school psychologists. The availability of services in the larger cities and in areas around them is satisfactory. In contrast, rural areas are poorly supplied with school psychologists (and with other types of psychologists as well). The reasons for rural areas not having school psychologists lie in the general social politics of Estonia (and form only a part of various rural areas' social problems). One reason is that schools are small and do not have the resources to hire a full-time school psychologist. As the distances between schools are long and transportation is not funded, people do not want to work in two or more schools in the countryside.

Although the official ratio is up to 600 students per 1 school psychologist, this is not mandatory and serves as a recommendation only. In reality, many schools do not consider this ratio when hiring a school psychologist. Most of the school psychologists have more than 600 children to serve (sometimes up to 1,200; the average number is 700–800 students). Smaller schools (with 300–400 students) hire school psychologists by offering half-time jobs.

In 2004, the official average monthly salary in Estonia was 7,287 Kroons (467 euros), whereas in education (including teachers and other staff members), it was 6,475 Kroons (415 euros; Statistical Office of Estonia, 2006). However, the salary of the school psychologist depends on the policy of each county. Most of the regions have equalized the salary with teachers' salaries. However, depending on the qualification and experience of a psychologist, it may be higher even in state schools, and it is even higher in the private sector.

In-service training courses are provided in several institutions and by various trainers. In universities, psychologists may participate in single courses in master's programs. This is possible in the program of the Open University, which offers bachelor's and master's degrees and arranges single modules and courses for in-service training. However, opportunities for career advancement in school services are practically absent.

Job stability is different in big towns (specifically, Tartu and Tallinn) and other areas. As mentioned, generally there are no possibilities of getting better (more highly valued and better paid) jobs inside the school system. In Tartu and Tallinn, young people work in schools during their master's studies but go on to find jobs outside the school system (e.g., in clinics, counseling centers, private practice). Therefore, job stability in these towns is quite low. In contrast, job stability in other areas is quite high. Only in rural areas, far from Tallinn and Tartu, is the age of school psychologists quite high.

The majority of school psychologists have stated that they are "mostly satisfied" with their work (Jimerson et al., 2004). They value the opportunity to plan and organize their own work and their own work schedule; they also value the responsibility that is directly connected to the decisions they make. Working in the school environment means dealing with different kinds of assignments, which makes the work appealing and challenging. On the other hand, the role confusion is great. During the past decade, many changes have occurred that have influenced the field of psychology and people's attitude toward it. As an outcome, school psychologists feel that their work is valued by their colleagues and by society. Unfortunately, the salary is not sufficient and does not offer security. Consequently, many professionals are overwhelmed by their various duties and often feel distracted.

Infrastructure of School Psychology

Two professional organizations serve the interests of school psychology and psychologists: the Union of Estonian Psychologists and the Union of Estonian School Psychologists. The Union of Estonian Psychologists was founded in 1988, with the goals of developing standards of psychology theory and practice in Estonia, serving the interests of Estonian psychologists, and raising the level of mental health of the Estonian people. The union participates in training psychologists, particularly in the areas of ethical knowledge and practice. Since 2003, the union has acted as the qualification granting body for school and clinical psychologists. The second professional organization, the Union of Estonian School Psychologists, was founded in 1992 with 30 members; today, it has 133 members. It unites psychologists working in schools and people who actively support the development of school psychology in Estonia. The main aims of the union are to support the improvement of children's and adolescents' mental health, inform others about the roles and activities of school psychologists in the country, serve the interests of its members, and organize in-service training. In addition, the members of the Union of Estonian School Psychologists have taken part in the work of the International School Psychology Association (see, e.g., Jimerson et al., 2004).

The Union of Estonian Psychologists has a newsletter in which school psychology issues are analyzed. Additionally, there is a monthly journal, *Education,* and the weekly *Teachers' Newspaper* in which school psychologists report about their work and research results. Issues of the journal *School Psychology International* and the International School Psychology Association newsletter are also available to union members.

In 1995, a job description for school psychologists was issued by regulation of the National School Board. It describes the main activities of school psychologists as the following: individual and group counseling of students, career counseling, consulting with teachers and parents about individual students' problems, and consulting with administration in planning school life and development projects.

One school psychologist should serve 600 students. If the number of students in a school is less than 600, the psychologist may work part-time. The professional standards for school psychologists were approved by the Estonian Qualification Center on April 9, 2003. The

accreditation of school psychologists according to these standards is carried out by the Union of Estonian Psychologists, which is the qualification granting body for school and clinical psychologists. The qualification standards are also described in Standards of Qualification for Teachers (2005). According to these standards, only people with at least a bachelor's-level education in psychology may work in schools as psychologists. However, as of March 2006, this standard had not been met. An ethical code for the members of the Union of Estonian Psychologists has also been developed. School psychologists additionally follow the code of ethics of the International School Psychology Association (Oakland, Goldman, & Bischoff, 1997).

Preparation of School Psychologists

Before 2002, higher education teaching was organized on three levels: bachelor's (4 years), master's (2 years), and doctoral (4 years). In accordance with the Bologna Convention, the new curricula were introduced in 2002; these comprise the following three levels of study: bachelor's (3 years), master's (2 years), and doctoral (4 years). Access to the second level requires successful completion of the first level.

To understand the situation in Estonian school psychological services today, a historical look is necessary, because current programs were recently developed, and some students still study under the previous programs. As there are no specific school psychology programs at the doctoral level, a description of only the lower levels' programs is provided. In Estonian universities, 1 credit is equivalent to 1.5 European credits.

Before 2002, the bachelor's studies of psychology required 160 credits. After completing the curriculum, students were given the degree of Baccalaureus Scientiarum. These programs were taught in the University of Tartu, the

University of Tallinn, and the University Nord. With this degree, it was possible either to start working or to continue studies at the master's level. Universities offered three types of master's-level curricula. The master of science curriculum enabled students to specialize in research fields; the students were given the degree of Magister Scientiarum in psychology. The master of applied psychology programs in clinical psychology and in school psychology (University of Tartu) required 80 credits.

The development of curricula in school psychology started in 1993 with Estonian psychologists cooperating with leading school psychologists from various countries. Attendance at the annual colloquium of the International School Psychology Association provided good information about, and support for, developing school psychology curricula. The curricula of several universities were discussed, and related articles and books were analyzed (e.g., Burden, 1994; Fagan, 1995; Farrell, 1995; Farrell & Lunt, 1994; Oakland & Saigh, 1989; Reynolds, Gutkin, Elliott, & Witt, 1984). Based on these analyses, the first in-service training program for practicing school psychologists in Estonia was developed. Twenty psychologists were taught according to this program at the University of Tartu in 1996–1997. Subsequently expanding this program and in cooperation with clinical psychologists, the first master's-level curriculum was developed. It was aimed at persons who had completed the curriculum and had acquired the necessary academic and practical skills to do their work rationally, systematically, and consciously and to be able to analyze their work and evaluate its effect. The model of school psychologist as scientist and practitioner was assumed. The new curricula (implemented in 2002) were developed, building on the first curriculum and on the feedback from the participants.

Accredited Psychology Programs

Currently, the bachelor's degree program in psychology requires 120 credits. The students

who have completed the curriculum receive the degree of Baccalaureus of Social Sciences. There are obligatory and optional courses; only the optional courses provide the opportunity to choose between a more theoretical or practical (including school psychology) orientation. Minimal duration of the curriculum is 3 years. The bachelor's degree program is offered at the University of Tartu, the University of Tallinn, and the University Nord.

The master's program in psychology enables students to specialize in one of the following fields: psychology, clinical psychology, school psychology, or social psychology at the University of Tartu and social psychology, counseling, or health psychology at the University of Tallinn. The curriculum requires 80 credits, and students who have completed one of these curricula are awarded the master of psychology degree. In addition to completing obligatory and optional courses, students must also write and defend a master's thesis. The minimal duration of the curriculum is 2 years. This level is needed to work as a practicing psychologist, including working in school.

There are specific degrees and professional credentials required to become a school psychologist. There are several ways to become a qualified school psychologist. The professional standards for school psychologists (Kutsestandard) state the following requirements and ways to obtain and maintain the certification: Qualification level III: bachelor's degree in psychology and at least 4 credits in school psychology courses; Qualification level IV: at least 3 years work experience, master's or bachelor's degree in psychology, and 40 credits in-service training in school psychology; Qualification level V: master's degree in psychology, 20 credits in-service training in school psychology, and at least 10 years work experience including publishing in educational or psychology journals.

The most straightforward route to becoming a school psychologist is to complete the master of psychology curriculum in school psychology in the University of Tartu. So far, nine persons have completed these studies. The other way to become a school psychologist is to complete bachelor's- or master's-level studies and participate in in-service training. Each year, there are about 30 state-paid places for psychology students at the University of Tartu and the University of Tallinn. In addition, at least the same number of students pay for their studies themselves. All these students may become school psychologists if they participate in school psychology courses either during or after their university studies and have practiced enough in school.

The following provides a description of the most direct way of becoming a school psychologist. These are the courses taught in the University of Tartu—the only university in Estonia that offers a master's-level program in school psychology. However, similar courses are also taught at the University of Tallinn. Studies comprise obligatory and optional courses. The obligatory courses at the bachelor's level are theoretical, but it is possible to choose more practice-oriented optional courses. On the master's level, there is a module in school psychology; additionally, students may choose courses from other modules. Thus, the description below includes the combination of courses related to school psychology (see, e.g., Cunningham & Oakland, 1998).

Core academic knowledge in psychology. Bachelor's-level studies include obligatory courses in numerous branches of psychology—developmental, personality, social, experimental, biological, sociocultural, cognitive, clinical, and motivational—as well as courses in neurophysiology, basic genetics, psychology of individual differences, basic psychometrics, psychopathology, neuropsychology, psychology and behavior of groups, and data analysis in social sciences. Students may also choose the 4-credit module in school psychology, including courses in the psychology of learning and students with special needs.

The following master's-level obligatory courses deepen the theoretical academic knowledge: personality and social psychology, individual differences, theories of development, history of psychology, neurochemistry, and methodology of studying personality. The module of school psychology includes courses in the psychology of children with special needs and special populations and theories and methods of clinical psychology.

Assessment services. The master's-level school psychology module includes courses in methods of individual assessment (including interviewing, observation, testing) and case studies. Assessment skills are practiced in the course of practical work in school (master's level, 80 credit hours). The theoretical background of assessment is taught in the academic studies described earlier.

Intervention. At the bachelor's level, students may choose between two optional courses: counseling psychology and practicum in counseling skills. Introduction to psychotherapy (with emphasis on the cognitive-behavioral approach) and consultation methods are taught at the master's level. Intervention is also discussed in the case study methods course. Students have the opportunity to practice these skills while in school (master's level, 80 credit hours).

Interpersonal skills. Also at the bachelor's level of studies, students may choose among the following optional courses: interpersonal skills, practicum in listening and communication skills, organizational psychology, and leadership and collaboration skills. These skills, and also professional decision-making skills, are practiced within the program (master's level, 80 credit hours).

Knowledge of statistical methods and research design. Both bachelor's- and master's-level programs include a course in psychology and social sciences research methods. As stated previously in this chapter, the model of psychologist as scientist and practitioner is emphasized. Students practice skills in research methods and apply their knowledge to specific purposes in the field of school psychology when writing seminar papers (4 credits, bachelor's level) or the master's thesis (20 credits). This thesis is a study that, utilizing scientifically valid methodology, (a) describes and analyzes some work-related problem (e.g., a case study or a developmentally oriented project for better organization of a psychologist's professional work), (b) develops and evaluates a new assessment tool, or (c) develops and evaluates a new intervention program or some other work of practical value.

Ethics of school psychology. Master's-level studies include a course in the ethics of psychology. Ethical dilemmas are also analyzed in the course on case study methods.

The education of school psychologists at the university level places an emphasis on theoretical foundations. The reason for this lies, first, in the general policy of university education according to the 3+2 curricula, with the bachelor's level designed to provide a foundation from which students can continue their master's studies in a variety of fields. This variability and possibility of choices facilitates flexibility and ease in finding future employment. Simultaneously, it also means that learning "on the job" and in-service training will become more important in the future.

The second reason lies in the small number of students specializing in school psychology in Estonia. If only a few students study school psychology, then it is necessary to integrate their studies with the studies of other specialists. In Estonia, as a rule, the curriculum in school psychology has been integrated with the curriculum in clinical psychology. As the work of clinical psychologists is more individual centered, this orientation has dominated the curriculum.

One way of improving the education of future school psychologists would be to introduce an internship into the program. This idea is described in the project of a framework for educating psychologists in Europe (Bartram et al., 2001). This project proposes a common framework for the education and training of practicing psychologists that would last 6 years, including three stages: bachelor's level, master's level, and one year of supervised practice (i.e., internship year). Today, the lack of supervision is one of the problems frequently mentioned by practicing school psychologists. Internship with on-site supervised practice, as recommended by Cunningham and Oakland (1998), would enhance the quality of school psychology preparation in Estonia.

Roles, Functions, and Responsibilities of School Psychologists

School psychologists perform a variety of activities, and their roles differ from school to school and from region to region. The activities in a specific school depend on the availability of other professionals (e.g., social workers, special teachers, social pedagogues) either in school or in the area. The most common activities are described in this section and listed in order of importance. This overview is based on results of the International School Psychology Survey, conducted in Estonia in 2003 (Jimerson et al., 2004; Kikas, 2003), and on an informal survey conducted in May 2004 (unpublished data).

Counseling. The most common activity performed by school psychologists is individual counseling. The aim of the individual work is to promote children's and adolescents' intellectual, academic, affective, social, personality, and vocational development and status. Social, family, and school resources are utilized in this counseling. Many psychologists work with student groups as well. Groups are usually based on the grounds of similar problems (e.g., children with behavioral difficulties or poor social skills). The most commonly used approaches in school counseling are cognitive-behavioral and behavioral therapy, solution-oriented therapy, and family therapy. Eclectic approaches characterize the work of many professionals. Approximately 30% of their time is spent performing these activities (Jimerson et al., 2004).

Consultation services. Approximately 20% of school psychologists' time is spent consulting with teachers and 20% of the time with parents or family members (Jimerson et al., 2004). Educating parents and helping them understand children's developmental peculiarities, but also providing support in crisis situations, are the main topics of consultation. Teachers have become more open to psychological help. Individual consultation practice is more common, but some school psychologists offer group consultation for teachers as well. In addition, cooperating with administrative staff (including consultations provided for the staff members) is becoming more widespread. It provides a great opportunity to influence school policy (e.g., how to treat children with special needs or academic problems).

The role of consultation is growing due to changes in the state policy concerning children with special educational needs. Today, inclusion of these children is more widespread than ever, which also results in the development and implementation of individual learning plans. The school psychologist has an important role here—first as an evaluator and later as a consultant. Also, measures are being introduced that would facilitate greater school attendance, decrease the number of school dropouts, and prevent pupils from repeating a year. These include the possibilities of assessing the problems earlier and making choices more accessible. For example, progress interviews are carried out yearly by a class teacher with the help of parents. In all these activities, school psychologists play an active role as consultants as well.

During the past few years, several school psychologists have lectured to groups of parents. Approximately 1% of their time is spent on this activity.

Testing and assessment models and methods. Assessment and evaluation are activities that receive somewhat less attention than counseling and consulting. Nevertheless, approximately 15% of psychologists' time is spent observing, interviewing, and testing children for academic, behavioral, social, and psychological weaknesses and/or disorders (Jimerson et al., 2004). Various methods and approaches are used, and the reliance on the ecological/systems approach is steadily increasing. This approach may include observations in various settings; behavior checklists; interviews with teachers and parents; questionnaires for children, teaching personnel, and parents; environmental assessment; and so on.

Because of its size, Estonia has no standardized tests. There are not enough resources to collect data all around Estonia and to update the norms as necessary; there also are no resources to pay for licenses. Although a wide variety of assessment tools are used, their usage is not coordinated throughout the republic, and the level of knowledge about these different tools is quite low among practicing psychologists. Some of these tools have been developed in universities as bachelor's and master's projects; others have been translated from different international sources and adapted in the course of practical work. Norms are collected and used locally. What follows is a description of frequently used assessment methods, starting with those used when assessing younger children.

Screening in the beginning of the first grade is also carried out in many schools. For this purpose, Krogh's (1978) Controlled Drawing Observation (developed in the late 1970s in Denmark) is used. It is a standardized group test, assessing the knowledge of elementary concepts (e.g., geometrical objects, numbers). Estonian school psychologists value this tool because it gives them an opportunity to assess children in the context of the classroom and encourages cooperation between the psychologist and the teacher. School psychologists make use of drawings and projective methods (e.g., completing stories or finishing sentences).

Assessing elementary school children's cognitive abilities, achievement, and social skills is performed in order to plan interventions (e.g., developing individual learning plans). This field is becoming more important in light of the policy of inclusion (i.e., incorporating students with special needs into mainstream schools). Several cognitive ability tests have been developed, based on the work and tests of Luria, Weschler, and Kaufman. Estonian versions take into account the specifics of Estonian language and culture. The Raven Coloured and Progressive Matrices have also been used in both practical and scientific work. The Beery-Buktenica Visual-Motor Integration Test is also sometimes used. Earlier, the adaptations of the tests by the Finnish psychologist O. Tasola were used.

For assessment of behavior and emotional problems, the Achenbach Child Behavior Checklists for parents, teachers, and adolescents are used. Personality, cognitive abilities, motivation, attitudes, and social skills are assessed in older children who come to visit a psychologist and discuss their problems. As a rule, these children would like to learn and understand more about themselves. In this work, tests are used as one way to gather information about a child. These tests include Cattell's Sixteen Personality Factor questionnaire, the Myers-Briggs personality test, and the Rosenberg self-esteem questionnaire.

Organizational and program development services. A few professionals are taking part in developing and evaluating curricula and other documents connected to educational and pedagogical issues. Psychologists involved in these activities spend approximately 1% of their time on them. The most common of the coordinated and developed programs in a school environment are connected with bullying, career counseling, health promotion, and prevention of drug use and addiction and HIV/AIDS. The time spent on these activities is approximately 1%.

Other activities. School psychologists have also mentioned the following activities: crisis intervention after a traumatic event in the school or in the community and preparing tests for school-entrance exams. Also, some psychologists report spending time investigating the satisfaction of parents with the school and teachers' opinions about school policy and satisfaction with their work and with other topics.

Current Issues Impacting School Psychology

Major problems related to the qualification system have emerged over the past few years. For example, the educational qualifications of several previously trained school psychologists do not meet the new standards. The situation produces insecurity among those psychologists and calls for solutions. Financial issues, including low salaries and poor working conditions, also have been underlying concerns for many years and can contribute to a lack of motivation. As mentioned earlier in the chapter, having too many tasks and assignments, including doing the work of a social worker or social pedagogue, can be challenging, but also overwhelming, for the school psychologist. Supervision is not available to many professionals, and this creates stress and burnout. The lack of supervision is more troublesome for younger people, sometimes leading them to resign from their positions.

Attempts have been made to address these challenges. The Estonian School Psychology Association has initiated negotiations with universities to find solutions for educating psychologists who are working but who lack the appropriate degree. The Estonian School Psychology Association has started to provide group supervision and encourages its members to gather together within regions to exchange information, knowledge, and support.

School psychologists in Estonia continue to debate about their roles. Although the variety of tasks provides psychologists with various opportunities and makes the work more interesting, it also results in feelings of role confusion and of being overwhelmed. If some level of conceptualization could be agreed on, it would be easier to describe the roles of school psychologists. Also, only after that would it be possible to provide a more integrated picture of school psychological services in the whole of Estonia. So far, the picture is quite fragmented.

References

Allik, J. (1992). Psychology in Estonia. *News from EFPPA, 6*, 7–10.

Bartram, D., Döpping, J., Georgas, J., Jern, S., Job, R., Lecuyer, R., et al. (2001, April). *A European framework for psychologists' training, version 5* (Report). Produced by the Project EuroPsyT. Retrieved July 20, 2005, http://www.europsych.org/framework/v5/

Burden, R. (1994). Trends and developments in educational psychology: An international perspective. *School Psychology International, 15*, 293–347.

Cunningham, J., & Oakland, T. (1998). International School Psychology Association guidelines for the preparation of school psychologists. *School Psychology International, 19*, 19–30.

Fagan, T. (1995). Trends in the history of school psychology in the United States. In A. Thomas & J. Grimes (Eds.), *Best practices in school psychology* (Vol. 3, pp. 59–68). Washington, DC: National Association of School Psychologists.

Farrell, P. (1995). Some reflections on the role of educational psychologists. In B. Norwich, I. Lunt, & V. Varma (Eds.), *Psychology and education for special needs* (pp. 129–141). Aldershot, UK: Arena Ashgate.

Farrell, P., & Lunt, I. (1994). Training psychologists for the 21st century. *School Psychology International, 15*, 195–208.

The Information Database on Education Systems in Europe. (n.d.). *The education system in Estonia (2003/2004).* Retrieved April 10, 2006, from http://www.eurydice.org/Eurybase/Application/frameset.asp?country=EE&language=EN

Jimerson, S., Graydon, K., Farrell, P., Kikas, E., Hatzichristou, S., Boce, E., Bashi, G., & International School Psychology Association Research Committee. (2004). The International School Psychology Survey: Development and data from Albania, Cyprus, Estonia, Greece and Northern England. *School Psychology International, 25*(3), 259–286.

Kikas, E. (1999). School psychology in Estonia: Expectations of teachers and school psychologists versus reality. *School Psychology International, 20*, 103–115.

Kikas, E. (2003). Pupils as consumers of school psychological services. *School Psychology International, 24*, 20–32.

Krogh, T. (1978). *Controlled drawing observation.* Holte: Søllerød Kommunens Skolevaesen.

Oakland, T., Goldman, S., & Bischoff, H. (1997). Code of ethics of the International School Psychology Association. *School Psychology International, 18*, 291–298.

Oakland, T., & Saigh, P. (1989). Psychology in schools: An introduction to international perspectives. In P. Saigh & T. Oakland (Eds.), *International perspectives on psychology in the schools* (pp. 1–22). Hillsdale, NJ: Lawrence Erlbaum.

Reynolds, C., Gutkin, T., Elliott, S., & Witt, J. (1984). *School psychology: Essentials of theory and practice.* New York: Wiley.

Statistical Office of Estonia. (2006). *Statistical database.* Retrieved April 20, 2006, from http://pub.stat.ee/px-web.2001/dialog/statfileri.asp

Laws and Acts

Eesti Vabariigi Haridusseadus [Republic of Estonia Law on Education], Riigi Teataja I 2004, 75, 524. Retrieved July 30, 2005, from https://www.riigiteataja.ee/ert/act.jsp?id=816786

Erakooliseadus [Private Education Institution Act], Riigi Teataja I 2005, 31, 229. Retrieved July 30, 2005, from https://www.riigiteataja.ee/ert/act.jsp?id=908848

Individuaalse õppekava järgi õppimise kord [Regulation of Learning According to Individual Learning Curriculum], Riigi Teataja L 2004, 155, 2329. Retrieved July 30, 2005, from https://www.riigiteataja.ee/ert/act.jsp?id=824971

Koolieelse lasteasutuse seadus [Law on Preschool Child Institutions], Riigi Teataja I, 2004, 41, 276. Retrieved July 30, 2005, from https://www.riigiteataja.ee/ert/act.jsp?id=754369

Koolipsühholoogi tegevusjuhend [Job Description for School Psychologists], Riigi Kooliameti

Käskkiri [Regulation of the National School Board] 77, April 18, 1995.

Kutseseadus [Professions Act], Riigi Teataja I 2003, 83, 559. Retrieved July 30, 2005, from https://www.riigiteataja.ee/ert/act.jsp?id=690522

Kutsestandard: Koolipsühholoog III, IV, V [Professional Standard: School Psychologist, III, IV, V]. Retrieved April 10, 2006, from http://www.kutsekoda.ee/default.aspx/3/content/118

Kutseõppeasutuse seadus [Vocational Educational Institutions Act], Riigi Teataja I 2005, 31, 229. Retrieved July 30, 2005, from https://www.riigiteataja.ee/ert/act.jsp?id=908863

Lasteaed-algkooli, algkooli, põhikooli ning gümnaasiumi eripedagoogide ja koolipsühholoogide miinimumkoosseis [Staff Minimum for Special Education Teachers and School Psychologists in Nursery-Primary School, Primary School, Basic School, and Upper Secondary School], Riigi Teataja L 2003, 4, 39. Retrieved July 30, 2005, from https://www.riigiteataja.ee/ert/act.jsp?id=238473

Pedagoogide kvalifikatsiooninõuded [Standards of Qualification for Teachers], Riigi Teataja I 2005, 6, 42. Retrieved July 30, 2005, from https://www.riigiteataja.ee/ert/act.jsp?id=839432

Põhikooli ja gümnaasiumi riiklik õppekava [National Curriculum for Basic Schools and Upper Secondary Schools], Riigi Teataja I 2004, 67, 468. Retrieved July 30, 2005, from https://www.riigiteataja.ee/ert/act.jsp?id=802290

Põhikooli ja gümnaasiumiseadus [Basic School and Upper Secondary School Act], Riigi Teataja I 2004, 56, 404. Retrieved July 30, 2005, from https://www.riigiteataja.ee/ert/act.jsp?id=784125

Põhikooli lihtsustatud riikliku õppekava (abiõppe õppekava) kinnitamine [Simplified National Curriculum for Basic Schools (Supplementary Learning Curriculum)], Riigi Teataja L 2004, 106, 1705. Retrieved July 30, 2005, from https://www.riigiteataja.ee/ert/act.jsp?id=792367

Rakenduskõrgkooli seadus [Applied Higher Education Institution Act], Riigi Teataja I 2005, 38, 297. Retrieved July 30, 2005, from https://www.riigiteataja.ee/ert/act.jsp?id=920764

Toimetuleku riikliku õppekava kinnitamine [National Curriculum for Students With Moderate and Severe Learning Disabilities], Riigi Teataja L 2004, 106, 1705. Retrieved July 30, 2005, from https://www.riigiteataja.ee/ert/act.jsp?id=790670

Ülikooliseadus [Universities Act], Riigi Teataja I 2005, 38, 297. Retrieved July 30, 2005, from https://www.riigiteataja.ee/ert/act.jsp?id=920734

11

School Psychology in Finland

Pirjo Laaksonen

Kristiina Laitinen

Minna Salmi

Context of School Psychology

Finland was a province and then a grand duchy (a territory ruled by a grand duke or grand duchess) under Sweden from the 12th to the 19th centuries and an autonomous grand duchy of Russia after 1809. Finland has been an independent democracy since 1917 and is located in Scandinavia in Northern Europe. Finland covers an area of 338,145 square kilometres and shares borders with Norway in the north and Russia to the East, with Sweden located across the Gulf of Bothnia to the west and Estonia across the Gulf of Finland to the south. Finland is officially bilingual, and its population of 5.2 million people consists of Finnish and Swedish speaking people plus a few small minority groups such as the Roma and the Sami. There are about 120,000 residents of foreign origin, and most of them originate from Russia, Estonia, and Somalia.

Regarding the age of Finland's population, 17% 14 years of age or younger, 69% are 15 to 64 years of age, and 16% are 65 years and older. The gross domestic product in 2004 was US$151.2 billion, US$29,000 per capita. Services (66%), industry (30%), and, to a lesser extent, agriculture and forestry (mainly paper and pulp; 3%) are the primary occupations (Statistics Finland, n.d.). The parliament consists of 200 representatives from a variety of political parties. The president is currently a woman, with a social democratic background. The best-known Finnish product of high technology is probably the cell phone made by Nokia. Finland also has many famous biotechnological experts and research groups. Social welfare, health, and educational services are provided by the municipalities and supported by the state.

The traditional objective of Finnish education policy has been to raise the general standard of education and to promote educational equality. A central aim is to provide all citizens with equal opportunity to receive education, irrespective of their age, domicile, financial situation, sex, or native language. Thus, preschool education, basic education, and upper secondary education are, in principle, free of charge: Tuition, welfare services, and school meals are provided free of charge at all levels. In Finland, nearly all comprehensive schools are owned and maintained by local authorities; very few schools are owned by the state. A few schools are privately owned, for example, by foundations.

Compulsory education begins at age 7. Almost all children attend preschool. After 9 years in basic education, students can continue either to general upper secondary education or to vocational upper secondary education and training, and, finally, to a polytechnic or university. The government's goal is to streamline the system and develop it in accordance with the principle of lifelong learning and to make it internationally compatible. The level of education in Finland has risen significantly since the 1960s, and especially the younger generation is now well educated. Parliament enacts laws on education and makes decisions regarding general principles of education policy. The government and the Ministry of Education implement these principles at the central government level.

Nearly all publicly funded education, from primary to higher education, is supervised by the Ministry of Education. Training related to national defense, law and order, and some aspects of communications and transport is administered by other ministries. Most existing private institutions are in the vocational sector, but they, too, rely heavily on public funding, and the education they provide is subject to public supervision. The universities are state institutions and funded directly from the budget; the central and local authorities provide most of the funds for the other educational institutions. The Ministry of Education is in charge of the administration of education, research, culture, youth issues, and sports and includes all universities. In matters related to comprehensive and upper secondary schools, vocational institutions, and adult education, the Ministry is assisted by an expert agency, the Finnish National Board of Education.

The Finnish National Board of Education is the national planning and evaluation agency responsible for primary and secondary education as well as adult education. However, institutions of higher education fall mainly outside its domain. The Finnish National Board of Education draws up and approves national guidelines for curricula and qualifications. It is also responsible for assessing the education system, with the exception of institutions of higher education. As in the other Nordic countries, education and culture in Finland are marked by the prominent role of local authorities in organising activities and providing services. Most comprehensive schools, upper secondary schools, and vocational institutions, as well as adult education institutions, are maintained by local authorities. They provide adult education, library services, and cultural and leisure activities (Finnish National Board of Education, 2005).

The numbers of Finnish school-age children enrolled in various levels of the school system are as follows: Basic education (ages 7–17), 593,100 students; general upper secondary education (ages 15–18), 121,300 students; vocational upper secondary education (ages 15–18), 183,300 students; polytechnics, 131,900 students; and universities, 174,047 students. The number of students in basic education has decreased by 0.7% since 2003. The number of students in special needs education is currently about 7% of the age cohort. The number of children with developmental dysphasia has increased the most. The integration within mainstream education is the legislatively recommended option for those who have special needs; thus, 42% of those children receive special needs education in an ordinary class, 33% in special classes within basic education schools, and 25% in special classes within special schools. During the school year 2003–2004, more than 126,000 pupils (approximately 20%)

received part-time special education because of moderate learning difficulties or adaptation problems. There was a 2% increase compared with the year before (Finnish Statistical Office, 2005).

Finland has a long tradition of developing special needs education. From a European point of view, Finland is seen as a multitrack country among systems of special needs education: Very inclusive models of support exist in Finland, including so-called part-time special needs education, separated special schools, and small special classes within the framework of an ordinary school. The number of learners in need of additional or special support has been increasing in Finland. The increase in numbers can be seen as a result of various factors, from changes in society to the improved methods of identifying students in need of special support. The move toward integration in Finland can be seen, for example, through the decreasing number of separate special schools. Yet, Finland is intending to preserve the present multitrack system of special needs education with special classes and special schools.

Origin, History, and Current Status of School Psychology

The first Finnish school psychologist began her work in Helsinki in 1938. Her post was later reorganised and connected to the Child Guidance Centre of the municipal schools in Helsinki. It was not until 1974 that local school authorities in Helsinki began to establish permanent posts for school psychologists. Parallel with the school reforms during the 1960s, a post for a school psychologist was established in the city of Lahti. The objectives of this post were to promote and enhance the school climate, school environment, and students' well-being and to engage in individual-centred work (Laaksonen, 1989).

These two work orientations, the individual-centred, clinically oriented and the systems-oriented one, have characterised Finnish school psychology for the past 30 years. In the 1970s,

local authorities began to establish permanent posts for school psychologists. In the early 1970s, the school departments were established in the State Provincial Offices; in three of these offices, the posts of regional school psychologists and one of a regional school social worker were also grounded. At the same time, the Finnish state had established a post for a senior adviser in student welfare affairs in the former National Board of Education. Her or his duty was to coordinate the work of school psychologists and school social workers throughout the country. The post holders in both regional governments and the National Board of Education had to coordinate the development of student welfare affairs according to the principles laid down by the student welfare committee in 1974. The regional civil servants supported the work of municipal school psychologists at a time when the number of school psychologists countrywide was approximately 55 (Ministry of Education and Culture, 1974).

During the economic recession of the 1990s, these posts, except for one in the former province of Uusimaa and the one in the National Board of Education, were abolished.

As a consequence, the development of school psychological and school social work became differentiated, depending on the size of the municipality. Supervision and training of municipal school psychologists and school social workers was nearly defunct in other provinces, with the exception of the former province Uusimaa. The nationwide collection of statistical data concerning their work also ceased. The development of school psychological work and social work at school became dependent on the financial resources of the municipalities. The major cities continued to develop the content of school psychological work. Minor municipalities with lesser resources turned to each other for cooperation. In addition, cross-sectoral working methods within the municipality were developed.

Most of the posts for school psychologists were established to promote the school reforms during the 1960s and 1970s. The education system changed to an integrated and free-of-charge school system—comprehensive schooling for all during the first nine grade levels. This formed the basic education for all students, including those with mental retardation. After the 9th or sometimes the 10th grade, school authorities are obliged to organise free secondary education for all students, the general upper secondary school leading to university studies and the vocational upper secondary school leading to working life.

Until the revision of the Child Welfare Act in 1990, the municipalities established posts for school psychologists with no support from the state. At that time, the number of school psychologists was about 123, and the posts were in 53 municipalities (only about 20% of the total number of municipalities). Over 90% of the school psychologist posts served pupils in southern Finland. The ratio of school psychologists to students was 0.47 per 1,000 in the southern provinces and 0.18 per 1,000 in the whole country (Kivinen & Sallila, 1992). The Child Welfare Act (1990) began a new period in school psychology, "a legalised one." The school psychologists and school social workers (school curators) were mentioned within the stipulations concerning child and family support for those pupils who had learning or adaptation problems at school. Furthermore, the Child Welfare Act also states that school psychologists and school social workers must participate in school planning and development activities and that the posts should be located in schools. However, the Child Welfare Act (1990) did not state that every municipality must have these kinds of services. Thus, the municipalities with sufficient financial resources established posts, but the smaller ones did not.

The third major event that has influenced the development of school psychology in Finland is the economic recession in the early 1990s. Basic financial and emotional security within so-called well-to-do-families was threatened. Research has shown that children's symptoms of emotional and social problems increased in the 5-year period after the recession (Laaksonen, 2002; Salmi, Huttunen, & Yli-Pietilä, 1996). The indicators describing the use of outpatient and inpatient psychiatric services for children and adolescents highlight the rise in the use of services that took place at the turn of the 21st century. Attention was then focused nationwide on mental health services for children and adolescents, and the state granted an extra supplement (nearly 12 million euros) to the municipalities for services for children and adolescents (Pirkola & Sohlman, 2005). In addition to this, some of the municipalities reacted to the increase in number of children's problems by establishing more student welfare posts (e.g., school psychologist and social workers at school; Sermilä et al., 2003).

The most recent event impacting school psychology services has been the revision of the Basic Education Act in 2003. This document stipulated for the first time what is meant by "student welfare": "Pupil/student welfare means action promoting and maintaining good learning, good mental and physical health and social well-being, and conditions conducive to these." A pupil is entitled to free pupil welfare necessary for participation in education. Pupil welfare shall encompass (a) pupil welfare provided for in the curriculum adopted by the education provider and (b) pupil welfare services comprising school health care referred to in the Public Health Care Act (1972) and support to education and parenting referred to in the Child Welfare Act (1983). Thus, the pupil/student welfare is defined in three separate laws in the Finnish legislation. The number of school psychologists did not increase dramatically after the Child Welfare Act's revision in 1990. Until 2004, the posts were primarily in the southern parts of Finland. The current data showing the number of school psychologists was collected by State Provincial Offices in October 2004. According to this survey, there are 158 school psychologists in Southern Finland Province (Etelä-Suomen lääni), of which 149 posts are full-time. In the country as a whole, there are 334 posts, of which

277 are full-time posts. The ratio of psychologists working per 1,000 students is 0.75 in the southern areas and 0.68 for the country overall. Many school psychological services are joint consultation or bought when needed, for example, services for several small cities or communities in rural areas. This means that the services are available only when the problems are very severe. Thus, preventive work is rare in this context (State Provincial Office of Southern Finland, 2005).

The term *school psychologist* applies to psychologists working in schools, in the municipal education departments, or in the social and health sector for schools. Nearly 50% of school psychologists work in municipal education departments. Although most of the posts are public, there are a few private schools and state schools (e.g., one institution for the blind, another for the deaf, and Steiner pedagogical schools) that have hired psychologists to work as school psychologists. The average salary of publicly working school psychologists is 2,640 euros per month. The salary of the school psychologist is a little less than for those psychologists working in the public child and family guidance centres (Finnish Psychological Association, 2005). The number of school psychologists and the availability of their services are much higher in the large cities such as Helsinki, Espoo, Vantaa, and Tampere than in the rural areas.

The municipalities in the metropolitan area of Helsinki and in other urban areas partially finance further training for their employees and also pay for school psychologists to attend specialisation courses (e.g., psychotherapy, neuropsychology). The school psychologists in smaller cities and rural areas have few opportunities for professional development. The State Provincial Office of Southern Finland organises seminars every year for all municipal workers working in student welfare (i.e., school psychologists, social workers, school nurses, special teachers, and head teachers). The school psychologists are usually directed by a psychologist in the office if there are several posts. Except in private schools, the school psychologist's work is not directed by the head teacher. The head teacher, school nurses, classroom teachers, and special education teachers are the main coworkers within the schools, and together they form the multiprofessional student welfare team. These multiprofessional teams operate in 80% of basic education schools (State Provincial Office of Southern Finland, 2005).

Infrastructure of School Psychology

The Finnish Union of Psychologists consists of psychologists working in different sectors of the workforce, with most psychologists working in public services. The union has registered 371 psychologists whose expertise is school psychology. As mentioned earlier, the actual number of school psychologists in Finland is somewhat smaller: There are 277 full-time school psychologist posts in the country overall. The remainder of these psychologists with expertise in school psychology work in health care centres or child and family guidance centres, and some complete school psychological evaluations, which the municipalities buy from private psychologists or neighbouring cities (Finnish Psychological Association, 2005; State Provincial Office of Southern Finland, 2005).

All school psychologists in Finland are trained clinical psychologists. The National Board of Medicolegal Affairs maintains a register of all health care professionals, including legislated psychologists. The psychologist must apply for the registration and, in addition, a separate registration if they work as a trained psychotherapist. The National Board of Medicolegal Affairs and the State Provincial Offices monitor the work of the health professionals and handle the administrative appeals related to the work of school psychologists in cases where the clients are not satisfied with the services or if they do not get services guaranteed by law. Only licensed psychologists or psychologists practising under the supervision of a licensed psychologist can carry out the work of a school psychologist.

Three basic laws guide the work of Finnish school psychologists. The most important guiding laws in Finnish school psychologists' work are The Basic Education Act (1998/2003), the Child Welfare Act (1983/1990), and the Primary Health Care Act (1972). In addition to these acts, there are laws regulating the work of all civil servants and the public services, which school psychologists must follow. Of special interest to the clients (pupils, students, and parents) are the laws of Patients' Rights and Consumers' Rights in Social Services. The Basic Education Act includes articles concerning the necessary psychological evaluations to be made before the child can be moved into or out of special needs education.

Finland has no professional journals in Finnish or English aimed solely for school psychologists. The Finnish Psychological Association publishes a monthly newsletter called *Psykologi*. The scientific discussion is contained on the pages of many international journals and the journal *Psykologia,* which is published by the Finnish Psychological Society.

Preparation of School Psychologists

In Finland, there is no specific university training programme for school psychologists, which means that almost all psychologists in Finland are trained to work as clinical psychologists. The period of supervised practice, which is included in psychology studies, often influences the individual's motivation and interests. Thus, many psychologists in training, who have been supervised by a school psychologist, wish to continue to specialise in this field. The average time spent in university studying to become psychologist is 5 to 7 years. The state financial support for 55 months is not often enough to enable students to complete their studies. The studies are completed in two phases: The first degree is in psychology and takes about 3 to 4 years. The second phase is the master's degree in psychology, and this requires another 3 to 4 years. Psychologists, including school psychologists, must have a master's degree in psychology and be certified by the National Authority for Medicolegal Affairs according to nationally recognised criteria (see http://www.teo.fi/uusi/engl_1.htm)

Finnish psychologists' university training consists of the core academic knowledge of psychology (e.g., development, learning and cognition, educational, personality, social, experimental, biological, statistics, and research design), assessment services (e.g., intellectual, academic, emotional, and social assessment), and intervention services (e.g., behavioral, affective, educational, and social systems). A focus on children and youth is not specifically handled within the context of classrooms and schools but generally within families, communities, and other systems. Students of psychology may major in a second subject, for example, from the educational sciences, medical sciences, or social psychology, in order to broaden the scientific background of their knowledge. Other obligatory courses for students of psychology in Finnish universities are those covering interpersonal skills, such as establishing trust and rapport, listening and communication skills, respect for the views and expertise of others, recognition of the assets and limitations of other professionals, and gaining a mature understanding of issues and effective methods to address them. Professional decision-making skills are not highlighted, because the training is rather academic and theoretical. Knowledge of statistical methods and research design is highlighted in the studies because the thesis, showing a student's research capacities, is obligatory before graduation. A few short courses cover legal and ethical issues related to psychological services; these issues also are incorporated in some other lectures. After 2 years of experience, a psychologist may apply for professional specialisation in one of the four fields, and after 4 years, he or she may obtain a psychology license. The possibility to continue to the highest academic degree, a doctorate in psychology, requires further training (emphasising science and scholarship) at the university.

Roles, Functions, and Responsibilities of School Psychologists

Prevention is the main reason behind the establishment of posts of school psychologists: Children should receive help with their learning or behavioural problems as early as possible. The post of school psychologist mainly serves pupils in the comprehensive basic education system, Grades 1 through 6. Only in some municipalities will clients come from the upper grades of basic education. The new Basic Education Act requires the municipalities to organise all services that children need in order to learn. Consultation with teachers has been the primary method for helping children. This takes place either in mutual conversation between the teacher and school psychologist or together with the child's caregiver.

In Finnish schools, problem solving, consultation, and planning intervention activities are often accomplished by a multiprofessional team (i.e., student welfare team). In most of the schools, the expert members of the group are the head teacher, the school nurse, and the special needs teacher. Not all student welfare teams have the expertise of the school social worker and school psychologist. The numbers of expert members, meetings, and issues handled by the student welfare team vary according to the size and grades of the school. The most usual issues handled in lower grades are learning difficulties, family problems, and special education needs. In Grades 6 and higher, absenteeism is often addressed (State Provincial Office of Southern Finland, 2005).

According to the National Core Curriculum (Finnish National Board of Education, 2005), the schools are also responsible for drawing up crisis intervention plans, creating procedures for the prevention of bullying, and planning school-home collaborations. Many student welfare teams have taken on this task.

In the majority of municipalities, the work of school psychologists is focused on the evaluation of, and consultation about, individual students' problems. The development of prevention and intervention programs for the entire school environment is possible only in larger cities where there are plenty of school psychologists. The education departments use the expertise of school psychologists in developing school supervising activities, the activities of the student welfare teams, further training of teachers, and curriculum planning. After the reforms in the education laws in 2003, the development of the curriculum in municipalities must be made in collaboration with the social and health care and education authorities. The participation of school psychologists, as experts in the planning phase of the curriculum process, is not yet used in all municipalities in spite of the fact that the student welfare activity (including school psychological work) is mentioned for the first time not only in the Basic Education Act but also in the National Core Curriculum. The latter regulation forms the basis for the municipal and school curricula.

Testing and assessment have been the basic tools used in Finnish school psychological evaluations, linked closely with discussions with the child's caregiver and teachers. Usually about 80% to 90% of the clients of school psychologists are helped by the consultation and negotiations grounded on these evaluations. The rest of the clients are referred for further evaluation and therapeutic treatment outside the schools, in child guidance centres or hospitals. The function of testing has developed simultaneously with teacher consultation. As knowledge about methods of testing and about medical, as well as neuropsychological, development has increased in relation to pupils with learning difficulties, the role of testing has also increased (although it was less popular in the 1980s). There has been a trend among school psychologists to concentrate on their own professional development either with individual students or on the development of systemic intervention within the school as a whole. These developmental trends have been associated with the general development of the school system and of the schools as organisations (Laaksonen & Wiegand, 1989; Sipilä-Lähdekorpi, 2004).

Tests commonly used by Finnish school psychologists to assess intellectual abilities include the Wechsler Intelligence Scale for Children–III, the Wechsler Preschool and Primary Scale of Intelligence, the Children's Neuropsychological Assessment (Psykologien Kustannus Oy, a Finnish test designed by Maarit Korkman et al.), the Visual-Motor Integration Test, the Raven Progressive Matrices, and the Bender-Gestalt Test. To assess behaviour and social skills, Finnish school psychologists use the Sentence Completion Test and observation (both classroom and small group observation). Most school psychologists do not often use projective tests, such as the Rorschach or the Children's Apperception Test that were often used 20 years ago. These tests are currently used more in the evaluation of the therapeutic interventions by psychologists working in child guidance centres and hospital clinics. Many school psychologists use the House-Tree-Person Test or the Draw-A-Person Test as a tool for gaining rapport with the child and for evaluating intellectual abilities using the Goodenough scoring method.

In many of the municipalities, the role of supervision is used to support the worker, to guarantee the quality of the work, and to protect the rights of the clients and the worker. So school psychologists are paid for being supervised. Again, this is often neglected by those municipalities that provide occasional services. For the past 10 years, many school psychologists have been active in developing crisis work in their municipalities, especially in the metropolitan areas. The origin of this kind of activity was highly supported by the Finnish Psychological Association in parallel with the National Suicide Prevention Program of the National Research and Development Centre for Welfare and Health (Upanne, Hakanen, & Rautava, 1999).

Current Issues Impacting School Psychology

Major challenges face school psychologists today, including the increasing number of students being referred to special needs education. The law demands that the evaluation of a child's special needs should be made by psychologists before a decision to transfer a child either to or from special needs education can be made. This transfer is seldom made without the permission of the child's caregiver. The development of regulations needed to accompany the reformed Basic Education Law are urgent in the following areas: (a) guaranteeing that student welfare services are provided to all schools, (b) defining the role and function of the student welfare team, (c) maintaining confidentiality in the field of student welfare, and (d) defining the role, tasks, and status of personnel working within student welfare services (i.e., school psychologists, school social workers, school nurses). At present, there is a cross-sector expert committee, set up by the Ministry of Social Affairs and Health, which is working to solve these questions.

References

Basic Education Act, 628 § 31 (1998/2003). Available online at http://www.finlex.fi/en/laki/kaannok set/1998/en19980628.pdf

Child Welfare Act, 683 (1983/1990). Available online at http://www.finlex.fi/pdf/saadkaan/E9830683 .PDF

Finnish National Board of Education. (2005). *National core curriculum for basic education* intended for pupils in compulsory education. Vammala: Vammalan Kirjapaino Oy. Available online at www.oph.fi (in Finnish)

Finnish Statistical Office. (2005). Educational statistics. Available online at www.tilastokeskus.fi/til/erop/index_en.html

Kivinen, T., & Sallila, S. (1992). Selvitys koulukuraattori ja psykologitoiminnan järjestämisestä kunnissa 1990–1992 [Survey on organising the school social work and school psychological activities 1990–1992] Sosiaali- ja terveyshallitus. [National Board on Social and Health Affairs]. *Tiedote Newsletter,* Issue No. 1.

Laaksonen P. (1989). Developmental phases in school psychological work: Reflections on the work of psychologists in Finland. *School Psychology International, 10*(1), 3–9.

Laaksonen, P. (2002). *Lasten ja nuorten hyvinvointi. Koulujen opetussuunnitelmallinen ja oppilashuollon tuki syrjäytymiskehityksen ehkäisemisessä. Kysely Etelä-Suomen läänin kouluille ja oppilaitoksille 1998* [Children and Youth's Welfare. The support systems of the curricula and student welfare in preventing exclusion]. Unpublished licensiate thesis, University of Tampere, Finland.

Laaksonen, P., & Wiegand, E. (1989). *Oppilasko ongelma? Oppilashuolto koulun systeemeissä* [Pupil the problem? Student welfare in the school systems]. Juva: Mannerheimin Lastensuojeluliitto Gummerus.

Ministry of Education and Culture. (1974). *Oppilashuoltokomitean mietintö* [Committee report on student welfare]. Helsinki: Author.

Pirkola, S., & Sohlman, B. (Eds.). (2005). *Mielenterveysatlas. Psykisk hälsa i Finland* [Atlas of mental health. Statistics from Finland]. National Research

and Development Centre for Welfare and Health. Saarijärvi: Gummerus Kirjano Oy.

Primary Health Care Act 66 (1972). Available online at http://www.finlex.fi/fi/laki/kaannokset/1972/en19720066.pdf

Salmi, M., Huttunen, J., & Yli-Pietilä, P. (1996). Lapset ja lama. STAKES. Sosiaali- ja terveyslan tutkimus- ja kehittämiskeskus. Raportteja 197 [Children and recession. National Research and Development Centre for Welfare and Health Report No. 197]. Jyväskylä: Gummerus Kirjapaino Oy.

Sermilä, P., Hallantie, M., Hyvén, A., Karppinen, A., Lindroos, P., Luotonen, A., et al. (2003). *Oppilas- ja opiskelijahuolto Helsingissä. Kehittämistyöryhmän muistio* [Pupil and student welfare in Helsinki. Report of the Helsinki Board of Education Developmental Task Force (Report No. B2)].

Sipilä-Lähdekorpi, P. (2004). *"It's a lot like the person who does it." The work of a school social worker in the upper level of comprehensive school* (Doctoral thesis, University of Tampere, 2004). Tampere: Oy FINN LECTURA AB.

State Provincial Office of Southern Finland. (2005). *Development of student welfare, order and punishments in the basic education system during the years 2001, 2003, and 2004* (National Summary Report). Available online at http://www.laaninhallitus.fi/lh/biblio.nsf/92F263CD4A3371A0C22570770030EB18/$file/SIVeril0105.pdf (in Finnish)

Statistics Finland. (n.d.). Available at http://www.stat.fi/index_en.html

Upanne, M., Hakanen, J., & Rautava, M. (1999). *Can suicide be prevented? The Suicide Project in Finland 1992–1996: Goals, implementation and evaluation.* National Research and Development Centre for Welfare and Health. Saarijärvi: Gummerus.

12

School Psychology in France

Jean-Claude Guillemard

Context of School Psychology

The French Republic, with a population of more than 60 million inhabitants, is one of the 25 countries that constitute the European Union. With a surface of 550,000 square kilometres, it is bordered on the west by the North Sea, the English Channel, and the Atlantic Ocean and on the south by the Mediterranean Sea. In the southwest, the Pyrenean mountains form the border with Spain, and the Alps form the eastern border with Italy and Switzerland. To the north, the tunnel under the English Channel offers direct access by train or by car to the United Kingdom. There are three other countries forming the border to the north: Belgium, Luxemburg, and Germany.

Despite its membership in the G8 (i.e., the Group of 8 wealthier countries in the world) and its gross domestic product of US$1.737 trillion, US$28,700 per capita in 2004, France, like other developed countries, experiences many economic and social problems. With an unemployment level of more than 10% and a very low level of economic growth (less than 2% in

2005), 6% of the population (3.5 million people, including 1 million children younger than age 15) live under the threshold of poverty according to French criteria (i.e., less than 50% of average income; average income in 2003 was €1,200 per month). In 2003, the cost of educating a child of pre-elementary age was €4,240 (equivalent to €2,620 in 1986); €4,540 for a child in a primary school (equivalent to €3,230 in 1986); €7,150 for a collège (junior high school) student (€5,040 in 1986); €9,750 for a general or technical lycée (high school) student (€6,440 in 1986); and €10,130 for a student in a professional lycée (€6,400 in 1986; Ministry of National Education, 2005). The French educational system, under the responsibility of the Ministry of National Education, is divided into three levels. The primary level includes pre-elementary (kindergarten) and elementary school for children ages 2 to 11 years. The secondary level includes collèges (junior high schools) for students ages 12 to 15 years as well as professional, technical, and general lycées (senior high schools) for students ages 16 to 18 years. The tertiary level includes preparatory classes, schools for engineers (Grandes Ecoles), teacher training schools, military schools, and universities. In 2000, the average class size in pre-elementary schools was 25.4 pupils; in elementary schools (Grades 1–5), 23.8; in secondary schools (collèges), 24.2; and in secondary schools (lycées), 27.6 (Ministry of National Education, 2005).

The number of handicapped children (i.e., children identified by a local special education commission as sensory, physically, or mentally/developmentally disabled) who benefit from an individual inclusion program in ordinary classrooms is about 52,000. There are about 115,000 children in special schools run by the Ministry of Health and special private schools that have an arrangement with state or local authorities. Also, 12,000 children are placed in classrooms that are integrated into hospitals, 3,000 are schooled in prison, and 4,500 are in specific classes for pupils who have been expelled from ordinary school for disruptive behaviour (*classes-relais*). In 1987, the number of children in special classes in elementary schools was 73,000 (Guillemard, 1989). The inclusive policy developed by the Ministry of National Education in 1990 explains the decrease in this number, down to 50,000 (Ministry of National Education, 2005).

Origin, History, and Current Status of School Psychology

The need for preparing qualified psychologists for service in French schools appeared at the end of World War II. After a successful trial period in Grenoble in 1945, involving the appointment of Bernard Andrey as the first school psychologist, a team of school psychologists began work in Paris in 1947 with Professor Henri Wallon (1869–1962). However, the application of psychology in schools actually began years before. As early as 1894, Alfred Binet, who was rightly considered to be the "grandfather of French

school psychology," created the Free Society for the Psychological Study of the Child. In 1897, he wrote a paper describing psychology in primary schools (Binet & Vaschide, 1897). In 1899, along with teacher Pierre Vaney, he opened a pedagogical and psychological laboratory in a Parisian primary school. In 1905, Binet was asked by the Ministry of Public Instruction (later renamed the Ministry of National Education) to study problems exhibited by children who could not follow the normal school curriculum. The Binet-Simon test was used to detect mentally retarded children and to direct them toward special classes. The first special classes for mentally retarded children opened in Lyon in 1906, and, in the following year, five special classes opened in Paris. In 1909, Marcel Foucault opened a laboratory of school psychology in Montpellier (in the south of France), and, in the same year, the first vocational guidance service was created (Foucault, 1923).

Although Wallon first opened a laboratory of child psychology in a primary school near Paris in 1923, he was not able to expand the project and develop school psychological services linked to a new democratic system of education until after World War II. According to Wallon (1952), school psychology's mission was to help all children. Its aim was not to discriminate or, by selection, to deny children the benefits of a culture that must belong to everybody. Instead, school psychologists were to study methods and techniques so as to promote the growth of the child and to promote high-quality education throughout the country.

In 1948, some school psychologists were appointed in secondary schools, and the number of practitioners was large enough to warrant holding the first national convention at Sèvres (near Paris) in 1949 and the second in Grenoble the following year. In 1951, the Ministry of National Education described the functions of school psychologists, and this text (Wall, 1958) was used as the basis for discussion at the First International School Psychology Colloquium organized by the United Nations Educational, Scientific and Cultural Organization (UNESCO) in Hamburg in November–December 1952 and at the Second International School Psychology Colloquium in April 1954, also in Hamburg (Wall, 1958). Despite these developments at the very moment when French school psychologists seemed to have an important part to play in the future development of the discipline on the international stage, their training and employment as a separate professional group ended, and they were sent back to primary schools as teachers. The official reason for this change was the need to fill vacant posts in primary schools after the postwar baby boom. However, the political reason was that the school psychology project was a part of the "Democratic Reform of the French School System" written in 1944 by Wallon and Langevin for the National Council of Resistance (the clandestine French government during German occupation), both authors being members of the French Communist Party.

Despite this development, the need for school psychologists increased substantially during the 1950s, chiefly due to an increase in the birth rate and the associated increase in the number of "maladjusted" children. For these reasons, the Ministry of National Education resumed training school psychologists with the main aim of using them to identify handicapped children in order to educate them in special classes and schools. As a result, the training initially focused on the use of psychometric tests and on theories of psychopathology.

During the late 1960s, much attention was focused on the significance of the school failure rate, affecting about 50% of all pupils between the first and fifth grades at the primary school level. The general belief held that, in relation to school failure, it was better to place the emphasis on prevention efforts rather than intervention. The subsequent success of a number of educational programs supported this belief. Thus, in 1970, the first prevention teams were established, called Groupes d'Aide

Psycho-Pédagogique (Psychopedagogic Aid Groups). They were, in theory, teams, each consisting of one specialist in school psychology, one in psychoeducation, and one in psychomotor development. Each Psychopedagogic Aid Group was intended to serve between 800 and 1,000 pupils, and, though based in one school, a particular group often had to work in several schools within a prescribed area. Moreover, school psychologists had to devote one third of their time outside the Psychopedagogic Aid Group area in assessing "maladjusted" children for special classes and schools.

The Psychopedagogic Aid Group system worked for 20 years without any change but also without important developments. The idea that every pupil could find support from a system based on a philosophy of prevention was actually never reached, and this strong republican French principle of equal opportunity for all was not applied in the schools. It was not surprising, therefore, that during the period 1980–1985, the Ministry of National Education ordered a national survey aiming to evaluate the effects of Psychopedagogic Aid Group action on pupils who had benefited from the support. The results were rather disappointing. A large proportion of pupils with learning difficulties, who had been registered in a Psychopedagogic Aid Group program, still had difficulties when beginning collège (junior high school) and still needed support from the Psychopedagogic Aid Group system, which was not available in secondary schools. However, the national survey acknowledged that all of the pupils who had benefited from Psychopedagogic Aid Group action were generally better integrated in the classroom and their self-esteem had improved. In other words, the members of the Psychopedagogic Aid Group had been effective in the area of emotional behaviour but not in areas related to their first mission: to improve learning skills.

The Réseau d'Aides Spécialisées aux Elèves en Difficulté (Special Support Network for Pupils With Difficulties) was designed to replace the

Psychopedagogic Aid Group system and to maintain preventative actions within the schools, but more generally it was incorporated into a major policy initiative aimed at providing inclusive education for all the children with specific educational needs (either moderate learning disabilities or severe handicaps). The Special Support Network for Pupils With Difficulties staff (always one school psychologist and two special education teachers) had to help teachers in their task to develop education for all, and, when necessary, they were expected to help pupils either in small groups or individually. Special classes were maintained for various categories of pupils who could not be included in mainstream classes.

The role and function of the Special Support Network for Pupils With Difficulties did not change until 2002, when an important circular was published in the Official Bulletin of the Ministry of National Education (Ministry of National Education, 2002b) reorganizing the system of special education within the general frame of inclusive education and meeting the specific needs of all children. In this text, the role of schools was reinforced, and they were given prescribed roles in relation to the assessment, provision, and monitoring of pupils who may require special help. The role of the school psychologist in this process was also clearly defined, although there are important differences from one Special Support Network for Pupils With Difficulties to another, according to geographical, historical, political, and economic factors.

The period from 1980 to 1990 was important for school psychology in France. The National Coalition of Psychologists' Organizations (in which the French School Psychologists Association was very much involved) had taken the important step of lobbying for the legal recognition of the title "psychologist." This action was successful, and, in 1985, a law was passed, legally recognizing the profession (French Government, 1985). Under this law, the title "psychologist" for professional use is exclusively reserved for persons who have earned a university degree in

psychology. These include degrees involving academic and professional courses in a 5-year-minimum program. Persons who illegally use the title "psychologist" professionally can be prosecuted (French Penal Code art. 259). The law encompasses all categories of psychologists and had many consequences for the profession of school psychology, including the following: (a) It obliged the employer of school psychologists (i.e., the Ministry of National Education) to modify and improve the selection and the professional training of its future employees. (b) It increased the recognition of school psychologists within the psychological profession, by associated professions, and among the public at large. It helped school psychologists build a professional identity and raise their professional self-esteem.

In France, there are three categories of psychologists working in schools: (1) school psychologists working in public primary schools (around 3,000), including a very small number who also work in child guidance centres and some who have a part-time private practice (in addition to their regular work in the public service); (2) vocational counsellor-psychologists working in secondary schools and universities (around 4,000), who are organized in Orientation and Information Centres that operate as a School Psychology Service; and (3) psychologists working in private Catholic schools (approximately 250).

With fewer than 3,000 school psychologists for 6,500,000 pupils in primary schools, the ratio is about 1 to 2,200. With about 4,000 vocational counsellor-psychologists for 5,000,000 students in secondary schools (not including university students), the ratio is about 1 to 1,250. With about 250 psychologists for 2,000,000 pupils in private Catholic schools, the ratio is about 1 to 8,000. According to the Association Française des Psychologues Scolaires (French School Psychologists Association), the number of vacant positions for school psychologists is between 200 and 400 (Association Française des Psychologues Scolaires, 2003).

School psychologists working in primary public schools are selected exclusively from among the teachers, and they keep this administrative status of teacher with the same salary scale when they become a school psychologist. In 2005, a new schoolteacher working in a primary school (elementary or pre-elementary) started at a salary of €1,100 per month. At the end of his or her career (following age 60), he or she may expect a (maximum) salary of €3,000 per month. Teachers who become school psychologists usually have at least 3 years of professional experience, which means their salary starts at about €1,500 per month, to which they can add a specific subsidy (as do all the special education teachers), which is approximately €1,000 a year (€80 per month). Teachers in secondary schools (and vocational counsellor-psychologists as well) have a similar salary scale, but they may expect various subsidies for specific work, which raises their salary significantly.

In the French school system, all the primary schools have, at least in theory, access to a school psychologist. The principal may request support from the school psychologist and from the Special Support Network for Pupils With Difficulties team. A pupil in a small school of the mountainous region of Grenoble or on an island of Brittany should also benefit from the support of a school psychologist. The reality is slightly different, and it is easier in Paris (or in any big city) than it is in a remote village of central France, for example, for a teacher (or a family) to call a school psychologist for help. There is a Centre for Orientation and Information in all medium-size towns where students can meet a vocational counsellor-psychologist or freely consult information on school and professional guidance. In each high school, there is usually a room where a student can meet with a vocational counsellor-psychologist once a week.

From informal enquiries made among school psychologists, it appears that the degree of job satisfaction is generally low. School psychologists often indicate that they are not recognized as psychologists by their employer, and the lack of a specific status of psychologist (rather than teacher) are the reasons given most often for this lack of satisfaction. They also indicate that they are overburdened by administrative tasks. They regret the lack of time to make in-depth assessments or to offer long-term psychological support. Some of them consider that they could be better used than they are and that their employer ignores their competencies.

Infrastructure of School Psychology

There are three associations for school psychologists:

1. Association Française des Psychologues Scolaires (French School Psychologists Association)

2. Association des Conseillers d'Orientation-Psychologues de France (French Association of Vocational Counsellor-Psychologists)

3. Association Nationale des Psychologues de l'Enseignement Catholique (National Association of Psychologists in Catholic Schools)

These three associations have frequent contacts and meet together in a coalition of six psychologists organizations. The Association Nationale des Psychologues de l'Enseignement Catholique was co-organizer, with the Association Française des Psychologues Scolaires, of the International School Psychology Association colloquium in 2001 in Dinan. Both associations are affiliated with the International School Psychology Association. The Association des Conseillers d'Orientation-Psychologues de France is a member of the International School and Professional Counselling Organization.

The Association Française des Psychologues Scolaires publishes a quarterly journal, *Psychologie*

& Education, and a newsletter, *Echanges,* which includes a biannual international supplement, *La Lettre Internationale de l'AFPS.* The Association des Conseillers d'Orientation-Psychologues de France publishes a journal, *Questions d'Orientation,* and a newsletter, *La Lettre de l'ACOPF.* The oldest psychological association in France, Societé Française de Psychologie (French Psychological Society), publishes two quarterly journals: *Psychologie Française* and *Pratiques Psychologiques.* The Syndicat National des Psychologues (National Union of Psychologists) publishes a newsletter, *Psychologues & Psychologies.* There is also a monthly private journal, *Le Journal des Psychologues,* which has many readers among school psychologists. The first manual in French describing the organization and the practices of psychologists working in the educational system was edited by the Association Française des Psychologues Scolaires (Guillemard & Guillard, 1997).

The law recognizing the title "psychologist" and defining the conditions (diplomas) was passed into law after a vote of the French Parliament in July 1985. All professional psychologists (including school psychologists) have to be registered on an official regional list *Automatisation des listes professionnelles* (Computerization of professional lists). Psychologists, but also nurses, social workers, and psychiatrists, must be registered on these lists. They have to renew their registration when they move to another region. In theory, only school psychologists (or vocational counsellor-psychologists in secondary schools) are allowed to practice psychological work in public schools. The Association Française des Psychologues Scolaires monitors the situation through its local delegates and informs the Ministry of National Education when nonqualified persons are illegally appointed.

Since the 1985 law recognizing the title "psychologist" and the circular defining the missions of school psychologists (Ministry of National Education, 1990), there have been no other official documents that refer exclusively to school psychologists. There are other circulars, for example, on special education and school inclusion, which give precise information about the school psychologist's work, his or her contribution to the integration process, and his or her working timetable. Another circular, on the identification and prevention of language difficulties (Ministry of National Education, 2002a), is strongly influenced by current theories in neuropsychology and has given the school doctors a central position in the identification and follow-up of children with oral or written language disorders. This circular indicates that the school psychologist may be required by the school doctor to assess cognitive skills using the Wechsler intelligence scales.

In addition to the law and circulars mentioned in the previous paragraph, several official documents have been published recently, all of which stipulate ways in which education services for children could be improved and all referring to the role of the school psychologist in this process. In particular, these documents make recommendations on how to build a more cohesive education system based on equality of opportunity and the reduction of school failure. They also introduce measures to empower people with disabilities and to give them more independence in how they organize their lives.

Preparation of School Psychologists

Following completion of the baccalaureat (end of secondary studies), psychologists are required to complete university training to obtain a degree. There are two different training routes for psychologists working in schools: one for school psychologists who work in primary schools and one for vocational counsellor-psychologists employed in secondary schools and universities. School psychologists working in public primary schools complete teacher training (2 years), then obtain teaching experience (minimum of 3 years), and subsequently complete studies at a school psychology training centre (1 year) to receive the school psychology diploma. Vocational counsellor-psychologists (those working in secondary schools) complete studies at a training centre (2 years) to receive a vocational counselling-psychology diploma. Vocational counsellor-psychologists are not required to be qualified and experienced teachers, though many are. Some work in public administration before beginning their professional training program (2 years). Psychologists working in the Catholic schools can enter the profession after having trained in the regular university system and completed a 2-year master's degree in psychology; these professionals hold the title "educational psychologist."

The general outline of all the programs in primary school psychology, delivered in six universities over one school year, is as follows:

Academic and practical courses (300 hours), covering the following content: psychology of cognitive and social learning; sociocognitive and socioemotional development of the child; cognitive, sociocognitive, and emotional functioning in real-life situations; theories and methods of psychological assessment (individual child assessment, groups in classrooms, institutional functioning); school integration; psychology of handicapped persons; psychopathology of children, youths, and adults (focusing on teachers); psychology and sociology of relationships in groups and organizations; school ergonomics; and professional ethics

Practicum (240 hours) in a psychological service, under the supervision of a school psychologist

Thesis (minimum 160 hours)

Training vocational counsellor-psychologists lasts 2 years, and an overview of the content is as follows:

Psychology of school and vocational counselling (500 hours), covering the following content:

psychological theories and applications; theories, practices, and methodology of school and vocational counselling; theories, practices, and methodology of counselling directed toward groups and organizations (assessment, collecting information, communication and cooperation with partners)

Sociological, economical, and organizational approaches of vocational counselling (350 hours), including sociology and economy of education; sociocultural aspects of school integration; structures and functioning of European educational systems, including historical and geographical, social and administrative aspects; sociology and economy of work (work environments, job description and sectors of activities; a perspective for counselors); relationship between professional preparation and employment; issues on social and professional inclusion; and professional ethics

Data collection and statistical treatment applied to vocational counselling (140 hours)

Practicum (20 weeks)

Thesis (50 hours)

Roles, Functions, and Responsibilities of Psychologists Working in French Schools

The mission of school psychologists in primary schools is described in a circular from the Ministry of National Education (1990). Through teamwork and partnership with teachers and families, the school psychologist's duties are to (1) prevent school difficulties (through teamwork with the Special Support Network for Pupils With Difficulties staff); (2) contribute to the conception and implementation of school projects; (3) conceive, implement, and evaluate programs of individual and collective support for pupils experiencing learning and behaviour difficulties;

and (4) contribute to the inclusion of handicapped children in regular schools.

In all of their work, school psychologists undertake assessment and observation and give psychological support to pupils while working closely with teachers and families. They aim to provide information after analysing the child's difficulties, to propose relevant strategies of support, and to facilitate the implementation of these strategies. School psychologists use testing in a rather moderate way; however, when a psychometric evaluation is needed (for special education provision), commonly used tests include, for cognitive skills, the Wechsler Intelligence Scale for Children–III (the fourth edition was adapted for use in France in 2005), the Kaufman Assessment Battery for Children–II, the Wechsler Preschool and Primary Scale of Intelligence–III, and the McCarthy Scales for Children. A French test, Echelles Différentielles d'Efficience Intellectuelle (Cognitive Skills Differential Scales), created by Perron-Borelli, is also used. Personality and projective tests used include the Thematic Apperception Test (Murray), Children Apperception Test (Bellak), Draw-A-Person Test (Goodenough), Draw-A-Family Test (Ionescu & Lachance), Tell a Story Test (Royer), and *Patte Noire* (Corman), a French adaptation of Blacky Pictures, in which the main character is a baby pig with a black leg instead of a dog. Tests of behaviour and questionnaires are not commonly used. School psychologists prefer to collect data through direct observation in the school setting and interviews with the child, the family, and the teacher. Many school psychologists are reluctant to use academic achievement tests. They collect data from teachers or from the Special Support Network for Pupils With Difficulties team members.

In their day-to-day work, vocational counsellor-psychologists' interventions concern mainly (1) psychological guidance, vocational advice and counselling, and interviews with students about orientation choices; (2) individual psychological and emotional assessment, through intelligence aptitudes and projective tests and interest questionnaires for students with learning difficulties and special needs before guiding them toward special education classes available in collèges and lycées; (3) group testing, offered for groups of students for vocational guidance; and (4) teamwork, that is, working with educational staff teams to follow up on educational projects.

The missions of educational psychologists working in Catholic schools, in partnership with others in the school community, contribute to the quality of the educational services offered to students in the French Catholic schools. The way they work is related to the needs of the schools and to their own competencies. They work with children, parents, and teachers with a particular focus on academic integration and guidance in the upper grades.

Current Issues Impacting School Psychology

Guillemard (1989) suggested that the major changes expected in the organization of school psychology in France were the following:

1. The unification of the two separate professions; school psychologists and vocational counsellor-psychologists

2. Government recognition of a specific status for school psychologists

3. A level of training for school psychologists in line with the requirement needed by other applied psychologists (5 years of study at a university)

4. A decline in the influence of psychoanalysis on professional practice with more importance being given to other theoretical approaches (e.g., cognitive, systemic, neuropsychological, organizational, and environmental)

5. A decrease in individual casework and an increase in organizational work and project planning

Unfortunately, in 2006, the situation for school psychology remains almost unchanged in spite of the publication of an important circular in 1990 defining the missions expected from school psychologists and a proposal, in 2004 (never implemented), to decentralize some public services, including vocational counsellor-psychologists.

In spite of numerous meetings between school psychologists' organizations and representatives of the Ministry of National Education—under either socialist governments or conservative governments—no meaningful government legislation has been passed to promote the development of unified psychological services for children. There are a number of possible explanations for this lack of progress. The first is historical. The origins of the vocational counselling system in secondary schools and the development of school psychologists in primary schools are different, and each had a different mission. Second, the idea that vocational counsellors have psychological tasks to fulfill is not always recognized by administrators, by users (e.g., families and teachers), and even by some counsellors themselves. Therefore, many school psychologists (especially those who consider or define themselves as clinical psychologists) are reluctant to consider vocational counselling as a psychological practice similar to theirs. Third, some school psychologists are afraid to lose professional freedom through being included in Orientation and Information Services under the leadership of a "chief psychologist."

The influence of psychoanalysis on school psychology has declined significantly since the 1990s. Cognitive psychology has become the major trend in the domain, and this is reflected in the training programs as is the rising influence of neuropsychology, although some are concerned that this approach is too close to the medical model of working.

Unfortunately, other approaches have still not attained the importance they deserve, in particular those with a systemic, environmental, and organizational orientation. These approaches would give school psychologists alternative tools and procedures to accomplish their mission (i.e., to contribute to school projects and to cooperate with professionals working in the school and local community; Guillemard, 2001).

A further problem has been the difficulty in establishing unified professional associations representing academic and applied psychologists across the country. Despite numerous attempts, very little has been achieved so far. This inability of French psychologists to establish a powerful national organization is the main obstacle that prevents the profession from reaching goals on which they all agree (e.g., on training, status, professional identity, and national and international recognition).

In conclusion, there are three main challenges that have to be faced in the coming years. The first concerns personnel: As long as school psychologists in primary schools are not recognized by their employer, namely the Ministry of National Education, as psychologists who are not, or who are no longer, teachers, their status will remain uncertain in the school community and in the local community. In addition, the ambiguous mission of vocational counsellor-psychologists, as part counsellor and part psychologist, does not facilitate the recognition of psychologists as a separate professional group in the eyes of the public or even among other applied psychologists.

The second concerns the organization of the profession. A political-governmental willingness, which has never occurred over the past 60 years, is needed to unify the profession of psychologist in the school from the kindergarten to the university. The psychologists' employer, namely the Ministry of National Education, which is responsible for the preparation of all psychologists through university programs, must prescribe a standardized route for training, recruitment, and employment. European regulations—especially the harmonization of professional degrees (the licence/master/doctorate system that is now available in most French universities) and the free circulation of professionals within the European Union—may help to speed this up.

The third challenge concerns school psychologists as individuals and their professional organizations. As long as psychologists remain unable to act collectively by forming an organization in which a majority of them could become members, their ability to influence their future is in jeopardy. There is a need for a cultural revolution within the profession in which individualism should be considered as a barrier to overcome in order to face the major challenges faced by the profession. In this respect, a cross-cultural vision of applied psychology and an international openness to different ways of thinking, through participation in International School Psychology Association colloquia, European Federation of Psychologists' Associations conventions, and other international professional events, are values that deserve to be cultivated within the community of French psychologists.

References

Association Française des Psychologues Scolaires. (2003, January 13). *Situation de la psychologie scolaire en France à l'aube du XXIe siècle* [School psychology in France at the beginning of the 21st century] (Report of the National Board of the AFPS). Quimper: Author.

Binet, A., & Vaschide, N. (1897). La psychologie à l'école primaire [Psychology in primary school]. *L'Année Psychologique, 4,* 1–14.

Foucault, M. (1923). *Observations et expériences de psychologie scolaire* [Observations and experiments in school psychology]. Paris: Presses Universitaires de France.

French Government. (1985). Loi n° 85-772 du 25 juillet 1985, article 44 DDOS portant diverses dispositions d'ordre social et concernant les personnes autorisées à faire usage du titre de psychologue [Law No. 85-772 of July 25, 1985, Article 44 DDOS on various social provisions and concerning persons authorized to use the title of psychologist].

Guillemard, J. C. (1989). School psychology in France. In T. Oakland & P. A. Saigh (Eds.), *International perspectives on psychology in the schools* (pp. 39–50). Hillsdale, NJ: Lawrence Erlbaum.

Guillemard, J. C. (2001). Psychologie des organisations et psychologie scolaire [Organisational psychology and school psychology]. In G. Masclet et al. (Eds.), *Les écoles et le management* (pp. 53–79). Saint Etienne: Aubin.

Guillemard, J. C., & Guillard, S. (1997). *Manuel pratique de psychologie en milieu educatif* [Practical handbook of psychology in educational settings]. Paris: Masson.

Ministry of National Education. (1990). Circulaire n° 90-083 du 10 avril 1990: *Missions des psychologues scolaires* [Circular No. 90-083 of April 10, 1990: Missions of school psychologists].

Ministry of National Education. (2002a). Circulaire n° 2002-024 du 31 janvier 2002: *Mise en oeuvre d'un plan d'action pour les enfants atteints d'un trouble spécifique du langage oral ou écrit* [Circular No. 2002-024, January 31, 2002: Implementation of a plan of action for children with oral or written language difficulties].

Ministry of National Education. (2002b). Circulaire n° 2002-113 du 30 avril 2002: *Les dispositifs de l'adaptation et de l'intégration scolaire dans le premier degré* [Circular No. 2002-113 of April 30, 2002: Plans for inclusive and integrated schools].

Ministry of National Education. (2005). *L'Education nationale en chiffres 2003–2004* [National education statistics, 2003–2004]. Retrieved July 25, 2005, from www.education.gouv.fr/ens/default.htm

Wall, W. D. (1958). *La psychologie au service de l'école* [Psychology for schools]. Paris: Bourrelier.

Wallon, H. (1952). Pourquoi des psychologues scolaires? [School psychologists—For which purposes?]. *Enfance, 5.*

13

School Psychology in Germany

Lothar Dunkel

Context of School Psychology

As Europe's largest economy and most populous nation, Germany remains a key member of the continent's economic, political, and defense organizations. European power struggles immersed Germany in two devastating world wars in the first half of the 20th century and left the country occupied by the victorious Allied powers of the United States, the United Kingdom, France, and the Soviet Union in 1945. With the advent of the cold war, two German states were formed in 1949: the western Federal Republic of Germany and the eastern German Democratic Republic. The democratic Federal Republic of Germany embedded itself in key Western economic and security organizations, the European Community (which became the European Union), and NATO, while the communist German Democratic Republic was on the front line of the Soviet-led Warsaw Pact. The decline of the USSR and the end of the cold war allowed for German unification in 1990. Since then, Germany has expended considerable funds to bring Eastern productivity and wages up to Western standards. In January 1999, Germany and 10 other European Union countries introduced a common European exchange currency, the euro. Today Germany is the fifth largest economy in the world, with a gross domestic product in 2004 of US$2.362 trillion, US$28,700 per capita.

Germany is located in Central Europe, bordering the Baltic Sea and the North Sea, between the Netherlands and Poland, south of Denmark. Germany has 3,621 kilometres of boundaries with nine neighboring countries: Austria, Belgium, the Czech Republic, Denmark, France, Luxembourg, the Netherlands, Poland, and Switzerland. It covers a total area of 357,021 square kilometres. The population was projected to become 82,431,390 by July 2005 (Central Intelligence Agency, n.d.). The following are estimated statistics for the year 2005. The age structure is birth to 14 years, 14% (male 51%, female 49%); 15 to 64 years, 67% (male 51 %, female 49%); 65 years and over, 19% (male 41%, female 59%). The median age is 42.16 years (total), 40.88 years for males and 43.53 years for females. There is a 0% population growth rate. The birth rate is 8.33 births per 1,000 population. The death rate is 10.55 deaths per 1,000 population. The net migration rate is 2.18 migrants per 1,000 population. Life expectancy at birth is 78.65

years, 75.66 years for males and 81.81 years for females. There are 231 inhabitants per square kilometre. The ethnic groups are German, 92%; Turkish, 2%; and other, 6% (made up largely of Greek, Italian, Polish, Russian, Serbo-Croatian, and Spanish). Traditionally, the two large religious groups are Protestants (34%) and Roman Catholics (34%). Muslims make up 4%, and the rest (28%) are unaffiliated or belong to other religious groups.

Each of the 16 states is autonomous with respect to its public education system. Thus, a general overview of the system is described here, which represents most of the states and most aspects within each state. Specific aspects of a particular state have to be omitted in this description. Preschool education is not considered part of the school system, and all formalized care and education up to the age of 6, such as the kindergarten, is the responsibility of agencies looking after families, children, and youth. Lately, with Germany ranking unexpectedly poorly in international comparative school studies, a closer connection between preschool and school education is being intensively discussed. One important aspect in that discussion is to move the quality level of education for preschool teachers up to the standards of schoolteachers.

Formal and compulsory schooling begins at age 6 and lasts for 10 years. The first 4 years are primary education, followed by 6 years of secondary education in three types or levels of schools: Hauptschule, Realschule, and Gymnasium. A fourth type of school, Gesamtschule, comprises the other three types of schools, intending to keep all children of one age level learning together and in one school system until Grade 10. The Hauptschule focusses on everyday practical experiences of children and youth and on students going into practical work and trades. The Realschule combines practical experience and theory and is directed toward students going into technical and administrative careers. The Gymnasium extends beyond Grade 10 to Grades 11, 12, and 13 (secondary II) and is a direct way to enter university. Its methods and content

have a scientific and theoretical orientation. To adapt to international standards, graduating from public school to enter university after 13 years is presently being changed to 12 years.

Berufsschule (sometimes also called Berufskolleg) is the name for a large variety of possibilities in further education after Grade 10. Anyone who wants to become a qualified worker goes through an apprenticeship in a company learning the practical parts and, at the same time, attends specific classes for the trade chosen in a Berufsschule, thus making for a dual system. Besides being part of the dual system together with the labor market, a Berufsschule also offers full-time schooling. In contrast to the scientific and theoretical secondary II education at the Gymnasium, the Berufsschule focusses on additional areas such as technology, economics, and administration; nutrition and home economics; social studies and public health; agriculture; decor and design; and natural sciences instead of the general academic subjects offered in theGymnasium.

The total number of students is 12.5 million (2003 estimate; Secretariat, 2005). At the end of Grade 4, parents have to choose one of the aforementioned types of schools (Hauptschule, Realschule, Gymnasium, Gesamtschule) for their child, taking into consideration the recommendation of the primary school. There are a lot of students who change from one type of school to another in the consecutive years. Most of these changes are from schools with higher qualifications to schools with lower qualifications. Moving from a school with lower to one with higher qualifications happens only rarely. The percentage of students attending the different types of institutions in Grade 8 is as follows: Hauptschule (23%), Realschule (25%), Gymnasium (30%), Gesamtschule (17%), and Special Education (5%). This distribution can be quite different in some states.

Special education focusses on eight areas and offers special schools in each year. The percentage of all special students in each area is as follows: learning disabled (53%), visually impaired and blind (1%), hard of hearing and deaf (3%), children with speech impediment (9%), physically and motor handicapped (5%), mentally handicapped (14%), emotionally and socially handicapped (8%), ill (2%), and no classification (4%). Individual care and attention is given to the question as to whether a child can best be taught in one of the special schools suited for his or her own needs or in a regular school and class with special assistance. The average class sizes are primary (22), Hauptschule (22), Realschule (27), Gymnasium (27), and special education (12). Student-teacher ratios are primary (20:1), Hauptschule (15:1), Realschule (19:1), Gymnasium (18:1), and Berufsschule–dual system (38:1).

All children and adolescents of school age who have to attend school do so. In elementary school, it is a rare exception for a child not to attend. Schooling is widely accepted and considered very important by the entire population. There are some rare cases recently of people having newly arrived in this country from other parts of the world who do not accept the value of schooling. From Grade 8 and following, there are some adolescents who are unwilling to continue to go to school and often do not attend for long periods of time or never attend again. The current system and methods that are used to help those who drop out or are absent and give them the proper kind of assistance need to be improved. Even more important, there is little interest in undertaking preventative actions to encourage adolescents to stay in school when their motivation wanes. With unemployment being quite high in some areas in the country, even among young adults, the goal to successfully finish school does not make much sense to some of them, as they do not have good prospects for employment.

Origin, History, and Current Status of School Psychology

It is known that William Stern demanded positions for school psychologists during the first conference on youth affairs in Hamburg in 1911.

A long controversial discussion followed for several years. The beginning of practical school psychology in Germany bears the name of Hans Lämmermann. He was the first person in Germany to carry the title of "school psychologist" and began his work in Mannheim in 1922. The idea to install this position was to introduce knowledge and methods of psychology from the universities directly into practical, everyday teaching. Intelligence and ability assessment, in order to guide students into the appropriate learning facility, was one of his major tasks. At the same time, these selective mechanisms later became reasons for criticism. Right from the beginning, Hans Lämmermann pursued his work at a high-quality level due to close monitoring from, and cooperation with, the university. In 1933, with the rise of the Nazis, the work of a school psychologist was not considered worthwhile, and Hans Lämmermann had to resign from his school psychology work and work instead as a special education teacher. There is no known school psychological work of any kind during the years of World War II. When peace came to Germany after 1945, the country was divided into a western part, strongly influenced by the United States, England, and France, and an eastern part, oriented toward Russia. Eventually two different Germanys evolved as politically independent entities until 1989, when reunification could be achieved. During these 44 years, two separate and very different kinds of school psychology developed in the two Germanys.

West Germany—Federal German Republic

Immediately after 1945, the western occupational powers introduced child guidance clinics to offer psychotherapeutic support to individual children. These clinics were not accepted very well by teachers and schools. In the west, school psychology started its existence again in the 1950s. Local initiatives in cities like Hamburg, Munich, Mannheim, Heidelberg, Stuttgart,

Fürth, and Cologne resulted in the opening of counselling centres staffed with school psychologists. The emphasis of their work was to assist individual students with any kind of school problems and to do general school career counselling. In contrast to that situation, some states started to employ school psychologists as an integral part of the school system with an emphasis on program development for crucial aspects of the school system, such as school readiness or student selective procedures and especially to support the school system in general through, for instance, teacher and school staff workshops plus the development of methods and materials.

Throughout the whole Federal German Republic, school psychology came into existence, and the number of school psychologists increased slowly. In 1965, there were 106 school psychologists in Germany; 10 years later, in 1975, there were 454. The settings in which they worked were generally not integrated into, or part of, the school system but were instead institutions of the local community administration.

A milestone in establishing school psychology in this part of the country was the Dortmund Resolution, put into effect after a nationwide meeting of school psychologists in the city of Dortmund. In order to integrate and coordinate the diversified activities in which school psychologists were engaged at that time, the following tasks were described (Ingenkamp, 1966): (a) individual counselling of students, including their teachers and parents; (b) continuing support and assistance for students; (c) school career counselling; (d) the monitoring and improvement of school psychological instruments; (e) promotion of good education and teaching; (f) incorporation of insights of psychology into education; and (g) coordination of the activities of different persons and institutions for one child. These guidelines were widely accepted and formed the base for school psychologists in their daily work.

Between 1969 and 1973, strong arguments for school psychology came from a number of government committees and panels working hard on reforming the German educational system. Plans were to have a ratio of 1 school psychologist for every 5,000 students. In addition, large school systems with more than 2,000 students should have one school psychologist. These goals were met in subsequent years only sporadically in a few parts of the country. As a whole, Germany has never been anywhere near achieving these self-set goals. Some of the reasons for this relate to the decreasing birth rate, the decreasing economic power of local communities, and the loss of importance of educational issues in overall politics (Sektion Schulpsychologie, 1977).

East Germany—German Democratic Republic

Developments in East Germany have been very different. Until 1973, school psychology did not exist. In November 1973, it was politically ordered that psychologists should be introduced into the educational system. The first result of this was the employment of psychologists in local committees that were responsible for advanced education and training for the local teachers. These school psychologists were given the task to "answer the questions and help solve the problems that are on the minds of teachers, educators, kindergarten teachers and the heads of institutions for national education" (Verfügungen und Mitteilungen des Ministeriums für Volksbildung Nr. 2/1979).

Until 1978, there was a fair amount of freedom to develop the field. After 1978, many rules and guidelines restricted the theories and methods that could be used, and mechanisms to control professional practice were introduced. Change came about in 1980, when the International Congress of Psychology was held in Leipzig. Until then, administrative leaders, economists, the socialist party, and leaders in education believed that the socialist ideology was a guideline for everything. After the International Congress, it could not be argued any longer that psychologists have special methods to provide for healthy, congenial, and efficient human interactions. The number of school psychologists increased, they were accepted into the educational system, and, within a rather rigid socialist system that largely ignored individual psychological conditions, they developed ways to assist teachers, students, and parents toward improved educational progress. Preschool education has always been an integral part of East German school psychology. This facilitated a smooth kindergarten-to-school transition. Diagnostic measures during early childhood and special training and remedial programs before entering schools took high priority, and some excellent programs (Breuer & Weuffen, 1990; Guthke, 1969; Roether, 1983) were developed.

A Unified Country

When East and West Germany reunited in 1989, there was an eager exchange and mutual visits to learn from each other, to hear about each other's history, and to understand the different structures and situations that school psychologists had in their daily job situations. A first large meeting of all school psychologists took place in 1994 in Rostock at the 11th meeting of the National School Psychology Association. In 2005, there were 982 school psychologist positions in the country, serving 12.5 million students. This makes for a school psychologist–student ratio of 1 to 13,000. This ratio is one of the poorest in all of Europe. There is no officially kept figure as to the female-to-male ratio in the profession. A good estimate, based on consultations with several key persons throughout the country, is that around 65% of all school psychologists are female and 35% are male. Lately, there seems to be a tendency for fewer men to enter the field. This can be judged from the students doing their practicum in school psychology.

Salaries for school psychologists are approximately €60,000 to €75,000 a year. Those in leading or key positions can earn from €70,000 to €95,000 a year. Due to the small number of school psychologists overall, there are very few top positions with top salaries. The salaries are exactly the same as those for teachers at the high school level and other professionals with a university degree (e.g., lawyers, architects, medical doctors) working in public service. Other people in education, such as social workers or teachers in elementary schools, earn less as their professional education has traditionally been considered to be of a lesser quality.

Access to a school psychologist differs depending on whether the location is an urban or a rural one. However, better access in urban areas is not always the case. There are regions where, even in larger cities, one school psychologist serves more than the average of 13,000 students. On the other hand, there are small towns close to big cities where local decision makers have been able to establish very favorable conditions.

As practice in school psychology in Germany covers a widespread area of activities, there is a lot of variation in the work that can be done. In addition, each school psychologist has a large degree of freedom as to which aspects of the job he or she wants to focus on. The other side of this coin is that the individual school psychologist may feel overburdened with all the expectations and duties to be fulfilled. Another stress factor is the small number of school psychologists overall and the resulting large number of students that have to be attended to. It seems likely that the majority of those in the field place importance on, and receive satisfaction from, the variety of professional activities available to them and the amount of freedom they have in deciding which of these activities to perform on any given day.

The Sektion Schulpsychologie (German School Psychology Association) describes, and thus defines, the field of school psychology in the following manner: "School psychologists are qualified psychologists. Additional qualification often consists of a complete teacher's training program with examinations for primary and secondary school teachers (prerequisite in some federal states), and many have completed training in vocational psychotherapy" (http://www.schulpsychologie.de/sektion/index.htm).

School psychologists support teaching at school by means of their scientific knowledge and psychological methods, and they promote the further development of the educational system. They see themselves as jointly constructing a system for education and vocational development that will provide the possibility of effective and rewarding activities to each school and the people working in it and satisfy the future demands by timely, future-oriented modelling of the content and conditions of schoolwork.

School psychologists maintain the necessary level of knowledge and competency by constantly furthering their own education and development. School psychology is directed not only to the problems of everyday school life but also to the design and development of the school itself. Thus, the aim of school psychological counselling may relate to the individual person or more to the institution as a whole. School psychological counselling means giving help for the sake of self-help, assisting people who look for advice in solving upcoming problems on their own behalf. The objective of consultation is determined by the client. School psychologists guide and help the client to find his or her own solution. School psychological counselling is always voluntary and free of charge and must never be compulsory. School psychologists have a profound knowledge of the "ins and outs of school" while being biased neither to the school nor to the interests of the parents and pupils. Their neutrality ensures the necessary mutual acceptance of changes. School psychologists are bound to a pledge of confidentiality.

Infrastructure of School Psychology

Because schools are managed by the individual states, school psychologists have tended to identify and organize themselves on a state level. All 16 states have a school psychologists' organization speaking for the interests of school psychologists

in that region. In the past few years, the Ministry of School Affairs in each region has more and more recognized those organizations as valuable partners Membership in these organizations is voluntary, and in some of them, only a small number of all school psychologists in that state are members.

On a national level, the Sektion Schulpsychologie im Berufsverband Deutscher Psychologinnen und Psychologen e.V. (German National School Psychology Association, part of the German National Psychology Association) represents the interests of all school psychologists. It is part of the national organization of all psychologists, representing all fields of psychology. The Sektion Schulpsychologie brings together the different interests of school psychologists from the various regions in the country and promotes a policy of bringing together the different regional organizations. The Deutsche Gesellschaft für Psychologie focusses on psychologists teaching and researching in the universities. Out of the 15 occupational subgroups, one focusses on educational psychology. In the past, there was very little contact among school psychologists, as the practitioners and educational psychologists as university professors and the contents of both fields were only minimally related to one another. More recently, there has been increasing openness and interest on both sides for contact and exchange.

Thirteen out of the 16 states require school psychologists to be qualified as a Diplom-Psychologe (equivalent to a master's degree in psychology). There are some exceptions to this, primarily due to the different university training that school psychologists in the German Democratic Republic had resulting in other kinds of diplomas. These were of the same quality but with a tendency for more paedagogical than psychological content.

The city-states of Hamburg and Berlin require school psychologists to be qualified as a Diplom-Psychologe and have credentials to teach in public schools. Bavaria nowadays only hires school psychologists with a special Bavarian school psychologist's education that can only be obtained in Bavaria. School psychologists are governed by a code of ethics, valid for all psychologists. This code of ethics was last revised by the Deutsche Gesellschaft für Psychologie in 2004 and by the Berufsverband Deutscher Psychologen in 2005. The school ministries in each state have established a set of regulations for school psychologists specific to the school structure and system in that Bundesland. These regulations are generally in accordance with the description of school psychology by the Sektion Schulpsychologie.

There is no particular journal focusing exclusively on school psychology. Journals in which school psychology issues are discussed and to which school psychologists contribute are *Zeitschrift für Entwicklungspsychologie und pädagogische Psychologie, Bildung und Erziehung, Erziehung und Unterricht, Pädagogik, Pädagogische Rundschau,* and *Psychologie in Erziehung und Unterricht.*

Preparation of School Psychologists

The basic requirement to become a school psychologist is a general diploma in psychology (equivalent to a master's degree in psychology). This is structured into two phases. During the first phase, emphasis is laid on establishing a methodical base through statistics, computer evaluation, and experimental design. Basic content during this phase covers areas such as cognition, learning, thinking and problem solving, memory, speech development, motivation, and emotions. Taking a look at related medical areas, such as physiology, genetics, or neurology, is usually the case. Furthermore, the fields of child development, personality, social psychology, theory building, and the history of psychology are covered at this time. The first phase ends with a variety of exams (Diplom-Vorprüfung) in the previously mentioned areas of study. Successful completion

allows for entering the second phase. In most universities, phase two focusses on three main areas: clinical psychology and psychotherapy, educational psychology, and industrial and business psychology. Within these fields, diagnostics, intervention techniques, evaluation, and scientific methods are the main topics. At the end of the second phase, a thesis has to be written, demanding independent and innovative scientific research. There is a minimum of eight semesters in which the courses of phase one and two can be covered. Following that, the exams can be taken, and the thesis needs to be written. These tasks can be overlapping.

Universities do not offer any kind of specific training or program geared toward becoming a school psychologist in particular. During training to receive a Diplom in psychology, there is the possibility of focusing on educational psychology within the second half of the program, often with a required course, exam, or both. But this makes up only a small portion of all courses that are required. Most universities require 12 weeks of practical in-service training under the supervision of a psychologist. These 12 weeks are usually served in two different institutions. Many school psychologists complete one of their practicums in the field of school psychology. Germany has approximately 100 universities with faculties for psychology.

Following the Bologna Agreement in 2003, the German university system is changing overall toward implementing internationally accepted programs for bachelor's and master's certificates. It is most likely that, in the near future, there will be specific programs to educate school psychologists at the master's-degree level. Presently, there is a general understanding in the field of school psychology that anyone entering the field with a general psychological background and qualifications must then learn and focus on the special techniques and methods needed in school psychology. If possible, a kind of "training on the job" through close contacts with experienced colleagues is a phase that promotes a newcomer to the field into someone identifying himself to the profession as being a school psychologist. Experience suggests that this phase lasts 2 to 3 years.

An exception to this is the program that some Bavarian universities provide for the training of Bavarian school psychologists. It follows the German tradition of teacher training for secondary education in which two school subjects are chosen for intensive studies. Students wishing to become school psychologists in Bavaria study school psychology and one other school subject. The areas covered in school psychology are, to a large degree, those areas described earlier in this section for a Diplom in psychology. When they finish university, they work primarily as a schoolteacher teaching their chosen school subject, and they act as school psychologist about 20% of their working time.

In 1985 (revised in 1992 and 1996), the Sektion Schulpsychologie formulated and recommended a desirable curriculum for school psychologists (Sektion Schulpsychologie, 1996). It can be seen as a guideline for anyone designing courses and in-service training programs or for individual school psychologists to evaluate their strengths and weaknesses and to be responsible for making individual arrangements for their own professional development. The curriculum calls for expertise with respect to three areas: the school as a company organization, group processes (be they students, parents, teachers, or mixed), and the individual as a person.

Specific knowledge for the school as an organization is called for in areas such as personnel development, school climate, designing innovative strategies, public relations, opening of schools, cooperation with outside agencies, system diagnosis, supervision, and evaluation. For group processes, some areas of expertise are diagnosing group processes, methods of interaction, group dynamics, presentation and moderation techniques, supervision, process evaluation, and conference techniques. With regard to working with individuals in school, expertise is to be demonstrated in personality theory, diagnosing and changing learning, working and social behavior, problem-solving methods, supervision, and counselling techniques. Regular in-service training is the responsibility of the ministries of education in each individual Bundesland. There is usually a good rapport between the ministry and the practicing school psychologists, and special and current issues considered important by the school psychologists are taken into account. The Sektion Schulpsychologie stages a 1-week national conference for school psychology (Bundeskonferenz für Schulpsychologie) every 2 years. This conference is where school psychologists learn about new developments in the field and promote school psychological issues. Each conference is summarized in a book, and there has been increasing international participation in the conferences.

Roles, Functions, and Responsibilities of School Psychologists

The tradition of German school psychology sees two main fields of work. One puts the focus on the situation of the individual student for whom school psychological assistance is requested and includes everything the school psychologist does to change the situation for that child. It is generally understood that the school psychologist is not the advocate for that child but rather the expert who gathers information and opinions from parents, teachers, and other experts or agencies on how best to serve the needs of that child. The other line of work focusses on schools in general and intends to produce service and action to support and strengthen the school as a system. The school as a living and developing organization can call on the school psychologist as the first and closest external expert to assist in accompanying a school as a whole, all teachers, a small group of teachers, a group of parents, or parts of the student body toward their self-set goals.

Most school psychologists have their offices in separate buildings outside of an individual school and serve a number of schools. They are not considered part of the organization of an individual school but take on the role of external experts and support and assist a school on a regular basis. Depending on the situation and the work to be done, school psychologists may have students, parents, or teachers come to their office, or they may decide to do their work within the school where they have no office. A small number of school psychologists work within the school, having their offices there and being part of the school staff.

School psychology in Germany covers all aspects of the definition of school psychological activity indicated by the International School Psychology Association. Diagnostics, testing, intervention, consultation, supervision, and organizational development are all practiced. This does not mean, however, that all of these activities are available in each school. With the ratio of school psychologists to students being 1 to 13,000 and many school psychologists working as individuals covering a large geographical area, only certain aspects and areas of work may be concentrated on by an individual school psychologist. This leaves issues and needs open that either cannot be filled or are covered by professionals such as social workers, different kinds of therapists, special education teachers, counsellors, medical doctors, and others.

A wide range of different tests are used. The most commonly used tests are listed here.

Achievement—Prüfsystem für Schul- und Bildungsberatung–R 4–6, PSB R 6–13 (Test System for School and Educational Counselling), Diagnostischer Rechtschreibtest (Diagnostic Spelling Test), Rechtschreibtest 7–8 (Spelling Test), Hamburger Schreibprobe (Hamburg Writing Test), Rechentest 9+ (Calculation Test), Zareki–R (Test for Math Problems)

Intellectual Abilities—Hamburg Wechsler Intelltigenztest für Kinder (Hamburg Wechsler

Intelligence Test for Children), Kaufmann Assessment Battery for Children–German Version, Allgemeines Intelligenz Diagnostikum (General Intelligence Diagnostics), Kognitiver Fähigkeitestest (Cognitive Ability Test), Coloured Progressive Matrices

Personality/Temperament—Persönlichkeitsfragebogen für Kinder zwischen 9 und 14 Jahren (Personality Questionnaire for Children Between Ages 9 and 14 Years), Angstfragebogen für Schüler (Anxiety Questionnaire for Students), Anstrengungsvermeidungstest (Achievement Avoidance Test), Familie in Tieren (Family as Animals).

Behavior/Social Skills—Körper Koordinations Test für Kinder (Body Coordination Test for Children), Motorik Test für vier- bis sechsjährige Kinder (Motor Test for Children 4 to 6 years old), Konzentrations-Leistungs-Test (Concentration-Achievement Test), and Test d2 K (d2 Test of Attention)

Current Issues Impacting School Psychology

Crisis intervention has become a pressing subject since the Erfurt incident in 2002, in which a former student shot and killed 15 students and teachers in a massacre in his former school and finally killed himself. This tragedy increased the ongoing efforts to prepare schools and the school system to respond to tragic events. Meanwhile, specially trained school psychologists form a network in each Bundesland, which enables specialists to be pulled together should the need arise. This network is extended beyond the Bundesländer and is also linked with other task force groups consisting of professionals from the police, fire departments, churches, and ambulance services.

At the same time, a large number of preventive measures have been taken, and special programs have been developed. Given that conflicts among people are normal and necessary in social settings, these programs encourage the idea of teaching everyone in school to use these conflicts as an opportunity for clarification, growth, and development. Due to Germany's history from 1933 to 1945, attending to students with special talents or gifted children has not been easy. The idea from those days of a "superior race" was automatically associated too closely with efforts that would pay attention to performance of excellence in any field. Since around 1990, this aspect of the German trauma has lessened and initiatives and programs to attend to gifted children have been promoted throughout the country. Because of the many years in which there was hardly any activity, there is a lot to be done. Despite the fact that Germany has a strong economic base, resources for the public service sector have continually decreased over the past years. In comparison with other public fields, school psychology has not been able to achieve a strong enough stand to withstand the cutbacks that have taken place on a general level. There has been a decrease in the number of school psychologists overall. Yet the picture is very heterogeneous, as there are some cities and regions where the number of school psychologists has increased. The age pyramid of school psychologists throughout the country is such that an estimated 80% of all personnel is 50 years and older. This indicates that there will be some dramatic changes within the next few years. There are areas where, within a time span of 3 to 4 years, approximately 50% of all school psychologists are expected to retire. Where public spending is frozen, this will mean a cutback in all school psychological services.

Because of Germany's poor international ranking in comparative school evaluations, there has been intense discussion throughout the country about how to improve the present school system and how to achieve better results. School psychologists need to take a decisive stand within this discussion to promote higher quality education with school psychologists contributing to the success of all students.

References

Berufsverband Deutscher Psychologinnen und Psychologen [German Psychological Association]. (1999). *Ethische Richtlinien der Deutschen Gesellschaft für Psychologie e.V. und des Berufsverbands Deutscher Psychologinnen und Psychologen e.V.* [Ethical principles of the German Psychological Society and the Association of German Professional Psychologists]. (Available in English online at http://www.bdp-verband.org/bdp/verband/ethic.shtml)

Breuer, H., & Weuffen, M. (1990). *Gut vorbereitet auf das Lesen- und Schreibenlernen?* [Well prepared for learning to read and write?]. Berlin: Deutscher Verlag der Wissenschaften.

Central Intelligence Agency. (n.d.). *World factbook: Germany.* Retrieved from http://www.cia.gov/cia/publications/factbook/geos/gm.html

Guthke, J. (1969). Lernfähigkeit und Leistungsdiagnostik [Ability to learn and diagnosing achievement]. *Probleme und Ergebnisse der Psychologie,* Vol. 27.

Ingenkamp, K. (1966). *Die schulpsychologischen Dienste in der Bundesrepublik Deutschland* [School psychological services in the Federal Republic of Germany]. Weinheim und Basel: Beltz.

Roether, D. (1983). *Vorschul-Lerntest* [Preschool learning tests]. Berlin: Psychodiagnostisches Zentrum.

Secretariat of the Standing Conference of the Ministers of Education and Cultural Affairs of the Länder in the Federal Republic of Germany. (2005). *Basic structure of the education system in the Federal Republic of Germany.* Bonn: Documentation and Education Information Service. Retrieved November 28, 2005, from http://www.kmk.org/doku/en-2005.pdf

Sektion Schulpsychologie. (1977). *75 Jahre Schulpsychologie in Deutschland* [75 years of school psychology in Germany]. Bonn: Deutscher Psychologen Verlag.

Sektion Schulpsychologie. (1996). *Curriculum für die Fortbildung von Schulpsychologen* [Curriculum for school psychologists in further education]. Münster: Author.

Verfügungen und Mitteilungen des Ministeriums für Volksbildung Nr. 2/1979 [Declarations and

Information of the Ministry of Education No. 2/1979]. Staatliche Schulberatung und schulpsychologische Angebote in Bayern (Landtagsbeschluss Nr. 15/2288) [School counselling and school psychology in Bavaria (Federal Parliament Resolution No. 15/2288)]. Bericht des Bayerischen Staatsministeriums für Unterricht und Kultus [Report of the Bavarian State Ministry of Education and Culture].

Additional Resources

Berufsverband Deutscher Psychologinnen und Psychologen e.V. [The German Psychological Association] http://www.bdp-verband.org

Deutsche Gesellschaft für Psychologie e.V. [Association of Educational Psychologists] http://www.dgps.de

Internet platform for school psychology in Germany http://www.schulpsychologie.de

Kultus Minister Konferenz—Statistik [Minister of Culture Conference—Statistics] http://www.kmk.org/statist/home.htm

Sektion Schulpsychologie [German School Psychology Association] http://www.schulpsychologie.de/sektion/index.htm

Statistisches Bundesamt [Federal Statistical Office] http://www.destatis.de/d_home.htm

14

School Psychology in Greece

Chryse Hatzichristou

Fotini Polychroni

Georgios Georgouleas

Context of School Psychology

Ancient Greek civilization reached its acme during the 5th century BC, giving birth to philosophy and poetry and offering foundations for science and modern Western civilization. Ancient Greek philosophers, especially Plato and Aristotle, were the first to mention psychological notions; the word *psychology* is of Greek origin, and the international symbol for psychological science is a letter of the Greek alphabet. During Hellenistic and Roman times, the Greek language was the main language used by philosophers and scholars. From the 4th to the mid 15th century CE Greece was part of the Byzantine Empire. After the fall of Byzantine Empire, Greece was conquered by the Ottomans and became a part of the Ottoman Empire for about 400 years. In modern times, Greece was recognized as an independent state in 1830 after the treaty of London, following the war of independence against the Ottoman Empire that started in 1821. During the 19th and 20th centuries, after several wars of liberation, northern Greece, the Northern Aegean Islands, Crete, and the Dodecanese Islands were incorporated within the modern Greek state. In 1974, Greece became a parliamentary republic, and, in 1981, Greece became the 10th member of the European Community, now the European Union.

The total population of Greece, according to the 2001 census, was 10,964,020 (males 49.5%). The population distribution by age is birth to 14 years, 15% (males 52%); 15 to 64 years, 68% (males 50%); 65 years and older, 17% (males 45%). Almost 93% of the inhabitants are of Greek origin, and 7% are immigrants (National Statistical Service of Greece, 2005). The landmass of Greece is 131,957 square kilometers. Greece, a peninsula of the Mediterranean Sea, lies at the southeastern part of Europe and shares borders with Turkey, Bulgaria, the former Yugoslav Republic of Macedonia, and Albania. Its geography is diverse, with a huge coastline of 16,000 kilometers and more than 3,000 islands, but there are also high mountains and river valleys in the mainland, especially in central and northern Greece. During the past century, the Greek economy has been marked by great changes and rapid development, with a gross domestic product in 2004 of US$226.4 billion, US$21,300 per capita (World Bank, 2005). Currently, the economy in Greece is largely oriented toward tourism, shipping, and commerce. Employment includes managerial and professional (24%); technical (23%); administrative support (11%); manufacturing (7%); services and sales (14%); and agriculture, cattle-breeding, and fishing (12%) (National Statistical Service of Greece, 2005). According to the 2001 census, 2,393,000 persons younger than 19 years old resided in Greece (i.e., approximately 22% of the population). Almost 530,000 were of age 4 or younger, 546,000 of ages 5 to 9, 588,000 of ages 10 to 14, and 729,000 of ages 15 to 19. Births decreased from 14.42 per 1,000 inhabitants in 1982 to 9.43 per 1,000 inhabitants in 2002 (National Statistical Service of Greece, 2005). Approximately 4% of children lived in single-parent families.

The educational system is highly centralized, and all schools follow the National Curriculum provided by the Ministry of Education regarding all aspects of the education process. In public schools, at all educational levels, education is free and course books are provided free by the State. There is a strong emphasis on education in Greek society. The pursuit of university studies is regarded highly by Greek parents, and there is family and societal pressure on children to succeed on the university entrance exam.

The educational system includes nursery school (ages 3–4 years), kindergarten *nipia-gogeio* (ages 5–6 years), primary education level: elementary school *dimotiko* (6 years, ages 6–12), secondary education level: junior high school *gymnasio* (3 years, ages 13–15), high school *lykeio* (3 years, ages 16–18) and technical schools, and tertiary education level: universities and technological educational institutes. According to 2003 statistical data from the National Ministry of Education, 142,051 children were enrolled in kindergarten, 652,052 in elementary schools, 341,048 in junior high

schools, and 371,329 in high schools and technical schools. Nine years of education (elementary and junior high school) is compulsory for all children, and approximately 95% of children complete the nine years. The numbers of children attending nursery school have increased over the past years. The percentage of children attending kindergarten reached 82% in 2002. Furthermore, 60% of these children entered kindergarten having been enrolled in nursery school the preceding year. The average class size during kindergarten is estimated at 24 to 25 students, during elementary school at 17 to 18 students, and during high school at 23 students (Eurydice European Unit, 2005).

Private schools exist in the primary and secondary education levels with students coming primarily from families who can afford to pay the tuition fees. Approximately 4% of kindergarten students, 8% of elementary school students, 6% of junior high school students, 7% of high school students, and 5% of technical school students attended private schools in 2002 (Eurydice European Unit, 2005). During the past two decades, the number of immigrant students has increased, with 7% of school-age children having immigrant parents and 2% of school-age children having "re-migrant" parents (Eurydice European Unit, 2005). Approximately 20,000 children received special education services in 335 special schools and 1,067 resource classes at all educational levels (i.e., primary, secondary, and technical) in 2004. Among these special education students, approximately 67% were classified as learning disabled, about 15% as mentally retarded, 4% with motor difficulties, and another 4% with sensory problems (Eurydice European Unit, 2005).

Origin, History, and Current Status of School Psychology

Psychology in Greece has its origins in ancient Greek philosophy. Greek philosophers, including Protagoras, Pythagoras, Socrates, Plato, and

Aristotle, introduced many psychological concepts and approaches in their attempts to explain human behavior and communication. For example, Aristotle investigated psychological phenomena, primarily in *De Anima*, "Peri Psychis," and touched on psychological topics about perception, thinking, and soul-body relations in *Parva Naturalia*, "Ta Physika." As a consequence, a number of psychological terms used today can be traced back to these philosophers' schools of thought. During a historical period of only a few hundred years, 25 centuries ago, the psyche of a man was explored in a systematic, logical, and scientific way by Greek philosophers (Romilly, 1992), making them the precursors of many theorists in modern psychology.

Fagan (1986) suggested that the history of school psychology in the United States can be divided into two general periods: the Hybrid Years (1890–1970), reflecting the early period of development of school psychology, and the Thoroughbred Years (1970–present), reflecting its more recent self-dependence and consolidation. Following Fagan's division, as described in Hatzichristou (2002), the history of psychology in the schools in Greece can be divided into two similar general periods: the Hybrid Years, ending with the 20th century, and the Thoroughbred Years, starting gradually in the new millennium. The evolution of school psychology in Greece closely resembles that of other countries: In the early years, the identity of psychology emerged gradually from the disciplines of philosophy, psychology, and education, and school psychology lacked specialized training and practice and professional recognition.

Despite the contribution of ancient Greek philosophy, the field of modern psychology and the applied areas of psychology (e.g., school psychology) developed slowly compared with the rapid developments that took place in some European countries and in North America in the second half of the 19th century and the beginning of the 20th century (Georgas, 1995). As a result of the strong connection between philosophy and psychology, psychology was studied as a major at the undergraduate level within departments of philosophy, psychology, and education in Greek universities in the 1980s. Gradually, starting from the end of the 1980s and the early 1990s, independent departments of psychology offering degrees in psychology were established at the University of Crete, the University of Athens, the University of Thessaloniki, and the Panteion University (in chronological order). At that time, many psychologists working in Greece were educated and trained in other countries (mainly in Europe and in the United States), and this had led to some difficulties due to the variety of their educational backgrounds.

The first 50 psychologists in the Greek public educational system were appointed in public special education schools and units in 1989 (Law 1566/85), and formal training of school psychologists began in Greek universities (see the section "Preparation of School Psychologists" in this chapter for a full description of programs). It is evident that, as in other countries, the preparation and training of school psychologists followed the need for the provision of school psychological services. Initially, graduate preparation in school psychology encountered a number of problems, mainly related to the faculty members being educated in different countries, the blending of training with clinical psychology, the lack of coordination between the university departments regarding the core school psychology program curriculum, and the lack of a clear definition of the specialty and the guidelines for provision of services (Hatzichristou, 2002). School psychology graduate programs progressively started delineating the different roles of school psychologists, emphasizing the importance of school-based provision of services in close collaboration with teachers (Paraskevopoulos, 1992).

In the last decade, the evolution of school psychology was related to several events, including the establishment of independent departments of psychology, the graduate programs in school psychology, the legislation that provided for posts for psychologists in the public special schools and the Centers for Diagnosis, Assessment, and Support, the provision of psychological services in the schools by Community Mental Health Centers, the notable increase of the relevant literature in Greek, the establishment of University Centers of School Psychology and the development of alternative models for the provision of school psychological services (Georgas, 1995; Hatzichristou, 1998, 2002, 2004a, 2004b).

In an effort to incorporate basic components defining school psychology and influencing its evolution, a conceptual framework of the evolution of school psychology was proposed by Hatzichristou (2002). The proposed framework synthesizes the following domains: (1) role and specialty definition–professional practice; (2) legal issues: (a) state and federal-national laws and statutes impacting psychology, education, and provision of services and (b) certification/licensure; (3) education/ preparation, accreditation; (4) scientific and professional associations; (5) scientific foundation for practice; and (6) professional identity.

There is a lack of official data regarding number, demographic characteristics, roles, and functions of school psychologists in different settings. There is a rough estimation of 400 psychologists working in public and private educational settings. No official data are available regarding the number of psychologists providing psychological services to children and families in community mental health centers, special need centers, hospital clinics, and non-governmental foundations. The majority of psychologists are employed by the Ministry of Education and work in public special schools and units and in the Centers for Diagnosis, Assessment, and Support as members of an interdisciplinary team. A smaller number of psychologists work in private schools, mental health centers, and special needs centers, which are typically located in large cities. Finally, psychologists work in university settings and private practice. Proportionately more psychologists work in urban areas (especially Athens

and Thessaloniki) and fewer in suburban areas. No reliable method exists for estimating psychologist-student ratios because there is a lack of relevant data in the Greek educational system.

The salary of school psychologists working in public schools and public centers depends on the number of years of experience that they have worked in the profession. The starting salary is about 1,100 euros per month on average for a psychologist working in a school setting. There is a gradual increase of salary, depending on years of experience, level of graduate studies, and family status (i.e., marital status, number of children). Psychologists working in the public education system are typically employed on a permanent basis (i.e., they are employed by the state as civil servants), and, as a consequence, attrition rates are very low or nonexistent. Opportunities for career advancement occur, as psychologists can take managerial positions after a set number of years of practice. There are also certain opportunities for professional development for school psychologists. In addition, psychologists may take a leave of absence to obtain a higher degree.

Infrastructure of School Psychology

There are two major psychology associations in Greece: the Association of Greek Psychologists and the Hellenic Psychological Society. The Association of Greek Psychologists was established in 1963 and is a member of the European Federation of Psychologists' Associations. Among the central aims of the Association of Greek Psychologists is advancing the scientific psychological research and upholding the high standards of the scientific and professional role of psychologists, protecting the profession of psychology, and informing and disseminating psychological knowledge to the public. Members of the Association of Greek Psychologists are practicing psychologists, of all specialties, working in public institutes, educational settings, and private practice. The majority of Greek psychologists are members of the Association of Greek Psychologists (about 1,400 members). The Association of Greek Psychologists has done much to enhance the interests of psychology, particularly in respect to public policy. Members of the Association of Greek Psychologists have been actively involved in several national and international committees and task forces. A major contribution of the Association of Greek Psychologists was publishing the *Ethics Code* (Association of Greek Psychologists, 1997), which addresses issues concerning standards of practice. The journal *Psychologika Themata* (Psychological Issues) is also published periodically by the Association of Greek Psychologists.

The second association, the Hellenic Psychological Society, was established in 1991, aiming at the promotion of research and teaching of psychology, the exchange of ideas among psychologists, teaching and conducting research in Greek universities and research institutes, and the support of psychological science. This scientific society is a member of the International Union of Psychological Sciences and includes about 500 members (with the majority being full members). Another aim of the Hellenic Psychological Society is to disseminate scientific psychological knowledge among the public and to promote the well-being of individuals, communities, and society in general. Psychologists who work in universities and research centers are typically members of this society. The minimum requirement for full membership is a doctoral degree in psychology. Task forces have been established within the Hellenic Psychological Society: Terminology, Crisis Intervention, International Affairs, Psychology and Media, and Ethics and Bioethics. The Hellenic Psychological Society has organized panhellenic congresses of scientific research every two years since 1989, in all fields of psychology, basic science, and applied psychology. Thematic conferences and seminars in areas such as school psychology, developmental psychology, social psychology,

cognitive science, personality, motivation, clinical and counseling psychology, and so forth have also been organized in collaboration with other national and international professional and scientific associations in the area of psychology and related disciplines. The Hellenic Psychological Society and the Association of Greek Psychologists organized the Fourth European Congress of Psychology in 1995 and are currently co-organizing the 26th International Congress of Applied Psychology, to be held in Athens in 2006.

Ten divisions of various specialties (e.g., social psychology, developmental psychology, organizational psychology, counseling psychology, clinical psychology), including the Division of School Psychology, were established within the Hellenic Psychological Society in 2000. Members can apply for membership in two divisions based on their areas of interest and work; there is no criterion of specialty training. The executive committee and the chairs of the divisions are elected biannually. Among the activities of the association is the organization of the biannual Panhellenic Conference of Psychological Research, in collaboration with a university department in a different city each time; the publication of the peer-refereed journal *Psychologia (Psychology)*, published four times a year; and a regular newsletter distributed to all members.

The Division of School Psychology of the Hellenic Psychological Society is an affiliate association of the International School Psychology Association. During the past few years, the division has organized symposia and workshops in the Panhellenic Conferences of Psychological Research held by the Hellenic Psychological Society and a number of other regional, national, and international conferences. It has also set up a work group on learning disabilities with the aim of reviewing theory and practice and clarifying issues regarding definition, assessment, intervention, and the role of school psychologist as a member of a multidisciplinary team, resulting in the publication of a special issue (Polychroni, Hatzichristou, & Bibou, eds., in press). It is envisaged that the published version of this work will increase public awareness on learning disabilities and become a position statement based on current scientific knowledge.

Hellinon Scholikon Psychologon Etaireia (The Greek Association of School Psychologists) is a professional association, its members mainly being practicing psychologists in special schools; specialization in school psychology is not a requirement for membership. Among the activities of the association is organizing seminars and conferences and, in general, advancing issues of the profession. In addition to the aforementioned associations, there exist other associations, which deal with issues of child education and support, such as the Society for Children's Mental Health and Neuropsychiatry, the Hellenic Pedagogical Society, the Society for the Psychosocial Health of Children and Adolescents, and so on.

In 2005, the 27th International School Psychology Colloquium was organized in Athens, Greece, by the International School Psychology Association and the Department of Psychology, University of Athens, in collaboration with the Hellenic Psychological Society, the Association of Greek Psychologists, the Division of School Psychology of the Hellenic Psychological Society, and the Greek Association of School Psychologists. The conference, the first on school psychology to be held in Greece, attracted a large number of Greek participants who were given the opportunity to present their work, both theoretical and applied, and interact and share common ideas and concerns with colleagues from around the world who worked in different settings. Throughout the conference, the importance of the role of school psychologists in the Greek schools and the increased need for a systematic provision of school psychological services in the Greek public educational system were made evident. Moreover, the large number and the enthusiasm of graduate students who attended the conference generated optimism and confidence for the future of school psychology in Greece.

Law 1566/85, regarding the structure and function of primary and secondary education, stated that 50 psychologists should be appointed and placed in special education schools and units. A recent law (2817/2000) of the Ministry of Education (March 2000) addresses educational policy issues regarding special education needs and the integration of students with special needs into regular schools. It also expands the provision of services of psychologists to regular schools. Centers for Diagnosis, Assessment, and Support are to provide services for students in the public schools, staffed by a multidisciplinary team comprising psychologists, psychiatrists, special education teachers, speech therapists, and occupational therapists. According to Law 2817/2000, 149 psychologists were to be appointed in the Centers for Diagnosis, Assessment, and Support. Despite the potentially large impact that this law may have for the future of school psychology in Greece, strong doubts have been voiced, especially because emphasis is again given to special education assessment and placement, thus perpetuating the "clinical model" that dominated school psychology in the earlier years. Moreover, no additional training in school psychology is required for psychologists employed in Centers for Diagnosis, Assessment, and Support. Thus, a considerable percentage of psychologists who work today in education have no training in school psychology but, instead, have training in clinical psychology and psychotherapy.

To practice as a psychologist in Greece requires a license, as regulated by laws enacted in 1979 and 1998 (278/79, 1331/B/98). This license is generic and requires at least a bachelor's degree in psychology. Currently, there is no specialty licensure for psychologists in Greece. A committee was formed in 2000 by the Ministry of Health to propose the specific qualifications needed for obtaining a specialty license in clinical, school, and organizational psychology.

Preparation of School Psychologists

Approximately 650 students are enrolled each year in the four psychology departments across the country. As mentioned earlier in this chapter, independent departments of psychology were created in four Greek universities in the late 1980s (University of Crete, Aristotle University of Thessaloniki, National and Kapodistrian University of Athens, and Panteion University of Social and Political Studies). Following that, graduate programs (school, clinical, organizational, and cognitive psychology) started in faculties. All graduate programs are organized by the relevant university departments and operate under the jurisdiction of the Ministry of Education.

The undergraduate studies leading to a *ptychion* in psychology (equivalent to a bachelor's degree) are 4 years long. The graduate studies leading to a *metaptychiako* (equivalent to master's degree) are 2 years, and for the doctoral studies 4 years (the first two years include the master's course). Access to the *didaktoriko* (equivalent to the doctorate) requires a successful completion of the master's degree (in cases where master's programs run in the respective departments). Attainment of a bachelor's degree typically requires (a) compulsory and optional courses and seminars in psychology (equivalent to 160 credits at the University of Athens), (b) internship in institutions of applied psychology (equivalent to 10 credits at the University of Athens), and (c) a dissertation (equivalent to 10 credits at the University of Athens).

There are two graduate programs in school psychology leading to a master's degree: (a) the Graduate Program of School Psychology, Department of Psychology, University of Athens and (b) the Graduate Program of School and Developmental Psychology, Department of Psychology, University of Thessaloniki.

The Graduate Program of School Psychology at the University of Athens started in 1993 (Acts 952/1993, 305/1996). Throughout the program, the importance of a scientist-practitioner model for professional preparation and practice is emphasized. Studies last four academic semesters. Attainment of the master's degree typically requires completion of 20 courses, an internship (800 hours in regular and special schools, mental health centers, counseling centers), a master's dissertation, and participation in research and educational activities. Each year, 15 to 20 students are accepted. Emphasis is given to a multidisciplinary approach, aiming at enhancing communication and collaboration among professionals of different specialties depending on their education and their role in the school setting.

According to the 2005–2006 program outline, the 20 courses are in accordance with the following domains of school psychology training and practice: (1) core academic knowledge of psychology: developmental psychology, school psychology, developmental neuropsychology, intelligence and learning, social psychology–small group dynamics, psychology of personality–developmental deviations; (2) assessment: assessment of cognitive skills, assessment of learning disabilities, assessment of personality and social assessment, assessment of school career guidance; (3) abnormal psychology and special educational needs; (4) intervention: counseling psychology, psychological consultation, prevention programs, psychotherapeutic interventions; (5) research methodology and advanced-level statistics; and (6) internship and supervision.

The establishment of the Center for Research and Practice of School Psychology, in the Department of Psychology at the University of Athens, has helped to link theory, research, training of graduate students, and implementation of intervention programs in schools as well as providing links between the university, schools, professional bodies, and institutions. In the context of a databased model of alternative school psychological services, several primary and secondary programs have been designed, implemented, and evaluated in educational settings in Greece and Cyprus (Hatzichristou, 2004a; Hatzichristou & Lampropoulou, 2004). At the primary prevention level, the program on Social and Emotional Learning in Schools was developed, implemented, and evaluated in primary and secondary schools, and different models of training of graduate students and teachers were put into practice (Hatzichristou, 2004c, 2004d).

The Graduate Program of School and Developmental Psychology, at the Department of Psychology, University of Thessaloniki, was established in 1993. Studies last four academic semesters and include theoretical courses, an internship (800 hours), research, participation in teaching and educational activities, and a dissertation. Seven students are accepted each year. Courses include Normal Development and Deviations, School Psychology, Research Methodology and Statistics, and Practical Applications of Developmental and School Psychology (course outline 2004–2005). In addition, a graduate program with a major in school psychology recently started at the Department of Psychology, University of Crete.

Representatives from Greek psychology associations have been involved in the EuroPsy project (2001–2003), funded under the European Union Leonardo Da Vinci Program, with the overall aim to develop a European diploma in psychology. The report indicates that there is a need to develop the transparency of qualifications and to develop new approaches to the specification of knowledge, skills, and competencies required by psychologists in Europe at the undergraduate and graduate levels.

Roles, Functions, and Responsibilities of School Psychologists

On the whole, there is a lack of national survey data concerning the roles, functions, and responsibilities of psychologists working in educational settings in Greece. The nature of their roles,

functions, and responsibilities depends on the context in which a psychologist works (e.g., in Centers for Diagnosis, Assessment, and Support, special schools, psychoeducational centers, or private schools) and the availability of other professionals (e.g., special education teachers, social workers, psychiatrists) as members of multidisciplinary teams. As a result, psychologists spend their time in diverse activities. In general, psychologists working in educational settings in Greece tend to devote a great percentage of their time to psychological assessment and counseling.

Two relevant studies provide data on the role and functions of psychologists working with children and families in various settings. A recent study commissioned by the International School Psychology Association Research Committee compared the training, roles, and responsibilities of school psychologists in different countries (Jimerson et al., 2004). The sample in Greece included 50 psychologists employed in educational settings. These psychologists reported devoting 20% of their time to psychoeducational evaluations, 20% to counseling students, 20% to consultation with parents/families, 10% to consultation with teachers and staff, 10% to providing direct interventions, 10% to administrative responsibilities, 5% to providing primary prevention programs, and 5% to conducting staff training and in-service programs. In addition, the International School Psychology Survey also revealed that, ideally, the specific sample of psychologists working in educational settings would prefer the following roles/responsibilities/activities (cited in rank order): (1) counseling students, (2) consulting with parents/families, (3) providing primary prevention programs, (4) conducting psychoeducational evaluations, (5) consulting with teachers and staff, (6) providing direct interventions, (7) conducting staff training and in-service/education programs, and (8) performing administrative duties.

In addition, according to the results of another relevant study (Besevegis & Giannitsas, 2000), psychologists employed in community mental health centers and special school settings placed more emphasis on the clinical model in terms of assessment and intervention. Specifically, the following conclusions were drawn:

1. Psychologists working in community mental health settings use a wide range of psychometric tools for assessment, whereas those working in special education settings primarily use checklists and the Wechsler Intelligence Scale for Children (third edition).

2. A limited number of psychologists have been trained in the use of psychometric tests.

3. The American Psychiatric Association's *Diagnostic and Statistical Manual of Mental Disorders* (fourth edition) and the International Classification of Diseases are used as the main classification systems in community health settings, though not in special education.

4. In terms of assessment, the psychodynamic and the systemic approach are followed; in the special schools, behaviorism is also used.

5. As the main problems for the multidisciplinary team, the psychologists reported the lack of means, limited support, need for a clear role definition, and different theoretical background of professionals with regard to assessment and intervention.

Typically, a school psychologist's role includes conducting psychoeducational evaluations; counseling individual students; consulting with parents and/or other family members, teachers, and staff; providing direct interventions; conducting staff training; delivering in-service programs; and fulfilling administrative responsibilities.

Psychoeducational evaluations are mainly carried out with students with learning or emotional difficulties. School psychologists typically evaluate a student's cognitive, social, and emotional levels of development using psychological assessment techniques (Besevegis & Giannitsas, 2000; Jimerson et al., 2004). In Greece, the Wechsler Intelligence Scale for Children, third edition, standardized in Greek by Georgas, Paraskevopoulos, Besevegis, and Giannitsas (1998), is the most commonly used instrument for assessing intellectual abilities. The "Athena" test (Paraskevopoulos, Kalantzi-Azizi, & Giannitsas, 1999) is used for screening as well as for assessing kindergarten and elementary school students' learning difficulties. Given that one of the most frequent roles of a school psychologist in Greece is to assess for learning disabilities and dyslexia in order for the student to qualify for educational support (e.g., he or she may opt to participate in oral examinations in secondary schools), psychologists follow a curriculum-based assessment process using nonstandardized, informal tools (text reading, free writing, dictation, written comprehension, etc.). Projective techniques (e.g., Rorschach, Thematic Apperception Test) as well as personality and temperament questionnaires (e.g., Inventory of Children's Individual Differences, Halverson et al., 2003) are used for personality assessment (Besevegis & Giannitsas, 2000; Hatzichristou, 2004b). Rating scales (e.g., Achenbach & Rescorla, 2004) are used in order to assess children's behavior and social skills. At this point, it has to be noted that translation and standardization of tests for assessment and research is a long process. Recently, an effort was made to collect the majority of assessment tools (translated, adapted, and/or standardized) currently in use by Greek psychologists (Stalikas, Triliva, & Roussi, 2002).

In addition, psychologists conduct individual counseling sessions with students and consultation with parents and/or other family members, as well as consultation with teachers and staff, focusing mainly on educational and/or emotional difficulties. Helping parents understand the way that they may actively participate in their child's development and to provide support in crises are the most common topics of consultation. Working with teachers in order to plan mainly individual educational programs and exchange information concerning children's performance is also very common. During the past few years, great emphasis has been given to the indirect model of service provision.

Direct intervention, used to promote children's cognitive and emotional development, may include teaching, counseling, and various therapeutic techniques (e.g., play therapy). Primary prevention programs include those that focus on promotion of mental health, social and emotional learning, prevention of drug abuse, and those that deal with immigrant students' adjustment difficulties. Conducting staff training and in-service programs, as well as supervising psychology students, also may be part of school psychologists' roles. Finally, psychologists must perform administrative tasks, such as keeping records of students with learning difficulties and special needs.

Current Issues Impacting School Psychology

During the past few years, the field of psychology has rapidly expanded in Greece, and a great deal of effort has been put into promoting the discipline of school psychology. There is an increasing need to respond to challenges currently impacting school psychology in the Greek educational system, concerning the interrelated domains of the conceptual framework (Hatzichristou, 2002), as described in this chapter. Another important topic is that of legislative issues, for instance, providing a specialty license (with a master's degree as a minimum level) and developing strategic planning regarding the provision of psychological services in the mainstream public schools (currently nonexistent). This could be accomplished by either expanding the role of school psychologist at the recently founded Centers for Diagnosis,

Assessment, and Support and/or by establishing new services. In addition, the topic of preparation and training is also a current issue. For instance, establishing more graduate programs of school psychology, including all recent developments regarding theory, research, and practice in school psychology, with a particular emphasis on the scientist-practitioner model and evidence-based interventions and the development of models connecting school psychology programs with the school community. Furthermore, it is essential to continue the efforts of the associations in the development of a specialty definition, standards of practice, guidelines for the provision of school psychological services, and position statements generated by task forces on advocacy issues for appropriate educational services for all children.

References

Achenbach, T. M., & Rescorla, L. A. (2004). Empirically based assessment and taxonomy: Applications to infants and toddlers. In R. Del Carmen-Wiggins & A. Carter (Eds.), *Handbook of infant and toddler mental health assessment.* New York: Oxford University Press.

Association of Greek Psychologists. (1997). *Ethics code.* Athens: Author. (in Greek)

Besevegis, E., & Giannitsas, N. (2000). The structure and function of mental health services for children and adolescents: An exploratory description of current status in Greece. In A. Kalantzi-Azizi & E. Besevegis (Eds.), *Themes of training and sensitization for mental health staff for children and adolescents.* Athens: Ellinika Grammata. (in Greek)

Eurydice European Unit. (2005). *The education system in Greece 2002/2003* (from Eurybase, information database on education systems in Europe). Retrieved September 5, 2005, from www .eurydice.org/Eurybase/Application/frameset .asp?country=GR&language=EN

Fagan, T. K. (1986). School psychology's dilemma: Reappraising solutions and directing attention to the future. *American Psychologist, 41,* 851–861.

Georgas, J. (1995). Psychology in Greece. In A. Schorr & S. Sarri (Eds.), *Psychology in Europe* (pp. 59–75). Göttingen, Germany: Hogrefe & Huber.

Georgas, J., Paraskevopoulos, I., Besevegis, E., & Giannitsas, N. (1998). *Greek Wechsler Intelligence Scale for Children, WISC-III: Manual*. Athens: Ellinika Grammata. (in Greek)

Halverson, C. F., Havill, V., Deal, J. E., Baker, S., Victor, J., Pavlopoulos, V., Besevegis, E., & Wen, L. (2003). Personality structure as derived from parental ratings of free descriptions of children: The inventory of child individual differences. *Journal of Personality, 71*(6), 995–1026.

Hatzichristou, C. (1998). Alternative school psychological services: Development of a databased model. *School Psychology Review, 27*(2), 246–259.

Hatzichristou, C. (2002). A conceptual framework of the evolution of school psychology: Transnational considerations of common phases and future perspectives. *School Psychology International, 23*(3), 266–282.

Hatzichristou, C. (2004a). Alternative school psychological services: Development of a model linking theory, research, and service delivery. In N. M. Lambert, I. Hylander, & J. Sandoval (Eds.), *Consultee-centered consultation: Improving the quality of professional services in school and community organizations* (pp. 115–132). Mahwah, NJ: Lawrence Erlbaum.

Hatzichristou, C. (2004b). *Handbook of school psychology*. Athens: Ellinika Grammata. (in Greek)

Hatzichristou, C. (Ed.). (2004c). *Program for the promotion of mental health and learning: Social and emotional learning in school* (Educational material for teachers and students in primary education). Tipothito: University of Athens, Center for Research and Practice of School Psychology. (in Greek)

Hatzichristou, C. (Ed.). (2004d). *Program for the promotion of mental health and learning: Social and emotional learning in school* (Educational material for teachers and students in secondary education). Tipothito: University of Athens, Center for Research and Practice of School Psychology. (in Greek)

Hatzichristou, C., & Lampropoulou, A. (2004). The Future of School Psychology Conference: A cross-national approach to service delivery. *Journal of Educational and Psychological Consultation, 15*(3–4), 313–333.

Jimerson, S. R., Graydon, K., Farrell, P., Kikas, E., Hatzichristou, C., Boce, E., Bashi, G., & International School Psychology Association Research Committee. (2004). The International School Psychology Survey: Development and data from Albania, Cyprus, Estonia, Greece and Northern England. *School Psychology International, 25*(3), 259–286.

National Statistical Service of Greece. (2005). *Census 2001*. Retrieved September 5, 2005, from http://www.statistics.gr/StatMenu_eng.asp

Paraskevopoulos, I. (1992). School psychology in Greece. Considerations and future perspectives. *Psychologia, 1*, 87–100. (in Greek)

Paraskevopoulos, I., Kalantzi-Azizi, A., & Giannitsas, N. (1999). *Athena test for assessment of learning difficulties*. Athens: Ellinika Grammata. (in Greek)

Polychroni, F., Hatzichristou, C., & Bibou, A. (in press). *Specific learning difficulties with an emphasis on dyslexia: Issues of classification, assessment and intervention*. Athens: Ellinika Grammata. (in Greek)

Romilly, J. (1992). "*Keep strong my heart,*" Odyssey u18. *The development of psychology in the Ancient Greek literature*. Athens: Asty. (in Greek)

Stalikas, A., Triliva, G., & Roussi, P. (2002). *The psychometric tools in Greece*. Athens: Ellinika Grammata. (in Greek)

World Bank. (2005). World Development Indicators database. Retrieved September 5, 2005, from http://www.worldbank.org/data/databytopic/GNIPC.pdf

15

Educational Psychology in Hong Kong

Shui-fong Lam

Context of Educational Psychology

Hong Kong, a metropolis at the southeastern tip of mainland China, was a British colony from 1842 to 1997. On July 1, 1997, it was returned to the People's Republic of China and became a Special Administrative Region. In the Joint Declaration with Britain, China promised that the socialist system would not be practiced in Hong Kong and that Hong Kong would enjoy a high degree of autonomy in all matters except foreign affairs and defense for 50 years, until 2047. Hong Kong continues to have its own legal system, currency, customs, and immigration authorities and its own way of life, shaped during the 155 years of British colonization. The colonization has carved numerous Western features in Hong Kong's social, economic, legal, and political landscape. However, Hong Kong has also preserved many aspects of Chinese culture. With the hustle and bustle of cosmopolitan city life, Hong Kong is well-known as a place where East meets West and the traditional merges with the modern.

With a landmass of 1,103 square kilometers and a population of 6.8 million, Hong Kong is one of the most densely populated cities in the world. In 2005, the population, by age, was birth to 14 years: 14.5%; 15 to 34 years: 28.2%; 35 to 64 years: 45.2%; and 65 years and older: 12.1%. The male and female percentages are 47.9% and 52.1%, respectively. Hong Kong is relatively homogeneous in its ethnicity. Over 95% of its residents are Chinese (Census and Statistics Department, 2006). Hong Kong consists of Hong Kong Island, Kowloon, the New Territories, and 236 outlying islands in the South China Sea. The Hong Kong climate is subtropical and the landscape is fairly hilly, with the population being mostly concentrated in the flat land along the coastal areas. On average, Hong Kong has 6,300 people per square kilometer, but the actual number is much higher because only 25% of Hong Kong's territories have been developed. The remaining 75% is set aside as country parks and nature reserves. The most densely populated district, Kwun Tong, has 50,820 people per square kilometer (Information Services Department, 2003).

Hong Kong's economy is characterized by its high degree of internationalization, well-established financial networks, and free trade. Hong Kong was rated as the freest economy in the world in the 2004 Index of Economic Freedom released by the Heritage Foundation (Miles, Feulner, O'Grady, Eiras, & Schavey, 2004). Over the past two decades, the Hong Kong economy has doubled in size with the gross domestic product growing at an average annual rate of 4.9%. In 2004, Hong Kong's gross domestic product was US$234.5 billion, and its per-capita gross domestic product was US$34,200. The population of the labor force is 3.23 million, with 31% in wholesale, retail, and import/export trades, restaurants, and hotels; 28% in community, social, and personal services, 15% in finance, insurance, real estate, and business services; 9% in construction; and 5% in manufacturing. The average annual wage is US$16,450 (Information Services Department, 2005a).

In 2005, 1.45 million children and teenagers (defined as aged 19 or younger) resided in Hong Kong. Children younger than age 5 accounted for 248,100, those between ages 5 and 9 years old accounted for 332,000, those between ages 10 and 14 accounted for 425,300, and those between ages 15 and 19 accounted for 445,100 (Census and Statistics Department, 2006). To sum up, children and teenagers made up 21.3% of the Hong Kong population. The majority of them lived with two parents; only 6.5% (96,100) lived with single parents (Legislative Assembly, 2005).

In 2004, Hong Kong had 130,200 kindergartners (ages 3–5), 446,600 primary students (ages 6–11), and 476,400 secondary students (ages 12–18), enrolled in 737 kindergartens, 759 primary schools, and 519 secondary schools, respectively (Education and Manpower Bureau, 2005). Schools in Hong Kong can be classified into three types according to their source of funding: government schools, subsidized schools, and private schools. Most schools are subsidized

schools operated by nongovernmental organizations, such as charity organizations and churches. About 92% of all primary schools and 79% of all secondary schools are government or subsidized schools (Census and Statistics Department, 2005), the remainder being private. Since September 1978, Hong Kong has provided 9 years of free and universal basic education. Children are required to be enrolled in school from age 6 to age 15 (Grade 9). Government and subsidized schools are financed entirely by government funding. In general, parents do not need to make contributions before their children attend Grade 10. However, parents who choose to send their children to private schools need to pay annual school fees that may range from US$6,000 to US$20,000. In recent years, increasing numbers of subsidized schools have joined the Direct Subsidy Scheme, a new initiative of the Hong Kong government. As of early 2006, 11 primary schools and 45 secondary schools had joined this scheme (Education and Manpower Bureau, 2006). In this scheme, subsidized schools are allowed to collect school fees from parents while receiving funding from the government. The school fees may be comparable to those of private schools. The average class size in Hong Kong is 19.6 for kindergartens, 32.5 for primary schools, and 38.2 for secondary schools. Total expenditure on education in the financial year 2004–2005 amounted to US$7.63 billion, 20.8% of the Hong Kong government's budget (Information Services Department, 2005b).

In 2004, Hong Kong had 8,500 students enrolled in 66 special schools (Education and Manpower Bureau, 2005), although it has been the government's policy to mainstream children with special educational needs wherever possible. They are placed in special schools only when the severity of their handicaps is such that they cannot benefit from the curriculum in mainstream schools. In 1997, the government launched a pilot project called the Whole School Approach to integration. Students benefiting from this project include children with mild grade mental handicaps (intelligence quotient 50–70), autistic disorders with average intelligence, visual impairments, hearing impairments, and physical handicaps. When they are placed in mainstream schools, they receive services such as school-based or center-based intensive remedial support in the basic subjects. Consultation is also provided to their teachers about their special educational needs. In 2003, the government piloted a new funding model for students with special educational needs. Under this new funding model, schools are provided with an Intensive Learning Support Grant and requested to adopt whole school approaches to support every student with special educational needs. In the 2004–2005 school year, 27,124 students with special educational needs were studying in mainstream schools. They made up 2.58% of the mainstream student population. They included students who might have been placed in special schools or who might have received support or no support in mainstream schools before 2004 (Education and Manpower Bureau, 2005).

Origins, History, and Current Status of Educational Psychology

School psychologists are called educational psychologists in Hong Kong, after the British designation. The profession of educational psychology is one of Britain's legacies to the educational system of Hong Kong. When first introduced to Hong Kong in the 1960s, educational psychology services closely followed the British model. Over the past 40 years, however, educational psychology has integrated with Hong Kong's local culture and has developed its own identity. Hong Kong is the first place in Asia with a recognized vocation in educational psychology and a postgraduate program for the professional preparation of educational psychologists.

The development of educational psychology in Hong Kong can be divided into five stages by landmark events.

Stage 1: The Establishment of a Special Education Section in the Education Department

Psychological services for students in Hong Kong began in 1959 when the Education Department of the Hong Kong government set up a special education section. This section monitored and regulated the work of nongovernmental organizations that provided services to students with special educational needs. During the 1960s and 1970s, there were only one or two psychologists who had received professional training abroad working in this section. They provided psychological services to students with learning, emotional, and/or behavioral problems, as referred by schools, parents, or other professionals. Nevertheless, because of the limited number of psychologists working in the schools during this period, their services consisted primarily of psychological and educational assessment of students with special educational needs (Hu, Oakland, & Salili, 1988).

Stage 2: The Establishment of a Local Training Program

Before 1981, all the educational psychologists in Hong Kong received their training in Britain. The small supply of educational psychologists had limited the development of services. After the University of Hong Kong set up a master's degree program in educational psychology in 1981, educational psychology services in Hong Kong expanded considerably. Between 1982 and 2004, this program produced 76 educational psychologists.

Stage 3: School-Based Psychological Services in Special Schools

Before 1986, almost all educational psychologists in Hong Kong were employed by the government. There were no school-based psychologists employed by nongovernmental organizations. All the psychological services to students were provided at the Special Education

Services Centers run by the government. The need for school-based psychological services in special schools was first raised in 1984 by the Joint Council for the Physically and Mentally Disabled of the Rehabilitation Division, Hong Kong Council of Social Service. A year later, the government approved the provision of educational psychologists for special schools. In 1986, nongovernmental organizations that operated special schools could hire one educational psychologist for every 30 classes of students with special educational needs.

Stage 4: The Extension of School-Based Psychological Services to Mainstream Secondary Schools

School-based psychological services were expanded further when the Hong Kong government announced the implementation of the Schools Support Scheme, as recommended in a report by the Education Commission, a government-appointed advisory body in education policy (Education Commission, 1990). The Schools Support Scheme aims to help students with emotional and behavioral problems who are enrolled in mainstream secondary schools. Under this scheme, school-based psychological services were extended to mainstream secondary schools. Nongovernmental organizations that operated subsidized secondary schools were entitled to employ educational psychologists according to a ratio of approximately 12 schools to 1 educational psychologist.

Stage 5: The Extension of School-Based Psychological Services to Mainstream Primary Schools

In 2001, the Hong Kong government declared a series of large-scale education reform measures that cover all stages of education from early childhood to continuing adult education (Education Commission, 2001). The impact of the reform on the future of Hong Kong

education, as well as the development of educational psychology in Hong Kong, has been tremendous. In the face of the drastic changes, educators felt the need for school-based professional support (Department of Psychology, 2001). In response to such needs that arose as a direct result of the education reform, the chief executive of Hong Kong announced, in his 2001 policy address, a series of plans to develop relevant services. One of these measures was to provide school-based psychological services to primary schools. Instead of expanding the team of educational psychologists within the government, the government invited nongovernmental organizations to bid for tenders to run the services. This move marks the beginning of the "contracting out" policy in the provision of school-based psychological services in Hong Kong. As of August 2005, there were 15 educational psychologists employed by nongovernmental organizations under this scheme. They provided school-based services to 91 primary schools with a ratio of 1 psychologist to 5 or 6 schools.

Two important threads run through the history of educational psychology services in Hong Kong. The first is the responsiveness of the profession to the needs of the society. The second is the changes in the service delivery model of educational psychology. In his review of international school psychology, Oakland (2000) pointed out that the growth of school psychology is likely to be more robust when the profession is responding to important national needs and priorities. The development of educational psychology services in Hong Kong bears out this observation. Because it has been responsive to the needs, agendas, and missions of Hong Kong education, the profession of educational psychology in Hong Kong has grown from nonexistence in the 1950s to a well-established profession in the millennium. The expansion of services in recent years during the painful process of education reform is the best illustration of this development.

Over the past four decades, educational psychology services in Hong Kong have evolved from center-based services to school-based services in both special and mainstream schools. This evolution implies significant changes in the service delivery model. Center-based services in the 1960s and 1970s were related closely to special education. They focused largely on the assessment of students with special educational needs. Since the introduction of school-based services in special schools in the mid 1980s, assessment has ceased to be the primary work of educational psychologists in these schools. Instead, they offer a wide range of services, including remedial intervention programs for students, consultation to teachers, and education programs for parents. The role of educational psychologists was extended further when school-based services were introduced into mainstream schools in the 1990s. The clientele of educational psychology is no longer restricted to the population with special educational needs. School-based psychologists now work with the entire population of students in a given school, with the scope of their services ranging from remediation to prevention, direct services to indirect services, and casework to systems work.

The changing role of the educational psychologist is reflected in the definition of educational psychology provided by the Division of Educational Psychology of the Hong Kong Psychological Society (2002). In its guidebook on psychoeducational services, educational psychologists are described as scientist-practitioners who can teach and conduct research in educational psychology as well as provide psychoeducational services to the public. Their services include psychoeducational assessment; intervention with children, adolescents, and their families; in-service training for teachers; and consultation with parents, teachers, and educational administrators.

In 2005, there were about 130 people in Hong Kong with qualifications to practice educational psychology. However, many of them worked in other capacities, such as teachers, education administrators, or college professors. As of August 2005, there were only 81 educational psychologists providing services in Hong Kong. The total number of students in kindergartens and primary, secondary, and special schools in Hong Kong was about 1,061,700 in 2005. This means an average ratio of 1 educational psychologist to 13,100 students. Among the 81 educational psychologists, 29 were center-based psychologists in the Education and Manpower Bureau in the government, 13 were school-based psychologists in special schools, 35 were school-based psychologists in regular secondary or primary schools, and 4 were in private practice. The majority (86.4%) of them were female. Two of them had doctoral degrees, and all others had master's degrees.

Salaries of educational psychologists in Hong Kong are uniformly in compliance with the master pay scale specified by the government. Novice educational psychologists start at an annual salary of US$37,200. Those with 10 to 14 years of experience earn approximately US$70,000, and those with 20 to 24 years of experience earn approximately US$107,000. This master pay scale does not apply to educational psychologists in private practice because they are self-employed.

Infrastructure of Educational Psychology

The Hong Kong Psychological Society was founded in 1968. In the past three decades, it has been active in promoting professionalism among psychologists in Hong Kong. In 1991, it published a code of conduct for the profession (Hong Kong Psychological Society, 1991). In 1995, it set up a registration board and encouraged psychologists in Hong Kong to register on a voluntary basis. To seek further regulation of the practice of psychology, the Hong Kong Psychological Society formed a working group in 1998 for the preparation of statutory registration of psychologists. The mission of this working group is to lobby the government to regulate the practice of psychology through legislation.

The Division of Educational Psychology, a division of the Hong Kong Psychological Society, was formed in 1987. Since its inception, the Division of Educational Psychology has been active in promoting educational psychology in Hong Kong. Its endeavors include lobbying the government for a better provision of educational psychology services, organizing continuing education activities for its members, and providing community services to the public.

Registration of Educational Psychologists

Despite the work of the Hong Kong Psychological Society and Division of Educational Psychology, the infrastructure of educational psychology is not strong in Hong Kong. In 2005, among the 130 individuals who had the qualifications to practice educational psychology in Hong Kong, only 71 joined the Division of Educational Psychology. Because the registration of psychologists is not mandatory in Hong Kong, many educational psychologists can practice without having either membership in the Division of Educational Psychology or registration with the Hong Kong Psychological Society. In 2005, there were only 38 registered educational psychologists in Hong Kong. The regulation of the professional practice of those who have not registered is left to their employers or clients. Until statutory registration is implemented, little can be done to improve this situation.

Laws Related to Special Education

Hong Kong does not have many laws governing special education. The most relevant one is the Disability Discrimination Ordinance (Chapter 487) of 1995. According to this ordinance, it is unlawful for an educational establishment to deny admission to or expel a student on the ground of disability. This ordinance facilitates the inclusive policy of the government in special education. As discussed earlier, the government launched the Whole School Approach to integration in 1997. Since then, more and more students with special educational needs have been placed in mainstream schools. This trend and the other changes arising from the education reform that started in 2001 have made school-based psychology services salient. Many educators turn to educational psychologists for professional support to accommodate students with special educational needs.

The Hong Kong Psychological Society publishes the *Journal of Psychology in Chinese Societies* twice a year. This is a peer-reviewed journal that publishes articles of general interest to psychologists working with or studying Chinese people. Educational psychologists who are members of the Division of Educational Psychology receive free copies of this journal. Although it may include topics in educational psychology, it is not a journal exclusively for the educational psychology profession. As all educational psychologists in Hong Kong are proficient in English, they also read journals from the West for professional development. In recent years, a considerable number of educational psychologists in Hong Kong have been striving to develop a literature of educational psychology that is relevant to the cultural context of Chinese societies. For example, in 2004, the Division of Educational Psychology published a practical handbook on educational psychology (Lam, 2004). This handbook is written in Chinese and consists of 38 articles on various practices in educational psychology.

Preparation of Educational Psychologists

According to the employment conditions specified by the Hong Kong government, educational psychologists are required to have a bachelor's degree in psychology and a master's degree in educational psychology. The master's degree must have an emphasis on professional training. The Educational Psychology Program at the

University of Hong Kong is the only program in Hong Kong that provides professional training in educational psychology. It had been accredited by the British Psychological Society until Hong Kong was returned to China in 1997. It is a 2-year full-time program with a scholar-practitioner's model at the master's level. It recruits applicants every other year and has the capacity to train 15 to 20 educational psychologists every 2 years. Applicants to this program are required to have a bachelor's degree in psychology and normally at least 2 years' work experience in educational settings. They must complete 14 courses, 1,500 hours of supervised internship, and an empirical research thesis before graduating. Courses cover the following core areas: psychological foundation (e.g., developmental psychology, children with special needs), educational foundation (e.g., curriculum and instruction, learning and motivation), assessment, intervention, research methods, and issues related to the profession (e.g., ethical and legal issues in educational psychology).

As for supervised internships, each student is placed in three different placement settings that include both mainstream and special education settings. Graduates of the program are not only expected to be practitioners providing services in school settings, but also scholars involved in the generation and dissemination of knowledge in educational psychology. To prepare competent scientist-practitioners, the program emphasizes research training and adopts a proactive and systems orientation that is in line with the service delivery model. This model addresses all levels of intervention that range from remediation to prevention, casework to systems work, and direct services to indirect services.

Roles, Functions, and Responsibilities of Educational Psychologists

Educational psychology services in Hong Kong have evolved into comprehensive services that differ greatly from those of the 1960s and 1970s. These services can best be conceptualized by a model described by Lam (2005). In this model, the services of educational psychologists are conceptualized as having three dimensions: intervention, target, and directness. There are three levels in the intervention dimension: remedial, preventive, and developmental. The three levels in the target dimension are individuals, groups, and systems. There are two levels in the directness dimension: direct and indirect.

Dimension 1: Intervention

Intervention includes all of the suggestions, activities, and planning that educational psychologists direct to their targets, be they individuals, groups, or systems. Remedial intervention focuses on treatment of problems or dysfunctions that have occurred, for example, anger control training for a student with aggressive behaviors. Preventive intervention focuses on prevention of dysfunction or problems that have either not occurred or are about to occur, for example, assertiveness training for a group of students at risk of being bullied. Developmental intervention focuses on enhancement and enrichment of positive qualities instead of elimination of problems, for example, leadership training for peer tutors in cooperative learning.

Dimension 2: Target

The targets of educational psychology services include individuals, groups, and the systems in which individuals and groups reside. At the individual level, the focus is the individual students, for example, counseling service for a student who has been referred for learning difficulties. At the group level, groups of students, teachers, educational administrators, or parents will be the targets, for example, of staff development workshops on accommodating student diversity. At the systems level, the targets are the systems in which the individual child resides, such as classrooms, schools, and families. Consultation with teachers on curriculum development is one of the services at this level.

Dimension 3: Directness

Interventions can be in the direct or indirect mode. Direct services are activities performed directly on the targets, for example, assessment and counseling for students who have been referred for academic difficulties. Indirect services are activities implemented around the targets in their environment. For example, to help students with specific learning difficulties, educational psychologists help teachers adjust their curricula and teaching methods.

In actual practice, the different dimensions and levels of the model are neither separate nor independent. An educational psychologist usually works simultaneously at different levels of the model to tackle a problem. For instance, if a school needs help in supporting a student with dyslexia, the educational psychologist may do any or all the following: conduct an assessment of the student's cognitive functioning and academic performance (remedial intervention and direct service at the individual level), discuss the case with the parents and teachers and give advice on how to teach the student (remedial intervention and indirect service at the individual level), and conduct a teacher workshop to promote teacher awareness of the needs of this group of students (preventive intervention and indirect service at the group level). Depending on the resources available at the school, the psychologist may also support the school in developing, for example, a reading program to strengthen the reading skills of all first graders (developmental intervention and indirect service at the systems level). Educational psychologists in Hong Kong can be flexible in providing services at different dimensions and levels according to the needs of their clients.

According to the findings of the International School Psychology Survey (Jimerson et al., 2006), educational psychologists in Hong Kong spend, on average, 23% of their work time on psychoeducational evaluations, 17% on counseling students, 11% on providing prevention programs, 32% on consultation with school personnel and parents, and 7% on conducting staff training for teachers. These findings are in corroboration with the service delivery model described by Lam (2005). There is a healthy balance between direct and indirect services. The results show that the educational psychology services in Hong Kong have moved away from the traditional model of direct services to a more comprehensive educational psychology services model.

Current Issues Impacting Educational Psychology in Hong Kong

The recent expansion of educational psychology services in Hong Kong is closely related to the education reform that was launched in 2001. Hong Kong's classrooms have become more heterogeneous than ever as a result of numerous measures implemented under this reform. The reform has changed the admission system and has allowed students with more diverse levels of ability to attend the same school. It is implemented against the background of an influx of new immigrant children from Mainland China that began in 1997, increased economic polarization with the Asian economic downturn in 1998, and a trend toward mainstreaming students with special educational needs since the mid 1990s. These new developments are pushing Hong Kong teachers into classrooms where students present an ever-expanding spectrum of needs, abilities, goals, backgrounds, and interests. Most of these teachers are not prepared to cope with the rapid growth in student diversity. They look to educational psychologists for professional support in this respect. The recent extension of school-based services into mainstream primary schools is a response to such a demand. The public has high expectations for the contribution of the profession to education. However, there is uncertainty as to whether the profession can really measure up to these expectations. Given that there are certain factors in the local environment that are not entirely favorable to the growth and development of the profession (e.g., poor ratio of psychologists to students), educational psychologists have to work especially hard to improve their services.

As of 2006, Hong Kong still does not have statutory registration for educational psychologists. As a strong regulatory system is lacking, there is no way to hold an educational psychologist accountable for unethical practice if he or she is not a member of the Hong Kong Psychological Society. There is also no way to ensure that a particular educational psychologist will engage in supervision and continuing professional development. In a survey, Lam and Yuan (2004) found that supervision for educational psychologists in Hong Kong was inadequate. The supervision tended to be administrative instead of professional in nature. There was a large variation among educational psychologists from different work settings in their participation in continuing education activities. The few educational psychologists in private practice participated the least in these activities. This unhealthy trend is alarming when there is mounting pressure for educational psychologists to provide quality services in an era of rapid changes. The need to establish a comprehensive regulatory system is urgent.

To integrate with local culture and develop a unique identity, educational psychology in Hong Kong requires research and scholarship that reflects Hong Kong's sociocultural conditions. Educational psychologists in Hong Kong have made some progress in this respect. However, there is still ample room for improvement. For example, although Hong Kong has some assessment tools with local norms, these are limited in number. They include the Hong Kong Wechsler Intelligence Scale for Children (Education Department & Hong Kong Psychological Society, 1981), the Raven Progressive Matrices (Education Department, 1986), Reynell Developmental Language Scales (Education Department & Medical and Health Department, 1987), Hong Kong Based Adaptive Behavior Scale (Kwok, Shek, Tse, & Chan, 1989), Hong Kong Torrance Test of Creative Thinking (Spinks, Ku-Yu, Shek, & Bacon-shone, 1995), Hong Kong Child Behavior Checklist (Leung, Ho, Hung, Lee, & Tang, 1998), and Hong Kong Specific Learning Difficulties in Reading and Writing (Ho, Chan, Tsang, & Lee, 2000). This handful of tools cannot meet the assessment needs arising from the multiplicity of reasons for referral. In many cases, educational psychologists have to fall back on tools developed in the West according to Western norms, such as the Bender Visual-Motor Gestalt Test (Bender, 1946), the Conners Rating Scales (Conners, 1990), the Childhood Autism Rating Scale (Schopler, Reicher, & Renner, 1988), the Leiter International Performance Scale (Leiter, 1948), the Merrill-Palmer Scale (Ball, Merrified, & Stott, 1978), and the Stanford-Binet Intelligence Scale (Roid, 2003). There is thus a stringent need to develop local tests or to standardize Western tests on local norms.

The "contracting out" policy in educational psychology services in recent years represents one attempt by the government to cut the budget in education. When services are contracted to nongovernmental organizations, the government can keep the budget low by competitive tendering procedures. The possible effects of such a policy may include low income and job insecurity for the service providers as well as fewer and diluted services to the public. The actual long-term effects of "contracting out" policy are yet to be seen, as the first contract was granted in 2002. However, educational psychologists in Hong Kong should be alert to the possible deleterious effects on their status and the quality of their services.

Hong Kong has long been suffering from a shortage of educational psychologists (Rehabilitation Advisory Committee, 1995). The recent expansion of the services into primary schools has exacerbated the problem. To ease the shortage of educational psychologists, the training program at the University of Hong Kong has increased its intake from 15 to 20 students by 2006 at the request of the government. However, the considerable increase cannot solve the shortage instantly. The problem may linger for years before it can be solved.

Since 1997, Hong Kong citizens have also been citizens of the People's Republic of China. In addressing national needs and priorities, educational psychologists in Hong Kong must now refer not only to Hong Kong but also to China as a whole. Psychologists are still rare in Mainland China. Most of the Mainland's school psychology services are conducted by individuals who are not formally trained specifically as school psychologists, for example, medical personnel, schoolteachers, and counselors (LaVoie, 1989; Zhang, 1992; Zhou, Bray, Kehle, & Xin, 2001). Facing the increasing need for psychological services for school-age children, educators and psychologists in Mainland China have begun to realize the importance of establishing training programs for school psychologists (Zhou et al., 2001). With experience accumulated over the past 40 years, educational psychologists in Hong Kong may be able to offer assistance to Mainland China in this respect. In fact, in 2005, a group of senior educational psychologists from Hong Kong volunteered to help the Sun Yat-sen University in Guangzhou to set up a school psychology program. This program is the first of its kind in Mainland China.

References

Ball, R. S., Merrified, P., & Stott, L. H. (1978). *Extended Merrill-Palmer scale*. Chicago: Stoelting.

Bender, L. (1946). *Bender Motor-Gestalt Test: Cards and manual of instructions*. New York: American Orthopsychiatric Association.

Census and Statistics Department. (2005). *Hong Kong digest of statistics of 2004*. Hong Kong: Government Printer.

Census and Statistics Department. (2006). *Hong Kong in figures: 2006 edition*. Retrieved April 21, 2006, from http://www.censtatd.gov.hk/FileManager/EN/Common/hkinf.pdf

Conners, C. K. (1990). *Conners Rating Scales manual*. Toronto: Multi-Health Systems.

Department of Psychology, University of Hong Kong. (2001, December). *Report on the survey of school-based professional support in primary schools*. Hong Kong: Author.

Division of Educational Psychology, Hong Kong Psychological Society. (2002). *A guide to the educational psychology services in Hong Kong*. Hong Kong: Author.

Education and Manpower Bureau. (2005). Figures and statistics. Retrieved July 25, 2005, from http://www.emb.gov.hk/index.aspx?nodeID=92&langno=1

Education and Manpower Bureau. (2006). *Direct subsidy scheme*. Retrieved April 21, 2006, from http://www.emb.gov.hk/index.aspx?nodeid=173&langno=1

Education Commission. (1990). *The curriculum and behavioral problems in schools* (Education Commission Report No. 4). Hong Kong: Government Printer.

Education Commission. (2001). *Reform of the education system in Hong Kong: Learning for life, learning through life*. Hong Kong: Government Printer.

Education Department. (1986). *Hong Kong supplement to* Guide to the Standard Progressive Matrices. Hong Kong: Government Printer.

Education Department & Hong Kong Psychological Society. (1981). *Hong Kong Wechsler Intelligence Scale for Children*. Hong Kong: Government Printer.

Education Department & Medical and Health Department. (1987). *Reynell Developmental Language Scales*. Hong Kong: Government Printer.

Ho, C. S. H., Chan, D. W. O., Tsang, S. M., & Lee, S. H. (2000). *The Hong Kong Test of Special Learning Difficulties in Reading and Writing*. Hong Kong: Hong Kong Specific Learning Difficulties Research Team & Hong Kong SAR Government.

Hong Kong Psychological Society. (1991). *Professional code of conduct*. Hong Kong: Author.

Hu, S., Oakland, T., & Salili, F. (1988). School psychology in Hong Kong. *School Psychology International, 9*, 21–28.

Information Services Department. (2003). *Hong Kong yearbook 2003*. Hong Kong: Government Printer.

Information Services Department. (2005a). *Hong Kong in brief*. Retrieved July 25, 2005, from http://www.info.gov.hk/info/hkbrief/eng/ahk.htm

Information Services Department. (2005b). *Hong Kong: The facts in education.* Retrieved July 25, 2005, from http://www.gov.hk/hkfacts/educat.pdf

Jimerson, S. R., Graydon, K., Yuen, M., Lam, S.-F., Thurm, J.-M., Klueva, N., Coyne, J., Loprete, L. J., Phillips, J., & International School Psychology Association Research Committee. (2006). The International School Psychology Survey: Data from Australia, China, Germany, Italy, and Russia. *School Psychology International, 27*(1), 5–32.

Kwok, J., Shek, D., Tse, J., & Chan, S. (1989). *A Hong Kong based adaptive behavior scale.* Hong Kong: City Polytechnic.

Lam, S.-F. (Ed.). (2004). *Practical handbook of educational psychology.* Hong Kong: Division of Educational Psychology, Hong Kong Psychological Society.

Lam, S.-F. (2005). The growth and development of school psychology in Hong Kong. In C. L. Frisby & C. Reynolds (Eds.), *Handbook of multicultural school psychology* (pp. 1107–1127). Hoboken, NJ: Wiley.

Lam, S.-F., & Yuan, M. (2004). Continuing professional development in school psychology: Perspective from Hong Kong. *School Psychology International, 25,* 480–494.

LaVoie, J. C. (1989). School psychology in the People's Republic of China. In A. Saigh & T. Oakland (Eds.), *International perspective on psychology in the schools* (pp. 165–175). Hillsdale, NJ: Lawrence Erlbaum.

Legislative Assembly. (2005). *Topic 15: Supports to single-parent families.* Retrieved July 25, 2005, from http://www.info.gov.hk/gia/general/200507/06/lcq15c.pdf

Leiter, R. G. (1948). *Leiter International Performance Scale.* Chicago: Stoelting.

Leung, P. W. L., Ho, T. P., Hung, S. F., Lee, C. C., & Tang, C. P. (1998). *CBCL/6–18 profiles for Hong Kong boys/girls.* Hong Kong: Chinese University of Hong Kong, Department of Psychology.

Miles, M. A., Feulner, E. J., O'Grady, M. A., Eiras, A. I., & Schavey, A. (2004). *2004 index of economic freedom.* Washington, DC: Heritage Foundation.

Oakland, T. (2000). International school psychology. In T. Fagan & P. S. Wise (Eds.), *School psychology: Past, present, and future* (2nd ed., pp. 355–382). Washington, DC: National Association of School Psychologists.

Rehabilitation Advisory Committee. (1995). *Report of the working group on the demand and supply of educational psychologists.* Hong Kong: Author.

Roid, G. H. (2003). *The Stanford-Binet Intelligence Scale* (5th ed.). Chicago: Riverside.

Schopler, E., Reicher, R. J., & Renner, B. R. (1988). *The Childhood Autism Rating Scale (CARS).* New York: Irvington.

Spinks, J. A., Ku-Yu, S. Y., Shek, D. T. L., & Baconshone, J. H. (1995). *The Hong Kong Torrance Test of Creative Thinking.* Hong Kong: Education Department.

Zhang, X. (1992). School psychology services in China. *School Psychology International, 13,* 143–146.

Zhou, Z., Bray, M. A., Kehle, T. J., & Xin, T. (2001). The status of school psychology in China at the millennium. *School Psychology International, 22,* 22–28.

16

School Psychology in Hungary

Nora Katona

Context of School Psychology

Located in Central Europe, Hungary is bordered by seven countries: Slovakia to the north, Ukraine and Romania to the east, Serbia and Croatia to the south, and Slovenia and Austria to the west. The terrain is mostly flat with some rolling plains, and there are hills and low mountains in the north. Hungary is 93,030 square kilometers, and, in 2005, the population of Hungary was slightly over 10 million. Its currency is the Hungarian Forint, and Hungary is a member of the European Union. The 2004 gross domestic product was US$149.3 billion, US$14,900 per capita, which is slightly more than half the average within the European Union. The annual economic growth is slower in comparison to other newly joining countries (MEH Elektronikuskormányzat-Központ, 2005). On the whole, Hungary is a moderately developed industrial-agricultural country, with approximately 65% of the national economy originating from service industries (mainly banking, economic services, and communal services), 25% from industrial activities, and 4% to 5% from agriculture and the building industry. In comparison to the average 4.2% of the gross domestic product spent on education in European Union countries, Hungary spends 5.4% on education and, within that, 1% on higher education (in comparison to the European Union average of 2%; MEH Elektronikuskormányzat-Központ, 2005).

Of the 10,117,000 inhabitants, currently 2,010,000 are of school age (3–22 years), and in the 2004–2005 academic year, 86.5% attended educational institutions full-time (Csernyák, Janák, Süpöl, & Zalánné Olbrich, 2005). Currently, compulsory education begins at age 6 and ends at age 16, but those beginning their compulsory education in the academic year 1998–1999 and later will now continue until they are 18 years of age (Ministry of Education, 2005).

Kindergartens typically accept children between the ages of 3 and 6. According to law, children have to attend 1 year of kindergarten before starting their elementary schooling. Students begin their elementary schooling between the ages of 5 and 7 years. Elementary schooling typically takes 8 years to complete.

Grades 9 through 12 are diversified according to levels of attainment, student motivation, and goals. In vocational or trade schools, students complete their general education studies (Grades 9–10) and begin learning a trade in Grades 11 and 12 (e.g., carpentry, cooking, etc.), ending their studies as a skilled worker. A secondary vocational or technical school is a combination of a trade school and a grammar school inasmuch as students have an opportunity to sit for levels A and O maturity exams and learn the basic elements of a chosen field; however, they only receive a skilled worker diploma if they continue their studies for a further year or two, typically gaining access to vocations tied to accredited postsecondary training programs (e.g., project manager, consumer services).

In grammar schools, the ultimate goal is to gain entrance to higher education by successfully taking levels Advanced and Ordinary maturity exams. Traditionally, grammar schools take 4 years to complete, but there are 6- and 8-year versions, as well. This means that the brightest students leave their local elementary school to continue their studies at these 6- or 8-year grammar schools. College studies take 3 years, whereas university-level studies take 5 years to complete. A typical doctoral program lasts 2 to 3 years and is to be completed after university studies.

Currently, special education needs are met in segregated institutions at the kindergarten, elementary, and secondary school levels in schools paralleling those of the majority. Serious efforts are being made to integrate as many special needs students as possible into the mainstream schools. In most places, as the first step, social integration is sought.

As a result of changes in the political system (Public Education Act No. LXXIX, 1993), the government had already made provisions for non-government-owned schools. Today, government-owned and -financed schools are still in the overwhelming majority, but there is a balance in foundational/private and denominational schools (Halász & Lannert, 2004). At the kindergarten level, 91% of kindergartens are government owned, 3% are denominational, and 6% are private schools or those owned by foundations. Among elementary schools, 92% are state owned, 5% are denominational, and 3% are owned by foundations or other private

entities. The number of denominational and private or foundation-owned institutions increases at the secondary level. The number of foundation-owned schools is evenly distributed among the three types of secondary schooling; an average of 17% of secondary schools belong in this category. Of all secondary schools, 7% are denominational; within that percentage, a disproportionately high 15% belong to the category of grammar schools, whereas only 3% belong to vocational/trade and 3% are secondary vocational/technical schools. Of the higher education institutions, 42% are state owned, 39% are denominational, and 19% are privately owned or are financed by foundations.

Throughout Hungary, the number of schools, average class size, and percentage of schools that are financed by the government are as follows: kindergarten, 3,405, 22.3, 91%; primary schools, 3,293, 19.8, 92%; secondary level, including vocational schools, 601, 25.3, 83%; technical schools, 794, 26.2, 76%; and grammar schools, 614, 28.8, 71%. In addition, there are 46 colleges, of which 28% are state owned, and of the 24 universities, 75% are state owned. Compulsory schooling starts in kindergarten, the first educational institution children attend. Due to the fact that, after World War II, two-earner families became the norm, the network of kindergartens became extensive. Currently, 327,000 children attend kindergarten, which is 87% of kindergarten-age children (3–6 years); only the last year of kindergarten is compulsory (Csernyák et al., 2005). Of this number, 1,500 have special education needs, and 75% of those students are educated in integrated settings with peers without special education needs (Csernyák et al., 2005). A brief summary of each of the schools is provided next.

Primary Education

The beginning of primary education is flexible; that is, children may enter when they are between the ages of 5 and 7 years. The majority of children enter at age 7. Primary schooling includes Grades 1 through 8. Since the beginning of the 1990s, the number of pupils entering primary education, in line with the demographic trends, has declined. Due to the steady decrease in the number of pupils entering first grade, there were fewer than 888,000 students in primary schools in the 2004–2005 school year, a mere 76% of the number in 1990–1991 (Csernyák et al., 2005). In the academic year of 2004–2005, 57,000 students of primary school age were recorded as having special education needs, the majority, 58%, in segregated classroom, institutions, or both (Ministry of Education, 2005). Forty-three thousand were diagnosed as having emotional and behavior adjustment problems.

In the year 2004, 118,000 students completed their primary education, and nearly all continued their studies into secondary schooling (Csernyák et al., 2005). According to data from 2003, 95% of students completed their primary education within the time limit for compulsory education (Csernyák et al., 2005), meaning that 6,000 did not complete the 8 years of primary schooling. Currently, 90% finish their primary education in the allotted time of 8 years—a figure that has remained stable for the past few years. Average class size is 20 pupils; this can be misleading as segregated special education classes have an average size of 12 pupils. Class sizes are regulated by maximum number of students. In Grades 1 through 4, it cannot be more than 21; in Grades 5 through 8, the maximum number is 27; and in secondary education, the maximum class size is 36. The performance of students during primary education is a factor in their acceptance to secondary schooling, with the most prestigious secondary schools holding entrance exams. Because of this, and because of the structure of secondary education, the Hungarian secondary education system is considered competitive and selective (Baranyi, 1997; Gazsó & Laki, 2004; Loránd, 1997).

Secondary Education

Secondary education includes four grade levels with three types of institutions. Secondary-level students are between the ages of 15 and 18 years.

The structure of secondary education changed significantly between 1990 and 2002. This is partly due to the revised compulsory schooling age as well as the revamped national curriculum. The revisions of the law on education also opened the way for starting alternative and private schools as well as loosening the rigid structure of 8 years primary and 4 years secondary education.

In the academic year of 2004–2005, a total of 571,000 students participated in full-time secondary education, which is more than the number indicated by population data (500,000 students ages 15–18), suggesting that retention and flexible dates for starting schooling have had a large impact on these figures. According to official data, 97% of 15- to 17-year-olds participated in secondary education, whereas the percentage of 18-year-olds participating in the education system was 76%, which is equal to the European Union average (Ministry of Education, 2005).

There are three types of secondary schools: vocational schools, secondary vocational/technical schools, and grammar schools. Changes in the demand for education are reflected in the changes in the distribution of pupils by school types. Of the 571,000 secondary students, almost 23% attend vocational schools, 43% are students of secondary vocational/technical schools, and 34% are in grammar schools. Of the 194,000 studying in grammar schools, 16% attended 8-year grammar schools, 18% studied in 6-year grammar schools, and 66% were in traditional 4-year grammar schools (Csernyák et al., 2005).

Vocational school. Students who attend vocational school complete their education in 4 years (Grades 9–12). In Grades 9 and 10, the prescribed national core curriculum knowledge elements are taught and completed with a vocational orientation. Vocational training is completed in Grades 11 and 12. At the end of their studies, students receive a diploma declaring them skilled workers in a vocation (e.g., carpenter, waiter, call-center operator). Of the

132,000 completing vocational studies full-time (Csernyák et al., 2005), 10,000 (8%) were diagnosed as having special education needs and 4,000 as having emotional and behavior/adjustment difficulties (Ministry of Education, 2005). The number and proportion of students attending vocational school has been declining since the early 1990s, whereas the number attending secondary vocational/technical schools appears to be increasing.

Secondary vocational/technical schools. By completing education in secondary vocational/technical schools, students may take maturity exams (and thus compete for entrance to higher education), and they also receive basic vocational training, although it does not give them a skilled worker diploma. Of the 245,000 full-time students, 800 are diagnosed as having special education needs, most of them integrated, and 2,000 as having emotional and behavior/adjustment difficulties (Besenyei et al., 2005). A majority of secondary vocational schools provide advanced training for an additional duration, 1 or 2 years (Grade 13 and/or 14), which leads to a diploma of advanced technical training specializing in a given field. Advanced training is tied to secondary education institutions, but is considered as tertiary education.

Grammar schools. Grammar schools provide education in core areas (e.g., reading, math, science), the acknowledged aim of which is to prepare students for entry into higher education. The opportunities provided by the 2003 revisions to the Public Education Act were utilized most frequently in this type of school. As a result, not only are traditional 4-year grammar schools (Grades 9–12) available; newer forms, such as the 6-year (Grades 7–12) and 8-year (Grades 5–12) grammar schools, also have emerged. The 6- and 8-year types are seen as a form of elite training and function as tools of early selection, the best and most able students leaving their primary school before the end of the eighth grade. The rapid growth in the numbers studying in 6- and 8-year

grammar schools has recently slowed, and only a minimal growth can be seen. In the academic year of 2004–2005, 66,000 students attended 6- or 8-year grammar schools, and, of these, 28,000 were of primary school age (Grades 5–8). In the academic year of 2004–2005, 193,000 full-time students attended these schools, with 800 students diagnosed as having special education needs, 77% learning in integrated settings, and 1,000 students identified as having emotional and behavior/adjustment difficulties (Besenyei et al., 2005). A total of 76,000 received education as full-time students in 2004: 48% in grammar schools and 52% in secondary vocational schools. Twenty-eight thousand students received skilled worker diplomas in vocational schools, and 27,000 received advanced technical degrees in secondary vocational/technical schools. Seventy-nine percent of those in secondary education attended public schools, 16% in schools financed by the church, and 5% in other private schools (Csernyák et al., 2005).

If we look at special education needs, we find that 2% of the population in secondary schooling has been diagnosed as having special education needs, the majority (87%) of whom attend vocational training, and segregation is the norm in this school type (84%). The remaining 13% of students with special education needs are equally distributed among secondary vocational/technical schools and grammar schools, with integration being common. Many factors contribute to the high degree of segregation. One can argue that one of the reasons for the high percentage of segregated schools and classrooms stems from a strong, well-established segregated system of education for students with special education needs. The other element, no doubt, is the feeling from teachers that they are inadequately prepared to face the challenge of integration. A third element is definitely the inappropriate environment, thought of by many as the most important (Avramidis & Norwich, 2002), including restrictions in the physical environment and insufficient support teams.

Tertiary Education

Entrance into tertiary education (i.e., higher education) requires matriculation (in most cases, ordinary level, also referred to as O level), although extra points can be earned by taking advanced, or "A"-level, matriculation. This can be crucial for getting enough points to be accepted. The tertiary level in higher education consists of college (bachelor's degree), university (master's degree), postgraduate training, and obtaining a doctoral degree. In the academic year 2004–2005, 226,000 full-time students participated in full-time higher education, which is nearly triple what it was in 1990. Of the 226,000 students, 212,000 were earning their first diploma, 7,500 were completing advanced training, and 5,800 were earning postgraduate or doctoral degrees in the academic year of 2004–2005 (Csernyák et al., 2005). Of the full-time students, 80% were financed by the state.

Origin, History, and Current Status of School Psychology

The silencing of psychology after World War II was broken in the late 1960s with the establishment of Educational Child Guidance Centers. These were originally established with the specific aim of serving the needs of school-age children, their teachers, and families. These institutions function under the auspices of the local council and have become well-established psychological and educational services. These centers became heavily clinically oriented, and teachers became dissatisfied as the centers concentrated more and more on serving families, making school issues secondary.

In the 1980s, when rigid political ideologies loosened and the education system became less indoctrinated, a project was set up with the mutual cooperation of the Ministry of Education and the psychology department of Eötvös Loránd University, Budapest, in 1986. As a result, the Ministry of Education provided funding for 30 school psychologists to be employed in schools for 2 years, and the psychology department of Eötvös Loránd University provided professional guidance. This project ended in 1988, and all of the schools opted to keep their school psychologists.

In 1987, a methodological base for school psychology was established at Eötvös Loránd University, the School Psychology Division was incorporated within the Hungarian Psychological Association in 1989, and the Hungarian School Psychology Association was formed in 1992. In this phase of development, school psychology was not codified; its existence was not officially recognized (Katona & Szitó, 1990). A major breakthrough occurred when Public Education Act No. LXXIX of 1993 was modified in 1996. The law used the title of "school psychologist," stipulated that school psychologists could be employed in educational institutions, and also stated that only those with a postgraduate degree in educational psychology or those with psychology and teacher diplomas could be employed as school psychologists. The colloquium of the International School Psychology Association, held in Hungary in 1996, was instrumental in heightening government officials' awareness of school psychology.

The 1996 revision of Public Education Act No. LXXIX defines who can be employed as a school psychologist, although there is no such degree offered in Hungary (Hunyady & Templom, 1990). The required postgraduate diploma is titled "Professional Educational Psychologist," but the term *school psychologist* is used to denote those persons who work in the field (i.e., in schools or kindergartens). A unique characteristic of Hungary is that "school" psychologists working in kindergartens are referred to as "kindergarten psychologists."

It is challenging to establish the precise numbers of school psychologists, as there is no requirement to provide this information. To further complicate the scenario, school psychologists can be employed by the schools, can be based in Educational Child Guidance Centers, or can be members of educational institutes based in county areas. In 1999, approximately 100 school psychologists were reported (Antalovits, 1999; Katona, 2000), and a nonrepresentative national survey in 2004 (Mező, Mező, & Józsa, in press) came up with 125 institutions (out of the 15,000 primary and secondary education institutions) stating they employed a school psychologist. Thus, it appears there are about 200 school psychologists in Hungary, predominantly female (90%) and with an average age of 32. Considering the number of children in compulsory education, this number of school psychologists would reflect a ratio of school psychologist per 7,300 children. In those schools that employ a school psychologist, this ratio is 1 to 1,000 to 1,500 children. Services of school psychologists are easiest to access in the center of the country and, in particular, within the capital city: More than two thirds of employed school psychologists work in this region. Going either east or west within the country, the number of school psychologists declines dramatically.

The salaries of school psychologists are determined by the fact that they are public servants, just as teachers are, and have a unified wage scale. With a university diploma, a school psychologist's net salary is 254 to 458 euros per month. This figure does not differ from the average salary for secondary school teachers or any other professional in the education system (at school level) who has a university diploma. With postgraduate training, a school psychologist's salary would be 260 to 469 euros per month. In both cases, the lower sum indicates a beginner's salary with an increase of 6% every 7 years (the inflation rate is 12%–15% annually). This level of income can be reached by other professionals and teachers if they have a degree in two subject areas. Teachers nevertheless may earn more than school psychologists if they work overtime or if they are willing to substitute for an absent teacher (neither is acknowledged in the case of school psychologists). Thus, the salaries of school psychologists are comparable to those of other workers in educational settings; however, the average salary is around half of the salary of those working in clinical settings and a third of those in private practice.

School psychologists can be found in all strata of education, including public, private, and special schools. Some are based directly in schools, some in Educational Child Guidance Centers, and some are employed by educational institutes. Those employed directly by schools are required to have 26 weekly contact hours; in other settings, this is 19 hours per week, although the law stipulates a 40-hour workweek in all settings. This act only states that school psychologists "may be" employed—it is not compulsory for educational institutes to do so.

Any psychologist in Hungary is free to take advantage of the numerous method-specific, accredited further training programs provided by associations or higher education institutions. Further training, free of charge, is provided on a monthly basis by the School Psychology Methods Center. Additional knowledge is provided by the journal of the Hungarian Psychological Association (*Psychology Review*), by the journal of the Psychology Department of the Hungarian Academy (*Psychology*), by the journal published by a consortium of universities (*Applied Psychology*), and by the series titled *School Psychology*, which is edited by the School Psychology Methods Center of Eötvös Loránd University.

Job stability is equal to that in Hungary as a whole (1.2% unemployed among those with university degrees), although, when financial restrictions affect education, it is usually support personnel—such as speech therapists, resource room teachers, and school psychologists—who are the first to go. Stability is higher where the school psychologist is employed via the Educational Child Guidance Center, but that is where the attrition rate is the highest, about 20% annually. One of the reasons behind this is that Educational Child Guidance Centers are predominantly based in clinical settings. Many who opt for being employed by the Educational Child Guidance Centers see this as an opportunity to get closer to a more prestigious clinical setting, but when confronted with the fact that they cannot change their position, they tend to seek employment elsewhere. As the financial and professional prestige of school psychology is relatively low, only those who are committed will remain employed in the field. One of the best indicators of job satisfaction is the attrition rate. Those staying tend to emphasize challenges, independence, and creativity as motivating elements.

Infrastructure of School Psychology

There are two professional organizations, the School Psychology Section of the Hungarian Psychological Society and the Hungarian School Psychology Association. There are no licensing requirements currently in place. One form of quality assurance is the fact that only diplomas resulting from nationally (governmental) accredited training programs are accepted, or foreign diplomas that have been adopted. By law, only those holding a master's degree in psychology can call themselves a psychologist. Only psychologists holding a postgraduate degree in educational psychology can be appointed as school psychologists.

Laws and regulations governing the work of a school psychologist include the basic law governing compulsory education, including special education services (i.e., Public Education Act No. LXXIX of 1993), which has been revised by the government on numerous occasions. The most current revision is the 21/2005 (VII–25) statute of the Ministry for Education and the 148/2005 (VII–27) government regulation both taking effect as of September 1, 2005. The changes mainly affect rules of matriculation and open up further possibilities for realizing integration. This law designates that independent special education committees are to diagnose special education needs and determine eligibility for services. The 2005 regulation of the Ministry for Education states that it will draw up new directives for the kindergarten and compulsory schooling of children with special education needs; currently, there are no such directives. Vocational training is ruled by the Vocational Education Act LXXVI of 1993.

Ethical standards, which have special sections regarding different applied fields and which are approved by the Hungarian Psychological Association, bind every psychologist.

Preparation of School Psychologists

A minimum of 5 years of studies in psychology is required to receive a master's degree in psychology. There are five universities in Hungary preparing psychologists; each year, 250 individuals receive their master of arts degree in psychology. Some universities offer specialization during the master's-degree program (usually in the last 2 years), but there are only two universities offering specialization in school psychology. Each year, 25 persons receive a master's with specialization in school psychology. University programs tend to be theoretically oriented, with two-thirds lectures and one-third practice and seminars. An additional 40 hours of field experience is built in, usually in the last 2 years of the master's-degree program.

By law, a psychologist may only practice independently if he or she has a postgraduate degree. A psychologist may apply to enter postgraduate training after a minimum of 1 year of supervised practice after receiving a master's degree in psychology. Postgraduate degrees typically take the form of in-service training; thus, postgraduate training cannot be done full-time. The postgraduate degree for school psychologists is titled "professional educational psychologist" and takes 2 years to complete. There is only one university that offers this postgraduate degree. Annually, about 20 persons receive their postgraduate degree in professional educational psychology. This postgraduate degree is not only necessary for school psychologists but also is an option, together with clinical child psychology, for those working at Educational Guidance Centers. In Hungary, those interested in applied fields and service tend to choose postgraduate training after obtaining their master's degree, and those theoretically inclined tend to enter doctorate programs. Currently, no doctoral-level training is offered specifically for school psychology.

As for the content of master's-degree training, biological bases and core academic knowledge of psychology takes up the first 3 years of university studies, which includes basic and extended scientific statistical knowledge. During these first 3 years, students complete research courses in the core fields, write research papers with appropriate statistical analysis, and take comprehensive exams in experimental psychology (which include the topics of learning, cognition, and memory), developmental psychology, and personality and social psychology. They also learn about basic intellectual, behavioral, emotional, and social assessment methods and basic information about applied fields, ethical issues, and professional interpersonal skills. A focus on children and youth is provided by studies in developmental and educational psychology within the context of families, school, classrooms, and communities. These issues are repeatedly addressed if a school psychology or educational psychology specialization is chosen in the last 2 years. In the last 2 years, applied fields predominate.

There is great diversity among universities regarding the amount of specialization and depth and breadth of studies. Studies of advanced assessment and intervention methods are thus geared toward the applied field concerned, as are professional decision-making skills and intervention methods. In assessment, all basic aspects are included: intellectual, behavioral, emotional, and social assessment methods. Intervention methods courses cover behavioral, affective, educational, and social systems approaches. Legal aspects are discussed in the framework of the specific applied field. In the course of postgraduate training, assessment and intervention approaches specific to the applied field are covered, and common legal and ethical issues are discussed.

The structure and therefore, to some extent, the content described in this section will change as of autumn 2006 as a result of Hungary's adhering to the Bologna agreement. According to the new the Higher Education Act No. CXXXIX, which was put into effect November 1, 2005, from autumn 2006 there will be separate bachelor's degree and master's degree levels. The bachelor's-degree level training takes 3 years to complete and results in a degree of "behavior analyst." A further 2 years of study in psychology is required to earn a master's degree in psychology. Those holding a master's degree in psychology are now acknowledged as psychologists.

Roles, Functions, and Responsibilities of School Psychologists

As indicated previously, special education committees diagnose special education needs; thus, school psychologists are relieved of these extensive assessment duties—school psychologists' primary activities involve screening, prevention, intervention, and consultation. The following headings are taken from an article by Oakland and Cunningham (1997) on the International School Psychology Association definition of school psychology.

Testing and assessment models and methods. Psychological, behavioral, social systems, and ecological models of testing and assessment are relied on. As cited earlier, by law, school psychologists are not responsible for official diagnosis of special needs; thus, screening predominates. Screening for school readiness is one of the major tasks performed by kindergarten and school psychologists alike. To assess various cognitive abilities, a composite method compiled by Porkolábné Balogh (1990) and the Massachusetts School Street Test is used; the Sindelar method also is used. If the need arises, testing for intellectual abilities is done before the referral to the special education committee. The Hungarian version of the Wechsler Intelligence Scale for Children, third edition, or the Hungarian version of the Woodcock-Johnson international edition, or the Budapest Binet is used to assess cognitive abilities. In the case of a teacher, parent, or self-referral, problem-specific testing and assessment are performed. In the field of personality and temperament, the Eysenck, Wartegg, and Picture Frustration tests are commonly used. A standard element in school psychological work is vocational and career counseling. This becomes an important issue in Grades 8 and 12, where value orientation and differential interest tests are used. Group screening procedures for anxiety and stress are frequently used, and the use of sociometry also is common. In the assessment procedure, structured observations play an important role. The development of reliable, curriculum-based assessment is an ongoing task, in part, because of the relatively frequent changes made to the curriculum in the past few years, as well as school psychologists' need for assessments linked with intervention.

Interventions. Interventions tend to emphasize prevention. One of the most common functions of school psychologists is to promote development to fulfill potential and minimize possible difficulties in school achievement. Another common function is to actively participate in drug prevention programs. Interventions utilize individually oriented and group focused approaches with direct and indirect services tending to be balanced. In direct, individually focused interventions, dynamic, focused short-term therapies and counseling are often used. Group approaches would be in the sphere of drug prevention or developmentally focused interventions.

Consultation. The responsibility of consulting with teachers and parents has been a primary duty of school psychologists from the very beginning when school psychological services were initiated (Porkolábné Balogh & Szitó, 1987). Consultation with colleagues working at community and regional levels is essential, with Educational Child Guidance Centers and special education committees being regular contacts for school psychologists.

Organizational and program development services. These types of services have currently surfaced, as the law requires that schools develop their own education profiles and curricula. As integration or inclusion is more and more sought after, the need for individual education planning has emerged, but these skills still need to be developed.

Supervision. Supervisory responsibilities are present where school psychologist teams have developed, mainly as a part of Educational Child Guidance Centers.

Current Issues Affecting School Psychology

One of the major challenges is to define and maintain an identity for the school psychologist. Testing and assessment are officially the role of committees and centers, whereas therapies are considered the domain of clinical child psychologists and the function of Educational Child Guidance Centers. An important step to be taken would be to develop a collection of adequate tools specific to school psychology. The strong integration and inclusion initiatives of the Ministry of Education imply possible growth and offer a potential identity for the school psychologist. There is consensus of professional and public opinion indicating that the intentions of the Ministry are only viable if appropriate support professionals are present in school, but financial restrictions in the field of education render this impossible (Huba, 2005; Kőpatakiné Mészáros, 2005; Vargáné Mező, 2003). Hence, the core of the problem is financial. Improving the skills of school psychologists in the area of program design and evaluation, curriculum-based assessment, and individual education plans could be instrumental in convincing the education administration to increase financing and, at the same time, facilitate competency among school psychologists. This issue is addressed by the further training plan of the School Psychology Methods Base, which provides regular in-service training to school psychologists. The aforementioned issues have become even more pressing, as the Ministry for Education has launched its project to develop and introduce competency-based teaching in the sphere of public education.

References

Antalovits, M. (1999). Az alkalmazott pszichológia Magyarországon [Applied psychology in Hungary]. *Alkalmazott pszichológia, 1*(1), 5–13.

Avramidis, E., & Norwich, B. (2002). Teachers' attitudes towards integration/inclusion: A review of the literature. *European Journal of Special Needs Education, 17*(2), 129–147.

Baranyi, K. (1997). Jobbra szelektív iskola [Selective schools for the better]. *Új Pedagógiai Szemle, 47*(1), 20–34.

Besenyei, R., Borbás, É., Csécsiné Máriás, E., Gardovszky, V., Hagymásy, T., Könyvesi, T., & Tuska, Z. (2005). *Statistical yearbook of education.* Budapest: Ministry of Education.

Csernyák, M. N., Janák, K., Süpöl, E., & Zalánné Olbrich, A. (2005). Data of education (Preliminary data of 2004/2005). Budapest: Hungarian Central Statistical Office.

Gazsó, F., & Laki, L. (2004). *Fiatalok az újkapitalizmusban* [Youth in new capitalism]. Budapest: Napvilág Kiadó.

Halász, G., & Lannert, J. (Eds.). (2004). *Education in Hungary 2003.* Budapest: National Institute of Public Education.

Higher Education Act No. CXXXIX. (2005). Retrieved November 30, 2005, from http://net.jogtar.hu/jr/gen/getdoc.cgi?docid=a0500139.tv

Huba, J. (2005). Integráció alulnézetbő l [A bottom-up view of integration]. *Fejlesztő Pedagógia, 16*(2–3), 12–16.

Hunyady, G., & Templom, J. (1989). *Pszichológus az iskolában = iskolapszichológus* [Psychologist in the school = school psychologist]. Budapest: Ministry of Education.

Katona, N. (2000). School psychology around the world and in Hungary. *Applied Psychology in Hungary, 2*(1–2), 39–45.

Katona, N., & Szitó, I. (1990). Hungarian school psychology. *School Psychology International, 11*(3), 203–208.

Kőpatakiné Mészáros, M. (2005). Hazai pályán a nemzetközi tapasztalatok alapján [Utilizing international experiences on home turf]. *Fejlesztő Pedagógia, 16*(2–3), 7–11.

Loránd, F. (1997). Az egységes iskoláról [On homogeneous schools]. *Új Pedagógiai Szemle, 47*(1), 3–20.

MEH Elektronikuskormányzat-Központ. (2005, May). Hungary.hu: Country info, Economy. Retrieved August 3, 2005, from http://www.magyarorszag.hu/angol/orszaginfo/gazdasag

Mező, F., Mező, K., & Józsa, H. (in press). Országos iskolapszichológiai helyzetfelmérés (2004/2005) [National survey of school psychology (2004–2005)]. *Alkalmazott Pszichológia.*

Ministry of Education. (2005, February). *Education in Hungary.* Retrieved July 22, 2005, from http://www.om.hu/main.php?folderID=137&articleID=2208&ctag=articlelist&iid=1

Oakland, T., & Cunningham, J. (1997). International School Psychology Association definition of school psychology. *School Psychology International, 18,* 195–200.

Porkolábné Balogh, K. (1990). Módszerek a tanulási zavarok csoportos szőrésére és korrekciójára [Group assessment methods to identify learning disabilities]. *Iskolapszichológia, 19.* Budapest: ELTE.

Porkolábné Balogh, K., & Szitó, I. (1987). Az iskolapszichológia néhány alapkérdése [A few basic questions of school psychology]. *Iskolapszichológia, 1.* Budapest: ELTE.

Public Education Act No. LXXIX. (1993). Retrieved October 30, 2005, from http://net.jogtar.hu/jr/gen/getdoc.cgi?docid=99300079.tv

Public Education Act No. LXII revising Public Education Act No. LXXIX. (1996). Retrieved October 30, 2005, from http://net.jogtar.hu/jr/gen/getdoc.cgi?docid=99300079.tv

Vargáné Mező, L. (2003). Gondolatok a gyógypedagógiáról [Thoughts on special education]. *Fejlesztő Pedagógia* [Special issue], pp. 4–16.

Vocational Education Act No. LXXVI. (1993). Retrieved December 15, 2005, from http://net.jogtar.hu/jr/gen/getdoc.cgi?docid=99300076.tv

17

School Psychology in India

Vijaya Dutt

Context of School Psychology

India is located in southern Asia, bordered by Pakistan to the northwest, China, Nepal, and Bangladesh to the northeast, the Bay of Bengal to the southwest, and the Arabian Sea to the southeast. India's geographical aspects comprise mountain ranges, deserts, a network of rivers, fertile agricultural plains, and dense hilly jungle areas. It is a large country spread over 3.28 million square kilometres with a federal structure of 28 states and 7 union territories with 32 languages and numerous dialects.

It is important to consider the country's physical, demographic, and economic characteristics. The population in 2005 was estimated at 1,080,264,388, which is approximately 15% of the world population. Although around 80% of the population is Hindu, India houses one of the world's largest Muslim communities (120 million Muslims). The population also includes Sikhs, Jains, Buddhists, Parsis, Christians, and Jews. The history of India reveals that it has been consistently bombarded with invaders from the Iranian plateau, Central Asia, Arabia, Afghanistan, and the west. These influences have produced a remarkable cultural and racial synthesis on the people of India.

The gross domestic product in 2004 was US$3.319 trillion, US$3,100 per capita. The majority of the labor force is employed in agriculture (60%), with fewer individuals in services and industry. India is a predominantly agricultural country, and about 75% of the people live in rural areas, many of which are remote and difficult to access (Dutt, 2004). There are approximately 200 million children who are 6 to 14 years old and should be going to school. However, only 100 million of these children have access to any kind of schooling (Tuli, 2004).

The elementary education system in India is one of the largest in the world with 2.9 million teachers and 888,000 educational institutions. Elementary education is the first stage traditionally found in formal education, beginning at about 5 to 7 years and ending at about 11 to 13

AUTHOR'S NOTE: The author thanks Neha Dutt for assistance in preparing this chapter.

years. All the states and union territories of India have adopted a uniform structure of school education, that is, the 10+2 system. In this system, at the end of Classes X and XII, the respective state boards of secondary and higher secondary education conduct public examinations (i.e., 10 + 2 more years of education). Previously, students only had to pass one board exam after Class XI and then go to college. However, there remains variation and flexibility within the states and union territories regarding the following issues: (a) number of classes constituting the primary, upper primary, high, and higher secondary school stages, (b) age for admission to Class I, (c) medium of instruction, (d) public examination, (e) teaching of Hindi and English, (f) number of working days in a year, (g) academic sessions, (h) vacation periods, and (i) fee structure.

On the legislative front, education is free and compulsory and a fundamental right for children from ages 6 to 14 years (Jha, 2004). In India, the different stages of education are as follows: the primary stage (Classes I–V), for children ages 6 to 10 years; the middle stage (Classes VI–VIII), 11 to 13 years; the secondary stage (Classes IX–X), 14 to 15 years; and the senior/higher secondary stage (Classes XI–XII), 16 to 17 years. At the end of Classes X and XII, the respective state boards of secondary and higher secondary education conduct public examinations.

The different types of educational services available for children in India, and mainly in the urban and semi-urban areas, are *regular*, as in regular schools up to the senior secondary level; *special*, as per the needs of children with disabilities; *integrated*, special and regular education merged in one school; and inclusive, regular schools to accommodate children with special educational needs with support services (Tuli, 2004).

The authority that runs a school determines the management of that school. For example, government schools are run by the central government, state government, or public sectors; local schools are run by the *Panchayati Raj* and local body institutions (e.g., municipal corporations/committees, cantonment boards); private aided schools are run by an individual or private organization, receiving grants from the government or local bodies; and, finally, private unaided schools are run by an individual or private organisation but do not receive grants from the government or local bodies (Nanavaty, 1973). The minimum age for admission to Class I of the primary school stage is between 5 and 6 years; this is true in all of the states and union territories, except in Mizoram, where there is no age restriction.

India's commitment to spreading knowledge among its citizens is reflected in Article 45 of its constitution: "The State shall endeavour to provide within a period of 10 years from the commencement of this Constitution for free and compulsory education for all children until they complete the age of 14 years." Despite efforts made by the government to promote education, about 35 million children in the 6- to 10-year age-group do not attend primary school, and statistics indicate that 9 out of 10 children do not complete their schooling: 37% of children drop out before reaching Class V, and the overall dropout rate in Classes I to X is over 68%. The rate of enrolment at the secondary level is half that of the primary level, indicating that a large number of students drop out at the initial stages of their education (Mago, 2005).

Large class size in schools is another factor that compounds some of the problems affecting the Indian education system. The class size could be anywhere between 40 and 75 children. Though there has been a considerable change in the Indian educational scenario, no more than 3% to 4% of the number of children with special education needs have access to education (Dutt, 2004). Indeed, according to the Janshala Report (Government of India, 2001), approximately 12 million of the 200 million children in the 6- to 14-year age-group have special needs, and only 1 million of these are attending school. The National Sample Survey Organisation survey, Disabled Persons in India, 58th round, 2002, states that in the 5- to 14-year age-group, 9,092 children per 100,000 children have some kind of disability (Mukhopadhyay & Prakash, 2004).

Origin, History, and Current Status of School Psychology

At the outset, it is important to know that the study of psychology in India does not have a long history, and, in fact, its importance as an essential service to schools is yet to be realised. As in the United States and the United Kingdom, psychology was studied for a long time as a part of philosophy (Menon, 1961). In fact, religion and philosophy have been the foundation stones of ancient Indian education, shaping the different systems of education at that time. Psychology has always been an integral part of Indian culture (e.g., the holy Geeta is an ancient book of psychotherapy but in a spiritual context). Religious books like the Vedas, Upanishads, and Puranas all had a strong influence on educational thinking, making ancient Indian philosophy almost as eclectic as modern philosophy of education (Nanavaty, 1973).

In ancient India's educational system, the teacher-student relation was important and very traditional. In fact, the teacher's home was the school (*ashram*), and the student actually lived with the teacher until the completion of his studies. The teacher was the pivotal and creative force behind the learning process. He became the student's "guru," father figure, and was sometimes even worshipped (Verma, 1968). The teacher was expected to have high moral values and qualifications, and the education system was based on the individualisation of instruction and direct interaction between the teacher and the student. During his stay in the *ashram*, the student was prepared for life and had to follow the strict rules of behaviour laid down by the teacher. It is evident from this that the teacher played a very crucial role in the overall development of the student.

There are many famous educationists and philosophers, who have greatly influenced and changed the landscape of the Indian education system. The contributions of a few of these eminent personalities will be reviewed, in order to get better insight into the dynamics of the present system. Raja Ram Mohan Roy (1772–1833), often known as the Prophet of Indian Renaissance, was a great secularist, humanist, reformist, and educationist. In fact, the history of modern education in India is supposed to have begun with him. He realized the importance of education as an instrument of advancement and progress, and he introduced English into the education system. Dr. Annie Besant (1843–1933) was the first woman educator in modern India and one of the greatest women education philosophers, who strove for secularism and nationalism. For her, education was a comprehensive science, aimed at training children in activity, emotions, and intelligence. She strongly believed that since people have to live in and perform certain functions in society, education must equip them with the necessary skills to perform those functions efficaciously. She emphasized the importance of understanding the emotions experienced by children and felt that it was the teacher's responsibility not only to bring out the best in the child but also to make the child aware of his or her latent worth and powers. Sri Aurobindo Ghosh (1872–1950) was a great naturalist, philosopher, educationist, and prophetic figure. He believed in the individual uniqueness of the personality of each child. According to him, a child is viewed as "a soul with a body, life energy and mind to be harmoniously and integrally developed" (Verma, 1968, p. 258). Therefore, the aim of education was spiritual in nature: to help in the awakening and development of the spirit in the mind and body of each individual.

The earliest departments of psychology started in Calcutta and Mysore Universities less than a century ago, but it was only after 1930 that psychology achieved independent status in undergraduate and postgraduate courses in other Indian universities (Menon, 1961). It was during the 1950s that educational psychology, industrial psychology, and the psychology of personality started gaining importance. The main areas covered under educational psychology were related to educational and vocational guidance, selections and placements for jobs, occupational information, reading and comprehension, and teachers' attitude toward their profession.

Vocational bureaus were started, run by both private and government agencies and the psychological institutes. They not only catered to the needs of the students, but some of them also conducted research on guidance problems (Krishnan, 1961). These institutes were established during the period 1950 to 1960 and were purely centre based. The staff were trained psychologists and rarely visited schools.

During the 20th century, academic psychology was influenced by behaviourism. This influence is still very much present, and academic psychology is still commonly defined as the science of behaviour. Indian culture has a rich reservoir of practical psychology and spiritual knowledge as its heritage, and psychology is viewed as a science of the soul and the science of consciousness. India is still recovering from 800 years of foreign rule, resulting in economic suppression. In spite of this, the spiritual and cultural influence on education is still strong (Matthew, 2001).

The average salary of psychologists working in schools is the same as the starting salary of teachers (i.e., between 11,000 and 15,000 rupees per month, approximately 180 to 250 euros). Salaries of psychologists working with nongovernmental organisations are not fixed. They depend on the inflow of funds that the organisation receives from various donations and resource deployment agencies. Those who are employed by government universities and community projects have a fairly regular income package, which can start anywhere from 15,000 rupees per month (approximately 250 euros), along with the additional perks extended to other government employees.

Infrastructure of School Psychology

In India, there are no organisations specifically for school psychology. However, there are a few mental health institutes and counselling and therapy training centers that train psychology students in doctoral degrees or diplomas in psychotherapy and counselling only for master's degree holders with a theoretical knowledge of psychology. The national and regional psychology associations in India include the Association of Clinical Psychologists, the Indian Association of Clinical Psychologists, the Indian Psychological Association, the Indian Academy of Applied Psychologists, the Indian Psychoanalytical Society, and the Rajasthan Professional Psychology Association. In India, a person can practice psychology with a master's degree; no license is required. However, the process of developing laws relevant to this field has begun. All professionals (including psychologists) working in the field of rehabilitation, which covers the area of special education, have to register with the Rehabilitation Council of India. Often, teachers take on the role of school psychologists, because there are very few school psychologists in India. Many teachers counsel schoolchildren along with their teaching assignments, though most of the time this is not carried out in an organised way. They are not trained school psychologists and do not have a degree in psychology. However, some of these teachers undergo courses in educational psychology and counselling during their teacher-training program (Mukhopadhyay, 2005).

The most common publications referred to by school psychologists are *The Journal of Counselling Psychology,* published by the American Psychological Association, and *RCI News Letter,* published by the Rehabilitation Council of India. School psychologists refer to very few journals, one of the reasons being that most of them do not have easy access to such literature.

Preparation of School Psychologists

To become a psychologist, a person has to study 3 years of psychology as a major subject at the bachelor's-degree level, and another 2 years to get a master's degree. In the second year of the master's program, the student needs to specialize in a particular area of psychology (e.g., clinical or educational). The curriculum varies depending on what area the student specialises in; for example, clinical psychology would include areas like abnormal psychology, psychological testing, and guidance and counselling. There are a number of courses on psychology in Indian universities, but none specifically for school psychologists. These include postgraduate courses, diploma courses, correspondence courses, specialised courses in clinical psychology, and specialised courses in guidance and counselling.

Information regarding the average number of school psychology students admitted into a program annually is not applicable, because presently no such courses are available. The same holds for information regarding the average number of school psychologists who graduate each year. Anybody who has graduated in psychology, with educational psychology, child psychology, or counselling and guidance as their concentration, can apply for a job as a psychologist in a school. However, people with additional qualifications, in particular, a doctorate, are preferred. A degree in psychology is essential in order to specialise in counselling.

Graduation in psychology requires 3 years of study and postgraduation a further 2 years. Diplomas, which usually are obtained in 1 year, equip novices with counselling techniques and can be done through workshops and regular classes and through distance education. The Indira Gandhi National Open University and National Council for Educational Research and Training offer a postgraduate diploma in guidance and counselling and a certificate in guidance, respectively. As there is no specific graduate program in school psychology, the National Council for Educational Research and Training is planning to start an international program in guidance and counselling for teachers in Delhi. This course will train teachers to counsel students regarding different issues, such as career-related problems and personal,

social, and value conflicts. It will be based on the "teacher-as-counsellor" model and will be a 6-month course, including an internship.

At present, some schools in the metropolitan cities have counsellors. Government schools have educational vocational guidance counsellors, who are in charge of two to three schools in a district (Banerjee, 2005). Once this course starts, it is expected that state governments will send their teachers for training in this area. One foreseeable problem is that of finding the requisite skilled workers to replace those teachers who go for training. This may deter schools from supporting teachers to attend this course. In India, school psychologists are generally known as counselling psychologists or counsellors. The psychological services available to schools are extremely limited in relation to the hundreds of thousands of schools spread throughout the country (Mukhopadhyay, 2005).

Roles, Functions, and Responsibilities of School Psychologists

The responsibilities of school psychologists are linked to the pressures of the present education system (i.e., the pressure to perform and do well academically) on both students and their parents. The educational counsellors have to intervene in cases where these pressures affect the students' performance. In addition to counselling students, they need to network with teachers, families, and, if need be, other professionals, such as doctors, psychiatrists, and child psychologists, to help the students cope with and overcome their problems. Some students go to vocational counsellors toward the end of their school life for help in planning out the right career path for them and guidance in making the right choices. Vocational counsellors provide them with information regarding the availability of courses, scholarship schemes, duration of courses, dates of entrance exams, financial assistance, and prospective employment opportunities. They guide students to opt for a specialisation most suitable to them. Job satisfaction has been found to be high among dedicated professionals in the field of counselling (Koda, 2001).

Some of the commonly used assessment and evaluation tests, apart from some teacher-made tests, are the Stanford-Binet Test of Intelligence, Raven's Progressive Matrices, Standard Progressive Matrices, Bhatia's Battery of Performance Tests of Intelligence, Differential Aptitude Test, Wechsler Intelligence Scale for Children, Wechsler Adult Intelligence Scale, Cattell's High School Personality Questionnaire, and Cattell's Sixteen Personality Factor Questionnaire. Only psychologists are permitted to administer these tests.

Current Issues Impacting School Psychology

In India, a visit to a psychologist carries a social stigma. This is due to the widely prevalent belief that any kind of therapy or counselling sessions for readjustment is related to some sort of mental instability. This often means that the psychologist is the last resort, rather than the first choice. Therefore, the success of a psychologist's practice depends, to a great extent, on the kind of society he or she works in. As mentioned earlier, some professionals in the teaching profession hold a bachelor's degree in psychology. This knowledge, together with the experiences they have in working with children, facilitates the development of a career as a school psychologist. Despite the fact that parents and children have proclaimed a desperate need for more support and guidance in the areas of severe learning disabilities and coping problems in mainstream schools, no positive steps have been taken to tackle this problem. Clinical psychologists who work in hospitals rarely visit schools (Farrell, 2005).

Another major area of concern is related to the present education system. Indian schools have an extremely rigorous academic curriculum. There is severe competition, and children are pressured to perform. Rote learning takes precedence over developing analytical skills and logical thinking. The ominously accelerated pace of teaching in the classroom, in order to complete the syllabus, is compounded with an increased burden of homework for the student. Most children have to be sent for private tuition after school hours, so that they can keep up with the pace of the class. Then, there is the added stress of learning a second and third language. As a result, extracurricular activities generally "take a backseat" to the academic frenzy in which most students are absorbed. In fact, every year, when the final examination results are declared, many students who fail or are disappointed with their marks commit suicide. The nation's schools should consider the gravity of the present problems and take necessary and prompt action to overcome them. In such an alarming scenario, the interventions of a school psychologist are urgently required. However, at present, there is no association of school psychologists, and, in fact, "the profession does not really exist" (Farrell, 2005, p. 2).

It is about time that schools and the education boards acknowledge their responsibility in building up a sense of security and self-worth in each child. All children should be accepted with all their shortcomings, varying intelligence levels, and disabilities and be encouraged to grow in a safe and invigorating environment leading to a feeling of success. One of the most destructive emotions is fear (Nath, 1964). Both teachers and parents must ensure that children develop in an emotionally stable environment and are armed with skills to tackle the heightened performance pressure. There should be a shift in focus, away from exam-oriented learning, to inculcate the joy of learning in students.

The teacher-as-counsellor model may not be effective in many schools due to the fact that the large class sizes make it difficult to promote adequate teacher-student relationships. Furthermore, not all teachers have sufficient knowledge of child and adolescent psychology. Therefore, they are not professionally equipped with the skills necessary to efficiently handle the multidimensional problems of the youth. The current effort of the government to implement inclusive education in all schools is another issue that has a considerable impact on school psychology. Most teachers, parents, and even students need to be counselled and sensitised to accept the presence of children with disabilities in their schools. The role that school psychologists play in ensuring a smooth transition and stress-free implementation of inclusive education is a crucial one. Having properly trained school psychologists in all schools is unquestionably among the most pressing needs of the day. Research in this area is not a priority at the moment. What is important is that the government should take the initiative and start an association for school psychologists and take the lead in establishing the profession.

References

Banerjee, R. (2005, April 26). Now go international, à la NCERT. *The Times of India* (New Delhi)

Dutt, V. (2004). *Strategic policy formulation to address the needs of people with multiple disabilities.* Paper presented at the National Seminar on Management of Inclusive Education, organised by the National Institute of Education, Planning & Administration, New Delhi.

Farrell, P. (2005). Letter from the president. *World Go Round, 32*(1), 1–2.

Government of India. (2001, January–March). Janshala report. Retrieved April 17, 2005, from www.un.org.in/Janshala

Jha, M. M. (2004). *From special to inclusive education: International perspectives and Indian policies.* Paper presented at the National Seminar on Management of Inclusive Education, organised by the National Institute of Education, Planning & Administration, New Delhi.

Koda, S. (2001, February 21). Rewards from a wise counsel. *The Hindu* [online newspaper]. Retrieved April 17, 2005, from http://www.hinduonnet.com/jobs/0102/05210021.htm

Krishnan, B. (1961). A review of contributions of Indian psychologists. In T. K. N. Menon (Ed.), *Recent trends in psychology.* Bombay, Calcutta, New Delhi: Orient Longman.

Mago, C. (2005, May 16). 90% kids drop out of schools. *The Times of India* (New Delhi), p. 11.

Mathew, V. G. (2001). *A short history of Indian psychology.* Retrieved April 17, 2005, from www.psychology4all.com

Menon, T. K. N. (Ed.). (1961). *Recent trends in psychology.* Bombay: Orient Longman.

Mukhopadhyay, B. B. (2005, June). Counselling tsunami hit children: Role of school psychologists. *World Go Round, 32*(3), 5.

Mukhopadhyay, S., & Prakash, J. (2004). *Managing inclusive education: Policy to implementation.* Paper presented at the National Seminar on Management of Inclusive Education, organised by the National Institute of Education, Planning & Administration, New Delhi.

Nanavaty, J. J. (1973). *Educational thought.* Poona: Joshi and Lokhande Prakashan.

Nath, P. (1964). *A vision of education.* Delhi: University Publishers.

Singh, J. P. (2004). *The educator.* Delhi: Rehabilitation Council of India.

Tuli, U. (2004). *Towards making inclusive education a reality.* Paper presented at the National Seminar on Management of Inclusive Education, organised by the National Institute of Education, Planning & Administration, New Delhi.

Verma, K. K. (1968). *Visions & voices.* India: Indian Publications, Ambala Cantt.

18

School Psychology in Ireland

Peadar P. Crowley

Context of School Psychology

The island of Ireland is situated in northwest Europe. The total area is 84,421 square kilometres, the Republic of Ireland comprising 70,282 square kilometres and Northern Ireland 14,139 square kilometres. The greatest length of the island is 486 kilometres, and the greatest width is 275 kilometers. The information in this chapter refers to the state named in the Constitution as Eire (Ireland in the English language), described as The Republic of Ireland in the 1948 Republic of Ireland Act, and generally referred to as Ireland. Ireland achieved its independence in 1922. The Constitution of 1937 and the 1948 Republic of Ireland Act severed Ireland's last formal links with Britain. The total population in April 2005 exceeded 4 million (Central Statistics Office, 2005a). The principal urban areas are the Greater Dublin Area (1,004,600, or 26% of the overall population of the state), Cork (186,200), Limerick (87,000), Galway (66,200), and Waterford (46,700). Although English is now the first language of the majority of the population, the Constitution names the Irish language as the first official language and English the second. Approximately 1.57 million persons aged 3 years and older were recorded as Irish speaking in 2002. According to the 2002 census, 88% of the population was Roman Catholic, 3% Church of Ireland (including Protestant), and 6% reported no religion or religion not stated. Approximately 21% of the population is aged birth to 14 years, and 16% is aged 15 to 24 years (Central Statistics Office, 2003).

Ireland is one of the fastest growing economies in the developed world; during the recent decade, the gross domestic product has nearly doubled. The gross domestic product in 2004 was US$126.4 billion, US$31,900 per capita. During the past few decades, the Irish economy has transformed from agrarian and traditional manufacturing to technology and international services based. In 2004, employment was mostly in services (66%), industry (28%), and agriculture (6%) (Economic and Social Research Institute, 2005).

Education in Ireland is compulsory from age 6 to 16 years (or until students have completed 3 years of second-level education) (Department of

Education and Science, 2004a). Although there is limited provision for preschool education in Ireland, primary (first-level) schools accept children on or after their fourth birthday. The typical primary school enrols pupils by age into eight age-groups or classes, ranging from junior infants, to senior infants, to first class, and on to sixth class. The vast majority of schools are state-funded but privately owned, often by church interests. The national curriculum, set by the National Council for Curriculum and Assessment, is child-centred and allows flexibility in timetabling and teaching methods. The great majority of pupils transfer to post-primary (second-level) schools at about the age of 12. The post-primary sector comprises secondary, vocational, community, and comprehensive schools. These schools follow the same state curricula and prepare students for the same state public examinations. These school types differ formally in the areas of ownership, management, and historical origins.

The majority of students (about 58%) attend secondary schools, 29% attend vocational schools, and 15% attend community and comprehensive schools. Secondary schools are privately owned, mostly by religious congregations, and publicly funded. After 3 years in the post-primary junior cycle (Years 1–3), students sit the state Junior Certificate examination. There are a number of programme options within the senior cycle of post-primary education, which generally extends for 3 years, from age 15 to 18. Before embarking on the Leaving Certificate programme, many students opt for the Transition Year programme, which provides a broad educational experience with a view to enhancing personal maturity through some academic work, work experience, entrepreneurial activities, and community involvement. The 2-year Established Leaving Certificate programme (Years 5 and 6) is the main senior cycle option. The Leaving Certificate Examination, managed by the State Examinations Commission, is taken at the end of the senior cycle, typically at the age of 17 or 18. The examination and the associated highly competitive points system (for access to third-level

education) occupy a prominent place in public discourse. In 2004, over 55,000 students took the Established Leaving Certificate Examination. An alternative route, the Leaving Certificate Applied, introduced in 1995, is a 2-year modular programme aimed at preparing students for adult and working life. It comprises three principal elements: vocational preparation, vocational education, and general education. About 3,500 students took the Leaving Certificate Applied in 2004 (Department of Education and Science, 2005a). Finally, the Leaving Certificate Vocational Programme can be described as a Leaving Certificate with a strong vocational dimension.

The third-level sector comprises mainly publicly funded universities, institutes of technology, and colleges of education (teacher training colleges). Recent years have seen the growth of private third-level institutions. There are seven universities in the state, three in Dublin, and one each in Cork, Limerick, Galway, and Maynooth, County Kildare. The technological institutes provide education and training in areas such as business, science, engineering, and music to certificate, diploma, and degree level. The number of third-level students increased by 105% in the past decade (Central Statistics Office, 2005b).

"Further education" refers to education and training which occurs after second-level schooling but which is not part of the third-level system. This includes a wide range of Post Leaving Certificate courses, with about 29,000 students, and the Vocational Training Opportunities Scheme, a second chance programme for about 5,000 unemployed persons.

In the school year 2003–2004, a total of 446,029 pupils attended 3,278 primary schools, 337,851 pupils attended 743 second-level schools, and 133,887 full-time students attended third-level institutions. Pupil-to-teacher ratios in 2003–2004 were 17 to 1 at primary level and 13.6 to 1 at second level. The average (ordinary) primary class size in the school year 2002–2003 was 24 (Department of Education and Science, 2004b).

The Irish educational system has traditionally been highly centralized, with the Department of

Education and Science exercising a great deal of influence over many aspects of the system (Coolahan, 1981). In recent years, a number of statutory agencies, such as the National Council for Curriculum and Assessment, the State Examinations Commission, and the National Educational Welfare Board, have assumed important functions. Regional offices of the Department of Education and Science have been established.

Each year about 13,000 children and young people leave school without having sat the Leaving Certificate Examination. Of these, some 2,400 leave before the Junior Certificate Examination (National Economic and Social Forum, 2002). The percentage of students who continue to be enrolled at age 17 years is about 83%. At primary level, students are absent for an average of 11 days out of 183. At post-primary level, students are absent for an average of 15 days each out of 167. Absenteeism is significantly worse in disadvantaged areas (National Educational Welfare Board, 2005). The National Educational Welfare Board was established under the provisions of the Educational Welfare Act 2000 (Government of Ireland, 2000a). The primary function of this independent statutory organisation is to ensure that each child in the state attends a recognised school or otherwise receives an appropriate education. The Board has a policy development role in relation to school attendance, and its educational welfare officers (currently numbering 73 and focussing only on priority areas) work closely with school personnel, parents, and others to encourage regular school attendance and to reduce absenteeism. The School Completion Programme is a Department of Education and Science initiative that targets schools with the highest levels of early school leaving and provides financial support and advice in the development of an integrated plan to facilitate graduation and associated interventions.

Research on education and psychology is primarily conducted in the third-level institutions. The Educational Research Centre at St. Patrick's Teacher Training College has had, for many years, a leading research role, especially in the fields of assessment and evaluation. A new specialist Children's Research Centre has been established in Trinity College, Dublin. A team drawn from the Children's Research Centre and the Economic and Social Research Institute has been appointed by the National Children's Office to undertake the recently announced National Longitudinal Study of Children in Ireland.

Promoting social inclusion is a public policy priority. The extent and consequences of educational disadvantage in Ireland are well documented. For example, the children of professional workers account for 15% of new entrants to higher education, substantially greater than their share of the population, about 9%, whereas the share of new entrants accounted for by children whose fathers' social class is "unskilled" is less than their share of the population subgroup, 3% compared with 5% (Fitzpatrick Associates & O'Connell, 2005). The Department of Education and Science has, following a review of existing measures, launched a programme titled Delivering Equality of Opportunity to Schools (Department of Education and Science, 2005b), which will integrate a number of existing programmes into a new School Support Programme. The School Support Programme will focus attention on 600 primary and 150 second-level schools with concentrated levels of educational disadvantage and will place a new emphasis on monitoring progress and the achievement of targets. Primary schools in the School Support Programme will provide enhanced access to early education and benefit from reduced class sizes.

The continuum of special educational provisions for students with disabilities ranges from placement in mainstream schools with additional supports to special class placement in mainstream schools to specialist support in special schools. This principle of a continuum of provision was first formally proposed in an Irish context in the Report of the Special Education Review Committee (Government of Ireland, 1993). The beginnings of special education in Ireland can be traced back to the mid 19th century when special services for persons with visual and auditory disabilities were set up by religious orders. In 1950, just one special school for pupils with "mental handicaps" had been given official recognition. The main growth of special schools took place in the 1960s and early 1970s. By 1993, about 0.9% of all primary and post-primary pupils were receiving their education in 114 special schools, 64 of which provided for pupils with mental handicaps. This figure of 0.9% for pupils segregated in special schools was low by the prevailing European standards. Many of these special schools were established by religious orders and community organisations, and these organisations, in turn, developed local psychological services. In the absence of mainstream school psychological services, these largely publicly funded "voluntary" services also provided psychological assessment services to mainstream pupils.

In October 1998, the government introduced an "automatic response" for children with special educational needs in primary schools, effectively implementing a policy of inclusion. For the first time, children with special educational needs were entitled to be automatically allocated resources (e.g., resource teaching, special needs assistants, and special equipment) in mainstream schools on the basis of assessed need. This announcement followed the publication in September 1998 of the blueprint for the National Educational Psychological Service (Government of Ireland, 1998b), and the new policy had a significant and unanticipated influence on the operation of the new psychological service.

Important Department of Education and Science reports on dyslexia (Government of Ireland, 2001b) and on autism (Government of Ireland, 2001a) were published in 2001. The National Council for Special Education was established in December 2003 to improve the delivery of services to children with disabilities. This independent statutory body has the following functions: to coordinate the provision of education and related support services with health boards, schools, and other relevant bodies; to provide a range of services at local and national levels in order that the educational

needs of children with disabilities are identified and provided for; and to carry out research and provide expert advice to the minister for education and science on the educational needs of children with disabilities and on related services. The council currently operates through a national network of 80 special educational needs organisers who are the key contact persons for parents, schools, health authorities, and other agencies. Additional special educational needs organisers are envisaged.

Teaching resources in mainstream primary schools for students with special educational needs are allocated on the basis of a working estimate of 10% of students being in need of learning support and 6% in need of resource teaching (i.e., having special educational needs). Students with "high incidence" disabilities, including borderline mild general disabilities (intelligence quotient 70–79), mild general learning disabilities (intelligence quotient 50–69), and specific learning disabilities (principally dyslexia) are provided with teaching resources on a general allocation model. This model allocates to schools additional teaching resources that are then deployed within schools at the discretion of school authorities. Students with "low incidence" special educational needs, arising from physical or sensory impairment, emotional or behavioural disturbance, autism, specific speech and language disorder, and moderate/severe/profound learning disability are allocated teaching resources on an individual basis, following appropriate professional assessment (Department of Education and Science, 2005c).

Origin, History, and Current Status of School Psychology

The 1960s in Ireland was a period of rapid change, including in education. Following the publication of the Government White Paper on Economic Expansion in 1958, there was an emphasis on education as an economic investment rather than a consumer service. An expanding economy needs and facilitates a growing educational sector. Headline reforms, following the publication of the Investment in Education Report (Department of Education, 1966), included the introduction of a school transport scheme and a free education scheme at second level.

The first school psychological services for mainstream schools in the state were established in 1960 by the City of Dublin Vocational Education Committee. Vocational education committees are public bodies that are responsible for vocational schools, community colleges (both second-level school types), and certain further education institutions and services. There are 33 vocational education committees throughout the state. The City of Dublin Vocational Education Psychological Service now consists of 10 psychologists providing services, on a time allocation basis, to 12 vocational schools, as well as colleges, and (since 1998) 22 education and training centres within the City of Dublin Vocational Education Committee area. A range of services is offered, including consultation with school staff, group and individual work with students (including counselling/therapy), liaison with other agencies, and supervision and training of certain professional staff. The biggest proportion of psychologists' time is devoted to working with pupils individually or in groups, followed closely by work with teachers, chiefly special needs teams and guidance counsellors. A growing involvement for the service is working with nonnationals. Psychologists in this service engage in ongoing professional development. Specific projects in which the service has engaged in recent years include a language development programme for adolescents and a research project in conjunction with the Crisis Pregnancy Agency.

The Psychological Service of the then Department (Ministry) of Education was established in 1965 with a brief to provide a guidance service to the newly established comprehensive schools, to develop standardised tests, and to conduct research. Psychological Service support was gradually extended to all second-level

schools, but psychologist-to-pupil ratios were very high, in some cases exceeding 1 to 20,000.

From 1960 until 1990, mainstream school psychological services were almost exclusively directed to second-level schools. There were many calls over the years, by the Psychological Society of Ireland (Psychological Society of Ireland, 1974) and others (Swan, 1981), for the establishment of comprehensive school psychological services. In the absence of school psychological services, assessment services for children attending mainstream schools were generally provided by clinical psychologists employed by the regional health boards (now reorganised into the Health Service Executive) and voluntary services, which are primarily publicly funded services for persons with special educational needs.

In 1990, a Pilot Project to Primary Schools was established by the Department of Education Psychological Service in two designated areas, one urban and one rural. The aim of the Pilot Project was to explore models for psychological services to primary schools. It developed a balanced model of casework, project work, the involvement of parents, and liaison with other agencies. It recommended enhanced psychologist-to-pupil ratios and team-based integrated (primary and post-primary) services. Services to primary schools developed from the mid 1990s.

In 1992, the County Dublin Vocational Educational Committee established its Psychological Support Service. The Psychological Support Service employs five permanent psychologists and two to three contract psychologists. Two of the permanent psychologists are employed to provide services to 22 second-level schools, and two are employed to work with other education and training centres. The Psychological Support Service also operates a High Support Learning Programme for students with complex special educational needs not attending mainstream schools and has allocated a psychologist and a learning support teacher to this project. Although the contract psychologists' work arises from self-financing projects, the entire service operates as a single team so that the specific skills of each psychologist are available, in principle, to all service recipients. As well as providing a consultation and advice service, the Psychological Support Service works with parents and students individually and in groups. The service emphasises training work with teachers and collaboration with other agencies. It operates a programme of further professional development for its staff and engages in a range of research and development activities. The Health Service Executive employs educational psychologists within its area community care programmes. Health service–funded learning disability services also employ educational psychologists.

The National Educational Psychological Service was established in 1999 and largely subsumed the Department of Education and Science Psychological Service. Development was initially rapid (National Educational Psychological Service, 2003a). The National Educational Psychological Service, which remains within the Department (Ministry) of Education and Science, is structured nationally into 10 regions (Department of Education and Science, 2005d). Within these regions, area teams of psychologists, led by senior psychologists, provide services to primary and post-primary schools.

The blueprint for the development of the National Educational Psychological Service (Government of Ireland, 1998b) envisaged 200 educational psychologists in the school system by 2004, 184 of whom would be in the National Educational Psychological Service. This report set out certain principles to govern the operation of the service. These include the need to achieve a balance between individual casework and more systemic support and development work. A general ratio of 1 psychologist to 5,000 students was envisaged. Currently about half of all primary schools in the state are on service from the National Educational Psychological Service, as are three quarters of post-primary schools. There is, however, considerable variation in coverage between counties. In relation to primary schools, this ranges from a low of 20% in receipt of a service from the National Educational Psychological Service to a high of 69%, while post-primary school coverage ranges from 13% to 100%. Broadly speaking, coverage is best in urban and disadvantaged areas and worst in rural areas.

In its Strategy Statement 2001–2004, titled *Working Together to Make a Difference for Children,* the National Educational Psychological Service (2001) describes its mission as "to support the personal, social and educational development of all children through the application of psychological theory and practice in education, having particular regard for children with special educational needs." As of 2005, the National Educational Psychological Service had 128 psychologists, of whom 76% were female. Once probated, psychologists in the National Educational Psychological Service become permanent civil servants. Salaries for psychologists employed in public service, including educational psychologists and Health Service Executive–employed clinical psychologists, are on a common scale from €47,877 to €75,515 for main grade psychologists (December 2004). The teachers' common basic salary scale (December 2004 without allowances) ranges from €27,164 to €52,796.

In 2001, the Department of Education and Science established a Scheme for Commissioning Psychological Assessments to provide a limited assessment service to schools without access to a comprehensive psychological service. This scheme, administered by the National Educational Psychological Service, permits schools to commission two assessments per 100 students per annum from psychologists in private practice. This panel, which may be regarded as an indicator of the number of psychologists in private practice available to the educational system, currently lists 158 psychologists.

Infrastructure of School Psychology

The term *educational psychologist* or *psychologist* (rather than *school psychologist*) is widely used in Ireland to refer to psychologists who work primarily in educational settings. As noted elsewhere, the title "psychologist" does not yet have statutory protection. The Psychological Society of Ireland is the professional body for psychology in Ireland. Established in 1970, the society now has over 2,000 graduate members. The Psychological Society of Ireland includes divisions of Counselling Psychology, Clinical Psychology, Health Psychology, Work and Organisational Psychology, and a newly established (in 2005) Division of Educational Psychology numbering 82 members. The Society publishes the *Irish Journal of Psychology* and the monthly *Irish Psychologist*. In the absence of a statute to regulate psychology, the Society established, in 1998, a nonstatutory register to promote high standards of behaviour, competence, and practice within the profession. A formal system of continuing professional development ensures that members continue to regularly update their knowledge and skills. The Psychological Society of Ireland's Code of Ethics is supported by its Board of Professional Conduct.

In addition to the *Irish Journal of Psychology*, educational psychologists rely primarily on publications from the United Kingdom, such as *Support for Learning, Educational Psychology in Practice, The British Journal of Educational Psychology*, and *The Journal of Child Psychiatry and Psychology*. Proposals to introduce statutory registration for psychologists (and certain other professions) are at an advanced stage, and the legislation is likely to be enacted in 2005. The Health and Social Care Professionals Bill (Government of Ireland, 2004a) provides for the establishment of a registration council and profession-specific committees. This mechanism will control entitlement to use the title "psychologist" and will deal with complaints relating to practitioner competence. There is diversity in the professional credentials required by different employing bodies. This is partially because postgraduate professional training in educational psychology was not available in Ireland before the 1990s. The Psychological Society of Ireland policy is that educational psychologists employed in the health service must have postgraduate training in educational

psychology. The requirements of the City of Dublin Vocational Education Committee and County Dublin Vocational Education Committee are consistent with this policy. Entry requirements for the National Educational Psychological Service have varied. The most recent recruitment criteria included eligibility for graduate membership of the Psychological Society of Ireland and a recognised postgraduate qualification in educational psychology, or 3 years experience working as a psychologist, or in special circumstances, a recognised teaching qualification, and 3 years teaching experience. It is likely that as the supply of educational psychologists improves, and with the advent of statutory registration, all newly recruited educational psychologists will have postgraduate professional training in educational psychology.

In addition to several recent statutes that impinge in a general way on the work of educational psychologists, namely the Data Protection Act (Government of Ireland, 1988), the Freedom of Information Act (Government of Ireland, 1997), the Equal Status Act (Government of Ireland, 2000b), and the Educational Welfare Act (Government of Ireland, 2000a), two statutes in particular directly influence the work of educational psychologists.

The Education Act (Government of Ireland, 1998a) was a major piece of legislation that consolidated certain rights and duties and put many existing educational functions and general provisions on a statutory basis. The Act requires that the minister for education and science ensure that all residents in the state, including persons with disabilities or other special educational needs, have access to support services and a level and quality of education appropriate to meeting their needs and abilities. Furthermore, the minister is responsible for the planning and coordination of such support services. Under the Act, it is the responsibility of each school to ensure that the educational needs of all students, including those with disabilities or other special educational needs, are identified and provided for. The Education for Persons With Special Educational Needs Act 2004 (Government of Ireland, 2004b) makes provision for the education of people with special educational needs and establishes the National Council for Special Education. The Act provides for the education of children with special educational needs in an inclusive environment, unless that is inconsistent with the best interests of the child or the children with whom the child is to be educated. The Act provides for the arrangement of assessments by schools, health authorities, or the National Council for Special Education and sets a timescale for such assessments. The school principal is required by the Act to have an education plan prepared for the appropriate education of the student, subsequent to the assessment. The National Council for Special Education may require a psychologist employed by the minister for education and science to join a team to prepare an education plan on behalf of the Council. The school principal, being supplied with necessary monies and support services, is required to implement the education plan.

Preparation of School Psychologists

There are two postgraduate training programmes in educational psychology in Ireland. The Psychological Society of Ireland offers a Diploma in Professional Psychology (Educational) on the basis of independent study. This programme, currently under review, is being undertaken by 14 trainees and is typically completed in 3 to 4 years. Since its inception in 1991, the diploma has been awarded to 14 psychologists. In order to successfully complete the programme, candidates must satisfactorily undertake 120 days placement in psychological services, complete a dissertation, pass four examinations, and submit several reports on casework and interventions with a range of client groups. Candidates without teaching qualifications or experience must complete a school placement. The diploma curriculum specifies both necessary knowledge and skills.

The core curriculum areas are as follows: (1) knowledge areas, including (a) cognitive development and learning, (b) physical, emotional, and social development, (c) education systems, professional and interprofessional issues, and (d) education for special needs; and (2) skill areas, including (a) teaching and school experience, (b) assessment and reporting, (c) skills and strategies for intervention, (d) consultation and training, and (e) research and evaluation.

University College Dublin has, since 1995, offered a master of arts in educational psychology. This 2-year programme (direct entry to Year 2 is possible for qualified teachers) is accredited by the Psychological Society of Ireland; currently, 12 students graduate per annum. Based within the education department, training is delivered mainly through lectures, seminars, and training placements. Following its recent accreditation (2005) by the Psychological Society of Ireland, the University College Dublin Master of Arts in Educational Psychology will become a 2-year programme for all participants. The domains of knowledge addressed are as follows: (a) foundation studies, which include educational psychology, developmental psychology, social psychology, social policy, special educational needs provision and legislation, occupational psychology, and counselling psychology; (b) knowledge of special educational needs/disabilities, which includes special educational needs and disabilities, aetiology assessment, and intervention; (c) nature of psychological interventions, which includes individualized planning, systemic and consultative interventions; (d) requisite skills for psychological interventions, which include psychometric assessment, report writing, counselling and communication skills, and professional and ethical issues; and (e) research, which includes research methodologies and statistical analysis. Students are required to complete 80 days of professional training placement and to submit a dissertation.

The duration of journeys to employment as an educational psychologist vary because of differing entry requirements and differing training programmes. (Notably, neither training programme in educational psychology requires prior teaching qualifications and experience.) Illustrative examples are (a) 3 years teacher training, 3 years teaching experience, 2 years postgraduate diploma in psychology, and a 1-year master of arts in educational psychology, totaling 9 years of study; (b) 3 years primary degree in psychology, 1 year teacher training, 3 years teaching experience, 1 year master of arts in educational psychology, totaling 8 years of study; or (c) 3 years primary degree in psychology, 1 year postgraduate training in counselling psychology, 3 years working as a psychologist, totaling 7 years. It is likely that the impending developments in the training of educational psychologists in the United Kingdom (moving in 2006 to 3-year doctoral training without the requirement of teaching experience) will have an influence on training models in Ireland. A number of the educational psychologists working in Ireland have trained outside the country, particularly in the United Kingdom.

Roles, Functions, and Responsibilities of School Psychologists

Educational psychologists typically provide a range of services to schools, including consultation and advice, training, and working with individual students. The National Educational Psychological Service model of service is one where consultation provides an overarching framework for service delivery. This model strikes a balance between consultation and casework about individual children, support and development work that involves systems-level consultation, and work of a preventative and developmental nature. In this service, a psychologist will typically provide service to about 20 schools, both primary and post-primary, but this number will vary according to the size and profile of the schools. Following an initial annual planning and review

meeting in each school, a programme of work for the year will be initiated. Support and development work with schools may address topics such as screening programmes, organisation and delivery of learning support and resource teaching services, promotion of mental health, and prevention of behavioural difficulties. Support and development work will often arise from individual casework.

In relation to individual casework, the National Educational Psychological Service Model of Service (National Educational Psychological Service, 2003c) envisages a three-stage process involving possible consultation and advice for class teachers and specialist teachers at Stages 1 and 2 and direct involvement at Stage 3. The educational psychologist will typically meet with parents and teachers prior to seeing a student. Direct involvement may involve observation of the student, consultation with parents and teachers, an assessment of the student's achievements, abilities, and needs, and the formulation of advice on interventions. The main psychometric instruments in use include the Wechsler Intelligence Scale for Children, the British Ability Scales, and the Wechsler Individual Achievement Test–United Kingdom. Dynamic assessment approaches are also employed. In the domain of social-emotional-behavioural functioning, the most commonly used assessment instruments are the Conners Rating Scales and the Child Behaviour Checklist. Guidelines on a continuum of support that will assist schools and psychologists in implementing provision for students with special educational needs, in a staged manner and corresponding to the model of service, are being developed.

Because National Educational Psychological Service psychologists are employees of the Department of Education and Science, they also provide certain services which arise from that status, for example, the provision of advice to the minister of education and science and to her department. Psychologists also furnish the State Examination Commission with recommendations on applications for reasonable accommodations in certificate examination for persons with specific learning disabilities. An important role for educational psychologists is the provision of support and advice to schools in relation to critical incidents that affect the school community. The National Educational Psychological Service has provided each school in the country with an information pack on responding to critical incidents (National Educational Psychological Service, 2003b). The National Educational Psychological Service also advises the National Council for Special Education on a range of issues.

In their work with schools, educational psychologists work collaboratively with principal teachers, class teachers, and specialist teachers, including learning support teachers, resource teachers, and guidance counsellors, as well as resource teachers for travellers, home school liaison teachers, visiting teachers for students with visual and auditory disabilities, and special needs assistants. Learning support teachers (formerly described as remedial teachers) work in both primary schools and post-primary schools. The learning support guidelines (Government of Ireland, 2000c) focus the attention of learning support teachers especially on those pupils who are performing at or below the 10th percentile on nationally standardised tests of English reading, mathematics, or both.

In mainstream schools, the role of resource teachers is primarily to support students with special educational needs. In the recent Department of Education and Science (2005c) guidance to schools, it is envisaged that both the learning support teacher and the resource teacher will work with students who have learning difficulties and those who have high incidence special educational needs under the general allocation model. Resource teachers are envisaged as providing support to students with low incidence special educational needs who have a specific allocation of resource teaching hours.

Guidance counsellors, located in the vast majority of second-level schools, are qualified teachers who successfully complete the Higher Diploma in Guidance and Counselling, a 1-year full-time university-based programme. The role of the guidance counsellor includes a number of related functions. In collaboration with other school staff, the guidance counsellor delivers educational and career guidance services. This role includes the provision of information, the promotion of career development, and engagement in group and individual educational and career counselling. Guidance counsellors employ a range of assessment tools, including the Differential Aptitude Tests and occupational interest tests and inventories (Darbey, 2003). In addition to their role in the area of career guidance, guidance counsellors also promote personal social development and provide individual and group counselling in both developmental and problem-solving contexts. The Institute of Guidance Counsellors is the relevant professional body, and the National Centre for Guidance in Education provides an information and advisory service.

Current Issues Impacting School Psychology

Emerging trends in Irish education that present challenges to school psychology services include the policy of inclusion and the needs of students for whom English is an additional language. There is also a clear need to improve the links between the many services for children. In light of the increasing number of support services to schools, there is a need to further clarify what are the most appropriate roles for educational psychologists in the educational system. The delineation of the most effective roles for educational psychologists should be followed by the active promotion of such roles. Operational challenges to school psychology services are to maintain a focus on providing services to all students while meeting the requirements of students with special needs. Few special schools and units are in receipt of a comprehensive school psychology service. Issues that are increasing in priority in Irish schools are the promotion of mental health, including the reduction of challenging behaviour and the prevention of suicide. Improving literacy skills is also a key objective. The capacity of psychological services to provide appropriate levels of service to all schools and other education centres is a matter that requires review.

References

Central Statistics Office. (2003). *Census 2002 principal demographic results*. Dublin: Stationery Office.

Central Statistics Office. (2005a). *Population and migration estimates*. Retrieved October 1, 2005, from http://www.cso.ie

Central Statistics Office. (2005b). *Statistical yearbook of Ireland*. Dublin: Stationery Office.

Coolahan, J. (1981). *Irish education: History and structure*. Dublin: Institute of Public Administration.

Darbey, L. (2003). *Assessment testing: Findings of a survey on the training needs of guidance counsellors in post-primary schools*. Dublin: National Centre for Guidance in Education. Retrieved September 12, 2005, from http://www.ncge.ie/reports/Assess_Test_Survey03.doc

Department of Education and Science. (1966). *Investment in education*. Dublin: Stationery Office.

Department of Education and Science. (2004a). *A brief description of the Irish education system*. Dublin: Stationery Office.

Department of Education and Science. (2004b). *Statistical report 2002/2003*. Dublin: Stationery Office.

Department of Education and Science. (2005a). *Key education statistics 1993/1994–2003/04*. Retrieved September 1, 2005, from http://www.education.ie

Department of Education and Science. (2005b). *DEIS (Delivering Equality of Opportunity in Schools): An action plan for educational inclusion*. Dublin: Author.

Department of Education and Science. (2005c, August). *Organisation of teaching resources for pupils who need additional support in mainstream primary schools* (Special Education Circular SP ED 02/05). Dublin: Author.

Department of Education and Science. (2005d). *National Educational Psychological Service*. Retrieved September 9, 2005, from http://www.education.ie

Economic and Social Research Institute. (2005). *Irish economy overview*. Retrieved September 9, 2005, from http://www.esri.ie/content.cfm?t=Irish%20Economy&mid=4

Fitzpatrick Associates & O'Connell, P. J. (2005). *A review of higher education participation in 2003*. Dublin. Higher Education Authority.

Government of Ireland. (1988). *Data Protection Act 1988*. Dublin: Stationery Office.

Government of Ireland. (1993). *The Report of the Special Educational Review Committee*. Dublin: Stationery Office.

Government of Ireland. (1997). *The Freedom of Information Act 1997*. Dublin: Stationery Office.

Government of Ireland. (1998a). *Education Act 1998*. Dublin: Stationery Office.

Government of Ireland. (1998b). *A National Educational Psychological Service: Report of Planning Group*. Dublin: Stationery Office.

Government of Ireland. (2000a). *Educational Welfare Act 2000*. Dublin: Stationery Office.

Government of Ireland. (2000b). *The Equal Status Act 2000*. Dublin: Stationery Office.

Government of Ireland. (2000c). *Learning support guidelines*. Dublin: Stationery Office.

Government of Ireland. (2001a). *Report of the Task Force on Autism*. Dublin: Stationery Office.

Government of Ireland. (2001b). *Report of the Task Force on Dyslexia*. Dublin: Stationery Office.

Government of Ireland. (2004a). *Health Care and Social Professionals Bill 2004*. Dublin: Stationery Office.

Government of Ireland. (2004b). *Education for Persons With Special Educational Needs Act 2004*. Dublin: Stationery Office.

National Economic and Social Forum. (2002). *Early school leavers* (Forum Report No. 24). Dublin: Author.

National Educational Psychological Service. (2001). *Statement of strategy 2001–2004: Working together to make a difference for children*. Dublin: Author.

National Educational Psychological Service. (2003a). *Report on NEPS 1999–2001*. Dublin: Author.

National Educational Psychological Service. (2003b). *Responding to critical incidents: Advice and information pact for schools*. Dublin: Author.

National Educational Psychological Service. (2003c). *Working together to make a difference for children: The NEPS model of service.* Dublin: Author.

National Educational Welfare Board. (2005). *School attendance at primary and post primary schools 2003/2004.* Dublin: Author. Retrieved September 12, 2005, from http://www.newb.ie/reports/attendance_2003.shtml

Psychological Society of Ireland. (1974). *A psychological service to schools.* Dublin: Author.

Swan, D. (1981). A psychological service in national schools in Ireland—A dream that is dying? *Irish Educational Studies, 1,* 143–155.

19

School Psychology in Israel

Bernie Stein

Context of School Psychology

The State of Israel, established in 1948 as a homeland for the Jewish people, has absorbed immigrants from many cultures and is now a unique multicultural society. Israel is located in the Middle East, bordered on the west by the Mediterranean Sea, by Lebanon on the north, by Syria, Jordan, and the West Bank on the east, and by Egypt on the southwest. The geography includes desert in the south, low coastal plains, and central mountains. Israel is 20,770 square kilometers with a population in 2006 of 7.1 million: 81% Jews and 19% Arabs. The gross domestic product for 2005 was US$141 billion, US$20,800 per capita. Public services, agriculture, manufacturing, finance, tourism, high-tech, and commerce represent the primary employment opportunities.

The total school-age population in 2006 was 1,379,897: 784,000 in elementary school (Grades 1–6), 254,400 in junior high school (Grades 7–9), and 346,765 in high school (Grades 10–12).

There are 4,395 schools, 51,871 classrooms, and 124,000 teachers in Israel. In addition, 481,000 3- to 5-year-olds attend kindergarten. School attendance in Israel is mandatory from age 5 through 16 and free through age 18. For children with special needs, education is free for ages 3 through 21. A recently enacted law extends free education to all children from the age of 3; however, due to budgetary constraints, its implementation has been confined, for the present, to some of the poorer urban areas. Preschool education comprises a network of institutions that includes 481,000 children ages 2 through 6 (in 2005–2006) attending municipal, public, and private kindergartens and day care institutions (80% in public kindergartens). Increasing emphasis on preschool education was prompted by strong interest in addressing developmental problems during early childhood. The early childhood education system aims to establish a shared foundation that includes developing language and cognitive skills, promoting learning and creative abilities, and

AUTHOR'S NOTE: The author would like to thank Sharona Maital for her helpful comments on an earlier draft of this chapter.

nurturing social and motor skills. Both school psychologists and developmental psychologists have played a major role in lobbying parliamentary committees to pass a law setting the age of 3 as the beginning of compulsory education in the country.

Maintaining educational institutions is the joint responsibility of the state and local education authorities. The state pays the teachers' salaries and covers the cost of the physical infrastructure, whereas the local authorities are responsible for school services, including school psychologists. Jewish parents can choose schools affiliated with one of three recognized educational trends: state (57.6%), state-religious (18.8%), or ultra-Orthodox (23.6%). The state system is equivalent to the standard educational system in most countries, whereas the state-religious system adds hours to the state curriculum devoted to the study of religious texts and to prayer. In the ultra-Orthodox system, nonreligious subjects are a very limited part of the curriculum, and most of the time is devoted to the study of religious texts. Arab children are educated in a separate network, where Hebrew is taught as a second language. Few educational institutions cater to both Jewish and Arab students.

The Compulsory Education Law was enacted in 1949, the year following the establishment of the State of Israel. Amendments enacted since then include a prohibition against discrimination on grounds of ethnic origin and a prohibition against discrimination in acceptance, placement, and advancement of pupils, as well as a prohibition against punishing pupils for parental actions or omissions. (An English summary of the most important laws relating to education in Israel can be found online at http://www.jewishvirtuallibrary.org/jsource/Education/edlaws.html)

The educational system includes both formal and informal frameworks. Formal education includes institutions at the preschool, primary, secondary (junior high and high school), post-secondary, and university levels. Informal education includes social and youth activities in various educational spheres that take place after school hours, such as extracurricular activities, assistance for children experiencing learning difficulties in school, sports activities, youth movements, and adult education. Of all pupils in high school, 95.4% complete 12 years of education, and 56% sit for the matriculation examinations at various levels. The matriculation certificate is a prerequisite for university entrance (together with a standardized test). The average class size is identified in the Ministry of Education publications as 25.5 in elementary schools, 31 in junior high schools, and 26.2 in high schools. However, these figures are misleading, because the average includes small special education classes (usually 8–12 pupils); thus, many elementary through high school classes have 35 to 40 pupils.

The Special Education Law was enacted in 1988. Although the state had provided special education services to children with special needs since its establishment in 1948, in 1988 a law was adopted that ensured these services to all individuals, ages 3 through 21 years, who require them. The disabilities covered by the law are deafness, blindness, children in hospital, mild to severe retardation, behavior disorders, cerebral palsy, learning disabilities, autism, delayed language development, and mental illness. Approximately 2% of pupils diagnosed with special needs now attend separate schools, pointing to a significant drop from 8% in the 1970s. The change reflects the policy that the Ministry of Education has adopted over the past 20 years, seeking to provide inclusive education for pupils with special needs and keeping the numbers attending separate institutions to a minimum. In the 2004–2005 academic year, 17,000 students received special education services in separate settings, about 25,000 students received special education services through local support and resource centers, and the remainder of students received special services within regular classrooms. (An English summary of the law can be found online at http://www.kinneret.co.il/benzev/yacov/sped law.htm)

Much of the work of the school psychologist is mandated by the Law of Special Education, and most of the pupils with special needs will only become eligible for help after undergoing a psychological evaluation. The school psychologist is a mandatory member in various statutory committees that decide on the placement of students. A child experiencing problems at school is tested by a school psychologist and, if deemed eligible for special education services, is referred to a local placement committee that also includes a school psychologist. The committees are instructed by the Ministry of Education to give priority to placing the child in a recognized school that is not a special education school. A child with special needs, a parent, or a representative of a public organization can appeal a decision of the placement committee within 21 days. The Ministry of Education must then appoint a seven-member board of appeal, which also includes a senior school psychologist, to confirm or overturn the placement committee's original decision. Special education laws have been extensively revised over the past 5 years, partly in response to parental advocacy demanding that children with special needs be included in regular classrooms. The Law of Inclusion, enacted in 2002, gives parents considerable rights with respect to placement and creates a multilevel hearing system. Decisions about special needs at the school level are made at a school-based, statutory committee meeting convened by the school principal, involving the school psychologist, who submits a psychological evaluation, as well as parents and teachers.

Origin, History, and Current Status of School Psychology

Local development of school psychology began when the first Center for Educational Psychology was established in Tel Aviv in 1936, under the auspices of the local municipality, and became the model for similar services elsewhere in Israel. The primary, and often the only, focus of their work was testing and placement. After 1948, freelance psychologists were employed by the Ministry of Education to travel throughout the country to test children experiencing difficulties at school and refer them to special education frameworks. The major thrust to the development of a statewide framework came in 1962, with the establishment of the Psychological and Counseling Service (known by its Hebrew acronym, SHEFI) at the Ministry of Education. Besides establishing the new profession of school counselor, this new department at the Ministry assumed the task of developing, planning, and implementing the work of school psychologists. The division of psychological and counseling services included the position of chief psychologist and established a crucial strategic decision: School psychology services would be provided under municipal auspices, to ensure that psychologists were employed by the local community and could serve as child advocates, rather than by the schools or by the Ministry of Education to serve the needs of the institution. This policy was mainly inspired by several Israeli psychologists who had recently returned from pursuing doctoral studies at American universities and had been influenced by two main trends: Gerald Caplan's ideas of preventive community psychiatry (Caplan, 1964) and Emory Cowen's Primary Mental Health Project (Cowen, Gesten, & Wilson, 1979). These theories introduced concepts of community mental health and a systemic approach to intervention in schools, in contrast with the views endorsed by the practitioners of the time, most of whom had trained in Europe before World War II. A major influence on an entire generation of young professionals was that of Kalman Benyamini, who served as the first chief psychologist when the Psychological and Counseling Service was set up, initiated the first courses in school psychology at the Hebrew University, and took over as director of the school psychology service in Jerusalem, implementing a systemic approach to work in schools. (For a comprehensive review of psychology in Israel, see Levinson, 1977.)

Much has changed since the first article on school psychology in Israel was published in *Psychology in the Schools in International Perspective*, Volume 2 (Ziv, 1977). The population of the country has almost doubled, and a substantial wave of immigration from the former Soviet Union has had a dramatic impact on the society. The school population has increased and so has the number of pupils in need of psychological intervention. Children of immigrants from Ethiopia and some of the Asian ex-Soviet Republics who came from widely different cultural backgrounds, and many without any prior schooling, posed special problems to teachers, challenging their tolerance of cultural differences. Schools have played a major role in the acculturation process, especially in the teaching of a new language, and psychologists were significant in helping the educational system deal with pupils manifesting learning, social, and emotional difficulties. Together with the difficulties involved in integrating an increasing and varied population, the country has also faced an ongoing conflict with the Palestinians during this period and has suffered sporadic waves of terrorism, which has left many physical and psychological scars in all sectors of society. School psychological services have grown proportionately to the population and, over the past 15 years, have more than doubled. At present, 270 municipal and regional services in the country employ 2,100 school psychologists.

The Psychological and Counseling Service currently budgets and supervises 270 school psychology services throughout the country. Financing is the shared responsibility of the Ministry of Education (two thirds) and the local municipalities (one third). There are 1,100 positions filled by 2,100 school psychologists employed by the local municipalities and regional councils (most psychologists work part-time). Nearly all the country's 284 cities and local and regional councils have a school psychology service. The country is divided into six districts; each has a district school psychologist employed by the Psychological and Counseling Service, who is responsible for overseeing the work of the services in the district.

During the past decade, an important area of development has been school psychology services for the Arab population. In 1995, only six Arab centers had school psychology services, both because Arab society was less open to psychology and because the country had very few Arab psychologists. Over 5 years, 40 new services were established in Arab and Bedouin centers employing more than 120 psychologists, and an Arab deputy chief psychologist was appointed to supervise them. The Arab society in Israel has gradually changed its attitude to psychology, and only staff shortages prevent further growth.

The current ratio of school psychologists to number of pupils is 1 to 1,500. The ideal ratio has been defined as 1 to 1,000. The percentage of women in the profession has increased over the years; when the last survey was taken, in 2002, 78% of school psychologists were female. In managerial positions, however, men outnumber women three to one. School psychologists are relatively young, the average age being 42.1 years ($SD = 8.39$ years). Increased demand for their services has led to a significant influx of younger psychologists into the school psychology services. This has resulted in a rather troubling development, given that approximately half the psychologists working in the system are either interns or unlicensed.

Close to 3,500 guidance counselors are employed directly by the schools. They deal mainly with learning problems and with the delivery of a number of prevention programs developed in the Psychological and Counseling Service over the years (drug and alcohol abuse, violence, child abuse), as well as with several other programs dealing with life skills training and sex education, implemented throughout the school system. The Psychological and Counseling Service also serves as a consultant to the minister of education and to decision makers in the Ministry with regard to educational policy issues.

The major development in the profession over the past 30 years is the transformation of conceptual foundations underlying the work of the school psychologist, involving a shift from an individual, child-centered approach to a systemic outlook that makes the school, rather than the child, the client. Instead of testing "problem children" and directing them to "appropriate" educational settings, schools are encouraged to address the pupils' special needs and keep them in regular schools, implicitly endorsing the motto of the well-known Polish educator Janus Korczak, who maintains that there are no bad children, there are only bad conditions. Psychologists consequently spend much less time in their clinics and more time working in the schools, going into classrooms, meeting with teachers, and helping their local municipalities to formulate educational policies. A further development is that school psychologists have assumed an active role, both in the schools and in the communities, in dealing with the aftermath of crisis situations (such as terrorist attacks, accidents, deaths, suicides, and natural disasters) and in setting up training programs to prepare school staffs to deal with future crises (Stein, 1997).

Psychology remains highly rated in occupational surveys and continues to attract some of the best students, thus ensuring that, barring some unforeseen development, it should retain this status in the future. Most comparative studies also find that psychologists report high levels of satisfaction with their work, and these findings were confirmed in an extensive 1996 survey of all school psychologists working in the Israeli system (Raviv, Mashraki-Pedhatzur, Raviv, & Erhard, 2002). Among 1,700 psychologists who were then working in 240 school psychology services throughout the country, findings indicated a high degree of job satisfaction, including a feeling that their work was appreciated by the people they worked with, that is, children, parents, teachers, principals, and public officials. When asked about the sources of satisfaction in their work, the following variables rated highly: good interpersonal relationships with colleagues; good working relationships with professionals in other fields, both in schools and in the community; good relations with teachers; good relations with principals; opportunities for in-service training and further education; and opportunities for professional advancement. Major sources of positive feelings were good interpersonal relationships with other staff members and excellent supervision and support systems. The following factors were mentioned as causes of dissatisfaction: too many demands on their limited time; too little time allocated for the tasks they were given; lack of support from their professional organizations; and poor university training that did not prepare them for the realities of their work.

In 2001, a survey of school principals obtained views concerning available psychological services (Erhard, 2001). Questionnaires were sent to all 2,928 elementary and secondary schools in the country; 53% of the principals responded. Kindergartens are administered by a different Ministry of Education department and were not included in the survey, which is unfortunate, given that school psychology services in Israel give priority to this age-group. Principals were asked: "What is your level of satisfaction with the psychological services provided at your school?" Answers were on a scale of 1 (*very dissatisfied*) to 6 (*very satisfied*). Results were very positive: 49.2% of the principals said they were satisfied or very satisfied with the psychological services provided to the school, 36.7% expressed moderate satisfaction, and 14.6% said they were dissatisfied or very dissatisfied with the service. A major factor of dissatisfaction was the limited extent of psychological services available to the school, mostly due to a lack of financial resources. A further, and perhaps vital, finding of this survey was that 89% of the principals said they wanted the psychologist to work more hours at the school; only 0.5% said they wanted the psychologist to spend less time at the school. School psychologists are more widely available in urban areas. The vast majority of school psychologists in Israel work in the public sector, although many of those in senior positions also work privately, mainly testing for learning disabilities.

Entry requirements to undergraduate psychology programs at Israeli universities include exceptionally high matriculation and psychometric scores. Admittance to a graduate program in clinical or school psychology is even harder, demanding very high grades at the undergraduate level. Only about 1 in 10 applicants is accepted, and training and internship are long and demanding. As described in the next section, after completing 5 to 6 years of study to obtain a master's degree, psychologists do an internship in an applied field such as school, clinical, developmental, or rehabilitation psychology for at least 2 years. They then present a written case study and take an oral exam. One would expect those who succeed in this lengthy process to feel that they belong to a privileged elite entitled to professional respect and adequate material reward. However, psychologists are one of the lowest paid professional groups in Israel (especially during the first years of in-service training), and their physical working environments are often of rather poor quality.

Infrastructure of School Psychology

The Israel Psychological Association is the sole professional organization for licensed psychologists. It includes sections for several subspecialties, including one for school psychology. Membership is voluntary, but most practicing school psychologists are members. The school psychology section organizes an annual 4-day seminar for school psychologists and conducts wage negotiations with employers. In 1977, the Law of Psychologists was enacted after prolonged lobbying by the Israeli Psychological Association. Through this law, the association sought to protect the public from people who lacked suitable academic training and were practicing as "psychologists." The law defined very clearly who may use the title of psychologist. The Ministry of Health was given responsibility for administering the law and issuing licenses to those who have

fulfilled the legal requirements. The law requires the Ministry of Health to set up a "Council of Psychologists" to oversee its implementation and suggest changes deemed necessary in the light of developments. The council includes 31 psychologists representing the various divisions of the Israel Psychological Association, the universities, and the major employers (the ministries of health, education, and welfare). The Council has professional committees to manage the training and licensing of specialists in the areas of school, clinical, developmental, rehabilitation, medical, and industrial psychology, as well as accrediting frameworks wherein psychologists can train for specialization. A special committee deals with complaints against psychologists and has powers to implement disciplinary measures for ethical or criminal offenses, including the withholding of licenses. As of 2005, the total number of registered psychologists was 8,600, of which 1,390 (16%) are licensed school psychologists. Many of the psychologists employed as school psychologists are not licensed as school psychologists.

Preparation of School Psychologists

To be licensed as a psychologist by the Ministry of Health, applicants are required to show that they have studied for at least 5 years and graduated with a master's degree from one of the five recognized universities in Israel (or at an equivalent institution abroad). They are then allowed to register at a recognized school psychology clinic and begin a training program for licensing. The law requires at least 2 years of full-time or 4 years of half-time work under supervision (at least 300 hours) and an oral examination at the end of the process. The trainee has to work and gain experience in the following areas: (a) individual diagnosis and evaluation of children and adolescents over a wide range of learning, behavioral, and emotional problems, using different kinds of tests, including specific tests for learning disabilities; (b) diagnosis and evaluation of group processes in the school system (at least 10 cases); (c) therapeutic interventions for children and their families (at least 30 cases); (d) psychological interventions in various educational frameworks: kindergarten, elementary school, high school, and a special education framework school; and (e) participation in in-service training programs (at least 100 hours). The final (oral) examination for obtaining licensing as a school psychologist requires that the candidate demonstrate proficiency in the following areas: (a) the school system—the school as the "client," systemic interventions, organizational interventions; crisis interventions; parent groups; (b) individual diagnosis and evaluation—learning disabilities, behavioral and emotional problems, and so on; and (c) therapeutic intervention—individuals, families, and groups.

The next phase of professional development is a license to supervise trainees. This process may begin only 3 years after being licensed as a school psychologist. The candidate must work half-time for at least 2 years in a recognized clinic, supervise at least two trainees, and be supervised by at least two licensed school psychology supervisors. A supervisor's license is granted on the basis of a written recommendation by the two supervisors who monitored the work. Psychologists with a master's degree in another field of psychology may also train to become school psychologists, but they either have to return to the university to attend courses in the subjects they did not study during their master's program or participate in specially tailored in-service training programs.

All five Israeli universities have master's-degree programs in psychology. Only one, however, offers a program in school psychology (Ben-Gurion University in Beersheba). The others have replaced their school psychology programs with master's programs in child clinical psychology, established in addition to their clinical psychology programs. The reason is that the status of clinical psychology has always been higher than that of other applied fields, and very few students were attracted to school psychology programs. As part of the child clinical master's-level practicum, however, students must also work in educational settings, and the program includes several courses in school psychology subjects. Many of these graduates end up working in the school psychology services because that is where most of the job openings are. There is a definite need for a separate profession of school psychology, but the reality of the profession in Israel is that it enjoys much lower prestige than the far more popular one of clinical psychology. The practical solution has been for school psychology to accept into its ranks psychologists with academic training in other applied areas and to train them in the field.

Each of the five university programs admits about 15 students a year, so that close to 75 school and child clinical psychologists graduate every year. Many psychologists have also entered the country as immigrants, and many opt to undergo the necessary training to become licensed to practice as school psychologists. Together with local psychologists, who have graduated locally in areas other than the educational and child clinical ones, they attend in-service training courses in four key areas: the work of the psychologist in the schools, psychological assessment, normal development and psychopathology, and treatment of children.

The academic and professional preparation provides training in core academic knowledge in psychology (development, learning and cognition, educational, personality, social, experimental, biological, statistics, and research design); assessment services (intellectual, academic, emotional, and social assessment); intervention services (behavioral, affective, educational, and social-systems); focus on children and youth (within the context of classrooms, schools, families, communities, and other systems); interpersonal skills (establishing trust and rapport, listening, and communication skills); professional decision-making skills; statistical methods and research design; and the services' legal and ethical basis. Training programs in Israel rely mainly on professional literature from the United States, but several Hebrew publications specifically aimed at school psychologists are available, although no Israeli academic journal deals with school psychology per se. There are doctoral programs in psychology at all of the five universities, but since the entrance requirement for work is a master's degree, the doctoral program is academic and not specific to applied areas such as school or clinical psychology.

Roles, Functions, and Responsibilities of School Psychologists

The typical activities, roles, and responsibilities of school psychologists include observations in classrooms; consultations with teachers, principals, and other professionals working in the schools; testing pupils referred for learning and behavior problems; participation in various mandatory frameworks; deciding on interventions and referrals of individual cases; and treatment (usually short-term) for children and/or their families. Other activities include preparing crisis response teams in schools or crisis interventions after a violent or traumatic event in the school or the community. In addition, all school psychologists in training receive at least one hour a week of individual supervision from one of the senior members of the clinic where they work, and also participate in in-service training seminars held on a regular basis.

The tests most widely used to evaluate intellectual ability are the Wechsler Intelligence Scale for Children, third edition, and the Kaufman Assessment Battery for Children, both of which have been standardized for the Israeli population (norms for these tests are currently being developed for the Arab population). Recently, the Wechsler Adult Intelligence Scale was standardized for high school students, and Israeli norms have been developed for several specific tests for learning disabilities. The Henrietta

Szold Institute has developed group tests of achievement for various age levels, as well as tests that identify gifted children. The most commonly used personality tests are the Rorschach and Thematic Apperception Test, although these are gradually losing in popularity and more emphasis is being placed on observations and interviews.

The 2002 survey (Raviv et al., 2002) found that, on average, school psychologists devoted three fifths of their time outside the psychological center to system-oriented activities such as consultation (with principals and teachers) and to administrative work, staff meetings, and supervision within the center. The rest of their time was devoted to clinically oriented activities such as diagnostic testing, individual therapy with children, and parent counseling. An interesting finding is that the school psychologists themselves envisage their desired role as that of a clinician who spends most of his or her time working with children in individual therapy, counseling with parents, and, to some extent, consulting teachers. The older and more experienced psychologists were found to spend relatively more time in organizational activities, supervising interns, and doing individual therapy.

Current Issues Impacting School Psychology

The most serious problem confronting the profession of school psychology is the concern about financing services in the future. There is a continuing possibility of privatization of school psychology services, mainly as a result of the government's neoconservative economic policies, which are gradually eroding the country's welfare state structure. In an attempt to preempt such a move, the Psychological and Counseling Service developed a "service basket" prescribing the essential services for which all children are eligible free of charge, mainly detailing the basic statutory services related to diagnostic work with children with special needs. This is a major achievement, in that it has helped to create a relatively uniform system of mandatory services throughout the country. Mandatory services include consultation with school personnel regarding pupils with problems; children at risk–systemic intervention in the community; diagnosis and evaluation of children with special needs (as mandated in the special education laws), and participation in the various placement committees at the school and district levels; therapeutic interventions with children at risk (up to five sessions); and crisis intervention at the individual, school, and community levels.

The service basket also delineates three further levels of service priorities, to be provided when the necessary personnel are available at the local school psychology service. These include participation in interdisciplinary committees that set up treatment programs for children with special needs; consultations with principals and teachers to promote social and emotional processes in the schools; consulting with municipal health and welfare agencies; participation in local educational steering committees; short-term therapy and counseling for children and parents; and diagnostic work to determine school readiness. Finally, the "service basket" lists services to be provided only if funded or paid for by the client. These include testing for giftedness and for special accommodations for students with learning disabilities; therapy beyond the first five sessions; group work with children; parent groups; and lectures and workshops for school personnel. Many school psychology services (especially the larger urban ones) now provide such additional services, using the income to supplement the budget of the school psychological service and offset the periodic budgetary cuts.

In October 2003, the government appointed a National Task Force for the Advancement of Education in Israel. The Task Force mandate was to conduct a comprehensive examination of the Israeli education system, recommend an inclusive plan for pedagogical, structural, and organizational changes, and spell out the means of implementing it (Ministry of Education, 2005). The impetus for reform came from public outcry at the alarmingly low achievements of Israeli pupils in the Program for International Student Assessment (PISA) studies of international comparisons. Although the report is very comprehensive, it says little about psychological services in the schools, leading to understandable anxiety within the profession and to extensive lobbying seeking to at least maintain current levels of psychological services in schools. The report sets a standard for services to be provided by the proposed regional educational administrations, including psychologists, charged with implementing and overseeing the reforms. The proposed ratio of pupils to psychologists is about 30% lower than the currently recommended ones. Instead of school psychology services functioning as separate organizational units under municipal auspices, the regional educational administrations will have a pool of psychologists to carry out their work as needed. The report makes no provision for psychological services for children with special educational needs, for children requiring psychological help with emotional difficulties, for dealing with crises in the school or the community, for prevention programs, for early identification of developmental problems in 3- to 4-year-olds, or for dealing with the emotional climate in schools. If this reform is implemented, it will pose a serious threat to the entire structure of school psychology in Israel. In an attempt to confront this crisis, school psychologists have invested efforts in several forums set up over the past 10 years to prepare position papers on several major issues: early childhood education, special education, learning disabilities, violence, and treatment of victims of sexual abuse. Some of these have been presented to the Ministry of Education, and some of the recommendations have been adopted as official policy, notably with respect to kindergarten retention and accommodations for pupils diagnosed with learning difficulties.

Seeking to improve postgraduate in-service training for all school psychologists, a group of senior school psychologists has established an Institute for Advanced Studies in School Psychology, with the support of the Psychological and Counseling Service. This is a comprehensive program that will offer courses in various areas of specialization, including management and financial skills. A further goal is to create more uniform standards of practice and to work with the professional licensing committee to establish advanced certification in subspecialties within school psychology.

One of the profession's most serious problems is that it lacks political influence and has been unable to offer a clear image of its input as a group with superior training, well appreciated in their working environment, and making a significant contribution to a troubled multicultural society. Another threat to school psychology derives from the difficulty of differentiating the profession from school counseling, especially because requirements for school counseling have been upgraded in recent years, and certification now requires a master's degree. Many counselors now also receive advanced training in group and family therapy. School psychologists are also increasingly required to deal with multidisciplinary teams that may include occupational therapists, expressive therapists (in art, music, or movement), learning disability specialists, and didactic assessors. In order to address these threats, the newly created Institute for Advanced Studies is running an ongoing symposium for both senior and junior psychologists dealing with the profession's future directions. Another related issue is that school psychology has always suffered from perceptions of inferiority vis-à-vis clinical psychology, aggravated by the law stipulating that only clinical psychologists are allowed to do psychotherapy. This has motivated many school psychologists in Israel to complete postgraduate courses and do clinical internships in order to be allowed to work as psychotherapists.

Despite the challenges facing the profession, and notwithstanding the pressing current concerns about statutory changes and budgetary constraints, opportunities are still available for further development. If suitably exploited, they could prove no less exciting to the future of school psychology in Israel than the significant achievements attained over the past 50 years.

References

Caplan, G. (1964). *Principles of preventive psychiatry.* New York: Basic Books.

Cowen, E. L., Gesten, E. L., & Wilson, A. B. (1979). The Primary Mental Health Project: Evaluation of current program effectiveness. *American Journal of Community Psychology, 7,* 293–303.

Erhard, R. (2001). *Survey of school principals' satisfaction with school psychology services.* Jerusalem: Ministry of Education. (in Hebrew)

Levinson, S. (1997). Psychology in Israel. *Psichologia, 6*(1), 109–120. (in Hebrew)

Ministry of Education, National Task Force for the Advancement of Education in Israel. (2005, January). *The National Education Plan: Because every child deserves more* (Dovrat Report). (in Hebrew)

Raviv, A., Mashraki-Pedhatzur, S., Raviv, A., & Erhard, R. (2002). The Israeli school psychologist: A professional profile. *School Psychology International, 23*(3), 283–306.

Stein, B. (1997). Community reactions to disaster: An emerging role for the school psychologist. *School Psychology International, 18*(2), 99–118.

Ziv, A. (1977). School psychology in Israel. In C. D. Catterall (Ed.), *Psychology in the schools in international perspective,* Vol. 2. Columbus, OH: International School Psychology Steering Committee.

20

The Service of School Psychology in Italy

Julia Coyne

Carlo Trombetta

Context of School Psychology

Italy is located in Southern Europe. As a peninsula, it extends prominently into the central Mediterranean Sea. It has an area of 301,230 square kilometers, including its islands of Sardinia and Sicily. Border countries are Austria, France, the Holy See (Vatican City), San Marino, Slovenia, and Switzerland. The population in 2005 was over 58 million. The reproduction rate is approximately 1.26 children per woman. Ethnic groups include small clusters of German-, French-, and Slovene-Italians in the northand Albanian- and Greek-Italians in the south. The religious profile is predominantly Roman Catholic, with some Protestants and Jews and a growing Muslim immigrant community. Italy ranks second only to Japan in having the highest population percentage of those over age 40. Those over age 60 compose 24% of Italy's population; by 2050, this number is expected to exceed 42%. The level of education among adults aged 25 to 64 is relatively low; 25% of this population left school before obtaining a primary school exit certificate. Of the remaining adult population that obtained primary school certificates and continued with secondary schooling, 42% obtained a high school diploma, and 9% obtained a university degree (Organization for Economic Co-operation and Development, 2003).

The total population of school-age students (ages 5–19) is 15 million, a 16% decrease from 1992 to 1999 (U.S. Census Bureau, 2001). The population aged 5 to 19 corresponding to formal education constitutes 15% of the country's population. Students between ages 5 and 14 enrolled in primary and lower secondary school (middle school/junior high) compose 10% of the total population, which is the lowest percentage in the European Union, having decreased at a substantial rate during the past two decades (Organization for Economic Co-operation and Development,

2003). The gross domestic product in 2004 was US$1.609 trillion, US$27,700 per capita. Services (63%) and industry (32%) account for the majority of employment opportunities, and unemployment is less than 7%.

During the past 20 years, although the number of school-age students has decreased by 22% (2 million students), school attendance has increased at all levels. The rate of passage from lower secondary school to upper secondary school was 82% in 1981, 98% in 2001, and 99% in 2002, reflecting a positive relationship between compulsory attendance and promotion to higher levels of education. This is largely attributed to Law 53 of 2003, which mandates that compulsory education is to begin at age 6 years and end at age 14.

The Italian State is obligated to provide a school system that is accessible to all young people, consistent with their attitudes and aspirations, regardless of economic and social circumstances. The Constitution provides for three types of schools: state schools, managed directly by the state; equal schools, which are run by organizations or private citizens that are officially recognized by the state and are therefore authorized to provide diplomas of legal value; and private schools, not authorized to provide diplomas of legal value. There are approximately 16,000 private schools, two thirds of which are nursery schools. In school year 2001–2002, there were 1,152,656 school-age students enrolled in private schools (Organization for Economic Co-operation and Development, 2003). According to the Organization for Economic Co-operation and Development (2001), the nationwide average pupil-to-teacher ratio for primary and secondary schools is 11 to 1. Primary education (elementare) lasts 5 years and is compulsory for all children ages 6 through 11. Classes are usually no larger than 25 students, with a limit of 20 students for classes in which students with special needs are included. In such classes, a support teacher is provided in order to facilitate integration and learning (United Nations

Educational, Scientific and Cultural Organization, 2004).

Lower secondary education (scuola media), or middle/junior high school, spans 5 years and is compulsory for all children ages 11 through 14. The requisite for admission is the certificate of exit from a primary school, usually earned by age 11. After passing the lower secondary school examination, students may choose to pursue courses of study lasting 3 to 5 years (United Nations Educational, Scientific and Cultural Organization, 2004).

Upper secondary education (scuola superiore), or high school, consists of all schools offering post-compulsory instruction. Following the state exams, taken after the third year of lower secondary school, students decide which track to follow. A student may choose pre-university training or professional training. Pre-university training (liceo) lasts 5 years. Course work at this level includes classical, scientific, linguistic, artistic, technical, or vocational studies. Vocational schools offer 3- to 5-year programs that terminate with a diploma. Professional training, on the other hand, provides a 4-year skill-based program without a diploma. These two choices are not mutually exclusive at the upper secondary level. It is possible to complete secondary school while gaining work experience, allowing a student to concurrently earn a diploma and prepare for university study while gaining professional training. On completing upper secondary school, students take a state examination to certify their level of academic achievement (United Nations Educational, Scientific and Cultural Organization, 2004). In 2001, the secondary school graduation rate was 70% (Istituto per lo Sviluppo della Formazione Professionale dei Lavoratori, 2003).

Origin, History, and Current Status of School Psychology

The origin of the relationship between psychology and education in Italy is difficult to clearly delineate. The psychocultural needs of Italy have varied tremendously throughout its history, and its cultural needs have influenced individual needs in countless ways in socioeducational contexts.

Early Italian educational psychology was influenced by research that attempted to explain to teachers the function of students' psychological life. Teacher training manuals and treatises were based on experimental research by Sergi (1873), Broffiero (1889), and Marchesini (1895). The emerging field of educational psychology gradually attracted anthropological investigations of how students' biographical information relates to learning in the scholastic environment (Pizzoli, 1909). This new strain of social scientific inquiry provided a new methodology for conducting original educational research, further legitimizing the field of educational psychology (Trombetta, 2003). Learning theory was applied in schools, which eventually brought a pedagogical perspective to the study of intelligence (Saffiotti, 1912, 1913, 1916).

Early educational decision making about individual needs was limited to biographical knowledge gained through familiarity with the child (Melzi, 1899; Montessori, 1906; Pastorello, 1904) and was based only on casual physiological and psychological observations (DeDominicis, 1909; Gullini, 1919; Massa, 1908). In 1898, the National Law for the Protection of Deficient Children was passed with the assistance of the well-known practitioners Montessori, Montesano, and Baccelli. In the 1900s, Montesano opened the Orthophrenic School, collaborating with Montessori, who then developed a program whereby previously institutionalized individuals with handicaps were taught to read and write. De Sanctis worked with children with different types of mental retardation, recognizing the role that learning difficulty, sociocultural disadvantage, and cognitive impairment played in scholastic performance. He designed methods to distinguish different levels of cognitive function and developed the first individualized education plans in Italy (Cornoldi, 1991).

Trombetta (1997) describes the historical shift of service provision from the private to the public domain as broad historical strands that contribute to our understanding of the development of school psychology in Italy. The strands begin with "closed assistance" in the period prior to Il Risorgimento (the Resurgence), gradually becoming the second strand, "open assistance," with the establishment of specialized schools, laboratories, and clinics. A growing awareness of the benefits of psychology in the educational context provided an impetus for service providers to contribute to school- and community-based initiatives that impacted cognitive and behavioral levels of performance. The third strand describes practitioners, whom Trombetta calls "single social operators," working directly in schools to provide various social and psychological services.

In 1962, a broad political change affected the three major subcultures of Italian life (secular-progressive, Catholic, and Marxist), resulting in significant changes to Italian education (White, 1991). This movement had a profound impact on the availability and provision of related services for children with disabilities by bringing psychological issues out of the institution to be dealt with in social realms. Oakland, Cunningham, Meazzini, and Poulsen (1991) trace the origins of the anti-institutional movement to its roots in England with the work of Maxwell-Jones, who developed planned environmental therapy; Szaz, who rejected the very premise of mental illness; and Laing, who outlined the dehumanizing effects of mental institutions. In Italy, this era is noted for its lack of precise theory-based referencing and for the anti-institutional movement from which Law 517, known as Basaglia's law, was influenced. Under this law, children with handicaps were deinstitutionalized and reintegrated into their home communities, making their care the responsibility of the local school systems and community health centers. There was an increase in the number of mental health initiatives in schools as provided by psychological practitioners referred to by Trombetta (1997) as "social operators."

Through the 1970s, there was no specific program to train psychologists to work in schools. Nevertheless, psychologists continued to assist in inclusionary efforts and to participate in the psycho-socio-medical team model, which was favored by the National Health Service at that time. Concurrently, the Ministry of Public Instruction developed a model of psycho-socio-pedagogical service delivery assigned to create psychopedagogues as the first professionals sanctioned to undertake such work in schools due to the increase in the number of reintegrated students. Subsequently, rather heterogeneous and disjointed psychological practices developed in terms of individual consultation in the school, which eventually developed into the concept of "psychology in the school rather than school psychology" (Rubini, 2001, p. 257).

Currently, two terms are used to describe those with psychological training who work in schools. They are *psicopedagogisti* (psychopedagogues), developed from the specialization in psychology formed in 1978 under Law 517 of 1977, and *freelance psychologists* with various specialties (such as developmental or educational), who work in schools on a consultative or contractual basis. According to the Order of Psychologists, the professional association of psychologists in Italy, those who qualify can exercise all the functions and activities inherent to being a psychologist practicing in schools. The only distinction, which is not obligatory, has to do with freelance psychologists who participate in the country's National Health Service. The term *psychopedagogista* (psychopedagogue) has been replaced by the term *psychopedagogical operator* according to Ministerial Ordinance 282, 1989. Though psychology services are delivered in public and private schools, universities, and clinics and also local health agencies, the title of "school psychologist" is not officially recognized in Italy.

There are no current reliable data available regarding the number or gender representation of those who deliver psychology services in Italian schools. Thus, discussions concerning average salaries, the ratio of school psychologists to students, opportunities for continuous professional development, and other issues important for understanding the profession of school psychology within Italy are not possible at this time.

Infrastructure of School Psychology

There are several national and regional professional organizations that specifically serve the interests of promoting school psychology service delivery in Italy. Among them are La Societa' Italiana di Psicologia dell'Educazione e della Formazione (Italian Association of Educational Psychology and Training, www .sipef.it), which promotes research and professionalism among educational practitioners and educators, and Societa' Scientifica Italiana di Studi e Ricerca per lo Sviluppo della Psicologia in Ambito Scolastico e Formativo (Italian Association of the Study of Research and Training in the Psychology of the Scholastic Environment, www.sirpas.it), an association dedicated to research on training school and educational psychologists to work in school environments.

Currently, there are no nationally recognized regulations regarding licensure of school psychologists. Depending on type of certificate and nature of the academic and professional program, those with a degree in psychology may practice various types of psychology in the schools, including clinical, developmental, general, social, and educational. In reference to laws or other regulations governing the general practice of psychology, and school psychology in particular, Abruzzo, in February 2004, was Italy's first region to legislate the service of school psychology. Its proposal was initiated in June 2001 when a work group was instituted to develop a definition and guidelines for the service of school psychology. A protocol of intent was submitted in July 2000 to the Ministry of Public Instruction, the Conference of the Principal Chairs of the Faculty of Psychology, the Italian Association of Psychology, the Italian Society of Educational and Developmental Psychology, and the National Association for Principals and Educational Directors. The Ministry of Public Instruction, the Unified Association of Italian Psychologists, and the Italian Society of Scientific Psychology signed Article 2 of the protocol in November 2000. The work group created a set of guidelines that reflect culturally and scientifically relevant information to promote the service of school psychology as conducted by trained school psychologists. Their activities specifically address areas of competencies in school psychology and how to evaluate them. These guidelines establish a basis for requesting and providing psychological intervention and assist practitioners in further articulating the field of school psychology (Rubini, 1991). It is surmised that the legislation, which guides school psychology service delivery, will likely remain at the regional, as opposed to the national, level.

There are several laws or other regulations, specifically designed to govern special education, which have implications for delivery of school psychology as well. Among the more pertinent ones are legislative mandates approved by the Decree of the President of the Republic (DPR). Examples include DPR 416, 1974, Article 4, which calls for specialists with medical, psycho-socio-pedagogical orientations to be of service to schools; Law 517, 1977, which calls for a more precise definition of psycho-socio-pedagogical competencies, together with the "necessary specialized integration" and "particular forms of support"; Law 426, 1988, which calls for the generic activity of "coordinator of scholastic service orientation" and "psycho-pedagogical operator of obligatory school"; and Law 104, 1992 (Italy's Legge Quadro [Framework Law]), which mandates the assistance, social integration, and rights of people with handicaps, referencing the generic description of the "psychopedagogical

operator" in Article 12, paragraph 5. In addition, there are several educational mandates that directly and indirectly impact the service of psychology in Italian schools. As school reform is an evolving process promulgated by legislation, school psychology has a continuous opportunity to further define itself as a profession. The most current education reform, known as *autonomia* (autonomy), is a continuation of the decentralizing process and is legislated by Law 59, 1997. With the *autonomia* reform movement, there were structural changes as well. The Ministry of Education was renamed the Ministry of Instruction, University and Research by Legislative Decree 258, 1999. Its major responsibilities include establishing overarching policies regarding general objectives for teaching and overseeing national curricular objectives. The Ministry is also responsible for establishing general guidelines for evaluating and recognizing credits and criteria for adult continuing education programs.

Autonomous schools provide students and their families with a specific education plan in response to their needs by implementing a *piano dell'offerta formativa* (plan of the formative/ educational offerings), wherein aspects of the curriculum that provide a sense of continuity, orientation, support, and compensatory skills are developed and modified to meet a student's specific needs. Teachers are trained to participate in developing, implementing, and monitoring the plan as well as evaluating data in light of individual academic credits and deficits. The student must develop a portfolio of competence under the auspices of the *profilo dell'offerta formativa*, which formalizes the learning experience.

The concept of autonomous schools also requires heightened attention to related service delivery such as special education remediation and direct instruction; this perspective requires revised models and methodology. This also presents new opportunities to further define the role of professionals who deliver psychological services in schools. Rubini (2001) addresses the need for increased school psychology service delivery in the context of autonomous schooling as consultants. School autonomy also calls for increased preparation of school personnel to be knowledgeable of psychology and theories of learning, to analyze professional development, to develop adequate competence in efficacy within a school system, to individualize the specific needs of a school system, and to monitor successful collaboration models. Such training of school personnel by school psychologists assists in the effective provision of site-based school psychology services. National and international professional journals relied on by school psychologists in Italy include *Psicologia dell'Educazione* (Educational Psychology), *Scuola e Psicologia* (Psychology and School), *Psicologia Scolastica* (School Psychology), *School Psychology International,* and *European Journal of School Psychology.*

Preparation of School Psychologists

Universities and private agencies are working to develop training models to address the need for increased psychological services in schools. Despite this sharper focus in professional training, the specific role of the professional school psychologist is not defined as clearly as in other countries (Gaillard, 2002). Trombetta, Rubini, and Carugati (2003) outline several historical reasons for this. Opposing dialogues among school stakeholders, politicians, and the national association of psychologists have contributed little to the clarification of the role of school psychology, which contributes to a larger sociopolitical debate that shifts the focus away from helping the child. The ambiguity of the role is further complicated by disparities in service delivery caused by historically weak connections between training programs in psychology and actual psychological service delivery in schools.

Four to 5 years of post–high school education are required to acquire a bachelor's degree in psychology, and an additional 1 to 2 years of specialization are required to deliver psychological

services in schools. Though private institutes also offer a master's degree in school psychology, graduates with a university master's degree are considered graduates in psychology with a 5-year diploma from an accredited university in the area of theoretical and professional orientation. Psychology master's programs historically appear to have been designed to function either primarily in the university in the academic domain or in the field in the practical domain, rather than a synthesis of both.

To address this disparity, master's degree programs, accredited by universities, were developed to prepare graduates to work in schools as professional school psychologists who are grounded in theory and trained to specifically work in schools. Such university degrees are known as master's degrees at the second level. This degree requires 60 formative university credits, available through enrollment in university programs such as the Service of School Psychology Program at the Libera Universita' Maria SS. Assunta (Free University of Santa Maria Assunta). The objective of Libera Universita' Maria SS. Assunta's master's program of the second degree is to train psychologists to function in schools as outlined by the school reform movement. To function effectively in a school, a professionally trained psychologist must interpret and operate within a rapidly changing educational system. This requires training in specialized consultation skills with respect to the academic system and personnel. Specific training in education program evaluation and methodologies differentiate professionals delivering psychological services in schools. The structure of the university program at Libera Universita' Maria SS. Assunta is grounded on principles established by the Societa' Italiana di Psicologia dell'Educazione e della Formazione (Italian Society of Educational Psychology and Training), which serves as a clearinghouse for best practices in educational and school psychology research, projections, and interventions, which are made available to school systems. In addition, the Italian Society of Educational Psychology and Training has designed a professional profile for effective training in school psychology that delineates the competence needed for working collaboratively. Under the auspices of the Italian Society of Educational Psychology and Training, school psychologists are trained to operate in the schools in the following five sectors of intervention: consultation, counseling, developmental activity, networking orientation, and organizational activities that promote the quality of scholastic function and evaluation.

University programs for master's degrees of the second level in school psychology usually require 300 program hours of theory, 300 hours of practicum in the schools, and 100 program hours dedicated to prepare for the final exam. Attendance is obligatory: A 75% attendance rate must be maintained. University instructors have specific competencies and training in psychology, education, instruction, and development. They generally have a background in education where they function as leaders and consultants, and they often are considered experts in organizational and professional training. Practicum supervisors have the practical experience needed for guiding their graduate students in acquiring institutional and organizational knowledge and learning about the daily life of the schools.

The first year of study in a program in school psychology such as the one at Libera Universita' Maria SS. Assunta's is usually organized into eight modules of 20 credits each, for a total of 500 hours, and culminates with the development of baseline competencies for providing school psychology services in the schools. The eight modules are assessment, evaluation, information about the student, information about the teacher, information about the class, schools as systems, school within communities, and practical experience. The second year of study is divided into two differentiated professional profiles (one for psychology for teaching and learning and another for psychology for organization and administration). Each specialty area is organized into seven modules. Because school psychology programs are newly established at the university level, data on graduate student characteristics are unavailable at this time.

Roles, Functions, and Responsibilities of School Psychologists

The 1991 work group that was developed by the Ministry of Public Instruction created a protocol that delineates the role of the school psychologist in Italian schools (Rubini, 2001). The group outlined five broad categories of professional activity for the school psychologist: counseling/consultation, training for specific interventions, orientation/connection with families, improving the organization of schools, and student evaluation.

Counseling and consultation are designed to provide far-reaching interventions to interact with elements that impact a student's scholastic environment. The principle objective in consultation is to identify and ameliorate the functioning difficulties of not only the individual student but also the diverse organizational levels of schools and classes and the relationship between schools and families. Through a variety of contexts (individual, single classes, or groups of classes), information is gathered regarding the states of well-being and academic level of achievement. In addition, consultants monitor the progress made by individual students through single case studies, classes, sections, small groups of teachers, small groups of students, and groups of parents. Consultation on behalf of the student consists of (a) the prevention and identification of scholastic or developmental disability and (b) the identification and monitoring of high risk indicators related to cognitive, personal, social, and motivational factors; resilience; school adjustment; and learning/personality styles. Guided communication is used to reinforce rapport and trust in small group settings, large group settings, or individually. School psychologists' consultations with teachers consist of supporting teachers' professional development, assisting in the analysis of difficult cases at the individual student level, understanding critical situations at the classroom level, and intervening to promote psychosocial well-being in the workplace. Consultations with parents consist of diagnosis and advocacy. Specific methods include collective theme work, group work, and role play.

Interventions require using proactive measures to predetermine and troubleshoot areas of conflict. A working knowledge of the school's surroundings, schedule, and curricular and extracurricular offerings increases the likelihood that the intervention will be effective. Problem solving and developing coping strategies are typical interventions with students. Effective interventions rely on the results of comprehensive evaluations focusing on the child-counselor relationship. Should a crisis develop, a strong relationship provides a foundation for an effective sociopsychological intervention. Professional competencies in this area include acute diagnostic ability and listening, observation, planning, cooperation, and targeted action.

Following the protocol of the Service of School Psychology, school psychologists develop the premise that collaboration and teamwork in the autonomous schools are essential and highly teachable. The supervisory model, with its emphasis on monitoring and feedback, is used to train nonpsychologist colleagues in psychological processing, which is a major goal of service. When teachers are given direct support by school psychologists, both parties may benefit: the teacher in enhanced collegial support and the school psychologist in enhanced visibility. To promote both personal and team development, the school psychologist may use behavior and personality scales, observations, role playing, microteaching, action research, questionnaires, and journaling. Improving the organization of schools relies on an effective multidisciplinary team. Personal development that enables better team functioning improves organizational performance.

Testing is one of the duties most often associated with the school psychologist. In the conceptualization of the Service of School Psychology, testing and evaluation of the student are restricted to that which is educationally relevant. When school psychologists evaluate a case, they examine many variables, along with test results, to obtain a clear idea of levels of the student's functioning. Such variables include class climate, daily rhythms, family issues, and the responsiveness and flexibility of the autonomous school system. Through interventions such as functional analyses of behavior and structured observations, data can be collected to assist in designing an individualized program for the student. During student evaluation, the school psychologist collects other data that are considered in conjunction with standardized test scores. An analysis of learning style, origins of motivation, and learning environment provide a global indication of the student's academic function in relation to ability.

Standardized tests that are widely used by Italian school psychologists include, but are not limited to, the Wechsler Intelligence Scale for Children–Revised (Orsini, 1993), Leiter International Performance Scale–Revised (Roid & Miller, 1997), Mental Structures 4–8 (Vianello, 1999), D70 Intelligence Test (Kourovsky & Rennes, 1973), and Analytic Intelligence Test (Mieli, 1960) for measuring intellectual aptitude. The Preschool Screening System (Hainsworth & Hainsworth, 1994) was translated into Italian and is used to screen for problems that would necessitate early preschool intervention. Tests for measuring calculation ability and generalized mathematical skills include the Ability to Calculate Arithmetic test (Fiore, Lucangeli, & Tressoldi, 1998) and the Test of Mathematical Ability (Rossi & Malaguti, 1994). Reading aptitude and achievement can be measured by tests such as New MT Tests of Reading for Elementary School, second edition (Cornoldi & Colpo, 1998) and New MT Tests of Reading for Middle School (Cornoldi & Colpo, 1995), the Analytical Test of Vocabulary (Boschi,

Aprile, & Schibetta, 1991), and the Linguistic Diagnostic Test from the Panlexia System (Kvilekval, 1998). Memory, attention, and learning are measured by instruments such as the Test of Learning and Memory (Reynolds & Bigler, 1995) and memory scales such as the Sintomatologia del Disturbo di Attenzione (Cornoldi, 1996). Results of diagnostic measures are discussed at meetings where a learning profile is created for the student, which integrates observational, historical, and evaluative material for educational decision making. As Italy's school reform moves toward local autonomy, school psychologists will play a greater role in training nonpsychologist colleagues and in implementing the five sectors of professional activity as outlined by the Ministry of Public Instruction Work Group.

Current Issues Impacting School Psychology

Recent studies have identified areas that impact the development and service delivery of school psychology. Dentici, Pagnin, and Agentero (2002) note that traditional psychological research is typically pursued in university laboratories to assist either medicine or the business world. The relationship between psychology and schools is more adapted to coping with behavior problems as they emerged as anomalies from the sociohistorical context, such as student behavior related to resisting authority in 1968, behavior surrounding advocating for inclusion rights for the disabled, drug abuse, social nonconformity, socially deviant behavior in school, and cultural issues related to immigration and assimilation. The researchers note that school psychology has rarely dealt with problems more inherent in the nature of the educational process such as cognitive development, the novice-expert continuum of learning theory, development of personal/professional/vocational interests, maintaining healthy peer relationships, understanding rules, values, prosocial skills, problem solving, and

teaching/ learning models. These aspects are perceived as traditional professional areas of pedagogy, pedagogues, or pedagogical specialists for their empirical, rather than practical, application.

Dentici et al. (2002) examined these and various perceptions of school psychology service delivery from among a sample of teachers and psychologists working in upper secondary schools in Pavia, a province in northern Italy. This study found teachers generally preferred programs focused on learning, cognitive strategies, social relationships, and personality problems. They also preferred an effective collaborative model between psychologists with practical school experience and teaching staff with a broader knowledge base in the psychology of adolescence.

The results of this study coincide with the guidelines set up by the Societa' Italiana di Psicologia dell'Educazione e della Formazione (Italian Society for Educational Psychology and Training) work group for the Service of School Psychology and have been used to pilot a psychological counseling program in the high school known as the Servizi Psicologici Educativi Scuola Secondaria (Psychoeducational Services in the Secondary School) project.

Initiatives are under way to address challenges in furthering school psychology in Italy. For example, in May 2001, a work group was developed to pilot a program in Pavia in conjunction with Servizio di Psicologia Scolastica (Service of School Psychology) according to its protocol of intent dated July 26, 2000, between the Ministry of Public Instruction, the Conference of Principals of the Faculty of Psychology, and various associations. In addition, the Department of Psychology at the University of Pavia and the Cairoli Institute are researching a proposal to establish local guidelines for psychological consultation and intervention, evaluation of the efficacy in terms of networking with schools, and the development of a central location of documentation and research. The second article of the protocol outlines five possibilities (the same five categories outlined for the development of professional competence in the role of school psychologists), which are professional activity regarding counseling/consultation, professional training, professional orientation and connection for and with families, school improvement measures, and evaluation of the students.

The data gathered for the Italian version of the International School Psychology Survey (Jimerson et al., 2006) provide some preliminary information regarding how school psychologists may utilize research findings and seek professional support. School psychologists identified a need for support in the following areas: classroom dynamics, family consultation, career counseling, relationships outside of school, professional recognition, collegial support, evaluations, and learning theory.

Presently, the areas of most urgent research needs within the field of school psychology are difficult to specify. Until the results of these and other major research initiatives become available, the current research needs in Italian school psychology will continue to be vague. Given the changes in schools toward greater local autonomy, there will be rich opportunities for more research projects. As school psychology in Italy continues to develop, opportunities for research will doubtlessly continue to be created. With the many initiatives and research efforts already under way, it is only a matter of time before enough data are generated to give us a deeper and more meaningful understanding about the needs of Italy's developing profession of school psychology.

References

Boschi, F., Aprile, L., & Schibetta, I. (1991). *Prove analitiche di vocabolario* [Analytical tests of vocabulary]. Florence: Edizioni O.S. Organizzazioni Speciali.

Broffiero, A. (1889). *Manuale di psicologia* [Manual of psychology]. Milan: Briola.

Cornoldi, C. (1991). *I disturbi dell'apprendimento. Aspetti psicologici e neuropsicologici* [Learning disabilities: Psychological and neuropsychological aspects]. Bologna: Il Mulino.

Cornoldi, C. (1996). *Impulsivita' e autocontrollo* [Impulsivity and self-control]. Trento: Edizioni Erickson.

Cornoldi, C., & Colpo, C. (1995). *Nuove Prove di Lettura MT per la Scuola Media Inferiore, Manuale* [New MT Reading Tests for Middle School, Manual]. Florence: Edizioni Organizzazioni Speciali.

Cornoldi, C., & Colpo, C. (1998). *Nuove Prove di Lettura MT per la Scuola Elementare–2* [New MT Reading Tests for Elementary School–2]. Florence: Edizioni Organizzazioni Speciali.

De Dominicis, S. (1908–1909). *Scienza comparata dell'educazione: antropologia pedagogica, sociologia pedagogica; storia della pedagogia* [Science compared to education: Anthropological pedagogy, sociological pedagogy, and history of pedagogy]. Turin: Streglio.

Dentici, O., Pagnin, A., & Agentero, P. (2002). I servizi psicologici nella scuola superiore: una ricerca sugli atteggiamenti degli insegnanti [Psychological services in high school: Research on the attitudes of teachers]. *Psicologia della Educazione e della Formazione, 4*(3), 375–406.

De Sanctis, S. (1909). Classi normale e asili-scuola [Normal classes and nursery school]. *Rivista Pedagogica II*, 218–220. Rome: Formiggini.

De Sanctis, S. (1912). Il problema dei fanciulli anormale [The problem of abnormal children]. *La Critica Medica, 13*. Rome: Formiggini.

De Sanctis, S. (1915a). Anormali psichichi: enciclopedia delle enciclopedie [Psychic abnormalities: Encyclopedia of the encyclopedias]. *La Pedagogia*. Rome: Formiggini.

De Sanctis, S. (1915b). *L'educazione dei deficienti* [The education of the deficient]. Milan: Vallardi.

Fiore, C., Lucangeli, D., & Tressoldi, P. (1998). *Abilita' di calcolo aritmetico* [Ability to calculate arithmetic]. Trento: Centro Studi Erickson.

Gaillard, B. (2002). *Place de la psychologie dans les systèmes éducatifs européens* [The place of psychology in European educational systems]. Rennes, France: Rapport e Recherche.

Gullini, G. (1919). *I castigati o "cattivi" nelle scuole elementari. Studio fisio-psychologico su 150 alunni* [The ones in trouble or the "bad ones" in elementary school: A psychophysical study of 150 school-age students]. Mondovì: Fracchia.

Hainsworth, P., & Hainsworth, M. (1994). *The Preschool Screening System* (P. Kvilekval & L. Sabbadini, Trans.). Pawtucket, RI: ERISys.

Istituto per lo Sviluppo della Formazione Professionale dei Lavoratori. (2003). *Rapporto ISFOL* [ISFOL Report]. Milan: Angeli.

Jimerson, S. R., Graydon, K., Yuen, M., Lam, S.-F., Thurm, J.-M., Klueva, N., Coyne, J., Loprete, L. J., Phillips, J., & International School Psychology Association Research Committee. (2006). The International School Psychology Survey: Data from Australia, China, Germany, Italy and Russia. *School Psychology International, 27*(1), 5–32.

Kourovsky, F., & Rennes, P. (1973). *D70: Scale of cognitive measurement.* Florence: Edizioni O.S. Organizzazioni Speciali.

Kvilekval, P. (1998). *Panlexia Linguistic Diagnostic Test.* Rome: Edizioni Scientifiche.

Marchesini, G. (1895). *Elementi di psicologia ad uso dei licei* [Elements of psychology and their use in high schools]. Florence: Sansoni.

Massa, S. (1908). Richerche di antropologia pedagogica eseguite nelle scuole elementare sopra i fanciulli 'i piu' studiosi e i non-studiosi' appartendosi alla stessa classe sociale [Pedagogical and anthropological research undertaken at elementary schools on studious and non-studious children]. *Rivista Pedagogica, 1,* 401–421.

Melzi, C. (1899). *Antropologia pedagogica* [Anthropological pedagogy]. Arona: Economica.

Mieli, R. (1960). *Test Analytico dell'Intelligenza* [Analytic Test of Intelligence]. Florence: Edizione O.S. Organizzazioni Speciali.

Montessori, M. (1906). *Antropologia pedagogica* [Anthropological pedagogy]. Milan: Vallardi.

Oakland, T., Cunningham, J., Meazzini, P., & Poulsen, A. (1991). An examination of policies governing the normalization of handicapped pupils in Denmark, Italy and the United States. *International Journal of Special Education, 6*(2), 386–402.

Organization for Economic Co-operation and Development. (2001). *Education at a glance, OECD indicators.* Paris: Author.

Organization for Economic Co-operation and Development. (2003). *Education at a glance.* Paris: Author.

Orsini, A. (1993). *WISC-R: Contribution of an Italian calibration.* Florence: Edizioni O.S.

Pastorello, A. (1904). *L'antropologia pedagogica e la rivoluzione scientifica in Italia* [Anthropological pedagogy and the scientific revolution in Italy]. Parma: Battei.

Pizzoli, U. (1909). *Pedagogia scientifica* [Scientific pedagogy]. Milan: Vallardi.

Reynolds, C., & Bigler, E. (1995). *Test di Mmemoria e Apprendimeno* [Test of memory and learning]. Trento: Centro Studi Erickson.

Roid, G., & Miller, L. (1997). *Leiter International Performance Scale–Revised.* Wood Dale, IL: Stoelting.

Rossi, G., & Malaguti, T. (1994). *Valutazione delle abilita' matematiche* [Evaluating mathematical ability]. Trento: Centro Study Erickson.

Rossi, G., & Malaguti, T. (1999). *Test GioMa Batteria di Prove per la Valutazione Precoce delle Abilita' e dei Disturbi di Lettura* [GioMa Battery for Early Detection of Ability and Disability in Reading]. Rome: Edizioni del Cerro.

Rubini, V. (2001). Relazione del gruppo di lavoro: Articolo 3 del Protocollo d'Intesa 2000 [Work group report: Article 3 of the Protocol of Intent, 2000]. *Psicologia dell' Educazione e della Formazione, 3*(3), 252–261.

Saffiotti, U. (1912). La psicologia sperimentale nell'indirizzo pedagogico moderno [Experimental psychology by way of modern pedagogy]. *Rivista Pedagogica, 5*(5), 22–35.

Saffiotti, U. (1913). L'échelle métrique de l'intelligence de Binet-Simon modifiée selon la méthode Trefes-Saffiotti [The measurement scales of intelligence of Binet-Simon, modified according to the Trefes-Saffioti method]. *Année Psychologique, 18,* 240–327.

Saffiotti, U. (1916). *La misura dell'intelligenza nei fanciulli: Esame critico delle proposte di misura fatte e contributo di indagini personali* [The measures of intelligence of children: Critical exams of proposals and measures undertaken and contributions of surveyed personnel]. Rome: Kappa.

Sergi, G. (1873). *Principi de psicologia di base delle scienze sperimentali, ad use delle scuole* [Principles of psychology with experimental science at the base of its use in the schools]. Messina: Capra.

Trombetta, C. (1997). *L'alleanza e il cambiamento. Storia e imagine del rapporto fra scuola e psicologia in Italia* [Alliance and change: Stories and images of the relationship between school and psychology in Italy]. Rome: Armando.

Trombetta, C. (2003). *Psicologia dell'educazione e antropologia pedagogica. Contributo storico-critico* [Psychology of education and pedagogical anthropology: Historical/critical contribution]. Rome: Kappa.

Trombetta, C., Rubini, V., & Carugati, F. (2003). Master universitari per gli psicologi scolastici: alcune riflessioni [University master's degree for school psychologists: Some reflections]. *Psicologia dell' Educazione e della Formazione, 5,* 403–420.

United Nations Educational, Scientific and Cultural Organization. (2004). *Statistical yearbook.* Paris: Author.

U.S. Census Bureau. (2001). *International database.* Washington, DC: Author.

Vianello, R. (1999). *MS 4–8.* Bergamo: Edizioni Junior.

White, S. (1991). *Progressive renaissance: America and the reconstruction of Italian education 1943–62.* New York: Garland.

21

School Psychology in Jamaica

Orlean Brown-Earle

Context of School Psychology

Jamaica gained full independence within the British Commonwealth in 1962 and currently includes 14 administrative divisions, referred to as parishes. Jamaica is the largest of the English-speaking West Indian islands. Situated in the Caribbean Sea, Jamaica covers an area of 10,991 square kilometres (4,411 square miles). Its greatest width is 80 kilometres (51 miles), from St. Ann's Bay to Portland Point. The distance from Kingston to the nearest point on the north coast, Annotto Bay, is 36 kilometres (22 miles). Historically, the Jamaican economy has had an agricultural base, dependent on a few staple export crops, primarily sugar and bananas. New economic development began with bauxite mining (after 1952) and the tourism boom in the 1950s and 1960s. Since the 1990s, tourism has become the major earner of foreign exchange. Jamaica's economic stabilization and adjustment process, which began in the 1980s, advanced significantly during the 1990s as the stages of deregulation and liberalization were accelerated. This included the liberalization of the foreign exchange market, market-determined interest rates, removal of price controls on goods, elimination of subsidies in products, lowering of fiscal borrowing requirements, and increased privatization of government-owned entities. The main impetus for economic growth has come from an expansion in the tourism industry, a rehabilitation of exports in agriculture, and a recovery in the bauxite/alumina industry (after a setback in the 1980s) and in the service sectors. With a 1.9% growth rate, in 2004 the gross domestic product was US$11.13 billion, US$4,100 per capita. Most labor force opportunities are in services (63%), agriculture (20%), and industry (16%).

As of 2005, the population of Jamaica was approximately 2,731,832, with an age composition as follows: birth to 14 years, 28%; 15 to 64 years, 66%; 65 years and older, 7%. The population growth rate in 2004 was 0.71%. Ethnic groups were divided as follows: Black, 90.9%; East Indian, 1.3%; White, 0.2%; Chinese, 0.2%; mixed, 7.3%; and other, 0.1%. The predominant religion is Protestant (61%), with Roman Catholics (4%) and others, including some spiritual cults, making up as much as 34%. The primary language is English. In 1995, it was estimated that 85% of the population older than 15 had attended school: 81% of males and 89% of females (Jamaican Information Service, 2005).

The Ministry of Education, Youth, and Culture is responsible for education policy (Jamaican Information Service, 2005). Tuition is heavily subsidized at the primary and secondary levels. A number of schools are run by churches and private groups, and many receive subsidies from the government. The mission of the Ministry of Education and Culture is to provide a system that secures quality education for all persons in Jamaica and achieves effective integration of education and cultural resources in order to optimise individual and national development. It also aims to devise and support initiatives striving toward literacy for all in order to extend personal opportunities and contribute to national development.

Primary goals of the Ministry include supporting student achievement and improving institutional performance to ensure that national targets are met; maximising opportunities to promote cultural development, awareness, and self-esteem for individuals, communities, and the nation as a whole; and devising and implementing more effective systems of accountability and performance management so as to win public confidence and trust.

Early childhood education is concerned with the development of children up to age 5. The institutions involved are day care centres, basic and infant schools, and infant departments in primary and all-age schools. A community-based sponsoring body manages basic schools, and the government's contribution is in the form of a subsidy—salary, nutrition, and class material. The Ministry's objectives in this area are to (a) continue the integration of day care into early childhood programs, (b) equip providers with skills to deliver stimulation and readiness programs, (c) assign one trained teacher to each of the 45 basic schools, and (d) upgrade resource centres.

Primary education is offered to children in Grades 1 to 6 of primary and in all-age schools. The educational offering at the primary level lays the foundation for the acquisition of knowledge, skills, and values for total development and continuing education. It is expected that each student within this age-group should be equipped with the following characteristics by the end of Grade 6: literacy and numeracy by global standards; competence in prerequisite knowledge and skills to access secondary education; and possession of a caring attitude toward self, others, and things. There are 346 primary, 356 all-age, and 90 primary and junior high schools providing for approximately 302,057 students.

The secondary education programme is concerned with educating students from Grades 7 through 13 in high schools. The focus of the programme is to improve the quality, efficiency, and relevance of the curricula. The main performance indicator at the secondary level is the examinations given by the Caribbean Examination Council, a body of educators in the Caribbean. There are 59 high schools, financed mainly by the government of Jamaica. These schools offer mainly academic subjects, although some offer a limited number of vocational subjects. Access to these schools is gained mainly on the basis of performance in the National Assessment Examination. The curriculum is a mixture of academic and vocational training, and students sit the same external examinations as those in traditional high schools. Technical/vocational education is offered to students at Grades 7 to 11, in the areas of art and craft, agriculture, business, home economics, and industrial arts. Technical/vocational education provides students with the skills, knowledge, and attitude that qualify them for job employment or entry into tertiary institutions. In addition to the schools identified under this program, technical/vocational education is offered in some high schools. Presently, there are 14 technical high schools, catering to 16,219 students.

Special education is provided mainly through private voluntary organisations in association with the government of Jamaica, which embraces those programs designed to meet the educational needs of children, 4 to 18 years old, identified as having mental, physical, and intellectual capabilities which deviate significantly from the norm expected of their age. The program aims to provide students with exceptionalities access to early childhood, primary, secondary, and tertiary education, in order to facilitate the development of their full potential. Schools for the Mentally Challenged, also known as Schools of Hope, are run by the Jamaica Association on Mental Retardation. These are attached to regular primary, all-age, and secondary schools. There are 29 institutions of this type, with an enrolment of 924 students and a teacher-pupil ratio of 1:10. There are 12 schools serving the hearing impaired population in Jamaica. Of this number, three are privately operated while seven are grant-aided; however, the Ministry of Education and Culture supervises them all. The schools cater to children from preschool through to the secondary level, with a total enrolment of 1,055 students and an academic staff of 95. The Salvation Army School for the Blind is the only school that caters to students who are blind or visually impaired. A deaf/blind unit is also attached. The school follows the regular school curriculum, and students who are successful in the National Assessment Examination move on to the secondary school system. The school is residential with an enrolment of 110 students. Provision is also made for children with learning and other mild disabilities in six special units attached to regular primary and all-age schools. The Hope Valley Experimental School offers education to nondisabled and disabled children and is the only institution that practices full integration. The number of children enrolled in this institution is 94.

The Mico College Child Assessment and Research Centre was established to ensure early detection of developmental disabilities in children and to prescribe corrective, instructional programmes to address the disabilities diagnosed. The Centre also runs a special program for gifted and talented children. The Centre offers diagnostic therapeutic services to thousands of children in Jamaica and the Caribbean and employs educational psychologists, school psychologists, and clinical psychologists to make psychoeducational assessments of their clients.

Origin, History, and Current Status of School Psychology

After the author sent out a questionnaire to determine if any of the psychologists who work in Jamaica were trained as school psychologists, it was realized that the author was the only trained doctoral-level school psychologist on the island. Many of the psychologists who responded to the survey who worked in consultative roles as school or educational psychologists were trained as clinical or counseling psychologists, and some had special education training that benefited them tremendously when called to help in academic settings. There is no position for a school psychologist within the Ministry of Education at this time. The author, who operates primarily as a private practitioner, has limited opportunities for professional development as there is no financial support for this.

The University of the West Indies offers a master's degree in psychological assessment, which allows individuals to practice as educational psychologists. The expansion of special education services was achieved through collaborative efforts of educators and educational psychologists. Northern Caribbean University and the University of the West Indies offer bachelor's degrees in psychology and counselling psychology, and the University of the West Indies additionally offers a master's degree in clinical psychology. Individuals who complete the undergraduate programs fall into a wide category of employment. Some of them immediately pursue a graduate education, as this will give them more opportunities. There are limited professional mobility opportunities for most individuals who complete the master's degree. Many find jobs in the field of counselling and others in academia.

Infrastructure of School Psychology

With regard to infrastructure, the Jamaica Psychological Society is currently developing guidelines for the role of the school/educational psychologist; these guidelines are tentatively titled the Jamaica Psychology Practice Act. The Practice Act is currently provisional and has been submitted to the local national body for supplementary medicine for final review and acceptance. This is groundbreaking work in Jamaica. The following is the proposed Jamaica Psychology Act.

Proposed Jamaica Psychology Practice Act

The practice of psychology affects the public health, safety and welfare of the citizens of Jamaica. Thus, the practice of psychology should be regulated to protect the public from the practice of psychology by unqualified persons and from unprofessional conduct by persons licensed to practice psychology. To this end, licensure to practice psychology will be granted at two levels: (1) Licensed Psychologist—a person holding a doctoral degree in psychology; (2) Licensed Psychological Associate—a person holding a master's degree in psychology. This licensure in intended for applied psychologists (i.e., clinical, counseling, school and applied-social psychologists) and not for academic and research oriented psychologists. This proposed Jamaica Psychology Practice Act in no way attempts to interfere with or inhibit the practice of other disciplines or other individuals providing services to the public, such as Social Workers, Counselors or Ministers. Rather, the Jamaica Psychology Practice Act is intended to regulate the practice of those individuals who specifically identify themselves as practicing psychologists or providers of psychological services. Lastly, the Jamaica Psychology Practice Act does not accredit or give licensure to graduate programs, but is intended to license individuals to practice psychology.

The Practice of Psychology: The Practice of Psychology means the practice of clinical psychology, counseling psychology, school psychology or applied-social psychology.

The Practice of Clinical Psychology includes: (1) *Testing and measurement,* which consists of the psychological evaluation or assessment of personal characteristics such as intelligence, abilities, interests, aptitudes, achievements, motives, personality dynamics, and psychoeducational processes. (2) *Diagnosis and treatment of mental and emotional disorders,* which consists of the appropriate diagnosis of mental disorders according to standards of the profession and the ordering or providing of treatments according to need. Treatment includes providing counseling, psychotherapy, marital and family therapy, group therapy, behavior therapy, psychoanalysis, hypnosis, biofeedback, and other psychological interventions with the objective of modification of perception, adjustment, attitudes, feelings, values, self-concept, personality or personal goals, the treatment of alcoholism and substance abuse, disorders of habit or conduct, as well as of the psychological aspects of physical illness, pain, injury or disability. (3) *Psychological consulting,* which consists of interpreting or reporting on scientific theory or research in psychology, evaluation, or engaging in applied psychological research, program or organizational development, administration, supervision or evaluation of psychological services. (4) The *evaluation of neuropsychological functioning* and treatment of neuropsychological disorders. (5) The rendering of expert psychological opinion and testimony.

The Practice of Counseling Psychology includes: (1) *Diagnosis and treatment of mental and emotional disorders,* which consists of the appropriate diagnosis of mental disorders according to standards of the profession and the ordering or providing of treatments according to need. Treatment includes providing counseling, psychotherapy, marital and family therapy, group therapy, behavior therapy, psychoanalysis, hypnosis, biofeedback, and other psychological interventions with the objective of modification of perception, adjustment, attitudes, feelings, values, self-concept, personality or personal goals, the treatment of alcoholism and substance abuse, disorders of habit or conduct, as well as of the psychological aspects of physical illness, pain, injury or disability. (2) *Psychological consulting,* which consists of interpreting or reporting on scientific theory or research in psychology, evaluation, or engaging in applied psychological research, program or organizational development, administration, supervision or evaluation of psychological services. In addition, depending on the individual's program of study and relevant supervised experience, some Counseling Psychologists, with training in psychometrics may be permitted to engage in: *Testing and measurement,* which consists of the psychological evaluation or assessment of personal characteristics such as intelligence, abilities, interests, aptitudes, achievements, motives, personality dynamics, and psycho-educational processes.

The Practice of School Psychology includes: (1) *Testing and measuring,* which consists of psychological assessment of children and adolescents in terms of intellectual ability, aptitudes, achievement, adjustment, motivation, personality or any other psychological attributes that directly relate to learning or behavioral problems that impact education. (2) *Counseling,* which consists of professional advisement and interpretive services with children and adolescents for amelioration or prevention of problems that impact education. (3) *Consultation,* which consists of educational or vocational consultation or direct educational services to schools, agencies, organizations or individuals. Psychological

consulting as herein defined is directly related to problems that impact education. (4) *Development of programs,* such as designing more efficient and psychologically sound classroom situations and acting as a catalyst for teacher involvement in adaptations and innovations.

Preparation of School Psychologists

There is no preparation program in Jamaica for school psychology. The lone doctoral-level school psychologist was trained in the United States of America. Most of the other psychologists are trained as clinical or educational psychologists and were trained in the United States, with a few trained in England and a smaller number trained in Jamaica.

Roles, Functions, and Responsibilities of School Psychologists

The roles and functions of the school psychologist include intervention services wherein the school psychologist works directly and indirectly with individuals, groups, and systems to promote educational development. Consultation services are provided primarily for educational and medical personnel but also for any other person or group who requests school psychology services. The school psychologist provides testing and assessment for infants, children, youth, and adults; determines etiology of disorders; and plans and evaluates intervention programmes where necessary. Supervision of counselling psychology and guidance counselling students at the graduate and undergraduate levels, along with participation in advocacy and research, is performed. Psychologists are members of multidisciplinary teams that determine if children are eligible for special education services. From the responses received from an informal survey conducted by the author of this chapter, the tests that are most commonly used include the Wechsler Intelligence Scale for Children, the Differential Ability Scales, Woodcock-Johnson Achievement Test, Sentence Completion, Behavior Assessment System for Children, Child Behavior Checklists, Revised Behavior Problem Checklist, Vineland Adaptive Behavior Scales, and the Bender Visual-Motor Gestalt Tests.

Current Issues Impacting School Psychology

Current issues in school psychology in Jamaica include the lack of school psychologists and the fact that there is no formal position for them within the educational system. The needs are great, especially with regard to helping children with special education needs. There has been strong advocacy for school psychological services from parent, teacher, and disability organizations over the years. The Ministry of Education has recently revised its policies and programs; thus, it is hoped that employment of school psychologists will be a part of the new focus on education, as the Ministry states that its goals include supporting student achievement and improving institutional performance in order to ensure that national targets are met.

References

Jamaica Information Service. (2005). *Education.* Retrieved October 10, 2005, from http://jis .gov.jm/gov_ja/education.asp/

Jamaican Psychological Society. (2005). Retrieved October 10, 2005, from http://members .jampsych.org/documents/ethicscode2004-jamaica.doc

22

School Psychology in Japan

Toshinori Ishikuma

Yoshinori Shinohara

Taketo Nakao

Context of School Psychology

Japan, an island chain in Eastern Asia, is between the North Pacific Ocean and the Sea of Japan, east of the Korean Peninsula. Japan's landmass is 377,835 square kilometers, and its population of 127.69 million is the ninth largest in the world. At 341 persons per square kilometer, its population density ranks fourth among countries with populations of 10 million or more. The climate varies from tropical in the south to cool temperate in the north, and the terrain is mostly rugged and mountainous. Japan has a constitutional monarchy with a parliamentary government representing 47 prefectures (i.e., states). Although the emperor retains his throne as a symbol of national unity, actual power rests in networks of powerful politicians, bureaucrats, and business executives. After three decades of unprecedented growth, Japan's economy experienced a major slowdown in the 1990s; however, Japan is currently a major economic power, both in Asia and globally. Japan is the second most technologically powerful economy in the world, after the United States, and third largest economy, after the United States and China. A notable characteristic that has bolstered the success of the economy is the collaboration of manufacturers, suppliers, and distributors in close-knit groups called *keiretsu*. The gross domestic product in 2004 was US$3.745 trillion, US$29,400 per capita. Among the labor force, 74% are in services, 25% are in industry, and 1% is in agriculture. Japan is among the world's largest and most technologically advanced producers of motor vehicles, electronic equipment, tools, steel, ships, chemicals, textiles, and processed foods. Robotics is also a key long-term economic strength, as Japan possesses 410,000 of the world's 720,000 "working robots."

Japanese children begin school when they are 6 years old; mandatory education is 6 years of elementary school and 3 years of junior high school. According to a recent survey (Ministry of Education, Culture, Sports, Science, and Technology, 2005), as of 2005, there are about 7,197,000 students in elementary schools, 3,626,000 in junior high schools, and 3,605,000 students in senior high schools. There are also about 7,000 students in unified lower and upper secondary education schools; these schools provide 6 consecutive years of education for junior high school and senior high school students. Although the maximum class size is 40 students, average class sizes are 26.1 in elementary schools and 30.7 in junior high schools. The size varies due to the policy of local (e.g., city) governments. During the past 30 years, the rate of junior high school graduates who go to 3 years of senior high school has been above 90%. In 2004, that number was 98%. About 52% of high school graduates attend 2- or 4-year colleges.

Japan provides special education services to students with special educational needs. The percentage of students who are in special schools (for the blind, deaf, mentally retarded, physically disabled, or health impaired) or self-contained special classes or who receive several lessons a week in resource rooms has increased during the past 15 years. Students with special education needs represented 1.5% of all pupils in compulsory education in 2003, up from 0.9% in 1993. The percentage changed toward an upward tendency from a downward tendency in 1990. As increasing numbers of children with a variety of problems are being identified, the number of children with disabilities receiving special education has grown. There are also questions concerning appropriate educational supports to be offered to students with learning disabilities, attention deficit hyperactivity disorder, and other challenges in regular classrooms and resource rooms, and how support should be provided to them (Ministry of Education, Culture, Sports, Science, and Technology, Survey and Study Committee on Special Support Education, 2003); at the same time, the number

of children with severe and multiple disabilities continues to increase.

Origin, History, and Current Status of School Psychology

In Japan, a formal system of school psychology has not been established; thus, presently the title "school psychologist" does not describe a profession in Japan. However, psychology services, such as those delivered by school psychologists in the United States and the United Kingdom, are also delivered in Japanese schools. In Japan, school psychology is defined as a field integrating education and psychology, where the practices and research regarding psychoeducational services to students are discussed and integrated to improve services helping each student deal with academic, psychosocial, health, and career problems, and to promote student development (Ishikuma, 1999; Matsuura, 2004). Thus, in Japan, the field of psychoeducational services represents what is referred to as school psychology in many Western countries.

In Japan, three types of personnel provide psychoeducational services: classroom teachers, teachers with psychoeducational roles or related professions, and "school counselors." Classroom teachers are expected to help students with school problems. Teachers in charge of classes help students with academic, psychosocial, health, and career problems through class management, teaching subjects, and leading classroom activities. They deal with almost everything that happens to their students, so they often contact parents to discuss students' needs and develop a support plan when problems occur. Class sizes are 40 students, maximum. Some teachers are expected to lead psychoeducational services because of their roles in schools and/or their profession (Oono, 1997). In Japanese schools, teachers belong to divisions that include schoolwide duties, such as students' organization activities and maintaining a safe environment. Teachers in the educational counseling division, student guidance division, and career guidance division are expected to provide psychoeducational services in the school. Also, special support education teachers and health teachers (school nurses) are teaching professionals, so there is a strong emphasis on psychoeducational services in their work.

Teachers in the student guidance and educational counseling divisions are expected to actively provide guidance and counseling services to students. Career guidance teachers provide students and classroom teachers with career information, whereas classroom teachers meet with students to talk about their career decisions. Special support education teachers are in charge of classes for special support education, and they often consult with regular classroom teachers about students in regular classrooms who have special education needs due to, for example, their learning disabilities or attention deficit hyperactivity disorder. Health teachers help students deal with physical and psychological health problems.

Finally, school counselors in Japan are hired in Japanese schools as part-time employees, for example, 1 day a week for 4 to 8 hours. As a part of a research project with government support, school counselors were employed, from 1995 to 2000, especially to manage nonattendance and bullying problems. Then, in 2001, prefectural governments began hiring part-time school counselors with financial support from the government. School counselors provide services such as counseling students, consultation with teachers and parents, and teacher education. Most school counselors are certified as clinical psychologists; some are certified as school psychologists. Clinical psychologists are certified not by government but by the Foundation of the Japanese Certification Board for Clinical Psychologists based on academic associations. In Japan, though clinical psychology is not a profession yet, clinical psychology certification has been recognized for mental health service providers. As of 2005, approximately 13,000 clinical psychologists are certified in Japan, and

their employment includes work as school counselors, as psychologists in hospitals, with companies, or as university faculty.

To be certified as a clinical psychologist, one must pass an examination consisting of a written section and an interview. To take that examination, one must satisfy certain conditions. Previously, completion of both a 2-year master's degree and at least 1 year of professional experience was required. The current requirement is completion of a designated graduate program. The required programs include a practicum and subjects such as clinical psychology, psychological interviewing, and psychological assessment, developmental psychology, family psychology, and social psychology. The designated graduate programs are classified into the first class and the second class, depending on the number of the faculty with clinical psychology certification and whether the university has the on-campus counseling center for training. After completing the program, graduates of the first-class programs are immediately eligible to take the examination; those of the second-class programs are required to have 1 year of clinical psychology practice experience before taking the test (Foundation of the Japanese Certification Board for Clinical Psychologists, 2005). As a result, school counselors provide services varying from psychoeducational to therapeutic, according to the training and experiences of school counselors and how the schools choose to use their professional skills.

As described earlier, psychoeducational services have been provided in the schools mostly by teachers, and recently, by school counselors as well. In Japanese literature, psychoeducational services have more recently been described as school educational counseling and school counseling, mainly for teachers' activities (Kokubu, 1987; Oono, 1997; Tagami, 1999). School clinical psychology has been described as focusing on school counselors' activities. "Educational counseling" is also used for children with disabilities; hence, it is part of the support system in the field of special education.

When the term *school psychology* was first used in Japan is not clear. However, a book titled *School Psychology* (Kobayashi et al., 1986) introduced school psychology services (of the type commonly described in the United States), including (a) psychological services in learning, including services for children with learning disabilities; (b) guidance and educational counseling; (c) school counseling and consultation; (d) education for children with and without disabilities; and (e) education and mental health services.

In 1990, the Japanese Association of Educational Psychology established the School Psychology Executive Committee, and the term *school psychology* has since been commonly used to refer to psychoeducational services for children's problems. The School Psychology Executive Committee examined whether the master's program includes specific subjects related to the practice of school psychology. The Committee worked with the Board of Education of prefectural governments to add the term *school psychology* to their advanced class certificates for teachers. Required subjects are educational psychology, developmental psychology, clinical psychology, education and psychology for children with disabilities, evaluation and psychological testing, school counseling, and student guidance and career guidance. Presently, 25 of 47 districts in Japan issue advanced class certificates to teachers with school psychology qualifications. In 1997, the Japanese Association of Educational Psychology began to certify school psychologists. In 2002, the Japanese Association of Educational Psychology, the Japanese Association of Special Education, the Japanese Association of Developmental Disabilities, the Japanese Association of Developmental Psychology, and the Japanese Academy of Learning Disabilities collaborated to establish the Japanese Organization of Certifying and Managing School Psychologists. Since 2002, the Japanese Organization of Certifying and Managing School Psychologists has certified school psychologists.

The advanced class certification of teachers and school psychology certification have been influenced by five factors: (a) increasing difficulty in solving school education problems such as nonattendance, bullying, and juvenile delinquency (Fukuzawa, Ishikuma, Onose, & Japanese School Psychology Association, 2004); (b) the need to improve special support education, especially for students with learning disabilities, attention deficit hyperactivity disorder, and high functioning autism (Ueno, 1984); (c) the increasing tendency of academic associations, especially the Japanese Association of Educational Psychology, to influence practice in schools (Ichikawa, 2003; Onose, 1996); (d) the introduction of school psychology practices of the United States to Japan (Ishikuma, 1994, 1999); and (e) publication of new books on school psychology (Ishikuma, 1999; Takano & Watanabe, 1998).

Ishikuma's *School Psychology: Psychoeducational Services by a Team of Teachers, School Counselors, and Parents* (1999) is one of the major references on school psychology in Japan. Seven chapters are about the theory of school psychology: toward a new paradigm of school education services; school psychology in the United States; school psychology in Japan; basic concepts of psychoeducational services; four kinds of helpers for psychoeducational services; three levels of psychoeducational services; and a national survey on needs for school counselors. Four chapters discuss school psychology practices: psychoeducational assessment as a base of psychoeducational services; counseling as a direct service to students; consultation with teachers, parents, and school organizations as team support to students; and uniqueness and future tasks of school psychology.

As of December 2005, 3,382 teachers, counselors, teacher consultants at the Board of Education, and university professors were certified as school psychologists (1,396 males, 1,986 females). Certification as a school psychologist in Japan does not directly lead to specific jobs; neither does it confer high status or high salary.

As a result, some school psychologists seem to have low satisfaction with what they gain from the certification. However, school psychology certification has started to gain attention, as many teachers and counselors with school psychology certification have attained high quality work, and the government and schools have recognized the importance of team support and the work of the coordinator. For example, it is recommended that a student support team of teachers, parents, and other school personnel (e.g., the special support teacher and/or the educational counseling teacher) work together to help students with difficulties in school life. Every elementary and junior high school in Japan names a special support education coordinator to promote special support education services. The coordinator's roles include consulting with teachers and parents, leading a special support coordination committee, and helping write an individualized instructional plan if needed. It is hoped that in more schools, teachers with school psychology certification will be appointed as special support educational coordinators and that counselors with school psychology certification will be hired as school counselors.

Infrastructure of School Psychology

The professional organization for school psychologists is the Japanese Association of School Psychologists, which is part of the Japanese Organization of Certifying and Managing School Psychologists. The Japanese Association of School Psychologists has 3,382 members in 31 regional associations. The Japanese Association of School Psychologists and some regional associations publish a newsletter. School psychologists have opportunities for professional development in workshops and group case supervision at national or regional levels of the Japanese Association of School Psychologists.

Also important are five academic associations that support the Japanese Organization of Certifying and Managing School Psychologists: the Japanese Association of Educational Psychology, the Japanese Association of Special Education, the Japanese Association of Developmental Disabilities, the Japanese Association of Developmental Psychology, and the Japanese Academy of Learning Disabilities. Those associations provide workshops for school psychologists and publish journals that discuss school psychology services, such as *The Japanese Journal of Educational Psychology* and *The Annual Report of Educational Psychology in Japan* by the Japanese Association of Educational Psychology. In addition to these associations, the Japanese School Psychology Association and the Japanese Society of Clinical Educational Psychology provide workshops and publish journals.

Preparation of School Psychologists

Those eligible to apply for school psychology certification are of five types. Type A: graduates of master's courses who finished the seven school psychology subjects and have 1 year of experience in psychoeducational services; Type B: teachers, special support teachers, or health teachers with 5 years of experience in psychoeducational services; Type C: counseling professionals with 2 years of experience in psychoeducational services (for graduates of master's courses and completed four or more out of the seven school psychology subjects) or with 5 years of experience (for graduates of master's courses not related to school psychology or for those with an undergraduate degree); Type D: university or college professors teaching subjects related to school psychology who have done enough research in the field of school psychology; and Type E: those who have certification or license as school psychologists or professions related to school psychology such as school counselors in other countries (Japanese Organization for Certifying and Managing School Psychologists, 2005). Applicants are required to complete a multiple-choice test on seven school psychology subjects and the theory and practice of school psychology, as well as an essay test on the topics of school psychology. Type A, D, and E applicants take only an essay test. All applicants also must submit a report on a supervised case.

In Japan, 4 years of higher education are required to enter a graduate program. Many graduate programs prepare school psychologists; as of 2005, more than 60 programs have been submitted to the Japanese Board of Certifying School Psychologists to help the process of school psychology certification. Thirty-three graduate schools (24 national, 1 prefecture, and 13 private) with master's-level programs now have courses for advanced class certificates for teachers with "school psychology" added. For school psychology certification, curriculum must include the following subjects, which are in three areas: (a) psychology: educational psychology, developmental psychology, and clinical psychology; (b) school education: student guidance and career guidance, education, and psychology for students with disabilities; and (c) psychoeducational service skills: evaluation and psychological testing (assessment), school counseling, and consultation.

Most graduate programs of school psychology are in education or human science fields, and graduate students take courses related to psychology and education. However, the Japanese master's-level programs in the fields of education emphasize teaching academic knowledge and guiding students toward a master's thesis; these programs follow the researcher model. We are now in a transition phase from the researcher model to the professional model, in which students receive more advanced skill training, which is related to providing psychoeducational services. According to the International School Psychology Association guidelines for the preparation of school psychologists (Cunningham & Oakland, 1998), the

programs in Japan need to improve courses to develop assessment, intervention, interpersonal relation, and professional decision-making skills. Additionally, courses should educate students about legal and ethical issues.

Roles, Functions, and Responsibilities of School Psychologists

Those with school psychology certification are expected to provide the following psychoeducational services in schools (Ishikuma, 1999, 2004).

Assessment. As student support team leaders, school psychologists perform assessment planning and integration of information regarding students' academic, psychosocial, career, and health problems. They also administer psychological tests, observe students in classroom activities, and interview teachers and parents. Psychological tests used for assessment of children include the Japanese versions of the Wechsler Intelligence Scale for Children (Azuma et al., 1998), the Kaufman Assessment Battery for Children (Matsubara, Fujita, Maekawa, & Ishikuma, 1993), and the Tanaka Binet Scale of Intelligence (Sugihara et al., 2003), as well as the Illinois Test of Psycholinguistic Abilities (Ueno, Ochi, & Hattori, 1992) for intellectual abilities. Though achievement is an important area for school psychologists to assess, individual tests for achievement have not been developed in Japan. So, group achievement tests (both norm-referenced tests and criteria-referenced tests) are used along with teachers' tests. Adaptive behavior scales, such as the Social Maturity Scale (Miki, 1980), are also used. For personality assessment, some school psychologists use the Sentence Completion Test and the Kinetic Family Drawing. They rarely use the Rorschach or Thematic Apperception Test, which are used by clinical psychologists. The ecological model is emphasized. Helping make individualized instructional plans for those with disabilities through comprehensive assessment is expected.

Consultation. School psychologists consult with teachers, parents, other educational personnel, and other school and community professionals to change the system of psychoeducational services in the school. School psychologists are expected to provide, in consultation, organizational and program development and leadership (especially in the area of special support education), crisis prevention and intervention, social skills training, and career education.

Interventions. School psychologists work directly with individuals and groups, providing counseling, classroom activities such as structured group encounters (Kokubu, 2000), skill training (Iida & Ishikuma, 2002), and academic guidance. Preventive services are emphasized, and crisis intervention is an important role for school psychologists.

Coordination. Coordinating psychoeducational services in the school to help students, schools, and the educational system is also a task performed by school psychologists. Because psychoeducational services are the collective work of teachers, counselors, and other personnel— without a school psychologist—the coordination of services in Japan is critical.

Practices of School Psychology

School psychology services are not delivered by a specific professional school psychologist but rather by a team of teachers with psychoeducational roles or related professions, teachers in general, and school counselors. In this section, we describe major models in school psychology services in Japan (Ishikuma, 1999, 2004).

All students have the right to receive psychoeducational services. Of course, classrooms and schools are also to be helped, and teachers and parents need help developing and implementing interventions. It is important to include the school system as the client.

The focus of school psychology services is threefold: (a) children as individuals: school life and mental problems; (b) enhancing environments: culture and function of classroom and school; and (c) interrelation of children and environment: matching learning and teaching styles, and child's behavioral style and expected behavior; fitness of child to environment (Kondo, 1994; Tagami, 1999).

School psychology services are conducted at three levels of psychoeducational services: primary, secondary, and tertiary (Cowen, 1977). As in the United States, this model is valuable in understanding how school psychology services are provided in Japan (Ishikuma, 1999; Oono, 1997). From a viewpoint of three levels of services, school psychology in Japan aims to provide services to all students. In the process of establishing the field of school psychology in Japan, researchers have consulted literature about school psychology and school counseling in the United States and other countries (Oono, 1997).

School psychology services are implemented through team efforts in Japan. Thus, the service system can be discussed at three levels (Ishikuma, 1999, 2004). The student support system is composed of a team, a coordination committee, and a management committee. The student support team includes the homeroom teacher parents, coordinator, health teacher, and other staff. Meetings are held as needed to collect information about the problem and to prepare an intervention plan. The student support coordination committee members include the special support education coordinator, teachers with guidance and/or educational counseling roles, special support education teachers, health teacher, administrators, and teachers related to the case or task. Meetings are held regularly to discuss the case or the action necessary to solve student problems and improve student support services. The student support management committee includes the principal, vice principal, and chief teachers of major divisions and grades. Meetings are held regularly, either independently or as part of school education management meetings, to make decisions about student support services. The Individualized Instructional Plan can be prepared by the student support coordination committee and the student support team.

Current Issues Impacting School Psychology

To discuss current issues impacting school psychology, and to promote school psychology services, it is helpful to consider the three critical steps of the paradigm shift suggested by Sheridan and Gutkin (2000). We next discuss issues of Japanese school psychology as they relate to each of these three steps.

The first step of the paradigm shift is to clearly understand major problems among Japanese students and in psychoeducational services. The most difficult problems in schools include nonattendance and bullying. In addition, special support education has recently begun to focus on students with developmental disabilities, such as learning disabilities and attention deficit hyperactivity disorder (Ministry of Education, Culture, Sports, Science, and Technology, Survey and Study Committee on Special Support Education, 2003).

Nonattendance has been a serious problem in Japanese education. In a national survey of basic schooling conducted for the 2004 school year, nonattendance is defined as a condition in which a student does not attend school for more than 30 days in one school year without any physical or economic reason (Ministry of Education, Culture, Sports, Science, and Technology, 2005). In the national survey, 23,310 elementary school students were classified as nonattendant. This is 0.32% of all

elementary school students. Nonattendant junior high school students number 100,007, which is 2.73% of all junior high school students. The total number of nonattendant students is 123,317—1.14% of all students who are in mandatory education.

Another national survey, conducted in 2002 (Ministry of Education, Culture, Sports, Science, and Technology, 2003), revealed that 6.3% of students in regular classes needed special educational support. The final report urges the government to modify "special education," which offers children with disabilities special schools or classes, depending on the classification and severity of disabilities, to "special support education" that provides relevant educational support according to their educational needs. Giving students with disabilities special support education boosts their functioning, minimizes their difficulties in life and in learning, and prepares them to participate in society.

Many Japanese students are having difficulties; this results in many challenges for schools. A strength of Japanese school psychology services is that teachers are expected to deliver these services through teaching and guidance so that students are helped in school life. At the same time, such heavy dependence on teachers is also a limitation of Japanese school psychology services. Quality and quantity of the services vary among teachers, because of inadequate training in school psychology. The lack of professionals to coordinate and lead psychoeducational services in schools is another serious limitation in Japan.

The second step of the paradigm shift is to examine the proposed paradigm to suggest reconceptualization and reorganization of school psychology services in Japan. The major models of school psychology services, as described earlier, are helping all students, helpers, and the system; focusing not only on students but on the environment and the interaction between students and the environment; providing primary, secondary, and tertiary prevention; and maintaining three levels of the system for psychoeducational services. Promotion of team support and effective coordination of psychoeducational services are critical in the second step; initiatives in school psychology services to address these tasks are examining and improving team support and coordination. In addition, publication of new books about school psychology should be added to the second step.

Team support in the school and in the community is receiving special attention as a means to help children with difficulties such as nonattendance, bullying, and delinquency, as well as with problems based on developmental disabilities. Team support is an important research topic in the field of school psychology in Japan. Tamura and Ishikuma (2003) have done research on a student support team that included a parent as a helper. The Ministry of Education, Culture, Sports, Science, and Technology, Division of Special Support Education (2004) has recommended the establishment of student support coordination committees in the schools to promote psychoeducational services for those with special educational needs. The functions of student support committees have been researched, and, after examining practices in a junior high school, Iechika and Ishikuma (2003) reported four student support committee functions: consultation, coordination in the school as well as between the school and the community, promotion of team support for students with additional need, and helping management.

Introducing the coordinator of psychoeducational services is a new challenge in promoting coordination. According to the Ministry of Education, Culture, Sports, Science, and Technology, every elementary and junior high school is to name a special support education coordinator. These coordinators are expected to coordinate services for children with special educational needs. In reality, students with special educational needs are not only those with disabilities but also those who have difficulties

in school life. So special support education coordinators are involved in coordinating psychoeducational services for students with academic, psychosocial, career, and health problems, while also consulting with teachers on understanding and helping children with disabilities. For example, the Educational Center in Kanagawa Prefecture has started to train teachers to become educational counseling coordinators who function as special support education coordinators and can deal not only with special support educational services but also with psychoeducational services in general. Research has been conducted on coordinators and coordination. For example, Seto and Ishikuma (2003) developed a scale of coordination activities and took a survey of teachers with psychoeducational roles, such as educational counseling and student guidance as well as health teachers and school counselors. As a result, they identified four activities (assessment and decision making, teaming with teachers and parents, consulting with other professionals, and coordination of opinions and activities) for coordination of team support for students with additional needs and four activities (collection of data about students and school, public relations, helping manage psychoeducational services, and networking) for coordination of psychoeducational services in schools.

Two publications about school psychology were created to organize school psychology practices. One is the series of four books planned by the Japanese Organization for Certifying and Managing School Psychologists (Matsuura et al., 2004). This publication, *School Psychologists: Theory and Practices*, includes theories of psychology and education that have contributed to school psychology and school psychology services in kindergartens to high schools. The other, the *Handbook of School Psychology*, by the Japanese School Psychology Association, discusses 109 keywords in the three domains of school psychology: psychology bases, education bases, and psychoeducational services (Fukuzawa et al., 2004). The publication of these books means that practitioners and researchers of school psychology in Japan have started to establish school psychology based on psychoeducational services in Japan.

The third step of the paradigm shift is to present specific moves by the profession toward the new paradigm. For future school psychology practice in Japan, three actions may be helpful. First, teachers with psychoeducational roles should be given more formal positions (e.g., special support education coordinator) than they have now, so that they can lead and coordinate services, including special support education. They also should be given a dedicated amount of time to fulfill this role. This action has already started. Second, the development of graduate programs for psychoeducational services is needed in order to prepare school psychology professionals and teachers with psychoeducational skills. Indeed, the Ministry of Education, Culture, Sports, Science, and Technology has started to reform the master's level of graduate programs in education from the academic and researcher model to the professional model. So, the development of graduate programs for school psychology services has the chance to be promoted through collaboration between the Japanese Organization of Certifying and Managing School Psychologists and other related organizations for psychoeducational services and the Ministry. Third, it is important to formally prepare school psychology professionals, whether those professionals are called "school counselors" or "school psychologists." Certification of school psychology professionals should be established by the government. This is currently a challenging task; however, the Japanese education system is moving toward collaboration among various professions rather than teachers providing all education services. Japan is trying to move toward a formally certified profession of school psychology to improve the quality of school life and welfare of all students.

School psychology has been developing and becoming a global profession in the field of psychology and education, although international development is still uneven (Oakland, 1993; Russell, 1984). In Japan, because there continue to be difficulties in school life, the development of school psychology services is an urgent task.

References

Azuma, H., Ueno, K., Fujita, K., Maekawa, H., Ishikuma, T., & Sano, H. (1998). *The Japanese version of Wechsler Intelligence Scale for Children–III.* Tokyo: Nihon Bunka Kagakusha.

Cowen, E. L. (1977). Baby-steps toward primary prevention. *American Journal of Community Psychology, 5,* 1–22.

Cunningham, J., & Oakland, T. (1998). International School Psychology Association guidelines for the preparation of school psychologists. *School Psychology International, 19,* 19–30.

Foundation of the Japanese Certification Board for Clinical Psychologists. (2005). *How to become a clinical psychologist.* Tokyo: Seishin Shobo.

Fukuzawa, S., Ishikuma, T., Onose, M., & Japanese School Psychology Association. (Eds.). (2004). *Handbook of school psychology.* Tokyo: Kyoiku Shuppan.

Ichikawa, S. (2003). What does educational psychology do? Its ideas and purposes. Japanese Association of Educational Psychology (Ed.), *Handbook of educational psychology* (pp. 1–7). Tokyo: Yuhikaku.

Iechika, S., & Ishikuma, T. (2003). A coordination committee for psychological and educational services in a junior high school. *Japanese Journal of Educational Psychology, 51,* 230–238.

Iida, J., & Ishikuma, T. (2002). Development of the School-Life Skills Scale–Junior High School Student Form. *Japanese Journal of Educational Psychology, 50,* 225–236.

Ishikuma, T. (1994). School psychologists and school psychology: New perspective on school education. *The Annual Report of Educational Psychology in Japan, 33,* 144–154.

Ishikuma, T. (1999). *School psychology: Psychoeducational services by a team of teachers, school counselors, and parents.* Tokyo: Seishin Shobo.

Ishikuma, T. (2004). Research and practices in school psychology in Japan: Moving toward a system of psycho-educational services. *Japanese Psychological Review, 3*, 332–347.

Japanese Organization for Certifying and Managing School Psychologists. (2005). *For applicants for the school psychologist: Manual and application forms 2005.* Tokyo: Author.

Kobayashi, T., Sato, S., Akiyama,T., Hayashi, S., Inui, M., Deguchi, N., et al. (Eds.). (1986). *School psychology.* Tokyo: Toshindo.

Kokubu, Y. (1987). *Basic issues on school counseling.* Tokyo: Seishin Shobo.

Kokubu, Y. (2000). *Structured group encounter.* Tokyo: Seishin Shobo.

Kondo, K. (1994). *Establishing relationships between teachers and children: School clinical psychology.* Tokyo: Tokyo University Press.

Matsubara, T., Fujita, K. Maekawa, H., & Ishikuma, T. (1993). *The Japanese version of Kaufman Assessment Battery for Children.* Tokyo: Maruzen Mates.

Matsuura, H. (2004). Definition and significance of school psychology. In H. Matsuura, K. Arai, S. Ichikawa, K. Sugihara, A. Katada, & N. Tajima (Eds.), *School psychologists: Theory and practices; School psychologists and school psychology* (pp. 72–83). Kyoto: Kitaouji Shobo.

Miki, Y. (1980). *Social Maturity Scale.* Tokyo: Nihon Bunka Kagakusha.

Ministry of Education, Culture, Sports, Science, and Technology, Survey and Study Committee on Special Support Education. (2003). *Final report on future of special support education.* Tokyo: Author.

Ministry of Education, Culture, Sports, Science, and Technology, Division of Special Support Education. (2004). *Guideline for development of educational system for students with learning disabilities, attention deficit hyperactivity disorder, and high functional autism in elementary and junior high schools (Tentative plan).* Tokyo: Author.

Ministry of Education, Culture, Sports, Science, and Technology. (2005). *School basic survey 2005.* Tokyo: Author.

Oakland, T. (1993). A brief history of international school psychology. *Journal of School Psychology, 31,* 109–122.

Onose, M. (1996). Research trend and survey on educational psychology: Review on a teaching and learning area from a school psychology approach to teaching. *The Annual Report of Educational Psychology in Japan, 35,* 88–99.

Oono, S. (1997). *Theory of school educational counseling.* Tokyo: Honnomori Shuppan.

Russell, R. (1984). Psychology in its world context. *American Psychologist, 39,* 1017–1025.

Seto, M., & Ishikuma, T. (2003). Coordinating team support for junior high school students: Ability and power factors. *Japanese Journal of Educational Psychology, 51,* 378–389.

Sheridan, S. M., & Gutkin, T. B. (2000). The ecology of school psychology: Examining and changing our paradigm for the 21st century. *School Psychology Review, 29*(4), 485–504.

Sugihara, K., Sugihara, T., Nakamura, J., Okawa, I., Nohara, R., & Serizawa, N. (Eds.). (2003). *Tanaka Binet Intelligence Scale.* Tokyo: Taken Shuppan.

Tagami, F. (1999). *Practices of school counseling: Helping non-attendant students by teachers in charge of class.* Tokyo: Kaneko Shobo.

Takano, S., & Watanabe, Y. (Eds.). (1998). *School counselor and school psychology.* Tokyo: Kyoiku Shuppan.

Tamura, S., & Ishikuma, T. (2003). Forming a core team (teacher, school counselor, and parent) to support a student: Parents as supporters. *Japanese Journal of Educational Psychology, 51,* 328–338.

Ueno, K. (1984). *Students with learning disabilities in the classroom.* Tokyo: Yuhikaku.

Ueno, K., Ochi, K., & Hattori, M. (1992). *The Japanese version of Illinois Test of Psycholinguistic Abilities.* Tokyo: Nihon Bunka Kagakusha.

23

School Psychology in Lithuania

Gražina Gintilienė

Context of School Psychology

Lithuania, a European country on the eastern coast of the Baltic Sea, is bordered by Latvia on the north, Belarus on the east and south, Russia on the west, Poland on the south, and 100 kilometers of Baltic Sea coastline on the west. The landmass of Lithuania is 65,200 square kilometers, and its population is over 3.5 million. The territory of Lithuania is divided into 10 counties, which consist of territories of the nine cities and 51 regional municipalities. The population is 83.5% Lithuanian, 7% Polish, 6% Russian, and 4% other. The official language is Lithuanian, and it, as the neighboring Latvian, belongs to the Baltic group of Indo-European languages.

In 1990, after a 50-year Soviet occupation, Lithuania proclaimed the restoration of its statehood, the roots of which date back to the early 13th century. In 2003, Lithuania had the fastest growing economy in Europe ("Baltic Tiger," 2003). In 2004, the country's gross domestic product was US$45.23 billion, 12,900 per capita, and unemployment fell from 11% in

2003 to 8% in 2005. Having such progress in its economy in 2004, Lithuania joined the European Union. Privatization of large, state-owned property is nearing completion. There remains a significant level of disparity in economic well-being between urban and rural districts. In terms of average disposable income, the rural population is 1.4 times poorer than the urban population.

Lithuania has a highly developed educational system. During the 2002–2003 academic year, 82% of learners ages 7 through 24 years were pursuing their education and training. Among 19- to 24-year-olds, 33% attended a higher education institution. In 2003, the percentage of gross domestic product allocated to education was 6% (Ministry of Education and Science, 2004). Lithuania's first post-communist Constitution (1992) Article 41 declares that every child younger than 16 must attend school. This ensures the individual's right to attend a state-funded, municipal, or private school and/or to move to another school of choice. A child starts first grade at 7 years old. Preschool and pre-primary education for children ages 3 to 7 years old is not compulsory. When enrolling in a state-funded or municipal school, individuals who reside within a territory are given priority. Children in some districts can choose their school according to language of instruction: Lithuanian, Polish, Russian, English, German, or French. The primary school curriculum is for Grades 1 to 4. Class sizes vary from 10 to 20 pupils in primary schools and from 20 to 30 students in the upper grades. The basic education curriculum consists of two educational content areas: one for Grades 5 to 8 and another for Grades 9 to 10. On completion of basic education, exams ascertain whether the basic level of education has been attained. Those who have attained the basic educational level then enter secondary education, which is a 2-year curriculum that focuses on profiling (e.g., humanitarian, real, technological, and artistic) and differentiation of the content of education offered by various types of schools (e.g., gymnasium, secondary, vocational, and other). Individuals who have completed secondary education take state- and/or school-level matriculation examinations. The results of state examinations are used to determine admittance to institutions of higher education (colleges, universities, and academies) throughout the country.

During the 2004–2005 school year, the total number of students at schools in general education in Lithuania was estimated at 563,063. Of these, 93% of the population graduated with basic education at age 16, and 80% of the population graduated with secondary education at age 18 (Statistics Lithuania, 2005). Special education needs pupils constitute 11% (58,837) of the general school population. At the beginning of the 2004–2005 school year, as many as 88% of pupils with special needs were taught at mainstream schools, 2% in special classes at mainstream schools, and 11% were taught at special schools or special boarding schools (Statistics Lithuania, 2005). Most children integrated into regular schools have speech and communication disabilities or specific cognitive disorders. Children with hearing impairments and mental retardation typically attend special schools.

Origin, History, and Current Status of School Psychology

The origins of school psychology in Lithuania are found in the early 1920s, when the Lithuanian Society for Psychotechnique and Vocational Guidance was established at the Experimental Psychology and Pedagogy Institute of Vytautas Magnus University in Kaunas. Its goals included helping to selecting candidates for study programs, assisting young people in finding their vocation, advising on different professions and occupations, selecting the most gifted or challenged children, and advising on special schooling and education (Gučas, 1937). With the outbreak of World War II and the subsequent occupation of Lithuania, the society's activities were halted. From 1946 until 1969, the training of professional psychologists was excluded from university programs. During this period, the specialization of psychology was available only in combination with the profession of Lithuanian language teacher. Most graduates who went into this profession followed a career in teaching or research. In 1969, Vilnius University was granted permission to train specialists in industrial and engineering psychology. This paved the way for the eventual training of specialists in educational and clinical psychology (Lapė, 1999).

Organized school psychological services in Lithuania began in the early 1980s, when the Section of Pedagogical Psychology was established within the Lithuanian Psychologists' Society. It is from this time that psychologists within the educational system began to be recognized. Spearheaded by members of this section, the first professional psychologists were employed by several Lithuanian schools open to participating in the experiment. In 1990, the Lithuanian Psychologists' Society played an important role in establishing the School Psychological Service Center in Vilnius. This center developed the first official documents regarding the main functions, duties, responsibilities, and rights of school psychologists. Within three years of the center's opening, three affiliates were opened: one in the city of Kaunas and one each in the regions of Prienai and Ignalina. The model for pedagogical psychological services was approved by the Ministry of Education and Science in 1995 (Valantinas, 1998).

This provided a 3-level system of service across the country. Level 1 was at the municipal level of pedagogical psychological services; Level 2 was at the specialized county level of pedagogical psychological services; and Level 3 was the Pedagogical Psychological Center. The Center had divisions around the country and worked with special needs children and adolescents at the county level. It also worked in cooperation with the municipal Pedagogical Psychological Services, using a multidisciplinary approach, to assess the special education needs of children. Within 4 years, 26 Pedagogical Psychological Services were established to serve schools and preschools at the municipal level. These covered about 50% of all municipalities (Aidukienė & Labinienė, 2003).

The 1990s saw the beginning of international cooperation among Lithuanian school psychologists. Initial efforts to introduce democratic changes to the Lithuanian educational system were summer schools for educators and psychologists, beginning in 1991, which were organized by the American Professional Partnership for Lithuanian Education society. Numerous projects with colleagues from Nordic countries have left lasting changes in Lithuanian education. Lithuanian school psychologists took an active part in the School for All program, supported by the Nordic Council of Ministers, and in the project Pedagogical Psychological Services for Democratization of Lithuanian Education, supported by the Danish Ministry of Education.

These, along with national projects, were catalysts for the rapid changes within the special education system that spurred the integration of children with special needs into mainstream schools and society. In 1999, 82% of pupils with special needs were taught in mainstream schools,

compared with 66% in 1993 (Aidukienė & Labinienė, 2003; Reklyte & Gintilienė, 1993). The developing integration led to a revision of the existing model for the provision of pedagogical and psychological assistance in 2003. Accordingly, the new model for further development of the system of special pedagogical and psychological support within the country, Pedagogical Psychological Center, was reorganized into the National Center for Special Needs Education and Psychology under the Ministry of Education and Science (for more information, see the Center's Web site, www.sppc.lt). The National Center for Special Needs Education and Psychology became responsible for coordinating the first and second levels of special pedagogical and psychological support, supporting the municipal pedagogical psychological services, training specialists, providing assessment materials, and supervising difficult cases.

During the past two decades, the number of psychologists working in educational settings has increased from several to 400. The term *school psychologist* is used in both broad and narrow senses. The broad sense refers to a professional with a master's degree in psychology (most hold a master's degree in educational psychology), who is recognized as a specialist in providing psychological assistance to children within the school and in school-related settings and services. The narrow sense refers to a professional psychologist who is employed directly by the school (kindergarten, primary, basic, youth, secondary, special, and vocational). The term *educational psychologist* is also used to refer to the professional who has completed a graduate program in educational psychology. The term *school psychologist* is most often used to identify professionals who work in educational settings, whereas the term *educational psychologist* tends to indicate those in academia. Neither term is defined in legislation. The Law on Education (2003) Article 20 states that "psychological assistance is provided and the prevention of psychological problems is undertaken by psychologists employed at psychological services,

Pedagogical Psychological Services, and schools." This law ensures that psychological assistance is available at (a) schools offering a preschool education program, (b) general education schools (except schools organized by hospitals for inpatients, schools for adult students, and training centers for adults), (c) schools providing art or sports education programs and carrying out formal education programs, (d) vocational schools, and (e) Pedagogical Psychological Services.

According to data provided by the National Center for Special Needs Education and Psychology (Specialiosios Pedagogikos ir Psichologijos Centras, 2006), during the 2004–2005 school year, 293 psychologists worked at mainstream and special schools and 22 worked in kindergarten. Another 105 psychologists were employed in 58 (of 60) municipal Pedagogical Psychological Services. In Lithuania, the average ratio is 1 psychologist to 1,420 schoolchildren. This ratio, however, is not consistent throughout the country. In Vilnius, the capital of Lithuania, 1 school psychologist serves some 1,050 children, whereas in the Vilnius region, 1 school psychologist may serve as many as 1,830 children. An especially problematic situation can be observed in the Siauliai County, where the ratio of schoolchildren to school psychologists is 3,000 to 1. Kindergartens have an average of 4,000 children per psychologist. The ratio of psychologists working in rural areas compared with those in towns is 1 to 24. Women dominate the field at a ratio of 23 to 1.

The average salary of a school psychologist working in public schools is equal to a special teacher's salary, which is slightly above the national average. The minimum salary is 250 euros (gross) per month for a school psychologist during the first four years after graduating from a master's-degree program in psychology. The school psychologist with 15 or more years of practice and a doctoral degree in psychology may earn the maximum salary of 430 euros (gross). School psychologists' earnings, therefore, depend on years of professional experience and qualifications.

Since 1997, the School Psychologists' Certification Committee, under the Ministry of Education and Science, has been overseeing and conferring certification for school psychologists. The clarification of requirements for qualification in school psychology has opened new opportunities for professional development. The legislation stipulates that the time provided for school psychologists to upgrade their qualifications, and remain certified, is equal to that allowed for teachers to do likewise. Consequently, an educational institution must offer a psychologist at least 5 days of qualification improvement courses a year. The dates for qualification courses are set by the head of the educational institution. Professional development is taken into consideration when a person applies for a higher qualification category or position. A system for continuing professional development, however, is not yet in place, so updating one's knowledge and skills often depends on a person's own initiative and financial situation. School psychologists usually prefer seminars organized by the National Center for Special Needs Education and Psychology and by the Teachers' Professional Development Center. Continuing education courses offered by universities are also popular among psychologists.

Infrastructure of School Psychology

During the Soviet period, the Lithuanian Psychological Society was a part of the Society of Soviet Union Psychologists, which was under the Academy of Science of the Union of Soviet Socialist Republics. In 1988, during the national liberation movement and 2 years before the restoration of Lithuanian independence, Lithuanian psychologists proclaimed their autonomy, and the independent Lithuanian Psychologists' Association was established (for more information, see the Lithuanian Psychologists' Association's Web site, ww.lps.vu.lt). In 1997, the Lithuanian Psychologists' Association joined the European Federation of Psychologists'

Associations. From its beginning, the Lithuanian Psychologists' Association has been prominent in promoting the development of psychological services in Lithuania. Its goals are to coordinate, and to attend to the quality of, these services and to promote the creation of a system to raise the professional qualifications of psychologists. The Lithuanian Psychologists' Association developed a Code of Professional Ethics for Psychologists (1996) and Regulations for the Use of Standardized Psychological Techniques (1997). These have established standards for psychological practice, including that of school psychology, in Lithuania.

Other organizations that have begun to work on behalf of schools include the Association of Directors of Pedagogical Psychological Services; the School Psychologists' Trade Union Divisions, under the Teachers' Trade Union; and the Methodical Council of School Psychologists, under the Municipal Education Department. The main legislation ensuring provision of psychological assistance to learners and strategies for prevention of psychological problems includes the Law on Education (new edition: 2003), the Law on Special Education (1999), and the Law on Fundamental Protection of Rights of the Child (1996). School psychology practice and psychological service within the educational system has been regulated by Ministry of Education and Science legislation, such as General Regulations for the Position of School Psychologist (2005); Description of the Requirements for the Position of School Psychologist Assistant (2005); Requirements for the Position of Psychologists Working at Municipal Pedagogical Psychological Services (2004); Description of the Procedures of the Provision of Psychological Assistance to Schoolchildren (2004); and the Procedure for Identification of Type and Degree of Disorders of Special Needs Persons and Designation of These Persons to Groups According to Special Education Needs (2002).

Requirements to be met by school psychologists are higher education, qualification (specialization) as a psychologist, at least a master's degree in psychology, or equivalent qualification (with no less than 200 credits in psychology earned during consecutive university study). Furthermore, school psychologists must have the ability to provide psychological assistance to students encountering a variety of psychological problems or having special educational needs in cooperation with teachers, special teachers, speech therapists, social pedagogues, other specialists, and parents, guardians, or tutors.

According to recent legislation, it is not mandatory to have graduated from an educational psychology program to become certified as a school psychologist. It is possible to become a school psychologist through other psychology graduate programs. Legislation does not preclude one from taking on the position of psychologist at a school or at Psychological Pedagogical Services if one has completed a master's-degree program in clinical psychology, health, or a related field.

The new Requirements for the School Psychologist Assistant Position (2005) allow a person with a bachelor's degree in psychology to provide certain psychological services under the supervision of a professional psychologist. Until now, the position of an assistant school psychologist could have been filled by specialists qualified as teachers in psychology. According to data provided by the National Center for Special Needs Education and Psychology (Specialiosios Pedagogikos ir Psichologijos Centras, 2006), 11.2% of those currently working in school psychology are not certified as psychologists. They either do not have a master's degree or are in the process of completing their studies.

Preparation of School Psychologists

Educational psychology master's-degree programs have been offered at Vilnius University since 1996, at Vytautas Magnus University in Kaunas since 1995, and at Klaipėda University since 2003. These programs were accredited by the Ministry of Education and Science in 2001.

Approximately 40 students graduate from these three programs each year. During their studies, students have to complete a program that requires no less than 60 credits. One credit is made up of 40 hours and includes lectures, seminars, course papers, home assignments, individual work, supervised practice, and a master's thesis.

The training requirements for becoming a school psychologist are a minimum of 6 years in psychology or, for those who graduated before 1996, a minimum of 5 years of study in psychology. Two-year master's programs are available only to those who have completed a 4-year bachelor's degree in psychology. Master's studies in educational psychology usually are less competitive than studies in clinical or organizational psychology.

Bachelor's-level students take courses covering core areas of knowledge in psychology including developmental, learning and cognition, educational, clinical, personality, social, experimental, biological, measurement, statistics, and research design. The holder of a bachelor's degree in psychology learns how to apply knowledge in psychology to solve psychological problems. The bachelor's psychology program covers a range of research techniques and theories. It includes courses on how to identify and assess questions of interest, carry out independent empirical research adhering to ethical guidelines and using a variety of data collection techniques, and interpret and relate data to different theories and communicate one's findings. Students also learn how to study independently and to work in groups.

The educational psychology master's-degree programs provide ample opportunities for students to relate theoretical knowledge to practical situations. The aims of the master's program are to impart basic knowledge in psychology in educational contexts, develop professional task-solving skills important for assessment and intervention, provide training in research techniques, develop skills for analyzing statistical data, and apply research to practice.

Students develop professional values consistent with psychological ethics and receive training in professional practice. However, only Vilnius University's master's-degree program requires 4 months of supervised professional practice in educational settings (primary, basic, and secondary schools and Pedagogical Psychological Services). A holder of a master's degree in psychology learns about the validity and reliability of psychological evaluation techniques and the scope of their application, and is able to gather information on difficulties encountered by students, families, and schools. Students in these master's programs learn how to (a) contribute to the prevention and intervention programs that promote the mental health of children and adolescents; (b) choose and apply relevant intervention methods, including consulting and counseling techniques; (c) analyze the counseling and intervention process; (d) evaluate outcomes and discuss them with clients; and (e) write psychological reports.

Roles, Functions, and Responsibilities of School Psychologists

Psychologists working at educational institutions provide a range of services for children, their families, and school personnel. The purpose of these services is to promote mental health and facilitate learning. Working directly in educational settings, school psychologists are familiar with the unique characteristics and current educational policies of the school system. School psychologists work with school- and municipality-based interdisciplinary teams, contributing their unique perspectives on child development and a research-based approach to problem solving. School psychologists combine different training and approaches to provide the most effective and comprehensive service to children and adolescents in schools. School psychologists support students and are able to prevent psychological problems that children face in schools and in the community.

School psychological service staff provide a range of diverse services to support students and their families when they face issues that affect students' learning, emotional status, and behavior in class. Among the responsibilities of psychologists working at schools and in-service settings are the following activities:

Consulting. School psychologists consult with school staff and community specialists on educational environment and other factors affecting students' learning. They consult with students, school staff, and parents regarding education and/or personal/social needs; provide information regarding community services available to students; make appropriate recommendations regarding students' vocational needs; and inform, assist, and make recommendations to parents, guardians, tutors, teachers, and others involved with the special needs child's education.

Assessment. School psychologists assess the child's strengths and difficulties to evaluate developmental, emotional, behavioral, and learning problems and special educational needs. The school psychologist assesses the child's level of maturity for schooling at the service center or school, or, in the event of severe mobility problems at home. Special education needs assessment is carried out by the Special Education Commission. It is based on a multi-team approach that includes the school psychologist. The psychologist on the team recommends specific learning skills and, if needed, psychological assistance. Assessment results are used to find the least restrictive environment that will best facilitate the children's education, according to the programs assigned by the Special Education Commission: modified, adapted, special, or individual. The tests commonly used in the psychological assessment process are the Wechsler Intelligence Scale for Children, third edition (for intellectual abilities); Strengths Difficulties Questionnaire and

the Achenbach System of Empirical Based Assessment (for emotional and behavioral problems); Kinetic Family Drawings, Incomplete Sentences, and the Adjective Checklist (for personality, social interactions). Observations, interviews, and informal assessment are also widely used.

Education. School psychologists educate children, their parents, guardians, tutors, or teachers about child development, education, and social and psychological problem prevention. Psychologists offer information and methodological assistance to teachers, specialists, parents, guardians, and tutors about the organization of education as it relates to children's psychological, personality, and educational problems and their solutions. Psychologists inform and implement the latest scientific findings in psychology. They work to create a positive attitude in the school community and society toward children experiencing various psychological, personality, or learning difficulties.

Prevention. School psychologists assess the need for psychological problem prevention programs that help prevent psychological, personality, and learning problems and foster the development of students with social and mental problems. They prepare, organize, and implement preventive measures and programs; they prevent and intervene during psychological crises at school (e.g., following a suicide or an act of violence).

Supervision. School psychologists engage in supervision to ensure the quality of psychological work, professional development, and assistance in complicated cases. According to legislation, graduates of psychology must work under the supervision of an experienced colleague for 1 year following completion of their studies.

Psychologists from the Pedagogical Psychological Services also provide group counseling for children who have experienced a trauma (e.g., from loss or violence) or who suffer from any type of dependence. Psychologists working at the National Center of Special Education Needs and Psychology are responsible for considering issues of psychological assistance in complicated cases. This may be necessary when a child's parents, guardians, or tutors do not agree with a decision concerning a psychological assessment made by the Special Education Commission or are dissatisfied with the quality of psychological service at a school or at municipal Pedagogical Psychological Services.

Current Issues Impacting School Psychology

Rapid political, economic, and social changes in Lithuania since 1990 have had a tremendous impact on the country's education system and on the development of school psychology. Legislative directives on psychological assistance in schools and school-related settings, the growing number of pedagogical psychological services, changes in educational psychology programs offered by universities, and increasingly close collaboration with colleagues from other countries have all created new opportunities for school psychologists. The growing role of the European Federation of Psychologists' Associations in developing guidelines to ensure the quality of professional psychologists in the educational system has also enhanced the profession.

Despite these advances, some issues regarding the provision of psychological assistance take top priority within the Lithuanian Psychologists' Association. Issues around accreditation and licensing need to be resolved. The establishment of a licensing system for psychologists is currently being discussed by the Lithuanian Psychologists' Association. The Lithuanian Psychologists' Association and universities should work together to establish accreditation standards and initiate program reviews and modifications for psychology study programs. The lack of national standards for preparing educational psychologists leads to variation among universities in terms of what is provided and required. The description of the basic competencies required for the European Certificate in Psychology from the European Federation of Psychologists' Associations and the Guidelines for the Preparation of School Psychologists developed by International School Psychology Association are sufficient to prepare students to be "good enough" school psychologists and could be used to establish national standards.

Opportunities for professional development of school psychologists are urgently needed. Adequate financing of school psychologists' continued training, qualification upgrading, and new qualification acquisition programs, in line with the needs of the education reform agenda, should be guaranteed. All psychologists working in educational settings should have the same opportunities to upgrade or acquire new qualifications. The existing system for certification of school psychologists is an issue. The role of psychologists in educational institutions needs to be clarified, and their functions need to be more precisely defined. Attention to training and upgrading qualifications is due. These considerations are included in the Provisions of the National Education Strategy 2003–2012, approved by the Lithuanian Parliament in 2003.

One of the many challenges school psychologists have been facing for a long time is psychological testing and assessment. It is an important area of psychological service, particularly for those working in multi-teams as members of the Special Education Commission at schools or pedagogical psychological services. Psychological testing in Lithuania during the past generation did not follow the same course as it did in many European, North American, or other countries. Testing was forbidden in the Soviet Union for a long time. This stopped the development of psychological testing in Lithuania until 2002, when the Wechsler Intelligence Scale for Children–III became the first intelligence test that was standardized in Lithuania. These scales were long awaited by school and clinical psychologists. School psychologists took an active part in the Wechsler Intelligence Scale for Children–III standardization process and attended special courses organized at Vilnius University for test users. This event changed some negative attitudes regarding psychological testing and assessment that had dominated among professionals. Today it is important to pool the forces of all psychologists, those in academia and those in practice, to develop psychological instruments. School psychologists have thus far taken an active role in the standardization of the Strengths Difficulties Questionnaire, Raven's Colored Progressive Matrices, and the School Maturity Scale. Nonetheless, psychological assessment remains problematic, as test adaptation or construction is relatively expensive because of the small number of test users who have relevant qualifications.

Despite the university's attempts to prepare more qualified specialists in educational psychology (the provision of psychological assistance at educational institutions), the number of such specialists, especially in rural areas, is extremely small. Educational institutions affiliated with the Special Education Commissions represent only a very small fraction of Lithuanian schools. The introduction of an inclusive practice in schools has created an increasing number of students who require psychological assistance, including assessment and consultation. The lack of specialists in some districts has forced Pedagogical Psychological Services to organize their work according to the practice model "refer, test, and place," which means that ongoing consultations and other follow-up activities are very limited.

The current challenges in meeting children's needs stimulate a search for new ways of interdisciplinary, interprofessional, and interservice cooperation. Educational systems, as well as health care services, require psychological support for projects designed for children's mental health provision. The first epidemiological study on the mental health of Lithuanian children and adolescents, conducted in 2003–2005, was a result of the close cooperation between the researchers from the Department of General Psychology and the Center of Child Psychiatry and Social Paediatrics of Vilnius University. It can also be viewed as an example of effective cooperation between school psychologists, clinical psychologists, and psychiatrists working as a team in close collaboration with schools and families.

The Lithuanian experience shows that, despite political interference, the dispersion of people throughout the country, and limited resources, the country has, in a short time, developed legislation and a system of psychological assistance to address schoolchildren's needs. Much work still needs to be done to improve, refine, and address shortcomings in the current system, training process, and core curriculum, but a road map has been charted to guide the process. The Lithuanian experience allows for, and welcomes, truly fascinating collaborative partnerships in cross-cultural research and the sharing of perspectives on curriculum and training.

References

Aidukienė, T., & Labinienė, R. (2003). Vaikų, turinčių specialiųjų poreikių, ugdymo tendencijų apžvalga tarptautiniame bei Lietuvos švietimo reformos kontekste (1990–2002) [Review of the trends in education for children with special needs in the international context and in the context of educational reforms in Lithuania (1990–2002)]. In J. Ambrukaitis, A. Ališauskas, R. Labinienė, & J. Ruškus (Eds.), *Essentials of special education. Handbook for pedagogy students* (pp. 31–49). Šiauliai: Šiauliai University Press.

Baltic Tiger [Electronic version]. (2003, July 17). *The Economist, 368*(833), 32. Retrieved March 8, 2006, from http://www.economist.com/displaystory.cfm?story_id=1929205

Gučas, A. (1937). *Pašaukimas ir darbas* [Vocation and job]. Kaunas: Lithuanian Society for Psychotechnique and Vocational Guidance.

Lapė, J. (1999). *Psichologų draugija ir js įtaka psichologijos raidai Lietuvoje* [Association of Psychologists and its influence on psychology development in Lithuania]. *Psychology: Research Papers, 19,* 124–132.

Ministry of Education and Science of Republic of Lithuania. (2004). *Education in Lithuania.* Vilnius: Author.

Reklyte, A., & Gintilienė, G. (1993, May). *Special education in Lithuania.* Paper presented at Special Needs Education in Europe for Children With Mental and Physical Disabilities Conference, Middelfart, Denmark.

Specialiosios Pedagogikos ir Psichologijos Centras [National Center for Special Needs Education and Psychology]. (2006). *Pedagoginių psichologinių tarnybų ir mokyklų psichologų apklausos rezultatų aprašymas* [Review of survey of psychologists from pedagogical and psychological services and schools]. Retrieved May 8, 2006, from http://www.sppc.lt/index.php?-984082152

Statistics Lithuania. (2005). *Education 2004.* Vilnius: Author.

Valantinas, A. (1998). The development of pedagogical psychological services in Lithuania. In *Contemporary problems in education* (pp. 48–54). Vilnius: Lithuanian Institute of Teachers' In-service Training.

24

School Psychology in Malta

Paul A. Bartolo

Victor Martinelli

Context of School Psychology

Malta was a British colony for 164 years. In 1964, it became independent; in 1974, it became a republic; and, in 2004, it joined the European Union. Malta consists of two main islands lying in the centre of the Mediterranean Sea, 93 kilometers south of Sicily and 288 kilometers west of Tunisia. Malta, Gozo, and three smaller islands make up a mere 316 square kilometers. Malta, the largest island, is 27 kilometers at its longest point and 14 kilometers at its widest point. With a population of 400,000, the Maltese Islands are the most densely populated (over 1,265 persons per square kilometer) country in the European Union. In 2004, its gross domestic product was US$7.2 billion, US$18,200 per capita. Its major industry is tourism (see Malta government Web site at www.gov.mt).

Malta's long cultural history extends to at least 5000 BC. The University of Malta is more than 400 years old, dating to the rule of the Military Order of the Knights Hospitallers of St John. Compulsory primary education for all children from age 5 through 14 years was introduced in 1946 and fully implemented by the early 1950s. In 1970, secondary education was extended to all students. In 1974, compulsory attendance was raised from age 14 to 16. In 1975, state-supported kindergarten centers for 4-year-olds were opened and, in 1987, were extended to 3-year-olds. More than 95% of children ages 3 and 4 attend school regularly.

The first education act was passed in 1974 and revised in 1988. These acts entitle every child to a public education (Zammit Mangion, 1992). In 1956, public special education services were initiated. All children with special needs now have the right to attend schools of their choice and are mainly in mainstream schools (Bartolo, 2001a). The education system serves about 70,000 students ages 3 through 16 years. Its structure is similar to that found in the United Kingdom. Children move from kindergarten (ages 3–4) to primary (ages 5–10), to secondary (ages 11–15), to sixth form or postsecondary vocational courses (ages 16–17). The Malta College of Arts, Science, and Technology offers postsecondary vocational courses. In addition, 10,000 students, including 700 international students, attend the University of Malta. State schools serve 64% of the school population. Another 24% attend church schools (which also are funded by the state), and 12% are in independent (private) schools. Only 0.41% of the total school population attends state schools for students with special education needs (i.e., hearing and visually impaired, multiple disabilities, severe intellectual disabilities, moderate intellectual disabilities, and emotional and behavioural difficulties).

Malta's educational establishment is similar to those found in many small countries. Malta has one central Department of Education that determines the funding, curriculum, and employment of school personnel in all state schools. Thus, policy and practice decisions affect all state schools. Attempts to establish separate autonomous clusters of schools are under way. Whereas administrators and educators in larger countries generally use their national policy and legislation to establish educational standards, the Maltese generally refer and defer to standards developed in other countries, initially to British standards; then, on becoming a republic, to United Nations standards; and, more recently, to European Union standards.

Until 1971, a very selective 11+ national examination system was used to certify educational attainment. Following the British educational practices, in 1972, the practice of grouping students in classes based on the results of the national achievement examinations (i.e., streaming) was abolished and replaced by a comprehensive system in which classes at all levels were grouped by age rather than educational achievement. However, preparations for this transition to mixed-ability classes were inadequate and partly responsible for an accelerated expansion of church and independent schools, which, at the time, had remained selective (Zammit Marmara, 2001). Consequently, in 1981, the practice of grouping students by age and having mixed-ability classes was abolished in favor of reinstituting the use of a national examination and streaming system. National examinations start in Year 4 primary (age 8 years), leading to the streaming of students on the basis of test scores obtained in five subjects: Maltese, English, mathematics, social studies, and religion. A similar end-of-year exam at age 10 is used to stream children into one of three secondary school ability streams: junior lyceums (higher achievers), secondary schools, and a number of other secondary schools for the lowest achievers, which teach a primary school curriculum. Approximately 50%, 45%, and 5% of students are streamed into each of these three levels, respectively. Schools for the lowest achievers are being phased out.

The curriculum for each subject is rigid, organized by year level syllabi and tied to the content of national examinations at each year level. Classroom instruction generally consists of whole-class teaching methods. Surveys of teachers and parents show that the majority is in favor of a streaming system (Bartolo, 2001b). Current thinking highlights the importance of academic competition as a way to prepare students for adult life (Bartolo, 2001b). Church and independent schools use a mixture of streamed and unstreamed systems. State schools admit students from a regional catchment area, while church and independent schools admit students from all localities in Malta and Gozo. During the past 15 years, a rival educational discourse has emerged, one that focuses attention on the rights of each child for a quality education, especially on the right of students with impairments for education in regular schools. These efforts have been fuelled by developments in Europe as well as local political and educational enterprise (Bartolo, 2001b).

The number of students identified as having special education needs is 1,785, or 2.57% of the total school population, including the 286, or 0.41%, who are in special schools. As of 2005, there were six special schools in Malta and another one for all categories of need on the smaller island of Gozo (Spiteri Borg, Callus, Cauchi, & Sciberras, 2005). The six special schools in Malta are the Helen Keller School for hearing and visually impaired students; the San Miguel School for students with multiple disabilities; the Guardian Angel School for students with severe intellectual disabilities; the Dun Manwel Attard School (Wardija) for students with moderate intellectual disabilities; the Mater Dei School for students with emotional and behavioural difficulties; and the St. Patrick's Crafts Centre. The special school on the island of Gozo is designated as a special annexe to a school and is part of a primary school building. All mainstreamed students with special needs are in regular classes, often supported by a learning support assistant, locally referred to as a "facilitator." The mainstreaming of the majority of children with special education needs has been made possible through the employment of 1,142 learning support assistants (Spiteri et al., 2005). There are no special classes in mainstream schools.

Origin, History, and Current Status of School Psychology

Educational psychology is relatively new in Malta. As in other domains, Maltese developments appear to have been influenced initially by British experiences. The first training of staff for educating children with special education needs occurred in the early 1950s when a teacher was trained as a speech therapist and, in 1956, became the first education officer for special education. This appointment coincided with the opening of the first state facility for children with hearing impairment within a mainstream school.

In 1961, two teachers were sent to the United Kingdom to complete a 1-year diploma on educating "handicapped children." Subsequently, one became the first educational psychologist in Malta, and the other was appointed as the second education officer for special education

(Bartolo, 2001a). At about the same time, a second teacher was trained as an educational psychologist in the United Kingdom and worked in the test construction unit of the Department of Education before joining the lecturing staff of the teacher training college. Thus, from 1971 to 1977, one educational psychologist was employed in the School Psychological Service within the Department of Education. Attempts to develop a relevant career structure failed, resulting in this single educational psychologist accepting the post of director in the Welfare/Social Services Department. The one and only post of educational psychologist lay vacant between 1977 and 1990. The few and fragmented educational psychological services offered were provided through the Health and the Social Services Departments.

The years 1984 through 1987 mark the next phase during which the Department of Education was faced with a number of teachers who returned after pursuing, on their own initiative, psychology programs overseas, particularly through the Commonwealth Scholarship Award program or through cultural agreements with various countries, including Italy and the former Soviet Union. Some trained as clinical psychologists or obtained a master's degree in academic educational psychology. None were fully trained as practicing educational psychologists. These personnel started delivering various psychological services following their placement in the special education section and, later, in the school guidance and counseling services within the Department of Education. They also urged the Department of Education to establish a school psychological service. Consequently, the two authors of this chapter were sponsored to complete their training as educational psychologists in two successive courses at the University of Manchester in the United Kingdom.

The first author was appointed educational psychologist in Malta in 1990. This appointment marked the formal beginning of the School Psychological Service, with its own office space and budget at the Department of Education and under the responsibility of the assistant director for support services. This appointment also marked the establishment of services provided by specifically trained educational psychologists, whereas the clinical psychologists previously serving in the embryonic School Psychological Service moved to the University of Malta and the Department of Public Health.

Most psychologists in the education system were trained in the United Kingdom. Thus, they always have referred to themselves as *educational psychologists*, consistent with terminology used in that country. On the other hand, the post in government employment has always been titled "school psychologist" with the corollary title "school psychological service," terms imported from Canada following the institution of the first educational psychologist post in Malta in 1971, the incumbent of which trained in Canada.

Despite attempts at developing the newly revamped School Psychological Service as a backbone to support services for schools, the continuing resistance within the Department of Education to establishing a career structure for educational psychologists hindered the expected development of the School Psychological Service. Thus, once again, the appointed educational psychologist and two other fully trained colleagues moved out of the education system in the 1990s, this time to an expanding psychology department at the University of Malta. The School Psychological Service continued to limp along, relying on educational psychologists who personally initiated their professional preparation, until Malta developed its own psychologist preparation program. Beginning in 1999, the University of Malta offered the first 2-year master's degree in psychology. Four trainees, sponsored by the Department of Education, later joined the only other psychologist in the School Psychological Service in 2001, and another joined 3 years later, resulting in six psychologists in the School Psychological Service.

The need for psychological services in education arose out of the increasing presence of students with special educational needs. In 1958, special schools were established and, by the 1980s, were serving all children with special educational needs (Bartolo, 2001a). In the 1990s, inclusive education policies expanded, and services were greatly enhanced through the establishment of a nongovernmental organization for providing multidisciplinary services for children with impairments. An educational psychologist initially led these services (Bartolo, 1994, 2000). Similarly, the establishment of a board to review requests for special provisions for children with special education needs within the Department of Education resulted in the involvement of educational psychologists to describe the extent of the learning difficulty and to provide advice on needed services (Ministerial Committee for Inclusive Education, 2000).

The drive to identify, understand, and serve the special education needs of students attending mainstream classes continues to be the mainstay of the School Psychological Service within the Department of Education. These educational psychologists are seen as an integral part of the process of identifying and evaluating student needs and, in many cases, serve as links between those providing services. The School Psychological Service recently established multidisciplinary teams, called Special Educational Needs Teams, in a number of schools. The inclusion movement also has impacted the examination system in Malta. Students with special needs may be tested under special arrangements, often based on an educational psychologist's report (Ministry of Education, 2002).

The Malta Union of Professional Psychologists attempted to create a common status for all psychologists in Malta and, in 1996, negotiated the first career/grade structure specific to all psychologists in government employment. The starting salary of a psychologist was pegged at the level of *professional officer 1* (having the same pay scale as a beginning physician) and rising within the government civil service grade structure. This structure has been reorganized such that the *psychologist grade* has been relegated to below that of a school guidance counselor and assistant head of school, positions that require less training. The maximum salary of a basic grade educational psychologist ranges from about US$21,000 to US$22,000 a year. Although educational psychologists report good job satisfaction in their work with their clients, they feel undervalued and underpaid. No educational psychologists work full-time in private practice.

There are only 11 educational psychologists in Malta; 7 are male. The number of female psychologists is increasing. In fact, the male-to-female ratio of psychologists who work in the Department of Education's School Psychological Service is 1 to 2, in favor of females.

Educational psychologists work in four different settings. Most are in state employment within the School Psychological Service and work in state and church schools. One works part-time with a major nongovernmental organization that serves students with special needs. Four form part of the teaching staff at the University of Malta, and a fifth also works part-time on the organization of special education arrangements within the university examination administration system. As there is considerable demand for psychoeducational services, because of the low ratio of psychologists to clients (about 1 per 11,500 students aged 3 to 17), most educational psychologists offer some services privately. One works part-time in a nongovernmental organization for children with disabilities.

About fifteen school counselors are employed within the Department of Education. They provide counseling services to secondary level students. They do not carry the title "psychologist," and they typically do not engage in testing except in relation to vocational guidance.

Because Malta is small, demarcations between urban and rural areas are not clear. Nevertheless, issues regarding limited availability of services in rural areas, prominent in larger countries, also are found on the small island of Gozo, which has a population of 25,000. The services of educational psychologists who work out of the centrally based School Psychological Service unit in Malta are less available to schools on Gozo. Traveling to the northern end of the island, queuing for the trip, and driving to the schools are time-consuming activities and result in fewer services to Gozo.

Opportunities for professional development are limited to conferences organized by the two psychology associations. Overseas opportunities are costly, as they involve airfare and living expenses. Additional continuing professional development is contemplated in light of the recently enacted Psychology Profession Act (2005). Most educational psychologists continue to acquire knowledge through journals and newsletters issued by the Division of Educational and Child Psychology of the British Psychological Society, including the *British Journal of Educational Psychology* and *Educational and Child Psychology,* and the European Federation of Psychologists' Associations' journal, *European Psychologist.* Educational psychologists also consult the reports of the European Federation of Psychologists' Associations' task force on school psychology (e.g., European Federation of Psychologists' Associations, 2001, 2003). The European Federation of Psychologists' Associations' metacode of ethics, adopted in 1995 (an important contribution to which was made by the South European Group of members within the European Federation of Psychologists' Associations at their meeting in Malta in November 1994), also constitutes the code of ethics for Maltese psychologists.

State employees, including psychologists, generally are appointed on a permanent basis. However, a number of educational psychologists left the service to teach at the university, a setting regarded as offering better work conditions than those available at the School Psychological Service. Unless a proper career structure is instituted, further attrition can be expected as current members fulfill their statutory period of service and look elsewhere for improved career opportunities.

Infrastructure of Educational Psychology

All educational psychologists are members of the Malta Union of Professional Psychologists, which was established in 1992 as both a trade union and a professional body. The Union is affiliated with a Maltese national federation of trade unions and remains the sole representative of the educational psychologist grade in collective and sector agreements with government. The Malta Union of Professional Psychologists, also serves as a member of international bodies, namely the European Federation of Psychologists' Associations and the International Union of Psychological Sciences.

Malta is the 16th European Union country to introduce the regulation of the profession of psychology. Maltese psychologists had requested this legislation some years ago because of the increasing number of unqualified psychologists offering services. The Psychology Profession Act of 2004, which became effective in February 2005, established the qualification of a psychologist as someone with a master's degree in psychology conferred by the University of Malta, or another qualification, as the Malta Psychology Profession Board may deem equivalent, plus 2 years of supervised practice. This requirement is consistent with that of the European Qualification in Psychology, except that it requires 2 years, rather than 1, of supervised practice. The law also provides for the possible future determination of specializations in psychology beyond the basic qualification: "The warrant . . . shall not entitle the holder thereof to exercise the profession of psychology in such areas of specialized psychology as may be prescribed by the Minister as requiring additional qualifications and, or, training . . ." (Psychology Profession Act, 2005, art. 3 (2)).

The proper implementation of these provisions will depend on the Malta Psychology Profession Board, which consists of six psychologists and an attorney. This board is instituting a process to "regulate the practice and the eligibility to practice the profession of psychology in Malta" (Psychology Profession Act, 2005, arts. 4, 5). Prior to this Act, the only board that issued licenses to psychologists in Malta (albeit only to clinical psychologists) was a Board Regulating Professions Supplementary to Medicine and included only one member to represent psychologists. Through the new Act, psychologists now officially lead and constitute the board that regulates psychology. Moreover, two members of the board are official representatives from each of the two psychologists' organizations in the country. Politicians still are responsible for appointing board members and implementing the board's recommendations. The board also is responsible for developing a code of conduct for psychologists.

Preparation of Educational Psychologists

Psychology only recently came of age in Malta. The development of courses for the training of psychologists by the University of Malta has been hampered by the coincidence of a period of funding restrictions at the University, after a period of great expansion in the early 1990s. At the same time, all full-time university courses are statutorily free. Thus, in 1996, when professional training at the master's level was proposed, funding had to come from nonuniversity sources, impeding its implementation. The first 2-year master's degree in psychology program, funded by three government departments, was finally offered in 1999. Funding problems remained. A second cohort of 11 students was enrolled in February 2005, after special arrangements were made to allow a degree of self-funding by students. There is as yet no assurance that a third cohort will be enrolled.

This 2-year master's program plus 2 years of supervised practice constitute the explicit standard of training required by the Psychology Profession Act of 2004 for acquiring the title "psychology." Thus, the period from entering an undergraduate program to obtaining a psychologist's license in educational psychology is at least 10 years: 3 years for a bachelor's degree in psychology (with honors), 1 year postgraduate teacher training, 2 years teaching, 2 years for the master's degree in psychology, and 2 years supervised practice. Some are lobbying to remove the teacher training and teaching experience requirements. They have been removed from the requirements for the projected European Qualification in Psychology professional qualification.

The preparation of all psychologists in Malta reflects the needs and history of this small island state. All areas of psychology were housed in the only Department of Psychology at the only university in Malta. Additionally, the market for psychological services in Malta is very small, by virtue of its population size. Thus, a decision was made to offer one professional training program for three specializations of psychologists: clinical, counseling, and educational. The number of trainees in the first cohort included three in clinical, four in counseling, and four in educational psychology. The 2005–2007 program accepted four, four, and three trainees, respectively.

The 2-year course consists of a total of 120 European Credit Transfer System (hereafter referred to as credits) credits divided as follows: 50 credits for theoretically oriented courses, 50 credits that offer practical training, 10 credits for research, and 10 credits for a final examination. In addition, trainees are expected to undertake 20 hours in personal development (University of Malta, 2005). The course attempts to promote interaction among the three specialization areas. Thus 20 of the 50 theoretical credits are common to the three streams. Another 4 credits are common to clinical and educational trainees, whereas clinical and counseling trainees share 22 credits. Thus, trainees receive a body of knowledge related to pharmacology (although psychologists in Malta do not have prescription privileges) as well as training in psychotherapy, topics not usually included in programs offered in the United Kingdom. The practice placements are in different environments; only educational trainees are placed in the School Psychological Service and other school-related

agencies. On the other hand, specialized fieldwork placements (e.g., assessment and family therapy) also are common.

The theoretically oriented courses for the educational specialization cover all the areas identified by Cunningham and Oakland (1998), with a core around understanding, assessment, and intervention with students with various forms of impairment, but also with an unusual slant toward clinical areas. The 50 theoretically oriented credits address the following: (a) knowledge of child development and special educational needs (14 credits on developmental psychopathology, students with developmental learning difficulties, physical and sensory impairments, communication difficulties, specific learning difficulties, socioemotional and behavioural difficulties, autism, and challenging behaviors); (b) knowledge of the context of development (10 credits on understanding contexts of development, disability issues and inclusive education, working with the child, parents, and teachers, and family therapy and systemic consultation); (c) assessment services (4 credits on psychological assessment of children and parts of other credits in special needs education and neuropsychology); (d) intervention services (10 credits on child and adolescent psychotherapy, psychopharmacology, information technology for special needs, part of the credits on different forms of impairment, family therapy and systemic consultation, group counseling and group psychotherapy, working with the child, parents, and teachers, and in-service training for teachers, parents, and other education professionals; (e) interpersonal skills and professional decision-making skills are covered as part of the credits in group counseling, group psychotherapy, and group supervision sessions, averaging an hour a week throughout the course; (f) knowledge of statistical methods and research design (4 credits on research methods and a supervised dissertation); and (g) knowledge of the legal and ethical basis for services (4 credits on professional ethics which are also addressed in individual and group supervision).

Educational psychologists usually provide pre- and in-service professional development for teachers. Virtually all educational psychologists have some involvement in tertiary education, usually in teacher education, general psychology, or meeting the needs of students with special needs. Courses for learning support teachers and assistants and inclusion coordinators have been coordinated by educational psychologists. An educational psychologist serves as the coordinator of a National Curriculum Focus Group aimed at implementing policy on inclusive education (Spiteri et al., 2005).

Roles, Functions, and Responsibilities of Educational Psychologists

The major role of educational psychologists is the provision of psychoeducational assessment services. Assessment is sought either for a diagnosis of learning difficulties or for the identification of resources to be provided for the child. This assessment often includes testing and may be carried out in multidisciplinary teams. One nongovernmental organization established in 1992 always has employed the services of a team of professionals, including psychologists, speech and language pathologists, and physio- and occupational therapists.

The School Psychological Service regularly uses a multidisciplinary approach by working in special educational needs teams in mainstream schools. These teams operate only in a few schools and normally comprise an educational psychologist, head of the school, school counselor, school social worker, speech and language pathologist, and school medical officer.

Testing and Assessment Models and Methods

Test use is problematic. Ability and aptitude tests as well as behaviour checklists are not normed on the Maltese population. Educational psychologists tend to use United Kingdom norms, when available. However, these norms

may not be appropriate for Maltese students and thus must be used cautiously. In addition, although Malta is formally bilingual and English is one of the official languages, Maltese is the first language of the large majority of the population. Thus, language-based items are likely to be culturally inappropriate for Maltese students. Attempts to translate language items into Maltese may further complicate test use. This situation places great responsibility on psychologists for understanding the constructs measured by tests, making judicious use of psychoeducational tests, and requiring care when interpreting scores, thus giving weight to a student's qualitative performance.

Educational psychologists use a wide variety of psychoeducational measures. These include the British Spelling Test Series (Vincent & Crumpler, 1997), Maltese Word Reading Test (Bartolo, 1988), and Neale Analysis of Reading Ability (Neale, 1997); intellectual ability tests, including the British Ability Scales–II (Elliott, Smith, & McCulloch, 1996), Differential Ability Scales (Elliott, 1990), and the Wechsler Intelligence Scale for Children (Wechsler, 1991); personality/temperament/behavior/social skills, including Vineland Adaptive Behavior Scales (Sparrow, Balla & Cicchetti, 1984), Bene-Anthony Family Relations Test (Bene, 1985), Brown Attention Deficit Disorder Scales (Brown, 1996), Childhood Autism Rating Scale (Aarons & and Gittens, 1992), Diagnostic Interview for Social and Communications Disorders (Wing, 1999), and Gilliam Autism Rating Scale (Gilliam, 1995), together with other assessment instruments including the Bracken Basic Concept Scale (Bracken, 1998), Dyslexia Screening Test (Fawcett & Nicholson, 1996), Phonological Assessment Battery (Frederickson, Frith, & Reason, 1997), and Sentence Comprehension Test (Wheddall, Mittler, & Hobsbaum, 1987).

Interventions

Given the heavy demands for psychoeducational assessment services, educational psychologists have limited time for direct intervention. Most rely on parents, teachers, and other school support staff to implement their recommendations. All children start school in the regular kindergarten. Thus, recommendations for them usually concern whether individualized instruction is needed, not placement. Recommendations often include advice on behavioral management and socioemotional support as well as teaching and learning strategies.

At the transition from primary to secondary school, educational psychologists are involved in decisions on special arrangements for examinations as well as placement decisions into the different types of secondary schools and levels of support required. Some educational psychologists also work directly with children and young adults, such as in cases of school phobia and emotional and behavioral difficulties. More recently, the School Psychological Service became engaged in supporting school staff and children in post-traumatic stress disorder after an accident on a school playground involving the death of a student.

Consultation Services

Virtually all educational psychologists, whether employed by the state or practicing independently, provide consultative services to teachers and learning support assistants, heads of schools and their assistants, and parents and other family members. They also provide consultative services to other professionals, including speech and language pathologists, occupational therapists, and occasionally pediatricians who work closely with them.

Current Issues Impacting School Psychology

Although the first educational psychologist was appointed in the Department of Education in 1971, the services offered by the Department of Education's School Psychological Service tend to be rather piecemeal. Educational psychology is still finding its feet. With regard to practice, the School Psychological Service is in a fluid situation. A need to restructure educational psychologists' status and conditions of work and to develop wider involvement at the system level instead of assessment for special examination arrangements is urgent (Martinelli & Scerri, 2000). The involvement of the School Psychological Service in the special educational needs multidisciplinary teams and in-service training needs to increase. Professional practice will improve, driven by the requirements of the Psychology Profession Act, if a peer supervision system is developed as part of continuing professional development. Current services by educational psychologists in nongovernmental institutions and the private sector often are fragmented due to their part-time status. This situation hinders the development of more permanent educational psychology service structures that would ensure the creation and continuity of high standards of service.

The training of psychologists poses other challenges. Only two cohort groups have been prepared, and there is no guarantee of future cohorts. Issues about entry into and the nature of the program have been contentious. Malta had followed the example from the United Kingdom that requires teacher qualification and experience as a prerequisite for becoming educational psychologists. Because this prerequisite has been removed from the European Qualification in Psychology professional qualifications, questions arise as to whether and how to implement the change. If the teaching qualification and experience are removed, then the 2-year master's program should be raised to a 3-year doctoral program that includes study and practice in teaching, learning, and other education issues. Finally, although the Psychology Profession Act of 2004 has allowed psychologists to take a momentous step forward by establishing standards of qualification, the task of establishing the roles and competencies of specialization in school psychology remains a challenge.

References

Bartolo, P. A. (1994). Hidma ma' genituri ta' tfal bi htegijiet specjali [Working with parents of children with special needs]. In R. G. Sultana (Ed.), *Genituri u ghalliema ghal edukazzjoni ahjar* (pp. 97–102). Malta: Mireva.

Bartolo, P. A. (2000). The development of inclusive education for children with autism in Malta. In M. G. Borg & P. A. Bartolo (Eds.), *Autism: The challenge of inclusion* (pp. 71–86). Malta: Eden Foundation.

Bartolo, P. A. (2001a). Meeting the diversity of student needs: The development of policy and provisions for the education of children with disability in Malta. In R. G. Sultana (Ed.), *Yesterday's schools: Readings in Maltese educational history* (pp. 203–233). Malta: Publishers Enterprises Group.

Bartolo, P. A. (2001b). Recent developments in inclusive education in Malta. *Mediterranean Journal of Educational Studies, 6*(1), 65–91.

Bartolo, P. A. (2005). Regulating the psychology profession in Malta. *European Psychologist, 10*(1), 76–77.

Cunningham, J., & Oakland, T. (1998). International School Psychology Association Guidelines for the Preparation of School Psychologists. *School Psychology International, 19,* 19–30.

European Federation of Psychologists' Associations (2001). *Reports 2001: Task force on psychologists in the educational system in Europe: Report to the General Assembly 2001 in London.* Retrieved May 11, 2006, from http://www.efpa.be

European Federation of Psychologists' Associations. (2003). *Working Group Psychology in the Education System: Report to the General Assembly 2003 in Vienna.* Retrieved May 11, 2006, from http://www.efpa.be

Martinelli, V., & Scerri, P. (2000). *Perceived effectiveness of educational psychologists as rated by primary school teachers in Malta.* Paper presented at the XXVII International Congress of Psychology, Stockholm, Sweden.

Ministerial Committee for Inclusive Education. (2000). *Inclusive education: Policy regarding students with a disability.* Malta: Ministry of Education. Retrieved May 11, 2006, from http://www.education.gov.mt/ministry/doc/pdf/policy_on_inclusion_of_students_with_disability_of_mcie.pdf

Ministry of Education. (2002). *Guidelines for special examination arrangements for candidates with particular requirements.* Malta: Author. Retrieved May 11, 2006, from http://www.education.gov.mt/ministry/doc/pdf/guidelines_of_special_examintions.pdf

Psychology Profession Act of 2004, Ministry for Justice and Home Affairs 471 (2005). Retrieved April 26, 2006, from http://docs.justice.gov.mt/lom/Legislation/English/Leg/VOL_15/Chapt471.pdf

Spiteri, L., Borg, G., Callus, A. M., Cauchi, J., & Sciberras, M. (2005, June). *Inclusive and special education review report 2005.* Floriana, Malta: Ministry of Education, Youth and Employment. Retrieved May 11, 2006, from http://www.education.gov.mt/ministry/doc/pdf/inclusive_edu.pdf

University of Malta. (2005). *M.Psy (2005–2007) handbook.* Malta: Author.

Zammit Mangion, J. (1992). *Education in Malta.* Malta: Studia Editions.

Zammit Marmara, D. (2001). The ideological struggle over comprehensive education in Malta. In R. G. Sultana (Ed.), *Yesterday's schools: Readings in Maltese educational history* (pp. 253–281). Malta: Publishers Enterprises Group.

25

Psychologists in Education in the Netherlands

Helen E. Bakker

Frida van Doorn

Context of School Psychology

The Kingdom of the Netherlands was established in 1815. In 1830, Belgium seceded and formed a separate kingdom. The Netherlands is located in Western Europe, bordering the North Sea on the west and north, Germany on the east, and Belgium on the south. The country is 41,526 square kilometers. Among its population of approximately 16,407,491 are 19% immigrants, approximately 53% of whom come from non-Western countries, mainly Turkey, Morocco, the Antilles Islands, and Indonesia (Statistics Netherlands, 2005). Thirty percent of the Dutch population is Roman Catholic, 20% is Protestant, 6% is Muslim, 3% practice other religions, and 41% are unaffiliated with a religion (Statistics Netherlands, 2005). The Netherlands has a prosperous economy, dependent mainly on foreign trade. The economy is noted for stable industrial relations, moderate unemployment

and inflation, a sizable account surplus, and its important role as a European transportation hub. The gross domestic product in 2004 was US$481.1 billion, or US$29,500 per capita. Industrial activity is predominantly in food processing, chemicals, petroleum refining, and electrical machinery. Among its working population, 4% are engaged in agriculture, 23% in industry, and 73% in services.

During the 2004–2005 school year, approximately 1,654,980 children, ages 4 through 12, attended primary schools, including special education; 924,780 children, ages 12 through 18, attended secondary schools; and 545,560 students attended some form of postsecondary academic or professional education (Statistics Netherlands, 2005). A core characteristic of the Dutch educational system is its freedom of education (Article 23 of the Constitution). This freedom, included in the constitution since 1848, guarantees the right to establish schools and to determine the principles guiding teaching, including religious, ideological, or educational beliefs. As a result, the Dutch system includes both public and private schools, serving about 30% and 70% of the students, respectively (Dutch Eurydice, 2005). Both public and private schools are funded by the government on an equal basis. The government also sets strict national standards for reading, writing, and arithmetic skills to be mastered in 8 years.

Since 1900, education has been compulsory for children from ages 6 through 12 (Leerplichtwet, 1969). Full-time education now is compulsory for ages 5 to 16. This period should include 12 years of schooling, including the full school year in which the child becomes 16. Children who leave school at 16 are obliged to continue schooling for one day a week until age 18. This is typically done in combination with work or job training.

In 2000, 17,500 students left secondary education without receiving a diploma or basic job qualification. This is about 10% of all students eligible to graduate from secondary school. About 60% of this group without qualification received a lower form of secondary education (Ministry of Education, Culture, and Science, 2003).

The Dutch education system includes three levels: primary education (ages 4–12); secondary education (ages 12–18), with three tracks (i.e., pre-vocational level, general secondary level, and pre-university program); and tertiary education (ages 16–24), which also includes three tracks (i.e., vocational level, professional education, and university). There are two types of schools, public and private. All schools are financed by the government. Public schools are also subject to local government supervision. Private schools get the same financial support as public schools; however, they are governed by a board. These schools are based on some kind of ideology, religion, or educational philosophy (e.g., Montessori Method, Pestalozzi, Dalton, and Jenaplan).

The system for primary education (ages 4–12) includes kindergarten (Grades 1 and 2)

through Grade 8. Although education is compulsory from age 5, most children start school on their fourth birthday. In 1988, the system changed radically under the influence of the inclusion movement. Regular schools for primary education and schools for children with special needs (in particular for children with mild mental retardation, learning disabilities, and behavior problems) were forced to become partners. In every region, consortiums of mainstream primary schools (both public and private) and aforementioned special schools (since then called *special primary schools* or *special basis schools)* were formed with the goals of making inclusion possible for more children, decreasing the number of children attending special schools (currently approximately 3%), decreasing the cost of special education, and having no more than 2% attend special (primary) schools. These goals are thought to be achievable by collaboration between schools, improved use of expertise from the special (primary) schools, providing consultation with professionals (e.g., psychologists), and sending peripatetic teachers from the special primary schools to their accompanying primary schools. Referral to special schools is possible only after a period of failed interventions, documented by an individual educational plan and evaluation. In most cases, children in special schools will remain there until they start secondary school, at which time they will be reevaluated and decisions will be made about the most desirable school setting.

The special primary schools are considered to be part of primary education and fall within the Primary Education Act (Wet op het Primair Onderwijs, 1998). Children with more severe special needs can attend schools within the Regional Centers of Expertise. This school system serves about 30,000 pupils, ages 4 through 12. Categories for special needs children fall into one of four clusters: for children with visual handicaps (cluster 1), auditory or communication handicaps (cluster 2), physical handicaps, mental retardation, or multiple handicaps (cluster 3), and behavior and psychiatric disorders (cluster 4). Schools are clustered around the above-mentioned special needs into Regional Centers of Expertise. Each Center is expected to provide schools and consultation to non-Center schools and to parents.

On granting a student access to special educational services by a Regional Center of Expertise school, parents may choose between placement in a special school or, with extra financial support, in a regular school. Thus, parents can choose an inclusive education setting for their child. Regular schools generally are obligated to accept these children unless they can justify why they cannot accommodate the special needs of a particular child. Acceptable reasons are not formally identified. This law has been in effect since August 2003. The first data available suggest that both the number of children identified as having special educational needs (defined as fitting the criteria for special education) and the number of children admitted to special schools have increased. The full effect of this law on the inclusion of students with severe special needs is unknown at this time. Within the Regional Centers of Expertise, schools are called *special schools,* and fall under the Centers of Expertise Act. The average class size is 21 in (regular) primary schools and 16 in special primary schools. Special schools within the Regional Centers of Expertise typically have 7 to 13 students per class, depending on the type of special needs.

All students in secondary education (ages 12 through 18) study the same national core curriculum (i.e., basic secondary education) during the first 2 to 3 years of secondary school. Tracking takes place from the start. Students expected to complete vocational training and those who will attempt the more academically advanced education designed to prepare them for professional careers attend either separate classes in broad schools, which accommodate students from various ability levels, or separate schools. The main secondary tracks are a 4-year pre-vocational secondary education program, a 5-year senior general secondary education program, and a 6-year pre-university education

program. Depending on the track, completing the core basic secondary education curriculum will take between 1 and 3 years.

The senior general secondary education program allows students to be admitted to professional schools. Some students also will complete the final 2 years of the pre-university program after finishing their senior general secondary education program.

Although the pre-university programs provide direct access to universities, some university programs require specific subjects to be taken during the student's pre-university training. In 2001–2002, 43% of the students in secondary education were enrolled in the basic secondary education (Years 1 and 2), 24% attended pre-vocational secondary education (*Voorbereidend Middelbaar Beroeps Onderwijs* [VMBO]; (Years 3 and 4), and 33% attended senior general secondary education (*Hoger Algemeen Voortgezet Onderwijs* [HAVO]) and pre-university secondary education (*Voorbereidend Wetenschappelijk Onderwijs* [VWO]; Ministry of Education, Culture, and Science, 2003).

Students with specific special needs are served by the Regional Centers of Expertise schools. Since 2002, additional educational services for special needs students may be provided under the Secondary Education Act. Low achieving students receive learning support in an enriched school environment. During 2002–2003, 97,000 students received such services. When it is expected that regular educational goals for pre-vocational secondary education (VMBO) may not be reached, students receive a curriculum that does not result in a graduation certification but instead provides direct vocational training (*Praktijk onderwijs* [PRO]). During 2002–2003, 23,000 students were in such a program. There are virtually no facilities for gifted students who need special education. Special schools typically provide a vocational education level.

Students preparing for university generally complete their secondary education at age 18 and then select between a school for higher professional education (sometimes called a university for professional education, i.e., *Hogeschool*) or a university program. The division between these two forms of tertiary education is strict. Recently, under the influence of the Bologna treaty, and in striving for a more uniform system of certification in Europe, the country is questioning whether both types of education should be brought closer together, making the transfer from one to another easier for students. Initiatives for collaboration between schools for higher professional education and universities currently are being taken. About 40% of the students in schools for professional education graduate within 4 years, 55% finish within 5 years, and 70% within 9 years. Completion rates at the university are 13% after 4 years, 30% after 5 years, 68% after 6 years, and 72% after 9 years (Statistics Netherlands, 2005).

Origin, History, and Current Status of School Psychology

School psychology is not officially recognized by title, and school psychologists are not specifically prepared as such by universities in the Netherlands. However, historically, psychologists have been involved in education in various roles and settings. Their first involvement, in the early 1920s, focused on testing students for possible placement in special education. At that time, both the Free University of Amsterdam and Amsterdam University had established psychotechnical (assessment) centers (Haas, 1995). In 1949, decision making by psychologists as to admission of children to special education was legally regulated by a royal decision (Koninklijk Besluit), an event some mark as the beginning of school psychology in the Netherlands (Wilmink, in Haas, 1995). Since then, the role of psychologists in education has grown steadily.

There is an extensive service network of centers for school advisory services (*schooladviesdiensten*). These were established by municipalities in the late 1950s and increased in number after about 1970 (Veldkamp & van Drunen, 1988). At this time, services were focused primarily on individual children. During the 1970s, the federal government began co-financing these services. At the same time, the services became more systems oriented. In 1981, the school advisory service centers secured federal governmental funding, a provision later incorporated in the 1986 Educational Services Act. All regions were required to maintain an educational advisory center to which all primary schools had access for services. Services included individual assessment, teacher consultation and training, and development and implementation of methods that strengthen the academic curriculum and promote social-emotional development. These services generally were performed by educational, developmental, and clinical child psychologists as well as by orthopedagogues (i.e., educational psychologists).

Funding for school advisory services soon will go directly to schools instead of to centers. Schools will be able to decide where and how to get needed support. Although this free market system may lead to increased quality because of the increased competition, it more likely will lead to a loss of the expertise that has been developed in the centers for school advisory services. The temptation to employ service delivery personnel who are less expensive, less experienced, and less qualified will thus lead to a decrease in the quality of service.

Psychologists who work in consortia of primary schools typically are involved in making decisions about whether students need special educational services in either primary schools or special primary schools. Those working in special primary schools assist in developing individual educational plans and consult with teachers and parents; their interests include issues important to individuals and groups; and they may provide social skill training or counseling. Psychologists who work in Regional Centers of Expertise elementary and secondary (special) schools are involved in assessment, the formulation and evaluation of individual educational plans, teacher consultation, and individual or group counseling (on a limited basis).

Historically, secondary education schools have rarely employed school psychologists. When they did, school psychological services typically were limited to students in special schools and involved assessment, limited counseling, teacher consultation, and educational planning. Students in regular schools who exhibited problems other than with learning were referred either to the mental health system or to another school with lower academic demands. School boards that decided to hire school psychologists would have to pay for their services. Currently, secondary schools, especially pre-vocational (VMBO) schools, increasingly offer some form of psychological or counseling service. Learning support services are available for children with defined special needs.

There is no formal training or licensing for school psychologists. Thus, psychologists with various forms of professional preparation work in educational settings, including developmental, educational (including orthopedagogues), or child clinical psychologists. Whether this group should be called "school psychologists" remains a topic of discussion. Some argue that this name unduly recognizes their expertise in the field of school psychology and would prefer to use the title "school psychologist." Others believe they are primarily developmental psychologists who work in educational settings. They typically refer to themselves as developmental, educational, or child and adolescent psychologists.

The Netherlands has a strong and easily accessible, governmentally funded mental health system. People seeking treatment pay only a small financial contribution, regardless of their level of income. Thus, mental health service within the school system is limited. As a result, school professionals focus on issues that more directly involve a student's school functioning. Teacher consultation, together with the exchange of information with and referrals to mental health

professionals, are important. Professionals in schools will need an outreaching attitude, and school officials must initiate mental health services for students, in that mental health professionals generally do not visit schools. Both a need and a trend exist for more collaboration between schools and mental health institutions to provide more support within the schools. Some pilot projects (e.g., through the National Center for Education and Youth Care [NIZW]) have established joint care teams within schools. Participating colleagues are optimistic, and their experiences seem promising.

Many professionals are involved in promoting the well-being of children within the educational system from kindergarten through high school. Although in the Netherlands school psychological services may not include all services as found in other countries, such services often are provided through other professionals. Four examples of other professionals providing related services follow.

Social workers. Social workers are commonly employed in schools for special education. They serve as members of the admission and guidance committee and are rarely employed in regular education. Social workers typically are the members of the committee that is responsible for making special educational service decisions within the consortium of primary schools. They also may be available on request from a school or mental health agency. Their assessment focuses on the home context. They may be involved in parent training or educational consultation and provide a communication link between schools and parents.

Internal guidance counselors. Internal guidance counselors are former teachers with advanced professional experience and, often, advanced training. Present in every elementary school, they provide assessment of achievement and consult with teachers on teaching, classroom management, and adaptive teaching issues.

Peripatetic teachers. Peripatetic teachers typically are teacher-trained professionals from a school for special education who provide consultation and sometimes offer individual remedial instruction in regular schools dealing with mainstreamed children with special needs.

Other psychologists. Finally, psychologists from mental health or youth care institutions may provide counseling or social skills training in schools, or in collaboration with schools, school consortia, or Centers for School Advisory Services. Some private practice psychologists who specialize in working with students with special needs are hired by schools to provide assessment or support services. Parents generally must pay for these services.

An estimate of the number of psychologists working in the area of education is difficult to determine. Earlier, an estimate of 1,500 psychologists for 2,400,000 pupils was given, suggesting a ratio of one psychologist per 1,600 students (European Federation of Psychologists' Associations, Task Force on Psychologists in the Educational System, 2001). However, the number of psychologists seemingly is estimated based on the number of members of the Education sections at the time of the Dutch Association of Psychologists. The number, 1,600, is likely to be larger. A 1988 study suggested that the Centers for School Advisory Services employed about 3,000 professionals, 80% of whom were educational specialists. That suggests that, at that time, about 2,400 psychologists and pedagogues were working in school advisory services.

Approximately 1,400 psychologists qualified to work as health care psychologists are employed in schools, among whom 7% are qualified as psychotherapists (van der Ploeg & Scholte, 2001). Training and certification standards do not require health care psychologist registration to work in schools. Thus, most psychologists who work in schools do not have this registration. Some are registered by the Dutch Association of Psychologists as Child and Adolescent Psychologists (NIP). This registration so far is directed more specifically toward work with children and youth than is the training program for health care psychologists. The number of school-based psychologists who do not have health care registration can be expected to rise, because opportunities to acquire this qualification are limited. The Dutch Association of Psychologists and colleague associations (e.g., the Dutch Association of Pedagogues/Educationalists [NVO]) are discussing ways to provide more specific and direct training for school psychologists.

A beginning salary for a psychologist in schools or in educational services, established by the governmental salary scaling system, is approximately 2,100 to 2,300 euros per month (payscale 10). A health care psychologist may earn from 2,845 to 4,300 euros. The maximum wage for a psychologist in education is approximately 4,000 euros (payscale 11). Psychologists who work for institutions or larger schools and have coordination or management responsibilities may earn up to 4,500 euros per month (payscale 12; Ministry of the Interior and Kingdom Relations, 2005).

Infrastructure of School Psychology

School psychology is not represented by a specialized professional organization. Among those working in schools, psychologists are represented by the Dutch Association of Psychologists and pedagogues by the Dutch Association of Pedagogues/Educationalists. Both organizations have divisions that focus on education. Within the Dutch Association of Psychologists, psychologists working in education are organized within the Youth Division, in the School Psychologists' section. This is a merger of two sections, Elementary/Special Education and Educational Psychology, which represents the field of education. The Educational Psychology section was originally formed in 1955, outside the association as a Research Group on School Psychology by a group of distinguished Dutch psychologists (e.g., A. D. Groot, P. van den Broek, J. Th. Snijders, S. Wiegersma) who were committed to education. In 1968, this organization joined the Dutch Association for Practicing Psychologists, now called the Dutch Association of Psychologists, and became the School Psychology section (Haas, 1995). In 1972, it was renamed Educational Psychology to better reflect the international developments in the field and to move away from an emphasis on the individual to the system level (Dudink, 2006). Over the past few years, the work of psychologists has been at the individual level. Thus, the discussion on the importance of working at the system level is still very important and has been at the core of the work of the Task Force on Psychologists in the Educational System in Europe (European Federation of Psychologists' Associations, Task Force on Psychologists in the Educational System, 2001, 2005). The Elementary/ Special Education section is a continuation of a Special Education section and will continue as the School Psychologists' section. The Dutch Association of Pedagogues/Educationalists also has an Educational Guidance section. On a different level, there is also an association for employers in educational advising (i.e., Edventure).

The Netherlands does not license school or other psychologists. Since 1993, the title "psychologist" has not been protected by law. Thus, everyone can use this title. In order to protect both clients and trained psychologists, the Dutch Association of Psychologists has a code of ethics and offers registration as a Psychologist NIP or a Child and Adolescent Psychologist NIP. Persons who use the title Psychologist NIP must have a master of science degree in psychology (previously a *doctorandus* degree, offered after 4 years of university training) and 6 months of supervised practice. The 1993 law on Professions in Healthcare (Wet op de beroepen in de individuele gezondheidszorg, 1993) requires professionals working in mental health settings to have additional training beyond the master's level. The section on health care psychologists was added in 1998 (Besluit Gezondheidszorgpsycholoog, 1998) and resulted in a 2-year training program for health care psychologists and title protection for health care psychologists. This law does not apply to psychologists working in education or special education. Formal assessment and classification of psychological or behavioral disorders regarding special education placement, as defined by the law on Regional Centers of Expertise, has been restricted to those with the title "Healthcare Psychologist," "Child and Adolescent Psychologist NIP," or "Orthopedagogue Generalist NVO" (Regeling Indicatiecriteria en Aanmeldingsformulier Leerlinggebonden Financiering, 2004). This creates an inconsistency in the current system: Although additional training and registration are required for those making formal decisions on admission, this additional training and registration is not required to work within the field. Professional associations are currently trying to find a solution for this inconsistency.

Schools for professional education recently have started programs in psychology directed toward preparing students for practice rather than toward academics and science. Professional associations strongly oppose this orientation as being insufficient for independent practice. However, since the title of "psychologist" is not protected, in some situations program graduates have been employed in schools to provide assessment services. Although this is legitimate within the law, the national and European professional associations strongly promote the belief that full academic training is needed for professional practice (European Federation of Psychologists' Associations, Task Force on Psychologists in the Educational System, 2001, 2005).

No Dutch journals feature issues selectively geared toward school psychology. The most read journals feature broader issues important to child and adolescent psychology. Articles in the most widely read journal, *Kind en Adolescent* (Child and Adolescent), typically feature empirical research performed in the Netherlands or other Dutch-speaking countries and may include cross-national studies. Topics include but are not limited to issues relevant to education. A parallel journal, *Child and Adolescent Practice*, is geared especially toward practical issues, and another journal provides an overview of translated internationally published articles relevant to Dutch practices (*Child and Adolescent Review*). Issues feature developmental psychopathology, assessment, prevention, and intervention.

Tijdschrift voor Orthopedagogiek (The Journal of Orthopedagogy) also is popular among colleagues in education. This journal is geared to a broad group of professionals, including psychologists, primarily within the educational context and with a focus on continuing professional education. General issues on policy and psychopathology also are included. The content is becoming more descriptive and less empirical. Finally, *School en Begeleiding* (School and Guidance) is specifically geared toward educational advisory services.

Relevant Laws and Regulations

School psychologists are expected to spend the limited time they have per student primarily providing diagnostic and consultation services, not treatment. Counseling and therapy are rarely provided in schools. The infrastructure does not mandate that school psychology services be placed within the school. Whether school psychology will become more integrated into the school infrastructure is unknown. School management and local and national policymakers commonly refer to social workers and psychologists working in the mental health system and restrict the school psychologist's intervention activities to working with students displaying learning difficulties.

During the past few years, many changes in special education have occurred in response to changes in laws governing this service: Primary Education Act (Wet op het Primair Onderwijs, 1998), Law on Centers of Expertise (Wet op de

Expertisecentra, 2003), and Adaptation of the Law on Secondary Education (Wet op het Voortgezet Onderwijs, 1998). Changes brought about by this legislation have greatly impacted students with special needs, the nature of special education services offered to them, and the procedures involved to qualify for special support. These changes also have had a great impact on school psychologists.

The current law on special education has a strict description and strict criteria for assigning children the right to special educational support (either in ambulatory support or special education). Assessment for classification, not treatment, is emphasized. Thus, much professional time and energy, including that of school psychologists, is spent on assessment and paperwork, leaving little time for consultation and guidance. In some instances, admission committees (independently organized from the schools) specify the tests to be used, a requirement that sometimes conflicts with the profession's ethical code. This issue currently is being discussed with policymakers.

The most recent changes in the law have led to a formal requirement for the formulation of an individual education plan. The Law on Centers of Expertise explicitly requires an individual education plan to be developed by the committee of guidance of the special school and agreed to by the parents. A first format was developed in 2002 (Struiksma & Bal, 2002). More specific guidelines are needed and have not been developed. As mentioned before, the funding for special support services was partly earmarked for centers for school advisory services. In 2006, this funding will be given to schools.

Preparation of School Psychologists

There is no specific training for school psychologists. The universities and professional organizations of psychologists strongly believe professionals should have a broad training in psychology, followed by specialization. Thus, the current training of psychologists working as school psychologists consists of a basic training as a *doctorandus* (4 years of academic training) or a master's of science degree (a 3-year bachelor's degree plus a 1-year master's degree) in developmental psychology or clinical child psychology. Within the specialty of orthopedagogics (educational psychology), students can specialize in learning difficulties or in education as a field of specialization at the master's level. Some master's programs in educational psychology are available, geared either toward individual development and instruction or toward more general system-related aspects (e.g., instructional methods, curriculum development).

Those who become school psychologists generally have been trained in one of the following programs: child and adolescent/developmental psychology, clinical psychology, clinical child psychology, educational psychology, or orthopedagogics. Within these programs, students may take some electives in topics directly relevant to the educational context. Students planning for a career in education/schools typically try to do their 420- to 630-hour internship within an educational context (e.g., an educational guidance agency, school for special education, center of expertise). Their thesis also may be related to issues in this specialty.

Receipt of a basic master's-level degree from a university is sufficient for professional practice. However, graduates are recommended to continue their professional training at first to the level of health care psychologist, child and adolescent psychologist NIP, or orthopedagogue generalist NVO. These are 2-year programs taken after obtaining the master's degree. This level will coincide with future requirements for the European Diploma in Psychology, which requires 5 years of academic training and 1 year of supervised practice (EuroPsy, 2005).

The option of a 2-year advanced program in child and adolescent psychology beyond the 4-year bachelor's/master's training, with an emphasis on the educational context, including supervised practice, is being reviewed. Since there is no specific training program in school psychology, the basic training includes all aspects needed to work as an entry-level professional psychologist (see criteria for European Diploma, EuroPsy, 2005; European Federation of Psychologists' Associations, Task Force on Psychologists in the Educational System, 2001, 2005).

Professional programs leading to a master's degree in child or developmental psychology generally are thought to include enough of a theoretical and academic basis to start a working career. Additionally, students generally acquire good knowledge of development and psychopathology, as well as basic knowledge and skills regarding individual assessment. However, acquisition of skills and knowledge specific to school psychology is generally insufficient, especially in consultation skills, knowledge regarding the school as a system (classroom, school, system), and laws and regulations. Assessment skills typically focus on child factors and not on the family or school. The degree to which students can apply these skills differs, depending on their master's program and their personal internship experiences.

Roles, Functions, and Responsibilities of School Psychologists

The Task Force on Psychologists in the Educational System in Europe has formulated functions and tasks for school psychologists in prevention, evaluation, and intervention. The different levels of work in the educational system are society, school system, group, and the individual.

Psychologists working in the school system primarily emphasize their work at the level of the school, the group, and the individual. Activities at the society level, whether they concern prevention, evaluation, or intervention, are more often left to researchers and policymakers.

Regarding training, the emphasis is on solid scientific training as a basis, whereas less importance is given to knowledge of school practice. This is, however, a growing concern among psychologists working in schools, since starting colleagues come prepared as scientists and general psychologists but know little of what actually goes on in the school setting. In the past 2 years, psychologists in the elementary/special education section within the Dutch Association of Psychologists and pedagogues of the Dutch Association of Pedagogues/Educationalists have worked hard to become official partners in the committees that discuss new legislation and practical translation of legal measures.

At the school system level, psychologists working in special schools have a clear role in continuing the professional development of teachers. The development and organization of school programs are considered to be their responsibility. Individual coaching of individual teachers is considered a luxury. The director of the school is responsible for decisions as to the need for coaching. It is offered by psychologists only under exceptional circumstances. School psychologists also may be involved in developing and implementing procedures regarding conflict management and aggression regulation. Evaluation is their main task. The implementation of national evaluation systems (*Leerling Volg Systeem* [Pupil Evaluation System]) and the translation of data into effective instruction decisions and individual educational plans take a large part of total work time. At the intervention level, school psychologists are working on the development of school crisis intervention teams. This is not a regular provision in the Netherlands.

Little work is done at the group level. In specific problem situations, school psychologists are asked to intervene and to help restore a healthy situation. Most schools do not use an organized approach to prevention or evaluation of group functioning. Social skills training (e.g., PATHS curriculum: Promoting Alternative Thinking Strategies; Greenberg, Kusche, Calderon, & Gustafson, 1987) is implemented in some schools. Treatment programs (e.g., the Friends program) for specific psychiatric disorders are used in some schools for special education on an experimental basis.

Services focus mainly on the individual level and include assessment, referral decisions, and teacher/team consultation. Evaluation services are emphasized, especially since the introduction of the new law on the Centers of Expertise (Wet op de Expertisecentra, 2002). Psychologists in schools play a central role in individual referral for intervention and intervention planning, especially regarding development of individual education plans. Social skill training or parent psychoeducation services also may be provided, albeit infrequently. Psychologists again assume a prominent role when evaluating the effectiveness of interventions.

Two main methodologies have been implemented widely: needs-based assessment (or handelingsgerichte diagnostiek; Pameijer, in press; Pameijer & van Beukering, 2004) and consultative pupil guidance (Meijer, 2000). The first emphasizes the importance of psychologist-client partnerships and is geared toward determining the special educational needs of the child. Its goal is to develop suggestions that will contribute to solving the referral problem, decreasing the problem behavior, or improving behavior and/or academic performance. Close collaboration with parents, teachers, and students is prerequisite for success. Needs-based assessment is geared toward perceived problem behavior in the child. However, because family and school factors may have an etiological role, assessment is transactional, and not just geared toward child factors.

A large number of tests and instruments are available. Because the children, as well as the reasons for assessment and transactional contexts, vary, naming them would be very difficult and not very informative. A listing of the instruments most widely used can be found in Evers et al. (2002) and Resing, Evers, Koomen, Pameijer, and Bleichrodt (2005).

Consultative pupil guidance is focused primarily on helping a teacher cope with or correct perceived problem behaviors in the classroom. Thus, the teacher and the diagnostician are partners. Individual child assessment typically is not done, although a combination of guidance and assessment (e.g., treatment oriented) may be necessary.

Most centers for school advisory services have adopted one or both of these two methodologies: needs-based assessment and consultative pupil guidance. In special schools and primary school consortia, many teams and individual psychologists have been trained in these methodologies.

Program development takes place at the centers for school advisory services and at national pedagogical centers and often involves school or educational psychologists.

Dutch psychologists recently have been participating in the training on crisis management developed by the International School Psychology Association. Unfortunately, some of these colleagues have had to use their newly acquired skills due to their involvement in crisis management activities. At the moment, the trained professionals are discussing the format in which they will continue their services. This may include active crisis management as well as training other colleagues and developing a protocol to guide this service. Collaboration with mental health organizations involved in crisis intervention and trauma will be important.

Current Issues Impacting School Psychology

The inclusion movement, spearheaded by new legislation and the implementation of a new structure of the educational system, has greatly influenced Dutch schools. Changes resulting from the movement have had a great impact on the work of psychologists in schools. For example, they spend much time classifying students, thus leaving little time to consider the factors

contributing to the problem or to help improve the quality of education. During the next few years, additional awareness of the importance of needs-based assessment is needed in order to make good placement and individual planning decisions. This, together with teacher consultation and program development, may help improve the quality of education and make inclusive education more of a reality.

An increase in the amount of aggression in schools is of great concern. Psychologists can play an important role by developing and implementing programs and by informing schools, parents, and policymakers about effective programs and interventions. This would enable them to shift their focus somewhat from assessment to prevention. Centers for pedagogy and those for school advisory services are involved in program development designed to prevent aggression. Psychologists can play a role in implementing these programs in schools.

Research is necessary to increase knowledge of what works and what does not. Programs may be developed, tried once, and then implemented without any further evaluation. On the other hand, promising programs may never get implemented because of limited funding. Psychologists, as experts, are responsible for making well-informed decisions, thus allowing money and other resources to be spent on programs that work. Evaluation of the effect of the current educational changes on the learning and development of children is needed, together with the willingness to translate the findings into practice, even if this means changes.

Some recent changes have had a positive influence on school psychology. School psychologists were forced to find consensus on best practices and referral procedures. The position of the school psychologist as the professional with expertise in assessment procedures has been more formally acknowledged in recent laws. School psychologists have started to participate more in discussions regarding policy making and educational system changes and are currently represented at various levels, informing policymakers on key issues and problems, providing suggestions for improvement, and collaborating on improving the current situation. Their participation has resulted in the publication of some articles and policy position papers, which have been directly offered to the Minister of Education (e.g., Werkgroep LGF, 2005). School psychologists must continue to voice their opinion and try to get a more formal position in policy making in the future.

The school psychologist is a scientist-practitioner, explicitly equipped to analyze problems using a theoretical base and able to translate that to the context of school and a particular educational situation. A clearer professional identity for the school psychologist is needed, one that is more closely aligned with the health care psychologist. How these two will relate to each other is unknown.

References

Besluit gezondheidszorgpsycholoog [Healthcare psychologist decree]. (1998). Zoetermeer: Ministry of Education, Culture, and Science.

Cox, A. (2005). *Achieving the Lisbon goal: The contribution of vocational education and training systems*. Country Report: Netherlands. Hertogenbosch: Cinop.

Dudink, A. (2006). Schoolpsychologie in historische context [School psychology in historical context]. In M. Taal & A. Dudink (Eds.), *School psychologie: de school als context voor ontwikkeling* [School psychology: The school as context for development]. Amsterdam: Boom.

Dutch Eurydice Unit, Ministry of Education, Culture, and Science. (2005). *The educational system in the Netherlands 2005*. Zoetermeer: Ministry of Education, Culture, and Science.

European Federation of Psychologists' Associations, Task Force on Psychologists in the Educational System in Europe. (2001). Report 1999–2001. Brussels: Author.

European Federation of Psychologists' Associations, Task Force on Psychologists in the Educational System.

(2005). Report 2003–2005. Brussels: European Federation of Psychologists' Associations.

EuroPsy. (2004). *The European diploma in psychology*. Brussels: European Federation of Psychologists' Associations.

Evers, A., van Vliet-Mulder, J. C., Resing, W. C. M., Starren, J. C. M. G., van Alphen de Veer, R. J., & van Boxtel, H. (2002). *COTAN Testboek voor het onderwijs* [COTAN test book for education]. Amsterdam: NDC/Boom.

Haas, E. (1995). *Op de juiste plaats: de opkomst van de bedrijfs- en schoolpsychologische beroepspraktijk in Nederland* [In the right place: The rise of the organizational and school psychology professional practice in the Netherlands]. Hilversum: Verloren.

Greenberg, M. T., Kusche, C. A., Calderon, R., & Gustafson, R. (1987). *PATHS curriculum*. Seattle: University of Washington Press.

Leerplichtwet [Compulsory Education Act] (1969). Zoetermeer: Ministry of Education, Culture, and Science.

Meijer, W. (2000). *Consultatieve leerlingbegeleiding: van theorie naar prakijk* [Consultative pupil guidance: From theory to practice]. Amersfoort: Christelijk Pedagogisch Studiecentrum.

Ministry of Education, Culture, and Science. (2003). *Facts and figures 2003*. Zoetermeer: Author. Retrieved December 26, 2005, from www.minocw.nl/english/figures2003

Ministry of the Interior and Kingdom Relations. (2005). *Salarisniveaus overheidspersoneel 2005* [Salary levels of government personnel 2005]. The Hague: Author.

Pameijer, N. K. (in press). Best practice in needs-based assessment in the Netherlands: A diagnostic model. *National Pages*, European Agency for Development in Special Needs Education, www.european-agency.org

Pameijer, N. K., & Beukering, J. T. E. van. (2004). *Handelingsgerichte diagnostiek: eenpraktijk-model voor diagnostiek en advisering bij onderwijsleerproblemen* [Needs-based assessment: A practical model for diagnostic assessment and recommendations regarding learning difficulties and behavioral problems]. Leuven: Acco.

Ploeg, J. D. van der, & Scholte, E. M. (2001). *De GZ-psycholoog in beeld* [The healthcare psychologists in the picture]. Amsterdam: Nederlands Instituut voor pedagogisch en psychologisch onderzoek.

Regeling indicatiecriteria en aanmeldingsformulier leerlinggebonden financiering (LGF) [Indication criteria and referral formula for pupil-bound financing]. (2004, March). In *Gele katern* (Vol. 6).

Resing, W. C. M., Evers, A., Koomen, H. M. Y., Pameijer, N. K., & Bleichrodt, N. (2005). *Indicatiestelling speciaal onderwijs en leerlinggebonden financiering: Condities en instrumentarium* [Indication for special education and pupil-bound financing: Conditions and instruments]. Amsterdam: Boom.

Statistics Netherlands [Centraal Bureau voor de Statistiek, Netherlands]. (2005). Statline. Voorburg: Centraal Bureau voor de Statistiek. Available online at statline.cbs.nl

Struiksma, A. J. C., & Bal, I. (2002). *Protocol handelingsplan bij leerlinggebonden financiering* [Individualized Education Plan protocol for personal pupil budgets]. Rotterdam: Pedologisch Instituut.

Veldkamp, T. A., & Drunen, P. van. (1988). *Psychologie als professie: 50 jaar Nederlands Instituut van Psychologen* [Psychology as a profession: 50 years Dutch Association of Psychologists]. Assen/Maastricht: Van Gorcum.

Werkgroep LGF. (2005). *Niet de procedure maar het kind centraal* [Not the procedure, but the child at the center]. Amsterdam: NIP/NVO.

Wet op de beroepen in de individuele gezondheidszorg [Individual Health Care Professions Act]. (1993). Zoetermeer: Ministry of Education, Culture, and Science.

Wet op de Expertisecentra [Centers of Expertise Act]. (2003). Zoetermeer: Ministry of Education, Culture, and Science.

Wet op het Primair Onderwijs [Primary Education Act]. (1998). Zoetermeer: Ministry of Education, Culture, and Science.

Wet op het Voortgezet Onderwijs [Adaptation Secondary Education Act]. (1998). Zoetermeer: Ministry of Education, Culture, and Science.

26

Educational Psychology in New Zealand

Terence Edwards

Jean Annan

Ken Ryba

Context of Educational Psychology

New Zealand is located in the southwest Pacific Ocean, approximately 1,600 kilometres east of Australia. The North and South Islands, together with numerous smaller islands, comprise a land area of 268,021 square kilometres. The two main islands comprise 113,729 square kilometres (North Island) and 150,437 square kilometres (South Island). Wellington, the capital city, is located in the southern part of the North Island. In June 2004, New Zealand's population was 4,061,400 (49% male) with approximately 76% residing in the North Island and 24% in the South Island. Auckland, located 658 km north of Wellington, is the largest city, and its region is home to 33% of New Zealand's population. The total population is expected to increase to 4.81 million by 2046 (Statistics New Zealand, 2005). In 2004, children ages birth to 15 (median age of 7.8 years) numbered 885,390, of which 282,420 were under age 5. New Zealand's population is diverse ethnically. The main ethnic groups are European (79%), Maori (15%), Pasifika (7%), and Asian (7%); percentages do not add to 100% because some people identify with more than one ethnic group. In 2001, the Auckland region was home to 181 ethnic groups and had the highest concentration of ethnic diversity. Twenty percent of New Zealanders were born overseas (in the Auckland region, 33% were born overseas).

Although New Zealand ranked 20th among 30 countries in a review by the Organisation for Economic Co-operation and Development in 2002, economic growth since the early 1990s has been substantial. In 2004, the gross domestic product was US$92.5 billion, US$23,200 per capita. The average annual growth in gross domestic product per capita has been higher than average for Organisation for Economic Co-operation and Development countries. From 1994 to 2004, New Zealand's economic growth has averaged 3.4%, which compares favourably to the 1.5% average for the previous decade. The primary industries in New Zealand are agricultural, horticultural, forestry, mining, energy, and fishing. Each plays an important role in employment and the export sector. These industries account for 7.6% of gross domestic product and contribute over 50% of New Zealand's total export earnings.

School attendance is compulsory for all children from age 6 to 16. Most children start school on their 5th birthday. Compulsory school years are classified from Years 0 through 12. The school year begins at the end of January and ends in mid-December. The school roll is recorded in July. Children ages 5 to 6 who begin school between July, after the school roll is recorded, and December 31 are in Year 0. Those who begin school between January and before the July roll count are in Year 1 (Ministry of Education, 2001).

The early childhood sector comprises day care centres, kindergartens, and play centres. Attendance is voluntary. Broadly speaking, the compulsory education sector is divided into primary, intermediate, and secondary schooling. In July 2004, 764,652 children attended school; 33% were in the Auckland region, and 3.8% attended private/fee-paying schools. The compulsory school sector includes state schools, state-integrated schools (i.e., schools that were private and now are integrated within the state system), private schools, special schools, and a correspondence school catering to students who for a variety of reasons (e.g., geographic isolation, health factors) are unable to attend a state school.

As of July 2004, there were 2,646 schools; among these were 1,179 full primary schools (Years 0–8, with 175,721 students), 816 contributing schools (Years 0–6, with 212,360 students), 127 intermediate schools (Years 7–8, with 62,115 students), 95 secondary schools (1) (Years 7–15, with 48,817 students), 243 secondary schools (2) (Years 9–15, with 215,705 students), 139 composite schools (Years 0–15, with 39,266 students), 46 special schools (Years vary by school, with 2,672 students), and 1 correspondence school (Years 0–15, with 7,996 students). In 2004, a total of 55,634 students left school. Although 40% of the students completed school within the highest academic attainment bands, 21% completed with little or no formal qualifications. Compared to their peers, students who are Maori and Pasifika consistently are underrepresented in the upper band figures and overrepresented in the lower band figures.

Origin, History, and Current Status of Educational Psychology

New Zealand has an abiding concern with and commitment to equity of educational provision. The 1877 Education Act specified education should be free, secular, and compulsory for all children of primary school age. However, systems of support for all students were not specifically instituted until 1920, after the Royal Commission on Backward Pupils in Schools detected the absence of adequate provision for students with special needs. Following this report, several special classes were established. However, almost 30 years elapsed before the services of educational (school) psychologists were developed to support these classes. The first educational psychology services were established in 1948 with the introduction of the psychological service by the Department of Education. Following its introduction, other educational support systems were established, specifically child guidance clinics in 1951 and the school guidance counsellor scheme in 1959. Such services initially were considered to be advisory.

As a government-operated internal agency, the psychological service comprised psychologists and secretarial staff. For more than 40 years, it delivered services to students with special needs, over time developing an increasingly stronger focus on holistic and developmental approaches to educational psychology practice (Bowler, 1997). However, in 1989, as part of wide-ranging government reforms, the service changed markedly in terms of its composition and operation. The implementation of recommendations from the Picot Report, delivered by the Taskforce to Review Education Administration (1988), involved significant modifications to the education system. The New Zealand government restructured its Department of Education and took the name Ministry of Education. New systems were developed to increase local decision making and to facilitate the deregulation of many aspects of education provision. Education was decentralised, leaving many decisions traditionally made at a national level to locally elected school boards.

The psychological service in its traditional form no longer existed and was replaced by a new agency, the Special Education Service, that comprised the members of previous educational support services, including advisors on deaf children, speech-language therapists, psychologists, and visiting teachers. In this restructuring, the Special Education Service became a *quango* (quasi-autonomous, nongovernmental organisation). This organisation was nominally independent of the Ministry of Education but continued to largely rely on government funding, which was disbursed in return for specified services. Other income was generated by the agency in the marketplace. Although this reform initially seemed to restrict opportunities to continue and further develop its developmental ecological practice, in effect, the multidisciplinary nature of the new service strengthened and expedited this process. By the early 1990s, the Special Education Service was a community-based, trans-disciplinary service that was operating nationally within a developmental perspective (Bowler, 1997).

Since February 2002, the Special Education Service has been reinstated as a government agency, operating again under the umbrella of the Ministry of Education. As this organisation is located in a section of the Ministry named Group Special Education, the organisation has become known by this title. Although Group Special Education is operated from a central national office, special education services, including educational psychology, are delivered from district offices throughout the country.

Most educational psychologists are employed by Group Special Education. This position allows them to consult with members of educational institutions as external agents. However, a few educational psychologists also have been employed by schools, or groups of schools, often in conjunction with the new Resource Teacher of Learning and Behaviour Service. Members of the Resource Teacher of Learning and Behaviour Service are qualified and experienced teachers who have acquired additional training in order to provide services to students with special needs. A few educational psychologists work privately. Regardless of their place of employment, educational psychologists must "recognise the limits of their own competence and provide only those services for which they are competent, based on their education, training, supervised experience, or appropriate professional experience" (New Zealand Psychological Society, 2002, p. 13).

The heavy workload constitutes one of the main challenges for educational psychologists, particularly those who work in Group Special Education. Several factors contribute to this. The ratio of educational psychologists to students is one important factor. Approximately 150 psychologists, mostly educational but some clinical, work in educational settings. This equates to a psychologist-to-student ratio of 1 to 5,100 for children ages 5 through 18. Psychologists within Group Special Education work with children and youth ages 22 and younger. Thus, a ratio based on numbers of school-age children likely underrepresents workload issues. In addition, as Group Special Education is funded to address only the most severe and difficult situations, educational psychologists spend much of their time working in highly complex and emotionally charged environments. Educational psychologists commonly are aware of discrepancies between their capacity to deliver psychological services and the demands of educational institutions. Anecdotal reports suggest that these experiences contribute to difficulties in staff retention and recruitment. To a degree, this situation also may have contributed to the development of a style of working in which educational psychologists have had to adjust their practice to distribute available resources fairly. For example, the work of educational psychologists usually is indirect and focuses on the development of systems to support students. Educational psychologists generally take a broad view of situations and focus on the most salient details. This approach, although developed for this particular context, also reflects and possibly influences a professional orientation that favors an ecological perspective among educational psychologists and many special educators.

Infrastructure of Educational Psychology

The practice of educational psychology is carried out by educational psychologists who generally work widely across educational, family, and community settings. Registration as a psychologist, including as an educational psychologist, occurs under the direction of the New Zealand Psychologists Board (http://www .psychology.org.nz/psychinnz/nzpb.html). The use of the title "psychologist" is protected by law. Professionals may use the title "psychologist" to represent themselves only if they are formally registered with the Board. Legislation governing all forms of psychology is found in the Health Practitioners Competence Assurance Act 2003, which replaced the Psychologists Act 1981.

All psychologists in New Zealand must be registered by the New Zealand Psychologists Board. The Board assesses the suitability of applicants. Minimally, applicants must have a master's degree in psychology from a tertiary educational institution accredited by the Board and must have completed an approved practicum or internship of at least 1,500 hours of supervised practice. Qualified psychologists can apply for registration under general and specific scopes of practice. The general scope is open to all applicants. Those who have undertaken study in specialist areas are eligible to apply to register in specific scopes of practice and, once approved, are entitled to use the designations "educational psychologist" or "clinical psychologist." Intern psychologists in postgraduate and doctoral psychology programs who are working with the public must apply for registration as "intern psychologists." The Board issues an interim practicing certificate with supervision conditions.

Under Section 40 of the Health Practitioners Competence Assurance Act 2003, the Board may establish and recognise competence programs, including cultural competence, for all psychologists or groups of psychologists. Formal academic training is provided by tertiary institutions. In-service training also is provided by many employers. The practice of educational psychology is formally defined as follows:

> Educational psychologists apply psychological knowledge and theory derived from research to the area of learning and development. By using psychological and educational assessments and applying interventions using systemic, ecological, and developmental approaches, they assist children, young persons, adults, and their families with learning, academic performance, behaviour, and social and emotional development. Such practice is undertaken within an individual area and level of expertise and with due regard to ethical,

legal, and Board-prescribed standards. (New Zealand Psychologists Board, 2004, p. 1)

The New Zealand Psychological Society is the national professional association for psychologists in New Zealand. The Society was established in 1947 and became incorporated in 1967. In 2004, the Society had 817 full members and about 200 student members (New Zealand Psychological Society, 2004). The Society is based in Wellington and provides representation, services, and support for members. The Society's several primary roles include representing psychologists to the public, the media, and the government; providing professional support and development to members; promoting high standards of ethical and professional practice; promoting the discipline of psychology as a science; and promoting and supporting biculturalism in the profession. A subdivision within the Society, the Institute of Educational and Developmental Psychology, specifically focuses on supporting and promoting the status of educational psychology.

The Society's *Code of Ethics for Psychologists Working in Aotearoa/New Zealand* (New Zealand Psychological Society, 2002) applies to all Society members and registered psychologists. It presents the principles and values to which psychologists should adhere and identifies the implications of these in terms of their application in professional practice.

At the time of the 1988 Picot Report, which recommended decision making be transferred to local communities, special education was seen as too complex and so was not included in these reforms. However, the deinstitutionalisation and inclusion movements contributed to a shift in special education from a deficit model to one that was more ecologically and contextually focused, including an increase in parental choice and self-managed schools. These and other changes presented pressures that resulted in a new policy, *Special Education 2000* (Ministry of Education, 1996), that provides for the individual funding and support of the 3% of the school population identified as having high to very high educational needs, and a further 5% to 8% of students needing support through resources allocated to schools or groups of schools (Ministry of Education, 2005). Educational psychologists work predominantly within two of the main initiatives under this policy: the Severe Behaviour Initiative, which targets students displaying difficult behaviour, and the Ongoing Resources Scheme (now called the Ongoing Reviewable Resources Scheme), for students who will have ongoing special needs throughout their schooling.

Various publications contribute to psychologists' general knowledge and practice. *Connections,* a monthly newsletter disseminating news, job advertisements, and information about professional development workshops and activities of interest to psychologists in general, is distributed to Society members. *The Bulletin,* a members-only periodical, is published twice per annum by the Society. *The Bulletin* contains short articles and feature sections on topics of general interest relating to psychologists' teaching, training, and practice, together with applications of the discipline of psychology to current social and political issues. The Society's *New Zealand Journal of Psychology* publishes articles that include data on national samples, articles that discuss the relevance of wider issues to the New Zealand social and cultural context, and articles relevant to the practice of psychology. *Kairaranga,* a New Zealand journal on educational practice, contains articles relevant to the practice of educational psychology and the education of children with special education needs. This journal is a joint effort between the Ministry of Education, the Resource Teachers of Learning and Behaviour, and selected New Zealand universities. Published twice yearly, *Kairaranga* attempts to link research and practice through evidence-based approaches. Career information for educational psychologists is available online from the Kiwi Careers Web site (http://www.kiwicareers.govt.nz/default .aspx?id0=103&id1=J25323), and employment opportunities for educational psychologists within Group Special Education are listed on the Ministry of Education Web site (www.minedu .govt.nz).

Preparation of Educational Psychologists

Massey University offers the only educational psychology training program in New Zealand. The program is located within the College of Education at Albany Campus in Auckland. The University of Canterbury offers a Master of Education program with an endorsement in Child and Family Psychology. Some of its graduates have been employed with Group Special Education within the Ministry of Education. Previous programs at the University of Auckland and the University of Otago are no longer offered.

Massey University's Educational Psychology Training Program offers distance education, flexibly delivering training in all parts of the country. Until their internship year, students can study either full- or part-time, attend block courses on campus, and complete assignments in their local areas. This program was established in 1998 and has graduated 100 educational psychologists.

Students are selected for this program after completing an undergraduate degree that includes foundation courses in both education and psychology. Students who have completed some or all requirements for a master's degree in education or psychology also may be accepted. The selection process considers an applicant's academic history, including performance in courses and the nature of their previous study, their background experiences in education, and the degree of professionalism they demonstrated in their work. After completing the first step in their preparation (i.e., obtaining a master of educational psychology degree), students are eligible to apply for the internship year, the Post Graduate Diploma of Educational Psychology. During this post-master's internship, students are engaged in

various types of work in their local areas, including both individual- and systems-level intervention across a range of referral circumstances and educational settings. As many as 30 students complete the Master of Educational Psychology program each year, and 15 to 20 students are admitted to the internship program. Not all students who complete the master's degree go directly into the internship program.

Each intern has a primary university-accredited supervisor who provides regular supervision on practical work. In addition, interns are encouraged to contact other members of the educational psychology community in order to access the broader range of knowledge required to enhance their work. Internships reflect a wide variety of placements. Some interns are supported by the Ministry of Education, which also provides access to fieldwork and supervision. Other interns are employed by schools in positions such as guidance counsellors or resource teachers of learning and behaviour. Others arrange their internships in a more freelance manner and engage in required work in a range of educational institutions wherein payment may occur on a case-by-case basis. Interns who access their casework in this way must arrange supervision from a university-accredited supervisor. Many educational psychologists participate in the community of practice (i.e., professional groups who engage in collaborative exchanges either face-to-face or electronically— e.g., Global School Psychology Network), thus enabling university educational psychology and special education programs to maintain professional relationships and promote professional development. Supervisors and graduates of the program generally remain in the online community, supporting dialogue between educational psychologists with varying levels of experience.

Educational psychology practice operates largely within an ecological paradigm. Educational psychologists working for the Ministry of Education, the largest employer of educational psychologists, describe their work as being ecological, emphasizing collaboration with learners, schools, families, and other agencies (Ministry of Education, 2004; Ryba, Annan, & Mentis, 2001). The Massey University training program encourages trainees to use ecological approaches in their practices. Graduates acquire knowledge of consultation, assessment, and intervention skills within a situational analysis framework, one that supports educational psychologists to work within the ecological perspective (Annan, 2005).

The goal of the educational psychology training program is to develop a student's knowledge and skill in 12 competency domains (Annan, Ryba, Mentis, Bowler, & Edwards, 2005). Taken together, these domains form a competency framework that serves as an outline for the program's curriculum. The development of this framework was informed, in part, by *School Psychology: A Blueprint for Training and Practice II* (Ysseldyke et al., 1997). The format of the curriculum retains its similarity with this U.S. model, although the content has been substantially modified to align it with the New Zealand context. The competencies are described next, along with an outline of the particular knowledge and skills required of graduating educational psychologists. These competencies, although developed for graduating psychologists, also have relevance for experienced psychologists, as they are congruent with the set of competencies required of educational psychologists under the Health Practitioners Competence Assurance Act 2003.

Consultation and collaboration. Graduating educational psychologists are expected to have well-established models of practice and demonstrate that they can apply these methods to the particular situations they will face in their work. Collaboration is an essential aspect of ecological practice and must influence decision making in all aspects of educational psychologists' work.

Assessment procedures. All decision making in educational psychology must be evidence-based. That is, each action taken by psychologists must be justified by psychological theory and research.

Psychologists use various methods to collect data and seek multiple independent sources of data. They also devise ways to demonstrate whether their projects are effective.

Problem-solving methods and decision making. Graduating educational psychologists must have consolidated effective problem-solving procedures. They must be able to articulate these processes and apply them effectively in applied settings. Educational psychologists also must be able to adopt leadership roles that allow them to collaborate effectively with the groups of people with whom they work. Problem-solving methods must be sufficiently developed to provide direction in professional activities.

Intervention. Educational psychologists must ensure that their interventions are guided by evidence-based analyses. Interventions must be consistent with psychological theory, local understandings, and the particular situations in which they are implemented. Psychologists must assess the extent to which interventions meet the objectives of their projects.

Reflective and ethical practice. Educational psychologists must demonstrate that they reflect on their work and make ongoing adjustments to their practices. The practices of educational psychologists evolve continually. Thus, they must actively review and, when needed, revise professional knowledge. Educational psychology work, whether during training or post-training, must be consistent with the *Code of Ethics for Psychologists Working in Aotearoa/New Zealand* (New Zealand Psychological Society, 2002).

Research and program evaluation. Educational psychologists are expected to have extensive knowledge of qualitative and quantitative research methods. This knowledge must be developed to the extent that psychologists can evaluate research reports as well as plan and conduct program evaluations. They must be able to construct research projects that align with the perspectives of the participants. Educational psychologists also are encouraged to contribute to the discipline's fund of knowledge through dissemination of research findings.

Diversity. Educational psychologists must be sensitive to the views of diverse groups of people who understand the world in different ways. They must develop knowledge of individual differences, abilities and disabilities, and the powerful influences of biological, cultural, socioeconomic, and political factors on development and learning.

Bicultural issues/Treaty of Waitangi. All psychologists are legally obliged to recognise and honor the principles of the Treaty of Waitangi (1840). This document, a covenant between the Maori and the Crown, is the founding document of the country. When working with Maori children, psychologists must collaborate with Whanau (extended family) at every point of the process. All psychologists must develop the skills and knowledge necessary to work effectively with Maori. Psychologists must collaborate with Maori to define and determine the issues to be addressed, to develop the processes of each project, and to co-construct interventions.

School systems organisation and policy development. Educational psychologists are supported by knowledge of general and special education systems. They must be able to facilitate the development of policies that create and maintain safe, supportive, and effective learning environments for children and others.

Developmental processes and issues. Knowledge of human development is fundamental to the practice of educational psychology. Educational psychologists must have knowledge of a range of theories of human development and be aware of their own views on this matter. They must be mindful of the influence of their own perspective on fieldwork. Educational psychologists must consider and analyse each situation in relation to

knowledge of human development, and their interventions must consider developmental factors.

Learning and teaching. Educational psychologists must be able to apply knowledge of theory and research in learning and teaching in ways that contribute positively to the learning of children and the work of teachers. They must develop a range of applicable assessment and intervention methods for the particular contexts in which they are used.

Knowledge management. Educational psychologists must be able to access, manage, and apply the knowledge required to carry out professional practice. Technical competencies include proficiency in oral and written communication, ability to access material from libraries or other repositories of information, technical skills in using the Internet, and ways to link with other professionals for the purpose of professional development.

Development in each of the competency domains begins well before students enter the training program. Many competencies are supported by courses selected for undergraduate study (e.g., research methods, applied behaviour analysis, developmental psychology, and theories of learning). Continued and focused development in each of the 12 competencies within the first and second year of the Master of Educational Psychology and the Post Graduate Diploma Educational Psychology programs is cyclical, with each stage building on the knowledge and skill developed previously. During their studies, students are required to maintain an ongoing professional development plan that indicates specific areas for development and documents learning in relation to each of the competencies. At the conclusion of their supervised internship, candidates for the Post Graduate Diploma of Educational Psychology are required to participate in a professional examination process conducted by a panel of educational psychologists. The panel reviews each trainee's academic and professional work for the year and conducts an oral examination in order to decide whether sufficient competence has been attained to begin practice as an educational psychologist. Successful candidates each receive from the university notification of course completion and a recommendation to the Psychologists' Registration Board for registration.

Roles, Functions, and Responsibilities of Educational Psychologists

Educational psychologists within Group Special Education provide a range of services at both the individual and system levels. Services fall into three bands, which include individual case referrals, system-level interventions and support, and third party contracts.

At the individual level, educational psychologists receive referrals for students who present with severe and extreme needs. Assessments focus on identifying problems and areas of need followed by the identification, implementation, and evaluation of appropriate support systems. Educational psychologists working at this level select appropriate assessment tools to support their work and the decision-making process. The selection of appropriate assessment tools is at the discretion of the practitioner. Although some school administrators request Group Special Education to conduct psychoeducational assessments, such assessments are not conducted as discrete pieces of work. Assessments occur only within the context of ongoing work with a student. Schools or parents who want to obtain psychoeducational assessments for children who seemingly do not evidence severe difficulties must obtain them from private practitioners.

Educational psychologists play a key role in the delivery of system-level intervention and support in such areas as whole school policy development (e.g., crisis prevention and response), school support and referral systems, programs designed to prevent violence, and curriculum adaptation. Educational psychologists also lead the traumatic incident teams that respond to crises in schools and the wider community when such events have a direct impact on the school community.

Group Special Education also is responsible for various service contracts with agencies that require input from psychologists. For example, the Independent Youth Benefit provides welfare benefits for young people estranged from their families. Educational psychologists working under Group Special Education are required to conduct an assessment in accord with established criteria to determine the eligibility of young people applying for this benefit. Psychologists also conduct assessments to determine eligibility for young persons to enroll in the correspondence school under a psychological/psychosocial category, when psychological and/or psychosocial issues prevent or limit attendance at the local school. Other contract work may include requests for specific training and in-service professional development.

Educational psychologists working in the state sector receive little if any funding or release time to conduct research and engage in other scholarly activities that inform the practice of educational psychology. However, they may be seconded to participate in Group Special Education service delivery and policy reviews that generate internal reports. Thus, educational psychologists are largely reliant on overseas literature to inform their practice.

Current Issues Impacting Educational Psychology

In order to acquire information for this chapter, we consulted educational psychologists from several districts to gain a clearer appreciation of current issues impacting the practice of educational psychology. Several key issues emerged, and prominent among these were concerns that centre on the implementation of the Health

Practitioners' Competence Assurance Act (2003). This legislation demands that psychologists must position themselves to demonstrate their competence in new ways, and at this time, the means of assessing competence are still being developed. Representatives of the educational psychologists' community are currently developing a competency document in which the current knowledge domains, shared among members of this group, are specified. The document is intended to indicate the particular skills required for translating psychological theory and knowledge into practice and the means by which the individual educational psychologist's practice can be evaluated. If the evaluation measures of other health-related disciplines in New Zealand serve as a guide, it is likely that portfolios of practice will become one means for the profession to gain insight into the practice of its members.

The way that the psychologists' community in general has responded to the Health Practitioners' Competence Assurance Act (2003) has been the subject of much debate in the educational psychology community. Although an educational psychology scope of practice has been designated, many psychologists have been disinclined to register under this scope, believing that the general scope, supported by the New Zealand Psychological Society's code of ethics (2002), offers sufficient protection to clients, as it requires all psychologists to practice within their area of training and expertise.

A more immediate matter for many educational psychologists is the perceived erosion of their traditional role in their workplaces. This is particularly the case for educational psychologist practitioners employed within the Ministry of Education, as their work often is decided by others. For example, the parameters of some third party contracts that are designated for delivery by psychologists within Group Special Education (e.g., Independent Youth Benefit assessments, correspondence school assessments) are negotiated with limited input from psychologists. The focus of these third party contracts also detracts from the core work of the practice of educational psychology, including work with students, teachers, and parents.

Educational psychologists working in private practice are in a better position to negotiate their fieldwork than are those working within Group Special Education. Government employees often find they are required to carry out tasks that are not within their knowledge and skill area, because those who negotiate the contracts regarding their work often have little knowledge of psychology/educational psychology. Many negotiators and managers of contracts are not psychologists and, in their efforts to maintain the viability of the organisation, at times agree to deliver services that require skills that psychologists do not have. In addition, some educational psychologists are concerned that they have some specialised skills that are not recognised, are not utilised, or are underutilised.

The boundaries between the roles of educational psychologists and other psychologists, and between educational psychologists and special educators, have been blurred. Employers assign positions and tasks, originally held by psychologists, to other education professionals, who have not have undertaken as thorough a level of training. It is not unusual for advertisements for a position previously held by an educational psychologist to call for applicants from a range of occupational groups. In addition to the obvious employment issues associated with such practice, educational psychologists also are concerned for public, practitioner, and organisational safety.

The vast majority of educational psychologists in New Zealand are employed by Group Special Education and therefore are required to adhere to two codes, the New Zealand Psychological Society's *Code of Ethics for Psychologists Working in Aotearoa/New Zealand* (2002) and the Ministry of Education code of conduct. In the main, these two codes do not conflict, but the ministry code requires psychologists to support their initiatives publicly. Such a requirement has the potential to place psychologists, who are in the business of critically evaluating systems of educational provision for children, in a position where the cost of working ethically could jeopardise their employment. Although the code of ethics (New Zealand Psychological Society, 2002) suggests that psychologists need to make decisions about which code should take precedence in such situations, psychologists are still placed in an ethical quandary.

The heavy workloads of educational psychologists contribute to further concerns for practitioner and client safety. The educational psychologists we consulted reported that they often do not have sufficient time to work as effectively as they know they can and should. Although they are required to carry heavy workloads, the code of ethics demands that they take personal responsibility for their practice. The issue of individual versus organisational responsibility continues to be debated within the general psychology community, but the Psychologists' Registration Board, charged with protecting the interests of the public and consumers of psychologists' services, has clearly indicated that the integrity of a psychologist's work is the responsibility of the psychologist. The Board will not accept organisational pressures as a just explanation for questionable practice.

Special Education 2000 policy was designed to meet a continuum of needs. The ways in which the different initiatives serve to separate rather than integrate practices of educational psychology is an ongoing issue (Ryba & Annan, 2000). Although the national policy for special education service delivery was sound in principle, its implementation had resulted in the fragmentation of support services (Wylie, 2001).

Current special education policy does not directly reflect the ecological perspective of contemporary educational psychology. Participation in system-level work is restricted, because this work is not directly supported in policy and funding provisions. However, educational psychologists work within the parameters of government policy and Group Special Education service

provisions in an effort to address a child's referral in ways that also consider broader and influential ecological and systemic factors. Educational psychologists have worked with schools to establish whole-school initiatives (e.g., behaviour support, peer mediation, learning support). This work generally is negotiated and funded independently by the school requesting the service.

In summary, a number of issues impact the practice of educational psychology in New Zealand, and readers may be familiar with many similar themes when working in countries that have limited resources yet ever-increasing service demands. The challenge for the profession and practice of educational psychology is to effectively manage the competing and often conflicting demands and restrictions in order to ensure safe, competent, and effective practice.

References

Annan, J. (2005). Situational analysis: A framework for evidence-based practice. *School Psychology International, 26*(2), 131–146.

Annan, J., Ryba, K., Mentis, M., Bowler, J., & Edwards, T. (2005). A blueprint for training educational psychologists in Aotearoa, New Zealand. *The Bulletin,* No. 103, 43–47. (Available from the New Zealand Psychological Society, http://www.psychology.org.nz/publications/bulletin.html)

Bowler, J. (1997). Educational developmentalists: The rise and demise of an emergent profession. *New Zealand Journal of Educational Studies, 32*(1), 25–36.

Ministry of Education. (1996, July). *Special Education 2000: Update one.* Wellington: Author.

Ministry of Education. (2001). *Schooling in New Zealand: A guide.* Wellington: Author.

Ministry of Education. (2004). *Professional practice in special education.* Wellington: Author.

Ministry of Education. (2005). *History of special education in New Zealand.* Retrieved August 10, 2005, from www.minedu.govt.nz

New Zealand Psychological Society. (2002). *Code of ethics for psychologists working in Aotearoa/New Zealand.* Wellington: Author.

New Zealand Psychological Society. (2004). *Annual report.* Wellington: Author.

New Zealand Psychologists Board. (2004). *Scopes of practice for psychologists registered in New Zealand.* Retrieved April 3, 2005, from http://www.psychologistsboard.org.nz/howto/nzgraduates/registrationinfo.html

Ryba, K., & Annan, J., (2000). *Analysis of the interface between specialist education services behaviour team and resource teachers of learning and behaviour.* Unpublished report on contract research for New Zealand Ministry of Education, Massey University, Department of Learning and Teaching, Albany.

Ryba, K., Annan, J., & Mentis, M. (2001). *Development of an integrated approach to practice for behaviour support.* Unpublished report on contract research for Specialist Education Services, Massey University, Department of Learning and Teaching, Albany.

Statistics New Zealand. (2005). *Projections overview.* Retrieved August 10, 2005, from http://www2.stats.govt.nz/domino/external/web/prod_serv.nsf/htmldocs/Projections+Overview

Taskforce to Review Education Administration. (1988). *Administering for excellence: Effective administration in New Zealand* (B. Picot, Chair). Wellington: Government Printer.

Wylie, C. (2001). *Picking up the pieces: Review of Special Education 2000.* Wellington: New Zealand Council of Educational Research.

Ysseldyke, J., Dawson, P., Lehr, C., Reschly, D., Reynolds, M., & Telzrow, C. (1997). *School psychology: A blueprint for training and practice II.* Bethesda, MD: National Association of School Psychologists.

27

School Psychology in Nigeria

Andrew A. Mogaji

Context of School Psychology

Nigeria is the most populous nation in the continent of Africa south of the Sahara, with an estimated population of 130 million. Its landmass is 923,768 square kilometers, and its climate is tropical. It was a British colony until its independence on October 1, 1960. Nigeria is bordered on the east by Cameroun Republic, on the west by Benin Republic, on the north by Niger Republic, and on the south by the Atlantic Ocean. The country is culturally diverse in such features as language, religion, food, marriage systems, trading systems, and ethnic tribes. The Hausa/Fulanis dominate the north, the Igbos dominate the southeast, and the Yorubas dominate the southwest. In 2004, the gross domestic product was US$125.7 billion, about US$1,000 per capita. Nigeria is oil-rich, which accounts for much of the national budget. However, the country has suffered economically as a result of political instability, corruption, inadequate infrastructure, and poor macroeconomic management. The administration has been restructured and revitalized since 2000. For instance, in 2003, the government initiated the deregulation of fuel prices and the privatization of the country's four oil refineries and instituted the National Economic Empowerment Development Strategy, a domestically designed and run program modeled on the International Poverty Reduction and Growth Facility for fiscal and monetary management. These initiatives have resulted in growth of the gross domestic product.

Between 1976 and 1980, Nigeria witnessed unprecedented growth at all levels of education: primary, secondary, and tertiary (Fafunwa, 2002). The launching of the Universal Primary Education Program by the federal government in 1976 led to rapid growth in pupil enrollment, from 6 million during the 1975–1976 school year to 8.7 million during 1976–1977 and 12.5 million during the 1979–1980 school year (Fafunwa, 2002). Between 1976 and 1978, the federal government made substantial grants available to the then 19 states in terms of capital and recurrent expenditures to help promote the success of this education program. During this period, education grants were poorly managed by some states that thought the grants constituted their own share of profits from the oil boom, resulting in the grant monies being diverted to noneducational projects.

The federal government subsequently reduced grants to the states when oil prices fell. Hence, state and local governments, as well as parents, were asked to assist in financing the Universal Primary Education Program. In 1980, revenue allocations were reduced by the federal government from 71% to 55%, and the shares of state and local governments were correspondingly increased. In addition, the federal government stopped funding primary education and passed this responsibility on to state and local governments. State and local governments began to default in payments of primary school teachers' salaries and allowances.

The reduction of grants led to gross shortages of almost everything. Most school buildings were dilapidated; some states owed teachers' salaries for more than 6 months; school buildings were not maintained; children read under trees; teaching aids, books, and furniture were lacking; and teachers were laid off to save costs. Primary education had collapsed in most parts of the country. The glaringly poor quality unavoidably affected the rest of the entire educational system. In response to the poor state of education, four commissions were set up to examine the problems of primary education. Between 1980 and 1988, government funds for financing primary education were derived from two sources, namely the local (10%) and state (35%) governments, which were derived from the federation account. In 1984, these conditions led to the federal government establishing the Fafunwa study group on the funding of education. The study group visited all 19 states of the federation and Abuja, the federal capital territory, and took written and oral evidence from individuals, groups, organizations, and state governments.

The study group made the following recommendations to the government. Primary education should be within the reach of every Nigerian child irrespective of the economic status of his or her parents. Salaries and allowances of primary school staff should be taken directly from federation sources. A compensatory sum should be made available for educationally disadvantaged states from federation sources. State governments should provide teachers with instructional materials. Local governments should provide furniture and see to the maintenance of the school buildings. They should also provide housing for teachers in rural areas and mobilize efforts for this purpose. Parents should assume the financial costs of textbooks, exercise books, writing materials, school uniforms, and midday meals for their children. State governments should aid parents who are unable to assume these costs.

Four years after the recommendations were made, the federal government agreed to pay 65% of the annual salaries of teaching and nonteaching staff at the primary school level; state governments would contribute 20%, and the local governments would contribute 15%. This led to the establishment of the National Primary Education Commission and the National Primary Education Fund, which led to money being deducted directly from the federal government's share of the federation account. The National Primary Education Commission was empowered to (a) prescribe the minimum standards of primary education throughout the country, (b) inquire into and advise the federal government on the funding of primary education in Nigeria, (c) receive the Nigerian National Primary Education Fund from the federal government and allocate the funds to the appropriate body designated by each state and the federal capital territory, and (d) collate periodic master plans for a balanced and coordinated development of primary education in Nigeria. The National Primary Education Fund recommended that class size be increased, on average, to 35 and 40 students per teacher at primary and secondary schools, respectively (Fafunwa, 2002; Federal Government of Nigeria, 2004). Secondary education enrollment increased from 771,366 in 1975–1976 to 3,608,215 in 1983–1984 (i.e., a 407% increase). This enrollment increase was consistent with the national education policy that secondary education should provide an increasing number of former primary school students with an opportunity for education of a higher quality, irrespective of their sex and social, religious, and ethnic backgrounds.

In 1977, the National Board for Technical Education was established to provide guidelines for the growth and development of technical and vocational education. The Board pioneered the idea of establishing minimum academic standards and established accreditation panels for this purpose. By 1990, there were 10 federal and 19 state polytechnic institutions, with a combined student enrollment of 60,000. With the Board's introduction of the minimum academic standards and entry requirements, all students pursuing the national diploma and higher national diploma-level courses achieved comparable levels of technical competence.

The introduction of the Universal Primary Education Program in 1976 was swiftly followed by the Universal University Education Program in 1978, which provided free university tuition. However, students continued to be responsible for paying for their lodging, meals, and books. Universities also witnessed unprecedented growth between 1970 and 1982. There were 6 universities in 1970; 13 in 1975; 21 in 1982; 22 federal universities, 9 state universities, and 6 colleges of education in 1990; and 24 federal universities, 19 state universities, 14 colleges of education, and two federal polytechnics with degree-awarding status in 2004. The 1979 constitution sanctioned private universities. In 2004, there were six private universities. In 2005, the federal government approved establishing more private universities.

Origin, History, and Current Status of School Psychology

Educational psychology and school psychology are two areas of applied psychology. School psychology focuses on applications of psychological methods, theory, and research in schools. On the other hand, educational psychology focuses on applications of psychological principles in all settings devoted to education; it is not restricted to the school environments. Hence, both educational and school psychology can be defined as applied areas of psychology that focus on the development, learning, motivation, instruction, and assessment of issues related to the teaching-learning process.

The content of educational psychology (e.g., development, learning, motivation, instruction) often forms the foundation for the preparation of school psychologists. Educational psychology generally is well taught in Nigerian universities and colleges of education. It was popular in all universities until the federal government enacted a policy that made guidance and counseling compulsory courses that had to be taught in tertiary institutions (e.g., colleges of education, polytechnics, and universities) and deemed that guidance and counseling services should be provided at all levels of education. The same policy also mandated continuous assessment in schools and stipulated that emphasis should be placed on promoting student development and the use of tools to assess students in three domains: cognitive (i.e., knowledge of particular subjects), affective (i.e., interest and positive attitudes toward the subjects), and psychomotor (i.e., acquisition of practical skills and display of industry).

Persons who have at least a master's degree in psychology are regarded as professional psychologists. Persons who specialize in psychology are regarded as practitioners in that area. No matter their area of specialization, university professors are assumed to be able to perform the roles of educational or school psychologists. For example, the author of this chapter is a personnel/organizational psychologist who also performs the role of a school psychologist because he is a university lecturer. He also does research with children, adolescents, and adults. Professional psychologists make use of psychological tests in their counseling and consultancy services.

Educational research generally involves finding solutions to educational problems and issues (e.g., the teaching-learning process in every school subject, evaluation of outcomes, administration and financial resources at every educational level; Obe, 2001). Some of these problems are evident in the lack of motivation on the part of students and teachers, cheating on examinations and mass failure among students, unwanted pregnancies among adolescent girls, and complaints that females are marginalized.

Guidance counselors began to focus on some of these problems with a view to prevention. Vocational guidance, an important service of guidance counselors, has been elusive because the government has failed to provide employment for most people. The industries and organizations that were supposed to provide employment are retrenching, and in some cases, when vacancies exist, they use favoritism and nepotism in the recruitment process. In such cases, recruitment and selection processes often lack objectivity.

These and other conditions have contributed to the negative attitudes of students toward the various subjects and attending class. Truancy has become prevalent. There have been instances of students drinking alcohol in beer parlors when they should have been in class. When such students did attend lectures, they challenged the authority of their teachers and in some cases threatened to beat them. Some students believe that, no matter what they do, teachers will fail them. When students fail, they commonly say the teacher failed them.

Because of these problems, the Nigerian Association of Educational Psychologists was formed. It is an association of persons interested in proffering solutions to the problems associated with the teaching-learning process. Members of this association agreed to work together with members of the Counseling Association of Nigeria.

There are very few publications on school psychology in Nigeria. The history and current status of school psychology services in Nigeria have been discussed by Jimoh (1986), Ezeilo (1989, 1992), and Mogaji (2003) from an impressionistic perspective (Mpofu, Peltzer, Shumba, Serpell, & Mogaji, 2005). In fact, all of these authors agreed that surveys on the status of school psychology in sub-Saharan Africa are scarce. The terms *educational psychology* and *school psychology* are used synonymously in many African countries, particularly in those with a British heritage (e.g., Nigeria, Zimbabwe, Malawi, and Zambia). Moreover, survey data suggest that school psychology services have the potential to make a difference in the quality of life and education of children in the region.

School psychology services grew from the widespread provision of general education services through the elementary primary school education and the availability of special education services. The availability of special education services in an African country is a reliable proxy indicator for the existence of, or potential for, school psychology in that country. School psychology services in developing countries tend to be narrowly defined to refer to psycho-educational support for school students with disabilities (Mpofu et al., 2005).

Moreover, Mpofu and his associates found that school psychology services were initially available to children of a middle-class background in metropolitan centers and less so to children in rural areas or those with special educational needs. Children with emotional-behavioral disabilities typically receive help from social workers, because they are basically perceived by the national governments as presenting primarily with social rather than educational needs.

Infrastructure of School Psychology

School psychology is a recognized profession in Nigeria (Mogaji, 2003), represented by the Nigerian Psychological Association, Nigerian Association of Educational Psychologists, Counseling Association of Nigeria, and the National Council for Exceptional Children. Neither the title nor the practice of school psychology is regulated. Other providers of school psychology services include clinical psychologists, school guidance teachers, special education teachers, and speech therapists/teachers.

Preparation of School Psychologists

In 1977, a national policy on education was established to spell out the philosophy and objectives that underlie the government's investment in education. With this educational policy, the federal government introduced the 6-3-3-4 system of education, meaning that students are encouraged to spend 6 years in the primary school, 3 years in the junior secondary, 3 years in the senior secondary, and 4 years in a university.

Students take entrance examinations that comprise verbal and quantitative aptitude tests, including tests of general reasoning, to gain admission into secondary schools. The West African Examination Council is the examining body that evaluates the degree of knowledge students have acquired in subjects of their choice. The Joint Admission and Matriculation Board is the examining body charged with the placement of students into the universities, polytechnics, and colleges of education. The testing unit of the Federal Ministry of Education is responsible for placing students with special needs education (e.g., those with speech impediments, vocational needs, or physical impairments) into classes according to their needs.

Some tests have been developed to measure students' academic aptitudes. For example, Obe's scholastic aptitude test (1980) is used to assess students' verbal and numerical aptitudes. The Torrance Tests of Creative Thinking (1974) are used to measure the creative talents of pupils in Nigeria. The Student Styles Questionnaire developed by Oakland, Glutting, and Horton (1996) is used to measure temperament and learning styles among Nigerian children. Even though school psychology is recognized as a specialty of psychology, misconceptions exist as to how it and educational psychology differ. Educational psychology is offered as a specialist course after one has obtained his or her first university degree. It is an area of specialization at the master's level like any other subfield of psychology that is offered in the department of psychology by the faculty of social sciences. The master's degree is a 12-month intensive program of academic work, including a 3-month internship experience or teaching practice under the supervision of an experienced professional person. Educational psychology is made up of four subfields, namely, guidance and counseling; measurement and evaluation; learning; and human growth and development. Educational psychologists strive to have students attend classes regularly and attend lectures. Moreover, they strive to identify students' problems with a view to proffering likely solutions.

Therefore, the focus of educational psychologists should be to carry out educational research. According to Barnes (1960) and other authors, educational researches may be classified in many different ways, such as by the field/discipline: educational psychology, curriculum studies, guidance and counseling, physical and health education, educational administration and planning, adult education, and sociology of education.

School psychology in countries surveyed by Mpofu et al. (2005) was loosely defined to refer to school guidance counseling (e.g., Botswana, Nigeria, Zambia), special education (e.g., Botswana, Nigeria), and professionals with psychology qualifications who worked in schools (e.g., Nigeria). In Nigeria, Malawi, South Africa, and Zimbabwe, school psychologists were found to be people with qualifications in educational psychology. School psychology (also called educational psychology) is an emerging profession in sub-Saharan Africa. It is generally unknown by ordinary citizens of countries in sub-Saharan Africa. Developmentally, school psychology services are evolving from the relatively more established services in special needs education and school guidance and counseling (Mpofu et al., 2005). Hence, those that can be regarded as school psychologists in Nigeria are numerous.

Due to the fact that school psychology practices in sub-Saharan Africa are in their infancy, there is variation in the use of the title "school psychologist" and in the practice of school psychology. In a majority of countries in sub-Saharan Africa, including Nigeria, professionals with school guidance and counseling or special education qualifications are regarded as school psychologists. The roles and functions of school psychologists vary by country. Countries with relatively stronger school guidance and counseling programs consider preventive health education and careers counseling a core function of school psychologists. Some countries consider special educational placement a core function.

School psychologists in 8 of the 12 African countries surveyed by Mpofu, Zindi, Oakland, and Peresuh (1997) worked as lecturers at universities or were with government social service agencies. School psychologists in 7 of the 12 countries had either undergraduate or graduate qualifications but no teaching experience. Mpofu et al. (2005) also reported that school guidance counselors led the list of allied service providers across the six countries, followed by special education teachers, clinical psychologists, and regular class teachers.

For a person to qualify as a clinical psychologist, he or she must possess at least a master's degree in clinical psychology (an area of specialization in psychology). This can be obtained after the 4-year bachelor's degree in general psychology. For a person to become a regular class teacher, he or she must possess either a degree in any teaching subject after a 4-year program at the university or at least a national certificate in education after a 3-year program at the college of education. The person can become a school guidance counselor if he or she specializes in guidance and counseling at any of the educational levels described above. Special education schools, such as the Federal College of Education (Special) in Oyo, and special education departments at the Universities of Ibadan and Jos were established by the federal

government to train and prepare middle-level managers of special needs education services.

Roles, Functions, and Responsibilities of School Psychologists

School psychologists provide consultative services in reference to academic and social behaviors as well as guidance and counseling (Mogaji, 2003). Special education assessment and placement is a primary job function for school psychologists. Career counseling is their secondary function. Their basic training and on-the-job training were perceived to be thorough (Mpofu et al., 2005). With the introduction of the 6-3-3-4 system of education, measurement and evaluation became an integral part of the teaching-learning process in Nigeria. Measurement and evaluation are used for the identification and placement of students into various classes.

Teacher-made curriculum-based achievement tests are constructed by teachers to measure learning outcomes of students in their classrooms. Nationally normed standardized achievement tests are available. Examples of these tests are those conducted by the Joint Admission and Matriculation Board (e.g., the Universities' Matriculation Examination) and the West African Examination Council (Junior/Senior Secondary School Certificate Examinations).

The Differential Aptitude Test is used to assist students in making vocational and educational decisions. Subtests include verbal reasoning, numerical ability, abstract reasoning, spatial reasoning, mechanical reasoning, clerical speed and accuracy, spelling, and sentence construction.

The Test Development and Research Unit, an arm of the West African Examination Council, has a series of tests that are used for selection into trade centers, teacher-training colleges, schools of nursing, civil aviation, federal training centers, secondary schools, common entrance, and employment and promotion in civil service, commercial, and industrial organizations. The Test Development and Research Unit also administers aptitude tests to Nigerian students on behalf of the Educational Testing Service (Obe, 1980).

The Vocational Interest Inventory (Bakare, 1977) is designed to indicate the type of work in which persons are interested and that they will enjoy. The Hare Self-Esteem Scale (Hare, 1985) assesses the influences of peer groups, school, and home on the self-esteem of school-age children. The Student Styles Questionnaire (Oakland et al., 1996) was used by Oakland, Mogaji, and Dempsey (in press) to measure the preferences of four bipolar traits—extroversion or introversion, practical or imaginative, thinking or feeling, and organized or flexible temperament styles—among Nigerian children.

Current Issues Impacting School Psychology

School psychology has tremendous potential yet also faces significant challenges. For example, poorly achieving students tend to lack motivation and could benefit from school psychology services (Mogaji, 2003). The growth of school psychology has been hindered by the lack of support by the federal government (Awanbor, 1995; Jimoh, 1986; Olowu, 1991). Its growth would be possible if a national policy of education that advocated the education of all children, regardless of disability, could be turned into law and enforced so that many children with disabilities could attend school. For example, special education legislation would reinvigorate school psychology services by empowering a significant majority of potential consumers of school psychology services, namely, children with disabilities and their families (Eleweke, 1999).

A lack of resources in test use, development, and research constitutes a major obstacle to a greater involvement of school psychologists in Africa, including Nigeria (Mpofu et al., 2005). Mpofu and his associates found that participants in their survey perceived a lot of potential for school psychology to develop in their countries with support by national governments, enhanced public awareness, more trained school psychologists, and greater investment in research on test use and development. Parental interests in meeting the special education needs of children were not sufficiently strong to warrant school psychology services. Most believe parents are superstitious and do not understand the actual causes of learning or behavioral problems in their children, resulting in their lack of involvement. In addition, parents are either unaware or ignorant of school psychology services. Mothers, not fathers, generally were more involved in attempting to meet the special needs of their children. Their use of community-based services for special educational needs was rare.

School psychology practices in the area of assessment and diagnosis should be adapted to local needs (e.g., sociocultural background of the consumers), and school psychologists should not disengage from the communities that they purport to serve. The apparent contextual disengagement from their practices by school psychologists could be a reflection of the values divide that exists between the goals and processes of education in African communities and the institution of schooling from Africa's Western European heritage. For example, cooperative learning and achievement with and for a group is highly valued by most communities in Africa but undervalued by the schools (Nsamenang, 1993). Schools in Africa are modeled after those of the West and place an emphasis on individual performance and achievement on tasks. School psychology practices are based on the same value system as the schools they work in and so seek to promote individual performance and achievement rather than cooperative learning (as in peer teaching and learning).

The contextual disengagement of school psychologists suggests that the professional preparation they received may have been deficient in cultural responsiveness (Jimoh, 1986). It may also be indicative of a lower stage of develop-ment in the indigenization of psychology in those countries (Mpofu et al., 2005).

A declining national economy resulting from mismanagement and the fall of oil prices limited the need for vocational guidance, a service provided by some school psychologists. School psychology was also hindered by inconsistencies in the standards of training across colleges, regions, and disability advocacy groups, as well as from poor remuneration (Awanbor, 1995; Ezeilo, 1989, 1992; Mogaji, 2003).

References

Awanbor, D. (1995). Ten years of the National Policy on Education in Nigeria: An assessment of policy on special education. *International Journal of Disability, Development and Education, 42,* 171–176.

Bakare, C. G. M. (1977). *Vocational interest inventory.* Ibadan: Ibadan University Press.

Barnes, J. B. (1960). *Educational research for classroom teachers.* New York: Pitman.

Eleweke, C. J. (1999). The need for mandatory legisla-tion to enhance services to people with disabilities in Nigeria. *Disability and Society, 1*(2), 227–237.

Ezeilo, B. N. (1989). School psychology in Nigeria. In P. A. Saigh & T. Oakland (Eds.), *International per-spectives on psychology in the schools: School psy-chology* (pp. 133–138). Hillsdale, NJ: Lawrence Erlbaum.

Ezeilo, B. N. (1992). The international school psy-chology survey: Implications for Africa. *School Psychology International, 13,* 155–161.

Fafunwa, A. B. (2002). *History of education in Nigeria.* Ibadan: NPS Educational Publishers.

Federal Government of Nigeria. (2004). *National policy on education.* Yaba, Lagos: NERDC Press.

Hare, B. R. (1985). *The HARE general and area-specific (school, peer and home) self-esteem scale.* New York: Free Press.

Jimoh, S. A. (1986). School psychology and the Nigerian cultural situation. *School Psychology International, 7,* 155–161.

Mogaji, A. A. (2003). *The current status of educational psychology in Nigeria.* Unpublished manuscript.

Mpofu, E., Peltzer, K., Shumba, A., Serpell, R., & Mogaji, A. (2005). School psychology in sub-Saharan Africa: Results and implications of a six country survey. In C. Frisby & C. Reynolds (Eds.), *Comprehensive handbook of multicultural school psychology* (pp. 1128–1151). New York: Wiley.

Mpofu, E., Zindi, F., Oakland, T., & Peresuh, M. (1997). School psychology practices in East and Southern Africa: Special educators' perspectives. *Journal of Special Education, 31,* 387–402.

Nsamenang, A. B. (1993). Psychology in sub-Saharan Africa. *Psychology and Developing Societies, 5,* 171–184.

Oakland, T., Glutting, J. J., & Horton, C. B. (1996). *Student Styles Questionnaire: Star qualities in learning, relating, and working.* San Antonio, TX: Psychological Corporation.

Oakland, T., Mogaji, A. A., & Dempsey, J. (in press). Temperament styles of Nigerian and U.S. children. *Journal of Psychology in Africa.*

Obe, E. O. (1980). *Educational testing in West Africa.* Lagos: Premier Press.

Obe, E. O. (2001). Towards funding educational research: Topic selection, proposal, justification and budget. *Lagos Journal of Educational Research, 1*(1), 1–15.

Olowu, A. A. (1991). Special students in "normal" secondary schools: Implications for counselling. *Nigerian Journal of Guidance and Counselling, 4,* 53–63.

Torrance, E. P. (1974). *Torrance Tests of Creative Thinking: Technical-norms manual.* Bensenville, IL: Scholastic Testing Services.

28

School Psychology in Norway

Roald Anthun

Terje Manger

Context of School Psychology

Norway has a population of 4.6 million (Statistics Norway, 2005b), of which 7.6% constitutes a heterogeneous immigrant population. The country's geographical area is 324,220 square kilometers (about two thirds is mountainous), with a coastline of 21,925 kilometers (including mainland, long fjords, and some 50,000 islands). Norway is a constitutional monarchy, and the economy is a combination of free market activity and government control. The government controls key areas, such as the vital petroleum sector. Norway is richly endowed with natural resources: petroleum, waterfalls, fish, forests, and minerals. The country is highly dependent on its oil production and international oil prices, with oil and gas accounting for one third of exports. Only Saudi Arabia and Russia export more oil. Norway is a member of the North American Treaty Organization and, in two referenda, decided against European Union membership. The gross domestic product in 2004 was US$183 billion dollars, US$40,000 per capita.

Approximately 909,000 children under the age of 15 and 289,043 between ages 15 and 19 reside in Norway (Statistics Norway, 2005b). Seventy-five percent of all children live with both biological parents, 17% live with only their mother, 3% live with only their father, 4% live with their mother and stepfather, and 1% live with their father and stepmother. Preschool or kindergarten programs are available for children ages 1 through 5. Compulsory education consists of the primary stage, which covers Grades 1 through 7 (ages 6–12), and the lower secondary stage, Grades 8 through 10 (ages 13–16). Grades 5 through 7 (ages 10–12) are sometimes called the intermediate stage. Classes are organized according to age and not according to subject or level of competence.

AUTHORS' NOTE: The authors would like to thank Professor Robert A. Wicklund for reading and commenting on an earlier draft of this manuscript.

Each school class typically remains together as a unit from the 1st through the 7th grade and, in many cases, to the 10th grade. Norway's population is geographically scattered, with numerous small school units in remote and sparsely populated areas. The country has about 1,000 primary schools that do not have separate classes for each age-group, owing to the small number of students. At the lower secondary stage, most schools are larger, with two or three parallel classes at each grade. Forty-seven percent of the compulsory schools have fewer than 300 students (Statistics Norway, 2005a).

All young people between the ages of 16 and 19 who have completed the 10-year compulsory school or its equivalent have a statutory right to a 3-year, full-time, upper secondary education. This education is intended to provide students with university entrance qualifications, vocational competence, or documented partial competence. Students and trainees who wish to obtain university entrance qualifications in addition to vocational competence may take additional courses after completion of technical or vocational training. The county is responsible for providing education, jobs, or vocational courses for young people who have the right to education but who are currently not in the schools and are not employed.

In 2003, 69% (205,172) of children between the ages of 1 and 5 and 85% of those between the ages of 3 and 5 attended preschools (Statistics Norway, 2004a). In 2004, 618,000 students attended the country's 3,189 primary and lower secondary schools (Statistics Norway, 2005a). In the same school year, 173,949 students attended the 474 upper secondary schools. Nearly 100% of the students completed compulsory education. Seventy-six percent of those who attended upper secondary schools in 1998 had finished within a 5-year period (Statistics Norway, 2004b).

Norway is divided into 19 counties and 435 municipalities (i.e., local authorities). The municipalities employ the teachers and are responsible for building and running preschools, primary schools, and lower secondary schools. Sixty percent of children attend public and 40% attend private preschools (Statistics Norway, 2004a). Only 1.6% of the student population attends private primary or lower secondary schools (Statistics Norway, 2001). The counties are responsible for upper secondary education. Five percent of the total student population attends private upper secondary schools (Statistics Norway, 2004b). The State, through its Ministry of Education and Research, is responsible for all education, including university and other higher education. The average class size in the public primary and lower secondary schools is 20.1 students (Statistics Norway, 2001), but many classes are smaller in rural municipalities. In upper secondary schools, the normal class size is between 25 and 30 students for general theoretical education and somewhat smaller for vocational training.

The Norwegian Education Act stipulates, "All students have the right to be taught according to their abilities and conditions." This principle applies equally to children with special educational needs and children with special abilities, be these theoretical, practical, physical, or aesthetic. The decision to provide all or part of a student's compulsory school education in the form of specially adapted teaching is made on an individual basis, in accordance with the Norwegian Administration Act. Figures from 2002–2003 reveal that 5.5% of the students in compulsory school have special needs. The percentage of students in special settings outside the compulsory school is estimated at 0.5% of the total number of students. Students with special needs are entitled to 3 years of full-time, upper secondary education along with other students. In addition, they may be given an extra 2 years of schooling at this level. Among upper secondary school students, 2.7% are educated in accordance with the special needs provisions.

Origin, History, and Current Status of School Psychology

School psychology services first were provided through private mental health agencies, modeled on the child guidance services in the United States.

These services were established by psychologists educated abroad, the most prominent of whom was Åse Gruda Skard, or "Mother Åse." Skard traveled, worked in many schools, and lectured publicly about the cause. In 1938, the first private agency for school psychology services was established in Oslo by Charlotte Bühler, who was inspired by Piaget. In 1939, the first public agency, in Aker, was opened. The further development of these services stopped during World War II and resumed in 1946. Development of the services was theoretically separated into two branches: one that promoted child mental health and one that focused on learning disabilities. This split orientation initially caused strife among professionals and has remained significant in determining the development of Norwegian school psychology and the country's Educational Psychological Services (Pedagogisk-psykologisk tjeneste).

Initial legislative milestones included laws that established special schools for students with general learning disabilities (1951) and later provided for them in local primary school (1955). Only larger municipalities established Educational Psychological Services before this legislation. Between 1956 and 1968, the number of Educational Psychological Service agencies rose from 12 to 82. The Primary and Lower Secondary Education Act, which stipulated that Educational Psychological Services be established in all districts, came into effect in 1969. This law served as an impetus to development of Educational Psychological Services, resulting in establishing 280 service agencies by 1984. Such services for the preschool and upper secondary school students were established by similar laws in the mid 1970s.

The first project examining the future organizations of Educational Psychological Services in 12 different model agencies across the country was initiated between 1969 and 1974 by the State Council for Experiments in Education. This project demonstrated that Educational Psychological Services could provide the necessary professional assistance needed to promote integration of special education students into the local schools. As a result, the Educational Psychological Services was made responsible for expert assessments of students needing special education. Subsequently, the law pertaining to special schools was repealed (1975). During the 1990s, the national special schools were transformed into resource centers. These later became part of the Norwegian Support System for Special Education.

White papers from the national education authorities throughout the 1970s and 1980s and the 1992 Program for Strengthening Educational Psychological Services helped shape school psychology significantly. Important investigations by Kiil (1989) and Støfring (1993) and several developmental projects and programs after 1990 also were milestones in school psychology development. Among these is the development of the Professional Center for Educational Psychological Services, the transactions pertaining to the closing of special schools and establishment of the Norwegian Support System for Special Education, the Program of Northern Norway, and the Competence Development Program for Educational Psychological Service Personnel and School Leaders. The Program of Northern Norway seems to have been the most important, by modeling collaboration in several types of networks. A competence development program (referred to in Norway as the Samtak program) was intended to prepare the Educational Psychological Services to assume responsibility for severely functionally disabled students locally and to do more system intervention work. The program was only partly successful. However, the Educational Psychological Services has been included in the latest revision of the Education Act (1998), which gives school competence and organizational development in the school system top priority. This move initiated major service provision changes.

Although the direct translation of the Norwegian school psychologist title *pedagogisk-psykologisk rådgiver* is "pedagogical-psychological counselor," the term *educational psychologist* is used much more often. In about the year 2000, when resource center positions were transferred to Educational Psychological Services, the total number of professionals employed by the 295 Educational Psychological Service agencies increased by 20%, to 2,100. According to numbers from the Norwegian Board of Education (2003), 45% of all professionals in the Educational Psychological Services were educational psychologists. Other Educational Psychological Service personnel include educational personnel at lower levels of special education (41%), social workers with different social education (6%), and miscellaneous professionals (8%). By the end of the 20th century, the male-female ratio of professionals had been reversed, going from two-thirds male to two-thirds female (Bræin, 1999). According to the Norwegian Psychological Association, in 2005, 325 members were educational psychologists, of which 72% were female (personal communication). Salaries among educational psychologists vary considerably with professional background, age, and specialization, with lower and upper limits estimated to be between US$45,000 and US$70,000 in 2005. Educational psychologists with a background in education and special education traditionally have received the highest salaries, although psychologists are now catching up. Educational psychologist salaries generally have not exceeded those for school personnel. Some municipalities have evaded this problem by redefining the contents and titles of positions.

Educational psychologists generally practice in Educational Psychological Service agencies. Some practice in the Norwegian Support System of Special Education and in higher educational institutions. Practicing educational psychologists work in both public and private schools. Some educational psychologists also travel to provide services on the Norwegian arctic islands Svalbard and at the Norwegian school on the Spanish Grand Canary Islands. About 30% of the Educational Psychological Service agencies are small entities in rural areas. Many do not have educational psychologists, only special teachers and social workers. About 23% of the agencies serving preschools and primary and lower secondary schools in 2003 were regional, versus 37% in 1996, covering about 64% of the municipalities. Educational psychologists often service both rural and urban areas and thus may be counted in both of them. The reduction in regional Educational Psychological Services reflects an ongoing shift to Educational Psychological Services combined with other public services, in 2003 covering 18.5% of the municipalities. The largest Educational Psychological Service agencies generally are situated in the biggest cities and have the largest number of educational psychologists. Twelve of 19 counties have separate Educational Psychological Services to serve upper secondary schools. In 2003, the ratio of students to educational psychologists was 1,250 to 1 and has been somewhat constant for a long period of time. On the other hand, the ratio of students to total number of professionals in the Educational Psychological Services has successively improved, with a mean ratio of 800 to 1 in 1996 and 640 to 1 in 2003.

Views as to opportunities for professional development of the educational psychologists differ. Some return to their respective specialization programs for continuing education programs, with the employer generally paying the costs. Compulsory in-service training and supervision are likely to be carried out as a part of one's existing professional assignments. The national school authorities offer courses for educational psychologists annually, at no financial costs to the agencies or their personnel. Sometimes the national school authorities arrange extensive educational projects or long-term programs. Individual professionals also may have the cost of external courses they choose to attend paid by the agency. Because the agencies have a high degree of administrative autonomy, they may hire other professionals to give courses, produce their own in-house educational programs, give each other supervision, or provide collaborative consultation in teams. Inexperienced educational psychologists have the right to 160 hours of supervision by colleagues.

Educational Psychological Service personnel generally view their high workload as the main limitation to professional development. Educational Psychological Services is usually considered by the school community at large to have a high turnover rate. About half of Educational Psychological Service personnel had 5 or more years of Educational Psychological Service experience, and 23% had only 1 year or less of such experience (Stubbe, 1994; Østrem, 1998). Furthermore, 30% had moved on to another Educational Psychological Service agency, and 10% had switched agency twice. Professionals who leave their service agency generally also leave Educational Psychological Services. In spite of the high turnover rate, vacancy is estimated to be continually falling, constituting 9% in 2001. The main reasons for educational psychologists to leave their jobs were low salary, high workload, and low professional challenges (Stubbe, 1994). In particular, many of the isolated educational psychologists in small rural agencies suffer from professional loneliness combined with extensive responsibility.

Infrastructure of School Psychology

The Division of School Psychology is a branch within the Norwegian Psychological Association. With nearly 4,000 members, the Norwegian Psychological Association represents approximately 90% of all psychologists licensed to practice in Norway (http://www.psykol.no). The organization is responsible for negotiating members' salaries and safeguarding working conditions and is affiliated with the joint Norwegian labor coalition for professional academic associations (*Akademikerne*), the European Federation of Professional Psychology Associations, the International Union of Psychological Sciences, and the Committee of Nordic Psychological Associations. The Union of Education Norway, which is a branch of the Confederation of Higher Education Unions, Norway, represents, among others, 1,400 members who hold master's degrees in education.

Norway has no specific degree programs in school psychology. Anyone qualified as a psychologist, with an education from Norway or abroad, may work as an educational psychologist. Psychologists hold about 50% of the educational

psychologist positions and are allowed to use their general professional title "psychologist." In addition, several master's-level programs in education and psychology may lead to qualification for an educational psychologist position. Psychologists are protected by the Health Personnel Act, and an application form for authorization and a license must be sent to the Norwegian Registration Authority for Health Personnel.

Educational Psychological Services activities in Norway are regulated by various acts of legislation. The key law is the Education Act (1998). Since the repeal of the Special School Act (1975), special education in Norway also has been regulated by the Education Act and associated national guidelines and regulations. Several other acts, such as acts regarding children, day care institutions, welfare services, municipality health services, social services, national insurance, public administration, and the freedom of information, also are important (Professional Center for the Educational Psychological Services, 2001).

The monthly peer-reviewed *Tidsskrift for Norsk Psykologforening* (Journal of the Norwegian Psychological Association) is intended to advance knowledge of the science and practice of psychology. The independent professional Division for Psychologists in School (*Forum for Psykologer i Skolen*), which is affiliated with the Norwegian Psychological Association and with the International School Psychology Association, is responsible for the journal *Skolepsykologi* (School Psychology). This journal promotes the knowledge and practice base of school psychology. In addition, the monthly journal *Spesialpedagogikk* (Special Education), published by the Union of Education Norway, contributes literature on students with special needs.

Preparation of School Psychologists

The pertinent degrees offered in Norway are in professional psychology, education at the master's level, and psychology at the master's level.

Annually, 240 students enter into one of four degree programs in psychology (at four of the five Norwegian universities). Approximately 200 students graduate each year. The reasons for the high graduation rate are primarily that the students admitted are stringently selected and the psychology programs are tightly structured.

The structure of the programs in education that qualify a psychologist is consistent with standards for the Norwegian Candidate (Candidatus Psychologiae) degree, which are set by the university programs and the Norwegian Psychological Association. In order to be admitted to the psychology programs, the student must have completed an introductory sequence of psychology courses, which requires one and a half semesters of full-time study in psychology. Admittance to the psychology program is based on a competitive grade point average from the introductory sequence.

The psychology programs are full-time, campus-based studies. They adhere to a scientist-practitioner model. This model emphasizes that the topics learned should be supportable empirically and theoretically and that they should be derived from a body of literature of high international standards. At most of the universities, the first $2\frac{1}{2}$ years are reserved for topics in psychological science (e.g., social, cognitive, biological, developmental, and personality) and research methods. The last $2\frac{1}{2}$ years offer practice-oriented education and supervised practice in various fields of applied psychology (e.g., clinical, work and organizational, neuroscience, educational, and psychosocial). All programs focus on children, adolescents, and adults. Interpersonal skills, assessment services, and knowledge of legal and ethical issues are emphasized. Students submit several research papers throughout the program and a thesis at the end. All universities have mandatory practice during the last $2\frac{1}{2}$ years. In addition, the University of Bergen has a compulsory 20 days of practice in Educational Psychological Services, supervised by a trained psychologist.

The psychology degree is generic. Thus, it offers few opportunities to acquire specialized education and training within a university program. Since 1959, the Norwegian Psychological Association has been responsible for specialization programs. These programs include at least 5 years of practice, supervision, courses, and the submission of a written paper in order to qualify as a specialist in the various fields of applied psychology. School psychology is one of eight areas that can be selected within the clinical psychology program.

All five universities and some colleges of education offer programs in education at the master's level, with specialization in such areas as counseling, special needs education, observation, and testing. The specialization is a limited part of more general programs in education. Thus, these programs are not comparable to programs in educational psychology at universities in some other countries. Furthermore, master's students acquire knowledge of scientific theory and research methodology, as well as training in the use of statistics and data analysis. The writing of a thesis is an integral part of the program. For example, students at the University of Oslo who specialize in educational psychological counseling must complete a supervised 10-week internship, a part of which may be served in the Educational Psychological Services, at a resource center for special needs education, or at another related organization. The University of Trondheim has, for a long time, offered a program leading to the master's degree in psychology, and other Norwegian universities are now offering such programs. There are several options for specialization in this master's program, and some specialization will qualify students for a position as an educational psychologist. The number of students who finish a master of education or a master of psychology program leading to a position as an educational psychologist is unknown.

In March 2005, a proposal for the establishment of a system of standards for the education and training of professional psychologists in Europe by means of a European Diploma in Psychology was circulated. The proposal was developed by a team of psychologists, also Norwegian, who represent a number of professional associations and universities. It is expected that future reform in the preparation of psychologists in Norway will be in line either with the proposal or with future versions of the document.

Doctoral programs in psychology are offered at four of the five Norwegian universities. Preparation involves 3 years of coursework, supervision, and a dissertation. Students who have mandatory teaching duties during the 3 years will be offered an extra year to finish their thesis. Similarly, all five universities offer a doctoral program in education for selected students who have finished their master's programs in education.

Roles, Functions, and Responsibilities of School Psychologists

From its inception, Educational Psychological Services has been the site of tension between separate interest groups: those interested in providing mental health services versus those interested in providing each special needs student with an individual education program. These aims reflect conflicting motivations, including the need to create sufficient numbers of professionally competent and independent Educational Psychological Service personnel while making a modest investment in their preparation compared with the great needs for intervention in the school system and families. Thus, the basic law gives Educational Psychological Services extended intervention authority and few rules and regulations for accomplishing its objectives.

Educational Psychological Services is defined as a counseling service and the backbone of the special education system (Professional Center for the Educational Psychological Services, 2001). The primary users are children and young people ages 3 through 19, together with adults needing special education. There are between 80,000 and 90,000 users per year (Norwegian Board of Education, 2003). The present Education Act has no specific expertise requirements for Educational Psychological Service personnel. Thus, the expertise needed to provide services must be determined on the basis of current caseloads and services to be provided. The *Handbook for the Educational Psychological Services* (Professional Center for the Educational Psychological Services, 2001, p. 23) points out that the main objectives according to the law are "expert assessment where the law demands it," "competence development for personnel and parents," "organizational development in schools and kindergartens," and "direct help" to primary users.

Between 1976 and 1996, changes in service have been considerable, with an activity increase of about 400%, with services provided basically by the same personnel resources (Bræin, 1999). More than 30% of the activities carried out in the 1990s were localized in schools and preschools, and more than 60% in the Educational Psychological Service agencies (Anthun, 1998; Bræin, 1999). Educational Psychological Services displayed less leadership and interdisciplinary functioning than expected, worked slowly and more indirectly through more help from parents and teachers, and provided more services to older students, with fewer student contacts and less collaboration with other public services.

According to the 2003 Norwegian Board of Education report, professionals in Educational Psychological Services would prefer to give more priority to promote competence and organizational development in schools. They also would prefer to provide more consultation to parents, kindergartens, and schools, and work less with individual assessment or treatment and expert reports. The activities and services delivered have not changed appreciably in recent years, despite the requirements of the 1998 law.

Although educational psychologists' particular roles are not defined satisfactorily, there is a clear implicit understanding of tasks that they need to perform. Psychologists often believe their work is too narrow or improper and does not match their particular expertise. The highly independent role of the Educational Psychological Service personnel, including no compulsory supervision and a heavy workload, are conditions that lead to much service variation both within and between districts. However, the basic casework process is the same.

Intervention and Consultation Services

Parents and authorized school personnel in principle are free to refer any student problem to Educational Psychological Services. Some Educational Psychological Services and schools have agreed on specific referral procedures in order to improve service quality. At present, Educational Psychological Services generally limit their services to problems in preschools, schools, and those associated with schoolwork at home. The next step in the process involves assigning the casework to one professional, who gathers information and counsels the parties at the same time, if possible. The kind of intervention and consultation chosen depends on the individual case and often will be directed to the school or home environment rather than to the student. The most recent national count of problem cases included sensory, 5.4%; motor skills, 3.6%; speech/communication, 8.1%; learning disability, 41.2%; socioemotional/ behavior, 24.3%; mental retardation, 15.0%; and others 2.4% (Anthun, 2002).

Considerable emphasis has been put on addressing the needs of individuals as early as possible in order to provide direct counseling and treatment for them. As much as 40% to 50% of all referrals to an agency may come from preschools. There are considerable differences in services at different age levels. Psychological counseling for students is more common at the upper secondary school level. Some Educational Psychological Service units at this level have been merged with another public service that works with students who fail or quit school (recently about 20%) and helps them get back into school, a job, or vocational courses.

Recently, such programs as Parent Management Training and Multisystemic Therapy have been undertaken by Educational Psychological Services and collaborating systems. The Marte Meo intervention method (Aarts, 2000) also has been applied often by Educational Psychological Services. Nearly one third of all Educational Psychological Service casework activity in the mid 1990s involved consultation with other professionals, such as colleagues (about 4%), school personnel (20%), or professionals outside the school (more than 7%); about 8% included parents in the consultation (Anthun, 1998; Bræin, 1999). Consultation methods usually are applied eclectically. Professionals also seem to prefer collaborative consultation.

Testing and Assessment Models and Methods

A common impression, that Educational Psychological Services activities consist primarily of assessment and testing, has been shown to be a myth (Anthun, 1998; Bræin, 1999). Testing represented not more than 11% to 13% of the activities of all professionals, with the majority being ability testing; personality tests also are used somewhat commonly, especially the screening of clients for disorders of psychological health problems. Change to more dynamic ability and achievement testing has been attempted.

By far the most common tests used by educational psychologists are Wechsler tests of intelligence. The Leiter International Performance Scale and the Raven Progressive Matrices also are used commonly. Less frequent are the Bender Visual-Motor Gestalt Test and scales by McCarthy, Goodenough, and Frostig, as well as the Children's Apperception Test and Thematic Apperception Test. The Rorschach rarely is used. Tests used by educational psychologists screening for psychological and social problems include the Child Behavior Checklist, the Personality Inventory for Children, and the Minnesota Multiphasic Personality Inventory. The Illinois Test of Psycholinguistic Abilities and Aston Index are used commonly by Educational Psychological Service personnel. Few tests are developed in Scandinavian countries, and even fewer have Scandinavian norms. A Norwegian test of attention/concentration/behavior (DATKON) is under development, and several Norwegian achievement tests are widely used.

Systemic and Developmental Activities

Since the 1970s, attempts to promote school organizational development have been part of the service repertoire. The Norwegian Education Act (1998) attempts to change special education organization in accord with the ongoing general educational system reforms. Educational Psychological Services has had limited success in making general changes in school system structure and function. Positive results take the form of supplements, including organizing guidance and language groups and promoting and supporting special teaching resource teams and meetings. These teams parallel the Intervention Assistance Programs in the United States (Ross, 1995) and have, in both nations, shown considerable success in the ability of schools to handle student cases and to reduce referral rates to the Educational Psychological Services (Anthun & Manger, in press).

Since 1970, toy guidance and toy lending have been among the standard services of Educational Psychological Services; they now are decreasing. Some agencies provide family therapy, and some collaborate with public health services. Programs developed by Olweus (1993) or Roland (1999) are widely used to prevent bullying and to create safer school environments. Educational psychologists take part regularly as supervisors or consultants, or apply the programs in their own individual cases. In the network linked to the Program of Northern Norway, some agencies were granted a special status to work directly with specialist services and professional development in a selected area. As an example, one agency has expanded its network to several universities and professionals abroad.

Kiil (1989) divided educational psychologist activities into three categories: direct work with individuals or groups, indirect work with individuals or groups, and system-changing work. He described professional development for educational psychologists using the same categories, indicating that responsibility for changing the school system was left to the one-third most experienced educational psychologists. Kiil found consultation concerning school organization development to be used commonly in the 1980s. During the 1990s, various projects and action research were implemented based on a central authority initiative.

Other Activities

Educational Psychological Services has been expected to be, and has been, a particularly independently managed municipal service. However, Educational Psychological Services is expected to engage itself in the municipal planning process and to make its own annual plan. One common routine is that the agencies evaluate their work and service delivery once or twice a year, often relying on consumers' evaluations. National authorities recently have issued an instrument to assist local Educational Psychological Service agencies in conducting evaluations.

Current Issues Impacting School Psychology

School psychology practice naturally is influenced by national legislation. Changes in the education system involve several paradigm shifts that have influenced the models of educational psychological services and related work. The most important is a shift from a medical or an individualistic model to a systemic model. Educational Psychological Services has had limited success in making a transition to more systemic models and in supporting changes in school system structures. The stability of school cultures and the Educational Psychological Services' lack of competence in system intervention work are most likely the main reasons for this limited success (Kiil, 1989; Stubbe, 1994).

The democratically oriented principle of inclusion has become the dominant paradigm for the development of the school. An important practical dimension derived from this idea is the principle of individual adaptation within a common classroom, curriculum, and teaching. However, within this context of an inclusive, democratic, and participatory ideal, there remains a school system that is characterized by segregation and compensation (e.g., Haug, 2000). Thus, a need for Educational Psychological Services and schools to cooperate in the development of more inclusive methods than the present school system offers is critical. Educational psychologists must be clear about what they can offer, and they must add practical value to schools and classrooms. They need to understand the classroom routines and dynamics and to provide recommendations that will meet the various and changing needs of all students. In line with these major challenges, the need for research on systemic work in the school and inclusive classroom methods is urgent.

Finally, the great variation in agency sizes and districts, personnel backgrounds, experiences, and different management models has resulted in a comparable variation in service delivery and quality. The shortage of educational psychologists in some areas of the country and the high employment turnover of professionals, who are being replaced by educational psychologists with minimal experience, represent challenges to service quality. Higher salaries and better working conditions may improve service quality. Both are issues that should be researched.

References

Aarts, M. (2000). *Marte Meo: Basic manual.* Harderwijk: Aarts Productions.

Anthun, R. (1998). Arbeidet med elevsaker i skolen [Casework at the school level]. *Skolepsykologi, 33,* 3–15.

Anthun, R. (2002). *School psychology service quality: Consumer appraisal, quality dimensions, and collaborative improvement potential.* Unpublished doctoral dissertation, University of Bergen, Norway.

Anthun, R., & Manger, T. (in press). Effects of special education teams on school psychology services. *School Psychology International.*

Bræin, O. (1999). Tidsstudier i PP-tjenesten i 1975, 1985 og 1996. En analyse av fagpersonalets arbeidsoperasjoner i Møre og Romsdal [Time studies in the Educational Psychological Services in 1975, 1985 and 1996: An analysis of the professionals' work in Møre and Romsdal]. *Skolepsykologi, 34,* 3–31.

Haug, P. (2000). Words without deeds: Between special schools and inclusive education in Norway. *Pedagogy, Culture and Society, 8,* 291–303.

Kiil, P. E. (1989). *Fra PP-tjenestens arbeidsfelt* [From the Educational Psychological Services' field of operations]. Hosle: Norwegian Institute for Special Education.

Norwegian Board of Education. (2003). *PP-tjenesten i Norge 2003. En tilstandsbeskrivelse* [The Educational Psychological Services in Norway 2003: A status description]. Oslo: Norwegian Board of Education.

Olweus, D. (1993). *Bullying at school: What we know and what we can do.* Oxford, UK: Blackwell.

Professional Center for the Educational Psychological Services. (2001). *Håndbok for PP-tjenesten* [Handbook for the Educational Psychological Services]. Oslo: Norwegian Board of Education.

Roland, E. (1999). *School influences on bullying.* Stavanger: Rebell forlag.

Ross, R. P. (1995). Best practices in implementing intervention assistance programs. In A. Thomas & J. Grimes (Eds.), *Best practices in school psychology* (pp. 227–237). Washington, DC: National Association of School Psychologists.

Statistics Norway. (2001). *Private grunnskoler* [Private primary and lower secondary schools]. Oslo: Statistisk sentralbyrå.

Statistics Norway. (2004a). *Barn i barnehager* [Children in preschools]. Oslo: Statistisk sentralbyrå.

Statistics Norway. (2004b). *Education statistics: Pupils in upper secondary schools.* Oslo: Statistisk sentralbyrå.

Statistics Norway. (2005a). *Education statistics: Primary and lower secondary schools.* Oslo: Statistisk sentralbyrå.

Statistics Norway. (2005b). *Folkemengde etter alder, kjønn, sivil status og statsborgerskap* [The population by age, sex, marital status and citizenship]. Oslo: Statistisk sentralbyrå.

Stubbe, A. (1994). *Hvordan har du det, PP-arbeider?* [How are you doing, educational psychological worker?]. Oslo: National Education Office Oslo & Akershus.

Støfring, E. (1993). *Idealer og realiteter i PP-tjenesten* [Ideals and realities in the Educational Psychological Services] (ODH Information Series No. 86-1993). Lillehammer: Oppland District College.

Østrem, K. (1998). PP-tjeneste med brukket rygg [Educational Psychological Services with a paralyzed back]. *Norsk Skoleblad, 16,* 26–28.

29

School Psychology in Pakistan

Shahid Waheed Qamar

Context of School Psychology

In 1947, the Islamic Republic of Pakistan emerged as an independent state. Pakistan has some of Asia's most magnificent landscapes; it stretches from the Arabian Sea in the south to spectacular mountain ranges in the north. Pakistan also is home to sites that date back to the world's earliest settlements, rivaling those of ancient Egypt and Mesopotamia. Located in South Asia, it shares its eastern border with India, its northeastern border with China, its southwestern border with Iran, and its western and northern borders with Afghanistan. A 1,064-kilometer coastline along the Arabian Sea forms Pakistan's southern boundary. The country's total area, 796,095 square kilometers, is nearly four times the size of the United Kingdom. From Gwadar Bay, at its southeastern corner, the country extends more than 1,800 kilometers to the Khunjerab Pass on China's border. Pakistan's climate is variable. Temperatures in the high mountain ranges in the north and northwest are extremely cold in winter but pleasant in the summer (i.e., April through September). The vast plains of the Indus Valley are extremely hot in summer and cold in winter. The coastal strip in the south has a temperate climate. Rainfall also is variable, generally sparse (13–89 centimeters), and monsoonal, principally in late summer. Pakistan is divided into four provinces: the North West Frontier, Punjab, Sindh, and Balochistan. The tribal belt (Federally Administered Tribal Areas) adjoins the North West Frontier Province. Azad Kashmir and Northern Areas are separate politically and administratively. Some Pakistanis in these areas receive assistance from the federal government through the Ministry of Kashmir Affairs and Northern Areas.

Pakistan's population increased rapidly from 1947 to 2005, growing from 32.5 million to 162 million. The average growth rate from 1951 to 1983, 3%, has declined to its current 1.9%. All but 3% of its population is Muslim. Pakistan's rural population decreased from 71% in 1981 to 68% in 1998, and its urban population increased from 29% to 32% during the same period. Provisions for health and educational services generally are marginal. Pakistan, an impoverished and underdeveloped country, suffers from internal political disputes, low levels of foreign investment, and a costly, ongoing confrontation with neighboring India. Pakistan's economic prospects, although still marred by poor human development indicators, improved in 2002, following the unprecedented inflows of foreign assistance that began in 2001. Foreign exchange reserves have grown to record levels, supported largely by rapid growth in worker wages.

Trade levels rebounded after a sharp decline in late 2001. Since 2000, the federal government has attempted to improve the country's economy and infrastructure through instituting macroeconomic reforms. However, economic progress is slow. Moreover, long-term prospects remain uncertain due to low levels of spending for development, high levels of regional tensions, and weak commitments to institute lender-recommended reforms, due to internal political tensions. Economic growth will be contingent on the success of the country's agricultural productivity, the price of foreign oil (which weighs heavily on Pakistan's economy), and the success of efforts to open and modernize its market economy. The country is in the second year of its $1.3 billion International Monitory Fund Poverty Reduction and Growth Facility program. The gross domestic product in 2004 was US$347.3 billion, US$2,200 per capita. Yearly program goals have been waived in recognition that political and economic reforms initiated by the federal government are difficult to implement.

Pakistan has three parallel yet completely separate education systems. All but some private schools are devoid of the basic meaning and concept of education in its sense of human development. Pakistan not only lacks the resources to use modern education methods, but it also lacks the desire. Its three-part education system consists of Madrasah System schools, in which mosques play the vital role, public schools under federal management and control, and private institutions. Each is discussed in the following paragraphs.

Students between the ages of 4 and 12 commonly attend Madrasah schools. These schools comprise a traditional and customary system that emphasizes religious education. It is devoid of qualities commonly found in a modern education system. For example, physical punishment is used to enhance learning. Its use is most common among orthodox religious scholars. The Madrasahs are numerous (approximately 13,763) and widespread across the country, and they have vigorous national support and the financial and other resources needed to grow. This system is oblivious of the content and methods common to school psychology. The government-supported public school system is a legacy from the British occupation of the subcontinent. The British changed an existing system to be consistent with methods used in their country. Successive Pakistani governments maintained the British system, one that has deteriorated over time, so that now it has a low status, lacking in both quantity and quality. Although this system is somewhat available throughout the country, it is most common in urban areas.

Primary schools, for children ages 5 through 9, number 251,299 (Ministry of Education, 2005). Among the total population in this age range (21,540,445), only 3,523,497 (16.71%) are enrolled in primary schools. Middle schools, for children ages 10 through 13, number 12,473. Among the total population in this age range (20,243,442), only 1,693,990 (8.3%) are enrolled in middle schools. High schools, for students ages 15 through 17, number 8,698. Among the total population in this range (18,400,873), only 1,218,653 (6.2%) are enrolled in high school. Thus, few students attend public schools, and the percentage declines as students' ages increase. The public education system is oblivious to school psychology. Nevertheless, public education leaders continuously criticize its antiquated nature, one hindered by a lack of financial, professional, and technical resources; lack of enthusiasm among poorly paid teachers;

and an attitude of indifference by the federal government.

Private educational institutions have recently been established, and their numbers are increasing. Students come from a select class, commonly called high gentry, who can afford luxuries and will spend handsomely to attain high quality educations for their children. Significant differences exist between the public and private schools in reference to class size (e.g., 50–60 vs. 20–25, respectively), salaries paid to teachers, and other qualities that affect teaching and learning. Although private institutions are advancing the cause of education, their impact is limited to a few students, which does not erase the larger impact of the generally low level of education students receive in public schools. A very few private schools recently recognized the importance of school psychology.

Origin, History, and Current Status of School Psychology

School psychological services are not in demand. Thus, no universities provide academic and professional programs to prepare school psychologists. Punjab University's master's-degree program in counseling and guidance, introduced in 1982, is one of the few that provides specialists with some background in applied psychology for work in education. Because school psychology and student counseling have been only recently and poorly recognized, the few jobs available in these fields are poorly paid positions (i.e., US$70–US$100 monthly) in public schools.

The profession of school psychology is in its introductory stage. Some professionals attempt to provide services typically performed by school psychologists. However, they generally lack proper academic and professional preparation and do not have links with psychology. They generally have only a working experience of general psychology. Those pursuing careers in psychology should anticipate a lack of job security. As a result,

the immediate future of psychology in Pakistan, including school psychology, appears to be dim.

Infrastructure of School Psychology

There is only one viable professional association for psychologists in Pakistan, the Pakistan Psychological Association. It mostly conducts workshops on issues important to clinical and social psychology. It seemingly has little interest in school and counseling psychology. Only one department of psychology, at Punjab University, offers a program for practitioners. Psychologists in Pakistan are not licensed. Thus, the profession is largely unregulated.

School psychology is not represented by a professional association, nor are its services regulated. Furthermore, plans for such regulation are unlikely in the foreseeable future. Postgraduate continuing education programs in school and counseling psychology are not available nor are professional journals that disseminate research and other forms of scholarship related to school psychology. Lack of resources for school psychology, due to lack of interest and awareness among governmental leaders and indifference from others, severely limits its development. Government, individual, and group efforts directed to prescribe a format to regulate school psychology and its professional roles are needed.

Preparation of School Psychologists

No public or private sector university prepares school psychologists. Some universities are introducing some elective subjects or courses at the master's level that may be relevant to the preparation of school psychologists. Compulsory subjects include the history and system of psychology, experimental psychology, social psychology, abnormal psychology, research methods, clinical psychology, child and educational psychology, and psychological measurement and testing. Optional subjects include cognitive psychology, neuropsychology, counseling psychology, industrial psychology, and military psychology.

Those preparing for careers as school counselors must take courses in child and educational psychology and counseling psychology. The courses identified in the preceding paragraph are taught within Punjab University's 2-year master's degree in psychology program. Various universities offer undergraduate degree programs in psychology, including Quaid-e-Azam University Islamabad, Jamia Karachi, Agha Khan University Karachi, Bahauddin Zakaria University Multan, and G. C. University Lahore. Thus, given an absence of school psychology programs, interested students are advised to specialize in school counseling.

Roles, Functions, and Responsibilities of School Psychologists

School counselors attempt to facilitate the learning process by promoting student achievement and guiding students through target-oriented goals. Goals are established, in light of students' inherent abilities, cognitive strengths and weaknesses, and aptitudes, to prepare them for careers consistent with their talents and interests. In this role, a school counselor conducts assessment and organizes testing of students, in part to identify gifted students. After identifying student talents, the counselor conveys this information and its implications for schooling and work to students. School counselors can be an integral part of a triangle linking parents, teachers, and students as they organize meetings with them to facilitate

understanding of a student's abilities. School counselors also may suggest remedial measures for students with learning problems. School counselors may arrange for students to work in pairs and groups so as to enhance their social skills. Additionally, school counselors may organize in-service teacher training programs to address general issues important to their responsibilities as teachers.

Current Issues Impacting School Psychology

The need to initiate social reforms favorable to psychology and to promote awareness of school and counseling psychology is obvious. In reference specifically to school psychology, government schools cannot afford to employ school psychologists, and private schools are unwilling to pay for their services. Thus, there is little incentive for students to choose school and counseling psychology as a career. Nongovernmental agencies can be helpful in promoting psychology and school/counseling psychology. Research on the potential impact of school psychology on Pakistani education also is needed. One bright spot is the government's establishment of the Student Counseling Center at Punjab University. Another is planned for implementation at G. C. University.

References

Board of Intermediate and Secondary Education Pakistan. (2005). www.bise.com.pk

Government of Pakistan. (2005). Islamic Republic of Pakistan official Web site. www.infopak.gov.pk

Ministry of Education. (2005). Education statistics. www.moe.gov.pk

University of the Punjab Lahore, Department of Psychology. (2005). www.pu.edu.pk

30

School Psychology in Peru

César Merino Soto

Maritza Díaz Casapía

Luis Zapata Ponce

Luis Benites Morales

Context of School Psychology

Peru's geographic and political structure has been highly influenced by its rich Inca tradition, Spain's colonization, and the 1821 Proclamation of Independence. The country includes 24 states as well as three geographic areas: coastal (in which Lima, its capital, is located, with 1% of the country's territory), mountains (29% of the territory), and forest (70% of the territory). Each state contains provinces (180 in all), and each province contains districts (1,747 in all). Differences exist in lifestyles and climates, as well as in educational and social expectations. Peru's landmass is 1,285,216 square kilometers, and Peru is the world's 20th largest country. It is bordered on the north by Ecuador and Colombia, on the east by Brazil, on the south by Bolivia and Chile, and on the west by the Pacific Ocean. The predominant language is Spanish, which is used by 80% of the population; Quechua, Aymara, and other native languages are used by the other 20%. The biological diversity of its fauna and flora, geography, and cultures, together with the economic inequality that extends throughout Peru, pose continuous challenges for psychology.

The population was 22 million in 1993 and nearly 28 million in 2005 (50% males). Nearly 8 million are indigenous, distributed in 65 ethnic groups, and live mainly in the coastal and forest regions. Peru's population constitutes 0.4% of the world's population and 5.4% of Latin America's population. Approximately 85% live in urban locations, 52% in the coastal region, 37% in the Andean Mountain region, and 11% in the Amazonian (forest) region. With respect to the population's age, those age birth to 14 years compose 37%, 15 to 64 compose 58%, and over 64 compose 5%. Annual population growth is expected to be 1.5% (Instituto Nacional de Estadística e Informática, 2001). Fertility among women living in urban areas is 50% of those living in rural areas.

There is a steep and progressive increase of informal businesses and employment, especially in urban areas. In 2004, the gross domestic product was US$155.3 billion, or US$5,600 per capita. Following years of inconsistent economic performance, the economy grew by an average 4% per year during 2002–2004. The exchange rate was stable and inflation was low. Children are often informally employed. Most employment opportunities are in the service sector (73%), with fewer opportunities in industry (18%) and agriculture (9%). Economic estimates are favorable, provided that inflation is reduced and economic growth is promoted. Nevertheless, existing poverty is expected to continue.

The first 12 years of education are compulsory. The education system is divided into four levels: preschool, elementary school, high school, and superior education. Subsystems of education include five modalities: children's education, special education, occupational education, adult education, and distance education. The education system includes preschool education for ages 3 to 5 or 6; primary or elementary education for ages 6 to 11, Grades 1 through 6; secondary or high school education for ages 12 to 16, Grades 1 through 5; special education; and occupational education. The country's postsecondary education system offers 1- to 3-year non-university options that include the preparation of teachers, technology specialists, and artists. University education extends from 5 to 7 years. And finally, adult education: This system is oriented to persons age 40 or below from low-income families who did not complete their studies in the school system. This educational system is intended to be responsive to the economic, social, cultural, ecological, family, and linguistic diversity common in some areas of Peru.

Until 2004 (Ministerio de Educación, 2005), there were 8.5 million students in all the modalities of education: 86% in public education programs; 97% (7.9 million) were regular and special education students of minor age; the rest were in adult education programs. Among minors, 83% were in public schools. Among registered children, 14% were in preschools, 52% in primary schools, 30% in secondary schools, 0.3% in special education, and 0.3% in occupational education for adolescents. The numbers of students in urban areas increased due to the migration of families from the countryside. School attendance for 6-year-old children has been emphasized (Instituto Nacional de Estadística e Informática, 2000). The number of persons engaged in education changes with age, with 95% attending primary school, and 88% attending secondary schools; 33% of those between ages 17 and 24 are enrolled in school. The number of students per school fluctuates between 500 and 4,000. Private schools average about 1,500 students, but the number is highly variable because it is dependent on the physical size of the school. The number of primary and secondary public school students per teacher averages 40; the pupil-to-teacher ratio is smaller in preschools. Small schools generally have one classroom per grade, whereas large schools may have eight or more.

Origins, History, and Current Status of School Psychology

Applied forms of psychology have been favored in Peru. Thus, the birth of school psychology occurred in light of applied needs to assess students' intelligence and to collect normative data about them at the primary and secondary levels. During its first period of development, contributions from school psychology came from individuals or small working parties (Alarcón, 1968), especially physicians and educators interested in children's intellectual development. This resulted in the first work published on normative data of the intellectual abilities of children in Lima: Chueca's 1920

Estudio sobre la Capacidad Intelectual de los Niños de la Ciudad de Lima (A Study of Intellectual Ability in the Children of Lima) (cited in Alarcón, 1968).

The second period began when Walter Blumenfeld, director of the Institute of Psychotechnics and Psychology at the Universidad Nacional de San Marcos (Sardón, 1968), published the first book on the psychology of learning (Blumenfeld, 1967) and influenced the development of the experimental approaches (León, 2005).

The adolescent period of Peruvian school psychology occurred with the definition of school psychology and a discussion of its role and functions in psychology alongside other psychology specialties. For example, during the 1970s and 1980s, the status of school psychology and its differentiation from other psychology specialties was discussed during presentations at national conventions (Tapia, 1975, 1983; Ugarriza, 1983). Some associated its identity with behavioral applications (Benites, 1985), whereas others emphasized evaluation services and other definitions of professional activity (Tapia, 1985). In 1972, the National Institute of Research and Educational Development was formed. This marked a key event for school psychology. The work of the National Institute emphasized psychologists' participation in evaluation of instructional programs, teacher training, and educational research. The interests of school psychology expanded, and school psychologists became more involved in important school-related work. The Department of Orientation for Students initiated special education schools and experimental early stimulation home-based programs. Research took other directions, including toward issues related to poverty (Majluf, 1984, 1986; Pollit, 1974) and cognitive learning (Meza, 1979, 1987).

The presence of school psychology is stronger in urban than in rural areas and in private than in public schools. A school psychologist is part of the school personnel in most of the larger private schools. Few work in public schools, and fewer work in rural areas. Nongovernmental organizations or private associations occasionally provide evaluation services, conferences with parents and students, and workshops in schools. Numerous new civil associations oriented to education are currently providing psychologists with clinical training, employment opportunities, and leadership roles.

School psychologists working in private schools are more likely to be satisfied with their work than those working in the public sector. This satisfaction is, in part, due to being paid more than those who work in the public sector. Their higher level of satisfaction also is due to recognition of the importance of their work. The locations in which school psychologists' work may be characterized by using a pyramid. They are most likely to work in private practice, decreasingly in private schools, public schools, special education schools, universities, and as consultants. Private practice services can address clinical or school problems with children and adults. The number of licensed specialties is not known. Nevertheless, approximately 60% are in clinical/health, 15% in education, including school psychology, and the others are in various specialties.

Approximately 90% of private schools employ psychologists. Many who work in private schools may not have suitable university training and instead obtain on-the-job training. Psychologists generally prefer private school employment, because it typically allows them to perform a broader range of services. Examples include assessment of children between ages 5 and 6 for school entrance and students for entrance to all grades; group and individual assessment of specific abilities; meetings to discuss academic and communication strategies with school personnel; preventive activities with parents, teachers, and students; evaluation of teaching activities; and general consulting activities.

The Ministry of Education is responsible for public schools. Only about 10% of public schools employ psychologists and other professional service providers to work with individual students. Employment favors those who work in educational technology and in other areas that may strengthen education's general infrastructure. The clergy is responsible for parochial schools. Religious congregations finance some but not all schools. Approximately 60% employ school psychologists. All schools that provide special education services employ school psychologists. Their work includes assessment, diagnosis, meetings with teachers and parents, and providing teacher workshops. Protection of special students from sexual and psychological maltreatment is currently an important topic.

Complete data are not available to accurately determine the number of school psychologists employed in various school settings. Nevertheless, approximately 25% of school psychologists work full-time in the schools. School psychologists also may provide services in the private sector (e.g., psychoeducational assessment and therapy, vocational counseling, training parents to address behavior problems). The profession of psychology is mostly female (75%). Among those who have master's and doctoral degrees, only about 0.5% are school psychologists licensed by the Association of Psychologists of Peru. School psychologists range in age from 22 to 60, with a mean age of 33. Few remain in school psychology practice for 20 or more years. They more likely have been in practice for 10 or fewer years.

Approximately 80% of psychologists work in Lima. Few work in rural areas. Psychologists often abandon school practice because of low pay, dissatisfaction with the nature of their work, and little recognition of its importance. Their pay is generally similar to that of teachers, whose pay is low relative to that of other professionals in other educational institutions. For example, psychologists often are paid US$200 to US$400 per month, whereas industrial/organizational psychologists earn approximately US$700. Salaries vary according to the type of school (private, state, parochial), amount of registered students, amount of hours worked, and type of contract (permanent or part-time).

Infrastructure of School Psychology

No professional association is devoted exclusively to school psychology. To some extent, the professional specialty chapters of the Association of Psychologists of Peru (Colegio de Psicólogos del Perú) fill some of this void. Standards for entrance into the profession of psychology and its regulation do not exist. The recently promulgated Law 28369 (October 28, 2004) addresses general services provided by psychologists, including assessment, evaluation, diagnosis, prevention, promotion, and treatment of psychological specialties; and the construction, administration, qualification, and interpretation of materials used to conduct psychological evaluations and interventions; the design and management of projects; and psychological research, consultancy, and consultants' activities in programs and projects. The specialty of school psychology has been recognized in these laws. The terms *school psychologist* and *educational psychologist* are used interchangeably in the applied setting. The Ministry of Education's organizational chart provides for the Oficina de Tutoría y Prevención Integral (Office of Protection and Prevention Education). School psychologists are included in the development, planning, and execution of activities of two of its programs, the Defensoría y Tutoría Escolar (Student Protection and Defense) for Children and Teenagers and the Program for Working Children. School psychologists also are involved in the following five features of the Tutoría y Prevención Integral (Protection and Prevention Education) program: prevention of illegal drug use; sexual education; culture of peace, human rights, and prevention of violence; ecology, environment, and prevention of disasters; and promotion of youth. However, to be included in these programs, school psychologists must apply for specific positions, as no position is specifically reserved for them.

No scholarly journals are devoted to school psychology. However, topics of interest to school psychologists can be found in other publications. Universities and professional associations publish journals, albeit not necessarily at regular intervals. Scholars often submit their manuscripts for publication to foreign journals.

Preparation of School Psychologists

Twenty-four universities are engaged in preparing professional psychologists. They have approximately 15,000 students. Those who complete program requirements receive an academic degree of Bachelor in Psychology. After obtaining this degree, students can begin an advanced course of study that leads to the title "psychologist" or "licensed psychologist." This work may require the completion of advanced training courses and professional experience, a case study, a thesis, and passing a proficiency exam.

Universities differ in their degree requirements. Not all universities require all the above work. Few universities provide programs that lead to a certificate in school psychology. In 2005, approximately 12,000 were registered as psychologists with the Association of Psychologists of Peru (Colegio de Psicólogos del Perú). Many other psychologists, in the thousands, are not registered with this association.

Some universities, the Association of Psychologists of Peru, and private organizations offer postgraduate professional development. Professional service models for schools psychology are influenced by traditions within clinical psychology. This is largely due to a lack of previous preparation for work in education among

psychologists. Programs traditionally have emphasized behavioral approaches and, more recently, cognitive-behavioral perspectives. Philosophic orientations of school psychology have evolved and now include reliance on psychodynamic, cognitive, behavioral, and humanistic theories.

Preparing to become a psychologist generally takes 6 years, as it requires an academic bachelor's degree followed by professional preparation. Although some psychologists merely have bachelor's degrees, their numbers are decreasing due to efforts by the schools of psychologists together with public recognition that those with less training are less prepared. The 6-year curriculum comprises 5 years of academic and preprofessional study and 1 year of professional practice or an internship. The first curriculum emphasizes foundation academic courses. Later, students take courses more directly related to their chosen careers. University programs are not externally controlled and thus enjoy considerable flexibility in the courses they offer. Of course, there are similarities in the programs. Some universities offer academic courses by specialty (clinical, educational, organizational, and social). Students preparing for careers as school psychologists take courses in educational psychology, instructional design, psychology of curricula, educational management, psychopedagogy, learning disabilities, educational technology, psychology applied to special education, early stimulation, psycholinguistics, educational planning, counseling, and tutorship, neuroscience, cognitive processes, and testing. With respect to training, the Association of Psychologists of Peru, universities, and nongovernmental organizations are working to improve and strengthen standards for professional preparation and practice. Psychology students in their middle or final academic training often engage in voluntary enlistment in schools and public or private organizations. This gives them the opportunity to interact with target populations when they participate in the development and implementation of research, evaluation, assessment, and intervention programs.

Roles, Functions, and Responsibilities of School Psychologists

The professional services provided by school psychologists vary in light of the needs of the schools in which they work. The seven most common services are described next.

Individual and group psychoeducational assessment. School psychologists ˙ organize and develop methods for evaluating new students or those referred for individual intervention. The evaluations tend not to use standardized multi-informant strategies. Standardized tests measuring aptitudes and intelligence are frequently used in psychoeducational assessment. Behavior and social adjustment is assessed with outdated or with clinical and/or informal methods.

Assessment activities generally use old instruments for which information on local validity and reliability is lacking. Emergent efforts are being made to adapt instruments for use in psychoeducational assessment. This work is not being documented in Peruvian scientific journals (Rocks, 1988). The Wechsler and Stanford-Binet intelligence scales are widely used to assess intellectual abilities. An assessment of visual-motor abilities relies on the Developmental Test of Visual-Motor Integration (Beery, 2000) or the Qualitative Scoring System for the Bender-Gestalt Test (Brannigan & Brunner, 2002), which is in the process of being developed (Merino, 2005). Academic achievement tests have been developed by the Unit of Educative Measurement, an office of the Ministry of Education. Standardized protocols of observation and scales are not widely used. However, some are using the Acting Out, Moody, Learning–Revised Scale (Cowen et al., 1996), the Strength and Deficit Questionnaire (Goodman, 2001), and the Behavior Dimensions Scale (Bullock & Wilson, 1989), as reported in Merino (2004a, 2004b, 2004c) and Livia and Ortiz (1993), respectively. Personality assessment tends to rely on the children's version of Eysenck's Personality Questionnaire.

Direct interventions. Individualized services are often provided by psychologists and other professionals outside of schools, thus allowing those working in schools to attend to other issues, including those associated with vocational guidance, behavior problems, low achievement, student violence, and teacher-student relationships.

Indirect interventions. School psychologists tend to use indirect intervention methods that allow them to work, individually or in groups, with parents, students, professors, tutors, and other personnel related to the student.

Research and evaluation. School psychologists rarely engage in research due to the lack of resources, academic preparation, and institutional value that schools place on such activity. They may be required to participate in the process of evaluating administrative and educational personnel with respect to their selection and efficiency. When working in smaller school settings, school psychologists are more likely to serve as consultants on interpersonal relationships among administrative personnel, students, and teachers.

Supervision and administration of services. School psychologists assume leadership within and between institutional efforts to coordinate and offer counseling services to students, monitor performance of these services, and improve communication between the components of the school system. Psychologists often supervise university students serving internships, to whom they delegate some tasks.

Prevention. Efforts to prevent possible psychological or physical maltreatment of children constitute a high national priority. Additional preventive activities are directed toward issues associated with violence, gangs, drugs, and, more recently, addictive behaviors with computer games. Some private schools organize local meetings of student leaders to provide preventive information in an effort to enlist their assistance in promoting prosocial behavior in students.

Program development and organizational services. School psychologists may be required to take part in a school system's efforts to improve and promote communication and to intervene at an organizational level. These roles take the form of consulting and training, and often include observations of relationships, events, and educational professionals of the particular school system; this is a dominant activity when problems arise in the school organization and personnel. Prevention programs at the organizational level are not common activities among school psychologists.

Current Issues Impacting School Psychology

The high ratio of students to psychologists is truly abysmal, a condition that delays the implementation of effective prevention and other intervention programs designed to diminish the prevalence of students at risk for academic failure and social maladjustment. In addition, school psychologists working in public schools do not have an important position in the school's administrative hierarchy. Although their perceived roles are socially worthy, they often encounter administrative barriers. For example, school psychologists often are not involved in a meaningful way in the evaluation of intervention programs. Persons responsible for these activities often have little preparation in evaluation or educational research. School psychologists have more training and experience to perform this important function although generally they have not enough training in

appropriate strategies of multivariate statistical analysis. Sometimes school psychologists are seen as being committed primarily to work with interventions that center on individual students. This perception often is accurate because clinic psychologists often are hired by schools.

Standardized tests are often used inappropriately because of poor academic preparation. Postgraduate statistics and psychometric courses needed to acquire background knowledge for using standardized tests are not popular among psychologists working in schools. The need for tests developed and normed on Peruvian children is apparent. Additional efforts that contribute to 21st-century methods for assessment, including those that go beyond diagnosis and prioritize interventions, are needed. Current information is needed on new standardized screening tests in behavioral and learning areas, as is information about differential diagnostic and screening objectives and methods. Several master's theses report research related to tests. However, this research rarely finds its way into journals.

Inadequate financial and work conditions also need to be addressed. They limit productivity, contribute to professional burnout, and result in many able persons leaving the specialty or performing in an apathetic manner. In addition, school psychologists are asked to perform varied tasks within schools, some of which are not related to their professional roles but to those of other professions (e.g., social workers).

References

Alarcón, R. (1968). *Panorama de la psicología en el Perú* [An overview of psychology in Peru]. Lima: Universidad Nacional Mayor de San Marcos.

Beery, K. E. (2000). *Prueba Beery-Buktenica del Desarrollo de la Integración Visomotriz* (4ta ed.) [The Berry-Buktenica Developmental Test of Visual-Motor Integration (4th ed.)]. México, DF: El Manual Moderno.

Benites, L. (1985). Psicología educativa: Un enfoque conductual [Educational psychology: A behavioral approach]. *Revista de Psicología, 1*(1), 33–39.

Blumenfeld, W. (1967). *Psicología del aprendizaje: Un libro para maestros y estudiantes* (4ta. ed.) [The psychology of learning: A book for teachers and students (4th ed.)]. Lima: Universidad Nacional Mayor de San Marcos.

Brannigan, G. G., & Brunner, N. A. (2002). *Guide for the Qualitative Scoring System for the modified version of the Bender-Gestalt Test.* Springfield, IL: Charles C Thomas.

Bullock, L. M., & Wilson, M. J. (1989). *Behavior Dimensions Rating Scale.* Itasca, IL: Riverside.

Cowen, E. M., Hightower, A. D., Pedro-Carroll, J. L., Work, W. C., Wyman, P. A., & Haffey, W. G. (1996). *School-based prevention for children at risk: The Primary Mental Health Project.* Washington, DC: American Psychological Association.

Goodman, R. (2001). Psychometric properties of the Strengths and Difficulties Questionnaire. *Journal of the American Academy of Child and Adolescent Psychiatry, 40*(11), 1337–1345.

Instituto Nacional de Estadística e Informática. (2000). Instituto Nacional de Estadística e Informática–*Encuesta Nacional de Hogares (ENAHO) 1995–1999, IV Trimestre* [National Institute of Statistics and Information Sciences–National Survey of Homes (ENAHO) 1995–1999, IV Trimester]. Lima: Author.

Instituto Nacional de Estadística e Informática. (2001). Perú: Estimaciones y proyecciones de población, 1950–2050 [Peru: Population estimates and projections, 1950–2050]. *Boletín de Análisis Demográfico, 35.* Retrieved July 20, 2005, from http://www.inei.gob.pe/Documentos-Publicos/Proyecciones_Libro.pdf

Köppitz, E. M. (1984). *El test gestáltico visomotor para niños* (10ma. ed.). [Visual-Motor Gestalt Test for Children (10th ed.)] Buenos Aires: Guadalupe.

León, R. (2005, June). *La tradición alemana en la psiquiatría y psicología peruana* [The German tradition in Peruvian psychiatry and psychology]. Paper presented at the 30th Interamerican Psychology Conference, Buenos Aires, Argentina.

Livia, J., & Ortiz, M. (1993). *Inventario de Problemas Conductuales y Destrezas Sociales de T. Achenbach* [Achenbach Inventory of Behavior Problems and Social Skills]. Lima: Psicología y Desarrollo.

Majluf, A. (1984). Rendimiento intelectual de niños infantes a adolescentes de clases socioeconómicas media y baja y de algunas provincias [Intellectual performance of young children to adolescents of middle and low socioeconomic levels in some counties]. *Revista de Psicología–PUC, 2*(1–2), 57–73.

Majluf, A. (1986). Diferencias de clase socioeconómica y de sexo en el desarrollo mental y postural en infantes de 8, 14 y 20 meses de edad en Lima [Socioeconomic and sex differences in the postural and mental development of infants of 8, 14, and 20 months]. In F. León (Ed.), *Psicología y realidad peruana: el aporte objetivo.* Lima: Mosca Azul.

Merino, C. (2004a). *Estudio psicométrico exploratorio de la escala AML–R* (Anxiety, Mood and Learning Scale–Revised) [Exploratory psychometric study of AML-R]. Unpublished manuscript, Asociación Civil Sembrar, Lima.

Merino, C. (2004b). *Estudio psicométrico exploratorio del BDRS (Behavioral Dimensions Rating Scale)* [Exploratory psychometric study of BDRS]. Unpublished manuscript, Asociación Civil Sembrar Lima.

Merino, C. (2004c). *Estudio psicométrico exploratorio del SDQ–P (Strengths and Difficulties Questionnaire–Parent)* [Exploratory psychometric study of SDQ-P]. Unpublished manuscript, Asociación Civil Sembrar, Lima.

Merino, C. (2005). Información normativa para la Prueba Gestáltica de Bender Modificada, con el Sistema de Calificación Cualitativa de Brannigan y Brunner [Normative information for the Bender-Gestalt Test from the Brannigan and Brunner Qualitative Scoring System]. Unpublished manuscript, Asociación Civil Sembrar, Lima.

Meza, A. (1979). Efectos de transferencia específica e inespecífica en los aprendizajes de conservación [Effects of specific and nonspecific transference on learning retention]. *Revista Peruana de Análisis de la Conducta, 1,* 34–55.

Meza, A. (1987). *Psicología del aprendizaje* [Psychology of learning]. Lima: Caribe.

Meza, A. (1988). Psicología educacional en el Perú [School psychology in Peru]. *Psicología y Sociedad, 1,* 17–94.

Ministerio de Educación. (2005a). *Estadística básica–2004* [Basic statistics–2004]. Unidad de Estadística Educativa. Lima: Author.

Ministerio de Educación. (2005b). *Presentación oficial* [Official presentation of the Ministry of Education]. Retrieved August 4, 2005, from http://www.minedu.gob.pe/umc/presentacion.php

Pollit, E. (1974). *Desnutrición, pobreza e inteligencia* [Malnutrition, poverty, and intelligence]. Lima: Instituto Nacional de Investigación y Desarrollo de la Educación.

Sardón, M. (1968). *Evocación de Walter Blumenfeld* [Memories of Walter Blumenfeld]. Lima: Prensas Industriales.

Tapia, V. (1975). *La psicología educacional como profesión en el Perú* [School psychology as a profession in Peru]. Paper presented at the first Peruvian Conference of Psychology, Lima.

Tapia, V. (1983). *La psicología educativa en el Perú: En busca de su identidad* [Educational psychology in Peru: In search of its identity]. Paper presented at the National Conference of School Psychology, Arequipa.

Tapia, V. (1985). Las dimensiones psicométrica y edumétrica de la evaluación del aprendizaje [Psychometric and edumetric dimensions in learning assessment]. *Revista de Psicología, 1*(1), 73–77.

Ugarriza, N. (1981). *El rol del psicólogo escolar* [The role of the school psychologist]. Paper presented at the second National Conference of Psychology, Lima.

Ugarriza, N. (1983). *La investigación en educación especial* [Research in special education]. Paper presented at the second National Conference for Special Education, Lima.

31

School Psychology in Puerto Rico

Frances Boulon-Díaz

Irma Roca de Torres

Context of School Psychology

Puerto Rico is an island in the Caribbean Sea that is part of the Major Antilles archipelago. The country is surrounded by palm-fringed beaches, and the central region includes mountains of volcanic origin, with a tropical climate and luscious, varied vegetation, rivers, and fauna. The country consists of approximately 9,104 square kilometers (about 100 miles long and 35 miles wide). It is densely populated, with almost 4 million people; about 25% of the population lives in San Juan, its capital, and surrounding area. The gross product in 2004 was US$53.380 million, US$13,5900 per capita. Services (55%) and industry (45%) are the major employment opportunities, and unemployment is estimated at 12% (Puerto Rico Planning Board, 2006).

The culture is influenced by various national and ethnic heritages. Early occupants include the Archaic and Taíno Indians, among others, who lived in Puerto Rico before its "discovery"

in 1493 (Figueroa, 1979). The Spaniards colonized Puerto Rico during the 16th century and introduced Spanish, the country's dominant language and one of two official languages (the other being English). Puerto Ricans often continue to refer to Spain as the "madre patria" or motherland. With the advent of slavery, Africans were forced to migrate to the Caribbean, forming highly influential communities, especially in coastal cities (Picó & Rivera Izcoa, 1991). After 1898, Puerto Rico was ceded to the United States of America by Spain at the conclusion of the Spanish-American War. Immigration of citizens from Cuba and the Dominican Republic has had significant influence on Puerto Rican culture, economy, and demography during the 20th century, especially since the 1960s.

Political domination by the United States encouraged efforts geared to acculturate Puerto Rican society into the "melting pot" or to bring it as close as possible to the ethos of continental U.S. communities. Granting U.S. citizenship to Puerto Ricans in 1917 was intended, in part, to promote closer ties between both countries. Thousands of Puerto Ricans have served in the armed forces. In 1952, the status of territory was changed to a commonwealth known as Estado Libre Asociado de Puerto Rico (Commonwealth of Puerto Rico), thus enhancing options for self-government while maintaining strong political and economic ties to the United States. English is taught in schools as a second language and is used intensely in business and intellectual communities. American citizens of Puerto Rico, native born or naturalized, have the right to vote for Puerto Rico's governor and legislature. However, while residing on the island, they may not vote for the president of the United States and they do not pay federal taxes.

The two dominant political parties differ regarding relationships with the United States. The New Progressive Party promotes full integration of Puerto Rico as a state of the Union, and the Popular Democratic Party defends the commonwealth status, arguing that it provides economic and political benefits of belonging to the United States while allowing for greater cultural autonomy and preserving the use of the Spanish language. The third political party, the Puerto Rican Independence Party, is committed to establishing an independent republic of Puerto Rico. Its leadership is very active in public discussion and action regarding social, political, economic, and cultural issues. The likelihood of this status option being favored in an election is low, having obtained less than 10% of the votes in each election held during the past 50 years.

Puerto Rico's educational system includes public and private schools. Public schools offer instruction at the following grade levels: elementary (kindergarten–Grade 6), intermediate (Grades 7–9), high school (Grades 10–12), and postsecondary. Postsecondary schools include those that offer technical or vocational, nonuniversity education (Department of Education, 2005). Vocational education also is available in schools that offer Grades 7 through 12. During the 2005–2006 school year, 1,538 public schools employed 47,328 teachers to serve approximately 666,978 students (Roldán Soto, 2005). Although the official government ratio of teachers to students is 1 to 14, most everyone doubts the accuracy of these figures. Teachers complain of having more than 30 students per classroom (R. Cibes, personal communication, July 22, 2005). Among the 666,978 students, 87,594 (13%) are registered to receive special education services (R. M. Santiago, personal communication, August 4, 2005).

The private education system consists of 525 schools that employ about 13,841 teachers to serve approximately 190,000 students (Consejo General de Educación, 2006; L. Piñero, personal communication, August 10, 2005). This system includes religious and nonreligious schools, institutions with kindergarten through Grade 12, and technical and specialized schools at the pre-college level. Thus, among students, approximately 75% attend public school and 20% attend private school. The remaining 5% include those who are homeschooled, homebound, or have abandoned school.

Education in Puerto Rico is ruled by Law 149 of June 30, 1999: the Organic Law of Education of Puerto Rico. It makes education compulsory for individuals ages 5 through 21. However, if a person graduates from high school before age 21, that person is not compelled to continue in school. Social workers are responsible for addressing school truancy. In spite of their efforts, 40% of children who start the first grade do not complete high school. In 2000, Puerto Rico had 906,368 children ages 14 years and younger (U.S. Census Bureau, 2000). In 2005, this age cohort will be ages 5 through 19, the expected ages of students.

Origin, History, and Current Status of School Psychology

During the late 19th century, college-level education was made available in Puerto Rico through private cultural centers that offered correspondence courses sponsored by universities within the Spanish empire (Roca de Torres, 2001). For example, the Ateneo Puertorriqueño, a society of intellectuals, continues to promote education and cultural activities in the 21st century. In 1900, the first postsecondary program of study, Escuela Normal (Normal School), was established. It offered a 2-year teacher preparation curriculum similar to an associate degree in education.

It is difficult to establish when school psychology emerged as a distinct specialty within psychological practice in Puerto Rico. In 1991, Irma Roca de Torres stated the practice of school psychology was just beginning. However, practices related to school psychology, such as test development and testing, had been carried out since the early decades of the 20th century. The practice of psychology in Puerto Rico is closely associated with education. The first professional school for teachers, Escuela Normal, was founded in 1900. This institution led to the creation of the University of Puerto Rico in 1903. The University of Puerto Rico was the first institution to offer college-level education. In 1900, a course in general psychology was offered to students at the Escuela Normal (Álvarez, 1994).

During the second decade of the 20th century, most psychology professors at the University of Puerto Rico had obtained master's degrees in educational psychology at universities such as Columbia and New York University in the United States or at European universities (Álvarez, 1994). Some of these professors translated tests to measure children's abilities, including the *Pintner Non Language Mental Ability Test* (Roca de Torres, 1991). This scale, translated in 1925 by psychologists working at the University of Puerto Rico and the Department of Education, was used to compare the mental abilities and academic achievements of Puerto Rican and U.S. children in Grades 3 through 8.

By 1933, a group of psychologists from the University of Puerto Rico, including Malvina Monefeldt, Fred C. Walters, Alfredo Silva, and Mercedes Chiqués, translated the 1916 Stanford Revision of the Binet-Simon Intelligence Tests (Roca de Torres, 1991). These early educational psychologists taught psychology courses and developed scales to use in their professional practices and research with children. Besides translating the Binet, they translated a general ability test for elementary school students and another for high school students; they also developed a reading achievement test and other achievement and aptitude tests (Álvarez, 1994; Roca de Torres, 2001) Their research interests included the teaching of English as a second language, learning processes, and cognitive abilities of Puerto Rican children (Álvarez, 1994). Their clinical practices and research are within the scope of current practice of school psychologists.

In 1949, the Department of Health developed the Children and Adolescents Mental Health Clinic and employed psychologists who served children referred from schools (Bernal, in press; Sumaza, in press). The master's-level training of psychologists employed at this clinic included courses related to clinical and school psychology. The psychologist's duties largely focused on evaluation and diagnosis (Hernández, 1985). During the 1950s, the clinic was transformed to a psychiatric hospital and employed two educational psychologists and one clinical psychologist. By 1954, one of the authors, Roca de Torres, remembers that her school, University of Puerto Rico Elementary and Secondary School, employed a psychologist in its guidance office to serve students with adjustment and learning difficulties. This psychologist, Ada Elsa Izcoa, had obtained a master's degree in clinical psychology from the University of Iowa (A. E. Izcoa, personal communication, July 12, 2005).

The development of the Division of Educational Research and Statistics (later the Office of Evaluation and Statistics) within the Department of Education, originally organized during the 1938–1939 scholastic year by Dr. Teobaldo Casanova, an educational and clinical psychologist, serves as another landmark in the development of school psychology (Roca de Torres, in press). Dr. Pablo Roca de León, who earned master's and doctoral degrees in psychology with a specialty in testing and guidance from the University of Texas, and Dr. Miguelina N. de Hernández, identified as the first graduate of a school psychology program to work on the Island, later developed this division. Dr. Hernández earned degrees at Columbia University and Purdue University. Drs. Roca and Hernández directed the Division during the 1950s and 1960s, respectively (Roca de Torres, 1991). This division (later known as the Office of Evaluation and Statistics) was responsible for developing many instruments to measure school achievement, vocational interests, and cognitive and visual-motor abilities, and for translating and adapting the 1937 edition of the Stanford-Binet Intelligence Scale (Roca, 1953) and the 1949 edition of the Wechsler Intelligence Scale for Children (Roca, 1951) for use with Puerto Rican children.

This office also developed or translated the following tests, among others: Draw-A-Person Test, Interamerican Cooperative Tests (in both English and Spanish), Puerto Rican Collective Test for Mental Capacity, Puerto Rican Test of Cognitive Ability, and the Raven Progressive Matrices (Roca de Torres, 1991). For further information on this topic, see Herrans (1985), Roca de Torres (1991), Rodríguez-Arocho (in press), and Rodríguez Gómez (2002).

During the 1960s and 1970s, the Child and Adolescent Mental Health Clinic employed additional psychologists. Some were appointed as psychological assistants, as they had taken graduate courses in psychology but had not finished a master's degree (Sumaza, in press). Starting in the mid 1960s, Head Start programs hired psychologists to perform various tasks including psychological evaluations, consultation to teachers, interventions with parents, organizational consultation about class functioning, and training for staff, teachers, and parents on children's development and related topics. This seems to be the first organized program of school-based interventions involving psychologists. Most psychologists working at Head Start programs were trained in clinical

psychology, as this was the dominant specialty offered by the newly established graduate programs available in Puerto Rico at the time.

During the 1980s, a consortium was organized between the University of Puerto Rico, Río Piedras campus, and Temple University in Philadelphia to prepare doctoral-level school psychologists through two methods. In one method, 10 students took several courses at the University of Puerto Rico taught by Temple University or University of Puerto Rico instructors holding adjunct teaching status at Temple. In 1984, this group moved to Philadelphia and took additional courses at Temple University for two academic sessions in order to complete a residency requirement. Later they worked on their dissertations with Temple University advisers and completed a 1-year internship in public or private schools in Puerto Rico. These tasks were done under the supervision of University of Puerto Rico–Temple University adjunct professors.

In the second method, students who completed a master's degree in clinical psychology at the University of Puerto Rico entered Temple University's doctoral program in school psychology. Each of the two programs resulted in nine students obtaining their doctoral degrees in school psychology. These school psychologists have been instrumental in developing programs in school psychology in Puerto Rican universities and hold various other professional leadership positions.

During the 1980s, several private schools started adding psychologists to their staff. Some served regular students in all classrooms, whereas others were assigned primarily to programs for students with learning problems. The psychologists performed evaluations, consulted with teachers, and presented workshops for teachers. Some of the initial students who worked as school psychologists in private schools were interns of the University of Puerto Rico–Temple University program.

The Interamerican University of Puerto Rico initiated a master's degree in school psychology at its San Germán campus in 1992 and at its metropolitan campus in 1979. This university initiated a doctoral program at both campuses in 2001. In 2005, the Interamerican University of Puerto Rico's San Germán campus graduated the first two doctorates in school psychology.

In 1992, Pontificial Catholic University of Puerto Rico began offering a master's degree in school psychology. The University of Puerto Rico, Río Piedras campus, offers a sequence of courses in school psychology leading to a certificate for those who complete the courses. A proposal to transform the sequence into a formal degree program is being developed by its Department of Psychology (M. Méndez, personal communication, October 2005). Turabo University at Caguas and Carlos Albizu University in Old San Juan plan to offer school psychology degrees at a later date.

Since the 1930s, the Department of Education has expressed its view that work performed by psychologists is important. Moreover, during this period, the Department employed some psychologists. One of them, Teobaldo Casanova, who had a doctoral degree in educational and clinical psychology, worked at the Division of Educational Research and Statistics in 1938 (Roca de Torres, in press).

According to Law 170 of August 12, 2000, psychologists employed by public schools must be licensed. However, by 2005, few public schools had employed full-time psychologists as required by this law. Although a degree in school psychology is preferred for those working in schools, those holding a psychology license may work in schools even if they have not been trained in school psychology. They must present evidence of training in testing and experience in school settings (Law 170 of August 12, 2000).

The Department of Education usually contracts with corporations of psychologists or individual psychologists to evaluate and intervene with children registered at the Register of Special Students or students referred by teachers (Sumaza, in press). They are given the title "psychologist" and may have been trained in clinical,

school, counseling, or other specialties of psychology, provided they have taken some courses in assessment and other clinical areas.

In 1995, the Department employed 10 psychologists full-time, 22 part-time, plus 30 doing contract work through seven corporations (Zambrana, 2000). Numbers employed vary each year. In January 2004, the Department employed five psychologists, mostly in administrative positions (Department of Education, 2004). Full-time employment at the Department of Education is rare, in part because salaries are very low. For example, the monthly starting salary for a licensed master's level psychologist is $1,776, similar to that for bachelor's-level teachers, who start at $1,500. Candidates with experience and a doctoral degree may earn up to $3,689 a month. Few psychologists are willing to work under such conditions. In contrast, psychologists at the Administration of Mental Health and Anti-Addiction Services may earn between $4,000 and $6,000 monthly. Police officers with a high school diploma, and perhaps associate degree–level training, earn initial salaries of $2,000 monthly.

In 2004, the Department of Education announced the availability of 50 full-time positions for psychologists to work in Quality of Life, a prevention program. Only two psychologists accepted positions, and one resigned after a year. The program has to rely on 22 psychologists who agreed to work part-time (R. Cibes, personal communication, July 22, 2005). Psychologists work 80 hours a month for $30 to $40 an hour and receive no fringe benefits (Asociación de Psicología de Puerto Rico, 2005).

Psychology became a licensed profession in 1983. As of June 2006, the Office of Certification and Registration of Health Professionals had licensed 2,710 persons to practice psychology as authorized by the Board of Psychologist Examiners of Puerto Rico. About 1,500 continue to renew their licenses every 3 years as required by law (Department of Health, 2003). Approximately 64% of licensed psychologists are females. Among psychologists who have a current license, approximately 10% identify their main workplace as schools (F. Medina, personal communication, August 15, 2005).

Infrastructure of School Psychology

Two associations represent school psychologists in Puerto Rico: Asociación de Psicólogos Escolares de Puerto Rico (Puerto Rico Association of School Psychologists), affiliated with the National Association of School Psychologists, and the Asociación de Psicología de Puerto Rico (Puerto Rico Psychological Association, affiliated with the American Psychological Association. The Puerto Rico Association of School Psychologists was founded in 1998 and has approximately 100 members. It was the driving force responsible for the approval of Law 170 of August 12, 2000, that requires the public school system to appoint psychologists as full-time employees of public schools. Many leaders and active members have degrees in school psychology from Temple University or the Interamerican University. Since its founding, the Puerto Rico Association of School Psychologists has organized a yearly conference at which the main speaker is usually the president of the National Association of School Psychologists (Huff, 2005). Local speakers also are invited to present on topics of interest to psychologists working in schools.

The Puerto Rico Psychological Association, founded in 1954, has approximately 900 members representing diverse specialties in psychology. It sponsors annual conventions, has organized numerous continuing education activities, and has been the most influential professional association for psychologists in Puerto Rico during the past 50 years. This organization publishes a newsletter and a peer-reviewed journal. It is actively involved in various programs sponsored by the American Psychological Association and has strong ties to the Interamerican Society of Psychology.

A major achievement of the Puerto Rico Psychological Association was the approval of Law 96 of June 4, 1983, which established licensing requirements for the private practice of psychology. This law requires an applicant to have a graduate degree in psychology from a program accredited by the Consejo de Educación Superior de Puerto Rico (Puerto Rico Council of Higher Education), when established in Puerto Rico, or an accrediting entity of similar quality in the United States, or by the American Psychological Association. Candidates for licensure must pass a written examination of 10 core subjects. Before taking the exam, candidates with a specialty in clinical psychology must have completed a doctoral degree, either a Ph.D. or Psy.D., and candidates with other specialties, including school psychology, must have completed a master's degree (Puerto Rico Board of Psychologist Examiners, 1992).

After passing the licensing exam, prospective licensees complete a registration process that includes presenting certificates from the police department verifying no record of delinquency, among other requirements. To maintain their license, psychologists must complete 45 continuing education hours related to the practice of psychology every 3 years. There are ample and diverse continuing education programs available. Universities, professional associations, and community service organizations sponsor most of these programs. Psychologists also may take American Psychological Association–approved courses outside of Puerto Rico.

Law 170 is a chapter within Law 149 of June 30, 1999: the Organic Law of the Department of Education. It also refers to Law 96, as it establishes that psychologists employed by public schools must be licensed. As a result, psychologists who have specialties in clinical, counseling, industrial, or social psychology, among others areas, may be hired to work in schools if they have training in basic skills needed for this work (e.g., can conduct intelligence and personality assessments). Professionals from other fields (e.g., teachers and social workers) may not be employed as school psychologists unless they meet the requirements to become licensed psychologists.

Puerto Rico is politically linked to the United States and receives U.S. funds for educational programs; therefore, federal laws governing education are enforced locally. As in the United States, Public Law 108-446, the Individuals With Disabilities Educational Improvement act of 2004, establishes important obligations for psychologists in the schools. The commonwealth law that describes the implementation of this act in Puerto Rico, Law 51 of June 7, 1996, Ley de Servicios Integrales para Personas con Impedimentos (Law for Integrated Services for Persons With Disabilities), is important for psychologists because it highlights the need for comprehensive psychological evaluations in order to establish a diagnosis. Law 408 of October 2, 2000, also known as the Mental Health Law of Puerto Rico, also assigns duties to psychologists by identifying them as mental health professionals who share responsibility for serving the public's mental health needs, including the provision of emergency care, when needed.

Compliance with Public Law 107-110, the No Child Left Behind Act, is a priority for the Puerto Rico Department of Education. Goals for improving achievement test scores of public school students through the scholastic year 2013–2014 have been established and are closely monitored (Colón Soto, 2005). Psychologists are active in various phases of this effort, especially providing services to special education students, such as testing, diagnosing, participating in individualized education and intervention planning, and training teachers in the Quality of Life program.

The first professional psychology journal published in Puerto Rico, *Revista Puertorriqueña de Psicología* (Puerto Rican Journal of Psychology), was founded in 1981 by the Puerto Rico Psychological Association. This peer-reviewed journal is published yearly and features articles in Spanish and English about research and theories on themes of general interest to psychology. The Puerto Rico Association of School Psychologists also publishes a newsletter, *Avances de la Psicología*

Escolar (Advances in School Psychology), which features professional issues, especially public policy discussions as well as research and theoretical articles of interest to psychologists working in schools. It is a valuable source for details on the history of school psychological services in Puerto Rico and professional issues related to the practices of school psychology.

Other professional journals used by psychologists and published on the Island are sponsored by universities. *Ciencias de la Conducta* (Behavioral Sciences) is published by Carlos Albizu University and features research in diverse settings by faculty and students of their graduate programs in general, clinical, and industrial/organizational psychology. Many of its issues are relevant to school psychology practice. The University of Puerto Rico publishes *Revista de Ciencias Sociales* (Journal of Social Sciences) at the Faculty of Social Sciences, which includes research by psychology professors and students. *Homines* (Humanity), published by Interamerican University's Metropolitan campus, features psychology, among other liberal arts subjects. It has served as a venue for publications by leaders in the practice of school psychology such as Irene Sumaza, Juana M. Rodríguez, Nelly Zambrana, and others.

Psychologists rely on journals published in Latin America and the United States, especially those published by the Interamerican Society of Psychology and the American Psychological Association. The Interamerican Society of Psychology publishes *Interamerican Journal of Psychology* and the newsletter *Interamerican Psychologist*. American Psychological Association members and nonmembers alike rely on *American Psychologist* and the *APA Monitor*. Those who belong to Division 16: School Psychology receive *School Psychology Quarterly*. A growing number of members of the National Association of School Psychologists rely on its publications, such as *School Psychology Review, Communiqué, Best Practices in School Psychology,* and others. Many National Association of School Psychologists documents are available in Spanish, and some are provided electronically, and free of charge (www.naspon line.org).

Publications for educators also are used by school psychologists. Some examples are *El Sol: Revista de la Asociación de Maestros de Puerto Rico* (The Sun: Journal of the Teachers Association of Puerto Rico), published by the Puerto Rican Teachers Association, and *Educational Leadership,* published by the American Society for Curriculum Development.

Preparation of School Psychologists

Two universities offer graduate programs in school psychology. The Interamerican University of Puerto Rico offers both a master's and a doctoral (Ph.D.) program in school psychology at two of its campuses, Metropolitan and San Germán. The Pontifical Catholic University of Puerto Rico offers a master's of education in school psychology at its Faculty of Education. Each of these graduate programs admits approximately 20 students yearly and graduates about 5.

Those applying to a graduate program in school psychology must have a bachelor's degree in any field, including at least 18 credits in psychology. Completion of a master's degree requires one to complete 53 credit hours at the Pontifical Catholic University of Puerto Rico and 62 credit hours at the Interamerican University of Puerto Rico. The master's degree requires approximately 3 years of full-time study. Degree holders then must pass a licensing exam and be granted a license to practice as a psychologist, thus allowing the psychologist to practice in any school or government agency or as a private practitioner.

Candidates who aspire to earn a doctoral degree after completing a bachelor's degree must take an additional 83 credit hours in school psychology, complete a 2,000-hour internship at schools, and write and orally defend a dissertation. This program typically requires 5 to 6 years of full-time study. Candidates who have master's degrees must take an additional 38 credit hours, complete the 2,000-hour internship, and write and defend a dissertation. This program typically requires 3 years of full-time study at the doctoral level.

Curricula for all academic programs of school psychology are ample, varied, and academically strong. They cover all areas suggested by Cunningham and Oakland (1998). The Interamerican University's master's program apparently places greater emphasis on research and statistics than does the Pontifical Catholic University of Puerto Rico program. On the other hand, this latter program is more oriented toward developing intervention skills. Both programs seem to prepare students well for their work in schools.

The master's program at Interamerican University of Puerto Rico requires the following courses for obtaining a master's degree in school psychology: general psychology, physiological psychology, developmental psychology, personality, cognition and learning, advanced statistics, measurements and test construction, research methods, applied research seminars I and II, professional ethics, interview techniques, cognitive assessment with practice, personality assessment with practice, role and function of a school psychologist, supervised practice I, II, III, and IV, applied behavior analysis for children and adolescents or an advanced seminar in school psychology, and a thesis or an additional course to substitute for it.

The master's program at Pontifical Catholic University of Puerto Rico requires the following courses: statistics applied to education, research and educational development, educational philosophy, advanced general psychology, behavior modification, learning, cognitive assessment with practice, personality tests with practice, personality development, psychotherapy, physiological psychology, psychopathology, human dignity, marriage and family, seminar in school psychology (ethics), an elective course, an internship that may be substituted for two additional courses, and a small thesis.

Pontificial Catholic University of Puerto Rico requires a one-semester practicum that consists of 15 hours of practice per week, under supervision at a school, or approximately 225 hours for the semester. Interamerican University of Puerto Rico requires master's students to complete four practicum courses, three of which require a minimum of 160 hours in school. Only the doctoral program at Interamerican University of Puerto Rico requires a 2,000-hour internship. All programs should add more training in educational assessment, ethics, and diversity.

Roles, Functions, and Responsibilities of School Psychologists

Psychologists working in schools and those serving students in their private practice devote most of their time to performing psychological and psychoeducational evaluations. Training teachers on behavioral issues (e.g., discipline, learning problems, mental health, and family issues) also composes an important part of their practice. Consultation with teachers and administrators is less frequent, yet it occurs, especially among psychologists employed full-time at private schools. As described previously, assessments that are commonly used include Draw-A-Person; Bender Visual-Motor Gestalt Test; Escala de Inteligencia Wechsler para Niños–Revisada, Puerto Rico (Wechsler's Intelligence Scale for Children–Revised, Puerto Rican Spanish Version); Children's Apperception Test; Raven's Progressive Matrices; and others. Universities conduct research on issues pertinent to students as exemplified by a series of studies on attention deficit disorder and cognitive processes (Bauermeister, 2000; Rodríguez-Arocho, 2003; Rodríguez-Arocho & Moreno-Torres, 2001; Sera & Rodríguez, 2002) at the University of Puerto Rico. Such projects provide services to the community and a research venue for completing graduate degrees. School-based research projects are found at the other universities with graduate programs in psychology.

Current Issues Impacting School Psychology

These early years of the 21st century are exciting and challenging for school psychology. Public support for including school psychological services in school systems is increasing. This increased support should be used to work on continued challenges, notably insufficient numbers of psychologists working as members of the school staff, inadequate supervision and remuneration of psychologists under contract to serve students, and poor quality of some services. The activism of the Puerto Rico Association of School Psychologists has been instrumental in promoting visibility through press conferences and radio and television appearances (Fajardo, 2003; Zambrana & Vargas, 2001), educating the public about the roles and functions of school psychologists.

The Puerto Rico Association of School Psychologists also has promoted the enforcement of Law 170 of August 12, 2000. The Association, with support from the Board of the Puerto Rico Psychological Association and the Puerto Rico Board of Psychologist Examiners, has coordinated numerous meetings, written requests, and publications and held press conferences to promote timely compliance with the law's plan for recruitment of school psychologists. The Federación de Maestros de Puerto Rico (Puerto Rico Teachers Federation) joined forces with the Puerto Rico Association of School Psychologists in efforts to persuade executives from the Department of Education to implement the Law (Bestard & Feliciano, 2003–2004).

As indicated earlier, the Department of Education has faced difficulties recruiting and retaining full-time psychologists due to inadequate salaries, contracts with few fringe benefits, delays in payment for services performed, and supervision by unqualified personnel. The board of directors of the Puerto Rico Association of School Psychologists currently considers the enforcement of Law 170 a high priority (Hornedo, 2005).

The Puerto Rico Psychological Association established a committee to address school psychology issues of interest to its members, including conditions at work, adherence to ethical and other best-practice standards in services to children, and issues affecting community and public policy. This committee intends to revise the *Professional Guidelines for Psychological Evaluations* (Miranda, 1991) in order to assist professional psychologists and graduate students in preparing reports and rendering quality services; designing and implementing an educational media campaign about psychologists' roles and functions in school settings; and reinforcing cooperation and formal agreements with organizations of school professionals, including the Puerto Rico Association of School Psychologists, educators, and other members of school staff. The latter goal is directed mainly to promote teamwork in school settings and mutual support for shared professional growth projects.

Possible ethical violations by unqualified and inadequately prepared psychologists who provide services to children constitute another ongoing concern. Such alleged violations, when presented in a formal complaint, may warrant sanctions under the provisions of the ethics code of the Puerto Rico Board of Psychologist Examiners. The complaint process is necessary and useful, yet it is remedial; preventive educational strategies need to be added and enhanced.

Psychologists in Puerto Rico have been licensed for over 20 years, during which time many changes have taken place, especially the accelerated growth of graduate programs described earlier. The need to update Law 96 of June 4, 1983, has been discussed frequently in conventions and meetings by leaders of local psychological associations. The last substantial amendment to this law (Law 47 of December 20, 1990), approved in 1990, resolved a controversy

related to licensing psychologists at the master's level. The original licensing statute, approved in 1983, indicated that after 11 years had passed, doctoral degrees would be required for licensure. The amendment, approved in 1990, determined that a doctoral degree would be required for psychologists whose specialty is clinical psychology. Psychologists graduating from other specialties may continue to be licensed at the master's level. Since this amendment was approved, graduate programs have increased in number, and five universities have established doctoral programs. Because opportunities to obtain doctorates in Puerto Rico are no longer scarce, one reason to maintain licensing at the master's level no longer is applicable. The Clinical Psychology Interest Group at the Puerto Rico Psychological Association established revisions of Law 96 of June 4, 1983, as a major goal for 2005 (Moreno-Velázquez, 2005).

Another indication of interest in modifying the licensing law occurred early in 2006. A proposal to license psychologists according to their specialty was drafted at the Puerto Rico House of Representatives. This proposal, known as P de la C 2285 (House of Representatives Project 2285) of January 2006, was the subject of a panel discussion held at Turabo University in Caguas, Puerto Rico, on March 16, 2006. The panelists were Representative Hector Ferrer, the author of the proposal; Dr. Dolores Miranda, representative of the Alliance of Directors of Psychology Graduate Programs; Dr. Vivian Rodríguez del Toro, president of the Puerto Rico Psychological Association; Ms. Edna Rodríguez and Dr. Gladys Altieri of Carlos Albizu University; and Dr. Frances Boulon-Díaz, president of the Puerto Rico Board of Psychologist Examiners. Drs. Rodríguez del Toro, Miranda, and Boulon-Díaz indicated the proposal should not be approved as drafted, but suggested further discussion on possible changes to Law 96 of June 4, 1983, and other issues related to the quality of psychological services in Puerto Rico. There was an exchange of ideas among those present; most disagreed with the proposal, but differences of opinion exist regarding new options for licensing psychologist practitioners in Puerto Rico (Maldonado, 2006; Puerto Rico Board of Psychologist Examiners, 2006). Discussion of new directions for the licensing of psychologists in Puerto Rico is expected to continue.

Some issues that have been presented to the Puerto Rico Board of Psychologist Examiners by licensed psychologists and students include that the license should not be the same for different levels of training and that distinctions among specialties should be defined more clearly (Rodríguez-Rivera, 2005). Revisions of the Puerto Rico Board of Psychologist Examiners' Bylaws and Ethics Code (Puerto Rico Board of Psychologist Examiners, 1992, 2003) are in progress. These revisions will address some issues related to the increasing complexity of psychological training and practice in Puerto Rico and provide clearer guidelines for providing specialized services.

Ideas regarding amendments to the licensing law are frequently discussed via Internet groups, at universities, and at professional meetings. Opinions differ regarding requirements for practice in different settings, including schools. Colleagues differ on available options for practice in multiple settings and on the desirability of restricting some jobs to those who have earned certain specialties or certifications. For example, clinical, counseling, and organizational psychologists are legally qualified to practice in schools if they are licensed. The ethics code requires they perform only services for which they have competence (Puerto Rico Board of Psychologist Examiners, 1992). There are doubts about the efficacy of self-imposed controls and of having the ethics complaint process as the only resource to control inadequate performance of duties by psychologists (Moreno-Velázquez, 2005). The Alliance of Directors of Graduate Psychology Programs, the Clinical Psychology and School Psychology interest groups at the Puerto Rico Psychological Association, the Puerto Rico Association of School Psychologists leadership, and other members of the community of psychologist practitioners and educators continue to rethink and debate these issues.

The need for test-related research and development is urgent. Issues include the reliability and validity of evaluations, accuracy and best practices when making diagnoses, and criteria used for placement decisions when data are sparse. Studies of such processes will provide foundations for decision making, especially regarding formulation of practice guidelines and policies.

Additional issues pertain to services for immigrant populations (e.g., from the Dominican Republic), parenting skills, communication and consultation with teachers, and efficacy of diverse teaching methods and learning styles in the classroom (M. Martínez-Plana, personal communication, February 22, 2005). Efforts are under way to collect and analyze samples of psychological evaluations in order to identify problems in applying and interpreting measurement tools.

We are optimistic for the future of psychological services in the schools. Universities are active in providing education and research opportunities to professionals eager to serve students better. Support from parents and school personnel is growing, as is public awareness of the need to provide students with enhanced opportunities for learning, personality development, and mental health. Academic success is readily identified as an essential resource for community development and quality of life. This is at the forefront of strategies to combat social problems such as poverty, violence, addictions, and other contemporary challenges (Boulon, 2005). At this exciting moment, information gathered in diverse environments and alternative solutions to problems contribute to our capacity for analysis and decision making.

References

Álvarez, A. I. (1994). La enseñanza de la psicología en la Universidad de Puerto Rico, Recinto de Río Piedras: 1903–1950 [Teaching psychology at the University of Puerto Rico, Río Piedras campus]. *Puerto Rican Journal of Psychology, 9,* 13–30.

Asociación de Psicología de Puerto Rico [Puerto Rico Psychological Association]. (2005, February). Grupos de interés [Interest groups]. *Boletín APPR, 27,* 1, 8.

Bauermeister, J. J. (2000). *Hiperactivo, impulsivo, distraído: Me conoces?* [Hyperactive, impulsive, distracted: Do you know me?]. San Juan: First Book.

Bernal, G. (in press). Desarrollo histórico de la psicología clínica en Puerto Rico [Historical development of clinical psychology in Puerto Rico]. *Revista Puertorriqueña de Psicología.*

Bestard, J., & Feliciano, R. (2003–2004, April–May). Unen esfuerzos la APEP y la FMPR [The APEP (Puerto Rico Association of School Psychologists) and the FMPR (Puerto Rico Teachers Federation) unite efforts]. *Advances in School Psychology, 6,* 3–4.

Boulon, F. (2005, March 3). De la violencia a la paz en las escuelas [From violence to peace in the schools]. *El Nuevo Día,* p. 93.

Colón Soto, V. (2005). *El psicólogo escolar frente al aprovechamiento académico* [The school psychologist faces academic achievement]. Unpublished manuscript presented at Interamerican University, Metropolitan campus, San Juan, Puerto Rico.

Consejo General de Educación [General Council of Education]. (2006). *Estadísticas* [Statistics]. Retrieved May 10, 2006, from http://www.cge.gobierno.pr/instesta.htm

Cunningham, J., & Oakland, T. (1998). International School Psychology Association guidelines for the preparation of school psychologists. *School Psychology International, 19,* 19–30.

Departament of Education. (2004, February 3). *Resumen de personal docente y no docente por categoría, región e isla con la nómina de enero del 2004* [Summary of teaching and nonteaching personnel by category, region and island with the payroll of January 2004]. Computing Center: Author.

Departament of Education. (2005). [Department of Education home page]. Retrieved August 12, 2005, from http://www.de.gobierno.pr

Department of Health, Information Systems Development Office]. (2003). *Informe de psicólogos registrados al 7 de noviembre de 2003* [Report of psychologists registered by November 7, 2003]. San Juan: Author.

Fajardo, R. (2003, November 6). Education urged to hire many more school psychologists. *The San Juan Star,* p. 17.

Figueroa, L. (1979). *Breve historia de Puerto Rico* [Brief history of Puerto Rico, Vol. 1]. Río Piedras: EDIL.

Hernández, R. (1985). Historia de los programas de salud mental en Puerto Rico [History of mental health programs in Puerto Rico]. *Homines, 3,* 22–31.

Herrans, L. L. (1985). *Psicología y medición: El desarrollo de pruebas psicológicas en Puerto Rico* [Psychology and testing: The development of psychological testing in Puerto Rico]. México City: Limusa.

Hornedo, N. (2005, May). Mensaje de la presidenta [Message from the president]. *Advances in School Psychology, 7,* 2.

Huff, L. (2005). *School psychologists helping children achieve: At school, at home, in life.* Paper presented at the seventh annual conference of the Puerto Rico Association of School Psychologists, Universidad del Este, Carolina, Puerto Rico.

Ley 96 del 4 de junio de 1983: Para reglamentar el ejercicio de la profesión de psicología en Puerto Rico [Law 96 of June 4, 1983: To regulate the practice of psychology in Puerto Rico].

Ley 51 del 7 de junio de 1996: Ley de Servicios Educativos Integrales para Personas con Impedimentos [Law 51 of June 7, 1996: Comprehensive Education for Persons With Disabilities Law].

Ley Número 149 del 30 de junio de 1999: Ley Orgánica de Educación de Puerto Rico [Law 149 of June 30, 1999: Organic Law of Education for Puerto Rico]. Retrieved August 5, 2005, from http:www.lexjuris.com/LEXMATE/educacion/lexeducacion

Ley 170 del 12 de agosto de 2000: Para crear el puesto de Psicólogo Escolar [Law 170 of August 12, 2000: To create the position of School Psychologist].

Ley Número 408 del 2 de octubre de 2000: Ley de Salud Mental de Puerto Rico [Law 408 of October 2, 2000: Mental Health Law of Puerto Rico].

Maldonado, L. (2006, March 19). *Reseña de actividad: Panel sobre P de la C 2285* [Review of panel discussion about House of Representatives Proposal 2285]. Retrieved March 21, 2006, from sociedadpsicologicapr@yahoogroups.com

Miranda, D. (1991). *Guías profesionales para la evaluación psicológica* [Profesional guidelines for psychological evaluations]. San Juan: Puerto Rico Psychological Association.

Moreno-Velázquez, I. (2005, April 25). *Letter to members*. San Juan: Puerto Rico Psychological Association.

Picó, F., & Rivera Izcoa, C. (1991). *Puerto Rico, tierra adentro y mar afuera: Historia y cultura de los puertorriqueños* [Puerto Rico, the land inside and the sea outside: History and culture of Puerto Ricans]. Río Piedras: Ediciones Huracán.

Puerto Rico Board of Psychologist Examiners. (1992). *Reglamento general* [General regulations]. San Juan: Departament of Health.

Puerto Rico Board of Psychologist Examiners. (2003). *Código de etica de psicólogos—Borrador* [Psychologists' code of ethics—Draft]. San Juan: Department of Health.

Puerto Rico Board of Psychologist Examiners. (2006, March 3). *Posición oficial de la Junta Examinadora de Psicólogos respecto al P de la C 2285 de enero de 2006* [Official position statement of the Puerto Rico Board of Psychologist Examiners about House of Representatives Proposal 2285 of January 2005]. San Juan: Department of Health.

Puerto Rico Planning Board. (2006). *Apendice Estadistico [Statistical Appendix]*. Retrieved July 3, 2006, from http://www.jp.gobierno.pr

Roca, P. (1951). *Manual Escala de Inteligencia Wechsler para Niños* [Manual for the Wechsler Intelligence Scale for Children–Spanish Version]. San Juan: Department of Public Instruction.

Roca, P. (1953). *Escala de Inteligencia Stanford Binet para Niños* [Stanford-Binet Intelligence Scale for Children–Spanish Version]. San Juan: Department of Public Instruction.

Roca de Torres, I. (1991). Estado actual de la evaluación psicológica en el área de la psicología escolar [Current state of psychological evaluations in school psychology]. *Puerto Rican Journal of Psychology, 7*, 43–54.

Roca de Torres, I. (2001). Problemas centrales para la formación académica y el entrenamiento profesional en psicología en Puerto Rico [Central problems for academic and professional training in psychology in Puerto Rico]. In J. P. Toro & J. F. Villegas (Eds.), *Problemas centrales para la formación académica y el entrenamiento profesional del psicólogo en las Américas* (Vol. 1). Buenos Aires, Argentina: JVE ediciones.

Roca de Torres, I. (in press). Reseñas biográficas de algunos precursores de la psicología de Puerto Rico [Biographical sketches of some pioneers of psychology in Puerto Rico]. *Puerto Rican Journal of Psychology.*

Rodríguez-Arocho, W. (2003). La relación entre funciones ejecutivas y lenguaje: Una propuesta para estudiar su relación [The relationship between executive functions and language: A research proposal]. *Perspectivas Psicológicas, 3*(4), 41–48.

Rodríguez-Arocho, W. (in press). La investigación de los procesos cognoscitivos en Puerto Rico: Hacia una integración de los hallazgos [Research on cognitive processes in Puerto Rico: Toward an integration of findings]. *Puerto Rican Journal of Psychology.*

Rodríguez-Arocho, W., & Moreno-Torres, M. (2001). El uso del lenguaje en niños y niñas con características del trastorno por déficit de atención e hiperactividad durante la planificación de una tarea [Language use in children with characteristics related to attention deficit disorder and hyperactivity during task planning]. *Interamerican Journal of Psychology, 35*(1), 143–162.

Rodríguez Gómez, J. R. (2002). *Compendio de pruebas validadas para Puerto Rico: Una antología multidisciplinaria* [Compendium of tests validated for use in Puerto Rico: A multidisciplinary anthology]. San Juan: Carlos Albizu University.

Rodríguez-Rivera, E. C. (2005). *Actitudes de los psicólogos/as licenciados/as de Puerto Rico hacia la licencia genérica en la práctica de la profesión de la psicología* [Attitudes of psychologists licensed to practice psychology in Puerto Rico toward the generic license]. Unpublished doctoral dissertation, Carlos Albizu University, San Juan, Puerto Rico.

Roldán Soto, C. (2005, August 3). A examen el sistema educativo [The educational system is tested]. *El Nuevo Día,* p. 12.

Sera, M., & Rodríguez, W. C. (2002). When language affects cognition and when it does not: An analysis of grammatical gender and classification. *Journal of Experimental Psychology: General, 131*(3), 377–397.

Sumaza, I. (in press). Breve historia de la psicología escolar en Puerto Rico [Brief history of school psychology in Puerto Rico]. *Puerto Rican Journal of Psychology.*

U.S. Census Bureau. (2000). *Table DP 1: Profile of general demographic characteristics: 2000 Geographic area: Puerto Rico.* Retrieved August 1, 2005, from http://factfinder.census.gov/

Zambrana, N. (2000). La psicología escolar en Puerto Rico: La experiencia hasta 1995 [School psychology in Puerto Rico: Experiences until 1995]. *Interamerican Journal of Psychology, 34,* 95–117.

Zambrana, N., & Vargas, I. (2001, March). Mensaje de la Junta Editora [Message from the Editorial Board]. *Advances in School Psychology, 3,* 1–2.

32

School Psychology in Romania

Margareta Dinca

Irina Holdevici

Luminita Monica Vlad

Aurora Frunza

Context of School Psychology

Romania is situated in the southeastern part of Central Europe and shares borders with Hungary, Serbia, Bulgaria, the Black Sea, Ukraine, and the Republic of Moldova. Romania is 237,400 square kilometres and has a temperate climate, similar to the northeastern United States, with four distinct seasons. Romania had a population of 22,329,977 in 2005. The ethnic breakdown is 89% Romanians, 7.5% Hungarians, 1.9% Romany (Gipsies), and smaller percentages of Ukrainians, Germans, Russian-Lipovenians, Turks, Tartars, Serbians, Slovakians, and others. Approximately 55% of Romania's population lives in towns and cities, and 45% lives in rural areas. The official language is Romanian with German and Hungarian also spoken in some counties,

including in schools and civil administration. The Romanian language is a Latin-based language, a continuation of the Latin spoken in ancient times in Dacia and Moesia—the eastern provinces of the Roman Empire. The main religions are Christian Orthodox (87%), Roman Catholic (5%), Protestant (5%), and Jewish (1%). There are 263 towns in Romania, 25 of which have a population of more than 100,000; eight cities have more 300,000 inhabitants. Among those in rural areas, 2,868,000 live in larger rural communities and 13,285,000 in smaller rural villages. There are 41 counties. The capital city, Bucharest, has a population of 1,934,449 (*Anuarul Statistic al României–2005*, 2006).

Romania's history is not marked by tranquillity. Various migrating people invaded Romania. Its historical provinces of Wallachia and Moldavia furiously resisted the invading Ottoman Turks. Transylvania was successively part of the Habsburg and Ottoman empires and then was briefly united with Wallachia, but it remained an autonomous province. Romania's post–World War II history, as a communist-block nation, is widely known, primarily due to the excesses of the former dictator Nicolae Ceauşescu. In December 1989, a national uprising led to his overthrow. The 1991 Constitution established Romania as a republic with a multi-party system, market economy, and individual rights of free speech, religion, and private ownership of property.

For centuries, Romania's economy was based on agriculture, and the region was known as Europe's breadbasket. During the 1930s, Romania was one of the main European producers of wheat, corn, and rye. In the 1950s, the communist system introduced and emphasized heavy industry. Although this shift toward heavy industry continues, agriculture remains economically important and employs about one third of the labour force. Since 1990, successive governments have concentrated on turning Romania into a market economy. The gross domestic product in 2004 was US$171.5 billion, US$7,700 per capita (*Anuarul Statistic al României–2005,* 2006).

The number of children of preschool age (3–6) is 883,339 and of school age (7–18) is 6,531,735. Thus, 7,415,134 people, 29.4% of Romania's population, are children (*Anuarul Statistic al României–2005,* 2006).

The Romanian education system includes public and private schools. Public education is free and includes the following school levels: Level 1, preschool education, with 629,703 students ages 3 through 6; Level 2, primary and secondary education, with 2,198,312 students ages 7 through 13; Level 3, high school education, with 740,404 students ages 14 through 18; Level 4, academic studies, with 596,297 students ages 19 through 24 in most cases. Older adults can study in regular school units if they are willing, but they rarely do. Higher education

(university level) extends over 4 to 6 years, depending on one's undergraduate degree (e.g., full-time study of 4 years for psychology and 6 years for architecture). In compliance with the Bologna Treaty, as of 2005–2006, the duration and structure of higher education changed, resulting in a 3-year undergraduate degree and a 2-year master's degree.

At age 13 and following their graduation from Level 2, students may select a parallel type of education, namely the vocational and apprenticeship program. Currently, 270,215 students are enrolled in this program. At age 18, following their graduation from Level 3 (high school), students may select another type of education, parallel to higher education, a post–high school and foreman program. It currently has 61,855 students (*Anuarul Statistic al României–2005,* 2006).

After 1990, private education, from kindergarten to the university level, increased in popularity, and the number of private schools increased as well. Many private schools were established, including Catholic schools and those based on American, British, German, Hungarian, French, Jewish, Lebanese, Albanian, and other national models. Most are designed for children from high-income families and those whose families come from abroad. University-level private education also has flourished in most big cities.

Before 1990, only large cities had special schools for children with disabilities. After 1990, private special schools were established in many cities. Graduates of such schools can pursue university-level studies. Ninety percent of students complete at least a compulsory education (i.e., from ages 7 to approximately 13, or Levels 1 and 2). The average age of high school graduates is 18 and of higher education (university) graduates is 24. The average class size in schools ranges from 25 to 30 students. The official number of students identified with special needs is 27,165. This figure underestimates the actual number of students with special needs. Families frequently do not release this information. Thus, accurate statistics are not available.

Origin, History, and Current Status of School Psychology

Between 1977 and 1990, faculties (e.g., departments) of psychology and the profession of psychologist were banned by the communist regime. In 1990, psychology faculties were reestablished within the existing universities (i.e., in Bucharest, Cluj Napoca, and Iassy). Additional psychology faculties later were established in several other large cities (i.e., Sibiu, Timisoara, and Craiova). Although universities do not provide specific programs for school psychology, school psychologists can prepare for their work through course work and practicum experiences. The nature of their preparation is discussed later in the chapter.

The terms *school psychologist* and *school counsellor* are used interchangeably to designate those who provide services similar to those provided by school or educational psychologists in other countries. In 1995, the Ministry of Education and Research decided that school counselling and guidance would be developed on three levels: pre-university, university, and outside university (i.e., in the labour, family, health, and military fields). Over 90% of school psychologists/counsellors work in public institutions. Approximately 650 school psychologists/counsellors work at the pre-university level, 450 at the university level, and 100 in other institutional structures of other ministries, associations, or private firms. Thus, there are 1,200 school psychologists/counsellors in Romania, among whom approximately 60% are between ages 25 and 40 and 80% are female (*Anuarul Statistic al României–2005*, 2006).

School counselling and guidance services are available at the pre-university education level either within the curricula (through education programs that provide differentiated school paths according to one's interests and skills) or at a student's request for special consulting services. School psychologists/counsellors are responsible for providing vocational and professional guidance and counselling to students and adults.

Pre-University-Level Institutions

School consulting. Services provided through school consulting services can be found frequently in schools having at least 800 students. These institutions are subordinated to the Ministry of Education and Research. Their main services include school counselling and orientation. The services are provided in groups or one-on-one as needed.

Interschool Offices for Psychopedagogical Assistance. Services provided through the Interschool Offices for Psychopedagogical Assistance are countywide and are found in the largest towns. Students studying in urban schools that do not have consulting services and students from rural areas may request services provided through these offices. The main services provided by these offices are school counselling and vocational/professional orientation and guidance. The services are provided in groups or on an individual basis, as needed.

University-Level Institutions

Consulting services available at the higher education level consist of providing information, guidance, and counselling to university students with regard to labour market trends. Services are provided in groups or individually, as needed. Vocational counselling, guidance, and information centres were established and coordinated by the National Agency for Employment, a department within the Ministry of Labour, following the Reform of the Technical and Vocational Education in Romania PHARE Project (1997), a project funded by the European Union. These centres provide counselling services to high school and university graduates who need to undertake training or retraining. The starting monthly salary for those meeting the minimum training requirements is approximately 100 euros per month. After 15 years, the monthly salary of those working in the public sector is approximately 250 euros and those working in the private sector is approximately 300 to 400 euros.

Infrastructure of School Psychology

Since 2004, the Commission for Educational Psychology, School and Vocational Counselling within the Romanian College of Psychologists has served as the national-level professional organisation that regulates school psychology. This Commission licenses school psychology practices and establishes and promulgates professional standards to licensed psychologists. Regional-level professional organisations also exist for those working in the Interschool Offices for Psychopedagogical Assistance and university consulting services for career information and counselling programs. Commissions for complex assessment of the personality of children and adolescents with disabilities and special education needs are operational.

School psychologists/counsellors are graduates from faculties of psychology, education sciences, sociology, or social assistance. Approximately 50% of psychologists working at the pre-university level hold a master's degree in one of the following: school guidance and counselling, cognitive-behavioural psychotherapies, school administration and management, or educational psychology. A bachelor's degree is needed to work as counsellor/psychologist at the pre-university level. These persons are employed as psychology teachers within schools, responsible for teaching together with counselling and guidance services. Those working at the university level and other school units have degrees from the aforementioned faculties plus at least 3 years experience in school psychology or other expertise (e.g., as legal adviser, economist, engineer). The coordinator of Consulting Services/Offices generally holds a doctorate. Irrespective of their background, school psychologists/counsellors usually are employed as teachers. Therefore, their services generally involve 25% teaching

and 75% counselling. High school graduates often work as assistants or secretaries in these Consulting Services/Offices.

The Law on Education No. 84/1995, adopted by the Romanian Parliament, regulates the activity of school psychologists/counsellors working within the institution subordinated to the Ministry of Education and Research. Article 49 of this law states, "In counties as well as in Bucharest, Centres or Consulting Services for Psychopedagogical Assistance shall operate, providing school and vocational guidance." In 2004, Law No. 213 established the Romanian Association of Psychologists and the Romanian College of Psychologists. The Commission for Educational Psychology, School and Vocational Counselling operates within the Romanian Association of Psychologists.

No professional journal or newsletter is dedicated to school psychology. Hence, these specialists rely on psychology or pedagogy sources. Among the most important are the *Journal of Pedagogy* (published by the Institute for Education Sciences of Bucharest), *Journal of Psychology* (published by the Institute for Psychology and Philosophy, Constantin Radulescu Motru of the Romanian Academy), and *Journal of Organisational Psychology* and *Journal of Social Psychology* (both published by Polirom). All are published semi-annually.

Preparation of School Psychologists

As noted previously, no university programs are dedicated to preparing school psychologists counsellors. However, bachelor-level preparation exists in the form of modules within the basic curricula of the faculties of psychology and educational sciences. Based on the principle of university autonomy, faculties decide on course content and the structure of training modules, which are similar to courses. The modules focus on the types of services practitioners need to provide. The curriculum for a school psychology module is intended to develop the competencies, knowledge, attitudes, and skills as follows: (a) basic competence in the areas of psychological evaluation, career counselling, personality knowledge, counselling methods and techniques, and cross-cultural approaches; (b) knowledge about the labour market, European policies regarding human resources, publicity, national policies for socioeconomic development, counselling theories, and adults' professional reorientation; (c) attitudes, including openness, empathy, flexibility, and respect for deontological norms; and (d) skills, including computer proficiency, efficient communication, group-work techniques, working in the community, psychotherapy, and career development. To attain the necessary professional abilities, school psychologists/counsellors selecting these modules need to acquire theoretical knowledge and engage in supervised practical training.

School psychologists/counsellors also may be prepared at the master's and doctoral levels. A master's degree in psychology takes three semesters, and the curriculum comprises the following topics: psychology of learning, school and vocational counselling, psychopathology, psychotherapy, psychopedagogy for the disabled, sociology of education, education for cultural diversity, counselling for children and adolescents, and group and family counselling. Doctorial programs take 4 or more years and result in the awarding of a doctorate in psychology, psychology and education sciences, or education sciences.

Continued postdoctoral training may involve participation in scientific meetings, work meetings, symposiums, and workshops accredited by the Romanian College of Psychologists' Committee for Educational Psychology, School and Vocational Counselling. One also can attend training courses provided by the National Centre for Secondary Teachers' Training or the European Union–funded programs (e.g., Information and Career Counselling and the National Resources Centre for Vocational Guidance Programs).

Graduates without a master's degree may be granted the right to practice school psychology, subject to their receiving proper supervision. A master's degree prepares one to serve as a supervisor as well as to practice without supervision. Those providing supervision in educational psychology, as well as school and vocational counselling, are employed on a contractual basis. A supervisor is a specialist who is licensed to practice, has at least 5 years experience in psychology and educational and vocational counselling, and holds a related doctoral degree.

Persons who work continuously in educational psychology or school and vocational counselling must reapply for licensure every 7 years by completing a dossier including new documents attesting to the applicant's participation in relevant training. If one discontinues one's professional work in educational psychology, school and vocational counselling for more than 5 years, one must submit a request to be licensed and be supervised.

Roles, Functions, and Responsibilities of School Psychologists

Common roles for school psychologists include counselling, consultation, and interventions. The functions and responsibilities of school psychologists include diagnosing students (at Levels 1, 2, and 3) with regard to their cognitive and personality development together with individual counselling for students, parents, and teachers on such issues as abilities, aptitudes, aspirations, choices, and interpersonal relationships.

For those working in the Interschool Consulting Services for Psychopedagogical Assistance and the county-level Centres for Psychopedagogical Assistance programs, counselling is provided only for Level 1 and 2 students, parents, and teachers, on such issues as students' abilities and aspirations or causes of interpersonal conflicts in school or family that negatively influence school activity and may lead to school failure. They also discuss specialisations offered through high school or vocational school programs.

Within high schools, consulting services provide information and counselling on such issues as performance on the school-leaving examination for various specialisations; opportunities for continuing education within post–high school training or universities; possibilities for vocational school graduates to continue studying in high schools or postsecondary schools, or in institutions at the post–high school level, or in higher education units; possibilities to directly join the labour market at the end of high school/vocational school; and information regarding various trades and opportunities for further development.

Current Issues Impacting School Psychology

The main problems faced by school psychologists and other specialists in psychology are generated by an incorrect representation of their role in the community. The long absence of the profession of psychology from institutional and community systems leads to confusions as to the roles and services of psychologists and how they differ from psychiatrists. In addition, the belief that only persons with severe mental health problems seek and need professional assistance is widespread. This attitude also hinders the acceptance of the roles of psychologists and their acceptance. Psychologists experience difficulty having their programs in institutions accepted because the managers lack information about that profession.

Other problems occur due to the dysfunctions of the national network for school psychology, including the small numbers of school psychologists; insufficient material resources; inconsistencies in the quality and nature of services nationally and internationally; and adult career guidance focused mainly on employment and too little on counselling. The Romanian Association of Psychology and the Commission for Educational Psychology, School and Vocational Counselling are newly formed. Thus, communication and collaboration among school psychologists/counsellors from different levels have been minimal and incidental, leading to a lack of synchronisation and discontinuity in services provided to clients. Special-needs persons represent the most disadvantaged group. With some exceptions, they are regarded mainly as medical cases. Students with minor or moderate levels of deficiencies generally remain in general education.

References

Anuarul Statistic al României–2005. (2006). Bucureşti: Amco.

Băban, A. (Ed.). (2001). *Consiliere educaţională* [Educational counselling]. Cluj Napoca: Ardealul.

Bucur, Gh. E., & Popescu, O. (Eds.). (1999). *Educaţie pentru sănătate în şcoli* [Education for health in schools]. Bucharest: Fiat Lux.

Jigău, M. (2001). *Consilierea carierei* [Career counselling]. Bucharest: Sigma.

Jigău, M. (2003). *Consilierea carierei la adulţi* [Career counselling for adults]. Bucharest: Afir.

Manolache, I. (1997). *Învăţare şi handicap* [Learning and handicap]. Bucharest: Licorn.

Radu, Gh. (1999). *Psihopedagogia dezvoltării copilului cu handicap* [Psychopedagogy for the development of pupils with disabilities]. Bucharest: Didactical and Pedagogical Publishing.

Salade, D., & Drăgan, I. (1998). *Ghidul învăţământului vocaţional* [School and vocational guidance]. Bucharest: Paco.

Tomşa, Gh. (1999). *Consiliere şcolară* [Counselling and guidance in school]. Bucharest: Viaţa Românească.

Verza, E., & Păun, E. (1998). *Educaţia integrată pentru copii cu handicap* [Integrated education of disabled children]. Bucharest: Didactical and Pedagogical Publishing.

33

Psychology in Education in the Russian Federation

Sergei B. Malykh

Daria A. Kutuzova

Svetlana V. Alyokhina

Context of Psychology in Education

The Russian Federation occupies the larger part of Eastern Europe and northern Asia. Covering over 17 million square kilometers, the Russian Federation is the largest country in the world. In the south and east, Russia borders on China, Mongolia, Korea, Kazakhstan, Georgia, and Azerbaijan. In the west, it borders on Norway, Finland, the Baltic States, Byelorussia, and Ukraine. The country is also bordered by three oceans: the Pacific, Arctic, and Atlantic. The Russian Federation consists of 21 autonomous republics, 49 regions, six territories, 10 autonomous areas, and one autonomous region. The Russian Federation is a multicultural country, with 160 national and ethnic groups. Russians compose about 80% of the population. Women (77.6 million) outnumber men (67.6 million). The official state language is Russian. Each autonomous republic is entitled to have its native language as the second state language. Among those who express interest in a religion, most Slavic believers are Russian Orthodox and most non-Slavic are Sunni Muslims.

The Russian Federation population is 144,526,000. The urban population (76%) is larger than the rural population (24%). The population is distributed unevenly, with 58 persons per square kilometer in Central Russia and 1 person per square kilometer in remote far east regions. Most of the population (80%) is concentrated in the European and Ural regions. Almost all (99.6%) of the adult population is literate. Despite its enormous territory, abundance of natural resources (especially fossil fuels), a well-developed industrial infrastructure, and high level of education, the contribution of the Russian Federation to the world's economy is small (1.36% in 1997, 1.04% in 2003), and the country ranks 60th in quality of life. The gross domestic product in 2004 was US$1.408 trillion, US$9,800 per capita. About 70% to 80% of the population composes the poorest stratum—those able to provide only for basic foods, clothing, and apartment rent. The economy has been in a state of transition from a controlled economy to a more free market economy following its change of political system in 1985 to 1991. The economy is dominated by heavy industry, especially metallurgy, chemistry, machinery construction, and power engineering. The timber industry is well developed. The country possesses the world's largest timber and natural gas resources, and its oil resources rank second.

Children age 17 and younger number about 26,015,000. The student population is about 16,000,000, among whom approximately 68% are in urban areas. Births are declining. Thus, in 2010, the student population is projected to be 36% lower than it was in 1995. The structure of the Russian educational system is hierarchical and consists of the following levels: kindergarten (noncompulsory, from ages 3 to 6 or 7; 94% of eligible children attend), primary general education (compulsory, free, guaranteed by the Russian constitution; from ages 6 or 7 to 9; 99% attend), basic general education (compulsory, free, guaranteed by the Russian constitution; ages 10–15; 91% attend); and complete general education (noncompulsory, ages 16–17; 70% attend). Those who are ages 15 to 17 may enter professional training colleges for a 3-year program. Individuals can enter a university immediately after completing general education classes as well as after professional training colleges.

Kindergartens and later schooling largely are public but may be private, with 98% of preschool children and 99% of primary and high school students attending public schools. Class size averages 25 in primary schools and 28 in high schools. The student-teacher ratio is 17 to 1 (United Nations Educational, Scientific and Cultural Organization, 2004). Systems that provide supplemental education (e.g., clubs for arts education, crafts, sports) have been deteriorating since the disintegration of the USSR (Union of Soviet Socialist Republics); the number of such clubs is decreasing, whereas those left are supported with less money, thus making supplemental education facilities less accessible to children.

A system providing special education exists at all education levels and serves about 3% of the total student population. Approximately 614,000 students with special educational needs are served in special schools and/or boarding schools. Among them, 9% are diagnosed with mild to moderate mental retardation, 69% are diagnosed with moderate to severe mental retardation, 9% have a hearing impairment, 6% have a visual impairment, 4% have a significant speech disorder, and 4% have motor system impairments. About 0.5% of children with special education needs are educated at home (Federal Agency on Education, 2005).

The Russian educational system is undergoing significant change, including the development of a system of continuous education that would ensure territorial, social, and academic mobility of the youth. This reform includes the following: (a) noncompulsory but strongly recommended preschool education, (b) profile education following general education during the two grade levels prior to university enrollment (i.e., students are sorted according to their motivation and aptitudes in reference to natural sciences, math and programming, and the humanities—subjects that often correspond with university programs), (c) developing a network of additional supplemental education establishments (e.g., clubs), and (d) national graduation examinations and transition programs to a two-level higher education system that includes both bachelor's and master's degrees. When implemented, the educational system would consist of preschool education (1 year), primary education (4 years), general education (5 years), and profile education as described in this paragraph (2 years).

Origin, History, and Current Status of Psychology in Education

The first attempt to create school psychological services, known as *pedology*, occurred after the 1917 revolution within a framework for establishing an interdisciplinary approach to provide for the physical and mental health of children. Pedologs initially attempted to use various tests and practical intervention methods with children and adolescents. However, in 1936, due to political changes, these services were frozen by a resolution of the central committee of the All-Russian Communistic Party of bolshevists, a resolution titled "About Pedological Perversions in the System of People's Commissariats for Enlightenment." The development of psychological science and practices was discontinued until the end of the 1960s, at which time the discipline of psychology and its practices were resumed. During the 1960s, schools began to reintegrate psychological services.

In the 1980s, efforts began to provide psychological services to education. At first, the activities of practicing psychologists were not systemic: They lacked rigorous organizational forms, the goals and tasks were not defined properly, and the science and technology did not exist. In 1982, the Scientific Research Institute of General and Pedagogical Psychology within the Academy of Pedagogical Sciences (currently the Psychological Institute of the Russian Academy of Education) started an experimental program of appointing school psychologists to work within the educational system. However, its fuller implementation occurred 6 years later, in 1988, when the State Committee on Education issued a decree calling for the establishment of the post of school psychologist in all educational establishments.

This decree established the legislative basis of school psychologists' work.

Beginning in the 1990s, drastic social and economic transitions in Russia led to acute psychological problems connected with ideological shift, various life changes, and the need to survive under conditions of societal and economic crises. These and other conditions increased interest in psychological science, especially in applied psychology. These years were marked by a rapid development of applied psychology. Many new posts for psychologists were established, many institutes and universities began to prepare psychologists, and an unprecedented number of high school graduates decided to major in psychology.

Similar increases in interest and growth were seen in psychological services. For example, in 1994 and 1995, two congresses of school psychologists were held. Participants expressed the view that psychological services should become an inalienable part of the state public educational system. The number of appointments for applied psychologists in education increased considerably. In May 2003, a third congress of school psychologists formally stated that the foundations of psychological services in education had been created.

This 2003 congress considered forming the Russian Federation of Psychologists in Education. The emerging association's Constituent Assembly was held in December 2003. Before being approved, the Society of Psychologists (that later became the Russian Psychological Society) reviewed various issues pertaining to the practice of psychology in schools.

The Russian Federation uses the term *psychologists in education* because their work is not confined to schools. School psychological services are regulated by the Provisions for the Practical Psychology Service of the Ministry of Education and Science of the Russian Federation (Order 636, October 22, 1999):

The Service is an organizational structure that consists of psychologists working at different regular educational establishments, specific educational establishments for children that require psychoeducational, medical and social assistance (psychological medical social centers, or PPMSC), psychological-pedagogical and medical-psychological commissions, scientific establishments, departments of universities, scientific-methodical offices and centers for education management, and other establishments providing psychological assistance to all the participants of the teaching/learning process.

The hierarchical structure for services presupposes a clear-cut differentiation of authority between administrative and professional components. In the near future, a newly created scientific methodological council will develop a strategy to further enhance psychological services. The current structure of services provided by practical psychology in education consists of three parts: (1) those engaged in practice (e.g., psychologists working at different educational establishments that require psychoeducational, medical, and social assistance, including psychological/medical/social centers for psychological emergency); (2) personnel preparation and professional development, including those who work in colleges, institutes, and universities; and (3) science and methodology, including those engaged in scientific research. The Psychological Institute of the Russian Academy of Education, the oldest psychological institute in Russia, plays a leading role in developing and providing scientific support for the psychological services in education.

Data gathered from 2002 to 2005 through surveys of psychologists working in schools in Moscow and in the Krasnoyarsk territory (which is an exemplary territory, occupying about 14% of Russia's landmass) and the city of Krasnoyarsk provide information on psychological services in education and the nature of the services. The research department of the Moscow City University of Psychology and Education and the Psychological Institute of the

Russian Academy of Education have been conducting surveys of psychological service in education (some results are presented in Malykh, Barsky, Kutuzova, & Malykhin, 2005; Rubtsov, Seliavina, & Malykh, 1999). The Moscow survey included 1,329 psychologists (66% of the total), and the Krasnoyarsk Territory and city survey included 560 psychologists (47% of the total). Data from these surveys are reported next.

The total number of psychologists in education in Russia is unknown. The final decision to employ psychologists at schools is made by school principals. The average ratios of students to psychologists (disregarding the type of educational establishment) are about 750 to 1 in Moscow and 500 to 1 in the Krasnoyarsk Territory. The average number of students per school is about 800 (ranging from 250 in rural areas to 1,500 in large cities). The average number of children attending kindergarten is about 110 per school and ranges from 80 to 150.

A psychologist often is assigned to one school and, during the school year, works with an average of 450 pupils (including group assessment). Significant numbers of students have no contact with psychological services. Although being responsible for 450 pupils may not seem burdensome in light of data from European countries and the United States, school psychologists in Moscow often complain that they have too many pupils with whom to work. The preferred psychologist-to-pupil ratio is about 1 to 300.

The following is a general portrait of psychologists in education. Most are female (95%), about 34 years old (standard deviation of 10 years), and have been a psychologist in education an average of 5 years (standard deviation of 4 years). Approximately 50% have 0 to 3 years of professional experience. The intention to leave the profession is higher for those with less experience. The average age of teachers is 40 years old. Thus, teachers tend to be older and more experienced than psychologists—conditions that are likely to influence the process of the psychologist's integration into, and acceptance by, the school staff.

The percentage of psychologists who first were trained as teachers is higher in the rural areas (76%) than in Moscow (29%). Rural area schools suffer from staff shortage. Thus, instead of hiring a graduate psychologist, school administrators are inclined to encourage a teacher to obtain additional psychological education and perform the duties of psychologists along with teaching. This combination of different professional roles leads to role conflict and occupational stress.

Psychologists working in educational systems earn an average of about US$2,500 annually (ranging from US$1,700 to US$3,700, depending on qualification, length of professional experience, and type of educational establishment). Teachers earn about US$3,500 annually. Psychologists and psychotherapists working full-time in private practice earn about US$8,700 annually. About 25% to 33% do private additional work (nonpsychological, e.g., sales) in addition to their school-based work. The second job provides income needed to help support themselves and their families. Most households are supported by wages earned by both parents. Few psychologists working at educational establishments engage in private practice in their leisure time, due, in part, to a lack of legislation for private psychological practice. For example, people are not sure whether they will be legally punished for not paying taxes on money earned from private practice. Thus, many choose not to venture into this field.

Among the survey respondents, 57% work at schools; 22% at kindergartens; 7% at the psychological medical social centers; and 14% at orphan asylums, boarding schools, special schools, education centers, and other educational establishments. According to the Education Law of the Russian Federation, Clause 55, psychologists work 36 hours per week, 18 hours on-site and 18 hours in methodical work (e.g., computing assessment data, completing logs, reading literature).

Psychologists spend the majority of their working time with children. Primary school pupils and older adolescents (ages 14–17) receive more services than do the younger adolescents (ages 10–13). The frequency of work with children of different ages at the psychological medical social centers varies depending on the region. Psychologists working in these centers in the rural areas work mainly with older adolescents in that the main issues include vocational choice, relationship troubles, and substance abuse. In contrast, those working in these centers in urban areas work mainly with preschool children, mainly on issues associated with abnormal development and school readiness.

Compared with their school-based colleagues, those working in psychological medical social centers are twice as likely to work with parents and less likely to work with teachers. Psychologists working in educational establishments work least often with administrators.

Among psychologists working at kindergartens, 83% work in one location and 17% in several locations. Among school psychologists, 88% work in one educational location and 12% in several locations. Those in psychological medical social centers work with several dozen educational establishments. Most educational establishments employ one psychologist. However, psychologists believe their work might be more effective if they could consult and collaborate with other psychologists several times a week. In the Krasnoyarsky Territory, 72% of psychologists work in urban and 28% in rural areas. Unfortunately, data on other territories within the Russian Federation are not available. The highest career achievement of a psychologist within school or kindergarten is the post of deputy headmistress and involves working with noncognitive aspects of education. Few psychologists attain this level; they are more likely to transition from school or kindergarten to a psychological medical social center or university.

Psychologists often report being dissatisfied with their work. The sources of their dissatisfaction are many: lack of collaboration with school staff, parents, and colleagues; the need to prove one's professional point of view in situations characterized by animosity; lack of defined requirements for structure and functioning of the psychological services, resulting in confusion and discrepancy between the image of profession obtained during training and the actual working conditions; role ambiguity and role conflict; lack of supervisory support; lack of power to influence the learning process and educational environment; low salary; lack of resources (e.g., time, equipment, room); inadequate self-organization and time management, especially few opportunities to model different interventions and assess their results; low self-confidence; lack of self-presentation and public relations skills; multicultural issues, including the need to work with children who do not speak Russian; and the noninclusive nature of the schooling system and society at large, thus provoking value conflict.

High numbers of psychologists, 28% to 30%, state their intentions to quit their job. The main reasons underlying the turnover intentions are, in descending order of importance, low wages, lack of necessary assessment measures, few opportunities for career growth, specific characteristics of the system and work of a particular educational establishment, role ambiguity, work overload, change of vocational preferences, lack of motivation among the school staff to collaborate with the psychologist, lack of contact with the professional community, burdensome paperwork, family circumstances (including pregnancy), and retirement age.

Infrastructure of Psychology in Education

The Russian Federation of Psychologists in Education, founded in 2003, holds annual conferences and maintains a Web site (http://www.psyinfo.ru). The interests of psychologists in education who work in the autonomous republics are served by the Ministry of Education and Science of the Russian Federation. Those who work in the autonomous regions are served by departments of education in their regions. The work of psychologists in education is regulated by the following legislation: The Education Law of the Russian Federation, edition of November 16, 1997, 144 (clauses 53, 54, 55, 56); the Provisions for Practical Psychology Service of the Ministry of Education and Science of the Russian Federation (Order 636, October 22, 1999); and the Provisions for Educational Establishments for Children in Need of Psychoeducational and Medical-Social Assistance (Decree 867 of the Government of the Russian Federation, July 31, 1998). Regulatory letters issued by the Ministry of Education and Science also impact services by prescribing psychologists' professional responsibilities in education, their salaries, and length of vacations.

Information relevant for psychologists in education may be found in the following journals and newsletters: *Voprosy Psikhologii* (Russian Psychological Enquiry), *Shkol'ny Psikholog* (School Psychologist Newsletter), *Vestnik Prakticheskoy Psikhologii Obrazovaniya* (Bulletin of Practical Psychology of Education), *Detsky Praktichesky Psikholog* (Child Practical Psychologist), *Psikhologiya Segodnia* (Psychology Today), *Vestnik Psikhosocialnoy i Korrektsionno-Reabilitatsionnoy Raboty* (Bulletin of Psychosocial Work and Rehabilitation), *Shkola Zdorov'ya* (School Health), *Psikhologicheskaya Nauka i Obrazovanie* (Psychological Science and Education), *Pedologiya: Novy Vek* (Pedology in the Twenty-first Century).

Several textbooks and handbooks were published during the past few years (e.g., Dubrovina et al., 2004; Ovcharova, 2003; Pakhal'yan, 2003; Semago & Semago, 2005).

Professional Preparation of Psychologists in Education

University programs in psychology prepare persons for applied practice or for scholarship (i.e., research and science). Those that emphasize applied practice are discussed first and most completely. Training that prepares those interested in working as a *school psychologist* or *psychologist in the educational system* does not exist as such. Psychologists are prepared in psychology faculties and departments at various universities and receive diplomas in one or more of the following specialties: 030300.62 Psychology (bachelor's degree), 030300.68 (master's degree), 030301.65 Psychologist/Psychology Teacher, 030302 Clinical Psychologist/Clinical Psychology Teacher, 050703 Teacher of Preschool Education and Psychology, 050706 Pedadogics and Psychology, and 050716 Special Psychology. There are 171 state and 175 private universities that prepare psychologists (Ministry of Education and Science of the Russian Federation, 2005). Young persons graduating from the 9th or 11th grades (i.e., ages 15–17) may enter a teachers college. Those who graduate from high school or a teachers college may enter a psychology or teaching faculty or department of some university. People entering a university from high school receive a 5-year program and thus normally graduate between ages 22 and 24 with the specialist degree. Alternatively, they may study 4 years to receive a bachelor's degree and then study 2 additional years to obtain the master's degree. Teaching experience is not required. Although no internship is provided, students engage in about 300 hours of supervised practical work during their education.

Many psychologists who work in the educational system majored in developmental, educational (pedagogical), and/or clinical psychology. Those specializing in developmental psychology generally take the following courses: problems of modern developmental psychology, active methods of vocational guidance, assessment and intervention in cases of disturbed parent-child relationships, assessment and intervention in cases of child abnormal cognitive development, intervention in cases of child abnormal development, methods of organization of personality, growth groups for adolescents, neuropsychological foundations for special education, psychological readiness to enter school, psychological foundations for optimization of learning and professional performance, psychological foundations for preschool developmental education, developmental psychology and design of educational programs, age-related consultation and counseling, psychology of abnormal development, psychology of family relationships, development and education of gifted children, and risk factors in child development.

Those specializing in pedagogical psychology generally take the following courses: school readiness and learning difficulties during the first school year; assessment and enhancement of motivation to learn; assessment and enhancement of learning skills; intelligence assessment basics; innovative practices in Russian pedagogical psychology; design, assessment, and redesign of the process of learning; psychological problems of worldview and attitude assessment and formation; and technical means to enhance teaching and learning.

Those specializing in clinical psychology generally take the following courses: psychopathology, neuropsychology, psychiatry, psychosomatic disorders, psychology of abnormal development, projective methods in clinical assessment, psychology of deviant behavior, psychopharmacology, personality disorders, prevention of substance abuse, basic theories and methods of psychotherapy, and methods of assessing normal and abnormal development. Most courses are based on the cultural-historical theory of Vygotsky, Luria, the activity theory by Leont'yev, and its application to developmental and pedagogical psychology, elaborated by Zaporozhets, El'konin, and Gal'perin.

A scientific degree is not required to work in the educational system. Only about 3% of those working in Moscow obtained the degree of Candidate of Sciences. Several people obtained the degree of Doctor of Sciences. None who work in the Krasnoyarsk Territory has a degree that prepares them as researchers and scholars in psychology.

The program in second higher education in psychology was designed for those who have a higher education degree in some other specialty and want to work as psychologists. These mainly are women in their 30s. This program extends over approximately 3 years and results in a specialist degree.

Opportunities to obtain advanced training in psychotherapeutic education also are available. This education occurs in nonuniversity settings and is obtained at the student's expense. Training includes individual and group psychotherapy and other forms of intervention and leads to qualifications as a psychotherapist or a counselor. Some schools and kindergartens do not distinguish between a university diploma in psychology and a psychotherapeutic certificate.

The highest level of education obtained by psychologists varies, with 43% receiving a first higher psychological education (university level, immediately after school), 14% receiving a second higher psychological education (university level, after graduating from some other specialty), 6% completing a 1- or 2-year program to requalify teachers or medical workers, 3% graduating from short-term programs (less than a year), and the remainder having more than one form of psychological training.

Regional differences exist in the percentage of those who received their first higher psychological education. For example, Krasnoyarsk City has the highest percentage (63%), whereas the rural areas have the lowest percentage (30%). The percentage of those with undergraduate degrees who work at educational establishments is higher in Moscow (13% for first higher psychological education and 3% for second higher psychological education) and lower in Krasnoyarsk city (3% for first higher psychological education students) and small towns of the Krasnoyarsk Territory (less than 1% for second higher psychological education students). As expected, psychologists who graduated from 1- or 2-year or even shorter programs are more likely to work in rural areas and small towns. Many psychologists working in rural areas and small towns obtain their education in psychology from nonuniversity sources (short-term courses). This method to obtain practical skills

and knowledge is not efficient. People resort to this kind of education because it is significantly less expensive than an intramural education when one considers travel and accommodation expenses.

Roles, Functions, and Responsibilities of Psychologists in Education

The most frequent professional services offered by psychologists at different types of educational establishments include the following: conflict resolution and mediation, individual child assessment, group assessment, psychological assessment of adults, individual or group rehabilitation and developmental games and exercises with children, consultation with children and adults, continuous professional education, reflection on and analysis of the psychologist's own work, psychologist supervision or peer group supervision, teamwork with teachers and parents (i.e., action planning systems), lectures on psychology for teachers and parents, paperwork, and scientific research.

The psychologists' work is dominated by accountability (which has little impact on professional motivation and therefore is rendered almost meaningless by psychologists) and individual intervention. Primary prevention and systems-level interventions within Russian society are underdeveloped. Differences in work assignments typically are due to age difference of children being served at various educational establishments. Differences also exist in rural and urban areas and between towns and the capital city. For example, those who work in rural areas and small towns are more involved with addictions, as these are locations in which teenage alcoholism is quite widespread, whereas those who work in large cities are more likely to be involved in work involving gifted children. More than 33% of the respondents have had to fulfill duties not connected directly with their professional work, 33% have substituted for teachers who are absent, 11% have served as class tutors, and 9% have served on student exam committees.

The six most frequent assignments for psychologists working at kindergartens involve speech disorders/difficulties, family problems, conflict with peers, lack of friends, behavior problems/lack of discipline, and anxiety and depression. The most frequent assignments for psychologists working at schools relate to learning disabilities/difficulties, behavior problems/lack of discipline, family problems, lack of motivation to learn, and lack of understanding of communication norms (e.g., autistic tendencies). The six most frequent assignments for psychologists working at the psychological social medical centers include family problems, learning disabilities/difficulties, conflict with peers, lack of friends, lack of motivation to learn, and anxiety and depression.

Psychologists who work in schools mainly work with students who display learning difficulties and behavior problems. Psychologists who work at psychological medical social centers mainly work with dysfunctional families and severe disability cases. Thus, their work usually requires higher qualification and/or specialization in clinical psychology or other specializations in psychology. The development and use of individual education plans is not common and usually is related to children with mental retardation or health problems.

The survey of assessment measures used with children and youth has identified 64 that are somewhat widespread, of which 33 were developed within other countries, imported for use, and typically lack Russian norms. As a result, many rely on projective methods. The most commonly used measures include the following tests. Those that assess intelligence include the Raven Progressive Matrices, Wechsler Intelligence Scale for Children, School Intelligence Development Test, Group Intelligence Test, and the Semago Assessment Kit. Projective tests include the Draw-Your-Family Test, Draw-A-Person Test, and the Children's Apperception Test.

Current Issues Impacting Psychology in Education

Issues that require immediate attention were summarized in the Program of Development of the Applied Psychological Services in Education, a statement prepared for presentation at the Third Congress of Psychologists in Education (held in May, 2003) and approved by the Ministry of Education of the Russian Federation. Key features of this document are summarized below.

Legislation. Regulations that contribute to a shared understanding of the psychologist's roles, functions, and responsibilities among various participants of the teaching/learning process and the community are needed. Their absence leads to role ambiguity, role conflict, and work overload for psychologists. A system of licensure, official evaluation of professional performance, and definitions of roles and functions should be developed.

Provision of assessment measures and instruments. Assessment measures and other scientific instruments that support practice are needed. Standardization of assessment measures and development of the necessary minimum assessment kit for psychologists in education is highly recommended. Models of psychologists' work with different educational strata are necessary.

Financial and technical support. Additional financial and technical support for the applied psychological services in education is needed.

Information. The dissemination of information relevant to building real and virtual professional communities is needed (e.g., informing students and psychologists about existing Web sites, journals, conferences, peer supervision groups, etc.). This goal is being partially achieved by the newly founded Federation and monitoring programs. The building of a peer and/or expert supervision system to provide support for young professionals entering the field is most urgently needed in order to maintain high standards for service.

Interdisciplinary and international collaboration. Interdisciplinary and international collaboration is necessary to enable psychologists to provide more services indirectly, to integrate themselves into the community, and to intervene at the levels of individuals, agencies, and the society.

References

Dubrovina, I. V., et al. (2004). *Prakticheskaya psikhologiya obrazovaniya* [Practical psychology of education]. Saint Petersburg: Piter.

Federal Agency on Education. (2005). *Education of Russia–2004.* Moscow: Author.

Malykh, S. B., Barsky P. I., Kutuzova, D. A., & Malykhin, P. A. (2005). School psychological services in Moscow. *School Psychology International, 26*(3), 259–274.

Ovcharova, R. V. (2003). *Prakticheskaya psikhologiya obrazovaniya* [Practical psychology of education]. Moscow: Academia.

Pakhal'yan, V. E. (2003). *Psykhoprofilaktika v prakticheskoy psikhologii obrazovaniya* [Preventive work in practical psychology of education]. Moscow: Per Se.

Rubtsov, V. V., Seliavina, L. K., & Malykh, S. B. (1999). Sistema psikhologicheskoy podderzhki obrazovaniya [The system of psychological support for education]. *Psikhologicheskaya Nauka i Obrazovaniye, 2,* 5–32.

Semago, M. M., & Semago, N. Y. (2005). *Organizatsiya i soderzhaniye deyatel'nosti psikhologa spetsial'nogo obrazovaniya* [Organization and content of activity of psychologists working in the special education system]. Moscow: Arkti.

United Nations Educational, Scientific and Cultural Organization. (2004). *Education for all: The imperative of quality.* Paris: Author.

34

Professional Educational Psychology in Scotland

Keith J. Topping

Elaine Smith

Wilma Barrow

Elizabeth Hannah

Claire Kerr

Context of Educational Psychology

Located on the northwestern rim of Europe, Scotland is one of four countries that make up Great Britain (along with England, Wales, and Northern Ireland). Scotland forms the northern part of the main island. Surrounded on three sides by sea, with the Atlantic Ocean to the north and west and the North Sea to the east, Scotland shares one land border, 60 miles long, with England to the south. Scotland covers an area of 31,500 square miles, is 274 miles long from north to south, and varies in breadth between

24 and 154 miles. Two thirds of the main land-mass consists of mountains and high plateaus. Scotland also has 790 islands, 130 of which are inhabited. Edinburgh is the capital, and Glasgow is the largest city.

The Scots originally were Celtic, Anglo-Saxon, Germanic, and Norse peoples. Today, Scotland has a wide mix of ethnic, linguistic, and cultural groups, including Jewish, Italian, Chinese, and Afro-Caribbean people and those from the Indian subcontinent. Until 1707, Scotland was an independent country. In 1603, King James VI of Scotland succeeded to the throne of England, thereby uniting the two

339

countries. In 1707, the union was formalized, and the Scottish Parliament dissolved. In 1997, the Scots voted in favor of devolution, and in May 1999, the Scottish Parliament was reconvened in Edinburgh. The Scottish Parliament has powers to decide matters relevant to Scotland, including education and law. The Westminster Parliament in London remains responsible for macroeconomic policy, defense, and foreign affairs. Until 1707, Scots was the official language of Scotland. However, the combined parliament decreed that English would be the official language. Thus, the use of Scots declined. Today, most Scots speak English. Around 58,500 Scots also speak Gaelic, a Celtic language similar to Irish, mainly in the north of the country and in the Western Isles.

The population of Scotland is just over 5 million, with 18% ages 16 and under, and 19% over 60. The overall population density is much lower than England's, and most of the population is concentrated in cities. Whilst traditional heavy manufacturing industries, fishing, and agriculture have declined, other areas have seen growth, including tourism, retailing, beer and whisky production, public and service sectors, and high technology industries. Employment is at its highest level in many years. Average earnings are currently £436 (US$765) per week. The gross domestic product per capita is £16,400, or US$28,730 (*Gateway to Scotland*, 2005).

Number of School-Age Children and Number of Students

Preschool children. As of January 2004, the number of children in preschool programs was 160,000, representing 100% of 4-year-olds, 85% of 3-year-olds, 50% of 2-year-olds, 25% of 1-year-olds, and 13% of those under 1 year (Scottish Executive, 2004a).

School-age children. As of September 2004, 722,359 students were enrolled in local authority (school district) schools: 397,853 were in primary (elementary) schools, 317,494 in secondary (high) schools, and 7,400 in special schools. A further 30,000 were enrolled in private fee-paying schools (confusingly called "public" schools in the United Kingdom). In addition, 545 children were being educated at home, due to parental choice, and 1,300 were receiving education at home or in hospital due to ill health or other circumstances. The population is declining, due mainly to falling birth rates. By 2014, the school-age population is projected to decrease by 14% (Scottish Executive, 2004b).

Number of students with special needs. As of September 2004, approximately 33,000 students were identified as having special educational needs (i.e., 4% of the school population): 14,500 were in secondary schools, 11,000 in primary schools, and 7,400 in special schools. More students are expected to be mainstreamed in the future (Scottish Executive, 2000, 2005).

Tertiary education. Half of all school-leavers go on to further education college (specializing in vocational training) or higher education (i.e., university). More females than males (3:2) enter tertiary education, with males more likely to become employed immediately (3:2). Further education colleges currently have more than 618,000 students enrolled in full- or part-time courses, with 90,000 in vocational training and the remainder in nonvocational courses. There are 208,000 students enrolled in Scottish universities, approximately 50,000 of whom come from outside Scotland. A further 28,000 Scots attend universities in other parts of Britain. More than 50% of Scots between 18 and 30 years have a qualification from a university or are studying for one. More than a quarter of Scotland's working population (18–64 years) has attended a university (Scottish Executive, 2004c).

Scotland's Education System

Scotland's education system always has been separate and different from that of England, Wales, and Northern Ireland. Since 1999, the first minister for Scotland and his ministers for education and enterprise and lifelong learning have been responsible for education. The Scottish Executive Education Department and the Scottish Executive Enterprise and Lifelong Learning Department are the corresponding administrative bodies. English is the main language of instruction, although Gaelic-medium education is used in some schools (Paterson, 1999).

Preschool education. Preschool education from age 3 through 5 is optional. A free nursery education is available in local authority, private, and voluntary centers for all children through the 2 years before they start primary (elementary) school (by age 5 and legally required after they reach their 5th birthday). A preschool curriculum framework guides development of key aspects of children's development.

Compulsory full-time education. Between ages 5 and 16, children attend school for a minimum of 11 years. Children must begin primary education by the entry date after their 5th birthday. There is only one entry date each year in August. Thus, some children start school at age 4. Children move on to secondary school after 7 years in primary school (school years are named P1 through P7) and receive a minimum of 4 years in secondary education (i.e., S1 through S4), until the leaving date nearest to their 16th birthday. About 75% of Scottish students remain at school for S5 and S6 and leave when they are 17 or 18. Education is free in state schools. On average, 4% of the school-age population attends fee-paying private schools, with a higher percentage attending private schools at secondary than primary levels.

Although children usually attend their local school, parents may request another school of their choice. This practice is more common in cities than in rural areas. The majority (85%) of Scotland's state schools are nondenominational (e.g., not religiously supported) schools. Most denominational schools are Roman Catholic. As

of September 2004, there were 2,217 primary schools, 386 secondary schools, and 186 special schools/units. Typically the maximum class size was 30 in P1 though P3 classes and 33 in P4 through P7 classes. Classes composed of different ages or years generally have 25 students. By 2007, the Scottish Executive Education Department plans to reduce the class size to 25 in P1 through P3 classes and to 20 in math and English classes in S1 through S2 (Scottish Executive, 2004b).

Post-compulsory education (for ages 16–18). Post-compulsory education is provided in secondary schools and in further education (vocational) colleges. Vocational training also is provided by independent trainers and on-site employers.

Tertiary education. Vocational further education, provided by more than 40 independent colleges, is funded through the Scottish Funding Council. Most students attend part-time.

Higher education takes place in 20 universities that offer undergraduate and postgraduate degrees. Study is usually full-time. Universities are funded by the Scottish Funding Council. Study through the Open University in Scotland also is possible. It currently offers distance learning courses to 15,000 students.

Origin, History, and Current Status of Educational Psychology

The terms *educational psychology* and *educational psychologist* (not *school psychology* and *school psychologist*) are commonly used in the United Kingdom. Professional educational psychology is the applied service-delivery form of academic educational psychology.

The statutory functions of educational psychology services in Scotland are unique in that they are broader than in many countries (MacKay, 1996, 1999). The functions are set out in the 1980 Education (Scotland) Act:

It shall be the duty of every education authority to provide for their area a psychological service, and the functions of that service shall include: (a) the study of children with special educational needs, (b) the giving of advice to parents and teachers as to appropriate methods of education for such children, (c) in suitable cases, provision for special educational needs of such children, and (d) the giving of advice to a local authority within the meaning of the Social Work (Scotland) Act 1968 regarding the assessment of the needs of any child for the purposes of any of the provision of that or any other enactment. (quoted in MacKay, 1999, p. 842)

The major difference between the duties of Scottish educational psychologists and those in England and Wales is that these duties are all mandatory, not discretionary. Educational psychologists in England and Wales often carry out a broad range of tasks, but the duties required by law are narrow and limited to the assessment of children and young people in relation to special educational needs. In Scotland, the work of educational psychologists extends to children from birth through age 19 and may extend to age 24. Thus, educational psychology practices are not restricted to school-based services.

History

In Scotland, educational psychology is rooted in the study of individual differences and the child guidance movement. Psychology first was offered as a subject in universities at the end of the 19th century. At that time, Francis Galton, who was interested in the scientific study of children, was researching individual differences, and he invited parents and teachers to bring their difficult-to-manage children for assessment and advice on treatment. In 1913, Cyril Burt, who shared Galton's interest in individual differences and the hereditary nature of intelligence, became the first professional educational psychologist in

Britain after being appointed to London County Council. He began using psychometrics to assess and possibly categorize children.

The child guidance movement started in Scotland in the 1920s (McKnight, 1978) with the appointment of a child psychologist to Jordanhill College and Glasgow City. He was responsible for training teachers to work with those with mental handicaps and as a psychological adviser to schools. Educational clinics were established by bachelor's-level psychologists in both Edinburgh and Glasgow universities to offer advice and support to teachers and parents on the management of children. These were the first child guidance clinics, although the first to be so called was the independent Notre Dame Child Guidance Clinic, established in Glasgow in 1931; it still provides services. These clinics relied on the services provided by a psychiatrist, educational psychologist, and social worker. Their work focuses mainly on emotional and behavioral difficulties (MacKay, 1999).

Legislative Influences

In 1937, Glasgow city established the first local authority child guidance service. Several other authorities followed. The Education (Scotland) Act (Scottish Office Education Department, 1980) empowered authorities to provide child guidance services with a range of functions, including determining which children required special educational treatment. Their functions became mandatory in the Education (Scotland) Act of 1969, when the terminology was changed from *special educational treatment* to *special education*. In 1980 and 1981, additional education legislation introduced the concept of *special educational needs*, thereby abolishing handicap categories, and introduced the *record of needs* (official individual educational plan) for children and young people with pronounced, specific, or complex special educational needs of a long-term nature. The role of the educational psychologist was extended to assessor and coordinator of this process.

In 1986, legislation renamed child guidance services as psychological services. Today, each of the 32 local authorities in Scotland has its own services. Some are known as educational psychology services, others as psychological services (but none as school psychology services). In 1995, the Children (Scotland) Act (Scottish Office, 1995) further defined the work of educational psychologists by extending the rights of children to have their views considered when decisions are being made about their care and education. More recently, the Standards in Scotland's Schools Act (Scottish Executive, 2000) espoused a "presumption of mainstreaming for all children" to promote social inclusion and raise educational attainment, thus highlighting areas where educational psychologists could make further contributions. The Education (Additional Support for Learning) (Scotland) Act (2004), implemented in 2005, supersedes much of the 1980–1981 legislation. It replaces the term *special educational needs* and the Record of Needs and introduces the concept of "additional support needs." This embraces a much larger and broader population of children and young people and requires different procedures and documentation.

The Beattie Report (Scottish Executive, 1999) reviewed the range of needs amongst young people requiring additional support to make the transition to post-school education and training or employment. It recommended the development of a post-school educational psychology service for ages 16 through 24, which would complement the assessment and advice provided by colleges and training providers, contribute to contextual assessment which is solution-focused and consistent with inclusiveness, support the transition process, contribute to strategic developments at the regional or national level, and improve the understanding, skills, and effectiveness of service providers through consultation, training, and action research.

Since 2004, 12 educational psychologists have been providing post-school psychological services as described above. Their effectiveness is being evaluated, and recommendations about the future of these services will be made in 2006. The Currie Report (Scottish Executive, 2002) also had a major influence on educational psychologists' services. It reviewed the provision of their services in Scotland and made a number of recommendations, including those detailed in later sections of this chapter.

Educational Psychology Service Delivery

Considerable geographical differences exist within Scotland. Thus, various models of service delivery can be found. The most common is the area model wherein an educational psychologist serves a general group of educational establishments and provides all needed services. Others use a sector model in which a psychologist or team of psychologists serves a particular sector (e.g., preschool, primary, secondary, or special provision). Some educational psychologists also may be responsible for work with a particular disability (e.g., hearing impairment). In a third model, the referral model, educational psychologists work with individual referrals as they arise. This model usually operates where staffing or geography does not lend itself to providing a school-based service (Scottish Executive, 2002).

The Association of Scottish Principal Educational Psychologists audits the profession in Scotland. (Association of Scottish Principal Educational Psychologists, 2005a). At the time of writing, the total number of established posts was 427.2 full-time equivalents, including 65.5 principal posts, 92.4 senior posts, 254.9 main grade posts, and 14.4 additional posts; minus 46.7 that were unfilled. The age profile of the educational psychologist is weighted toward the older end; 55% are over age 50 and another 22% are between 40 and 49. The majority of younger educational psychologists are female and thus more likely to take career breaks to meet family needs. A demographic time bomb is evident. Among undergraduate students, 70% of psychology students are female, and unsurprisingly, 65% of educational psychologists are female. However, more males than females occupy principal post positions (34:29.8), slightly more females than males are in senior post positions, (46.1:43.8), and many more females than males are in main grade positions (162:48.2). Educational psychologists' salaries range from £34,113 (US$59,900) for newly qualified persons in their first year of practice to £55,713 (US$97,836). This is similar to other local authority education officers and managers. Some educational psychologists work in private practice on a self-employed basis and can earn more.

Infrastructure of Educational Psychology

The main representative body for psychologists in the United Kingdom is the British Psychological Society. Founded in 1901, it received its Royal Charter in 1965 when it was "charged with national responsibility for the development, promotion and application of psychology for the public good" (British Psychological Society, 2005b). The Scottish Branch, one of eight regional groups within the British Psychological Society, serves all members in Scotland. In 2001, a Glasgow British Psychological Society office was opened. There is recognition that Scotland has a context distinct from the rest of the United Kingdom, with its own parliament, legislation, and public policy. The Scottish Division of Educational Psychology, one of 10 Divisions within the British Psychological Society, serves the interests of educational psychologists in Scotland. It promotes educational psychology through dissemination of information, maintenance of professional standards, postgraduate training, and monitoring induction of probationer psychologists.

Powell (2005) provides an overview of the history of regulation of psychologists in the United Kingdom. In 1987, the Royal Charter was amended, allowing for the establishment of a voluntary register of chartered psychologists. Although the British Psychological Society considered and rejected proposals for statutory regulation by the Health Professions Council, Powell notes that the Society is not opposed in principle to regulation and has developed a range of self-regulation procedures. These include procedures for admission to a register, fitness to practice and professional conduct procedures, and requirements for continuing professional development. However, a major drawback of the current system is its voluntary nature. Psychologists are not required to register. A psychologist who is removed from the register may still practice.

The generic title "Chartered Psychologist" is used by psychologists who are registered. Legitimate use of the term *Chartered Educational Psychologist* requires the individual to be a member of an Educational Psychology Division in one of the four United Kingdom regions. Educational psychologists are usually employed by education authorities that stipulate that they should have a postgraduate qualification in educational psychology (currently a 2-year full-time program at a master's-degree level in Scotland) and be eligible for chartered status with the British Psychological Society. Educational psychologists are required to follow the British Psychological Society professional Code of Conduct (1985) and the British Psychological Society Ethical Principles for Conducting Research With Human Participants (1992).

The Education (Additional Support for Learning) (Scotland) Act 2004, enacted in November 2005, had major implications for special education services and the practice of educational psychology in Scotland. The term *additional support needs* replaced the term *special educational needs. Additional support needs,* a broader term, refers to any young person who, for whatever reason, requires additional support for learning. Possible barriers to learning include physical, social, emotional, family, and care circumstances. The Act imposes duties on education authorities to establish systems to identify and meet the additional support needs of young people. It imposes duties on other agencies (e.g., social work services and health boards) to work with education authorities.

The majority of young people with additional support needs will have individualized educational programs. For the minority of "children or young people who have enduring, complex or multiple barriers to learning and require a range of support from different services outwith *[i.e., outside or beyond]* education" (Education [Additional Support for Learning] [Scotland] Act, 2004, p. 24, italics added), *Coordinated Support Plans* will be developed. The Act extends the rights of parents of young people with additional support needs for whom a Coordinated Support Plan is required. Those ages 16 and over have the same rights as their parents. Every education authority has a duty to provide a free independent mediation service for parents of young people with additional support needs. Independent tribunals hear formal appeals relating to Coordinated Support Plans. The Scottish Division of Educational Psychology (2005a) welcomed the new Act but raised questions pertaining to implementation. The Division proposes that assessment for additional support needs to be embedded in a staged process coordinated by school personnel and that the Coordinated Support Plan incorporate available learning and care plans, thereby improving uniformity of practice across the 32 authorities.

The main professional journals read by educational psychologists are *The British Journal of Educational Psychology* (published by the British Psychological Society), *Educational Psychology in Practice* (Carfax Publishing), *Educational and Child Psychology* (produced by the Division of Educational and Child Psychology and published by the British Psychological Society), *Educational Psychology in Scotland* (produced by the Scottish Division of Educational Psychology and published by the British Psychological Society), *The Psychologist* (published by the British Psychological Society), and *Debate* (produced by the Division of Educational and Child Psychology and published by the British Psychological Society).

Preparation of Educational Psychologists

Two full-time 2-year professional training programs prepare educational psychologists (i.e., certify their fitness to practice) at the universities of Dundee and Strathclyde. Both programs are accredited by the British Psychological Society and are delivered in partnership with Scottish local authority psychological services, which provide practical placements. These programs admit and graduate in alternate years. Minimum requirements for entry are an undergraduate honors degree in psychology which meets the criteria for the Graduate Basis for Registration as defined by the British Psychological Society, at least 2 years experience working with children and young people, and high competence in the English language.

Training is firmly rooted within study of the discipline of psychology. Effective application of this to educational issues at child, class, family, school, community, school district, and national levels is necessary for competent practice. Training is underpinned by the scientist-practitioner and reflective-practitioner models. Practitioners are encouraged to be critical, self-aware, and reflective in their practices. The British Psychological Society Code of Conduct and Ethical Principles (British Psychological Society, 1985, 1992) also inform training. A philosophy emphasizing equality of opportunity and the celebration of human diversity underpins a collaborative problem-solving approach.

The two graduate programs integrate academic study, practice-based learning, and research components, and are delivered at a postgraduate master's level. The curriculum promotes the development of attitudes, skills, and knowledge in relation to (a) normal and exceptional child development, (b) assessment and intervention methods, both at individual and systemic levels, (c) the range of contexts and systems within which children and young people function, (d) research and evaluation methodologies, and (e) transferable andinterpersonal skills. Although a range of theories is introduced, social-interactive, ecological, organizational, and systemic theories predominate.

Local educational psychology services provide supervised practice placements for students. The weekly pattern involves 2 days of academic work at the university, 2 days of practical placement, and 1 day of independent study. Practice learning is supplemented through additional full-time but short-term placements in psychological services. These programs lead to professional qualification as an educational psychologist with a master's degree in educational psychology. They also lead to eligibility for registration as a chartered psychologist after a probationary year of supervised practice in employment. Currently, 27 trainees are in the Dundee program (www.dundee .ac.uk/fedsoc/mscedpsy/), and 24 are in the Strathclyde program. Students who will subsequently work in Scotland receive financial support from the central Scottish government during training, covering university tuition fees and living expenses. The number of funded places and level of funding provided have increased progressively over the years in response to demographic projections of an aging profession, the extension of services to age 24, and recognition of the importance of the work done by educational psychologists.

The British Psychological Society Subject Benchmarks in Educational Psychology (2005a) delineate the required core competencies in knowledge, understanding, and professional skills for practice in the United Kingdom. The training committee of the Scottish Division of Educational Psychology monitors quality and standards of training in Scotland and has developed a core developmental curriculum for training programs (Scottish Division of Educational Psychology, 2005b). It includes the following:

1. Promote effective communication and interpersonal skills (e.g., consultation, negotiation and interpersonal skills with a range of young people and adults in a variety of contexts, and skills to manage and contribute to meetings, including delivering presentations and working collaboratively).

2. Promote development within contexts (e.g., understanding the impact of barriers to learning across a range of contexts together with knowledge and understanding of local and national policy and legislation).

3. Facilitate change via assessment and intervention (e.g., knowledge and skills in utilizing problem-solving models in a collaborative manner to facilitate change, with an understanding of a range of assessment and intervention approaches and their effectiveness mediated by contexts, and an ability to gather and synthesize needs assessment information, and plan, execute, and evaluate interventions).

4. Promote research and evaluation (e.g., skills in conducting research and in using research critically to inform practice and policy in an evidence-based manner).

5. Acknowledge frameworks for professional practice (e.g., skills and frameworks for working within and across many interfacing contexts, drawing on psychological theories, legislation, and an understanding of organizations and consultation models).

6. Prepare providers to display autonomy in the delivery of core elements.

Existing programs differ somewhat in their learning and teaching approaches and emphases. For example, the Dundee program adopts a problem-based learning approach and places more emphasis on a research thesis.

Three routes exist for optional extension of training to the doctoral level, two of which are available by distance learning and research. They offer full- or part-time study. They do not certify fitness to practice as an educational psychologist.

These include a professional doctorate in educational psychology (www.dundee.ac.uk/fedsoc/research/degrees/DEdPsy/), an accelerated or regular doctorate in educational psychology (www.dundee.ac.uk/fedsoc/research/degrees/PhDEdPsy/), and a continuation doctorate in educational psychology for those completing the 2-year master's programs in Scotland.

Roles, Functions, and Responsibilities of Educational Psychologists

Educational psychology services in Scotland constantly face new opportunities and challenges. Legislative and policy developments reflect an underlying philosophical shift from a deficit model to one of rights and entitlement, resulting in significant impacts on the role of educational psychologists. Key developments influencing their practice are listed here.

Integrated or "joined-up" working. Attempts are made to coordinate service delivery across agencies working with children and young people, enabling planning for and delivering holistic assessments and interventions whilst minimizing the intrusion in the lives of children and their families.

Promotion of social inclusion in education. Educational psychologists have a key role in supporting and developing inclusive approaches to the education of all children and young people.

Development of post-school psychological services. Educational psychologists assist vulnerable young people to make successful transitions into adulthood.

Consultation with children and young people and their parents. Educational psychologists endeavor to help these client groups participate actively in bureaucratic and legalistic decision making regarding their own futures.

Nationally, information on the roles, functions, and responsibilities of educational psychologists were set out in the Review of Provision of Educational Psychology Services in Scotland (Currie Report; Scottish Executive, 2002). Educational psychologists operate at various systemic levels: the individual and family, the school or other establishment (e.g., community family centre), and the wider local authority. Within each level, educational psychologists have five core functions—assessment, intervention, training, consultation, and research—in which they operate at the levels of child and family, school or establishment, and local authority (school district). In practice these overlap, as in the following examples: (a) consultation at the level of child or family (e.g., home visit to parents or other domestic carers) to discuss supporting a child's learning at home; (b) intervention at the level of school or establishment (e.g., contribution to an entire school peer-support initiative); and (c) research at the level of local authority or council (e.g., design, implement, and evaluate a systemwide initiative on thinking skills).

Local authority psychology services differ in the range of functions they perform and the extent to which they operate at all levels. Some services emphasize entire schoolwide or authority-wide practice. Others emphasize work with individuals and families. Differences also exist in the degree of professional autonomy afforded to individual psychologists—qualities that also contribute to variety in practice. The following section discusses how some core functions of psychologists work in practice.

Assessment

Educational psychologists are involved in assessing learning, behavior, and social/emotional functioning. Historically, psychometric approaches have been emphasized. However, ecological and social-constructivist theories now inform assessment. An increasing number of educational psychologists use approaches such as dynamic assessment (the child's learning in response to adult mediation is assessed; e.g., Lidz, 1987), play-based assessment, curriculum-based assessment, and direct observation. The Additional Support for Learning Act (2004) gives parents the right to request psychological assessment. The Association of Scottish Principal Educational Psychologists has produced assessment guidance (Association of Scottish Principal Educational Psychologists, 2005b) in an effort to encourage a more coherent approach to such requests. This allows for a variety of approaches but emphasizes that assessment should be contextualized, minimally intrusive, able to inform intervention, and take into account the views of the child or young person.

Many educational psychologists no longer use psychometric tests at all, and many more use them very sparingly in conjunction with observational and other ecologically valid and dynamic forms of assessment. Tests of achievement are more likely to be given by teachers than psychologists, and they include group and individual norm-referenced tests of reading, spelling, and mathematics (e.g., Neale Reading Test, National Foundation for Educational Research [NFER] 5–16 Group Reading Test). General intellectual tests administered individually by psychologists include the British Abilities Scale and the Wechsler Intelligence Scales. Personality tests have rarely been used. A variety of behavior and social skills checklists are used (e.g., Spence social skills checklist), but these are mostly criterion-referenced rather than standardized.

Approaches to Intervention

Some services use consultation as the main model of service delivery (Wagner, 2000), with the goal to provide the most efficient, effective, and least intrusive methods for deploying scarce psychological resources. This targets support for those closest to the child or young person. There is debate about the place of individual therapeutic intervention. Some educational psychologists would like to do more but systemic or other

administrative work pressures (the Currie Report; Scottish Executive, 2002) discourage engagement in therapeutic services. Interest in approaches that identify and build skills and strengths has grown, including solution-focused brief therapy (de Shazer, 1988), person-centered planning (Mount, 1992), and video interactive guidance (www.cpdeducation.co.uk/veroc/). These can be used at individual and systemic levels. Practice also can develop to reflect local needs or contexts (e.g., the use of eye movement desensitization and reprocessing, developed following the specialist training of a small group of psychologists in the aftermath of a critical incident in a primary school in Dunblane (O'Connor, 1999).

Research

The need to further develop the research role of educational psychologists has been well documented (MacKay, 2002). A national program funded by the Scottish central government supports groups of psychologists to conduct research relevant to the profession (e.g., on resilience; see www.ltscotland.com/pdp). A number of services now employ research assistants and operate bounded research and development projects to ensure that time and resources are protected for this purpose.

Supervision of Educational Psychologists

There is no single model of supervision. Supervision can be formal and/or informal, peer based, and/or hierarchical. Psychologists trained in particular techniques, such as video interactive guidance, receive additional specific supervision.

Current Issues Impacting Educational Psychology

Many interesting issues await future clarification. These include whether the latest round of legislation will consume more or less psychological time in procedural or administrative work concerning special needs, rather than direct service delivery; whether the specialty will move to doctoral preservice training, and if it does, whether this will this be cost-effective; and whether doctoral preparation and any increased focus on administrative tasks are in conflict.

Educational psychologists wrestle with other questions. As boundaries between children with and without special needs blur, given an inclusive mainstreamed environment, will educational psychologists be effective in promoting educational attainment and enhance social competence for all children? Major national curriculum reviews are under way in both Scotland and England. One wonders to what extent educational psychologists are contributing to these efforts. Issues include how educational psychologists can meet the challenges of delivering effective services for 16- to 24-year-olds, what are the needs of such clients, and what are the most relevant applied psychology services.

What is the unique added value of educational psychologists, and what distinguishes their services from those provided by other applied psychologists and indeed from other professions? Are they experts who can inform clients what to do (and if so on what evidential basis?), or are they postmodern facilitators of change (if so, how do they differ from other facilitators)? What assessments should be used for what purposes in the light of conflicting views on the reliability, validity, impact on practice and policy, and cost-effectiveness of different forms of assessment?

Given that educational psychologists are few in number, how should their time be allocated to the needy and less needy and to different systemic levels of service? Does equal opportunity imply offering an equal service or ensuring equal and effective outcomes from services? These and other issues merit rigorous scholarship, not merely opinionated debate.

However, there are other, more outward-looking research questions needing answers. What are the most effective ways of raising achievement and enhancing social competence for different populations and contexts? For these, to what extent are interventions linked with positive outcomes? What interventions have a durable impact under less than ideal circumstances? What evidence of cost-effectiveness is there?

Although psychological services may not be able to mount research on all or many topics, they need to be persistent and critical consumers and disseminators of research gathered systematically rather than haphazardly or selectively. However, research and other forms of scholarship are only the beginning. Knowledge transfer to many other stakeholders in ways that impact practice and policy also is needed. How to effectively apply social psychology for this purpose also merits further study.

References

Association of Scottish Principal Educational Psychologists. (2005a). *ASPEP national staffing survey.* Unpublished document.

Association of Scottish Principal Educational Psychologists. (2005b). *Educational psychology assessment in Scotland.* Unpublished document.

British Psychological Society. (1985). *Code of conduct for psychologists.* Retrieved July 13, 2005, from http://www.bps.org.uk/the-society/ethics-rules-charter-code-of-conduct/code-of-conduct/a-code-of-conduct-for-psychologists.cfm

British Psychological Society. (1992). *Ethical principles for conducting research with human participants.* Retrieved July 13, 2005, from http://www.bps.org.uk/the-society/ethics-rules-charter-code-of-conduct/code-of-conduct/ethical-principles-for-conducting-research-with-human-participants.cfm#principles

British Psychological Society. (2005a). *Benchmarks for applied psychology.* Retrieved July 5, 2005, from www.bps.org.uk

British Psychological Society. (2005b). *Welcome to the Society.* Retrieved July 6, 2005, from http://www.bps.org.uk/the-society/welcome-to-the-society/welcome-to-the-society_home.cfm

de Shazer, S. (1988). *Clues: Investigating solutions in brief therapy.* New York: Norton.

Education (Additional Support for Learning) (Scotland) Act. (2004). Retrieved July 11, 2005, from http://www.opsi.gov.uk/legislation/scotland/acts2004/20040004.htm

Gateway to Scotland. (2005). Retrieved June 24, 2005, from http://www.geo.ed.ac.uk/home/scotland/scotland.html

Lidz, C. (1987). (Ed.). *Dynamic assessment: An interactional approach to evaluating learning potential.* New York: Guilford Press.

MacKay, T. A. W. N. (1996). The statutory foundations of Scottish education psychology services. *Educational Psychology in Scotland, 3,* 3–9.

MacKay, T. A. W. N. (1999). Psychological services and their impact. In T. Bryce & W. Humes (Eds.), *Scottish education* (2nd ed.: *Post devolution*). Edinburgh: Edinburgh University Press.

MacKay, T. A. W. N. (2002). Discussion paper: The future of educational psychology. *Educational Psychology in Practice, 18*(3), 245–253.

McKnight, R. K. (1978). The development of child guidance services. In W. Dockrell, W. Dunn, & A. Milne (Eds.), *Special education in Scotland.* Edinburgh: Scottish Council for Research in Education.

Mount, B. (1992). *Person-centered planning: A source book of values, ideas, and methods to support person-centered development.* New York: Graphic Futures.

O'Connor, M. (1999). EMDR: A specific intervention for the treatment of trauma. *Critical Events for Schools PDP 1998–1999.* Retrieved July 14, 2005, from http://www.ltscotland.com/pdp

Paterson, L. (1999). Educational provision: An overview. In T. Bryce & W. Humes (Eds.), *Scottish education* (2nd ed.: *Post devolution*). Edinburgh: Edinburgh University Press.

Powell, G. (2005). President's column. *The Psychologist, 18*(7), 194.

Scottish Division of Educational Psychology. (2005a). *Response to consultation on the* Education (Additional Support for Learning) (Scotland) Act 2004–*Draft code of practice.* Retrieved July 7, 2005, from http://www.bps.org.uk/publications/consultation-papers/consultation-papers_home.cfm?action=details&paperID=191

Scottish Division of Educational Psychology. (2005b). *Core curriculum for initial training programmes in educational psychology.* Unpublished manuscript.

Scottish Executive. (1999). *Implementing inclusiveness: Realising potential* (The Beattie Report). Edinburgh: Author.

Scottish Executive. (2000). Standards in Scotland's Schools Act. Edinburgh: Author.

Scottish Executive. (2002). *Review of provision of educational psychology services in Scotland* (The Currie Report). Edinburgh: Author.

Scottish Executive. (2004a, July). *Pre-school and childcare statistics 2004* (Statistics Publication Notice Education and Training Series). Retrieved June 24, 2005, from http://www.scotland.gov.uk/stats/bulletins/00346-20.asp

Scottish Executive. (2004b, November). *Provisional pupil numbers 2004, projections and children educated outwith school 2003/04* (Statistics Publication Notice). Retrieved June 24, 2005, from http://www.scotland.gov.uk/stats/bulletins/00378-02.asp

Scottish Executive. (2004c). *Tertiary education: Education and training in Scotland National Dossier 2004 Summary.* Retrieved July 11, 2005, from http://www.scotland.gov.uk/library5/education/etsnd4s-08.asp

Scottish Executive. (2005, April 12). Pupils in Scotland 2004. *Statistical Bulletin.* Retrieved July 11, 2005, from http://www.scotland.gov.uk/Publications/2005/04/11114958/50011

Scottish Office. (1995). The Children (Scotland) Act. Edinburgh: Author.

Scottish Office Education Department. (1980). Education (Scotland) Act. Edinburgh: Author.

Wagner, P. (2000). Consultation: Developing a comprehensive approach to service delivery. *Educational Psychology in Practice, 16*(1), 9–18.

35

School Psychology in the Slovak Republic

Eva Gajdosová

Gabriela Herényiová

Context of School Psychology

Slovak people belong to the Slav tribes that settled near the Danube River in the 5th century and established their kingdom, the Empire of Samo. The Great Moravian kingdom of the 8th century marks the beginning of the first well-known Slovak state. King Svatopluk, being progressive, began to educate his people by providing religion, education, and new information in their own language, not in Latin and Greek. In addition, he invited scholars, including Cyril and Metod from Byzancia, to his kingdom. Scholars prepared the Old Slavonic script, translated the Bible and other religious books into the Old Slavonic language, and began converting the Slovaks to Christianity. Schools were established. The Great Moravian kingdom was destroyed in the early 10th century.

The Slovak people lived under foreign occupation until 1918, when the Austrian-Hungarian monarchy was dissolved. In 1918, after World War I, the independent autonomous state of Czechoslovakia was founded. In November 1989, massive demonstrations throughout Czechoslovakia brought an end to the communist rule that had begun in 1945. A non-communist government took office, and the country's new leaders began the difficult process of transforming Czechoslovakia's political system, re-creating a market economy, and reorienting foreign policy. The country's first multiparty elections were held in June 1990. During the early 1990s, Czech and Slovak government leaders began to disagree on economic and political issues. Parliamentary elections held in June 1992 brought a leftist government to power in Slovakia, and a center-right group won control in the Czech Republic. Later that year, the leaders of the two republics decided to divide Czechoslovakia into two independent nations. A new constitution of Slovakia, adopted in September 1992, went into effect when Slovakia became an independent sovereign country in January 1993. The constitution declares Slovakia to be a parliamentary democracy. The first parliamentary elections of independent Slovakia were held in 1994.

Slovakia has both a president and a prime minister. The president is elected by the people for a 5-year term and is responsible for naming a prime minister to head the government. The prime minister typically is the leader of the party with the majority of seats in parliament or the head of a coalition. The president also appoints a cabinet with the advice of the prime minister. Slovakia has a single-chamber parliament, the Slovak National Council. Each of the parliament's 150 members is elected to a 4-year term by popular vote. All citizens over the age of 18 are eligible to vote in Slovakia. Judicial authority is vested in various courts, starting with the highest courts, the Constitutional Court and the Supreme Court, and going down to those at regional and district levels.

Slovakia is divided into four regions: Bratislava, West Slovakia, Central Slovakia, and East Slovakia. The capital of the Slovak Republic, Bratislava, with 446,880 inhabitants, is the country's largest city, and is the location of most political, government, economic, education, and research institutions. Other important cities include Kosice, an industrial city with 234,840 inhabitants; Nitra, a food processing center with 89,788; Presov, known for electrical engineering, with 87,788; Banska Bystrica, a mining and manufacturing area, with 85,000; and Zilina, a business center, with 83,883 inhabitants. The gross domestic product in 2004 was US$78.89 billion, US$14,500 per capita.

The Slovak Republic lies in central Europe and shares borders with five countries: the Czech Republic, Poland, Ukraine, Hungary, and Austria. Slovakia's central position within Europe allows it to serve as a crossroads connecting the north with the south and the west with the east. The building and expansion of a transportation network have allowed Slovakia to join with important European towns and regions. Slovakia is a mountainous country with 80% of its territory 750 meters or more above sea level. The country is characterized by a variety of elevations, flora, and fauna. Some have described it as a country of highlands, given its Carpathian, Tatra, and Fatra mountains, along with the national park of Law Tatras. The Danube is its most significant river. The country has rich mineral resources and abundant thermal waters. With four seasons, January is the coldest month and July the warmest. The Slovak Republic's population of 5,336,207, of whom 52% are women, comprises various ethnic groups, including 86% Slovak, 11% Hungarian, and the remaining 3% Romany, Czech, Rumanian, Ukrainian, or German. The density is 110 inhabitants per square kilometer. Approximately 57% of the population lives in urban areas.

About 68% consider themselves Roman Catholics. Protestant churches, including the Lutheran Church, the Slovak Evangelical Church, and the Reformed Christian Church, also are common. The Orthodox and Uniate churches maintain active followings among Russians and Ukrainians in eastern Slovakia. Most of Slovakia's Jewish community was decimated during World War II. Religion plays a major role in everyday life, with 73% declaring church membership. Even when under communist control, which explicitly opposed religious practice, most Slovaks baptized their children, were married and buried according to religious traditions, and practiced their faith in other ways. Many individuals have no religious affiliation, probably resulting, in part, from 50 years of Communist party rule and its forceful fight against religious attitudes and practices.

Slovakia has established a good educational system that consists of elementary and secondary schools, together with universities. Schools are supported by the state, by churches, or privately. Children can begin school at about age 3, in the nursery schools. Primary school is attended by 650,000 children ages 6 through 15. This 9-year attendance span is intended to provide time for pupils to decide on their future careers, which are furthered through the system of different kinds of secondary schools, including the gymnasia, secondary technical schools, vocational schools, and apprentice centers. The 8-year gymnasia, schools providing general education, were introduced some years ago. Talented children generally are given an opportunity to develop their knowledge and skills by means of a demanding curriculum. On completing their secondary education, students must pass an exit examination that assesses language, additional subjects on which they elect to be tested—those with which they would like to continue—and either mathematics or foreign languages. Slovakia has 28 institutions of higher education.

The country's oldest university, Academia Istropolitana, was founded in 1465. It later became Comenius University of Bratislava. The University of Mining, created in 1735, was the first institution to specialize in mining internationally.

Slovak children are raised primarily in families that consist of a mother, father, and siblings. At about 20%, the divorce rate generally is lower than in many countries, although it is higher in large cities (e.g., Bratislava's divorce rate is 33%–50%). Slovak society has accepted international conventions that promote human rights in its constitution (No. 460/1992) as well as the Rights of the Child in the Convention on the Rights of the Child in the Slovak Republic in 1993.

Origin, History, and Current Status of School Psychology

During the 1930s, school psychology began to appear in Czechoslovak psychology. Psychologists Stejskal and Ohera (Hvozdík, 1986) proposed a concept of school psychological services that included psychodiagnostic services, the selection of primary school pupils for secondary school, work with talented and gifted children, and attention to behavior and learning problems. Unfortunately, further development of school psychology was interrupted during World War II. After that war and through the 1960s, conditions were unfavorable for psychology, including school psychology. During this socialist period, many psychological institutions were closed or abolished, and psychology was oriented only toward Soviet socialist psychology. The use of the discipline of psychology, as found in literature from the United States and Western European countries, was forbidden.

During the 1970s, after Dubcek's Spring, "socialism with the human face" began, leading to debates on the nature of school psychology services and school psychologists' work. Several educational psychologists working in universities in Bratislava and Kosice proposed concepts governing the work of school psychologists and prepared school psychologists in a 5-year program that emphasized training, mainly in the study of educational psychology plus another subject (e.g., English, biology, arts). During the 1970s, professors advocating this form of preparation conducted longitudinal research to examine the need for school psychologists to work with pupils, teachers, and parents in some primary and secondary schools in Bratislava and Kosice. This study verified the need for such services, thus initiating university training programs for school psychology. Unfortunately, in 1975, these programs were discontinued due to an unfavorable climate for such programs following the occupation of Czechoslovakia by Russian soldiers in 1968. During the late 1970s and 1980s, one could not utilize Western ideas and methods in the study and practice of psychology.

In 1989, during the Czechoslovak Velvet Revolution, the fight for freedom and democracy was successful and so ushered in a new period. Many progressive, modern, and humanistic ideas, thoughts, and conceptions started to be realized in Slovak society, politics, economy, culture, and education. The 1990s were favorable for the development of school psychology, including the preparation of young school psychologists for practice. Support for this development came from teachers, parents, and students, and later, from the Ministry of Education.

In 1991, the School Psychology Association of Czechoslovakia was established with support from the International School Psychology Association. The first members of the School Psychology Association of Czechoslovakia were university teachers from Slovak universities in Bratislava, Kosice, and Banská Bystricam, and later, from Prague and Hradec Kralove, in the Czech republic. In 1993, an International School Psychology Association colloquium was held in Banská Bystrica, a town in central Slovakia.

During this period, the potential importance of school psychological services became apparent once more. Various problems were occurring at schools (e.g., nonattendance, juvenile delinquency, academic failures, behavior and learning difficulties), and some issues (e.g., selection and services for gifted and talented pupils, creativity development of pupils, career choice guidance) could best be addressed through professional psychological services. In 1991–1992, the School Psychology Association of Czechoslovakia, at the request of the Ministry of Education, developed a new model for the work of school psychologists in schools and other school institutions based on information provided by the International School Psychology Association and the experiences of its members. The model specified the main missions and tasks of the school psychologists in schools; the vertical and horizontal structures of the school psychologist's work; the forms, methods, procedures, and approaches of this work; their services to pupils, teachers, parents, school administration, and other institutions responsible for the welfare of children and adolescents; professional and methodological guidance; descriptions of their responsibilities in light of their functions and salary; and methods to promote cooperation with school managers, teachers, and pupils (Gajdosová, 1992).

In 1992, the authors of this chapter prepared a curriculum for training school psychologists in the Department of Psychology, Philosophical Faculty, Comenius University in Bratislava. It was to begin a new era for the training of school psychologists. During these years, information on school psychologists' activities was published in conference reports, journals, and books, including university textbooks. The monographs *The School Psychologist and His or Her Entrance Into the Humanization of Our Schools* (Gajdosová, 1998a) and *The School Psychologist* (Gajdosová, 1998b) became important to efforts to advance school psychology.

The introductory parts of these two monographs present a detailed characterization of new concepts of school psychologists' work in Slovakia, including their work in identification, diagnosis, prevention, and intervention activities. Consultation with teachers and parents and cooperation of the school and the family were emphasized. The school psychologist was described as having a humanizing presence in schools, leading to improvements of the psychological well-being of pupils and teachers. Other books published in the Slovak Republic (e.g., Gajdosová & Herényiová, 2002; Hvozdík, 1999) addressed issues important to school psychology. Concepts that may guide school psychologists' activities in the schools during the first part of the 21st century are described by Rosa, Turek, and Zelina (2002).

Infrastructure of School Psychology

The 1990s can be characterized by two interlocking developments: the development of school psychology in Slovakia, namely as an independent applied psychological specialty, as well as the development of school psychologists' activities in schools, pedagogical-psychological counseling centers, children's centers, and children's homes. In 1990, the School Psychology Association of Czechoslovakia was established. Its basic goals have been to assist in the proper utilization of psychology in the context of education and training; to support communication between psychologists, teachers, counselors, special educators, and social workers attempting to improve the education and training of children and adolescents in various types of schools; to promote the utilization of school psychological services in schools; to cooperate with organizations and institutions having similar goals in their programs concerning the development of care of children and adolescents; to develop and initiate educational and developmental programs to ensure high professional standards for school psychologists; and to publish a professional journal, other professional publications, psychodiagnostic methods, congressional proceedings, and other materials from professional events.

Membership in the School Psychology Association of Czechoslovakia is open to every psychologist, including graduates of psychological studies in combination with other specialties and psychology students (albeit nonvoting). Associate members may include teachers and other professionals making use of psychological services in the schools, school establishments, and other educational institutions. The structure of this association includes provisions at local and eventually regional levels, as well as through committees, an executive committee, and the congress. The Association functionaries include a president, president-elect, past president, secretary, and two other members of the executive committee. Despite the division of Czechoslovakia into the Slovak and Czech Republics in 1993, the School Psychology Association of Czechoslovakia continued its unified activities and was becoming registered in both republics: as the association of School Psychology of the Slovak Republic and as the Association of School Psychology of the Czech Republic. Every 3 years, the presidency of the Association rotates between candidates from the

Czech or Slovak Republics. Presidents of the School Psychology Association were A. Furman (later president of the International School Psychology Association), E. Gajdosová, J. Mares, J. Zapletalova, and G. Herényiová.

The development of new concepts in school psychology has made contributions that were later used as a legislative base by the Slovak Ministry of Education. During 1991 and 1992, representatives from the Association of School Psychology, educational-psychological counseling centers, and the Ministry of Education met in an effort to resolve multiple controversial issues concerning school psychology. This collaboration led to the preparation of the Law on School Institutions (No. 279/1993). This law, approved in October 1993, allowed the employment of school psychologists as permanent employees of schools or educational-psychological counseling centers. In January 1996, regulations from the Ministry of Education (No. 43/1996) were equally significant for school psychology. These regulations described the work of school psychologists and specified their activities in relation to pupils, educators, parents, or legal representatives of pupils, and the school. The formulation of the school psychologist's work in this regulation enables psychologists to develop the scope and contents of their activities, reflecting the specific conditions of the school and their own professional and personal dispositions. The Association publishes its journal, *School Psychologist*, twice yearly. It was initiated by members from the Department of Psychology, Philosophical Faculty at Comenius University. The journal has contributed to the further development of school psychology in Slovakia.

Although all of the conditions described above are favorable to installing school psychology services in schools, small numbers of school psychologists, about 150, are employed directly in schools. An additional 250 school, counseling, and clinical psychologists work in educational-psychological counseling centers that provide once-a-week services in two to three nearby schools. At present, due to financial reasons, the headmasters cannot afford to employ their own school psychologist in spite of growing problems in schools. Approximately 160 school psychologists work in state and private schools. Their salaries are about 400 euros a month.

Preparation of School Psychologists

School psychologists employed in schools or educational-psychological counseling centers may receive their preparation through computer-assisted study of psychology or teacher training programs in which psychology is studied in combination with another subject (e.g., psychology and biology, psychology and arts, psychology and English) culminating in completing a four-semester postgraduate program in school psychology at Comenius University.

In 1993, school psychology training was started by the Department of Psychology, Comenius University following legislation authorizing this preparation. The preceding period can be divided into three stages. During the first stage, the 1970s, school psychologists were trained at the university in educational psychology plus another subject (pedagogy, philosophy, foreign languages). Thus, school psychologists gained teacher's certificates, because they presumably would be teaching the other subject part-time. During this period, attempts to establish school psychology in schools were not successful. During the second stage, beginning in the early 1990s, prospective school psychologists completed either a 5-year course of study that combined psychology with pedagogy, without receiving a teacher's certificate, or a 4-year course in psychology, specializing in school, counseling, and educational psychology. A few school psychologists were employed in secondary schools during this period. During the third stage, beginning in the late 1990s to the present, following the passage of the Law on Educational Institutions and Regulations of Ministry of Education, the Department of

Psychology, Philosophical Faculty, Comenius University, Bratislava, began preparing school psychologists in a 5-year program in psychology. Program features are discussed below.

A student's graduate study in psychology is ensured through the selection of optional courses (lectures, seminars, exercises). During the first three years of psychological study, which lead to a bachelor of arts degree, students take basic theory and methods courses, including compulsory courses in general psychology, developmental psychology, psychology of personality, experimental psychology, social psychology, educational and school psychology, clinical and counseling psychology, organizational psychology and psychological methodology, psychodiagnostic services for children and adults, sociology, philosophy, education, statistics, and computer technology.

Social-psychological training of students is compulsory during semesters (terms) four through six, with the goal of promoting metacognition skills, further awareness of others, and the acquisition of social skills. Students receive applied psychological practice experience in preschools, primary and secondary schools, and other establishments. After the sixth term, students must take and pass the first state final examination of basic psychological knowledge to gain a bachelor's degree. Students may continue in their studies at the magister's (i.e., master's) level only on passing this exam.

Compared with the preceding 3 years of study that focus on acquiring basic psychological knowledge, the next 2 years focus on preparing for one's intended work and lead to a magister's degree. Compulsory subjects include psychology of counseling, psychology of management, clinical psychology, and psychotherapy. Optional courses are chosen on the basis of student interests, preferences, and future specialization. Students may select from among the following subjects or themes: forensic psychology, political psychology, preventive programs, family therapy, matrimonial counseling, relaxation techniques, art therapy, conflict resolution, and Adlerian psychology.

Students pursuing a magister's degree who want to specialize in school psychology may select such courses as a career guidance program for teenagers, an emotional intelligence program for children, psychodiagnostic methods in the school psychologist's work, or bullying at schools. Knowledge and skills related to these topics may be applied by working in primary and secondary schools with individuals, small groups, classes, teachers, and vocational counselors (e.g., providing assessment and intervention services with children and youth within the context of classrooms and schools). Students may help evaluate the maturity of children entering first grade, engage in some preventive programs with pupils, or consult with parents under the supervision of the university teachers and school psychologists working in these schools. Preventive and developmental programs commonly appear in ethics or civic education classes. Students also participate in research conducted within the Department of Psychology, especially research on issues important to clinical, social, organizational, counseling, and school psychology. During their final year, students write a thesis, are enrolled in a diploma seminar, and may take some optional courses. The second state final examination, taken at the end of their studies, assesses general psychology, developmental psychology, psychology of personality, methodology, and two of the following psychological subjects: clinical psychology, counseling psychology, school psychology, educational psychology, social psychology, and organizational psychology. On graduation, students are awarded the title "magister in psychology."

Continuing education programs for psychologists working in practice are offered by departments of psychology at the universities that organize short courses in psychology (50–100 hours in duration) and specialized courses in psychology (about 240 hours in duration), resulting in certificates that do not award additional degrees or titles. The postgraduate course resulting in the doctor of philosophy degree and

title may have an internal or external form. Students selecting the internal form study for 3 years, during which time they are members of the department of psychology of the university and are required to help teach selected courses and lessons. Students selecting the external form study for 5 years, during which time they work in psychological institutions. Both programs terminate with a final exam and dissertation defense.

Since 1995, students completing their university study of psychology can take specialization courses in school psychology that lead to certification in school psychology. Specialization requires 240 hours and ends with a thesis defense and three exams: one on school psychology and conception of the work; another on psychodiagnostic methods; and a third on prevention, consultation, counseling, and correction. This program emphasizes four spheres of knowledge and skills: learning difficulties, behavior difficulties, career orientation and guidance of pupils, and prevention programs (e.g., tolerance, effective conflict resolution, emotional intelligence, career guidance).

Roles, Functions, and Responsibilities of School Psychologists

School psychologists generally assume responsibility for providing psychological and educational counseling. Educational counselors also provide these services in educational-psychological counseling centers and the Educational Counseling Board within the Ministry of Education. As employees of the school administration, they report to school administrators. Their work is guided, directed, and sometimes supervised by administrators of the educational-psychological counseling center. These centers are located in each of the country's 78 regions. Their work conforms to regulations of the Slovak Psychological Association and the School

Psychology Association of Slovak and Czech Republics. School psychologists generally work in one school, but they may work in two to three schools. Their main missions are to promote the safety, well-being, and social development of pupils and to facilitate the implementation, evaluation, and improvement of comprehensive social and emotional education, beginning in preschool and continuing through high school.

School psychologists attempt to work cooperatively with all components within the school system that may influence pupils' academic success. Thus, they contribute to solving school problems and participate in the development and implementation of training of teachers, parents, and children. Their work is intended to promote pupils' development, including their mental health and social-emotional development.

The vertical structure of a school psychologist's work occurs within a hierarchical structure of school management. School psychologists attempt to work cooperatively with school administrators, teachers, educational counselors, special educators, physicians, nurses, pupils, and their parents. The horizontal structure of their work is differentiated according to the focus of their services (e.g., helping overcome a pupil's learning or behavior problems, assisting with occupational choices, and promoting social climates, interpersonal relationships, and educational and psychohygienic conditions at the school).

School psychologists perform the following tasks in an effort to improve school effectiveness. In reference to pupils, they acquire an understanding of pupils' personalities, abilities, interests, attitudes, personality characteristics, and motivation to learn; identify gifted and talented pupils; and work with pupils who are failing, those learning below their capabilities, and those with behavior problems. They work in cooperation with teachers, parents, educators, counselors, and other professionals. They participate in the construction and implementation of

programs to promote matrimony and parenthood, mental health, and interpersonal relationships.

School psychologists provide teachers and other educators with consultations to improve applications of psychological knowledge and to promote teachers' education and training; counseling services to help address stress associated with teaching; and help in solving interpersonal problems. In reference to parents or legal guardians, school psychologists provide consultation services, assisting them in promoting their children's development, especially their learning, personalities, decision making, and vocational and occupational choices.

In reference to schools and school systems, school psychologists propose ways to improve the quality and raise the effectiveness of the school as a system; participate in developing and implementing systems interventions intended to promote the personality development of pupils and students; provide services that promote professional orientation and occupational choice; promote the welfare of the gifted and talented; provide partnership and matrimonial counseling and education; provide services intended to promote professional and personal growth of teachers; and provide services intended to increase the effectiveness of personal and social management and organizational development.

Slovak school psychologists may use one or more of the following tests in their work.

- Tests that assess achievement include the Reading Test by Matejcek, Sturma, Vagnerova, and Zlab, the Reading Discrimination Test by Raiskup, the Bourdon Test, the Questionnaire of Self-Evaluation of School Achievement by Matejcek, and the Screening Test for Reading and Writing.
- Tests of school maturity are also used; these include the Picture Test of School Maturity by Krogh, the Goppingen Test of

School Maturity, and the Jirasek-Kern Test of School Maturity.

- Tests that assess intelligence and other aptitudes include the Wechsler Intelligence Scale for Children, third edition, the Intelligence Structure Test by Amthauer, the Culture Fair Intelligence Test by Cattell, the Test of Intellectual Abilities by Vonkomer, the Test of Intellectual Potentials by Rican, the Torrance Figural Test of Creative Thinking, the Woodcock-Johnson Test of Cognitive Abilities, and Coloured Progressive Matrices by Raven.
- Tests that assess personality and temperament include the Eysenck Personality Questionnaires for children and for youth, the Cattell Sixteen Personality Factor Questionnaire for youth, the Test of Semantic Choice by Dolezal, the Adjustment Inventory by Bell, the Tree Test by Koch, the Draw-A-Person Test by Goodenough-Harris, House-Tree-Person, Rosenzweig Picture Frustration Test, and the State-Trait Anxiety Inventory for Children by Spielberger.
- Measures that assess behavior and social skills include the Achenbach Child Behavior Checklist, the Connors Rating Scale for Teachers and Parents, the Rating Scales of School Behavior, and the Scale of Risk Behavior by Mezera, Skerik, and Kubice.
- Measures that assess social climate, relations, and status include the Schutz Fundamental Interpersonal Relations Orientations, the Sociometric Rating Questionnaire by Hrabal, and the Social Climate at Schools by Kollarik. Measures of career interests include the Hierarchy Interests Test by Hrabal, the Secondary Schools Questionnaire by Hrabal, the Interests Orientation by V. Hrabal, the Holland Test of Interests, and the Picture Interest Test for Career Guidance by Blaskovic.
- Measures that assess family qualities include the Adolescent on Parents Questionnaire by Matejcek and Rican, Parents Education Styles Questionnaire by Cap and Boschek, and the Scale of Family Relations by Hargasova and Kollarik.

Current Issues Impacting School Psychology

The major issues impacting school psychological services include the following. First, additional financial support is needed to allow schools to employ their own school psychologists. Second, the psychological community should work to accredit psychologists who have teacher training and experience. These graduates would make suitable school psychologists since they are trained in pedagogy and often have teaching experience. They are well prepared to work with teachers, educators, and pupils. Third, additional work is needed to publicize school psychology and the work of school psychologists, especially prevention services. Various issues need further attention, including the qualification of school psychologists, supervision of their work, psychodiagnostic methods necessary for the identification of pupils with behavior difficulties, work with Roma pupils, the integration or inclusion of mentally and physically handicapped children into schools, and the development of tolerance among pupils.

References

Gajdosová, E. (1992). The current status of school psychology in Czechoslovakia. *Psychologie Erziehung, 18*(1), 127–135.

Gajdosová, E. (1998a). *Skolsky psycholog a jeho vstup do humanizacie nasich skol* [The school psychologist and his or her entrance into the humanization of our schools]. Bratislava: Príroda.

Gajdosová, E. (1998b). *Skolsky psycholog. Specialne otazky skolskej psychologie* [The school psychologist: Special issues related to school psychology]. Bratislava: Comenius University.

Gajdosová, E., & Herényiová, G. (1999). The school psychologist's work in developing the emotional intelligence of pupils. *World Go Round, 26*(2), 8–10.

Gajdosová, E., & Herényiová, G. (2002). *Skola rozvijania emocionalnej inteligencie ziakov* [The school of emotional intelligence development in pupils]. Bratislava: Príroda.

Hvozdík, J. (1986). *Zaklady skolskej psychologie* [Foundations of school psychology]. Bratislava: Slovak Pedagogical Publisher.

Hvozdík, S. (1999). *Vybrane kapitoly zo skolskej psychologie* [Selected chapters of school psychology]. Presov: Presov University.

Rosa, V., Turek, I., & Zelina, M. (2002). *The National Program of Education of the Slovak Republic for the next 15 years.* Bratislava: Iris.

Schwaryová, M. (2004). *Regiony Slovenska* [Regions of Slovakia]. Bratislava: Veda.

36

School Psychology in South Africa

Berenice Daniels

Lynette Collair

Nadeen Moolla

Sandy Lazarus

Context of School Psychology

South Africa lies at the southern tip of the continent of Africa. With a landmass of 1,219,912 square kilometres, the country is nearly three times larger than the state of California in the United States and more than twice as large as France. It consists of nine provinces: Western Cape, Eastern Cape, Northern Cape, North West, Free State, Gauteng, KwaZulu-Natal, Limpopo, and Mpumalanga. In 2001, during the last census, its population was approximately 44 million (Government Communication and Information System, 2003). More than half live in urban centres, the largest of which are Johannesburg and Cape Town. There are 11 official languages.

English is mostly used in business and government. The landscape varies dramatically across the country. South Africa is bordered on the west side by the Atlantic Ocean and on the east side by the Indian Ocean, and many picturesque beaches line the coast. In addition to its scenic attractions, South Africa has a mild and sunny climate. In 2004, the gross domestic product was US$491.4 billion, US$11,100 per capita. The majority of job opportunities are in services (45%) and industry (30%). Unemployment is high (50%).

South Africa has had an indigenous population for at least 100,000 years. The region first was colonised by the Dutch in 1652 and later by the British. The Union of South Africa came into being in 1910. Although segregationist policies existed earlier, racial segregation became firmly entrenched when the National Party assumed power in 1948. From 1948 to 1994, South Africa was one of the few countries in which a minority controlled the government under a policy called *apartheid* (from the Afrikaans word for "apartness"). The people of South Africa were divided into four main groups: White, Black, Coloured (i.e., "mixed race"), and Indian/Asian. People were classified on the basis of appearance and known ancestry. Whites made up about 10% of the population, controlled Parliament, administered the laws, and ensured that all the best areas, schools, jobs, and other resources were reserved for them. Blacks, who made up about 77% of the population, Coloureds (10%), and Asians (3%) were not allowed to vote and were subjected to harsh laws, deprivation, and lack of basic provisioning. The stated goal of the government was separate development of each group. However, Blacks were given the fewest resources, Coloureds and Asians slightly more but still fewer than what Whites received. The people in each group were forced to live in separate areas, and the children went to separate schools. There were massive inequalities and inconsistencies among the different segregated education departments. Education support services, including school psychological services, were most accessible to "White" learners.

Much began to change following the April 1994 election of the first democratic parliament after a protracted struggle for liberation that resulted in many organisations banned and people imprisoned and dying for their participation in the struggle. The first president of the democratic South Africa, Nelson Mandela, was freed in 1990 after 27 years in prison. Since 1994, there has been considerable change and transformation in South Africa to enable it to move toward becoming a nonracial, democratic country with a culture of human rights, respect for justice, and rule of law. Although great strides have been made, much still needs to be done to eradicate the legacy of apartheid.

South Africa has the most advanced economy on the African continent, including some world-class features. It has one of the top 10 stock exchanges in the world. South Africa is a country of contrasts, with a sophisticated financial and physical infrastructure, high-quality telecommunications, and electricity supply networks. However, these resources are often lacking in rural and disadvantaged areas.

Given its history of inequalities and the wide disparities of wealth, South Africa currently is facing its second revolution, namely, the challenge to transfer economic ownership to the formerly disadvantaged people through meaningful participation in the economy and skills acquisition. Under the leadership of President Mbeki, who took over from Nelson Mandela in 1999, South Africa also is committed to spearheading an African renaissance based on cooperative governance, extending democracy, and economic development throughout the subcontinent. Although many challenges still face the country, including the effects of globalisation, the digital divide, poverty, crime, HIV/AIDS (human immunodeficiency virus/acquired immunodeficiency syndrome), and creating conditions for sustainable development, South Africa has succeeded in laying the foundation for the nation's individual and collective human potential to come to fruition. School psychology has a significant role to play in helping heal the wounds of the past, addressing the barriers to learning and development, and unleashing the potential of its children.

In 2002, there were 13,531,695 learners (a generic term for pupils and students) in educational institutions (Department of Education, 2004). Public ordinary schools provided education for 86% and private independent schools for 2% of these learners. Public ordinary schools are of three types: primary, middle/intermediate, and high schools. In 2002, there were 17,197 primary, 4,698 middle/intermediate, and 5,752 high schools. The remaining 12% of learners were in other types of educational institutions, which included 3,486 early childhood development centres, 1,895 adult basic education centres, 50 further education and training colleges, and 370 special education schools. There also were 36 higher education institutes, universities, and universities of technology (formerly known as technikons) that were attended by 677,913 learners, accounting for 5% of the total learner population.

Formal education in South Africa is structured according to three levels: the general education and training band, the further education and training band, and the higher education band. The general education and training band includes the foundation phase (Grades R–3), intermediate phase (Grades 4–6), and senior phase (Grades 7–9). The preschool or reception year (Grade R) is being progressively implemented; it was started in 2002 and will be available in all schools by 2010. The first year of compulsory schooling is Grade 1. The age of compulsory school attendance begins the year the child turns 7, although children may begin school from age 5.5 years. The earliest age a learner may legally leave school is 15 or at the end of Grade 9.

The further education and training band is from Grades 10 to 12 in schools. Learners who choose to exit the schooling system at Grade 9 may continue their education at a further education and training college, which provides a more practical or technical education. Learners proceeding to Grade 12 who wish to continue into a higher education institute need to pass Grade 12 with a matriculation endorsement. The percentage of Grade 12 learners who receive matriculation endorsement is about 16% of the total who write the examination. If a learner starts school in Grade 1 at the age of 6 and does not repeat a grade, the average age of completing secondary school would be 18. However, the dropout rate is high: Only about 50% of learners who begin Grade 1 complete a secondary or equivalent education (Department of Education, 2004).

Primary schools generally are from Grades 1 through 7 and secondary schools from Grades 8 through 12. A number of middle/intermediate schools serve learners from Grades 7 or 8 through 9. State funding is provided to support a ratio of about 39 learners per educator in primary schools and 33 per educator in high schools. Principals and other members of the school management team are, however, included in these figures. Learner-to-teacher ratios increase when the management team does not, or is unable to, assume their full teaching load or where a shortage of classrooms exists, which is the case in many of the disadvantaged schools. School fees are payable at public schools. Fees are set by school governing bodies in consultation with parents. Recently, there has been a move to eliminate fees in certain schools in very poor communities; if this occurs, those schools will then receive additional state funding. More affluent public schools usually employ extra educators paid for by the parents via school fees, thereby reducing learner-to-teacher ratios.

There are 370 special education schools that serve 79,589 special needs learners, about 0.6% of the total school-age population (Department of Education, 2004). These mainly are learners with some form of disability (e.g., deafness, blindness, cerebral palsy) or those who have specific learning or behaviour difficulties. Schools tend to be located mainly in the former White areas, although integration of learners from other population groups has occurred.

Data on all aspects of special needs and specialised support are not being routinely kept. This sector has been quite separate and marginalised throughout the history of education. With the promulgation of the new policy in *White Paper 6: Special Education. Building an Inclusive Education and Training System* in 2001, this sector is slowly being brought into the mainstream. Thirty school districts have been chosen to field-test the recommendations of *White Paper 6* (Department of Education, 2001). Two of these districts have been selected to develop holistically as model districts: Metropole South, an urban district in the Western Cape Province, and Siyanda, a rural district in the Northern Cape Province. Although data for all nine provinces are not readily available, some data on school psychological services have been obtained for these two districts.

In 2002, there were 100,242 students who completed qualifications for higher education. Major fields of study were science, engineering, and technology (39%) and business and management (39%). Humanities and social sciences accounted for 15% of total graduates and education for 15%. Only 7, 856 students obtained master's or doctoral qualifications (Department of Education, 2004). The higher education system is currently being restructured to facilitate an increased participation rate, more comprehensive institutions, addressing of race and gender inequities, and additional support for postgraduate programmes and research (Government Communication and Information System, 2003).

Origin, History, and Current Status of School Psychology

The term *school psychologist* is used internally in the Department of Education to refer to those who provide psychological services to schools. Some are trained as psychologists and therefore are registered under the Health Professions Council of South Africa, a statutory body that is discussed later. Some school psychologists are registered in the educational psychologist category, and others may be in other categories, in particular, counselling and clinical psychology. In addition to the registered psychologists, there are those employed in school psychology posts who have an honours, bachelor of education, or equivalent 4-year degree trained as psychometrists or counsellors and registered with the Health Professions Council of South Africa. The minimum qualification to work as a school psychologist in a school or district is registration as a counsellor or psychometrist. School psychologists may work in education districts as part of district-based support teams, at education department head offices, and at special schools (also called schools

for learners with special education needs). Registered educational psychologists may work in the aforementioned formal education support system as well as in private practice, private schools, public ordinary schools paid for by parents via school governing bodies, nongovernmental organisations, universities, on the corporate sector. These distinctions are important to note when trying to understand the origin, history, and current status of school psychology in South Africa. In particular, knowledge of how educational psychology and guidance and counselling have emerged within both the psychology profession and education contexts during the past century is important.

Education became the first field of practice for psychological intervention via psychometry (Louw, 1986). Schools were introduced to psychological testing in 1912, given the need to determine the extent of mental retardation in schools and to assess and diagnose children who required special classes and schools. In 1937, the first psychologist was appointed in what is now the Western Cape Province (Normand, 1993). The focus within the field of educational psychology in schools on testing and particularly on the development of instruments that would measure intelligence remained until the 1960s.

Alongside these developments, vocational guidance developed as an important school psychology service. The development and application of test batteries for vocational guidance began in 1922. In 1927, programmes for vocational guidance in primary and secondary schools were established. In 1936, the first education guidance officer was appointed in what is now Gauteng province. Personal issues, educational decisions, career choices, and remedial and therapeutic interventions were emphasised.

From 1948, with the coming to power of the Nationalist government and its apartheid ideology, the country's education system began to be divided along racial lines. Education for Coloured, Indian, and Black learners was controlled nationally, whereas education for White learners was managed by provincial departments of education. Each White provincial department had its own system for allocating school psychologists. For example, in the early 1990s, there was about one school psychologist for every 5 to 10 schools in the Cape Province. Other education departments had much lower ratios. For example, in some Black areas there were ratios of 1 school psychologist to about 50 schools. School psychology services, particularly vocational guidance, were strongly influenced by ideology, such as job reservation and the intention to maintain the existing socioeconomic order.

Early in 1990, immediately preceding the radical change of government and the beginning of the dismantling of apartheid, the different threads of school psychology, including the focus on special needs and guidance and counselling, were investigated as part of the National Education Policy Investigation, which included a focus on support services. Policy proposals covering the various areas of school psychology were presented in this report (National Education Policy Investigation Report, 1992). In 1998, the Ministerial National Commission for Special Needs in Education and Training and National Committee for Education Support Services presented the minister of education with a report outlining policy guidelines for these interconnected areas (Department of Education, 1997). Most of the recommendations in this report were embraced in *White Paper 6* on special education (Department of Education, 2001).

After 1994, school psychologists from the former segregated education departments who had worked at school clinics, child guidance clinics, education aid centres, area offices, and head offices were brought together in nonracial provincial education departments, usually into district-based or provincial teams. The qualifications, experience, and previous workload of the school psychologists differed widely. From the more advantaged ex-departments, there were the often highly qualified school psychologists who had time for much individual work and diagnostic, curative interventions. At the

other end of the scale were school psychologists who often were less qualified and focused mainly on group interventions, for example, group intelligence testing.

In 1997, the National Commission for Special Needs in Education and Training and the National Committee for Education Support Services report estimated that about 50% of learners could be considered to experience barriers to learning and development (Department of Education, 1997). The report stated that "special needs" often arise as a result of barriers within the curriculum, the institution, the system of education, and the broader social context. Therefore, it was considered more appropriate in the South African context to use the expression "barriers to learning and development" than "special needs." Barriers include socioeconomic factors and disabilities as well as language and communication, emotional, behavioural, and learning difficulties. With such a high prevalence of barriers and a shortage of specialists (particularly in disadvantaged and rural areas), models focusing on individualised specialised support for learners are no longer considered to be appropriate. Systemic barriers need to be identified and addressed as well. School psychologists have had to change their roles and responsibilities, and this change has presented major challenges for those who had provided primarily individually based services. School psychologists are attempting to redefine their roles and functions within a transformed education support system. This effort is supported by various national and provincial programmes aimed at facilitating the implementation of the new policy (Department of Education, 2001).

White Paper 6 (Department of Education, 2001) states that the education support service would have, as its core, district-based support teams whose primary function would be to support teaching, learning, and management by building the capacity of schools and other learning institutions to recognise and address learning difficulties and to accommodate a range of learning needs. Institutional-level support teams, also called Teacher or Education

Support Teams in some provinces, are being created to address barriers. The primary function of this team is to put in place properly coordinated support services within the school. These teams receive support from the education district support teams, other government departments, those in the community who have skills and expertise, and other sources.

In this context, the role of specialised support service staff, including school psychologists, has had to shift from being reactive, problem oriented, and deficit based to being preventative, developmental, and asset based, providing assistance to support and develop capacity to address barriers to learning. This includes capacity-building through the facilitation of workshops aimed at building understanding of and addressing barriers, consultation with institution-based teams, and participation in task teams to improve curriculum access. Specialised staff also provide services such as assessment or counselling of learners who have been identified by the institution-based team as needing this kind of support.

A radical curriculum transformation occurred alongside policy developments affecting school psychology. This included the transformation of guidance and counselling into the now formally recognised learning area of Life Orientation—a compulsory subject at all levels of schooling. Linked to this development is the major national focus on HIV/AIDS education and other strategies located within the context of the Health-Promoting Schools framework (Department of Health, 2000).

Detailed statistics on school psychologists were not easily available from all provinces. In the Western Cape, which is probably the province with the most school psychology resources, in 2004, 76 school psychologists worked as part of district support teams. Thirty of these were registered as educational psychologists, 11 as counselling psychologists, and 1 as a clinical psychologist. The rest were psychometrists or counsellors. (B. Phillips, Western Cape Education Department, personal communication, September 2005). Each school psychologist

served about 20 schools. By way of contrast, in the Northern Cape, which is a sparsely populated rural province spread over vast distances, out of 9 school psychologists, 3 were registered educational psychologists and each of the 9 served about 40 schools (H. Abbas, Northern Cape Education Department, personal communication, September 2005). The numbers of learners for whom school psychologists are responsible in the Western Cape and Northern Cape is approximately the same. Rural schools are small, more homogeneous, and far apart, whereas most of those in urban areas are large, close together, and have diverse populations.

In a district, the highest post level is usually that of director. Below the level of the education director are five post levels. Post level 4 usually is the highest level, reserved for a specialist in school psychology. Those school psychologists who progress higher than post level 4 are involved in more generalised education management. Senior school psychologists are appointed at this level with a salary range between R170,000 and R317,000 (US$25,475–US$46,410). School psychologists who are members of district support teams usually are appointed at post level 3, with a salary range between R140,000 and R203,000 (US$20,497–US$29,745). School psychologists at special schools usually are appointed at post level 2, with a salary range between R117,000 and R162,000 (US$17,130–US$23,718). In comparison, teachers are appointed at post level 1, heads of departments at post level 2, deputy principals or principals of small schools at post level 3, and principals of larger schools at post level 4. In the Western Cape Province, in which one of the proposed national model districts is located, a work-study investigation is being conducted on all specialised support service posts as a result of *White Paper 6*. Proposals have been tabled which may lead to the adoption of revised job descriptions for school psychologists and other specialised staff as well as new staffing models. This is discussed in more detail later in the chapter. This is the first work-study investigation since 2000, when the district-based support teams were constituted. In the interim, no school psychology posts were lost. This job stability for school psychologists may, however, not be the same in all provinces.

Infrastructure of School Psychology

As previously discussed, school psychologists are either registered educational, clinical, or counselling psychologists, or psychometrists. The registration of all school psychologists as registered psychologists would be preferable, ideally in the category educational psychology. However, in the two provinces surveyed, only about a third of school psychologists were registered educational psychologists. All psychologists, including educational psychologists, are required by law to register with the Health Professions Council of South Africa. This Council is a statutory body, established by the Health Professions Act 56 of 1974. Its purpose with regard to the health professions is to determine the standards of professional education and training and to promulgate and maintain standards of ethical and professional practice. The Professional Board for Psychology is one of several professional boards within the Health Professions Council. The Professional Board for Psychology is responsible for carrying out the duties of the Health Professions Council of South Africa with regard to psychology. The Professional Board for Psychology is mandated to exercise control and authority in terms of training of psychologists, psychometrists, and counsellors. Therefore, it evaluates all professional psychology training programmes for accreditation. Programs in educational psychology are reevaluated for accreditation every 5 years.

In September 2005, 1,178 psychologists were registered with the Professional Board for Psychology as educational psychologists (E. Wood, Health Professions Council of South Africa, personal communication, September 2005). Of these, 72% were female, and 84%

work in three of the nine provinces that have a higher density of urbanisation: Gauteng (55%), KwaZulu-Natal (13%), and the Western Cape (17%). As previously mentioned, educators with additional training in psychometry also are employed by the provincial education departments as school psychologists. They are required to register as psychometrists or counsellors with the Professional Board for Psychology of the Health Professions Council of South Africa. In 2005, 2,088 were so registered.

A professional association, the Psychological Society of South Africa, is a separate entity that is responsible for the professional interests of practitioners. Although many psychologists are members of the association, membership is not compulsory. There is no national association of school psychologists or journal specifically dedicated to school psychology; rather, there are associations and journals for psychology generally. All psychologists, including educational psychologists, are subject to the code of conduct for psychologists prescribed by the Professional Board for Psychology. The code of conduct pertains to such aspects as professional competence; professional relations; privacy, confidentiality, and records; fees and financial arrangements; assessment activities; therapeutic activities; psycho-legal activities; advertising and public activities; teaching, training, and supervision; research and publication; and resolving ethical issues. Psychometrists and counsellors also are subject to a code of conduct and guidelines regarding their scope of practice as established by the Health Professions Council of South Africa. Apart from being registered with the Health Professions Council of South Africa, the Department of Education, as the employer of school psychologists, requires them to be registered as educators with the South African Council of Educators.

A system of continuous professional development is being introduced for all registered psychologists that will compel them to engage in a stipulated minimum of professional development activities annually in order to remain registered with the Health Professions Council. The education departments offer workshops for school psychologists; higher education institutions offer modules that can enhance capacity, skills, and expertise; and conferences are held that may include suitable presentations and workshops.

Preparation of Educational Psychologists

Students wanting to pursue a master's in psychology must have an honors degree in psychology or education as well as education experience. Should they intend to specialise in educational psychology, they are required to have a professional teacher's qualification before being admitted to the master's programme. To qualify as educational psychologists, students must complete an accredited master's programme in educational psychology or psychology with a specialisation in educational psychology and an approved 1-year internship. The master's-degree qualification is a postgraduate degree awarded after a minimum of 5 years of university study. The master's-degree programme generally constitutes 1 year of coursework followed by a 1-year supervised internship and a mini-thesis. Thirteen universities offer full- or part-time accredited master's programmes that lead to registration as educational psychologists. Some universities offer a specialised master's programme in educational psychology. An example of such a programme is the one offered at Stellenbosch University. Those offering a specialisation within a general master's programme in psychology, which prepares students as clinical, counselling, or educational psychologists, usually reserve a few places for educational psychology students. An example of such a programme is one offered at the University of the Western Cape.

The goal of the specialised master's programme in educational psychology is to develop students both professionally and academically. The programme consists of coursework and a research component. The research component encompasses a thesis, which contributes 50% toward the final mark. The coursework is offered full-time over 1 year or part-time over 2 years. The thesis can be completed simultaneously with the coursework or as soon as possible thereafter. The degree is awarded on completion of the coursework and thesis. The completion of at least the coursework allows students to access internships in educational psychology service settings, such as those at universities, within the Department of Education, or in private practice. The internship has to include learning opportunities in assessment, therapy, and community involvement. Completion of an approved internship is a prerequisite for registration.

The programme aligns competencies with those prescribed by the Health Professions Council of South Africa for educational psychologists. Competencies include the identification, assessment, diagnosis, planning, and implementation of services in response to educational and psychological needs of learners, schools, families, and communities.

The content of the programme may vary in focus and emphasis, depending on whether it is a specialised educational psychology master's programme or a programme that offers a specialisation within a more generic training programme. The programmes offered at Stellenbosch University (i.e., specialised educational psychology master's degree) and the University of the Western Cape (i.e., psychology master's degree with specialisation in educational psychology) include the following core curricula: psychopathology in children and adults; educational and psychological assessment (e.g., intellectual, academic, personality, behavioural, systemic); educational and learning support; approaches to psychotherapy/counselling/emotional assistance; methods to facilitate development in school and community contexts; research methods (i.e., theoretical and methodological traditions, developing research proposals, qualitative and quantitative approaches to research, data collection and analysis, writing the thesis); a practicum and fieldwork to develop skills related to core competencies relating to the theoretical modules (i.e., integration of knowledge, skills, and values acquired in the theoretical work with professional practice); and special educational needs (i.e., inclusive education, understanding educational psychology as a science and profession, understanding special needs, with an emphasis on disabilities and high risk).

The second year comprises an internship at an institution accredited by the Professional Board for Psychology. A thesis is a required component of the master's degree in psychology and composes 50% of a student's grade.

The preparation of educational psychologists is labor-intensive and underscores a lack of human and material resources to prepare sufficient numbers of professionals to service the needs of an already undersupplied school population. Training institutions are challenged to review degree structures as well as the content and process of training (Donald, 1991). Donald recommends shorter programmes that focus strongly on basic and accessible mental health services in schools, with a strong emphasis on community and family interventions, intersectoral collaboration, and proactive, preventative, and consultative work with teachers and schools. Others (e.g., Suffla & Seedat, 2004) advocate the need to adopt a community psychology orientation in the training and practice of psychology. This is particularly needed for those choosing to work in schools where there are high client-practitioner ratios.

Roles, Functions, and Responsibilities of School Psychologists

School psychologists deliver both direct and indirect services. Services include counselling or therapy with individuals and/or groups of learners; psychoeducational assessments; and working with, and supporting the efforts of, parents, educators, principals, and others involved in working with children. Such work includes workshops; individual or school systems consultation, often via Institution-Level Support Teams; and developing and supporting collaborative initiatives. Prevention services are becoming more important, with emphasis on mental health promotion and the establishment of health-promoting schools.

Assessment techniques used include standardised instruments and tests constructed by the school psychologists themselves. Achievement is assessed through the use of various locally developed scholastic tests that assess reading, spelling, and mathematical ability. Portfolios of learners' work often are used, thus providing curriculum-based assessments. There is an emphasis placed on this type of assessment in *White Paper 6*. Intellectual abilities may be assessed through the use of the Junior South African Individual Scale and the Senior South African Individual Scale–Revised. Personality and temperament are assessed through the use of the Draw-A-Person Test, Kinetic Family Drawings, Kinetic School Drawings, Children's Apperception Test, Thematic Apperception Test, High School Personality Questionnaire, Sixteen Personality Factor Questionnaire, Children's Personality Inventory, and the Murphy-Meisgeier Type Indicator for Children. Behaviour and social skills may be assessed through the Connors Rating Scales. Other assessments may include the Survey of Study Habits and Attitudes, the Beery Test of Visual Motor Integration, the Bender-Gestalt Test, and genograms.

The draft report of the work-study investigation in the Western Cape, based on *White Paper 6*, has formulated the following job purpose and proposed the following roles and responsibilities for school psychologists working as part of district-based support teams. Their job purpose is to provide psychoeducational and psychotherapeutic/counselling support within a whole-school context to educators, parents, and learners through institution level support teams. Their proposed roles and responsibilities include designing and developing learning and developmental programmes, conducting psychoeducational assessments and evaluations, providing therapeutic interventions, developing schools and other role players' knowledge and understanding on psychosocial and related issues that create barriers to learning and development, providing community outreach, and promoting organisational and systems development. Currently, there is no standardised national job description for school psychologists. Thus, school psychology practices may differ considerably among provinces and even among districts.

Thirty districts in the country are field-testing proposals expressed in *White Paper 6* (Department of Education, 2001). Some have already started implementing a more consultative preventative model of specialised support service provision. School psychologists accustomed to the old model of service delivery that focused mainly on assessment for placement in special classes and schools and provision of psychotherapy with individuals have had to undergo a major reorientation. School psychologists are not the only staff responsible for addressing barriers. They collaborate with other staff that compose district-based support teams (e.g., learning support advisers, social workers, HIV/AIDS advisers, curriculum advisers, therapists, circuit managers, information technology advisers, administration advisers) who have also had to adjust to new service delivery models and methods. The manner in which school psychologists may work in the 30 districts identified for field-testing of the new policy is described next.

Each school psychologist will be part of a district-based support team that services a cluster of schools. Each school has an institution level support team the members of which are interested educators, one preferably a member of the school's management team. After a teacher has been unsuccessful in addressing the learning barrier after trying various interventions, she or he may request that the institution level support team recommend additional methods that may be helpful. If the difficulty still is not overcome, the district support team may be requested to join the institution level support team in a consultancy role. The district team usually includes a school psychologist. As a result of these discussions, a school psychologist may arrange a workshop to assist educators to better address the barrier, work with a group of learners, do an assessment, assist with curriculum adaptation, network with other government departments or community organisations to find assistance for the school, or refer the learner to a special school or specialised programme or to the management of the district for systemic intervention through the use of an existing or new programme. Traumatic incidents or emergencies (e.g., child abuse or a shooting incident) are somewhat common in some crime-ridden areas. Following these events, a school psychologist or social worker is involved directly, and a referral to an educational support team is bypassed.

With schools becoming more integrated in South Africa, school psychologists have found working with learners who speak languages different from their own to be quite a challenge, particularly when engaging in direct work such as assessments or counselling. Presenting workshops, "giving away" skills to educators (which has been the purview of the specialists), relying less on psychometrics and more on learners' work and portfolios to make an assessment of the barrier, and working in a multidisciplinary or multifunctional team have also been very challenging for some.

Due to the high level of need and the shortage of human resources, the previously used model for delivering school psychological services has become untenable. Many school psychologists who have made the shift to the new model report a higher level of job satisfaction and a feeling that they are making a difference to educators and learners, to their colleagues on the team, and, in some cases, to the education system as whole.

Current Issues Impacting School Psychology

The numerous challenges currently impacting school psychology can be clustered into two broad categories: resource challenges and challenges related to the changing role of school psychologists in the South African context. The lack of human and financial resources at various levels in the education system has a negative impact on the preparation and training of educational psychologists at tertiary institutions and also affects the employment opportunities of school psychologists within state-supported institutions. This has resulted, in a serious shortage of educational psychologists, given the needs of learners, their families, educators, and schools. The fact that a large number of individuals employed as school psychologists lack proper professional qualifications presents an added complexity with regard to the capacity of such human resources to deliver support services within education.

The changing role of educational psychologists presents serious challenges at the level of school psychology training and practice. The academic and professional preparation of educational psychologists requires shifts in perspective and focus. Serious consideration must be given to how professionals can be equipped to meet the vast educational, psychological, and social needs in the schools and homes of the majority of children. A call for a new service delivery model—one that is preventative, consultative, and community based—is clear, and training programmes must take cognizance of these approaches (Donald, 1991; Pillay, 2003; Sharratt, 1995).

Furthermore, a move to more broad-based styles of practice will be difficult unless changes occur in the demands and expectations of educational leaders who employ educational psychologists, parents, teachers, and even educational psychologists themselves. To this end, the transition to a new service delivery model that incorporates a more consultative approach, the implementation of inclusive education, and advocacy on the part of educational psychologists as to what they have to offer in multidisciplinary settings are crucial. Despite all of these challenges, in those locations where educational psychology has become more attuned to the current realities, it is being heralded as leading the vanguard for a contextually relevant, progressive application of psychology and psychological practice in South Africa.

References

Department of Education. (1997). *Quality education for all* (Report of the National Commission for Special Needs in Education and Training & National Committee for Education Support Services). Pretoria: Government Printer.

Department of Education. (2001). *White paper 6: Special education. Building an inclusive education and training system.* Pretoria: Government Printer.

Department of Education. (2004). *Education statistics in South Africa at a glance in 2002.* Pretoria: Government Printer.

Department of Health. (2000). *Guidelines for the development of Health-Promoting Schools/sites in South Africa.* Pretoria: Government Printer.

Donald, D. R. (1991). Training needs in educational psychology for South African social and educational conditions. *South African Journal of Psychology, 21*(1), 38–44.

Government Communication and Information System. (2003). *South Africa Yearbook 2002/03.* Pretoria: Government Printer.

Louw, J. (1986). *This is thy work: A contextual history of applied psychology and labour in South Africa.* Unpublished doctoral thesis, Amsterdam University, the Netherlands.

National Education Policy Investigation Report. (1992). *Support services.* Cape Town: Oxford University Press.

Normand, P. (1993). *The practice of educational psychology.* Unpublished doctoral thesis, University of Stellenbosch.

Pillay, J. (2003). Community psychology is all theory and no practice: Training educational psychologists in community practice within the South African context. *South African Journal of School Psychology, 33*(4), 261–268.

Sharratt, P. (1995). Is educational psychology alive and well in the new South Africa? *South African Journal of School Psychology, 25*(4), 211–216.

Suffla, S., & Seedat, M. (2004). How has psychology fared over ten years of democracy? Achievements, challenges and questions. *South African Journal of School Psychology, 34*(4), 513–519.

37

School Psychology in South Korea

Hyunhee Chung

Hyeonsook Shin

Context of School Psychology

South Korea is located in the southern part of the Korean Peninsula, in the northeastern corner of the Asian continent. South Korea's neighbors are North Korea to the north, Japan across the Sea of Korea (also known as the East Sea) to the southeast, and China across the Yellow Sea to the west. The area of the peninsula is 222,154 square kilometers, of which about 45% (99,313 square kilometers) constitutes the territory of South Korea. In 2004, the population was estimated to be 48,598,175. The average age has changed, largely due to falling birth rates and rising life expectancies. According to a 2004 estimate, 20% of the population is younger than age 15, 71% is 15 to 64, and 8% is 65 or older. By 2030, more than 20% of the population is expected to be 65 or older. South Korea's economy underwent a profound transformation during the latter half of the 20th century. Per capita income in South Korea grew 100-fold in four decades. South Korea is now a nation with one of the highest rates of Internet access, a leader in semiconductor production, and a global innovator in consumer electronics. In 2004, the gross domestic product was US$925 billion, US$19,200 per capita. The unemployment rate is estimated at 3.6%.

As of July 2005, an estimated 11,984,000 children (or 25% of the country's population) were under age 18 (National Statistical Office, 2005). During the 2004 school year, 1,984,265 students were enrolled in schools, among whom 689,414 were in elementary schools, 597,120 in middle schools, 594,474 in high schools, and 103,257 in colleges or universities. The education system consists of 6-year elementary schools, 3-year middle schools, 3-year high schools, and 4-year colleges or universities that offer undergraduate and graduate education leading to master's or doctoral degrees. There also are 2- to 3-year junior colleges and vocational colleges.

Elementary school attendance is compulsory, with an enrollment rate of almost 100%. In 2004, there were 5,541 elementary schools (5,466 public, 75 private). The majority of elementary school children (98.8%) attended public schools. The average number of students per teacher was 26.2. On completing elementary school, children ages 12 through 14 attend middle schools. In 2004, there were 2,888 middle schools, and 80% of the students attended public schools. The student-teacher ratio for middle schools was 19 to 1 in 2004 and 42 to 1 in 1970.

There are two types of high schools: vocational and general. Applicants for vocational high schools select the school they want to attend and are admitted through examinations administered by each school. As of 2004, there were 729 vocational high schools with 514,550 students. Among general high schools, several specialize in art, physical education, science, or foreign languages. Courses at general high schools tend to prepare students to enter universities. As of 2004, there were 1,351 general high schools with a total enrollment of 1.23 million students, 53% of whom attended public schools. The average number of students per teacher was 14.

Education is compulsory through the ninth grade. Although preschool education is not compulsory, its importance has been increasingly recognized. Since 1999, the federal government has instituted a nationwide project to subsidize kindergarten tuition for children from low-income families, thus providing underprivileged children with increased opportunities for preschool education and thereby establishing a more equitable educational environment. In 2004, 99.7% of middle school graduates advanced to high schools. Among high school graduates, 89.8% of those who graduated from general high schools and 62% from vocational high schools continued their education in institutions offering advanced education (National Statistical Office, 2005). The dropout rate was 0.7% for middle school students, 1.2% for general high school students, and 3.4% for vocational high school students.

Higher education offers several types of institutions: colleges and universities with 4-year undergraduate programs (6 years for medical and dental colleges), 4-year teachers' universities, 2-year junior vocational colleges, and a correspondence university, open universities, and miscellaneous schools of collegiate status with 2- or 4-year programs such as nursing and theology. As of 2004, there were 411 institutions of higher education, with 3.56 million students and 64,019 faculty.

As of 2004, 141 special schools had an enrollment of 23,762 students. They included 6 schools for students with psychological problems, 12 for students with visual impairments, 18 for students with hearing impairments, 20 for students with physical impairments, and 85 for students with mental retardation. In addition, 28,002 students with disabilities received special education in 4,366 special classes in regular schools. These schools provide general education and vocational transition programs designed to prepare students for productive employment and independent lives.

Origin, History, and Current Status of School Psychology

The history of school psychology in South Korea goes back to the late 1980s. In 1987, Dr. Sang-Cheol Han, an educational psychologist, created the first graduate-level school psychology program within the Department of Psychology at Yonsei University in Seoul. Although this program later became a combined program (school/counseling), it served a leading role in the development of school psychology in South Korea. Over the past two decades, the school psychology program at Yonsei University has produced at least 5 doctoral-level school psychologists and more than 40 master's-level school psychologists.

In 1995, Dr. Hyunhee Chung joined the school psychology program at Yonsei University as an instructor, after having finished her doctorate in school psychology at Rutgers University in New Jersey. In 2000, Dr. Chung took a faculty position in the school counseling program at Keimyung University but continued to collaborate with Dr. Han to establish the school psychology profession in South Korea. In 2002, Dr. Hyeonsook Shin, who had obtained her doctorate in school psychology from the University of Minnesota, joined the faculty at the Chonnam National University and began teaching both undergraduate and graduate students in school psychology.

Despite the pioneering efforts by Dr. Han and support from Drs. Chung and Shin, the specialty of school psychology has developed slowly, due, in part, to an absence of laws and regulations governing school psychologists' professional roles, limited professional resources for training, undeveloped professional associations, lack of credentialing systems, and a limited job market for school psychologists.

However, school psychology reached a turning point in 2002, when the Korean School Psychology Association was founded as the 12th division of the Korean Psychological Association. Although the Korean Society for School Psychology, which was initiated by educational psychologists in Busan, already existed, its impact was largely regional. Therefore, the Korean School Psychology Association has been consistently recognized as the first national-level professional organization established by psychologists with interests in school psychology. Dr. Han served as the first and second president of the Korean School Psychology Association, and Dr. Chung is currently serving as the third president.

The Korean School Psychology Association has approximately 60 registered members (as of May 2006). About half have a doctoral degree in school psychology or related areas such as counseling, clinical, developmental, and educational psychology. The remaining members are graduate students at Yonsei University, the Chonnam National University, Keimyung University, and other universities. Almost 100% of the members work and reside in large cities. Most members with a doctoral degree are university or college faculty. However, some work as practicing psychologists at public or private counseling centers for youth.

The term *school psychology* has been used to describe the specialty itself and also the university training programs. There is no official job title such as "school psychologist." Psychological services similar to those provided by school psychologists in the United States are performed by teachers called "school counselors" or "professional counseling teachers" in Korean schools, including special schools. This situation poses a serious challenge, as it lowers the quality of services received by students and limits job opportunities for school psychologists and other professional psychologists who are well trained and want to work in school settings.

Infrastructure of School Psychology

Psychology, in general, has developed a relatively strong infrastructure at both the national and regional levels. The Korean Psychological Association, a national professional association of psychologists, has 11 divisions: Health Psychology, Developmental Psychology, Social Issues, Personality and Social Psychology, Industrial and Organizational Psychology, Counseling Psychology, Consumer and Advertising Psychology, Experimental Psychology, Women's Psychology, Clinical Psychology, and School Psychology. School psychology is now at the initial stage of developing its infrastructure at the national level.

Two professional associations serve the interests of scholars, graduate students, and practicing psychologists in school psychology. The Korean School Psychology Association was established as a national-level division of the Korean Psychological Association in 2002. The

Korean Society for School Psychology was originally established in 1995 as a regional division of the Korean Society for Educational Psychology.

In contrast to school psychology, which is still in its infancy, clinical, counseling, and educational psychology divisions have a long history and have established both national- and regional-level professional associations. Although faculty and students in school psychology primarily are affiliated with the Korean School Psychology Association, they also participate in the activities of other professional associations serving the interests of counseling, clinical, and educational psychologists (e.g., Korean Clinical Psychology Association, Korean Counseling Psychological Association, Korean Counseling Association, Korean Society for Educational Psychology). For example, the Division of School Counseling and the Division of Child and Adolescent Counseling at the Korean Counseling Association attract the interests of scholars and students in school psychology.

Currently, only two journals are published with the goal of disseminating information that advances the knowledge and practice of school psychology. *The Korean Journal of School Psychology* is the official journal of the Korean School Psychology Association. The *Journal of School Psychology* is the official journal of the Korean Society for School Psychology. Both journals are published biannually.

Graduate students and scholars in school psychology also read the official journals of clinical, counseling, developmental, and educational psychology associations (i.e., *Korean Journal of Clinical Psychology, Korean Journal of Counseling and Psychotherapy, Korean Journal of Counseling, Korean Journal of Developmental Psychology,* and *Korean Journal of Educational Psychology*). Those who are interested in youth counseling and community mental health also read the *Korean Journal of Youth Counseling*, published by the Korean Youth Counseling Institute.

In South Korea, the official job title of "school psychologist" and licensure of such do not exist. Thus, no statistical data or records regarding their activities and professional affiliations are available. No national or regional laws govern the credentialing or licensing of school psychologists. Except for a few professionals (e.g., youth counselors, mental health clinical psychologists, and school counselors), most psychologists are licensed through the credentialing processes of the professional associations with which they are affiliated. For example, clinical psychologists obtain their licenses (Professional Clinical Psychologist, Clinical Psychologist Level 1, Clinical Psychologist Level 2) in accordance with the licensing regulations of the Korean Clinical Psychology Association. Counseling psychologists obtain their licensure (Counseling Psychologist Level 1, Counseling Psychologist Level 2) in accordance with the licensing regulations of the Korean Counseling Psychological Association. Counselors obtain their licenses (Supervising Professional Counselor, Counselor Level 1, Counselor Level 2) in accordance with the licensing regulations of the Korean Counseling Association.

Since 2004, the Korean School Psychology Association has worked to establish credentialing and licensing regulations for school psychologists. The licensing board of the Korean School Psychology Association expects to finish preparing credentialing and licensing regulations for school psychologists and ethical/professional standards by the end of 2006. The Korean Society for School Psychology is also currently in the process of developing regulations for the licensure of school psychologists.

As of 2006, credentialing/licensing requirements and ethical/professional standards for school psychologists and laws and regulations for school psychological services do not exist. However, the *Guidelines for Psychological Testing* (Korean Psychological Association, 1998), which provides specific guidelines for the development and use of psychological tests in clinical, school, and industrial settings and for assessment of people with disabilities, is expected to influence the regulation of school psychological services, in particular, assessment services in schools.

Compared with most psychologists (including school psychologists) who would be certified and licensed through the credentialing and licensing processes of their professional organizations, youth counselors, mental health clinical psychologists, and school counselors (also known as professional counseling teachers) are licensed under the laws and regulations of national ministries. Regulations from the Ministry of Culture and Tourism govern the credentialing and licensing of youth counselors (Levels 1, 2, and 3), those from the Ministry of Health and Welfare govern the credentialing and licensing of mental health clinical psychologists (Levels 1 and 2), and those of the Ministry of Education and Human Resources Development govern the credentialing and licensing of school counselors (Levels 1 and 2).

In South Korea, those who want to work as school counselors in elementary and secondary schools need to earn teacher certificates before applying for school counselor licenses, and employment in schools is possible only in accordance with the laws and regulations of the Ministry of Education and Human Resources Development. Thus, the licensure of school counselors is governed by the Elementary and Secondary Education Law of the Ministry of Education and Human Resources Development. This law also stipulates the placement of itinerant school counselors at educational administrative organizations and facilities at city and provincial areas. Some roles and functions of school counselors in South Korea resemble those of school psychologists in the United States.

In addition, several other national laws and regulations have implications for psychologists in general and for school psychologists in particular. For example, laws and regulations of the Ministry of Education and Human Resources Development (e.g., laws governing gifted education, school health, special education, and early childhood education) have implications for the professional practice of psychologists in general (e.g., screening, assessment, therapy, consultation).

Although special education laws and regulations in South Korea do not delineate the roles and functions of school psychologists in particular, or those of psychologists in general, they do have important implications for the roles and functions of school psychologists, because they include stipulations on the following practices. Current special education laws and regulations stipulate eight disability categories (visual impairments, hearing impairments, mental retardation, physical disabilities, emotional disorders, speech and language disorders, learning disabilities, and health impairments); psychological services such as psychotherapy, counseling, and assessment for students with disabilities and their families; supportive services for regular education teachers in inclusive classrooms; and placement of therapeutic education teachers in schools.

Preparation of School Psychologists

In South Korea, many universities offer programs to prepare psychologists. However, only two universities, Yonsei University and the Chonnam National University, offer graduate-level programs for students majoring in school psychology.

At Yonsei University, students majoring in school psychology are admitted into the combined program of school and counseling psychology. Four to five school psychology students are admitted annually into the master's program and one or two students into the doctoral program. From 1987 to 1997, the average number of students who completed the school psychology program at the master's level was one or two each year. However, it increased to eight in 2002. Since 1997, when the first doctorate in school psychology was granted by Yonsei University, one or two students each year have completed their doctorates in school psychology at Yonsei University. Compared with Yonsei University, Chonnam National University's school psychology program has a relatively short history. Chonnam National University began its school psychology program in 2002. As of May 2006, only one student has completed a master's degree at the Chonnam National University.

The school psychology program at Yonsei University is in the Department of Psychology, whereas the school psychology program at the Chonnam National University is in the Department of Education. Accordingly, curricula for the school psychology programs at the two universities are somewhat different.

The Department of Psychology at Yonsei University requires 30 semester credits for the completion of a master's degree in school psychology and 60 semester credits for the completion of a doctoral degree. Thirty of the 60 semester credits required for the doctoral degree can be earned through the master's program. Regardless of the degree level and the specialization program, all students are required to take two core courses (advanced psychological statistics and experimental design) and then are free to take other courses offered in the department. School psychology majors usually are advised to take school psychology courses; these courses cover the following areas: intervention, assessment, consultation, research methods, ethical issues, advanced school psychology, and a seminar on psychological services in the school. In addition, students pursuing the master's degree also are required to earn 6 practicum credits. Practicum and/or internship credits are not required for those pursuing doctoral degrees.

The Chonnam National University school psychology program requires master's students to earn at least 24 semester credits and doctoral students to earn at least 36 semester credits. School psychology students are required to take basic core courses (i.e., research in education, qualitative research methods in education, quantitative research methods in education) and professional practice of school psychology courses (i.e., assessment in school psychology–intellectual domain, assessment in school psychology–affective domain, remedial instruction for learning problems, school psychological interventions–affective domain, and

school-based consultation). School psychology students also are advised to take foundations of school psychology courses (i.e., seminars in school psychology issues; school psychology research), psychological foundations courses (i.e., child neuropsychology, developmental psychopathology, child and adolescent psychology), related courses (e.g., understanding of exceptional students, positive psychology in education), or counseling psychology courses. Each course is 3 credits.

In South Korea, school psychology programs provide graduate students with courses on assessment services and intervention and consultation services. The most common areas of assessment and the tests used to assess those areas are the following (all tests are Korean versions): (a) intellectual abilities (Wechsler Preschool and Primary Scale of Intelligence, Wechsler Intelligence for Children, Wechsler Adult Intelligence Scale, Kaufman Assessment Battery for Children, Pictorial Test of Intelligence, and Draw-A-Person Test); (b) achievement (Basic Learning Skills Test); (c) personality (Minnesota Multiphasic Personality Inventory, Minnesota Multiphasic Personality Inventory–Adolescent, Personality Assessment Inventory, Personality Inventory for Children, California Psychological Inventory, Sixteen Personality Factor Questionnaire, Thematic Apperception Test, and Children's Apperception Test); (d) emotion, behavior, and social skills (Child Behavior Checklist, Youth Self-Report, State-Trait Anxiety Inventory–KYZ, Beck Depression Inventory, Children's Depression Inventory, sentence completion test, and projective drawing tests such as the House-Tree-Person Test and the Kinetic Family Drawing Test); and (e) others (Bender Visual-Motor Gestalt Test, Symptom Checklist-90–Revised, interviews, and behavioral observations).

As of May 2006, no school psychology graduates had secured positions as school psychologists in schools, as there is no such job title. A few graduates are practicing privately, providing consulting or counseling services. Others work as counselors at community counseling centers or as researchers at universities or government-funded centers. Because credentialing and licensing regulations for school psychologists have not been established, students majoring in school psychology only have to complete the academic and practicum requirements of the program for which they have registered. Except for master's students at Yonsei University, practicum/internship requirements are not enforced. Students usually seek to acquire necessary practicum experience on an individual basis through case conferences and workshops provided by professional organizations.

Roles, Functions, and Responsibilities of School Psychologists

The Korean School Psychology Association delineates the roles of prospective school psychologists in accordance with the scientist-practitioner model. The roles of school psychologists are characterized within five broad service delivery systems: assessment, intervention and prevention, consultation, program development and training, and research. However, because no one is working with the official job title of "school psychologist" in South Korea, the roles, functions, and responsibilities of school psychologists described next are given by the Korean School Psychology Association only as guidelines for the delivery of school psychological services and the preparation of school psychologists.

Assessment services for children and adolescents are provided so that data are collected and decisions are made about the children and adolescents. Prevention and intervention services are provided for students experiencing maladaptive problems and those at risk. A recent survey (Shin, Kim, & Lyu, 2004) revealed that secondary school teachers in South Korea strongly acknowledge the necessity and importance of prevention and intervention services

(particularly for juvenile delinquency, career indecision, emotional problems, school adjustment problems), among other school psychological services. Consultation services are provided to help parents and teachers enhance healthy adjustment of children and adolescents who display various problems (e.g., developmental delays, learning problems, social skills deficits, and emotional and behavioral problems). Program development and training services are provided mainly to develop competence enhancement programs for normally developing students and to develop therapeutic/counseling programs for maladaptive students and their teachers and parents. Research is conducted to gain a deeper understanding of the problems of children and adolescents, to develop reliable and valid assessment methods and procedures, and to test the effects of intervention and prevention programs.

Current Issues Impacting School Psychology

During the past two decades, school psychology has improved slowly yet significantly. The founding of a national-level professional organization, the Korean School Psychology Association, with its own academic journal, constitutes the most salient achievement and a big step toward establishing its future. However, the Korean School Psychology Association is new and faces many challenges and problems (Chung, 2000, 2003; Shin, 2003).

First, the Korean School Psychology Association must promote professionalism by developing standards and guidelines for the delivery of school psychological services and the preparation of school psychologists. The Association also should attempt to develop regulations for the licensure of school psychologists that lead to certified or licensed school psychologists serving national interests. In addition, the number of graduate-level training programs should be increased.

Second, the term *school psychology* is unfamiliar to South Koreans. Since school psychology, and psychology in general, has roots in Western culture, the term *school psychology* is not an easy concept for those who have limited experience with that culture. Therefore, the Korean School Psychology Association should consider selecting a term that conveys the concept in a way that is consistent with Korean culture. Once the term is selected, the Association needs to disseminate information about school psychology to laypeople as well as to professionals through various means (e.g., printed materials, the Internet, seminars, workshops).

Third, the Korean School Psychology Association should make an effort to form close relationships with other professional associations and individuals. The Division of School Psychology remains the Korean Psychological Association's newest division. Thus, many Korean Psychological Association members do not have a clear understanding of school psychology and the goals of this division. By providing a clear description of school psychology and communicating more with other divisions within the Korean Psychological Association (e.g., counseling, clinical, and developmental psychology), the Korean School Psychology Association should be able to attract more Korean Psychological Association members into its division and maintain good relationships with other associations. In addition, the Korean School Psychology Association should develop close relationships with other related disciplines (e.g., special education, child psychiatry, school social work) and government officials or policymakers in education or health fields.

References

Chung, H. (2000). Breaking fresh ground: A school-based primary prevention in Korea. *Journal of Prevention & Intervention in the Community, 19*(2), 109–114.

Chung, H. (2003). *School psychology: Concepts and roles.* Paper presented at the annual convention of the Korean Psychological Association, Seoul, Korea.

Korean Psychological Association. (1998). *Guidelines for psychological testing.* Seoul: Author.

Ministry of Education and Human Resource Development. (2004). *Annual report on special education 2004.* Retrieved August 10, 2005, from http://www.moe.go.kr/assembly/assembly11.html?Menu_Code=11

National Statistical Office. (2005). *Statistics on youth 2005.* Retrieved August 9, 2005, from http://www.nso.go.kr/nso2005/bbs/report/report10/view.jsp?content_id=3055

Shin, H. (2003). *Historical development of school psychology in the U.S. and its implications.* Paper presented at the annual convention of the Korean Psychological Association, Seoul, Korea.

Shin, H., Kim, I., & Lyu, J. (2004). Current status of school counseling and the necessity of school psychological services perceived by secondary school teachers. *The Korean Journal of School Psychology, 1*(1), 53–77.

Additional Resources

Information on Professional Associations

Korean Clinical Psychology Association: http://www.kcp.or.kr

Korean Counseling Association: http://www.counselors.or.kr

Korean Counseling Psychological Association: http://www.krcpa.or.kr

Korean Psychological Association: http://www.koreanpsychology.or.kr

Korean School Psychology Association: http://www.schoolpsych.or.kr

Korean Society for School Psychology: http://www.schoolpsychology.or.kr

Information on Laws and Regulations

http://www.klaw.go.kr
http://www.korea.net
http://www.moleg.go.kr

38

School Psychology in Spain

José Carlos Núñez

Julio Antonio González-Pienda

Context of School Psychology

Spain is located in southwest Europe, separated from Africa by the Strait of Gibraltar, and borders France in the north and Portugal in the west. Its surface area is 505,992 square kilometres, and it has a population of 40,341,462. Only 37% of the population is under age 31; 14% are between birth and 14 years old. Spain's gross domestic product in 2004 was US$937.6 billion, US$23,300 per capita. Sixty-four percent of the labor force is in service industries; 30% is in construction, mining, and manufacturing; and 4% is in agriculture. Unemployment is high, about 11%. Forty-two percent of the working population has finished compulsory education (10th grade).

The Spanish educational system is structured according to the following phases and ages (Ministerio de Educación y Ciencia, 2004): infant education (birth to age 5), primary education (ages 6–11), compulsory secondary education (ages 12–15), post-compulsory secondary education (ages 16–17), and university education (over age 17). During the 2004–2005 academic year, 1,419,307 were enrolled in infant education, 2,494,598 completed primary education, 1,876,322 studied compulsory secondary education, 1,148,658 took part in post-compulsory secondary education, and 29,283 attended special education programs. Thus, 6,968,168 participate in non-university studies, of whom 4,708,942 (68%) attend public schools and 2,259,226 (32%) attend private or semi-private schools. The average number of students per class is 20 in infant education, 21 in primary education, and 25 in compulsory secondary education.

During 2004, Spain devoted 5.4% of its gross domestic product to education. The state contributes approximately 80%, and families pay the remaining 20%. Families with lower incomes have access to scholarships, with the full cost of the education of these families' children paid by the state. During 2004–2005, the government established scholarships for 466,804 students, totalling €752,331. Spain's population recently has increased as a result of immigration. During the 2004–2005 academic year, 389,726 children age 16 or younger from immigrant families attended school. Most (51%) come from South America and Central America, 25% from other European countries, and the remainder from North America and other regions of the world.

Students with special educational needs constitute 2.5% of the total population, among whom 81% attend normal schools. Students with physical disabilities (e.g., hydrocephaly) are most frequent (64%), followed by those with autism and serious personality disorders (13%), motor disabilities (e.g., cerebral palsy; 7%), hearing impediments (5%), and vision impediments (3%); 9% have multiple disabilities.

Origin, History, and Current Status of School Psychology

Different periods characterise the history of school psychology (Muñoz, García, & Sánchez, 1997). The first period, 1880 to 1920, is marked by interest in the study of individual differences and the usefulness of tests for diagnosis and treatment planning for children who displayed psychological problems. Thus, from its beginning, school psychology has been strongly linked to special education. The second period, 1920 to 1955, is marked by the impact of the mental health movement, in which psychological services were provided to treat children's disorders in and out of school. These efforts helped extend the focus of school psychology services to children with emotional, affective, and social problems, not merely those with learning problems. During the third period, 1955 to 1970, efforts to provide knowledge about psychology to teachers and to link this information to pedagogical practices became prominent. During the 1970s, some psychologists began to question the use of traditional service delivery models that focus on individual therapy. They began using alternative models based on more current cognitive learning theories; systemic,

organisational, and ecological theories; and community psychology in their attempt to emphasise the contexts both of learning and of the educational system.

Thus, school psychology emerged following the development of scientific psychology. School psychology as such emerged as a consequence of the application of psychological knowledge to the academic setting. Interest in applying psychology to school-related issues and to professional guidance initially contributed to this development. During the 1970s, many universities established departments of psychology, resulting in the graduation of students who added significantly to the availability of professional psychologists. The need to apply psychological knowledge and technology, including psychoeducational interventions, became increasingly apparent.

Thirty years ago, no school psychologists worked in public education. There currently are 3,600; 52% are men. School psychologists compose 38% of all psychology professionals. Nearly 90% work in urban areas. Psychologists working in rural areas are becoming progressively scarcer. School psychologists generally work in public schools: in early attention and infant education teams, interdisciplinary sector teams for primary education, specific teams (hearing-impaired students, motor-impaired students, disruptive conduct), and guidance departments. School psychologists also work in private schools, in private practice, and in centres for reeducation and academic support that support diverse interventions (e.g., speech therapy, parent education, training in basic skills). Most centres provide numerous high-quality professional services for children.

One must pass a competitive examination to become a psychologist and engage in work. Those working in the public sector receive an annual salary of approximately €26,600, an amount that changes according to the number of years one works, the position one holds, and other job-related conditions. As government employees, their jobs are more stable than those in the private sector. Those working in the private sector earn about 20% more, but their employment is more competitive and less stable. School psychologists tend to be moderately satisfied with their work due more to the perceived importance of their services than to the amount of money they earn.

Infrastructure of School Psychology

In 1970, the General Law of Education established school and vocational guidance services. Vocational guidance counsellors initiated the practice of using psychology in schools. However, the Ministry of Science and Education did not sanction these services until 1977. These services included personal, professional, and school guidance; advice and support for students, teachers, and parents; diagnosis of students with special educational needs; and research. These functions were linked to guidance models current at that time. Services were extensive and not well defined, and given the lack of personnel and the small number of teams in each of the 17 autonomous territories in Spain, they were incapable of significantly influencing school systems.

Following the first democratic municipal elections in April 1979, municipal psychopedagogic services were created. The services provided by psychologists in schools were the same as those provided by the health and social service sectors. Municipal psychopedagogic services were widely influenced by preventive models from health areas and offered specific curriculum support activities for children who were academically delayed or experienced a long illness. Following the 1977 National Plan for Special Education and the 1982 Social Integration Law for the Handicapped, a new framework for providing psychoeducational services was created: multi-professional teams (e.g., psychologists, pedagogues, speech therapists, social workers, and physicians) linked to special education. They were responsible for the initial student evaluations and decision making as to special education eligibility and services. Their services focused on prevention, multi-professional evaluation, identification of needs, guidance, and monitoring.

In 1979, the Spanish Constitution was established and, according to Article 49, the government was encouraged to work on "policies of prevention, treatment, rehabilitation, and integration of the physically and/or mentally handicapped, affording them any special attention that they might require." In 1982, the Law for the Social Integration of Handicapped People further developed Article 49 by establishing the principles of service normalisation and division, integration, and individual attention. That same year, the Royal Decree 334/85 for the Arrangement of Special Education set in motion planning measures to "guarantee that those students with special educational needs will be able to reach the general educational goals established at the highest level possible." Following this decree, experimental programs were established, designed to integrate students with permanent special educational needs, first in regular primary education schools and, after 1992–1993, in compulsory secondary education schools.

These efforts led to new work for school psychologists. On the one hand, the functions of the Ministry of Education and Science teams focused on diagnostic assessment in order to establish the correct placement of students in schools and on providing support for the newly acknowledged projects and to establish the correct placement and integration of students into schools. On the other hand, the functions of the school and vocational guidance (Servicios de Orientación Escolar y Vocacional) and the multi-professional teams (Equipos Multiprofesionales) were unified. They provided general services in regular schools and specific services in integration and special education schools. Their priorities included integration of regular and special needs children, attention to issues impacting families, diagnosis, and prevention of academic failure. They operated under the same organisational and operational model.

Organic Law 1/1990 for the General Regulation of the Educational System (Ley Orgánica de Ordenación General del Sistema Educativo; Law 10/03/1990) extends the principles and objectives stated in the Constitution and the above-mentioned royal decrees to include the establishment of guidance services. Guidance is described as activities inherent to the teaching-learning process, not external to it, as occurred in the 1970 General Education Law (Ley General de Educación de 1970). As a result, guidance no longer was considered to be a process in which an expert helps those who are less experienced.

In accordance with Ley Orgánica de Ordenación General del Sistema Educativo, the educational guidance model was elaborated by the following principles. Guidance services are provided at three levels: individual services, those provided by a guidance department, and those provided within more extensive geographic areas. Moreover, as noted above, guidance services are inherent to educational activities and thus take place within normal educational activities. Services comprise two aspects, educational and vocational, and are intended to have both therapeutic and preventive outcomes. A systemic perspective in psychoeducational intervention is adopted.

Various professional journals offer scholarships. The following journals discuss more general issues that are relevant for psychology or education: *Papeles del Psicólogo* (Papers of the Psychologist), *Revista de Psicología General y Aplicada* (Journal of General and Applied Psychology), *Estudios de Psicología* (Studies of Psychology), and *Psicothema*. School psychologists may be more interested in articles that appear in the following journals: *Revista de Educación* (Journal of Education), *Infancia y Aprendizaje* (Journal for the Study of Education and Development), *Cultura y Educación* (Culture and Education), *Cuadernos de Pedagogía* (Journal of Teaching), *Revista Española de Pedagogía* (Spanish Journal of Teaching), *Bordón* (Support), *Revista de Investigación Educativa* (Journal of Educational Research), and *Revista de Psicología y Educación* (Journal of Psychology and Education). Numerous textbooks also are available on various topics, including school and educational psychology, learning, teaching, special education, school guidance, and diversity.

Preparation of School Psychologists

Spanish universities have 29 faculties of psychology, some in health sciences and others in legal and social sciences. These faculties have 45,000 students, with 8,000 to 10,000 entering each year, 60% of whom complete their degrees, typically after 5 years. The number of students admitted to the various departments differs considerably. Some departments are very selective, limiting new enrolment to no more than 110, whereas others allow almost all qualified students to enter.

Psychologists typically receive a 5-year degree, referred to as a *licentiate*. Each academic year is divided in two 4-month periods (i.e., fall and spring semesters). Syllabi in the various psychology faculties are not uniform. Programmes typically extend over 5 years and allow students to specialise in a number of applied specialties (clinical, school, work-organisational, and social intervention), and are divided into two cycles of 3 and 2 years each. The first cycle emphasises basic academic courses, and the second emphasises courses related to a student's specialisation. Syllabi are organised according to three types of courses: compulsory, optional (courses that prepare students for their chosen specialty and from which they select certain courses), and elective (courses that cover preparation for other specialties). Thus, students can tailor their academic preparation to best suit their academic and professional interests. Students perform a practicum (15 credits, equivalent to 150 hours), which requires them to apply their knowledge in professional settings, including schools, health centres, penitentiaries, and other public or private enterprises.

The preparation of psychologists generally focuses on the following academic courses: basic psychological processes, developmental psychology, psychology of learning, personality psychology, social psychology, group and organisational psychology, physiological psychology, basic neuroscience, neuropsychology, data analysis, research designs, psychometrics, psychological assessment, educational psychology, learning disorders and disabilities, psychosocial intervention, psychopathology, and intervention and treatment techniques, among others. Students who desire to weight their curriculum in favour of school psychology also can choose other subjects, such as instructional psychology, psychological bases of attention to diversity (in which various disabilities and developmental disorders are studied), school guidance, study strategies and techniques, and so forth.

After completing their basic education, students may decide to engage in a third cycle for 2 years, which leads to theoretical, practical, and research specialisations. Students have recently been encouraged to pursue quality doctorate programmes called *programas de doctorado de calidad*. After completing their regular studies (licentiate and/or doctorate), those who want to work as school psychologists in public institutions must pass a competitive examination, which involves a 2- to 3-year preparation period that normally takes place in specialised centres or academies and in the Official Colleges of Psychologists. University degree programmes are being reviewed throughout European Union countries in an attempt to unify requirements for professional practice. This review is likely to result in changes in the manner in which students are prepared as psychologists at both undergraduate and graduate levels. However, its impact cannot be determined at this time.

Roles, Functions, and Responsibilities of School Psychologists

As noted earlier in the chapter, the 1990 General Organic Law for the Reform of the Educational System requires an educational model in which the teacher plays a central, though not exclusive, role in improving educational quality. Due to their extensive, important, and complex roles, teachers need support services from other professionals. This support staff may include various specialists, including the school psychologist, speech therapist, physiotherapist, and social worker. Despite their differences, these specialists must work collaboratively as educational teams at each school. This is the context in which both general and individual psychoeducational interventions can be provided by school psychologists and other specialists.

In order to achieve these goals, psychoeducational interventions must be fully integrated into the educational institutions. School psychologists perform specific intervention functions. Their work must aid that of other education professionals. Teachers participate in these interventions by assuming specific responsibilities (e.g., tutorial functions). Thus, distrust and disorganisation between teachers and psychologists are to be avoided so that everyone makes the best use of the psychologist's professional intervention.

School psychology is committed to providing the following seven services (Álvarez, Núñez, González, & López, 2003; González-Pienda, González-Cabanach, Núñez, & Valle, 2002; Marchesi, 1993; Ministerio de Educación y Ciencia, 2004; Sampascual, Navas, & Castejón, 1999; Sanz, Fernández, Campos, Pereto, & González, 1991): diagnostic-intervention, prevention, guidance to assist in professional and vocational decision making, work to improve the dispensation of educational services, family planning, community outreach, and teaching and research. Each of these is discussed in this section.

Before the implementation of the General Organic Law for the Reform of the Educational System, school guidance followed a clinical model. Its goal was to provide direct assistance to students who displayed emotional, adaptation, behavioural, or achievement problems, together with aid, to make decisions about their choice of studies. As of 1990, under the General Organic Law for the Reform of the Educational

System, the work of the school psychologist and other members of the guidance team is a continuous effort that is integrated into the educational process. In this sense, when referring to guidance and tutoring, the rule says that

> guidance in general, and also educational support or specialised psychopedagogical intervention carried out by the guidance department, are part of the curriculum, of the curricular development, and should be understood as an integral educational offer aimed at all aspects of learning and maturation of the student's personality and therefore also should be a personalised offer. (Ministerio de Educación y Ciencia, 1992, p. 18)

This model of work implies the following principles (Sampascual, Navas, & Castejón, 1999):

1. Guidance services should be targeted at all the students and not only at those who have special educational needs (e.g., disabilities, handicaps, etc.); the receipt of guidance services is the right of all the students at their different stages and educational levels.

2. Guidance services should be continuous and systematic throughout the entire educational process (as they are a part of the educational process itself), and therefore they cannot be understood as a series of separate and precise actions.

3. Guidance is an interdisciplinarian task that involves all the members of the educational community (therefore, it must be integrated into the Programación General del Centro Educativo [General Programming of the Educational Centre] and will be understood as a cooperative activity).

4. Guidance services should attend to all the needs of the student (e.g., personality, affective, intellectual needs) and should cover and promote all aspects of the student's development.

5. Guidance services should understand individual differences and should focus on helping students acquire the abilities and skills that will lead to their self-guidance.

6. Therefore, from this perspective, guidance implies a global intervention in the entire educational process, including aspects of centre organisation and functioning, collaboration with teachers in the design of the instructive process, and specific, precise interventions on individual problems that may appear. Thus understood, the model of intervention is a mixed model that adopts traits from different models (clinical-medical, psychometric, humanist, and constructivist).

Diagnostic-Intervention Services

School psychologists attempt to detect, prevent, and address physical, psychological, and social problems (e.g., mental subnormality, affective or personality disorders, enuresis, sleep and eating disorders, behaviour problems, violence, school and family conflicts). Identification begins as early as age 3, when infant education starts. When necessary, school psychologists evaluate children in reference to the educational goals and the ability of the people responsible for helping children achieve these goals. A school psychologist may decide to conduct an evaluation in order to diagnose or rule out problems. Based on this evaluation, a school psychologist may suggest interventions designed to improve students' educational competence and the educational services they receive, to resolve individual and group problems, and to propose specific solutions to the difficulties noted during the evaluation.

School psychology initially utilised a clinical-psychometric model, so there was an extensive tradition in the use of psychological tests. Various commercial firms adapted important tests to the Spanish population. Among them, TEA Ediciones (www.teaediciones.com) markets more than 300 tests, many of which were developed in Spain. Some of these tests were developed in other countries (especially the United States). Thus, school psychologists have access to a wide variety tests that assess cognitive, personality, and social characteristics, study strategies and techniques, and achievement, as well as tests related to instruction, family, and the school-family relationships.

Prevention Services

Preventive services may involve modifying a child's social and educational environments so as to avoid or lessen developmental disorders of an educational or social nature. School psychologists may offer advice or professional assistance to teachers and to others to prevent specific educational problems (e.g., school adjustment difficulties, learning disorders and difficulties, social problems, maladaptive attitudes, and inadequate study habits). Additionally, they may engage in programs designed to overcome pervasive disorders (e.g., health, emotional and sexual behaviours, drug dependency).

Guidance Services to Assist in Professional and Vocational Decision Making

School psychologists help students make decisions about professions or vocations. This work involves conducting evaluations, conferring with others to determine a person's competencies, and clarifying professional or vocational goals. This enables persons to understand their strengths and limitations and guides their training and decision making.

Work to Improve the Applications of Educational Services

School psychologists work to adapt students' educational environments, so students receive more or improved educational services. In this work, school psychologists informally examine the teacher's skills and abilities together with other resources in the class or school. Possible interventions include adapting instruction to

students' learning styles, supporting and assessing teachers, checking their general activity (e.g., adapting plans to students' psychosocial and learning characteristics), and appraising the teachers' adaptations to people and/or to special educational situations and attention to diversity.

Family Planning Services

School psychologists realise that both schools and families exert considerable influence on children's development. Thus, family services, including assessment and interventions, are warranted at times. Services may include helping parents understand their children's development and resulting needs, providing information about various psychological and educational issues (e.g., discipline, study planning and supervision, development of self-esteem, and communication abilities), providing parent training, improving family relationships, and supporting and participating in school programs.

Community Outreach

The characteristics of a community also have a significant impact on a student's development. School psychologists are aware of cultural conditions that may affect a student's social and emotional development and thus may help better link school and community resources, better utilise or improve community services, or work with others to create and sustain them.

Engagement in Reflection, Research, and Teaching

School psychologists engage in activities designed to promote understanding of one's individual contributions and those of the specialty through reflection and research. The goals of these activities are to improve the use of knowledge and technical resources together with an in-depth study of school psychology theory and practices. Through teaching, school psychologists attempt to spread their knowledge to other education professionals, students and their parents, and other professional groups.

More on School Guidance

From a more detailed perspective, school guidance services provided by school psychologists and other professionals occur on three levels: (a) in the classroom wherein guidance services are provided by teachers, especially by the tutor teacher; (b) at school within its guidance department; and (c) at a systems level at which an interdisciplinary team coordinates programme services (Álvarez, Soler, & Hernández, 1998; Álvarez, Soler, González-Pienda, Núñez, & González-Castro, 2002; González-Pienda, Álvarez, Fernández, & González, 2003; Marchesi, 2001). The school psychologist is a part of the guidance department. Thus, some of the main functions in which the psychologist is directly involved (e.g., related to the school as an educational centre, to the student, to the teacher, or to the family) are discussed below.

School-related services include the following: collaborating on the development of educational projects (e.g., general curriculum, specific educational programmes, teacher training); evaluating key educational provisions (e.g., its administration, curriculum adaptations, psychopedagogic interventions); contributing to education through action research; collaborating on educational activities both in and out of school; promoting cooperation between school and family; contributing specialised psychopedagogical services with support from the interdisciplinary team; and promoting professional and vocational guidance services, especially in secondary schools. The educational projects provide a general framework that gives shape to an educational centre and defines the way in which diversity will be attended to (e.g., how the specific needs of each student at the centre will be met in order to promote his or her personal growth and cognitive, social, and affective development). The school psychologist is actively involved in these endeavors.

Student-related services include the following: promoting guidance services for all students; providing individual and diversified academic and professional guidance services that promote vocational maturity and decision making; helping at-risk students and those making transitions (e.g., admission in a new school, change from one grade to another, selection of courses, and transition to adult and working life); providing support and encouragement to students who might need it; and contributing to the introduction of innovative educational methodologies.

Teacher-related services include the following: transmitting information on the psychopedagogical evaluation of students; counselling teachers about practical matters of groups (e.g., efficient ways to provide instruction to groups of students in the classroom); the flexible treatment of students with diverse aptitudes, interests, and motivations; coordinating tutorial work and assessing the tutorial function; facilitating the in-class use of specific instructional techniques related to work habits, study techniques, how-to-think teaching programmes, abstract symbols handling, and similar techniques; collaborating in guidance unit activities; assisting teachers in improving their interpersonal relations and use of group dynamics and management, assessment interviews, and leadership; providing technical guidance on formative and guidance evaluation processes and activities; and collaborating with teachers to detect developmental or learning problems or difficulties.

Family-related services include the following: promoting tutor-family relationships to solve problems that have an impact on children, guiding families so as to improve their ability to responsibly educate and guide their children, and engaging families in school activities and programmes.

Current Issues Impacting School Psychology

School psychologists represent approximately 40% of all working professional psychologists. However, the progressive growth of this specialisation involves certain difficulties that must be addressed. The main difficulties come from three areas: administrative work (e.g., issues concerning professional acknowledgement, recruiting methods); definition of role, profile, and functions (the progressive improvement of traditional clinical-medical practices and the emergence of the social demand for intervention in various areas leads to the need for a constant debate about the issues of the school psychologist's role); and ethical issues (e.g., when school psychologists find themselves in a situation in which there may be a conflict of interest between addressing the needs of students and conforming to the expectations of the local educational system).

Last, the school psychologist currently faces a big challenge in the ever-changing dynamics of the educational world due to technological and social advancements. Reforms planned in the European Union attempt to answer new questions and, furthermore, to create a structure that starts with theoretical training, stresses the practical aspects of the psychologist's professional activity, and emphasises research and scientific activity in daily professional practice.

References

Álvarez, L., Núñez, J. C., González, P., & López, C. (2003). Los equipos de orientación: Asesoramiento para el desarrollo de estrategias de aprendizaje en educación infantil [Guidance teams: Counselling for the development of learning strategies in early childhood education]. In L. Álvarez & G. Fernández (Coords.), *Equipos y departamentos de orientación* (pp. 13–20). Madrid: CCS.

Álvarez, L., Soler, E., González-Pienda, J. A., Núñez, J. C., & González-Castro, P. (2002). *Diversidad con calidad. Programación flexible* [Diversity with quality: Flexible programming]. Madrid: CCS.

Álvarez, L., Soler, E., & Hernández, J. (1998). *Un proyecto de centro para atender a la diversidad* [A project for a centre to attend to diversity]. Madrid: SM Ediciones.

González-Pienda, J. A., Álvarez, L., Fernández, G., & González, P. (2003). El departamento de orientación: Asesoramiento para la elaboración de adaptaciones grupales [The guidance department: Counselling for the elaboration of group adaptations]. In L. Álvarez & G. Fernández (Coords.), *Equipos y Departamentos de Orientación* (pp. 101–122). Madrid: CCS.

González-Pienda, J. A., González-Cabanach, R., Núñez, J. C., & Valle, A. (Coords.). (2002). *Manual de psicología de la educación* [Handbook of educational psychology]. Madrid: Pirámide.

Marchesi, A. (1993). Intervención psicopedagógica en la escuela [Psychopedagogic intervention at school]. In J. Beltrán, V. Bermejo, D. Prieto, & D. Vence (Eds.), *Intervención psicopedagógica* (pp. 383–399). Madrid: Pirámide.

Marchesi, A. (2001). Dilemas y condiciones de las escuelas inclusivas [Dilemmas and conditions of inclusive schools]. In A. Sipán (Coord.), *Educar para la diversidad en el siglo XXI* (pp. 143–152). Zaragoza: Mira.

Ministerio de Educación y Ciencia. (1992). *Orientación y tutoría. Educación secundaria* [Guidance and tutorship: Secondary education]. Madrid: Secretaría de Estado de Educación.

Ministerio de Educación y Ciencia. (2004). *Proyecto de Ley Orgánica de Educación* [Organic Education Law Project]. Retrieved July 26, 2005, from http://www.mec.es/mecd/jsp/plantilla.jsp?id=31&area=estadistica

Muñoz, A. M., García, B., & Sánchez, A. (1997). La psicología en la escuela: Aportaciones a la historia de la psicología escolar [Psychology at school: Contributions to the history of school psychology]. *Psicología Educativa, 3*(1), 7–126.

Sampascual, G., Navas, L., & Castejón, J. L. (1999). *Funciones del orientador en primaria y secundaria* [The guidance counsellor's functions in primary and secondary education]. Madrid: Alianza Editorial.

Sanz, L. M., Fernández, A., Campos, F., Pereto, M., & González, P. (1991). El rol del psicólogo escolar [The school psychologist's role]. *Papeles del Psicólogo, 51*, 51–52.

39

School Psychology in Switzerland

Lukas Scherer

Heinz Bösch

Paul Zeberli

Context of School Psychology

Switzerland is located in Central Europe, with a western border of France, northern border of Germany, southern border of Italy, and eastern border of Austria. Its landmass is 41,000 square kilometers, a high percentage of which is the Alps. Switzerland is divided into 29 regional provinces, referred to as cantons. Its population, about 7.3 million (47% male; Bundesamt für Statistik, 2006), is varied culturally and uses four official languages: German, French, Italian, and a Roman-oriented language (Romansch). Among its population are 465,000 primary school students (6% of the population), 295,000 secondary school students (4%), and 400,000 students in higher education or apprenticeships (4%), about 90,000 of whom are attending a university. Persons ages 20 through 39 constitute 28% of the population; 40 through 64, 34%; and over 64, 16%. Approximately 42% of marriages end in divorce. Households average 2.24 persons. Switzerland has a prosperous and stable market economy, along with low unemployment (3%), a highly skilled labor force, and a per capita gross domestic product larger than many of the Western European economies. In 2004, the annual gross domestic product was about US$251.9 billion, with an average per capita income of US$33,800.

Attendance in Grades 1 through 9 is compulsory. Each of the 26 cantons (i.e., regional states or provinces) has its own educational system. All provincial educational directors attempt to coordinate their different systems with the goal of achieving an educational system that is similar throughout the country. Nevertheless, educational conditions differ, especially between the French- and Italian-speaking cantons. Schools are governed locally and are supervised by elected representatives.

The following description applies mainly to school systems within German-speaking cantons, where the majority of the population lives. Children enter school at age 6 or 7 and remain there for the next 9 years. The dropout rate is low, less than 1%. Most students attend public school. The number of students who attend private schools (5%–10%) is small but increasing. Depending on the canton, primary education extends for 4 to 6 years, and secondary education extends for 3 to 5 years. Secondary school students are grouped in two to four academic ability levels. After completing primary or secondary school, students with high achievement may elect to enter a gymnasium. Approximately 15% to 20% of students pass an exam and attend a gymnasium. Graduation from a gymnasium is a commonly used pathway to enter a university. Most students enter an apprenticeship after completing secondary school. Apprenticeships are popular because they promote technical and professional skills as well as provide further education in specific schools. Apprentices often work on the job for 3 days and attend school for 2 days. During their apprenticeship, persons can apply to enter a university program in applied sciences.

Switzerland has a well-developed system for students with special needs. About 5% of primary school students (http://www.bista.zh.ch/vs/VS_Stufen.htm) receive special education services through inclusive, small classes, or separate institutions. Public school special education classes typically average about 10 to 14 students. They include students with minor learning disabilities, behavior problems, and non-German-speaking immigrant children. Most public schools provide forms of inclusive education. In some subjects, students with learning disabilities obtain their instruction in small groups. Several different institutions (e.g., special needs schools, apprenticeships for handicapped children in protected institutions) specialize in serving some children with special needs, including those with intellectual, physical, language, or attention deficit disorders. During the past few years, the average class size for all students has increased, going from about 20 students in primary school and fewer in secondary schools in the 1980s to current levels of 25 to 27 in primary grades and 22 to 24 in secondary grades.

Origin, History, and Current Status of School Psychology

School psychology in Switzerland started in 1919 in Geneva (Caglar, 1983; Wall, 1956), where Claparède first used the term *school psychology* (Gerber, 1994). In 1920, the first school psychology service was established in Bern and was called an educational consultation center. In Basel, the first service was in 1927, 1939 in St. Gallen, and 1942 in Lucerne. Until the mid 1960s, school psychology was mainly administered by teachers with further education; from about 1975 on, more persons educated in psychology were working in school psychology (Gerber, 1994). The development of school psychology was closely associated with the growth of special education, especially the need to evaluate students who were experiencing school-related difficulties, leading to diagnoses, special education placement, and interventions. A law that required students to be assessed by school psychologists contributed importantly to school psychologists' employment in German-speaking areas. During the past 15 years, school psychology has been accepted, especially by parents who see that their children are receiving additional and needed educational services.

The term *school psychologist* typically is used in German-speaking areas. In Bern, the terms *educational adviser* or *educational psychologist* are used. The Swiss Association for Child and Youth Psychology prefers the use of *child psychologist* or *psychologist for youth.*

Across Switzerland, there are about 800 school psychologists, 60% of whom are females. Some 650 are members of the Swiss Association for Child and Youth Psychology. Although annual salaries differ between the cantons, they often begin at approximately US$50,000 and go up to US$100,000 for those with the most experience. Most school psychologists are employed by public institutions organized by local schools or, in some areas, by the cantons. Some school psychologists work as consultants in special public schools and psychiatric institutions. School psychologists work more frequently in urban than rural areas. The ratio between school psychologists and students is lower in rural than urban areas. The ratio of school psychologists to students varies from 1 to 1,000 to 1 to 6,000. Many school psychologists have been employed in their positions for many years. They often feel overwhelmed from working overtime, and some experience professional burnout.

Infrastructure of School Psychology

School psychology is represented by regional, district, and national professional associations. The Schweizerische Vereinigung für Kinder- und Jugendpsychologie (Swiss Association for Child and Youth Psychology) serves as its national association. Membership in this association requires a person to have a university degree in psychology and employment as a school psychologist. Associations have their most important impact at the provincial level—the location of school systems. Although school psychologists do not hold a professional license, they can use the restricted and protected terms *child psychologist* or *psychologist for youth* (Swiss Federation of Psychologists, www.psychologie.ch) that refer to the specialization of school psychology. These titles are

awarded after completing a graduate program of 750 hours. Some cantons require school psychologists to hold the title "child and youth psychologist" or "educational psychologist." Few regulations govern school psychology practice. Those that impact their practice generally address services provided to special needs students, especially assessment services.

The Swiss Association for Child and Youth Psychology sponsors one semiannual journal for school psychology, *Psychologie und Erziehung* (Psychology and Education). The Swiss Federation of Psychologists publishes *Psychoscope* (Psychology Review), which includes articles on education and school psychology.

Preparation of School Psychologists

Preparation to become a school psychologist takes, on average, 5 to 6 years to obtain a graduate degree. The University of Lausanne offers the only graduate program designed specifically for school and vocational counseling. This program has few students. School psychologists must obtain a master's degree. Most obtain a graduate degree in applied, clinical, or child psychology.

A degree from the University of Applied Psychology in Zurich requires 4 years and currently offers the degree of Diploma in Clinical Psychology. After 2007, this university will offer a master's degree. Although the nature of the courses to prepare school psychologists are not regulated, every psychologist who completes a master's degree may be employed as a school psychologist. The Swiss Federation of Psychologists prefers school psychologists to use the title "child and youth psychologist." However, the use of this title is not regulated in law. Efforts by the canton of Zurich to regulate school psychology have been successful: The last vote on public schools resulted in school psychology being included in the law for the first time. The specific nature of its regulations will be determined later. The canton of Bern requires school psychologists to complete a 2-year graduate education program in educational psychology.

University programs in psychology typically require 2 years of basic education (e.g., statistics, personality psychology, applied psychology, clinical psychology, child psychology, developmental and social psychology). On completing these courses, students decide to specialize in one of the following areas: clinical, applied, child, developmental and social, or personality psychology. Students also select two additional subjects for studying (e.g., psychopathology). During the last 2 years, psychology students have considerable flexibility in designing their programs. Students also complete applied courses and a 3- to 6-month internship. The canton of Bern requires a 1-year internship following the completion of a master's degree. Some agencies that employ school psychologists require additional preparation in psychotherapy. On beginning their work, school psychologists often take additional courses, including supervision, in order to further advance their knowledge and professional abilities.

During the 1990s, the Swiss Association for Child and Youth Psychology (www.skjp.ch) strengthened a specialized postgraduate education program by clarifying and adding requirements for those who desire to hold the title "child and youth psychologist." To enter this program, a psychologist must have a university degree in psychology. This postgraduate program requires 750 hours of coursework, including 300 hours in diagnosis, counseling, and developmental and organizational psychology, and another 150 hours of supervised work. Psychologists can select other relevant courses for an additional 150 hours. Finally, 150 hours are reserved for research.

School psychologists, as well as general psychologists, take courses in cognitive, applied, personality, developmental, educational, social, and philosophical psychology; statistics and research methods; intervention methods; and counseling. Additional program requirements may include neuropathology, neuropsychology, psychopathology, pharmacology, psychotherapy (e.g., systemic approach, psychoanalysis, cognitive-behavioral psychology), and special education. Although testing and other assessment methods are acquired through coursework, most school psychologists acquire these skills during their practicum and internship experiences in schools, psychiatry clinics, or child care centers. Little attention is devoted to legal and ethical issues. All cantons require a university degree for employment (Milic, 2001).

Roles, Functions, and Responsibilities of School Psychologists

A school psychologist may be responsible for multiple schools within a community or for a particular school district within a city. Their basic responsibility is to promote student development in all areas of public schools (regular education, special education, boarding schools). Their roles include assessing students and recommending interventions (e.g., learning support, special local education). This work requires them to meet with the student, parents, other caretakers if needed, and teachers to review the assessment results and recommendations. About 40% of their time is devoted to assessment; 30% to meetings and consultation; 20% to administrative work, intervention, organizational tasks, and prevention activities; and 10% for continuous education and informal meetings in schools. Implementation of interventions is less common but does happen with individuals, families, or at the systems level. A study in the canton of Zurich (Milic, 2001) found that school psychologists spent the majority of their time assessing children (57%). School psychologists are supervised by experienced colleagues. School psychologists regularly consult with other professionals as well as local and state educational authorities.

Commonly used tests include the Kaufman Assessment Battery for Children, Wechsler

Intelligence Scale for Children–III, Cattell Culture Fair Test, personality tests including the Wartegg Test and the Zulliger Test (a form of Rorschach Test for children), and the Draw-A-Tree/Person/Family tests. In addition, school psychologists commonly use several sentence-completion forms to assess personality, questionnaires to assess behavior problems and attention-deficit/hyperactivity disorder, and tests to assess psychomotor skills, visual perception, and memory. Student achievement is assessed, including spelling, through the Salzburger Lese- und Rechtschreibe Test and Diagnostischer Rechtschreibe Test; reading, through the Zürcher Lesetest and Zurcher Leseverständnis Test; and math tests for certain grades (Rechentest for Grades 1–4).

Current Issues Impacting School Psychology

In some cantons (i.e., Bern), school psychological services are regulated by law. Professional associations representing school psychology are attempting to establish laws that require the use of school psychology services in some German-speaking cantons that do not have such laws. In addition, school psychologists are beginning to be employed in family care centers.

The legalization of services and specifying the nature of school psychology professional preparation programs are important issues in those areas that lack such policies. School psychology is unlikely to obtain these goals at this time. Some changes in school law will occur in the coming years, at which time school psychologists must help ensure their services are acknowledged in the law.

References

Bundesamt für Statistik [Federal Bureau of Statistics]. (2006). Retrieved May 11, 2006, from http://www.bfs.admin.ch/bfs/portal/de/index/themen/bevoelkerung/sprachen_religionen/blank/kennzahlen0/sprachen.html and http://www.bfs.admin.ch/bfs/portal/de/index/themen/bildung_und_wissenschaft/bildung/bildungssystem/kennzahlen0/lernende_r/uebersicht.html

Caglar, H. (1983). *La psychologie scolaire* [School psychology]. Paris: Presses Universitaires de France.

Gerber, J. (1994). *Geschichte der Schulpsychologischen Dienste der Deutschschweiz* [History of the school psychology services in the German-speaking part of Switzerland]. Unpublished dissertation, University of Zurich.

Kaser, R. (1993). *Neue Perspektiven in der Schulpsychologie: Handbuch der Schulpsychologie auf ökosystemischer Grundlage* [New perspectives in school psychology: Handbook of school psychology on the basis of ecosystemical thinking]. Bern: Haupt.

Milic, A. (2001). *Die Schulpsychologischen Dienste im Kanton Zürich* [School psychology services in the canton of Zurich]. Zürich: Bildungsdirektion des Kantons Zürich.

Wall, D. (1956). Psychologie im Dienst der Schule [Psychology in the schools]. Hamburg: UNESCO-Institut für Pädagogik.

40

Psychological Services in the Schools in Turkey

Nevin Dölek

Z. Hande Sart

Psychological services in Turkish schools date back to the 1950s and were largely influenced by the advances and developments in the field of psychological counseling in the United States. Professionals providing psychological services in the schools are typically referred to as *psychological counselors*. There are no undergraduate or graduate programs in school psychology offered in the universities. For this reason, the term *psychological services* is used in this chapter.

Context of Psychological Services in the Schools

The Republic of Turkey (Türkiye Cumhuriyeti) was founded in 1923 from the Anatolian remnants of the Ottoman Empire. Under the leadership of Mustafa Kemal Atatürk during the 1920s, the country adopted wide-ranging social, legal, and political reforms. A bi-continental country, Turkey is located mainly in the Middle East and partly in Southeast Europe. The actual area of Turkey is 814,578 square kilometers, of which 790,200 are in Asia and 24,378 are in Europe. Turkey is bordered by Bulgaria and Greece on the west; Georgia, Armenia, Azerbaijan, and Iran on the east; and Iraq and Syria on the south. Turkey's location is where the three continents of Asia, Africa, and Europe are closest to one another. The mainland of Turkey, Anatolia, is called "the cradle of civilization," because it hosted many civilizations, including the Hittite, Phrygian, Lydian, and Trojan civilizations, the Seljuk, the Ottoman Empire, and others.

Turkey's total population in 2002 was 67.8 million, estimated at 70.41 million in 2006; its population is the second largest in Europe. The estimated population distribution by age is birth to 14 years, 25.5%; 15 to 64 years, 67.7%; 65 years and over, 6.8% (http://www.die.gov.tr). Seventy percent of the population is younger than 35 years. Students, in private and public institutions from preschool to higher education, constitute 25% of the population. More than 60% of the population resides in cities (Tunalı, Ercan, Başkent, Öztürk, & Akçiğit, 2003). The majority of the population is of Turkish ethnicity and speaks the official language of the country, Turkish. Other minorities include the Abkhaz, Albanians, Arabs, Armenians, Assyrians, Bosniaks, Circassians, Greeks, Georgians, Jews, Kurds, Levantines, and Zazas. Nearly 99% of the population is Muslim, although Turkey is the only Islamic country that includes secularism in its constitution and guarantees complete freedom of worship to non-Muslims.

Since World War II, the Turkish economy has been transformed by the growth of modern industry and commerce and the consequent decline in the share of agriculture in its national income. In 2004, Turkey's gross domestic product was US$508.7 billion, US$7,400 per capita. Agriculture still accounts for more than 35% of employment. The largest industrial sector, however, is textiles and clothing, which accounts for one third of industrial employment. However, other sectors, notably the automotive and electronics industries, are rising in importance. Employment percentages are 36% agriculture, 23% industry, and 41% services (http://www.die.gov.tr). During the past decade, the Turkish economy has suffered from several major shocks, including two Gulf Wars, an economic crisis, the delayed impact of the Russian crisis, and two devastating earthquakes in the industrialized regions of western Turkey. These resulted in substantial fluctuations in the standard of living. Notably, between the end of 2000 and the beginning of 2003, the number of unemployed individuals doubled (Akkök & Watts, 2003; Tunalı et al., 2003).

According to the results of the 2000 Census, 27,429,570 children (defined as the population under 20) resided in Turkey (http://www.die.gov.tr). Children under age 5 account for 6,584,822, those between ages 5 and 9 account for 6,756,617, those between ages 10 and 14 account for 6,878,656, and those between ages 15 and 19

account for 7,209,475. Thus, children under 20 make up approximately 40% of the population.

The educational system in Turkey includes formal education and nonformal education. Formal education includes pre-primary education, primary and secondary education, and higher education institutions. Pre-primary education includes optional education of children between ages 36 and 72 months who are too young for compulsory primary education. Primary education for children between ages 6 and 14 is compulsory for all citizens, boys and girls, and is free in public schools. Primary education institutions provide 8 years of education, at the end of which graduates receive a primary education diploma. These include public institutions (primary schools, boarding schools, schools for children with disabilities) and private institutions (Turkish, foreign, minority, and international primary schools). Secondary education includes all institutions of general, vocational, and technical education for a period of at least 3 years following primary education. However, educational reform, starting with the 2005–2006 school year, has extended secondary education to 4 years. Among higher education institutions are universities, faculties, institutes, higher education schools, conservatories, vocational higher education schools, and application-research centers. Nonformal education includes services such as teaching reading and writing and continuing education opportunities for students to acquire the concepts and habits of collective living, supporting, helping, and working and organizing collectively.

In Turkey, all aspects of schooling, including educational programs, curricula, and the selection of teachers and resources are performed under the supervision and control of the Ministry of National Education. According to the Constitution, everyone has the right to receive formal education. During the 2001–2002 academic year, the total numbers of students and teachers were 16,090,785 and 578,805, respectively (Akyüz, 2001). Ratios of students to teachers at each level of the education system were pre-primary (256,392:14,520), primary (10,310,844:375,511), secondary (2,312,271:138,785), and nonformal (3,211,278:49,989). Paralleling changes in the school system, the Ministry of National Education is also making changes to the goals, programs, and organizations of nonformal education by shifting its focus from formal or nonformal education to continuing education. As of 2005, 16 types of nonformal education institutions, such as public training centers, apprenticeship training centers, practical schools of art for girls, industrial practical schools of art, open primary education, open high schools, and vocational and technical open schools, are now functioning within the Ministry of National Education system and are providing services to people of all ages.

Across the education system, over 90% of students are enrolled in public school systems. Enrollment rates in the 2000–2001 academic year were 100% in pre-primary education, 100% in primary education, and 64% in secondary education (22% in vocational education and 42% in general high schools). In the academic year 1997–1998, the overall average number of students per classroom was 43; in 2001–2002, this figure dropped to 39, and in cities, it was reduced from 61 to 48. There are 578,800 teachers employed in 58,900 public, private, and special education institutions. In the formal education system, 96% of the schools, 98% of the students, and 95% of the teachers are in public institutions. Education services are also provided in special education schools for children and adolescents in five disability groups, namely, visual impairment, hearing impairment, orthopedic impairment, mental retardation, and chronic illness. In the academic year 2001–2002, 17,600 students were educated, and 3,100 teachers were employed in 347 special education schools and institutions.

Origin, History, and Current Status of Psychological Services in the Schools

The necessity for psychological services within the educational system was formally recognized by a decree from the Ministry of National Education in 1953, which resulted in the establishment of the first center for psychological services in Ankara in 1955. For diagnostic and educational purposes, the Test and Research Bureau, established by the Ministry of National Education in 1953, started to standardize tests of intelligence, personality, and achievement (Doğan, 1998). In 1958, the Ministry of National Education issued a bylaw that changed the name of the Psychological Services Centers to Guidance and Research Centers in order to specifically emphasize the need for guidance and research (Öner, 1977). The period between 1955 and 1960 marked the beginning of guidance and counseling services in Turkey and thus the establishment of psychological services in its schools. Within the framework of this movement, psychological services in schools were defined by the functions of those employed by the Ministry of National Education at Guidance and Research Centers.

The impact of the testing movement constituted a second force in the growth of psychological services. According to the report prepared by Öner (1977), group tests of mental and educational abilities were initiated in guidance centers and in schools; individual tests of mental and personality characteristics quickly became standard procedures in psychiatry or mental health clinics (cited in Dölek, Inceoğlu, & Özdemir, 1989). The establishment of guidance and counseling services in junior and senior high schools was mentioned in the Second Five-Year Developmental Plan that was implemented between 1968 and 1972 (T. C. Başbakanlık Devlet Planlama Teşkilatı, 1967). In the Third Five-Year Developmental Plan, covering 1973 to 1977, the importance of guidance in education was further emphasized (T. C. Basbakanlık Devlet Planlama Teşkilatı, 1973). In the Basic Law of National Education, guidance and counseling services were deemed necessary in schools. In accordance with the decisions taken at the meeting of the Ninth National Council of Education in 1974, a 2-hour weekly guidance program was included in the curriculum of junior and senior high schools (T. C. Milli Eğitim Bakanlığı, 1985).

During the period of establishment of under-graduate programs in counseling (1982–1995), Turkish universities began accepting students in a 4-year bachelor of education program. In 1989, the Psychological Counseling and Guidance Association was founded by a group of educators in Ankara. The Association began to publish the *Journal of Psychological Counseling and Guidance* in 1990 and added a newsletter, *Psychological Counseling and Guidance Bulletin*, in 1997. The Turkish Psychological Counseling and Guidance Association held the First National Psychological Counseling and Guidance Congress in 1991. The ethical standards of the counseling profession were established in 1995 (Psikolojik Danısma ve Rehberlik Derneği, 1995). In 1992, the International School Psychology Colloquium was held in Istanbul, which motivated international involvement among colleagues. The Turkish Psychological Counseling and Guidance Association became affiliated with the International School Psychology Association at that time. In 1996, the Higher Education Council, in collaboration with the World Bank, developed 4-year undergraduate and master's degree guidance and counseling programs under the National Education Development Project for Pre-service Teacher Education (YÖK/World Bank National Education Development Project Pre-service Teacher Education, 1996).

The two major earthquakes in 1999 had a profound influence on the development and nature of psychological services. On August 17, 1999, an earthquake caused destruction equal to that of approximately 400 nuclear bombs when it hit the Marmara region of western Turkey (Sağlamer et al., 1999). According to information from the General Directorate of Disaster Affairs of the Ministry of Public Works and Settlement, a total of 18,373 lives were lost, 48,901 people were injured, and 800,000 were left homeless by the widespread destruction (İşte Depremin Bilançosu, 2000). Social Services and Child Protection Organization reported that 1,400 children lost their mothers, fathers, or both (Deprem, 2000). Less than 3 months later, another massive earthquake, rated 7.2 on the Richter scale, hit Duzce and Bolu in the region just east of the first disaster area. It left another 100,000 homeless, 8,845 dead, and 4,948 wounded. The psychological impact was immense, as Turkey was still struggling to cope with the first disaster when the second struck. Schools were also affected greatly: 178 teachers and 1,387 students died, 1,605 schools were damaged, and 102 schools collapsed (İşte Depremin Bilançosu, 2000; T. C. Başbakanlık Kriz Yönetim Merkezi, 2000).

Hundreds of mental health professionals (psychologists, psychiatrists, counselors, and social workers) focused, from the beginning, on the need for psychosocial support to children and their parents. These professionals worked in earthquake areas on a volunteer basis for many months. Priority was given to helping children. A few days after the earthquake, psychosocial support activities were already taking place in children's centers in the disaster areas. These were initiated by nongovernmental organizations and universities and later supported by the United Nations International Children's Fund and the Ministry of National Education. Yet, a need for empowering professionals with effective crisis response tools was felt soon afterward. For this reason, efforts were concentrated on organizing immediate training programs for mental health professionals, including those working in schools. Within several months, many programs were provided by experts from different countries.

One of the training programs for mental health professionals was delivered in İstanbul, through the Helpers Assisting Survivors of Natural Disasters project, an initiative of the Community Stress Prevention Center of Kiryat Shmona, Israel. Another was organized by the Turkish Psychology Association on the Eye Movement Desensitization Reprocessing approach. The International School Psychology Association and the National Emergency Assistance Team members of the National Association of School Psychologists in the

United States provided a series of training programs on crisis intervention for school counselors, school psychologists, and school principals. This series was sponsored by the Foundation for the Advancement of Counseling in Education in Turkey. As a result of these programs, the Foundation for the Advancement of Counseling in Education, in cooperation with the Department of Education in the province of Istanbul, developed a project to assist the schools to prepare for crisis situations. This project aimed to (a) establish crisis intervention units at Guidance and Research Centers in various provinces of Istanbul, (b) form interschool crisis support groups with the participation of the principals from 15 schools in the same province, and (c) set up a school crisis response team in each school to develop skills in crisis intervention and assist in its effectiveness. The first achievement of this project was to train 180 principals, 50 psychologists or counselors working at Guidance and Research Centers, and 15 psychological counselors as trainers on crisis preparation, crisis management, and crisis response in schools.

The Turkish Ministry of National Education, in collaboration with the United Nations International Children's Fund, other United Nations agencies, and the Turkish Psychological Association, developed a comprehensive Psychosocial School Project to assist schools in disaster areas. To implement such a large-scale project, a strong infrastructure was developed. The Ministry of National Education in Ankara appointed a project team from within the Ministry and a professional National Expert Team representing some of the key resource institutions in Turkey (Ministry of National Education & UNICEF, 2001). The projects contributed to an increased acceptance and recognition of the importance of counseling services within Ministry of National Education, as well as in the school system.

School psychological service professionals gained a huge amount of experience from these unfortunate events and now have a better working plan to help in times of crisis. There is growing awareness in Turkey of the need for crisis plans and for school safety programs. In addition, there is a higher appreciation of the work done by mental health providers both inside and outside of the schools. These events led many universities to initiate courses on crisis intervention in counseling programs.

In response to inquiries made by the authors, an officer of the Ministry of National Education (H. Şen, personal communication, July 2005) reported that by the 2005–2006 school year, the total number of professionals working for psychological services was 11,327 (5,782 females, 5,545 males). Approximately 53% of these professionals are serving at the primary school level, and 37% are working at the secondary school level. Only 79 psychological counselors are reported to be working in rehabilitation centers for children with mental retardation and autism. In 2005, there were 133 Guidance and Research Centers with a total of 917 professionals (527 females, 390 males) serving students. There are almost no psychological services in schools in rural areas, but Guidance and Research Centers in city centers also serve students referred by rural schools (Ministry of National Education, n.d.).

More than half of the professionals currently employed to deliver psychological services in the school system have a bachelor's degree in guidance and psychological counseling (58%) or psychology (8%); the rest come from a diverse variety of bachelor's degree programs, such as educational sciences, child development, educational management, special education teaching, pedagogy, sociology, and philosophy. The ratio of students to psychological counselors appears to be about 4,500 to 1. Salaries of psychological services personnel working in public schools and Guidance and Research Centers are determined by the Ministry of Finance and the Ministry of Work and Social Security, because they are considered to be state workers. Most receive payment equal to that of teachers, averaging about US$600 to US$900 per month, depending on years of experience. Those working in the private schools earn about US$800 to US$1,500 per month (http://www.iskur.gov.tr). Job stability for those working for public schools and for Guidance and Research Centers is high, because their rights are protected by the laws for state workers. Work contracts in private schools are usually for one year, to be renewed every year. This creates considerable anxiety for professionals working in private schools. Increasing numbers of private schools and universities create new job opportunities, yet job security is not stable in private institutions.

The organization of in-service training for psychological counselors is the responsibility of the Ministry of National Education. However, professional associations and private counseling centers also have active roles in organizing in-service training. The Ministry of National Education encourages psychological counselors working in public schools and Guidance and Research Centers to pursue graduate studies by enabling them to work, while going to school, without any reduction in their salaries. On the other hand, most of the private schools provide financial support for the in-service training of their psychological counselors. Although many psychological counselors hope to find employment outside the school system (e.g., in private counseling centers) when they complete their master's or doctoral studies, the number of psychologists and counselors in private practice is still limited.

The Infrastructure of Psychological Services in the Schools

Three national organizations work on behalf of psychologists and psychological counselors in Turkey. The Turkish Psychological Association was founded in 1976 and has approximately 1,600 members. It is the only professional organization that represents the science and the profession of psychology in Turkey. The Turkish Psychological Counseling and Guidance Association, which was founded in 1989, serves the counseling profession in Turkey. The Foundation for the Advancement of Counseling in Education is a nonprofit organization that aims to advance the development of psychological services in schools and help cultivate the profession in higher education institutions.

Turkish national education has been determined in accordance with the Constitution of the Turkish Republic, the Basic Law of National Education No. 1739, and the Law for Unification of Education and the Law for Eight-Year Compulsory and Uninterrupted Education No. 4306 (www.meb.gov.tr). To overcome the problems in the field of special education and to improve the quality of education for students with disabilities, Act 573 was enacted in 1997. According to Act 573, all individuals with disabilities have the right to be educated. Accordingly, children with disabilities who were previously disregarded or restricted from exercising their educational rights are given the opportunity to benefit from education (Ministry of National Education, 1997).

Role definitions, tasks, and functions of guidance and psychological counselors in the schools and of professionals working at Guidance and Research Centers are regulated by a Ministry of National Education decree. The most recently revised decree, dated May 2001, declares that school psychological services in Turkey are mainly performed by the guidance and psychological counseling offices in primary and secondary schools and Guidance and Research Centers of the Ministry of National Education (T. C. Milli Eğitim Bakanlığı, 2001b).

Preparation of Psychologists Working in the Schools

As of 2004, approximately 4,290 students were enrolled in counseling psychology undergraduate programs. Approximately 695 students apply yearly for the bachelor of arts degree in these programs. The distribution of students enrolled in guidance, psychological counseling, and psychology departments at the undergraduate and graduate levels are as follows. In the 2003–2004 academic year, a total of 695 students from 34 universities graduated from undergraduate guidance and psychological counseling programs; 450 students from 23 universities graduated from undergraduate psychology programs. Also in the 2003–2004 academic year, only 57 students at the master's level and 12 students at the doctoral level graduated from guidance and psychological counseling programs, and only 89 students at the master's level and 10 students at the doctoral level graduated from psychology programs (www .osym.gov.tr).

In contrast to international practices in the field of school psychology, no school psychology program exists at the undergraduate and graduate levels. Since 1982, the number of programs in psychological services has been increasing at both the undergraduate and graduate levels. However, there is great discrepancy among the courses offered and in course content from one university to another (Akkoyun, 1995). Some programs emphasize a psychological base in their training; others underscore educational sciences. In addition, there are no formally recognized requirements for professional certification and no procedures for official accreditation, and there is no agreement on a job title or a definition of psychological counseling (Doğan, 1998).

Although there are no established accreditation standards to guide the preparation of psychological counselors, most of the universities use the scientist-practitioner model. For example, Bogazici University in Istanbul provides specialization at the master's level in guidance and psychological counseling (Bogazici University, n.d.). The program emphasizes both theory and technical competence and has three areas of focus: (a) theoretical, with specialized focus on culture, community, development, and special education (e.g., personality theories, adoloscent psychology, early intervention,

cultural issues, educational psychology, and psychological assessment); (b) research (e.g., program development and evaluation, research methods, and applied research); and (c) field practice (internship) using different kinds of assessment tools, skills, and intervention methods under supervision, classroom observations, consultation, testing, and interviews. The Master of Arts in Guidance and Psychological Counseling program in the Department of Educational Sciences is a 2-year program consisting of 30 credit hours of coursework spread over four semesters and includes a thesis and an oral thesis defense. Students are also required to complete fieldwork. The successful completion of the program leads to the master of arts in educational sciences degree (www.boun .edu.tr). The program in the Middle East Technical University, Ankara, emphasizes (a) core courses on research methods and educational statistics; (b) courses in psychological counseling and guidance (e.g., counseling children, assessment, career development counseling, crisis counseling, counseling in higher education, principles and techniques of counseling, field practices, and group counseling); and (c) elective courses (e.g., ethical issues in counseling, theories of counseling, mental health issues, and guidance) (Middle East Technical University, n.d.).

Roles, Functions, and Responsibilities of Psychologists Working in the Schools

According to the Decree of Guidance and Psychological Counseling Services, Guidance and Research Centers were to be established in cities and towns in Turkey (T. C. Milli Eğitim Bakanlığı, 2001a). These centers are designed to coordinate the activities of guidance and psychological services in the primary and secondary schools in the city where they are situated and to identify students with special needs and carry out necessary interventions and placements. Professionals on the Guidance and Research Centers' interdisciplinary teams include psychological counselors, psychologists, special educators, social workers, and program development specialists.

The stated functions of these centers are to conduct research for the purpose of developing better educational methods and strategies at schools, to study local problems in educational institutions, to submit reports to Ministry of National Education representatives in the city, to coordinate the yearly programs rendered by guidance and psychological counseling units in schools, to identify needs and organize in-service training for guidance and psychological counselors working in schools, to carry out individual and group counseling and therapy services for students with emotional and behavioral problems and their parents (who are referred by the schools), to identify students with special educational needs, to prepare individual educational programs, and to apply individual and group tests at the centers. In carrying out their function of remediation for students with problems, the centers are expected to refer children with extreme problems to the medical centers located at nearby university hospitals. It seems that the responsibilities and functions of Guidance and Research Centers resemble the tasks of school psychologists in Western countries (Dölek et al., 1989).

The scope of psychological services in schools is quite extensive. The most frequent direct services to students involve vocational and academic guidance and personal counseling. Other direct services include testing, group counseling, and consultation with teachers and parents. Diagnosing emotional and behavioral problems in pupils and applying interventions are given priority. Identifying learning disabilities and providing curriculum-based interventions to teachers in order to modify behavioral and academic problems in the classroom are tasks that are seldom performed. Few materials are available for remedial work in the subject

area. Those working in private schools may also take part in selecting students at the primary level, even at kindergarten. For that purpose, psychological counselors in primary schools use standardized or nonstandardized assessment techniques, observations, and interviews with applicants for kindergarten and first grade. In private schools, psychological counselors often are also responsible for organizing seminars, lectures, and group guidance on children's development and needs for parents and teachers. Referrals are generally made by teachers and involve behavioral, emotional, and/or learning problems, but services usually focus on individual counseling or working with parents rather than working with teachers. Generally, teachers report that they do not receive adequate support. Students are often referred to professionals in therapy centers or hospital mental health clinics; these professionals are usually psychiatrists who are mostly medication-oriented or psychologists in private practice who apply therapeutic approaches.

In 2001–2002, the Ministry of National Education published a report about the tests commonly used in Guidance and Research Centers. According to the report, tests used include Beier Sentence Completion, Bender Visual-Motor Gestalt Test, Children's Apperception Test, Cattell Intelligence Test, Denver Developmental Screening Test, Leiter International Performance Scale–Revised, Peabody Picture Vocabulary Test, Stanford-Binet Intelligence Test, Stanford-Binet Intelligence Test for children with visual impairment, and the Wechsler Intelligence Scale for Children–Revised.

Current Issues Impacting Psychological Services in Turkey

From the beginning, according to the laws and bylaws regulating psychological services, in schools and in Guidance and Research Centers, counseling was not seen as a separate unit but as a supplementary unit of the Special Education Department of the Ministry of National Education. This attitude can create two situations: one in which counselors specialize in different disciplines, such as sociology, special education, and philosophy, and a second in which psychologists, counselors, and special education specialists are appointed by the Ministry of National Education to provide psychological services in the schools without any distinction between their roles and functions.

The debate on how to organize psychological services in the schools and how to train professionals in this area has been ongoing; no consensus has yet been attained. Although many of the school psychology practices in other countries are also carried out in Turkey, either by guidance and psychological counselors in the schools or by Guidance and Research Centers, no independent and well-defined specialization in school psychology exists in Turkey. This leads to ambiguity in role definitions and conflicts among counselors, psychologists, special educators, and social workers. Furthermore, the Ministry of National Education appoints professionals who specialize in disciplines other than psychological counseling and psychology, such as sociology, education, and philosophy, to provide psychological services in schools. This creates another problem with the advocacy of professional rights. Significant numbers of psychological counselors labor under inadequate work conditions. They frequently lack adequate supervision, secretarial support, appropriate assessment techniques, and adequate time in which to perform duties. Other work-related difficulties include a lack of economic resources and a lack of knowledge among school personnel and parents about the nature of work school psychological personnel can perform.

Many professionals working for psychological services in the school system report problems with teachers and school administrations. Conflicts are associated with the diffusion of their professional roles within schools, making compromises between organizational limitations and professional standards, and receiving little personal recognition for contributions to the progress of individuals or schools. On the other hand, a sense of comradeship among psychological counselors is strong, peer supervision is a common practice, and contact with professional colleagues is frequent.

The quality of psychological services in Guidance and Research Centers and schools is largely affected by the limited number of standardized counseling tools, such as interest, aptitude, intelligence, and personality tests, and sufficient literature and research in the field. Although there is a great demand for graduate studies, the number of programs and number of students accepted each year at the graduate level are currently very limited. According to the Bologna Declaration of the European Union (1999), Turkey should reform its higher institutional programs to be consistent with the European Union standards; eventually this will promote change in the infrastructure of psychological services in the schools. Interest and motivation in the profession are still high among psychological counselors. This is an important and positive factor favoring the continuing development of psychological services for the children of Turkey.

References

Akkoyun, F. (1995). Psikolojik danışma ve rehberlikte ünvan ve program sorunu: birinceleme ve öneriler [The problem of the relationship between the job title and the training programs in psychological counseling and guidance: A review and recommendations]. *Psikolojik Danışma ve Rehberlik Dergisi, 2*(6), 1–28.

Akkök, F., & Watts, A. G. (2003, March). *Public policies and career development: A framework for the design of career information, guidance and counselling services in developing and transition countries. Country report on Turkey.* Washington, DC: World Bank.

Akyüz, Y. (2001). *Türk Eğitim Tarihi.* Istanbul: Alfa.

Bogazici University Educational Sciences Department. (n.d.). *Graduate programs.* Retrieved August 8, 2005, from http://ed.boun.edu.tr/eng_lisan sustu.asp

Bologna Declaration of the European Union. (1999). Retrieved August 8, 2005, from http://ec.europa.eu/education/policies/educ/bologna/bologna_en.html

Deprem, 1400 çocuğu yetim ve öksüz bıraktı [The earthquake left 1,400 children orphaned]. (2000, January 21). *TRT Haber.* Retrieved June 15, 2000, from http//www.trt.net.tr.herevamsonuc.asp?haberno=10986

Doğan, S. (1998). Counseling in Turkey: Current status and future challenges. *Education Policy Analysis Archives, 6*(12). Retrieved August 8, 2005, from http://epaa.asu.edu/epaa/v6n12.html

Dölek, N., İnceoğlu, D., & Özdemir, N. (1989). School psychology in Turkey. In P. A. Saigh & T. Oakland (Eds.), *International perspectives on psychology in the schools.* Hillsdale, NJ: Lawrence Erlbaum.

Işte Depremin Bilançosu [Here is the cost of the earthquake]. (2000, August 17). *Hürriyet,* p. 20.

Middle East Technical University. (n.d.). Retrieved August 8, 2005, from http://www.eds.metu.edu.tr/

Ministry of National Education. (n.d.). Retrieved February 9, 2006, from http://orgm.meb.gov.tr/Istatistikler/istatistik2006/istatistikler 2006.htm

Ministry of National Education, Directorate of Special Education and Guidance and Research Services. (1997). Special Education Regulation 573. Ankara: Author.

Ministry of National Education & UNICEF. (2001). *Turkish Ministry of Education–UNICEF Psycho social School Project: Assessment and evaluation, September 1999–June 2001, Turkey.* Ankara: Author.

Öner, N. (1977). *Psychology in the schools in international perspective, 2* (International School Psychology). Columbus, OH: U.S. Department of Health, Education, & Welfare National Institute of Education. (ERIC Document Reproduction Service No. ED147257)

Psikolojik Danışma ve Rehberlik Dernegi. (1995). *Psikolojik danışma ve rehberlik alanında calişanlar icin etik kurallar* [Ethical standards for counselors]. Ankara: 72 TDFO.

Sağlamer, G., Barka, A., Sağlamer, A., Boduroğlu, H., Kara Doğan, F., Ansal, A., et al. (1999, August 17). *Kocaeli Depremi: Istanbul Teknik Universitesi ön değerlendirme raporu* [Kocaeli earthquake: Istanbul Technical University preliminary evaluation report]. Retrieved from http://www.basbakanlik.gov.tr/krizyönetim/merkezi/kocaelideprem.htm

T. C. Başbakanlık Devlet Planlama Teşkilatı [Republic of Turkey, Prime Ministry State Planning Institute]. (1967). *Kalkınma Planı: Ikinci Beş Yıl 1968–1972* [Developmental Plan: Second Five-Year Plan 1968–1972]. Ankara: Başbakanlık Devlet Matbaasi.

T. C. Başbakanlik Devlet Planlama Teskilatı [Republic of Turkey, Prime Ministry State Planning Institute]. (1973). *Yeni Strateji ve Kalkınma Planı: Üçüncü Beş Yıl* [New Strategy and Developmental Plan: Third Five-Year Plan]. Ankara: Başbakanlik Devlet Matbaasi.

T. C. Başbakanlik Kriz Yönetim Merkezi. (2000, August 17). *Depremler 1999* [Earthquakes 1999]. Ankara: Author.

T. C. Milli Eğitim Bakanlığı [Republic of Turkey, Ministry of National Education]. (1985, December 16). *Tebliğler Dergisi* [Journal of Announcement], *48*(2201). Ankara: Author.

T. C. Milli Eğitim Bakanlığı [Republic of Turkey, Ministry of National Education]. (2001a, March 17). *Tebliğler Dergisi* [Journal of Announcement], 24376. Ankara: Author.

T. C. Milli Eğitim Bakanlığı [Republic of Turkey, Ministry of National Education]. (2001b, May). *Tebliğler Dergisi* [Journal of Announcement], 2524. Ankara: Author.

Tunalı, İ., Ercan, H., Başkent C., Öztürk, O. D., & Akçiğit, U. (2003). *Background study on labor market and employment in Turkey.* Prepared for the European Training Foundation.

YOK/World Bank National Education Development Project Pre-service Teacher Education. (1996). *Teacher education: Guidance and counseling.* Ankara: Author.

41

School Psychology in the United Arab Emirates

Mohammad Adnan Alghorani

Context of School Psychology

The United Arab Emirates was established as a constitutional federation on December 2, 1971, and Sheikh Zayed bin Sultan Al Nahyan, known as the founder of the United Arab Emirates, was elected as its first president. The federation consists of seven emirates: Abu Dhabi, Dubai, Sharjah, Ajman, Umm al-Qawain, Ras al-Khaimah, and Fujairah. The United Arab Emirates is located on the Arabian Gulf and borders Saudi Arabia on the south and west, Qatar and the Arabian Gulf on the north, the Indian Ocean on the east, and Oman on the east and south. The area is 83,600 square kilometers (32,278 square miles). The land in the south and west of the country consists mainly of sand dunes and salt flats with an occasional oasis. The sand dunes in the north yield to gravel plains formed by the Hajar Mountain range. The mountains themselves rise to a height of more than 3,000 meters and extend from the United Arab Emirates south into Oman. The east coast

is a fertile plain, and the rainfall and subterranean water in that region have facilitated the practice of agriculture for thousands of years. Unspoiled beaches stretch for kilometers along the east coast, and over 100 islands and numerous shallow inlets are on the Arabian Gulf side.

The population of the United Arab Emirates has increased by approximately 1,745% during the past 25 years. Its growth has been one of the highest in the world. Its population in 1965 was estimated at about 111,000 (United Nations, 1966). In 1970, prior to the establishment of the federation, the population was 248,000. Since then, population growth has been rapid. It increased to 558,000 in 1975, to 1.042 million in 1980, to 1.379 million in 1985, to 2.411 million in 1995, to 3.511 million in 2002, and to 4.330 million in 2004 (Ministry of Information and Culture, 2005b).

The rapid population increase is due mainly to a massive influx of foreign labor (Al-Aesawi, 2005). At least 100,000 visas have been processed every year during the past decade. Infant mortality rates have declined (in 1994, there were 16.6 per 1,000 live births) and fertility rates have increased, resulting in 2.94 children per woman. The estimated population distribution by age is as follows: 25% for age 14 and younger (52% males), 55% for ages 15 to 39 (71% males), 18% for ages 40 to 59 (80% males), and 2% for age 60 and above (60% males). The country's population is largely urban (85%) (Ministry of Economy and Planning, 2004). The emirate of Abu Dhabi constitutes nearly 40% of the total population. About 80% of United Arab Emirates inhabitants are foreign-born workers and their dependents, including those from other Arab countries, Iranians, South and East Asians, and Westerners (Central Intelligence Agency, 2005). Only 20% are United Arab Emirates citizens.

The economy is open. The gross domestic product in 2004 was US$63.67 billion, US$25,200 per capita (Central Intelligence Agency, 2005; United Arab Emirates Embassy in Ottawa, 2005). The wealth of the country is based on oil and gas production (about 30% of the gross domestic product). The economy has become more diversified and less dependent on oil and gas production. The gross domestic product composition by sector reflects the following percentages: agriculture, 4%; industry, 58.5%; and services, 37.5%.

According to 2004 estimates, children age 19 and younger account for 32% of the population. Children age 4 and younger number 368,651, ages 5 to 9 number 379,091, ages 10 to 14 number 346,283, and ages 15 to 19 number 270,364. During the 2002–2003 academic year, approximately 595,000 students attended 1,208 public and private schools. Private education served 290,000 in 464 schools with 16,822 teachers. Public/state education served 305,000 in 744 schools with 23,874 teachers.

When the United Arab Emirates federation was established, only a very small portion of the population had access to formal education. Since then, state-funded educational opportunities have blossomed. Primary school education is compulsory for all United Arab Emirates citizens, both boys and girls. Education is free from primary through college in government-supported schools and university. Students are segregated based on gender beginning in the first grade. However, about 5 years ago, the Ministry of Education initiated the only female-administered schools, where boys and girls are not segregated from first to fifth grades. The private education sector has also increased substantially, in part because state-funded schools became limited to citizens. Private schools serve about 40% of students attending kindergarten, primary, and secondary schools. Private schools are not required to segregate students based on gender; therefore, some do and others do not.

The country's four-tier educational structure was established in the early 1970s. It has developed over the years and it is currently as follows: kindergarten (ages 4–5), first circle (ages 6–10, Grades 1–5), second circle (ages 11–14, Grades 6–9), and secondary (ages 15–17, Grades 10–12) (Ministry of Information and Culture, 2005a). The educational system provides opportunities for students to follow one of the following types of education:

1. General education: Students specialize in either a liberal arts track or a science track, starting in Grade 11. Students who graduate from Grade 12 are awarded secondary school leaving certificates.

2. Vocational education: Students specialize in an agricultural, industrial, or commercial track, starting in Grade 10. Students are awarded a technical secondary diploma on completing these programs.

3. Religious education: This begins in Grade 6.

Staff-to-student ratios established by governmental policy (Ministry of Education, 2005b) are 1 to 20 at kindergarten and first circle levels and 1 to 15 at second circle and secondary levels.

The current staff-to-student ratios are well within these ranges.

The Ministry of Labor and Social Affairs supervises centers for children with special needs. These centers serve children with hearing, visual, and physical disabilities and others with special needs (e.g., autism). The percentage of people with disabilities is thought to be similar to worldwide averages (i.e., 8%–10% of the population). Developments in this area are rapid. For example, in Abu Dhabi, a large center with 70 classrooms and 20 training workshops is being constructed. The Ministry of Education and Youth, together with the Red Crescent Society, opened a center for children with autism of Abu Dhabi, the first of a number of such centers planned by the Ministry.

Origin, History, and Current Status of School Psychology

The origin of school psychology in the United Arab Emirates can be traced to school social services and special education. In 1972–1973, social services were provided in schools by three *social specialists* (Al-Khayat, 2005). The number of social specialists has increased substantially, reaching 247 in 1980–1981 and 883 in 2004–2005. They have attended to problems affecting students' regular attendance in classes and academic performance. Prior to 1980, these social specialists were also expected to handle students' psychological needs and problems, which they were neither educated nor trained to handle. In his study about psychologists and social workers' expectations about the latter's didactic interventions with students, Abdulmajeed (2000) reported that psychology graduates expect school social specialists to use psychological measures. However, they are not qualified to do so; for example, social specialists lack the knowledge needed to work with children diagnosed with epilepsy or schizophrenia or those who were abused. Therefore, in 1980, the Ministry of Education established two offices of psychological services, one in Abu Dhabi and one in Dubai, in which psychology specialists who held bachelor's degrees were hired to attend to referrals from social specialists, to make home visits, and to refer cases to community psychological and psychiatrist clinics. Psychology staff helped social specialists provide services to normal students in schools, especially related to regular attendance, proper discipline, and other qualities that characterize a healthy school climate.

The rapid growth of special education also contributed to the development of school psychological services. Special education classes began in 1979–1980 (Al-Jalahmeh, 2002). In 1979, there were 5 special education classes; in 2000, there were 247 classes serving 1,844 students. This increase required qualified staff to assess children and to qualify them for special education services. Psychology staff played an important role in this growth. Psychology staff also helped special education specialists by evaluating students to determine if they qualified for special education services.

The work of psychology staff was not limited to the previously mentioned functions. They increasingly attended to other issues by addressing students' coping problems and learning difficulties and consulting with teachers and parents through workshops on various issues—for example, teaching students academic and social skills, training parents about childrearing, and helping teachers with techniques for classroom management, disciplining skills, and dealing with students' individual differences.

In 1980, the Ministry of Education and Youth established a research center to investigate issues related to the interests of the school community and to support the work of social specialists and psychological specialists in schools. Psychology staff working in schools were given the title "psychological specialist." However, the term *psychological* carries the stigma that being seen by a professional for a psychological evaluation or intervention means a person must be insane. Therefore, people are reluctant to visit a psychologist or be referred to one. As a result, the Ministry of Education and Youth has considered changing the title to "educational counselor."

In 1980, when the two offices of psychological services were established, the staff attempted to meet the heavy demands from schools. Initially, there were only a few staff, so they were not assigned to specific schools; instead, they responded to schools' requests for services. Psychological specialists were first assigned to schools in 2001. Each was assigned to 10 schools. In 2003, each psychological specialist was assigned to five schools, varying from three to four urban schools and one to two rural schools. In 1994–1995, 26 psychological specialists served public schools; of these 26, 5 women and 2 men were United Arab Emirate citizens who had started work in 1992–1993. By 2005–2006, 64 psychological specialists (25 men and 39 women) served 744 public schools with 305,000 students. At the current rate of 1 psychological specialist per 5 schools, less than 50% of the public schools are served. The Department of Social and Psychological Welfare within the Ministry of Education and Youth projected a need for 150 psychological specialists (85 women and 60 men) in order to satisfy the ratio of 1 psychological specialist for every 5 public schools. During the process of writing this chapter, the Ministry of Education and Youth has announced its need to hire a few hundred psychological specialists, so that one is appointed in each school. In general, male specialists are assigned to male-specific schools, and female specialists are assigned to female-specific schools. However, depending on the need of the school districts and the preference of the specialists, they may serve students of the opposite sex.

A survey of demographic and professional practices conducted by the International School Psychology Association was distributed to psychology specialists (Alghorani, 2005). Data from this survey indicated annual salaries reported for 18 psychological specialists averaged US$33,722 and fell within the range of US$17,330 to US$50,649. The Department of Social and Psychological Welfare reported that the average annual salary of psychology specialists was US$39,933.

The specialty of school psychology has not been established in the United Arab Emirates. However, the following are various services provided to children, especially by psychology staff and generally by holders of degrees in the various programs of social sciences. These service providers work in public and private schools, hospitals, private consultancy centers, juvenile centers, humanitarian and charity organizations, and centers for children with disabilities.

The ratio of students to school psychologists varies depending on the latter's assignments. Currently, each psychology specialist works in five public schools. Therefore, the ratio depends on the number of students in the schools to which one is assigned. Some schools have fewer than 100 students, whereas others have more than 1,000. As previously noted, 64 psychology specialists presently serve 320 schools. During academic year 2002–2003, 305,000 students attended one of the 744 schools. Thus, the number of students per school averaged 410, and the ratio of students to psychology specialists averaged 2,050 to 1.

The Department of Social and Psychological Welfare provides an extensive program of professional development to its staff. On average, the psychological specialists are offered six to seven workshops annually, each of which lasts 3 to 4 days. Such training is offered by university professors or professionals from abroad. Moreover, the psychological specialists are encouraged to present papers at national or international conferences. With regard to job satisfaction, though the psychological specialists suffer the stigma of the term *psychology* in their title, they enjoy the advantages of being called *specialists*. Additionally, they enjoy autonomy in their work, as they do not have to report to school principals, except when they need to leave a campus early. For all other administrative, professional development, and evaluation-related issues, they report directly to the specialized department in the school district office.

Infrastructure of School Psychology

Professional organizations that serve the interests of psychology specialists in the United Arab Emirates are in the initial stage of development. In 2003, the Emirates Psychological Association was founded. A group of counselors is attempting to found another professional organization, which might be called the Emirates Association of Counseling and Career Practitioners but is publicized as Counseling Arabia. In January 2005, the author of this chapter created an Internet medium to promote communication among psychology specialists. The link to this Web site is http://groups.yahoo.com/group/Arab_School_Psychology/. Both associations and the Web group plan to serve the interests of psychologists and school counselors.

No laws regulate the practice of psychology. However, three ministries issue licenses to provide such services. The Ministry of Health issues licenses to those prepared to work in medical settings such as hospitals and medical clinics. The Ministry of Education issues licenses to those prepared to work in educational and/or psychological private consultation centers. The Ministry of Labor issues licenses to those prepared to operate a private center that serves children with special needs.

No professional journals specifically address issues important to the work of psychological specialists. One newsletter, *Our Psychological Health,* first published in 2005 by the Department of Social and Psychological Welfare, Ministry of Education, addresses some of their needs.

Preparation of School Psychologists

In 1976–1977, the Department of Psychology was established within the College of Education at United Emirates University. During 1995–1996, it was moved to the Faculty of Humanities and Social Sciences. Its initial function was to be a service department, offering courses that supported other departments within the College of Education and beyond. More recently, it has become larger and more specialized, and it has acquired its own focus.

The current psychological specialists, who are UAE citizens, are graduates of the United Arab Emirates University's Department of Psychology, which offers the only bachelor of arts program in psychology. The remaining psychological specialists are mainly from Lebanon, Jordan, Palestine, Sudan, and Egypt. Not all psychological specialists graduated from psychology-related programs. Some have degrees from other programs, including philosophy. They mainly work as high school teachers of psychology and have been transferred to work as psychological specialists.

The numbers of students registered in the department of psychology during the last 3 years is as follows: 115 in 2002–2003, 105 in 2003–2004, and 52 in 2004–2005. Not all graduate with a degree in psychology. Some drop out, and others transfer to other departments. Eight men and 188 women graduated from the program during the academic years 2001–2002 and 2003–2004. Among those who graduated in the class of 2001–2002, 1 of 2 men and 7 of 83 women are employed. Approximately 45 women (about 54%) are unemployed, and 6 are awaiting employment. Data on 35 women are not available. For the class of 2002–2003, 4 men are employed and 1 is not. No women are employed. The employment status of 17 women is unknown. No data are available for the class of 2003–2004.

Psychological specialists typically complete their bachelor's degree in about 4 to 5 years. The following describes the bachelor's degree program in psychology at the United Arab Emirates University up to academic year 2003–2004. The program was developed to be consistent with a scientist-practitioner model, that is, the science of psychology was featured over its practice. The program consisted of courses totaling 132 credit hours, 48 of which were university and college requirements. The remaining 84 hours were psychology courses, which were distributed as follows: 45 credit hours in required specialized courses, 21 credit hours in elective specialized courses, 12 credit hours in supporting courses, and 6 credit hours in free electives.

The 45 credit hours of required specialized courses, considered the core academic knowledge of psychology, include general psychology, developmental psychology, social psychology, introduction to psychological statistics, physiological psychology, introduction to inferential statistics, cognitive psychology, abnormal psychology, psychological measurement, psychological tests and measurements, research methods in psychology, experimental psychology, applied research, and Practicum I (which involves working 7 weeks in schools) and Practicum II (which involves working 7 weeks in hospitals).

The 21 credit hours of elective specialized courses consist of two of the following four courses: clinical psychology, industrial psychology, counseling psychology, and forensic psychology; and five of the following nine courses: differential psychology, psychology of learning, psychology of personality, neuropsychology, organizational psychology, methods of psychotherapy, advanced experimental psychology, mental and neuropsychological tests, and behavior disorders. The 12 credit hours of supporting courses consist of fundamentals of biology and school counseling plus two of the following five courses: introduction to sociology, social problems, introduction to social work, educational psychology, and introduction to special education. The above-described program is tailored for a general bachelor's degree in psychology. Thus, there is no specific focus on well-established practical training courses on intellectual, academic, emotional, or social assessment or interventions. Moreover, courses are not designed solely to focus on children and youth, on decision-making skills, or on the legal and ethical foundations for service.

Roles, Functions, and Responsibilities of School Psychologists

The job description of psychological specialists includes the following roles:

1. Planning for the identification of students referred for possible learning difficulties and behavioral disorders

2. Planning interventions for students with learning difficulties

3. Assessing students who may have learning difficulties, using standardized tests

4. Referring students needing specialized psychological attention and submitting reports on them

5. Organizing guidance and counseling programs for students

6. Participating in school committees, including those responsible for admitting and registering new students, transferring students to special education classes, and focusing on high-achieving students

7. Participating in standardizing tests

8. Providing lectures, seminars, and workshops to students, teachers, and parents with the goal of increasing their awareness of psychological issues and knowledge

9. Following the recommendations of specialized professionals about particular cases

10. Evaluating the programs and activities that one develops and implements

In practice, psychological specialists assess, especially for special education, intervene somewhat, consult, and provide group counseling. Their role is primarily preventive.

Psychology specialists use few psychological tests when attempting to assess whether a child qualifies for special education classes. They currently use the following tests: the Wechsler Intelligence Scale for Children–III (either the Kuwaiti or Egyptian standardization), the Non-Verbal Intelligence Beta III scale, the Goodenough-Harris Test of Psychological Maturity, the Raven Coloured Progressive Matrices, the Porteus Tests, the Vineland Adaptive Behavior Scale, the Emotional Intelligence Scale, and the Students Temperament Styles. Most measures were normed on United Arab Emirates students and are used in each of the 20 special education assessments done by each psychology specialist per year. Psychology specialists also take part in the assessment of students' vocational interests.

Current Issues Impacting School Psychology

School psychology in the United Arab Emirates is in its infancy. The following challenges are hindering its development. No graduate programs specialize in preparing professionals to work with children and youth. Existing psychology specialists are not prepared to properly deliver psychological services and thus do not serve as marketing advocates for the specialty of school psychology. A comprehensive plan for professional development for existing psychology specialists does not exist. Tests and other assessment methods are minimal and are not sufficient to allow psychology specialists to properly fulfill their roles.

As stated earlier, the Ministry of Education's goal of assigning one psychology specialist to five public schools requires doubling employment. However, all new hiring is presently directed to meet the most pressing need, which is for additional classroom teachers. As a result, psychology specialists are not being hired, and instead, high school psychology teachers are being transferred to the department of social

and psychological welfare to work as psychology specialists. Such a maneuver obviously imposes on this new staff a dire need for training.

Many initiatives could help to promote school psychology. A proposed master's degree program in clinical and counseling psychology could provide opportunities to improve the competency of psychology specialists. The author of this chapter has proposed a master's degree program in school psychology that, if accepted, could be a major turning point in the development of school psychology in the United Arab Emirates. Efforts to develop additional standardized tests that are normed on this population are gaining momentum, as some university faculty members, the Psychological Welfare Department within the Ministry of Education, and other government and community organizations are collaborating on selecting education, vocational, and psychological tests compatible with the history and cultures of United Arab Emirates society. Finally, the newly born psychological organizations are attempting to recruit and service the interests of psychology specialists and thus, eventually, are likely to contribute to their professional development. Research on most issues important to school psychology is needed, especially on the identification of students with educational and psychological problems.

References

Abdulmajeed, H. S. (2000). Psychologists and social workers' expectations about the latter's didactic interventions with students. *Journal of Humanities and Social Sciences, 16*(1), 1–52.

Al-Aesawi, F. M. (2005). UAE population growth between 1975 and 2002: The geographical implications. *Journal of Humanities and Social Sciences, 21*(1), 359–412.

Alghorani, M. A. (2005). *Demographics of psychological service staff in UAE.* Paper presented at the 27th International School Psychology Colloquium, Athens, Greece.

Al-Jalahmeh, A. (2002). *Special education classes and resource rooms in UAE schools: A statistical study.* Dubai: Ministry of Education.

Al-Khayat, A. H. (2005). *Historical background of the development of social and psychological services in UAE educational system.* Paper presented at the first Arabian Gulf Conference about Social and Psychological Service and Education, Kuwait.

Central Intelligence Agency. (2005). *The world factbook.* Retrieved August 15, 2005, from http://www.cia.gov/cia/publications/factbook/index.html

Ministry of Economy and Planning. (2004). *Population and vital statistics.* Abstract retrieved August 8, 2005, from http://www.uaeinteract.com/uaeint_misc/pdf_2005/index.asp

Ministry of Education. (2005a). *The history of education in UAE.* Retrieved August 10, 2005, from http://www.moe.gov.ae/history/history1.htm

Ministry of Education. (2005b). *Statistics about education in UAE.* Retrieved August 10, 2005, from http://www.moe.gov.ae/pdf_statistics/pdf_stc.htm

Ministry of Information and Culture. (2005a). *UAE Education Centre.* Retrieved August 13, 2005, from http://www.uaeinteract.com/education/

Ministry of Information and Culture. (2005b). *UAE yearbook 2005.* Dubai: Trident Press. Retrieved August 10, 2005, from http://www.uaeinteract.com/uaeint_misc/pdf_2005/index.asp

United Arab Emirates Embassy in Ottawa. (2005). *About the U.A.E.'s economy.* Retrieved August 15, 2005, from the UAE Embassy in Ottawa, Canada, Web site: http://www.uae-embassy.com/uae-economy.htm

United Arab Emirates University. (2005). *History and degree program of psychology.* Retrieved May 13, 2006, from the UAE University, College of Humanities and Social Sciences, Program of Psychology Web site: http://www.fhss.uaeu.ac.ae/Divisions/Society&Behavior/Psychology/Psychology_Goals.htm

United Nations. (1966). *Statistical yearbook.* New York: Author.

42

School Psychology in the United States

Shane R. Jimerson

Thomas D. Oakland

Context of School Psychology

The American colonies sought independence from England in 1776 and were recognized as the new nation of the United States of America following the Treaty of Paris in 1783. During the 19th and 20th centuries, 37 new states were added to the original 13 as the nation expanded across the North American continent. The United States includes 50 states, the District of Columbia, Puerto Rico, and various territories. In 2005, its population of 295,734,134 was distributed by age as follows: birth to 14, 21% (males 51%); 15 to 64, 67% (males 49%); and 65 and over, 12% (males 42%). Ethnic diversity is reported as White, 77%; Black, 13%; Asian, 4.2%; American Indian and Alaska Native, 1.5%;

Native Hawaiian and other Pacific Islander, 0.3%; and other, 4%. The landmass of the United States is 9,158,960 square kilometers. The United States borders both the North Atlantic and the North Pacific Oceans and lies between Canada and Mexico. The United States is about three tenths the size of Africa; half the size of Russia; half the size of South America (or slightly larger than Brazil); slightly larger than China; and about two and a half times the size of Western Europe. Its geography is diverse, with vast central plains; mountains in the west; hills and low mountains in the east; and mountains, river valleys, and volcanic topography in Alaska.

During the past century, the growth of the U.S. economy has been somewhat steady, producing a gross domestic product of over US$11.7 trillion,

AUTHORS' NOTE: Portions of this chapter were derived from Oakland (2000) and Oakland, Faulkner, and Annan (2005).

US$40,100 per capita in 2004 (Central Intelligence Agency, 2005). The United States is among the leading industrial nations, highly diversified, and technologically advanced in such areas as petroleum, steel, motor vehicles, aerospace, telecommunications, chemicals, electronics, food processing, consumer goods, lumber, and mining. Employment includes managerial and professional, 31%; technical, sales, and administrative support, 29%; manufacturing, mining, transportation, and crafts, 24%; services, 14%; and farming, forestry, and fishing, 2%.

In 2002, 72 million children (defined as the population under age 18) resided in the United States (Fields, 2003). Children under age 6 account for approximately 23 million, those between ages 6 and 11 years account for approximately 24 million, and those between ages 12 and 17 account for approximately 24 million. Thus, children under age 18 make up 26% of the U.S. population. Sixty-nine percent of children live with two parents, 23% live with only their mother, 5% live with only their father, and another 4% live in households with neither biological parent present.

The educational system includes nursery school (ages 3 and 4), kindergarten (ages 5 and 6), Grades 1 through 12, and an extensive postsecondary system that includes vocational and technical schools, community and junior colleges, senior colleges, and graduate schools in universities. Approximately 90% of students are enrolled in publicly supported education programs. Kindergarten through Grade 5 typically is considered elementary school. Grades 6 through 8 usually are called middle school or junior high school, and Grades 9 through 12 constitute high school; together, they are considered to be secondary schools. Results of the 1999 U.S. Census indicated that 4.6 million children were in nursery school, 3.8 million in kindergarten, 16.8 million in Grades 1 through 4, 16.1 million in Grades 5 through 8, and 15.9 million in Grades 9 through 12. At the kindergarten through high school levels, enrollment numbers tend to mirror closely the population count in those ages, with close to 100% enrollment of the population ages 5 through 16 because of compulsory attendance requirements. Average class size during elementary school is estimated at 20 to 25 students. Class size during kindergarten generally is somewhat smaller and during middle and high school is somewhat larger.

The number of children attending nursery school has increased over the past 40 years, growing from approximately 0.5 million in 1964 to more than 4.5 million in 1999. Public kindergarten is available in most states. Among children enrolled in kindergarten, the majority are White non-Hispanics (60%), followed by Blacks (16%), Hispanics (17%), and Asians and Pacific Islanders (5%). The percentage of children attending kindergarten all day increased from 11% in 1969 to 58% in 2000. Furthermore, the majority of these children (59%) entered kindergarten with previous school experience, having been enrolled in nursery school the preceding year. Among elementary and secondary students, approximately 64% are White non-Hispanic, 16% Black, 15% Hispanic, and 5% Asian and Pacific Islander and other races. The school-age population is expected to become more diverse. During the past two decades, both births and immigration have contributed to increased numbers of students. During this period, births increased from 3.6 million to 4.0 million annually. Immigration also has added to school enrollment, with 20% of school-age children having at least one foreign-born parent; 5% of school-age children are themselves foreign born.

There also are private and parochial (e.g., religious-supported) schools. Children from families with higher incomes are more likely to be enrolled in them. Whereas 4% of children from families with incomes under $20,000 attend private schools, 14% of those from families with incomes of $40,000 or more attend such schools. Approximately 10% of students attend private or parochial school, a figure that has remained relatively stable since the 1970s.

The annual dropout rate (i.e., during a given year, students who withdraw from school prior to graduating from high school and are not enrolled in alternative educational programs) is approximately 4% to 5%. For example, during the 1-year period ending in October 1999, about 520,000 (4.7%) of all 10th- through 12th-grade students dropped out of high school. This rate has remained the same since 1997. The annual high school dropout rates of Blacks (6%) and Hispanics (7%) have been higher than that of White non-Hispanics (4%), while female and male dropout rates are relatively similar (4% and 5%, respectively). Whereas 9% of high school students from families with incomes below $20,000 dropped out of school during this 1-year period, 2% of those from families with incomes of $40,000 or more left school before graduation. Overall, roughly 15% of students do not complete high school (Kaufman, Alt, & Chapman, 2001). The percentage of 18- through 24-year-olds who completed high school in 2000 further reveals the disparate educational trajectories among diverse groups. Only 64% of Hispanic students and 84% of Black students completed high school in 2000, compared with 92% of White non-Hispanic and 95% of Asian and Pacific Islander students. Approximately 15 million students are enrolled in colleges and universities.

More than 6.5 million children receive special education services. During the 2000–2001 school year, nearly 12.5% of all students were classified as needing special education (Jamieson, Curry, & Martinez, 2001). Among these special education students, the percentage classified as displaying a learning disability has increased from 22% in 1977 to 46% in 1998 and in 2005 was approximately 50%. Spending for special education approximates $50 billion annually, or 21% of the budget for kindergarten through 12th-grade education. Approximately 55% of students who received special education services graduate with a high school diploma.

Origin, History, and Current Status of School Psychology

The origins of school psychology within the United States can be traced to child development, clinical psychology, and special education (Fagan, 1992; Fagan & Wise, 2000). The first psychological clinic, established at the University of Pennsylvania by Lightner Witmer in 1896, generally is seen as marking the origin of school psychology. Witmer envisioned the preparation of pedagogical or psychological experts to work with children who did not benefit from ordinary educational methods. He later embodied this vision by serving as a school psychologist (Fagan, 1986). School psychology and other applied areas of psychology grew slowly during the following 50 years. Psychology departments, dominated by experimental scientists, generally were not interested in applied psychology.

The distinction of holding the first title of "school psychologist" belongs to Arnold Gessell, who was employed in 1915 by the state of Connecticut as a school psychologist following the receipt of doctoral degrees in psychology and medicine (Oakland, 1993). Before 1920, there were an estimated 100 to 150 school psychologists (Walter, 1925). Only a few were qualified psychologists (Wallin, 1914). Standards for preparing, credentialing, and licensing school and other applied psychologists did not begin to appear until the 1920s, initially in New York and adjacent states. In 1950, only 10 universities offered specific programs for preparing school psychologists.

Four national conferences focused on the future of school psychology; these were held in Thayer, 1951; Spring Hill, 1980; Olympia, 1981; and Indianapolis, 2002. Each discussed current and future demands for school psychologists, and the specialty's ability to meet those demands, and offered ideas for maximizing the benefits to children and schools (see D'Amato, 2003; Fagan & Wise, 2000; Sheridan, 2004, for further discussion of these conferences).

Current Status

The American Psychological Association (www.apa.org) and the National Association of School Psychologists (www.nasponline.org) have approved definitions of *school psychology*. There is considerable consistency in these definitions. The American Psychological Association's archival definition of the specialty of school psychology follows.

School psychology is a general practice and health service provider specialty of professional psychology that is concerned with the science and practice of psychology with children, youth, families; learners of all ages; and the schooling process. The basic education and training of school psychologists prepares them to provide a range of psychological assessment, intervention, prevention, health promotion, and program development and evaluation services with a special focus on the developmental process of children and youth within the context of schools, families, and other systems. School psychologists are prepared to intervene at the individual and systems level, and develop, implement, and evaluate preventive programs. In these efforts, they conduct ecologically valid assessments and intervene to promote positive learning environments within which children and youth from diverse backgrounds have equal access to effective educational and psychological services to promote healthy development. (American Psychological Association Council of Representatives, 1998)

As of 2005, an estimated 32,300 school psychologists practice in the United States (Charvat, 2005). They work in all 50 states and are most numerous in states with large populations and in the Northeast, upper Midwest, and the West (e.g., New York, New Jersey, Illinois, Ohio, California). As is true of other countries, proportionately more are found in urban and suburban than in rural areas (Fagan & Wise,

2000). Approximately 41% of school psychologists have a master's degree, 28% have a specialist degree, and 30% have a doctoral degree (Curtis, Chesno Grier, Walker Abshier, Sutton, & Hunley, 2002). Their average age is 45, and, on average, they have 13 years experience as a school psychologist. Ninety-three percent are White, approximately 2% are Black, 3% are Hispanic, and 72% are women. The ratio between school psychologists and students is estimated to be approximately 1 to 1,680. Between one fourth (Thomas, 2000) and one third (Curtis, Chesno Grier, et al., 2002) of school psychology positions in the United States meet the ratio of 1 school psychologist for every 1,000 students, as recommended by the National Association of School Psychologists.

School psychologists work in numerous settings, including public and private schools, special schools, centers, and private practice. Seventy-eight percent are employed in public school settings. Among them, most work within the context of special education. Some work in university settings (7%) and private practice (5%). Smaller numbers work in mental health clinics, hospitals, and other medical settings and in research centers. School psychologists enjoy many employment opportunities. However, recent economic downturns in a few states have decreased the funding for education and related services. Thus, there are fewer resources to employ school psychologists and other educational professionals in these states. However, employment opportunities are very strong nationally.

Salaries vary somewhat across the country and are influenced by number of years of experience. School psychologists working in elementary and secondary schools average about $54,500 per year (Bureau of Labor Statistics, 2004). Those with 10 to 14 years of experience earn approximately $74,000, and those with 20 to 24 years of experience earn approximately $96,000 (Pate, Frincke, & Kohout, 2003). On average, individuals in the United States with doctoral degrees earn about $89,400 and those with master's degrees average $62,300 (Day & Newburger, 2002).

Infrastructure of School Psychology

School psychology has developed a strong infrastructure at the national and state levels. The American Psychological Association does much to enhance the interests of school psychology, especially with respect to public policy. In addition, its Division of School Psychology advocates for school psychology within the American Psychological Association and nationally. School psychology also has its own national professional association, the National Association of School Psychologists, with more than 23,000 members. Other national organizations working on behalf of school psychology include the Council of Directors of School Psychology Programs, the National Association of State Consultants in School Psychology, the Society for the Study of School Psychology, and Trainers of School Psychology.

School psychologists report belonging to a variety of different professional organizations: Approximately 72% belong to the National Association of School Psychologists, 74% to state school psychological associations, 32% to the National Education Association, 31% to local teacher unions, 20% to the American Psychological Association, 13% to the American Psychological Association's Division of School Psychology, 9% to the American Federation of Teachers, and 8% to the Council for Exceptional Children.

State laws govern the credentialing and licensing of school psychologists. In most states, only credentialed school psychologists are allowed to work in the schools as school psychologists. States typically also have separate laws that govern the licensure of psychology. State departments of education generally regulate the practice of school psychology within education. State boards of examiners of psychologists generally regulate the practice of psychology as well as school psychology when practiced outside of education; some also regulate its practice within education. A national certification process allows school psychologists to become certified and licensed in more than one state. Credentialing requirements for school psychologists are discussed in the next section.

School psychology practice is influenced heavily by federal legislation that becomes established in policies promulgated by state education agencies and carried out by local education agencies (Oakland & Gallegos, 2005). These include the 1964 Civil Rights Act, Individuals With Disabilities Education Act, Section 504 of the Rehabilitation Act of 1973, Family Education Rights and Privacy Act of 1974, and the No Child Left Behind Act of 2002.

For example, in 1975, the U.S. Congress passed Public Law 94-142 (Education of All Handicapped Children Act), subsequently codified as the Individuals With Disabilities Education Act. This initial legislation specified the receipt of federal funds required to develop and implement policies that assure a free appropriate public education to all children with disabilities. Amendments to this Act (e.g., Public Law 105-17 and Public Law 108-446) have provided further guidelines regarding the education of children with disabilities. In addition, Public Law 107-110, the No Child Left Behind Act of 2002, emphasizes a school's accountability for promoting achievement, local control and flexibility, expanded parental choice, and use of effective research-based instruction. Such legislation has important implications for the preparation and practices of school psychologists. For example, both the No Child Left Behind legislation and the Individuals With Disabilities Education Improvement Act of 2004 underscore the importance of implementing instructional strategies supported by empirical evidence. Moreover, the Individuals With Disabilities Education Improvement Act of 2004 allows schools to discontinue use of a discrepancy formula to identify students with learning disabilities and to refer students for possible learning disabilities only after they do not show progress following intensive services. Given the recency of this legislation, its full impact on school psychology practices will not be known for years.

All professions are expected to establish uniform and recognized standards governing professional, scientific, educational, and ethical issues. Various standards that exemplify the profession's values and principles and that serve the needs of service providers, clients, educators, the society, and legal bodies have been developed (Oakland, 1986). Standards prepared by the American Psychological Association include *Psychology as a Profession* (American Psychological Association, 1968), *Guidelines for Conditions of Employment of Psychologists* (American Psychological Association, 1972), *Ethical Principles in the Conduct of Research With Human Subjects* (American Psychological Association, 1973), *Standards for Educational and Psychological Testing* (American Educational Research Association, American Psychological Association, & the National Council on Educational Research, 1999), *Guidelines and Principles for Accreditation of Training Programs in Professional Psychology* (American Psychological Association, 1996), "Ethical Principles of Psychologists and Code of Conduct" (American Psychological Association, 2002), and *Petition for Reaffirmation of the Specialty of School Psychology* (American Psychological Association, 1997).

In addition, the Division of School Psychology (American Psychological Association, Division 16) has addressed various issues concerning standards in the following position papers: *Guidelines to Work Conditions for School Psychologists; Test Protocols in Relation to Sole Possession Records; School Personnel Qualified to Provide Psychological Services to Pupils/Students, School Staffs, and Parents; School Psychology Internship;* and *State Legislative Mandates for School Psychological Services Encouraged.*

The National Association of School Psychologists also has established standards. They include *School Psychology: A Blueprint for Training and Practice II* (Ysseldyke et al., 1997), *Principles for Professional Ethics* (National Association of School Psychologists, 2000b), *Guidelines for the Provision of School Psychology Services* (National Association of School Psychologists, 2000a), and *Standards for the Credentialing of School Psychologists* (National Association of School Psychologists, 2000c). Four national professional journals are intended to advance the knowledge and practice base of school psychology: *Journal of School Psychology, School Psychology Quarterly, Psychology in the Schools,* and *School Psychology Review.* Several school psychology journals that also are received by many school psychologists include *The California School Psychologist, School Psychology International, Canadian Journal of School Psychology,* and the *Journal of Applied School Psychology.* Sixteen secondary journals and 26 tertiary journals also contribute to the field's literature (Reynolds & Gutkin, 1982, pp. 1169–1172). Numerous textbooks also discuss school psychology. Newsletters from the National Association of School Psychologists (i.e., *Communiqué*), the Division of School Psychology (i.e., *The School Psychologist*), and various state associations also contribute to the dissemination of information among school psychologists.

Preparation of School Psychologists

Approximately 8,500 students are enrolled in the nation's 218 school psychology programs. Approximately 1,900 students graduate yearly with one of three degrees: master's, specialist, or doctorate. In contrast to prevailing international practices (Oakland & Cunningham, 1999), no school psychology programs exist at the undergraduate level. Attainment of a master's degree typically requires a 1- to 2-year program of 10 to 15 semester-long courses. Preparation at the specialist level typically involves a 3-year program that includes 20 or more semester-long courses and a 1-year supervised internship. Preparation at the doctoral level typically involves a 4- to 6-year program that includes 3 years of coursework (30 to 40 semester-long courses), a 1-year supervised internship, and a dissertation.

Approximately one third of the school psychology programs offer doctoral-level preparation, whereas the remaining two thirds offer preparation at the master's or specialist levels. A number of programs offer both specialist and doctoral degrees. There are no national qualifications for admission into school psychology programs. Each program specifies its own admission criteria. Applicants generally must obtain at least an average score on the internationally administered Graduate Record Examination. Because all school psychology programs are at the graduate level, all students must first complete an undergraduate degree (e.g., bachelor of arts, bachelor of science). Although undergraduate degrees in psychology and education make candidates more competitive for admission, degrees in these fields are not required. Successful applicants often have experience working with children, and some have been teachers. However, a teaching credential is not required to become a school psychologist.

Efforts to prepare school psychologists have been influenced heavily by accreditation standards promulgated by the National Association of School Psychologists and the American Psychological Association. Quality school psychology programs adhere to these standards. Programs offering only specialist degrees tend to be consistent with the National Association of School Psychologists standards, and those offering doctoral-level degrees often are consistent with both the American Psychological Association and the National Association of School Psychologists standards. The National Association of School Psychologists standards are summarized in the next section.

Prevailing Philosophy Guiding Preparation and Practice

Current professional research literature as well as legal and ethics codes establish standards for practice. Furthermore, a prevailing view, particularly among advocates of doctoral-level school

psychology, emphasizes the importance of a scientist-practitioner model for professional preparation and practice. This model advocates the belief that applications of psychology, including school psychology, should be supported empirically and theoretically and derived from a body of literature held in high esteem. This scientist-practitioner model emphasizes the importance of reciprocal relationships between scholarship and practice within psychology; each contributes to the other. Thus, school psychologists are expected to contribute to science and to base their practices on it.

There are diverse perspectives as to whether school psychology belongs in psychology or education. Some view school psychology as a specialty within the profession of psychology whose research base is derived largely from the discipline of psychology. Others view school psychology as a profession separate and independent from psychology and more clearly allied with education. Those who work in schools frequently identify closely with their colleagues in education. However, much of the scholarship and technology used in their work comes from psychology. Furthermore, legal and financial issues that often transcend both psychology and education increasingly govern practices. For example, federal legislation (e.g., the Individuals With Disabilities Education Act) delineates regulations to which states must adhere in order to receive federal funds. These regulations include numerous guidelines regarding individual education plans, appropriate means of determining whether students may have access to special education services, the education of children with disabilities, and evidence that students are receiving support (e.g., school psychology) services.

Training standards delineated by the National Association of School Psychologists (2000d) have impacted the curriculum and structure of most school psychology programs that offer the specialist degree and many that offer the doctoral degree. These training standards address program structure, domains of school psychology training and practice, field experience and internship, performance-based program assessment, and program support and resources. The National Association of School Psychologists standards

> serve to guide the design of school psychology graduate education by providing a basis for program evaluation and a foundation for the recognition of programs that meet national quality standards through the National Association of School Psychologists program approval process. (2000d, p. 7)

The domains of school psychology training and practice are (1) data-based decision making and accountability; (2) consultation and collaboration; (3) effective instruction and development of cognitive/academic skills; (4) socialization and development of life skills; (5) student diversity in development and learning; (6) school and systems organization, policy development, and climate; (7) prevention, crisis intervention, and mental health; (8) home/school/community collaboration; (9) research and program evaluation; (10) school psychology practice and development; and (11) information technology. Students in specialist programs approved by the National Association of School Psychologists complete a 3-year program, including a 1,200-hour supervised internship. Many programs also offer a master's degree en route to the specialist degree.

Through addressing these training standards, programs emphasize (a) core academic knowledge of psychology (e.g., development, learning and cognition, educational, personality, social, experimental, biological, statistics, and research design); (b) assessment services (e.g., intellectual, academic, emotional, and social assessment); (c) intervention services (e.g., behavioral, affective, educational, and social-systems); (d) focus on children and youth (e.g., within the context of classrooms, schools, families, communities, and other systems); (e) interpersonal skills (e.g., establishing trust and rapport, listening and communication skills, respect for the views and expertise of others, recognition of the assets and limitations of other professionals, and a mature understanding of issues and effective methods to address them); (f) professional decision-making skills (e.g., the ability to consider important qualities that characterize the child and the contexts within which the child is being raised, being informed by research, and being motivated by problem-solving orientations that consider the viability of alternative courses of actions); (g) knowledge of statistical methods and research design (e.g., often prepared within one of two models: as a good consumer of research and other forms of scholarship or as a scientist and practitioner); and (h) knowledge of the legal and ethical basis for services (e.g., laws, administrative rulings, and other regulations as well as ethics codes governing practice).

Roles, Functions, and Responsibilities of School Psychologists

School psychology services may be characterized within six broad delivery systems. The following provides a brief description of each.

Individual psychoeducational evaluations frequently are conducted on students referred for possible special education services. School psychologists typically evaluate a student's cognitive (i.e., intelligence and achievement), affective, social, emotional, and linguistic characteristics while utilizing educational and psychological assessment techniques.

Direct services are utilized to promote academic, social, and emotional development through tutoring, teaching, and counseling.

School psychologists provide *indirect services* to students by working individually or with groups of parents, teachers, principals, and other educators who are responsible for direct interventions. Indirect services may involve assessments, participation in child study teams, in-service programs, consultation, and collaboration.

Research and evaluation activities are intended to assist professionals in education and psychology to develop a body of literature on which to base their practices.

Supervision and administration services enable school psychologists to administer pupil personnel and psychological services. In this capacity, they are responsible for conceptualizing and promoting a comprehensive plan for these services, for hiring and supervising personnel, for promoting their development, and for coordinating these services with other psychological and social services provided in the community.

Prevention services are designed either to prevent the occurrence of problems or to minimize their deleterious impact should they occur. Prevention programs often focus on drug and alcohol abuse, suicide, dropouts, school violence, and pregnancies.

The specialty of school psychology is prepared to provide the aforementioned services, with individual school psychologists providing them in varying degrees. The responsibilities of a particular school psychologist rarely encompass all areas and domains described in the previous paragraphs. The quantity and nature of services often differ for preschool, elementary, and secondary students. Nationally, school psychologists devote about 5% of their time to preschool, 60% to elementary, 20% to middle school, and 15% to senior high students. Also, national survey data reveal demographic and regional variability in current roles, job satisfaction, assessment practices, and system reform attitudes and beliefs of school psychologists (Curtis, Hunley, & Chesno

Grier, 2002; Curtis, Hunley, Walker, & Baker, 1999; Hosp & Reschly, 2002; Reschly, 2000).

Tests commonly used to assess achievement, intellectual abilities, personality and temperament, and behavior and social skills vary across the United States. The following is a brief list of some of the most commonly used tests. Achievement tests include the Woodcock-Johnson III Tests of Achievement, Peabody Individual Achievement Test–III, Wechsler Individual Achievement Test–II, and the Wide Range Achievement Test 4. Intelligence tests include the Wechsler Intelligence Scale for Children–IV, Wechsler Preschool and Primary Scale of Intelligence–III, Woodcock-Johnson III Tests of Cognitive Abilities, Differential Ability Scales, Comprehensive Test of Nonverbal Intelligence, Kaufman Assessment Battery for Children–II, and the Universal Nonverbal Intelligence Test. Measures of personality and temperament include the Minnesota Multiphasic Personality Inventory–Adolescent, Personality Inventory for Children–II, and the Student Styles Inventory. Measures of social and emotional behaviors include the Behavior Assessment System for Children–II, Child Behavior Checklist, Social Skills Rating Scale, Beck Youth Inventories of Emotional and Social Impairment, and the Conners Parent and Teacher Rating Scales–Revised. Measures of adaptive behavior include the Adaptive Behavior Assessment System–II and the Vineland Adaptive Behavior Scale–II.

School psychologists who work mainly in special education typically devote about 32% of their time to students with learning disabilities, 22% to those with behavioral and emotional problems, 14% to those with mental retardation, and 16% to the general school population (Smith, 1984). School psychologists also devote smaller amounts of time to students who are talented and gifted (4%) and to those exhibiting acuity (3%), physical (2%), and speech (2%) disorders. When asked how they actually spend their time and how they would prefer to spend their time, school psychologists indicated they actually spend about

54% but would prefer to spend 40% of their time in assessment activities, they spend 23% but would prefer to spend 30% of their time in interventions (e.g., counseling, program development), they spend 18% but would prefer to spend 23% on consultation, and they spend 1% but would prefer to spend 4% on research (Smith, 1984).

Current Issues Impacting School Psychology

The National Association of School Psychologists and other organizations have advocated for the preparation of more school psychologists. There may be a shortage of school psychology practitioners (Curtis, Hunley, et al., 2002), particularly in some areas of the country. In addition, large numbers of school psychology faculty positions remain unfilled. The numerous openings and reshuffling of current faculty reflect a lack of doctoral graduates entering academia. This is particularly disconcerting for the future of school psychology, including the preparation of school psychologists and scholarship.

The recent federal legislation described earlier places an emphasis on implementing evidence-based interventions to facilitate academic achievement and allows for the implementation of response-to-intervention strategies in identifying special needs of students. Thus, school psychology programs are likely to increasingly emphasize these topics. Also, in light of federal legislation, some graduate programs have begun to focus more narrowly on efforts that promote academic achievement.

References

American Educational Research Association, American Psychological Association, & the National Council on Educational Research. (1999). *Standards for educational and psychological testing.* Washington, DC: Author.

American Psychological Association. (1968). *Psychology as a profession.* Washington, DC: Author.

American Psychological Association. (1972). *Guidelines for conditions of employment of psychologists.* Washington, DC: Author.

American Psychological Association. (1973). *Ethical principles in the conduct of research with human subjects.* Washington, DC: Author.

American Psychological Association. (1996). *Guidelines and principles for accreditation of training programs in professional psychology.* Washington, DC: Author.

American Psychological Association. (1997). *Petition for reaffirmation of the specialty of school psychology.* Washington, DC: Author.

American Psychological Association. (2002). Ethical principles of psychologists and code of conduct. *American Psychologist, 57,* 1060–1073.

American Psychological Association Council of Representatives. (1998). *Archival description of school psychology as a specialty in professional psychology* (Minutes of the Council of Representatives Meeting, February 1998). Washington, DC: Author. Retrieved December 20, 2005, from Division of School Psychology Web site: http://www.indiana.edu/~div16/G&O.htm

Bureau of Labor Statistics. (2004). *Occupational outlook handbook, 2004–2005 edition, Psychologists.* Retrieved May 27, 2004, from http://www.bls.gov/oco/ocos056.htm

Central Intelligence Agency. (2003). *The world factbook.* Retrieved October 1, 2005, from http://www.cia.gov/cia/publications/factbook/index.html

Charvat, J. L. (2005). National Association of School Psychologists study: How many school psychologists are there? *Communiqué, 33,* 12–14.

Curtis, M. J., Chesno Grier, J. E., Walker Abshier, D., Sutton, N. T., & Hunley, S. (2002). School psychology: Turning the corner into the twenty-first century. *Communiqué, 30*(8), 1.

Curtis, M. J., Hunley, S. A., & Chesno Grier, J. E. (2002). Relationships among professional practices and demographic characteristics of school psychologists. *School Psychology Review, 31*(1), 30–42.

Curtis, M. J., Hunley, S. A., Walker, K. J., & Baker, A. C. (1999). Demographic characteristics and professional practices in school psychology. *School Psychology Review, 28*(1), 104–116.

D'Amato, R. C. (Ed.). (2003). Proceedings of the Multisite "Futures" Conference. *School Psychology Quarterly, 18*(4).

Day, J. C., & Newburger, E. C. (2002, July). *The big payoff: Educational attainment and synthetic estimates of work-life earnings* (Current Population Special Report No. P23-210). Washington, DC: U.S. Department of Commerce Economics and Statistics Administration, U.S. Census Bureau.

Fagan, T. K. (1986). The historical origins and growth of programs to prepare school psychologists in the United States. *Journal of School Psychology, 24,* 9–22.

Fagan, T. K. (1992). Compulsory schooling, child study, clinical psychology, and special education: Origins of school psychology. *American Psychologist, 47,* 236–243.

Fagan, T. (2002). Trends in the history of school psychology in the United States. In A. Thomas & J. Grimes (Eds.), *Best practices in school psychology* (4th ed., pp. 209–221). Bethesda, MD: National Association of School Psychologists.

Fagan, T. K., & Wise, P. S. (2000). *School psychology: Past, present and future* (2nd ed.). Bethesda, MD: National Association of School Psychologists.

Fields, J. (2003). *Children's living arrangements and characteristics: March 2002* (Current Population Report No. P20-547). Washington, DC: U.S. Census Bureau.

Hosp, J. L., & Reschly, D. J. (2002). Regional differences in school psychology practice. *School Psychology Review, 31,* 11–30.

Jamieson, A., Curry, A., & Martinez, G. (2001). *School enrollment in the United States: Social and economic characteristics of students* (Current Population Report No. P20-533). Washington, DC: U.S. Census Bureau.

Kaufman, P., Alt, M. N., & Chapman, C. D. (2001). *Dropout rates in the United States: 2000* (NCES Publication No. 2002-114). Washington, DC: Government Printing Office.

National Association of School Psychologists. (2000a). *Guidelines for the provision of school psychology services.* Bethesda, MD: Author.

National Association of School Psychologists. (2000b). *Principles for professional ethics.* Bethesda, MD: Author.

National Association of School Psychologists. (2000c). *Standards for the credentialing of school psychologists.* Bethesda, MD: Author.

National Association of School Psychologists. (2000d). *Standards for training and field placement programs in school psychology.* Bethesda, MD: Author.

Oakland, T. (1986). Professionalism within school psychology. *Professional School Psychology, 1*(1), 9–28.

Oakland, T. (1993). A brief history of international school psychology. *Journal of School Psychology, 31,* 109–122.

Oakland, T. (2000). International school psychology. In T. K. Fagan & P. S. Wise (Eds.), *School psychology: Past, present, and future* (2nd ed.). Bethesda, MD: National Association of School Psychologists.

Oakland, T., & Cunningham, P. (1999). The futures of school psychology: Conceptual models for its development and examples of their applications. In C. R. Reynolds & T. B. Gutkin (Eds.), *The handbook of school psychology* (3rd ed., pp. 34–53). New York: Wiley.

Oakland, T., Faulkner, M., & Annan, J. (2005). School psychology in four English-speaking countries. In C. Frisby & C. Reynolds (Eds.), *Comprehensive handbook of multicultural school psychology* (pp. 1081–1106). New York: Wiley.

Oakland, T., & Gallegos, E. (2005). Legal issues associated with the education of children from multicultural settings. In C. Frisby & C. Reynolds (Eds.), *Comprehensive handbook of multicultural school psychology* (pp. 1048–1078). New York: Wiley.

Pate, W. E., Frincke, J. L., & Kohout, J. L. (2003). *Report of the 2003 APA Salary Survey.* APA Research Office. Retrieved November, 2, 2005, from http://research.apa.org/03salary/home page.html

Reschly, D. J. (2000). The present and future status of school psychology in the United States. *School Psychology Review, 29*(4), 507–522.

Reynolds, C., & Gutkin, T. (Eds.). (1982). *The handbook of school psychology.* New York: Wiley.

Sheridan, S. M. (Ed.). (2004). Proceedings of the Multisite Conference on the Future of School Psychology [Special issue]. *School Psychology Review, 33*(1).

Smith, D. K. (1984). Practicing school psychologists: Their characteristics, activities, and populations served. *Professional Psychology: Research and Practice, 15,* 798–810.

Thomas, A. (2000). School psychology 2000. *Communiqué, 28*(2), 28.

Wallin, J .E. W. (1914). *The mental health of the school child.* New Haven, CT: Yale University Press.

Walter, R. (1925). The functions of a school psychologist. *American Education, 29,* 167–170.

Ysseldyke, J., Dawson, P., Lehr, C., Reschly, D., Reynolds, M., & Telzrow, C. (1997). *School psychology: A blueprint for training and practice II.* Bethesda, MD: National Association of School Psychologists.

43

School Psychology in Venezuela

Carmen León

Silvana Campagnaro

Milena Matos

The Context of School Psychology

Venezuela is located in the northern part of the South American continent. It was discovered in 1498 by Christopher Columbus and conquered and colonized by the Spanish kingdom. In 1811, Venezuela declared its independence from Spain, and after many wars, the country was finally liberated from Spain in 1824. Subsequent civil battles occurred during the remainder of the 19th century. Toward the beginning of the 20th century, Venezuela achieved social and political stability, based on a democratic government that fostered the construction of a modern country, including a universal educational system, social development, and better training. Despite these efforts and the country's abundant natural and economic resources, Venezuela remains underdeveloped; its poverty level has increased dramatically during the past 7 years and, at 61%, is high. Opportunities for a better quality of life, that is, education, health services, employment, housing, social security, and recreation, are distributed unequally.

Venezuela has a privileged geographical position, with a landmass of 916,445 square kilometers, and borders on the north with the Caribbean Sea, on the east with the Atlantic Ocean and the Federated Republic of Guyana, on the south with Brazil and Colombia, and on the west with the Republic of Colombia. The territory is divided into 23 states and the District Capital, Caracas. Venezuela is geographically diverse, with ocean coasts and tranquil beaches, islands, snow-covered peaks in the Andean Mountains, high mountains in the Coastal Range, vast rocky tablelands, fertile valleys, sand dunes, plains, and tropical jungles. The Angel Falls is the highest waterfall in the world, and the Orinoco River is the third longest in Latin America.

Under the 1999 national constitution, the present government is a democratic-participant system, consisting of five public powers: executive (president, vice president, executive cabinet, state governors, and municipality mayors), legislative (National Assembly with one deputy chamber), judicial (Supreme Court of Justice), electoral (National Electoral Council), and moral (attorney general, public defender, and general inspector). Theoretically, these authorities are independent of each other, and their goal is to guarantee the people's well-being. The official language is Spanish, and there is religious freedom. As of 2001, Venezuela's population was 24,765,581, with a density of about 25 persons per square kilometer. Two thirds are concentrated in 40% of the national territory. An accelerated urbanization process has elevated the urban population percentage from 40% in 1950 to 88% in 2001. Only 12% of the population is rural and indigenous and lives under very poor economic conditions, with few opportunities for schooling and health services. The projected population for 2005 is 26,577,423, distributed mainly along the northern coastal borders and in the District Capital. Three states in the southern part of the country encompass more than half of Venezuela's total territory and 7% of its population.

Venezuela is one of the world's largest oil producers and exporters, and its economy is largely dependent on its oil industry. Venezuela produces and exports other raw materials, such as gas, aluminum, iron, bauxite, gold, and coal, and it also exports hydroelectric energy. Nevertheless, it depends on imported foods and manufactured products to satisfy internal demands. The government controls the value of its currency, the bolivar, which, in recent years, has been devaluated dramatically in spite of high oil export revenues. This has had a direct adverse impact on the population's purchasing power and diminished the quality of life. In 2004, the gross domestic product was US$145.2 billion, US$5,800 per capita.

The population is basically young. According to the population distribution obtained in the most recent census, taken in 2001 (National Statistics Institute, n.d.), 60% of the population was 29 years or younger; the difference in the number of males compared with the number of females was insignificant. Population studies do not consider ethnic differences. The distribution of persons under age 18 is as follows: 11% age 4 or younger; 11% between ages 5 and 9; 11% between ages 10 and 14, and 10% between ages 15 and 19. Approximately 907,694 individuals displayed some kind of special need.

The Venezuelan school system is structured according to educational levels and modalities. There are four levels: (a) Initial education consists of a nursery level for children between birth and age 3 and a preschool level for children between ages 4 and 6. (b) Basic education comprises three stages: I, from first to third grades (7–9 years); II, from fourth to sixth grades (10–12 years); and III, from seventh to ninth grades (13–15 years). (c) Diversified and professional middle education for ages 16 to 17 is provided over 2 years. (d) Superior education for those 18 years and older grants several degrees: high technical degrees (such programs are provided over six academic semesters); pre-graduate university level leading to a professional title or license usually obtained in 5 years (except for medicine and veterinary, which require 6 years); graduate degrees leading to such titles as "diplomat," "specialist," or "master"; and finally, doctoral degrees.

The Venezuelan educational system offers the following modalities: special education, education for the arts, military education, religious education, adult education, and extracurricular education. The curriculum offered by special education is very important to school psychologists, because its goal is to meet the special needs of children and adolescents, including those with mental retardation, sensory deficits, learning difficulties, autism, and physical impediments, and to provide education for the gifted. The educational system also offers support programs in early intervention, education and work, social integration programs within regular schools, and language rehabilitation centers.

Among the 907,694 Venezuelans with special needs, only 11%, or 101,577, receive special education services (Ministry of Education, Culture, & Sports, 2004). Education is mandatory until Level III of basic education (i.e., until about age 15). Education is under the guardianship of and guaranteed by the federal government. Educational programs are offered in public and private institutions. Public schools are classified as national, state, or municipal. Private schools may be either religious or lay, depending on which organization manages them. All schools must comply with the federal government's educational curriculum. Each school year lasts 180 days, with a daily minimum of 5 hours of activities. The average age to begin school is 4 years for preschool and 7 years for first grade. The average class size is 35 children in public schools, but it varies in private schools. In special education, efforts are made not to exceed 15 children per classroom.

According to Bravo (2005), 33% of the entire population was registered in some area of the educational system. In 2003, 402,993 children repeated a grade, most frequently the first and seventh grades of basic education. These two are transition grades in which the teaching-learning patterns change significantly. Among the children who began basic education in 1993–1994, only 66% later entered seventh grade, and 51% later entered ninth grade. These numbers underscore the need to strengthen school psychology as a specialty, because it can serve as a resource to support the children's educational process until they are ready to be integrated into their social and work life.

The economic, social, and educational reality in Venezuela requires that every effort be made to guarantee a quality education for children and adolescents. A United Nations Educational, Scientific, and Cultural Organization report (2000) emphasized the need to increase the number of children receiving and completing formal education and that education should not differ based on sex. The need to educate children from low-income families, make early intervention efforts, and later promote the students' integration into the world of work also were highlighted. Thus, faced with these daunting challenges, ones that hold true for most Latin American countries, school psychology constitutes a potentially important specialty, one that could prove socially beneficial.

Origin, History, and Current Status of School Psychology

School psychology was born out of practical need, which was followed by academic and professional preparation. Applied psychological services first were offered as a means of satisfying educational needs and later those related to special education, which then became part of regular education (Oakland, Feldman, & León, 1994). Some historic milestones include the following. In 1912, special education services were provided to children with extreme deficiencies. In 1940, the first school counseling service was created in a private educational institution managed by Jesuits. In 1956, the first school psychology program was established at the Central University of Venezuela. In 1957, a second program was established at the Andrés Bello Catholic University. Thus, in Venezuela, as in many other countries, the practical need to solve problems within the educational context came first and was followed by the creation of the academic and professional preparation programs.

In 1978, professional psychology was strongly energized when the Professional Practice of Psychology Law was approved in 1978. It included the creation of specific professional societies, which resulted in the further strengthening of the Venezuelan Society of School Psychology (1969), the first freestanding professional association of school psychology in America. Simultaneously, the third school psychology program was created outside the capital, at the Rafael Urdaneta University in Maracaibo. Years later, four other school of psychology programs were created: Bicentenaria de Aragua in Maracay in 2000, Arturo Michelena in Valencia in 2001, Yacambú in Cabudare in 2004, and Universidad Metropolitana in Caracas in 2004. The creation of programs demonstrates the importance of psychology in addressing the need for such services in light of Venezuela's complex economic, social, and educational conditions.

The initial relationship between academic/ theoretical psychology and applied psychology was described by Oakland, Feldman, and León (1994) as strong, and Oakland and Cunningham (1992) concluded that although school psychology services throughout Latin America were weak, the situation was better in Venezuela and Brazil. Unfortunately, this period, characterized by significant accomplishments for school psychology, has been followed by a sluggish phase of development. This could be related to the interaction of several factors, including the socioeconomic and political situation (which has weakened professional organizations) and a lack of graduate programs in the specialty. To overcome these problems, school psychologists have attempted to develop various academic efforts such as seminars, courses, workshops, and, most recently, specialized research. The goal is to meet the nation's growing social and educational needs (e.g., high poverty levels, a large urban marginal population, and high dropout rates).

In discussing the status of school psychology in Venezuela, León, Campagnaro, and Matos (2004) identified its most frequent functions, the conceptual base for educational intervention programs, and the international scholarships that support this work. The goal was to systematize achievements, pinpoint challenges, and promote professionalism in this specialty.

To prepare for writing this chapter, the authors recognized the need to systematize the data collection to enable them to objectively describe the current status of school psychologists in Venezuela. Thus, they created a professional network consisting of 112 school psychologists, 23% of whom responded to the survey. Although practice-related information may not be comprehensive, its veracity has been supported by information obtained from other sources, including data obtained from directors of the seven schools of psychology.

Infrastructure of School Psychology

All Venezuelan psychologists are required by law to be members of the Federation of Psychologists. Regionally, 18 professional associations promote training and professional development. School psychology is represented by the Venezuelan Society of School Psychology. A scientific and professional society, it was founded in 1969 to promote the development of school and educational psychology in order to improve the scientific and professional level of its members; promote the exchange of information among those dedicated to studying, teaching, and applying school and educational psychology; and encourage research and development of new methodologies (T. Jimenez, Venezuelan Society of School Psychology, personal communication, May 2005). School psychologists must comply with the Professional Practice of Psychology Law (1978) and with the ethics code implied in it. Other related laws include the Constitutional Law of Education (1999), which applies to regular and special education, and the Constitutional Law for the Protection of Children and Adolescents (1998).

Little official information exists about Venezuelan school psychologists; the following profile is based on information acquired through the network described in the previous section. Most professionals are female and earn an annual salary of $7,000, slightly more than other educational professionals. Most work in private schools, some in public municipal schools and in special education, and some have private practices. Seventy-seven percent work with the general school population; 23% work with special education students. The preschool population is the most frequently served (28% work in public schools and 62% in private schools). Among those working in basic education, 41% work in public schools and 55% in private schools. Only 18% receive professional supervision. This means that 82% work independently of supervision, and 78% work collaboratively with other psychologists, learning specialists, language therapists, and occupational and social workers.

Most professionals work in urban settings with children from middle and high socioeconomic levels. The proportion of school psychologists per student varies according to the educational institution. The ratio between school psychologists and students is more favorable in private than in public schools. In regular education, the ratio is 1 to 600, and in special education, it is 1 to 65. Some aspects that interfere with professional satisfaction are low appreciation for school psychologists, the many professional roles they must assume, low salaries, and the large numbers of students they must serve. These conditions diminish productivity.

Preparation of School Psychologists

The country has seven schools of psychology, all of which are independent units with administrators that report to their respective deans. All are located in regions with large populations. As previously noted, three schools have relatively long histories (e.g., the first founded in 1956), and four were created more recently (2000, 2001, and two in 2004). The Central University of Venezuela offers the only major in school psychology.

At the undergraduate level, most universities offer a general program designed to prepare students to obtain licenses as psychologists. Undergraduate programs extend over a 5-year period with an emphasis on academic courses for approximately 60% of the time and on applied experiences for the remaining 40%. Theoretical courses generally include the following: basic

psychological concepts, 45%; research methods, 17%; assessment, 13%; legal basis, professional ethics, and other themes, 4%. With respect to preparation for professional practice, 10% is spent in activities related to children (e.g., human development, child assessment, child psychopathology, school psychology), 8% with adolescents (e.g., human development, clinical assessment, clinical psychopathology, counseling, family therapy), 12% with adults (e.g., human development, clinical psychopathology, counseling, family therapy), and 5% with the elderly (e.g., human development, clinical assessment, counseling, family therapy). Time also is dedicated to practicing with professional instruments and tools. The three oldest school psychology programs offer a theoretical course in school psychology that includes a supervised practice for at least one year. After completion of their undergraduate programs, students may participate in graduate studies in related fields, as no university offers a master's or a doctoral degree in school psychology.

Professionals working in the schools of psychology number 262 (73% are female). Staffing patterns vary among the programs. Of those with the longest history, one school serves 909 students, with 30 full-time, 35 half-time, and 17 hourly professors. Another school, serving 770 students, has 1 full-time and 29 hourly professors. A third, serving 354 students, has 3 full-time, 2 half-time, and 51 hourly professors. Among the professors, 19 hold a doctoral degree, 86 hold a master's degree, 42 have a specialist degree, and others have a psychology degree (or license) with no graduate studies. Thus, although each university has its own staffing patterns, professors hired on an hourly basis are predominant. This staffing pattern has the advantage of utilizing professors who practice psychology and who can better apply theory and research to their daily work. Unfortunately, the staffing pattern does not provide time or other forms of support for research and other scholarly engagements.

Thus, Venezuela has the professional resources needed to strengthen graduate programs, including one or more graduate programs in school psychology. Among the practitioners who responded to the survey, 70% had completed graduate programs nationally or internationally. This indicates the existence of qualified professionals in the field to support future graduate programs. A total of 9,087 students graduated from three of the seven universities. They constitute approximately 0.3% of Venezuela's 2005 population of 26,577,423. Therefore, the ratio between psychologists and the population is very low: 1 psychologist for every 2,924 inhabitants. The numbers of psychologists are not adequate to meet Venezuela's need for psychological services. Interest in the study of psychology is high. During the past 5 years, among all seven universities, 6,135 candidates have been admitted to psychology programs and 1,710 obtained degrees in psychology. In the four recently created universities, 1,323 students are registered. The newest schools of psychology, funded 5 years ago, will graduate their first students in 2005.

Those working to obtain a license or a doctorate have conducted some research related to school psychology. However, little of their work has been published. Works pertinent to this chapter's theme include Sánchez's (1979) study of the history and current status of school psychology in Venezuela from 1958 to 1978, León's (1987) model for school psychology services in municipal schools, Oakland, Feldman, and León's (1994) discussion of the origin of and perspective on school psychology in Venezuela, and León et al.'s (2004) review of the status of school psychology.

Opportunities for school psychologists' continued professional development are limited. For example, opportunities to participate in professional development or continuing education courses are rare. Only one university, the Rafael Urdaneta University, offers a graduate program in educational psychology, and another, the Central University of Venezuela, offers one in the psychology of teaching. School psychologists have neither the time nor the other forms of support needed to engage in research and other scholarly activities.

Roles, Functions, and Responsibilities of School Psychologists

School psychology services are thought to involve planning primary prevention programs, counseling students, counseling teachers and administrative personnel, counseling parents and families, direct intervention with students, psychoeducational evaluations, staff training, and administrative responsibilities, as well as some other services. On average, 17% of a professional's time is devoted to counseling teachers and staff, 16% to counseling parents and families, 13% to individual interventions, 12% to administrative responsibilities, 11% to psychoeducational evaluations, and the remaining time to various other activities. Thus, school psychology practices seem to focus most on counseling different members of the educational community, especially adults, while direct intervention with children seems to play a secondary role. These data indicate a need to prioritize professional involvement in basic prevention and counseling activities to help meet the needs of the country's large population, one with multiple needs and limited financial resources.

One of the roles school psychologists fulfill is the psychoeducational assessment of the school-age population. The most frequently used strategies to evaluate academic achievement are curriculum-based tests and portfolio reviews, adapted to the educational level. There are no standardized achievement tests, due to the high cost of the validation procedures. School psychologists also use many observational methods, such as Modelo Octogonal Integrador del Desarrollo Infantil (Octagonal Integrative Model of Child Development; León, 1992, 2003), which is a structured observational scale designed to assess child development; it includes strategies for observation and interviewing.

In Venezuela, the law does not require validation, normalization, and standardization of assessment instruments with Venezuelan data; thus, most assessments are used with the original psychometric technical properties. Frequently used standardized tests include the Wechsler Intelligence Scale for Children–III and the Kaufman Assessment Battery for Children (intellectual abilities); the Bender-Gestalt Test (Koppitz version) and Berry's Visual Motor Integration Test (perceptual-motor assessment); the Draw-A-Family Test, Kinetic Family Test, Kinetic School Test, Human Figure drawing, and Children's Apperception Test (emotional maturity). To assess behavior and social adaptive skills, various scales and questionnaires are used, such as the Vineland Adaptive Behavior Scales, the Child Behavior Checklist, and Escadita (Escala Diferencial de Trastornos de Atención [Differential Scale of Impulsivity, Attention and Hyperactivity]), which is a scale made ad hoc.

Current Issues Impacting School Psychology

School psychologists have identified several external threats to their practice. These include low salaries, usurpation of their posts by other professionals, low numbers of psychologists working in institutions, work overload, lack of supervision, little support among specialists, students' low levels of academic performance, and Venezuela's precarious economic conditions. These threats discourage professional growth and development. Among perceived internal threats, they identified limited opportunities for evaluations of their professional performance, few chances to obtain grants for research, and professional burnout related to the previously identified external conditions. This information underscores the need to promote professionalism and to join efforts to enhance the importance of school psychology services.

The directors from the seven programs expressed a different perspective. They identified the need to strengthen graduate courses in order to update the knowledge of licensed professionals as the most important issue. The need for validated intervention programs that are effective in a context characterized by poverty and the low academic level of high school graduates also is critical. The directors consider this last issue as vital in order to provide an opportunity for school psychology to demonstrate its ability to serve the nation and to respond to a much needed restructuring of communities around the academic institutions. During this process, school psychologists should assume an important role in improving the educational system and identifying and serving children with cognitive, emotional, and social needs.

Limited graduate program resources restrict research and other scholarships, due in part to reduced access to international literature and to scarce opportunities to engage in the research that would help professionals improve their daily practice. There are no specialized journals in school psychology. However, other journals provide empirical and theoretical articles relevant to practice, including *Behavioral Analogies* (published by Andrés Bello Catholic University), *Behavior* (published by Simón Bolívar University), and *Psychology* (published by Central University of Venezuela). Some directors report access to international journals in some libraries. However, subscriptions are not maintained on a regular basis due to their cost, thus limiting professional knowledge and improvement.

Applied research is considered fundamental to school psychology. The most important research-related issues include the development and evaluation of intervention strategies to determine their effectiveness in the Venezuelan reality; the design, adaptation, and validation of tests and other instruments; the management of school violence; and interventions with high-risk groups. Applied practice cannot be based only on theory, because school psychologists must validate the methods and tools that they commonly use in their daily professional work. Thus, universities that offer school psychology programs face the challenge of providing continuing education, specializations, and master's and doctoral programs. These unsettled issues will require cooperation among academic institutions.

Although school psychology remains unable to fully meet the needs of students, especially those attending public schools, progress has been achieved. A body of specialized professionals has developed strategies to help solve individual and group problems, detect difficulties in early stages, and promote primary prevention programs for the well-being and mental health of citizens. The nation's sociopolitical situation requires their continued professional contribution in order to transform present threats into opportunities. Their participation is both useful and vital.

Perhaps the greatest challenge lies in uniting efforts among universities to fortify professionalism by offering professional development and continuing education courses, graduate programs, research, and professional publishing opportunities adjusted to Venezuela's economic, social, and cultural reality. Recognition from all psychological associations as to the value of school psychologists' work is needed. Finally, sharing responsibilities and activities with other professionals working within the school context is imperative, as it will lead to the formation of professional, cooperative teams (Minke, 2000) capable of dealing with issues important to education and psychology (Oakland & Cunningham, 1999).

References

Bravo, L. (2005). *La escolaridad en el período 1999–2004* (Papel de trabajo No 1 para discusión) [Education in the period 1999–2004 (Working Discussion Paper No. 1)]. Caracas: Universidad Metropolitana.

León, C. (1987). *Hacia el modelo CEPE: Un centro de psicología escolar en cada Municipio* [The CEPE model: A school psychology center in each county]. Unpublished work presented at Andres Bello Catholic University, Caracas.

León, C. (1992). El Modelo Octogonal Integrador de desarrollo Infantil: Sus implicaciones para evaluación e intervención a nivel de prevención primaria y secundaria [The octogonal integrative model of child development: Implications for primary and secondary prevention]. *Analogías, 1994*(1), 96–111.

León, C. (2003). *Secuencias de desarrollo infantil* (4th ed.) [Phases of child development (4th ed.)]. Caracas: Publicaciones Universidad Católica Andrés Bello.

León, C., Campagnaro, S., & Matos, M. (2004). Psicología escolar [School psychology]. In G. Peña (Ed.), *Introducción a la psicología II. Áreas de aplicación.* Caracas: Publicaciones Universidad Católica Andrés Bello.

Ley del ejercicio de la psicología, Gaceta Oficial de la República de Venezuela Año CV. Mes XII No 2306. 11 de Septiembre de 1978. Caracas [Professional practice of psychology law, Official Gazette of the Republic of Venezuela].

Ley orgánica de educación, Gaceta Oficial de la Republica de Venezuela No 36.787. 15 de Septiembre de 1999 [Constitutional education law, Official Gazette of the Republic of Venezuela].

Ley orgánica para la protección del niño y adolescente, Gaceta Oficial de la República de Venezuela No 5.266 Extraordinaria. 2 de Octubre de 1998 [Constitutional law for the protection of the child and adolescent, Official Gazette of the Republic of Venezuela].

Ministry of Education, Culture, & Sports. (2004). Annual Report V. CXXVIII-N°CXXIV. Caracas: Author.

Ministry of Education, Culture, & Sports. (2005). *Estimado de la matrícula estudiantil para el período escolar 2004–2005* [Estimate of student registration for the school period 2004–2005]. Retrieved July 7, 2005, from http://www.inegov.ve/condiciones/educacion/asp

Minke, K. (2000). Preventing school problems and promoting school success through family-school-community collaboration. In K. Minke & G. Bear (Eds.), *Preventing school problems, promoting school success.* Bethesda, MD: National Association of School Psychologists.

National Statistics Institute. (n.d.). *Census 2001* (Data summary). Retrieved from http://www.ine.gov.ve/poblation/distribution/asp

Oakland, T., & Cunningham, J. (1992). A survey of school psychology in developed and developing countries. *School Psychology International, 13,* 99–130.

Oakland, T., & Cunningham, J. (1999). The futures of school psychology: Conceptual models for its development and examples of their applications.

In C. Reynolds & T. Gutkin (Eds.), *The handbook of school psychology* (3rd ed.). New York: Wiley.

Oakland, T., Feldman, N., & León, C. (1994). La psicología escolar en Venezuela: Tres décadas de progreso y un futuro con un gran potencial [School psychology in Venezuela: Three decades of progress and a future with great potential]. In R. Sousa, L. Da Silva, & S. Weschler (Eds.), *Psicología escolar. Campinas,* Brazil: Editorial Atomo.

Rodríguez, J., Yépez, A., & Campagnaro, S. (1997). *Estudio psicométrico epidemiológico de la escala de calificación diferencial del TDAH (Escadita)–versión escuela y versión hogar* [Psychometric epidemiological study of the scale of differential qualification of the TDAH (Escadita)–school and home versions]. Unpublished manuscript, Universidad Católica Andrés Bello, Caracas.

Sánchez, L. (1979). *20 años de psicología en Venezuela 1958–1978* [20 years of psychology in Venezuela]. Unpublished manuscript, Universidad Central de Venezuela, Caracas.

United Nations Educational, Scientific, and Cultural Organization. (2000). *U.N. millennium development goals.* Geneva: Author.

44

School Psychology in Zimbabwe

Elias Mpofu

Magen M. Mutepfa

Regis Chireshe

Joseph M. Kasayira

The term *educational psychologist*, not *school psychologist*, is used in Zimbabwe. Thus, the terms *school psychology* and *school psychologist*, as used in this chapter, refer to educational psychology and educational psychologist, as used in Zimbabwe.

The Context of School Psychology

Zimbabwe is a landlocked Southern African country that borders Botswana, Mozambique, Namibia, South Africa, and Zambia. The country stretches 725 kilometers from north to south and 835 kilometers from east to west and covers an area of 390,600 square kilometers. The

quality of the national road network has declined significantly in recent years due to neglect by local authorities and the central government. Thus, many rural schools are inaccessible by car. The country has 10 administrative regions. Its economy is largely agricultural; tourism and mining are also significant industries. The country has a small and thriving industry in crafts such as basket weaving, woodcarving, and tinsmithing, which mostly markets to tourists. In 2004, the gross domestic product was US$24.37 billion, US$1,900 per capita. The population of Zimbabwe is approximately 11,900,000, of which 51% are females. The population growth rate averaged about 3% per annum during the past two decades, and may have leveled off due to HIV/AIDS (human immunodeficiency virus/acquired immunodeficiency syndrome).

The HIV/AIDS prevalence rate is 1 in 4 in adults. Most Zimbabweans (or about 80%) live in rural areas and speak Shona. The minority culture groups are Ndebele/Nguni, Venda, Tonga, Asians, and Whites. Zimbabwe has one of the youngest populations in the world, with about 38% of the population between ages 10 and 38.

Eighty percent of Zimbabwean children have living mothers and fathers; however, about 50% of children live with extended family members. The cultural practice of living with extended family has deep cultural roots among indigenous Zimbabweans who subscribe to strong collectivistic family values (Mpofu, Chireshe, & Gwirayi, in press). Females head one third of the households. A growing number of teenagers also are assuming leadership of their households after losing their parents and other family members to the HIV/AIDS pandemic and in the absence of reliable government social welfare programs or extended family with resources. The average Zimbabwean child works to make money for the family by farming, livestock rearing, or marketing.

Zimbabwean education has three administrative levels: elementary (Grades 1–7), junior high (Grades 8–9), and high school (Grades 10–13). About 3,339,000 students attend primary and secondary (or high) school. Nearly 85% complete primary schooling. The age for enrollment in first grade is 5 years and 6 months. High school begins at age 13 years. About 65% complete the minimum 4 years of high school. Students preparing for specialist programs at colleges or universities take an additional 2 years of advanced classes. Zimbabwe's national literacy rate of 85% is one of the highest in the world.

The teacher-pupil ratio is 1 to 40 in primary schools, 1 to 33 in junior high schools, and about 1 to 25 in senior high schools (Education Secretary's Circular No. P.17 of 2004). Private schools have higher teacher-pupil ratios, between 1 to 9 and 1 to 25. The teacher-pupil ratio in special needs education classes is 1 to 19 for children with mild to moderate mental retardation, 1 to 7 for those with severe mental retardation and/or deafness or hearing impairment, and 1 to 10 for those with visual impairment or physical disabilities. In 2004, 14,115 students received services for mental retardation, 50,000 for learning disabilities, 1,634 for hearing impairments, and 2,635 for blindness or visual impairment (Education Management Information Systems, 2004; Mpofu, 2004c). Because physical disabilities are not as well documented by state social agencies as cognitive and sensory disabilities, the number of children with physical disabilities attending school is unknown.

The World Health Organization (1980) estimates that at least 10% of children have disabilities. Applying this figure to Zimbabwe, about 300,000 Zimbabwean children can be expected to have disabilities. However, the prevalence of disabilities usually is higher in developing countries like Zimbabwe. Assuming that the World Health Organization estimate is accurate for Zimbabwe, the approximately 70,000 Zimbabwean students with disabilities attending school constitute only about 25% of those with disabilities.

The Zimbabwe Ministry of Education, Sport and Culture has a School Psychological Services and Special Education Department, whose primary responsibility is the educational placement of students with disabilities. It provides free school psychology services to all students in the country and educates parents/guardians and teachers about special educational needs in children. The School Psychological Services and Special Education Department also provides a diverse range of counseling services. Five institutions of higher education offer teacher certification programs in special needs education and other school psychology-related services. Compared with those of its neighbors and other African nations, Zimbabwe's education system is relatively advanced.

Origin, History, and Current Status of School Psychology

The development of school psychology can be traced to 1971, when psychology as a profession was regulated statutorily, and the regulations made enforceable through the Zimbabwean (then Rhodesian) courts of law (Kasayira, Chireshe, & Chipandambira, 2004; Mpofu & Khan, 1997). From 1890 to 1980 Zimbabwe was the British colony of Southern Rhodesia. Under Zimbabwean law, the official title is "educational psychologist." During the British colonial period, school psychological services were available to White, Asian/Indian, and mixed race (or Colored) students only (Mntungwana-Hadebe, 1994; Mpofu & Nyanungo, 1998). Schools were segregated by race. White students and others of non-African origin were regarded as suitable for skilled positions in the colonial economy and more deserving of educational support than their Black peers. The colonial regime educated Blacks primarily to be drawers of water and hewers of wood (Mills, 1970; Mungazi, 1990, 1991; Zvobgo, 2000). Thus, there was no need to invest in specialized educational support for Black children. Christian missionaries provided schooling to a minority of Black students at community schools built with the assistance of denominational churches. They also provided school psychology-related services to some Black students attending schools at church mission stations. However, following national independence from colonial rule in 1980, school segregation was abolished, and school psychology services were extended to Black students.

A number of national and international events other than attainment of national independence also marked the evolution of school psychology in post-colonial Zimbabwe. For example, the passing of the Education Act in 1987 and the Disabled Persons Act of 1992 were major milestones in advancing school psychology. The maturation of the national disability rights movement in the post-colonial period

was another positive development for school psychology. School psychology also developed from the partnership between the state and the University of Zimbabwe to train educational psychologists and from the support of international development agencies. The Education Act of 1987 extended the right to schooling to all Zimbabwean children. After its enactment, school psychologists provided community outreach and education, efforts that led to increased enrollment of children with disabilities in schools. They also provided in-service education to teachers and administrators on special needs education and programming. The Disabled Persons Act of 1992 was intended to remedy inequities in the provision of social services to people with disabilities, including the provision of education services. School psychologists provide services consistent with the intent of the Disabled Persons Act, including providing advice on attitudinal and physical-structural barriers to educational opportunity for students with disabilities.

By the mid 1990s, there were more than 40 disability advocacy movements in the country, most led by individuals with disabilities (Chimedza, 2000). Disability advocacy movements in the post-colonial period demanded full civil rights for individuals with disabilities, including equal access to educational, social, and health services (Chimedza & Peters, 1999; Mpofu, 2000; Mpofu & Harley, 2002). They sought educational services responsive to the needs of persons with disabilities, including comprehensive school psychological services (Peters, 2001). School psychologists allied with the disability civil rights movement in helping children with disabilities obtain access to educational opportunity equal to that of their nondisabled peers.

International aid agencies, including the Swedish International Development Agency, the Canadian International Development Agency, and the Norwegian Psychological Association, provided the major financial and other resources critical to the development of school psychology. They funded outreach activities, continuing education for school psychologists, transportation, test procurement, test development, and educational technology. The Swedish International Development Agency, in particular, was the biggest single sponsor of school psychological services from the mid 1980s to the late 1990s, at which time its cooperation agreement with the Zimbabwe government ended.

In 1980, the extension of school psychological services to formerly Black schools occurred when there were very few licensed psychologists to work in the newly enfranchised schools. The vast majority of licensed school psychologists in service in colonial Zimbabwe (then Rhodesia) were trained in foreign countries (e.g., England, South Africa). Formal programs to train school psychologists were unavailable. In response to that need, the Zimbabwe Ministry of Education, Sport and Culture and the University of Zimbabwe (which, at that time, was the only university in the country) developed a cooperation agreement to train school psychologists to meet the national need. Thus, in 1983, the University of Zimbabwe offered for the first time a master of science degree program in educational psychology. Six trainee psychologists from the Ministry of Education, Sport and Culture composed the first class. On graduation, they added to the nucleus of licensed psychologists prepared to train more school psychologists through an internship program established by the School Psychological Services and Special Education Department. Currently, 32 school psychologists, 18 men and 14 women, serve as school psychologists; 9 of the 32 are in private practice. Between 1985 and 2000, the Zimbabwe Ministry of Education, Sport and Culture also developed a number of policies to guide the work of school psychologists. These were important for advancing the professionalization of school psychologists and their services. Some of the key policy documents are described later.

A chief psychologist is the director of the Zimbabwe School Psychological Services and Special Education Department. Two deputy directors, one for School Psychological Services and another for Special Needs Education, assist the chief psychologist in his or her functions. Four education officers responsible for school programs in hearing impairment, blindness and visual impairment, mental retardation, and guidance and counseling also are members of the School Psychological Services and Special Education directorate. The School Psychological Services and Special Education director is located at the Ministry of Education, Sport and Culture at Harare.

A principal educational psychologist heads the School Psychological Services and Special Education Department in each of the 10 administrative regions. Each administrative region has a complement of four to five school psychologists, six to eight remedial tutors, a guidance and counseling officer, one or two speech therapists or and a research assistant. However, most regional offices do not have a full complement of staff due to the financial constraints of the central government and job attrition.

School Psychological Services and Special Education personnel provide services on a peripatetic basis (i.e., they visit schools for the purposes of consulting and providing services). In 2004, the ratio of school psychologists to students was 1 to 145,955. The ratio vastly exceeds that of 1 to 700 recommended by the United Nations Economic, Social, and Cultural Organization (Wall, 1956). Many Zimbabwean students with special educational needs never receive the services of a psychologist. Help is more likely from teachers and parents or guardians. Since the late 1990s, when the program of cooperation between the Zimbabwean and Swedish governments was terminated, inadequate levels of funding further curtailed the delivery of school psychological services.

School psychologists in private practice typically work from home-based offices, learning enrichment centers, or colleges. The Health Professions Authority of Zimbabwe licenses their work premises. Currently, school psychologists in private practice obtain payment for their services from their clients. Unlike Zimbabwean clinical psychologists, school psychologists do not have reimbursement plans with health maintenance organizations.

School psychologists are compensated at a level comparable to that of their colleagues in the Zimbabwean education sector (Chigwamba, 2004a, 2004b). Salaries of school psychologists compare favorably with those of colleagues of similar grades in the Ministry of Education, Sport and Culture. For instance, the 2005 basic school psychologist annual salary is 4,183 to 4,518 euros, which is the same as the deputy headmaster and about 1,000 euros more than senior teachers and remedial speech teachers. A director of school psychology currently receives between 10,598 to 11,445 euros, which is the same as the provincial education director.

There are several opportunities for the professional development of school psychologists. The School Psychological Services and Special Education Department provides continuing education, and the Norwegian Psychological Association provides short-term training at Norwegian universities in neuropsychological assessment and rehabilitation. Visiting school psychologists from the international community also provide continuing education on an ad hoc basis in partnership with the Zimbabwe Psychological Association or the School Psychological Services and Special Education Department. During the 1990s, school psychologists received training in test development from Canadian professors with a grant from the Canadian International Development Agency. The Canadians also provided training in the assessment of children with autism and other atypical disorders with funding from the Canadian International Development Agency. In 1986, a few Zimbabwean school psychologists received advanced training in test development from the United States Educational Testing Service.

Other professional development opportunities include teacher certification through the vocational and technical colleges. Most opportunities for professional development are realized with the help of internship agencies. In a few instances, professional development opportunities are available from psychological associations and research centers in South African and Western countries. During the past decade, the International Union of Psychological Science, International Test Commission, International Association of Cross-Cultural Psychology, and International School Psychology Association sponsored conference attendance or participation of at least six school psychologists from Zimbabwe.

The job attrition rate among school psychologists is high, primarily because other employers need their skills and are able and willing to offer more compensation. For example, during the past decade, school psychologists filled about 75% of the academic positions in psychology at higher education institutions. Human resources departments in not-for-profit and for-profit organizations also heavily recruited school psychologists. Since the late 1990s, high caseloads, understaffing, underfunding, and other unsatisfactory professional conditions have further accelerated the rate of job attrition. During the past decade, job attrition at the senior levels has had a major negative impact on the quality of training and on the availability of school psychological services (Mnkandla & Mataruse, 2002).

During the past three decades, significant advances have been made in developing the infrastructure of school psychology, including training, management, supportive legislation, and community outreach. However, despite its relatively long history, school psychology services in Zimbabwe are not widely available (Mpofu, Peltzer, Shumba, Serpell, & Mogaji, 2005).

Infrastructure of School Psychology

Although Zimbabwe has only 32 practicing school psychologists, they constitute the largest professional specialty within psychology (Nyanungo, 2002). There are more school psychologists than clinical psychologists. Their professional associations, the legislation and policies that influence their work, the roles of professionals in the education system who perform school psychology-related functions, as well as the availability of published scholarship, are discussed below. Organizations that service the interests of psychologists include the Health Professions Authority of Zimbabwe and the Zimbabwe Psychological Association. The Health Professions Authority of Zimbabwe maintains a register of school psychologists, licenses the physical premises for their practice, and regulates their practice (Chireshe, 2005; Mpofu & Khan, 1997). The Zimbabwe Psychological Association provides a professional identity as well as education and training for all psychology specialties. The Zimbabwe Psychological Association has regional chapters, enabling psychologists throughout the country to participate in its activities. School psychologists also are represented on the Public Service Commission, a government agency for all professional grades within the Zimbabwean civil service.

The educational and civil rights legislation that influences the work of school psychologists was discussed in an earlier section. Other legislation related to the provision of school psychological services includes the Children's Protection and Adoption Act of 1996 and the Sexual Offences Act of 2001. The Child Adoption and Protection Act provides for the establishment of juvenile courts and the protection, welfare, and supervision of children and juveniles. School psychologists promote the acquisition of behavior management skills by service providers at rehabilitation facilities for child offenders. The Sexual Offences Act attempts to prevent the sexual exploitation of young persons and people with mental retardation. School psychologists provide counseling services to sexually abused children and expert testimony to courts on the intellectual functioning of abused children with mental retardation (Mpofu, 2004a).

A number of Ministry of Education, Sport and Culture policy statements direct the activities of school psychologists in school and community settings. For example, the Education Secretary's Circular Minute No. P.12 of 1987 provides guidelines on remedial programs for students with learning disabilities. The Education Secretary's Circular Minute No. P.36 of 1990 provides procedures for the educational placement of students with special needs. The Education Secretary's Circular No. P.5 of 2000 provides procedural guidelines for counseling abused children and their families. The Education Secretary's Circular Minute No. P.3 of 2002 provides guidelines on inclusive education and education for community participation and makes provision for guidance and counseling services for high school students.

Personnel in the Zimbabwean education system who provide school psychology-related services include remedial tutors, speech therapists, education officers for guidance and counseling, and research assistants (Mpofu, 1999; Oakland, Mpofu, Glasgow, & Jumel, 2003, 2005; Peresuh & Barcham, 1998). Remedial tutors help teachers develop, implement, and evaluate remediation plans for students with learning disabilities. Speech therapists work with teachers and families to diagnose speech and language disorders in children and train teachers to provide speech programs in schools. Special needs education teachers provide leadership for educating students with special needs. They work with regular class teachers, the school administration, and school psychologists to develop and manage educational programs for students with special educational needs (Mnkandla & Mataruse, 2002).

Education officers for guidance and counseling services work with high school counselors to provide guidance and counseling services to students. Research assistants carry out studies on special needs education as well as provide community outreach programs. They also help school psychologists organize continuing education workshops for school psychologists, remedial tutors, speech therapists, and special education personnel.

There are no professional journals specifically for school psychologists. School psychologists who publish their research work do so in educational journals such as the *Zimbabwe Bulletin of Teacher Education, Zimbabwe Journal of Educational Research,* and *Zambezia.* A small cohort of Zimbabwean school psychologists publish their scholarship in international journals such as the *British Journal of Educational Psychology, Educational and Child Psychology, Educational and Psychological Measurement, European Journal of Psychological Assessment, International Journal of Psychology, Journal of Genetic Psychology, Journal of Psychology in Africa, School Psychology International,* and the *South African Journal of Psychology.* The Zimbabwe Psychological Association newsletter, *Feedback,* has intermittent circulation and is a useful source of information on developments in psychological research and practice. Efforts are under way by the Norwegian Psychological Association to host a Web site for the Zimbabwe Psychological Association, thus providing a source of information on psychology.

Preparation of School Psychologists

Most school psychologists are trained within the country (Mpofu & Khan, 1997). Many hold University of Zimbabwe qualifications either at the undergraduate or graduate level. Two main programs prepare school psychologists: a full-time 3-year internship program under the School Psychological Services and Special Education Department in the Ministry of Education, Sport and Culture, and a master of science degree in educational psychology at the University of Zimbabwe (Mpofu & Khan, 1997; Nyanungo, 2002). Few school psychologists have teaching qualifications, a desirable quality recommended by the United Nations' Education, Social, and Cultural Organization (Wall, 1956). The quality of training of school psychologists has been rated as marginal to adequate in surveys of Zimbabwean special education personnel and school psychologists (Mnkandla & Mataruse, 2002; Mpofu et al., 2005).

The master of science degree program in educational psychology enrolls about 10 students biennially. Program availability depends on the availability of lecturers with requisite qualifications at the University of Zimbabwe and an adequate number of qualified students. This program graduates about 8 students every 2 to 4 years. The internship program through the School Psychological Services and Special Education Department has at least six trainees at any one time. On average, the School Psychological Services and Special Education internship program graduates about two licensed school psychologists per year. The number of trainee psychologists in this internship program depends on the availability of licensed school psychologists to supervise the trainees at the 10 regional offices. The availability of licensed psychologists varies from time to time due to job attrition and availability of financial resources from the central government to hire more psychologists.

Following high school, 6 to 7 years of education are required to qualify as a school psychologist. All school psychologists are required to hold an honors degree in psychology. This is achieved after 3 to 4 years of college (Mpofu & Khan, 1997). The University of Zimbabwe, Zimbabwe Open University, and Midlands State University offer honors degrees in psychology. This degree is a required entry to both the 3-year full-time internship program and the master of science degree in educational psychology program at the University of Zimbabwe. The University of Zimbabwe is the only institution currently offering this degree.

Trainee school psychologists taking an internship with the School Psychological Services and Special Education Department have both pedagogic instruction and internship experience in special needs education and child rehabilitation. The internship training experiences include child assessment, report writing, teacher, school, and parent consultation, special needs education programming, the administration of special needs programs, child advocacy, and legal aspects of school psychology practice. Trainee school psychologists have fieldwork placements at institutions that serve children with disabilities, mainstream school settings, vocational training centers, children's rehabilitation centers, organizations for or of persons with disabilities, and outpatient psychiatric settings. Trainee psychologists are placed on a rotation of internship experiences that includes direct service experiences with children with learning disabilities, hearing impairment, physical disabilities, speech and language disorders, behavioral disorders, and visual impairment. Each rotation lasts about 6 to 8 weeks.

Trainee school psychologists are required to produce an internship portfolio for evaluation by the Psychological Practices Advisory Committee of the Health Professions Authority of Zimbabwe. The Psychological Practices Advisory Committee is composed of five licensed psychologists with school, clinical, organizational/industrial, and academic psychology backgrounds. The portfolio should include evidence of continuing education, papers presented at professional seminars and workshops, assessment reports, child placement reports, and research reports. In addition, the portfolio should include letters of recommendation to register from at least two licensed school psychologists who provided professional supervision

to the trainee school psychologist during the 3-year period.

Roles, Functions, and Responsibilities of School Psychologists

Some roles assumed by school psychologists were discussed previously. This section discusses the following primary roles: consultation and advocacy, assessment, professional training, resource mobilization, and research.

Consultation and advocacy. School psychologists work with students, parents, educators, and other mental health services to develop environments that support student learning and well-being. They work closely with other professionals, such as remedial teachers, rehabilitation specialists (e.g., physical and occupational therapists), social workers, physicians, audiologists, and speech specialists. School psychologists also network with governmental and nongovernmental organizations interested in the welfare of children (Kasayira et al., 2004; Mpofu, 2004c). Some of the nongovernmental organizations with which school psychologists work are Childline, Justice for Children, Child Protection Society, Girl Child Network, and the Zimbabwe Institute of Systemic Therapy. These organizations provide counseling, accommodation, and legal representation to children at risk or with trauma.

Assessment. School psychologists assess students prior to conferring with them, teachers, parents, and other school officials regarding current and future learning needs. Assessments often occur after a referral by a teacher and/or a parent through the school. However, parents may directly request that their child be assessed by a school psychologist (Mpofu, 2003). The specific assessment functions carried out by school psychologists include screening for educational problems, counseling, and rehabilitation progress.

Specific assessment procedures used by Zimbabwean school psychologists include task-oriented tests, observations, and self-reports. For example, school psychologists use curriculum-based assessment, which is a type of task-oriented test (Mpofu, 1996; Mpofu & Nyanungo, 1998). Using curriculum-based assessments, school psychologists determine the child's learning difficulties after evaluating his or her performance on actual curriculum tasks. School psychologists use observation-oriented tests to assess a child's functioning in any domain of interest for educational advisement. Using self-reports and interviews helps psychologists provide counseling services. Tests of school achievement commonly used by Zimbabwean school psychologists include the Wide Range Achievement Test–Revised, Daniels and Diack's Spelling Test, Daniels and Diack's Graded Test of Reading Experience, Word Graded Reading Test, the Burt Word Reading Test, Schonell's Reading and Spelling Tests, Basic Arithmetic Skills, and Vernon Graded Arithmetic (Mutepfa, 2005). The Ministry of Education, Sport and Culture developed diagnostic tests for local and indigenous languages and also for mathematics (Mpofu & Nyanungo, 1998).

Psychologists use imported tests of ability to assess learning potential. For example, they use the Wechsler Intelligence Scale for Children–Revised, British Ability Scales, Wechsler Preschool and Primary Scale of Intelligence, Stanford-Binet Intelligence Scale, and Kaufman Assessment Battery for Children–Revised. Only the Wechsler Intelligence Scale for Children–Revised has some Zimbabwean norms, albeit only for urban children. School psychologists typically rely on achievement tests to determine a child's learning ability and use imported ability tests with a minority of students from a middle-class background or with strong English language skills. In general, psychologists do not do any personality testing with children due to the probable invalidity of Western tests in an African setting (Mpofu et al., 2005; Mpofu & Nyanungo, 1998). Nonetheless, the Vineland Social Maturity Scale is used by school psychologists who consider it to have some relevance in assessing social skills (Mutepfa, 2005).

Professional training. School psychologists also serve in a number of training and supervisory roles (e.g., supervise school psychology interns). However, they often lack needed training in supervision and rely on what they experienced during their own internships. School psychologists also have supervisory roles over early childhood education programs within their administrative districts and, as previously described, supervise education professionals providing psychology-related programs in school settings.

Resource mobilization. School psychologists function as allies for communities to access resources for special needs children. For example, through community outreach programs, school psychologists educate communities about the availability of special needs education programs from the Ministry of Education, Sport and Culture and also from rehabilitation centers. They also educate communities about the availability of assistive devices for children with orthopedic disabilities and sensory disabilities from the Zimbabwe Ministry of Health and Child Welfare or nongovernmental agencies. School psychologists help establish networks of parents with children who have experienced deprivation so as to enable them to learn from one another about resources and opportunities for child rehabilitation in the community, regionally, or nationally (Mpofu, 2003; Mpofu & Mapfumo, 1989).

Research. School psychologists carry out research on strategies to promote effective learning in schools. From that research, they learn how best to assist teachers, parents, and schools regarding the effective delivery of special needs education programs. Increasingly, school psychologists are involved in research on the psychosocial effects of HIV/AIDS on children and their families. The results from such research have formed the basis for seeking help from international agencies to support HIV/AIDS and poverty relief efforts in their jurisdictions and the delivery of appropriate health interventions.

Current Issues Impacting School Psychology

School psychologists face several challenges to the development and provision of services. Previously discussed challenges include underfunding by the central government, high job attrition, and the consequent erosion of the quality of training. The diminished financial resources result from a decision by the central government to not assume the financial responsibilities that formerly were provided by the Swedish International Development Agency. Sadly, there currently are no plans to provide resources at or above the same level. The Zimbabwean economy is currently on a decline due, in part, to politically motivated sanctions on the nation by the major Western countries coupled with the effects of years of economic mismanagement by the central government.

School psychological services currently are provided free of charge. A possible solution to the problem of resource insufficiency is to levy service fees to people in middle to high income brackets whose students receive school psychological services and to provide school psychology services at no cost only to students from families who fall below a means test. Supplemental to fees for services, the Ministry of Education, Sport and Culture could levy a school psychological services fee on all schools located in the more affluent suburbs or on large farms. Zimbabwean private schools, patronized by the elite, also receive free services from the School Psychological Services and Special Education Department. These schools could be required to hire their own school psychologists or pay a service levy to the Ministry of Education, Sport and Culture. In addition, the School Psychological Services and Special Education department can engage in externally funded research. This fee-for-service strategy and other such options, if properly managed, would generate the additional resources needed to make school psychological services available to more students across the nation.

The availability of resources for school psychologists to carry out their job functions and a quadrupling of the number of school psychologists per region would reduce job attrition due to frustrations associated with resource scarcity and case overload. In 2005, the School Psychological Services and Special Education Department hired 30 trainee psychologists, a record number. Thus, the central government seemingly is becoming more mindful of the importance of school psychology services and more willing to commit resources to the School Psychological Services and Special Education Department. However, the shortage of supervisors for the trainees could frustrate the trainees, resulting in early job attrition. The department has a history of neglecting trainees in their professional development needs (Kasayira, 2005; Mnkandla & Mataruse, 2002). It could, however, recruit school psychologists from private practice to assume some training responsibilities. Furthermore, the Ministry of Education, Sport and Culture could reactivate its dormant school psychologist training partnership with the University of Zimbabwe. The state–University of Zimbabwe partnership has experienced a stranglehold due to attrition of qualified faculty. However, a plan to offer the master of science degree program on an annual basis and use part-time adjunct faculty would add to the availability of training to new or unlicensed school psychologists.

Attrition to private sector employment opportunities is unlikely to be remedied soon. Nonetheless, compensating school psychologists at a competitive level vis-à-vis the private sector would enhance retention. Initiatives are in place for the Zimbabwe public service to review the compensation levels for school psychologists and to make them more competitive with those in the private sector.

Many Zimbabwean students with disabilities and their families are unaware of the availability of school psychology services and the type or relevance of the services (Mpofu, Zindi, Oakland, & Peresuh, 1997). Moreover, families holding strong indigenous cultural beliefs about disabilities prefer to seek services from traditional healers, often in place of psychologists (Mpofu, 1994, 2000, 2003). At the same time, people in many developing countries, including Zimbabwe, may be starting to accept scientific perspectives about disabilities (Mallory, Nicholls, Charlton, & Marfo, 1993; Mpofu, 2002). Consequently, a segment of the population holds both indigenous-cultural and modern views toward disabilities. They also flexibly utilize the services of both traditional healers and psychologists (Mpofu, 2000; Piachaud, 1994). School psychologists need to be comfortable working across epistemological lines regarding disability and health.

Creating awareness among the general public and some schools as to the availability and quality of school psychological services constitutes a long-standing problem. The outreach program of the School Psychological Services and Special Education Department has been helpful, yet currently is crippled due to a lack of funding. The School Psychological Services and Special Education Department has produced simple flyers to distribute to the community and schools, but their distribution has been unsystematic and no thought has been given to their impact. The use of radio broadcasts to reach the greater Zimbabwean population also has been considered. The long-term success of the outreach effort will depend, in part, on the ability of the Department to actually deliver the services that it claims to provide; this, in turn, depends on the availability of resources.

Among the major issues for research by school psychologists is the practice of culturally sensitive school psychology (Mpofu, 2003; Mpofu et al., 2005). For example, many Zimbabwean students and their families believe that spiritual forces cause disabilities; thus, effective interventions should address these agents (Mpofu, 2000, 2003; Ngwarai, 1995). Mpofu (2003) demonstrated how Zimbabwean indigenous notions of the causation of behavioral disorders could be integrated into a multilayered treatment regimen, thereby also addressing perceived intercession by ancestral spirits. School psychologists need to carry out research on enhancing the interface between Western paradigms of disability, and their related interventions, and local, indigenous paradigms.

The development of valid assessment procedures for students receiving school psychological services is urgently needed. School psychologists rely too much on Western tests and concepts. These tests may lack validity with many students, which leads to diminished credibility of services based on results (Mpofu, 2005; Mpofu & Nyanungo, 1998). Results from test data that have poor validity could misguide interventions and be harmful to students. The department has been developing reading tests based on the local curriculum (Mutepfa, 2005). This project, if successful, could be a good step toward the availability of contextually relevant tests. Mpofu (1996, 2004a, 2004b, 2004c) recommended research into the use of task-oriented measures using widely available school curriculum materials to address the perceived relevance of assessment by students, parents, and teachers.

Zimbabwe's school psychological services are probably some of the most advanced on the African continent, and the work of school psychologists in Zimbabwe has developed appreciably over the past three decades. The potential for school psychology in Zimbabwe is great, dependent on improved managerial functions, increased support by the central government, and application of contextually relevant research to guide practice.

References

Chigwamba, C. (2004a). *Appointment, performance advancement, regarding transfer, promotion, and training procedures for nongraduate remedial tutors in the Public Service.* Harare: Public Service Commission.

Chigwamba, C. (2004b). *Approved key scale for the year 2005.* Harare: Public Service Commission.

Children's Protection and Adoption Act. (1996). Harare: Government Printers.

Chimedza, R. (2000). *Study of disability organizations.* Copenhagen, Denmark: Danish Council of Organizations of Disabled Persons.

Chimedza, R., & Peters, S. (1999). Disabled people's quest for social justice in Zimbabwe. In F. Armstrong & L. Barton (Eds.), *Disability, human rights, and education* (pp. 7–23). Buckingham, UK: Open University Press.

Chireshe, R. (2005). *Infrastructure of school psychology.* Unpublished manuscript, Masvingo State University.

Disabled Persons Act. (1992). Harare: Government Printers.

Education Act. (1987). Harare: Government Printers.

Education Management Information Systems. (2004). *Summary table of education statistics: First term statistics of 2004.* Harare: Ministry of Education, Sport and Culture.

Health Professions Authority Act. (2000). Harare: Government Printers.

Kasayira, J. M. (2005). *Origin, history, and current status of school psychologists in Zimbabwe.* Unpublished manuscript, Midlands State University.

Kasayira, J. M., Chireshe, R., & Chipandambira, K. (2004). *Educational behaviour.* Unpublished manuscript, Zimbabwe Open University, Harare.

Mallory, B. L., Nicholls, R. W., Charlton, J. L., & Marfo, K. (1993). *Traditional and changing views of disability in developing countries: Causes, consequences, and cautions.* Durham, NH: World Rehabilitation Fund.

Mnkandla, M., & Mataruse, K. (2002). The impact of inclusion policy on school psychology in Zimbabwe. *Educational and Child Psychology, 19,* 12–23.

Mills, M. G. (1970). *Annual report of the secretary for African education for the year ended 31st December 1969.* Salisbury, Rhodesia: Author.

Mntungwana-Hadebe, J. A. (1994, September). History of special education in Zimbabwe. *Teacher in Zimbabwe Newsletter,* pp. 7–12.

Mpofu, E. (1994). Counsellor role perceptions and preferences of Zimbabwe teachers of a Shona cultural background. *Counselling Psychology Quarterly, 7,* 311–326.

Mpofu, E. (1996). The differential validity of standardized achievement tests for special educational placement purposes: Results and implications of a Zimbabwean study. *School Psychology International, 17,* 81–92.

Mpofu, E. (1999). Learning disabilities: Theories, practices and applications in the Zimbabwean context. In M. Peresuh & T. Nhundu (Eds.), *Foundations of education in Africa* (pp. 147–166). Harare: College Press.

Mpofu, E. (2000). Rehabilitation in international perspective: A Zimbabwean experience. *Disability and Rehabilitation, 23,* 481–489.

Mpofu, E. (2002). Psychology in Africa: Challenges and prospects. *International Journal of Psychology, 37,* 179–186.

Mpofu, E. (2003). Conduct disorder in children: Presentation, treatment options, and cultural efficacy in an African setting. *International Journal of Disability, Community and Rehabilitation, 1*(3). Retrieved July 17, 2005, from http://www.ijdcr .ca/VOL02_01_CAN/articles/mpofu.shtml

Mpofu, E. (2004a). *Counseling people with disabilities.* Harare: Zimbabwe Open University.

Mpofu, E. (2004b, October). *Equitable assessment practices: An African perspective.* International Test Commission, The College of William and Mary, Williamsburg, Virginia, United States.

Mpofu, E. (2004c). Learning through inclusive education: Practices with students with disabilities in sub-Saharan Africa. In C. de la Rey, L. Schwartz, & N. Duncan (Eds.), *Psychology: An introduction* (pp. 361–371). Cape Town, South Africa: Oxford University Press.

Mpofu, E., Chireshe, R., & Gwirayi, P. (in press). Adolescence in Zimbabwe. In J. Arnett (Ed.), *Encyclopedia of adolescence.* New York: Routledge.

Mpofu, E., & Harley, D. (2002). Rehabilitation in Zimbabwe: Lessons and implications for rehabilitation practice in the United States. *Journal of Rehabilitation, 68*(4), 26–33.

Mpofu, E., & Khan, N. (1997). Regulations for psychological licensure in Zimbabwe: Procedures, problems, and prospects. *World Psychology, 3,* 211–226.

Mpofu, E., & Mapfumo, S. (1989, June). Rehabilitation and community education: What can the teacher do? *Special Education Teacher's In-Service Course.* Alvord Public Service Training Centre, Masvingo, Zimbabwe.

Mpofu, E., & Nyanungo, K. R. L. (1998). Educational and psychological testing in Zimbabwean schools: Past, present, and future. *European Journal of Psychological Assessment, 14,* 71–90.

Mpofu, E., Peltzer, K., Shumba, A., Serpell, R., & Mogaji, A. (2005). School Psychology in sub-Saharan Africa: Results and implications of a six country survey. In C. R. Reynolds & C. Frisby (Eds.), *Comprehensive handbook of multicultural school psychology* (pp. 1128–1151). New York: Wiley.

Mpofu, E., Zindi, F., Oakland, T., & Peresuh, M. (1997). School psychology practices in East and Southern Africa: Special educators' perspectives. *The Journal of Special Education, 31*(3), 387–402.

Mungazi, D. A. (1990). *Education and government control in Zimbabwe: A study of the commissions of inquiry, 1908–1974.* New York: Praeger.

Mungazi, D. A. (1991). *Colonial education for Africans in Zimbabwe: George Stark's policy in Zimbabwe.* New York: Praeger.

Mutepfa, M. (2005). *Roles, functions, and responsibilities of school psychologists in Zimbabwe.* Unpublished manuscript.

Ngwarai, R. (1995). *Down syndrome: Etiological perspectives and help-seeking of parents of children with Down syndrome in Zimbabwe.* Bachelor of Education Special Education dissertation, University of Zimbabwe, Educational Foundations Department.

Nyanungo, K. L. R. (2002). *Psychology, the public, and other professions.* Harare: Zimbabwe Open University.

Oakland, T., Mpofu, E., Glasgow, K., & Jumel, B. (2003). Diagnosis and administrative interventions for students with mental retardation in Australia, France, United States, and Zimbabwe 98 years after Binet's first intelligence test. *International Journal of Testing, 3*(1), 59–75.

Oakland, T., Mpofu, E., Glasgow, K., & Jumel, B. (2005). *Learning disabilities in four countries.* Manuscript submitted for publication.

Peresuh, M., & Barcham, L. (1998). Special education provision in Zimbabwe. *British Journal of Education, 25,* 75–80.

Peters, S. (2001). The situation of disabled people in Zimbabwe and directions on change (Interview with R. Mupindu). In R. Chimedza & S. Peters (Eds.), *Disability and special needs education in an African context* (pp. 149–162). Harare: College Press.

Piachaud, J. (1994). Strengths and difficulties in developing countries: The case of Zimbabwe. In N. Bouras (Ed.), *Mental health in mental retardation* (pp. 382–392). Cambridge, UK: Cambridge University Press.

Wall, W. D. (1956). *Psychological services for schools.* New York: New York University.

World Health Organization. (1980). *International classification of impairments, disability, and handicaps: A manual of classifications relating to the consequences of disease.* Geneva, Switzerland: Author.

Zvobgo, R. J. (2000). *Colonialism and education in Zimbabwe.* Harare: Sapes Books.

SECTION II

Synthesis Chapters

45

School Psychology Internationally: A Retrospective View and Influential Conditions

Thomas D. Oakland

Shane R. Jimerson

The profession of psychology and its various specialty areas, including school psychology, can be understood best through considering some of its international dimensions. This chapter acknowledges some persons and events that provided a foundation for the professional practice of psychology, discusses qualities that must be in place for the emergence of the profession of psychology, explores important facets regarding the preparation and education of school psychologists, discusses the roles and responsibilities of school psychologists, and delineates important external and internal conditions that impact the development of the specialty of school psychology around the world.

School psychology is one of several professional specialties within psychology and is not a separate discipline or profession. Professional practices within school psychology are derived from the theory, research, and technology within the discipline of psychology—to which school psychology has made important contributions—together with the instrumental experiences of its seasoned practitioners.

AUTHORS' NOTE: Appreciation is expressed to Thomas Fagan for his careful and thoughtful review of this chapter.

Philosophical and Experimental Foundations of Psychology

The seeds of psychology were sown in the writings of Plato, Socrates, Aristotle, and other Greek philosophers, given their thoughtful considerations and deep insights into the nature of human behavior. Psychological theory, research, and technology began to emerge formally during the middle of the 19th century. In 1879, Wundt established the first laboratory for the study of psychology in Leipzig, Germany. Others soon followed, including Galton's laboratory in London, devoted to the study of individual differences. Binet and Simon, working in their physiological-psychology laboratory at the Sorbonne in Paris, developed an important test of children's intelligence. Its revisions continue to be used internationally (Oakland & Hu, 1992). The influence of Freud, Jung, Adler, Bowlby, Piaget, and other practitioner philosophers was immense. The work and writings of Itard and Sequin were important in stimulating interest in children with special needs.

Collectively, their theories characterized human behavior in ways that allowed practitioners to describe and explain behavior. Their influence on research and practice was significant. Thus, many of the theoretical and empirical foundations for the discipline of psychology can be traced to Europe. Around the beginning of the 20th century, a number of very able graduate students in the United States sought quality graduate degrees by working with leading professors in Germany or England, given the advanced status of psychology in these regions at that time.

The Emergence of the Profession of Psychology

Professional practice requires at least four qualities: a need for services; a sufficiently mature discipline that provides relevant theory, research, and technology; university-based programs to prepare practitioners; and educated practitioners who are willing to devote their professional lives to gain the instrumental knowledge needed to serve the public well. These four conditions emerged during the first half of the 20th century.

A need for services. Recognition of a need for psychological services occurred first. The need for psychological services typically is recognized first when societies are experiencing significant changes, in both institutions and personal relationships. Changes created by the industrial revolution during the 19th century elicited a need for psychological services. Prior to this period, persons often lived in personalized family-centered communities. Their economies often were dependent on small family-run farms or other small businesses. Immediate and extended family members or close friends cared for one another. Few professional services were available. Children generally were taught to follow in their parents' footsteps—boys to carry on the family business and girls to become wives, mothers, and homemakers. Education was informal, home based, and practical.

The industrial revolution forever changed this long-standing and prevailing lifestyle for many families. Many moved from small communities or farms to larger industrial cities, seeking a better life, including more professional services. The introduction of child labor laws, jobs that required formal education, mandatory elementary education, and compulsory attendance laws had a profound impact on children. For example, once children were in school, individual differences often became more apparent and potentially deleterious to both the social fabric of schools and the children's educational opportunities.

Additionally, some families did not adjust well to a large urban environment, resulting in family discord and division. More children became abused, neglected, orphaned, on wards or of the court and in other ways warranted public attention. Professionals with expertise in human behavior and the social sciences were needed to assist children and their families as well as education, courts, and other social services to address changes resulting from this transition.

A sufficiently mature discipline of psychology. A discipline typically evolves over time, acquiring new knowledge that contributes to new theories and technologies. There is no objective standard to use when deciding if a discipline is sufficiently mature to be used as a basis for professional services.

The professions of psychology and social work began to emerge in Europe and the United States toward the beginning of the 20th century. Four forms of school psychological services were typical (Wall, 1956). School psychologists provided primary prevention programs in one or more schools. Another service delivery system emphasized the coordination of services between the school and community. A third system relied on community-based child guidance clinics. A fourth system focused on research on child growth and development. Each delivery system was designed to meet prevailing social needs within a community.

University-based programs. Prior to the mid 1950s, few psychologists were prepared as school psychologists and instead had obtained an undergraduate degree in general psychology or a master's degree in clinical psychology. The term *school psychology* first appeared in print in 1898 in an article by Hugo Munsterberg in the context of a practitioner serving in a consultant role between child and experimental psychologists and the classroom teacher (Fagan, 2005a). The second appearance documented in the literature was in 1910 when a German psychologist, W. Stern, suggested the need for psychologists to work in schools in a fashion parallel to the work of school-based physicians (Fagan, 2005a). It is thought that in 1918, Gesell, a U.S. physician and psychologist, became the first professional to hold the title *school psychologist* in the United

States (Fagan, 2002, 2005a). In 1896 Lightner Witmer established the first psychology clinic at the University of Pennsylvania that served the needs of children.

The growth of school psychology programs during the first half of the 20th century was slow. For example, in 1940, there were approximately 500 school psychologists in the United States, mainly in the states of New York and Pennsylvania (Fagan & Wise, 2000). In contrast, the growth of school psychology programs after World War II was significant.

World War II had a deleterious impact on almost all institutions within Europe. For example, financial and professional resources needed to reestablish its schools were in short supply. In 1948, the United Nations Educational, Scientific and Cultural Organization (UNESCO) convened an international conference of representatives from 43 countries to discuss methods needed to promote desired educational services, including school psychology services (United Nations Educational, Scientific and Cultural Organization, 1948). The conference recommended the establishment of research institutes to improve the quality of teaching and school achievement as well as programs to prepare guidance specialists and school psychologists. A follow-up conference (Wall, 1956) reaffirmed the need to improve guidance services, educational methodology, teaching practices, and school psychology services. European countries that became leaders in school psychology (e.g., Denmark, France, Sweden, and the United Kingdom) assumed an active role in these United Nations Educational, Scientific and Cultural Organization meetings and were some of the first European countries to develop school psychology services.

In the United States, the growth of school psychology followed on the heels of the growth of clinical psychology. Although the practice of clinical psychology emerged during the first two decades of the 20th century, events following World War II had a decisive impact on clinical psychology and its services. Following the war, the U.S federal government provided considerable financial support to universities to create doctoral programs in clinical psychology and fund graduate students contingent on their performing their internships in Veterans Administration hospitals. The goal of this support was to help meet the psychological needs of thousands of World War II veterans. The 1949 Boulder Conference helped establish standards for the preparation of clinical psychologists in the United States (Boulder Conference, 1949; Raimy, 1950).

The Thayer Conference in 1954 (Cutts, 1955) helped establish standards for the preparation of school psychologists in the United States (Fagan, 2005b). The conference was instrumental in defining psychological services, establishing two levels of graduate preparation, delineating the primary functions of practice, and suggesting desired personal and professional qualities. In the United States, the passage of the Education for All Handicapped Children Act (P.L. 94-142, 1975), which later became the Individuals With Disabilities Education Act, had a decisive impact on increasing the number of school psychologists needed to implement this special education legislation and the nature of their services. The 1981 Education Act in the United Kingdom had a similar impact on the growth of school psychology there.

Educated practitioners. There are an estimated 500,000 psychologists internationally, among whom 100,000 work in the United States (Bureau of Labor Statistics, 2006). The ratio between psychologists and the population is 1 to 3,000 in the United States and 1 to 1,800 in Europe. The strength and growth of psychology are particularly strong in Europe, with an estimated 277,000 graduate students in psychology (European Federation of Psychologists' Associations, 2006).

In the United States, between 1940 and 1970, the number of school psychologists increased from 500 to 5,000. Thirty years later, in 2005, there were more than 32,000 school psychologists

in the United States (Charvat, 2005). As is true for other professionals, most work in urban areas; fewer work in rural areas (Hosp & Reschly, 2002; Oakland, 2003).

A 1990 survey of school psychologists in 54 countries found approximately 87,000 school psychologists (Oakland & Cunningham, 1992). Given their increase in some countries, 100,000 school psychologists may be a more accurate current estimate.

A country's gross national product was found to strongly influence services. School psychologists were found most commonly in high gross national product countries. Additionally, high gross national product countries averaged about 2,000 school psychologists, whereas low gross national product countries averaged about 300. The yearly incomes of school psychologists averaged US$17,000 in high gross national product countries and US$3,000 in low gross national product countries. A country's gross national product also influenced the ratio between school psychologists and students. The average ratio was 1 to 3,500 in high gross national product countries and 1 to 26,000 in low gross national product countries. At the time of Oakland and Cunningham's study, school psychologists typically were female (62%), in their 30s, and had been practicing 10 years (Oakland & Cunningham, 1992). The results of later surveys of school psychologists in 10 countries confirm that the majority of school psychologists continue to be female (Jimerson et al., 2004; Jimerson et al., 2006).

Many countries offer both undergraduate and graduate preparation in school psychology. High gross national product countries are more likely to offer master's degree programs, whereas low gross national product countries are more likely to offer undergraduate degree programs. Almost all school psychologists obtain a 4-year undergraduate degree in psychology; few obtain degrees in education.

In 1990, doctoral school psychology programs were available only in the United States. Since then, doctoral school psychology programs have been established in Brazil, England, and New Zealand. Among faculty who teach in school psychology programs, most hold a master's degree and fewer have a doctoral degree. Seventy percent teach full-time and 30% teach part-time. Thus, graduate students aspiring to become university professors in school psychology commonly obtain a master's degree, in part, because doctoral school psychology programs may not be available. Faculty salaries in low gross national product countries often are very low (e.g., they averaged US$4,000 in 1990). Thus, faculty in low gross national product countries typically need additional employment to maintain a middle-class lifestyle (Oakland & Cunningham, 1992).

Different titles, similar services. School psychologists use various professional titles. "Psychologist" is most common. "Educational psychologist" is used commonly in countries associated with the British Commonwealth. "School psychologist" is used in the United States and is common in other countries.

Preparation of School Psychologists

The 1990 international survey of school psychologists (Oakland & Cunningham, 1992) found considerable similarities in their preparation. Most school psychology programs offer a curriculum that relies heavily on five areas: courses that focus on core areas of psychology, assessment and intervention, interpersonal skills, professional decision making, and legal and ethical issues. Core areas within the discipline of psychology include psychology of learning and cognition, research design, and statistics, as well as biological, developmental, educational, experimental, personality, and social psychology. Assessment and intervention services typically focus on intellectual, academic, emotional, and social qualities through the use of behavioral, affective, educational, and social-systems models. Interpersonal skill development typically focuses on effective collaboration, consultation, and leadership development. Legal and ethical issues are addressed by being embedded within other courses or as a stand-alone course. Courses in research design and statistics are more likely to emphasize the role of the school psychologist as a good consumer of the literature rather than as a contributor to the literature through scholarship.

Nature of School Psychology Services

The nature of school psychology services is determined by two broad conditions: the preparation school psychologists receive and society's need for services. School psychologists should not offer services for which they are unprepared. However, educators and others responsible for determining the nature of school psychological services may limit their work to a few critical areas. Thus, school psychology services differ between countries. In general, school psychologists provide assessment services and may provide direct (e.g., counseling students, tutoring) and indirect (e.g., teaching psychology, teacher and parent consultation, and in-service teacher training) services. Their services may focus on primary, secondary, or tertiary prevention efforts with individuals, groups, or systems (e.g., a school or school system).

The nature of school psychological services within a country necessarily reflects the level of development and acceptance of the discipline of psychology within the country, the development of the profession of psychology, and the need for services (Catterall, 1976, 1977, 1979). For example, school psychology commonly is found in countries in which the discipline and general profession of psychology are strong (e.g., Australia, Canada, Israel, New Zealand, United States, and Western Europe) and is not found in countries in which the discipline and profession of psychology are not strong (e.g., Arab countries, India, and the People's Republic of China). Additionally, school psychological services generally occur after a country develops universal education for boys and girls from Grades 1 through 12 and establishes special education services. As previously noted, a country's gross national product also influences school psychology services (Oakland, 2000).

Professional services often are provided in the context of an unwritten social contract between a profession and society. The social contract allows the profession to establish university-based professional preparation programs, select applicants for the programs, determine their preparation, establish standards for entrance into the profession, conduct research, and engage in other activities that further the profession. The social contract also requires the professional to serve everyone: urban and rural, rich and poor, male and female, young and old. The profession of psychology often is regulated by external standards, including laws, administrative regulations, and ethics statements. The degree to which external regulations govern a profession can be used as a gauge of its commitment to its social contract as well as its professional development.

The nature of services provided in 53 countries (i.e., the United States was excluded) participating in the 1990 survey (Oakland & Cunningham, 1992) was analyzed in light of the degree to which they were externally regulated (Cunningham, 1994). Six clusters were identified. Some examples follow. School psychology had few if any external regulations in eight countries (i.e., Burkina Faso, Papua New Guinea, Greece, Iran, Yemen, Niger, South Korea, and Ethiopia). These constituted cluster one. Services in these countries typically focused on biologically based conditions (e.g., providing basic care to children with mental retardation). School psychology was somewhat more externally regulated in cluster three (e.g., Italy, People's Republic of China, Poland, Russia), where psychological services had been heavily influenced by socialism. School psychological services in cluster six (i.e., Denmark, England, Israel, New Zealand) had the highest degree of regulation. School psychological services in these countries were similar and provided a broad range of services, including those for individuals, groups, and systems (see Cunningham, Chapter 46, this volume).

Conditions That Will Influence School Psychology's Future

The future of school psychology will be influenced strongly by five external conditions (i.e., a country's cultural history and current conditions, economy, geography, and language, as well as national needs and priorities) and by five internal conditions (i.e., degree of professionalism, definition of school psychology's scope and functions, its legal status, its engagement with education, and scholarly and technical contributions). Each is discussed in this section.

External Conditions That Influence School Psychology

A country's cultural history and current conditions. A country's cultural status often reflects long-standing historical national policies. For example, the national policies of some countries lead to their being engaged with other countries, sharing knowledge and technology, valuing various beliefs, and engaging in other activities that lead to cultural pluralism. In these countries, psychology can be expected to grow by serving national values.

In contrast, national policies of other countries lead to their not engaging with other countries and instead remaining insular. Examples include the Soviet Union as well as many countries in the Middle East and sub-Saharan Africa (Friedman, 2005). In these countries, psychology is not strong and is likely to remain weak. School psychology is strong only when psychology is well accepted and serves national needs and values.

Additionally, the discipline of psychology has a decidedly Western emphasis. For example, individual differences, the keystone of the discipline of psychology, are more important in Western cultures than in some other cultures. Thus, a discipline dedicated to the study of individual differences will be seen as less relevant in countries that favor collectivist beliefs. Psychology and thus school psychology will be more acceptable when its theory, research, and technology extend beyond its current dominant (e.g., Israeli, North American, Western European) scholarship to include theory, research, and technology from countries in which psychology is emerging.

A country's economy. Psychology and school psychology generally are stronger when a country's economic resources are stronger. Countries that have a higher gross national product tend to have well developed educational institutions (i.e., preschools through postdoctoral education), provide services to children with special needs, educate both boys and girls, have a larger percentage of professionals, and provide higher incomes to professionals. Psychology is likely to be strong in these countries. In contrast, people in low gross national product countries often struggle to find sufficient money for food, clothing, and shelter. Psychology and school psychology cannot be sustained under these conditions.

A country's geographic location. Geographic qualities have influenced the development of psychology. Psychology tends to be strong or weak regionally. For example, it is strong and thriving throughout most of Europe and weak and generally nonexistent throughout Africa. Countries that are contiguous often develop in like fashion. A country's geographic distance from the epicenters of psychology often has helped define its acceptance. However, the availability of knowledge to anyone who has a word processor, an Internet connection, and knowledge of English removes many of the previous barriers to knowledge. Thus, a country's geographic isolation is becoming less of a major

barrier to the discipline of psychology and to knowledge of school psychology.

A country's language. Many of the earliest writings in psychology were in German and French. English has become the international language of science. More scholarly journals are published in English than in any other language. International conferences typically use English. Thus, knowledge of English has become a prerequisite to scientific and professional knowledge. The growth of psychology, including school psychology, will be most rapid in those countries that either use English as their first language or teach English as their second language. Thus, in most parts of the world, psychologists are expected to know English. Those who do not know English are less likely to have access to current knowledge.

A country's national needs and priorities. The issues that fuel the development of strong disciplines and the nature of related professional services always reflect national needs and priorities. For example, school psychology became established in Western Europe and the United States in response to national needs and priorities. The initial and continued acceptance of psychology and school psychology depends, in part, on practitioners' ability to communicate their relevance in meeting important national needs. For example, psychology is acquiring a strong foothold in the People's Republic of China by assisting in its economic development—a national need and priority. Clinical psychology's acceptance is growing in Japan, in part, in response to helping the country deal with gender role changes—a national need and priority. School psychology is not strong in either of these two countries. Its growth may be furthered following the recognition that it too can help address national needs and priorities. Addressing the educational and psychological needs of students and promoting the well-being of children are important ways in which school psychologists can facilitate educational success and contribute to the public health of a country.

Internal Conditions That Influence School Psychology

School psychology's degree of professionalism. The social contract between psychology and society must be acknowledged in order for the profession and its specialty areas, including school psychology, to be strong. Psychology, including school psychology, must work to develop and institute high professional and legal standards governing the education, including continuing education, of psychologists, ethics that serve the public, a commitment to serve persons from all walks of life, and a commitment to provide services to the public that are effective and highly regarded—even indispensable.

The strength of a profession within a country is directly related to the strength of its national professional association(s). A sufficiently large workforce precedes the development of professional associations. Psychology is strong only in countries with well-developed professional associations. This holds true for school psychology too. Professional associations are needed to assume leadership for developing high standards and then working to ensure they are met.

The presence of strong international associations within psychology and its specialty areas is a good barometer of its health and vitality internationally. Two strong international associations represent psychology. The International Union of Psychological Sciences was founded in 1951 to serve as an association of national psychological associations of which approximately 70 are members. In contrast, membership in the International Association of Applied Psychology consists of individual psychologists engaged in the practice of psychology. The International Union of Psychological Sciences and the International Association of Applied Psychology alternate in sponsoring international conferences every 2 years. Psychology also is strengthened through various regional associations (e.g., in the Americas, Asia, and Europe).

School psychology also has had a viable international presence through the International School Psychology Association. The International School Psychology Association has established a code of ethics (Oakland, Goldman, & Bischoff, 1997), defined the specialty (Oakland & Cunningham, 1992), and recommended a model professional preparation program (Cunningham & Oakland, 1998). Its small membership of individuals (approximately 400 to 500) and 30 national associations of school psychologists currently limit its impact (see Oakland, Chapter 47, this volume). School psychologists in various parts of the world see considerable potential for the International School Psychology Association to have an important role by providing workshops and other training activities during its annual colloquium, facilitating collaboration among international colleagues, and promoting the exchange of information, resources, and research internationally (Jimerson et al., 2004; Jimerson et al., 2006).

Definition of school psychology's scope and functions. A profession must define itself clearly to be credible to other professions and the public. Thus, professional associations must take leadership in preparing statements that define the nature and scope of services and their functions. The definition of school psychology's scope and functions should be aspirational, yet achievable. It serves to establish the parameters of school psychological services to be consistent with its social contract.

School psychology's legal status. School psychology is strong in countries that have laws requiring the provision of, and financial support for, its services. A national definition of school psychology's scope and functions typically is prerequisite to establishing such a law. Moreover, this action typically requires the presence of a strong national association.

School psychology's engagement with education. School psychologists straddle two fences: psychology and education. Educated mainly in the discipline of psychology, they strive to apply its theory, research, and technology, together with their personal instrumental knowledge, to issues important to both children and youth and, more narrowly, to students. Educators typically determine educational policy and hold the purse strings for services. Educators may or may not welcome the services of school psychologists. Thus, the nature of relationships between education and school psychology is critical to the welfare of school psychology.

The first author met recently with a group of school principals in a Central American country to discuss how school psychology services may better assist them. Some principals were critical of school psychologists for not being team players and not contributing to the overall objectives of their schools. Their comments serve to remind us that a social contract exists between school psychology and education. School psychologists must work in ways that benefit the institution of education or face the possibility of having other specialists serve in their stead. While being a team player is important, school psychologists also need to be critical of services that do not serve students well and be an objective voice to the schools.

School psychology's scholarly and technical contributions. As noted previously, professional practices within psychology, including school psychology, are derived from the discipline of psychology. School psychology is not merely a consumer of this discipline, as it has made important contributions to its theory, research, and technology. Moreover, the discipline of psychology expects the specialty of school psychology to serve as an active and important conduit to children and youth, especially within the context of education (Oakland, 2003).

Results of an international survey of school psychologists in 10 countries revealed that school psychologists are more likely to identify external challenges than internal challenges to the profession (Jimerson et al., 2004; Jimerson et al., 2006). Prominent external challenges include lack of money to properly fund services and the low status of school psychology. Prominent internal challenges include deficiencies in research and evaluation methods, professional leadership, and supervision.

The Future of School Psychology Internationally

The need to expand the discipline beyond its somewhat narrow Western influences requires school psychologists in non-Western countries to become more engaged in research and development efforts. These efforts may be aided by establishing partnerships between well-established scholars in school psychology and those living and working in countries in which school psychology is emerging. Together, they can combine resources to help address important issues in developing countries with a degree of scientific rigor that may otherwise not be achievable. Other chapters in this handbook provide information and insights regarding the specialty of school psychology internationally. Its growth, in part, is contingent on the degree to which collaboration occurs among international colleagues.

References

Boulder Conference. (1949). *Minutes of the Executive Planning Committee on the Boulder Conference on Graduate Education of Clinical Psychologists–1949* (Shakow Papers, M1383). Akron, OH: University of Akron, Archives of the History of American Psychology.

Bureau of Labor Statistics. (2006). *Occupational outlook handbook, 2006–07 edition—Psychologists.* Retrieved May 19, 2006, from http://www.bls.gov/oco/ocos056.htm

Catterall, C. D. (Ed.). (1976). *Psychology in the schools in international perspective,* Vol. 1. Columbus, OH: International School Psychology Steering Committee.

Catterall, C. D. (Ed.). (1977). *Psychology in the schools in international perspective,* Vol. 2. Columbus, OH: International School Psychology Steering Committee.

Catterall, C. D. (Ed.). (1979). *Psychology in the schools in international perspective,* Vol. 3. Columbus, OH: International School Psychology Steering Committee.

Charvat, J. L. (2005). National Association of School Psychologists study: How many school psychologists are there? *Communiqué, 33,* 12–14.

Cunningham, J. (1994). *A contextual investigation of the international development of psychology in the schools.* Unpublished doctoral dissertation, University of Texas at Austin.

Cunningham, J., & Oakland, T. (1998). International School Psychology Association guidelines for the preparation of school psychologists. *School Psychology International, 19,* 19–30.

Cutts, N. E. (Ed.). (1955). *School psychology at mid-century.* Washington, DC: American Psychological Association.

European Federation of Psychologists' Associations. (2006). *Status and future of psychologists in Europe—and EuroPsy.* Retrieved May 19, 2006, from http://www.efpa.be/news.php?ID=30

Fagan, T. K. (2002). Trends in the history of school psychology in the United States. In A. Thomas & J. Grimes (Eds.), *Best practices in school psychology–IV* (Vol. 1, pp. 209–221). Bethesda, MD: National Association of School Psychologists.

Fagan, T. K. (2005a). Literary origins of the term, "school psychologist," revisited. *School Psychology Review, 34*(3), 432–434.

Fagan, T. K. (2005b). The 50th anniversary of the Thayer Conference: Historical perspectives and accomplishments. *School Psychology Quarterly, 20*(3), 224–251.

Fagan, T. K., & Wise, P. S. (2000). *School psychology: Past, present, and future.* Bethesda, MD: National Association of School Psychologists.

Friedman, T. (2005). *The world is flat.* New York: Farrar, Straus & Giroux.

Hosp, J. L., & Reschly, D. J. (2002). Regional differences in school psychology practice. *School Psychology Review, 31,* 11–30.

Jimerson, S. R., Graydon, K., Farrell, P., Kikas, E., Hatzichristou, C., Boce, E., Bashi, G., &

International School Psychology Association Research Committee. (2004). The International School Psychology Survey: Development and data from Albania, Cyprus, Estonia, Greece and Northern England. *School Psychology International, 25*(3), 259–286.

Jimerson, S. R., Graydon, K., Yuen, M., Lam, S.-F., Thurm, J.-M., Klueva, N., Coyne, J., Loprete, L. J., Phillips, L., & International School Psychology Association Research Committee. (2006). The International School Psychology Survey: Data from Australia, China, Germany, Italy and Russia. *School Psychology International, 27*(1), 5–32.

Oakland, T. (2000). International school psychology. In T. K. Fagan & P. S. Wise (Eds.), *School psychology: Past, present, and future* (pp. 355–382). Silver Spring, MD: National Association of School Psychologists.

Oakland, T. (2003). International school psychology: Psychology's worldwide portal to children and youth. *American Psychologist, 58*(11), 985–992.

Oakland, T. D., & Cunningham, J. L. (1992). A survey of school psychology in developed and developing countries. *School Psychology International, 13,* 99–129.

Oakland, T., Goldman, S., & Bischoff, H. (1997). Code of ethics of the International School Psychology Association. *School Psychology International, 18,* 291–298.

Oakland, T., & Hu, S. (1992). The top ten tests used with children and youth worldwide. *Bulletin of the International Test Commission,* 99–120.

Raimy, V. C. (Ed.). (1950). *Training in clinical psychology* (Boulder Conference). Englewood Cliffs, NJ: Prentice Hall.

United Nations Educational, Scientific and Cultural Organization, International Bureau of Education. (1948). *School psychologists* (Publication No. 105). Paris: Author.

Wall, W. D. (Ed.). (1956). *Psychological services for schools.* New York: New York University Press for the United Nations Educational, Scientific and Cultural Organization Institute for Education.

46

Centripetal and Centrifugal Trends Influencing School Psychology's International Development

Jacqueline L. Cunningham

As the new millennium heralds unprecedented interconnectedness among the peoples of the world, the international expansion of school psychology promises to become psychology's portal to children and youth worldwide (Oakland, 2003). In his award address, as the 2003 recipient of the American Psychological Association's Award for Distinguished Contributions to the International Advancement of Psychology, Thomas Oakland offered this hopeful vision on the basis of the professional and scientific maturity believed achievable by school psychology internationally. Forces both internal and external to a discipline govern the course of its development (Altman, 1987; Danziger, 1990). An extensive survey undertaken in 54 countries throughout the world (Oakland, 1992; Oakland & Cunningham, 1992) formed the basis of an empirical study by the author (Cunningham, 1994), which sought to determine the influence various intraprofessional and extraprofessional forces exert on the development of school psychology internationally. The purpose of this chapter is to summarize this research and discuss implications of the findings. Improved understanding of the influences governing growth in international school psychology is needed if the field is to be guided toward its most fruitful outcomes.

A Guiding Orientation: Altman's Contextual/Transactional Model of Disciplinary Development

An analysis by Altman (1987) provided the theoretical orientation on which the 1994 study of school psychology's international development was based. According to Altman, interplays between centripetal and centrifugal trends, emerging both intraprofessionally and extraprofessionally, form the sociopolitical contexts within which a discipline evolves. Centripetal trends are unifying and are most likely to thrive within stable times. In the United States, they characterized the period of psychology's development prior to 1900 and to the 1960s when consolidation on many fronts, both intraprofessionally and extraprofessionally, led to theoretical, methodological, philosophical, and institutional unity. With the changing lifestyles and pluralism that began to characterize society in the 1960s came the challenges to a traditional philosophy of science and the centrality of administration and governance that emerged during this period and which continue to this day. Disciplinary development is conceptualized in Altman's contextual/transactional model as the inevitable transactions that arise within a total system of intraprofessional and extraprofessional forces and that provide the momentum for systemic change. Prior conceptualizations of school psychology's international development were based on lineal analyses. In Catterall's (1976, 1977, 1979) four levels of development model, progress was closely identified with the influence a country's socioeconomic status exerts in moving school psychology toward increasingly exemplary levels of professional salience. Because the view of progress captured in such a model is unidimensional, it cannot represent the various trajectories school psychology may follow in establishing itself within diverse world contexts (Oakland & Cunningham, 1999). This is particularly the case as a global economy replaces one that had been characterized by differences in wealth between Western and non-Western nations. A more promising grounding for the detailed scrutiny of the power bases influencing school psychology's international development rests on contextual analyses.

The 1992 International School Psychology Survey (Oakland & Cunningham, 1992), which represented 54 countries, furnished the database used in the 1994 study. A 17-page questionnaire containing 475 items, field-tested under the auspices of the Standards and Practices Committee of the International School Psychology Association (Oakland, 1989), had been developed in the late 1980s for the survey. The questionnaire became available in both English and French. A French version was considered helpful for enlisting the participation of francophone African countries that usually are not represented in surveys of this type. Their participation was considered important to getting a full conceptualization of the sources of influences that contribute to the emergence of psychology in developing nations. The questionnaire items addressed five broad areas of inquiry: characteristics of school psychologists; nature of school psychology services; legal, political, and professional regulation; research issues; and perceived future trends. A sixth area requested information about the expert respondent representing each country. Certain sets of items required dichotomized yes/no responses, whereas others required ratings on a 3-point scale (little, some, very). Some items required open-ended statements by the respondent. The items paralleled those used in surveys on the status of school psychology undertaken by the United Nations Educational, Scientific and Cultural Organization and the International Bureau of Education in 1948 and in 1954 (Wall, 1956). The 1994 study was exploratory in its intent to identify the mechanisms underlying the development of school psychology internationally and to find support for Altman's model in its interpretations of the findings.

Defining Levels of Professional Autonomy

The first step in conducting the study was to define a level of professional autonomy for each of the countries. Methods of naturalistic inquiry (Lincoln & Guba, 1985) were used to rate each country's similarity to another in terms of

EXTRAPROFESSIONAL POWER BASE

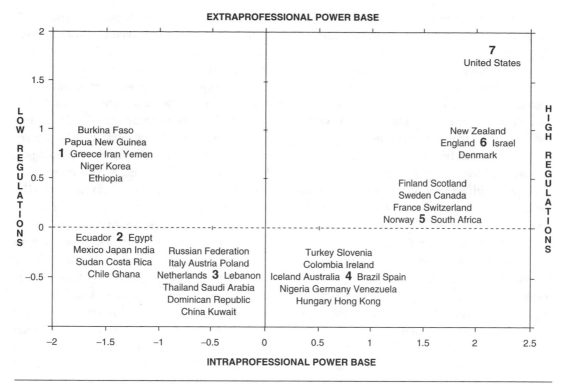

Figure 46.1   Configuration of professional autonomy showing a two-dimensional configuration consisting of a strong curvilinear dimension

indicators of autonomy of school psychology in the respective country. These ratings of similarity formed the proximity data that were analyzed by a nonmetric model of multidimensional scaling for ordinal data (Kruskal & Wish, 1978). The program used for this analysis was Multidimensional Scaling from Statistical Analysis System (Statistical Analysis System Institute, 1992). Figure 46.1 presents the professional autonomy configuration that was obtained from the multidimensional scaling analysis. The horseshoe shape of the distribution indicates a circumplex rather than unidirectional model as representing the relationship that existed between the proximities in the data and the distance between points. The finding revealed a two-dimensional rather than a lineal pattern of relationships existing among the countries with regard to their similarities in professional autonomy. The horizontal axis appears to represent low

versus high regulation, and the vertical axis appears to represent an extraprofessional versus an intraprofessional power base.

Intraprofessional power bases are needed to establish standards of training in a specialty and accreditation of its educational program but are supplemented by extraprofessional power bases when a country's legislature protects the right to autonomous practice. The 13 countries in the upper right quadrant (labeled 7, 6, and 5) appear to have reached strong levels of professional autonomy, characterized by strong extraprofessional power bases credentialing appropriately qualified practitioners and accrediting training programs by societally sanctioned accrediting bodies.

Twelve countries in the lower right quadrant (labeled 4) appear to have strong intraprofessional power bases regulating training and other standards, whereas intraprofessional power bases exist but more weakly support the establishment of standards in 20 countries located in the lower left quadrant (labeled 3 and 2). Eight countries located in the upper left quadrant appear to have no intraprofessional power bases regulating training and practice, although there may be self-defined individuals who have the authority to practice as school psychologists.

Although the two-dimensional, circumplex solution yielded by multidimensional scaling is in keeping with Altman's model, strong curvilinear trends are noted in the arrangement of the seven "neighborhoods" that represent clusters of countries that are highly similar to one another in terms of professional autonomy. Thus, Catterall's stage model also is represented in the analysis. Countries in neighborhoods 5, 6, and 7 (upper right quadrant) tend to have higher gross national products per capita as well as lower population growth rates than do the other groups. Their favorable socioeconomic status sustains the extraprofessional power bases that differentiate them from other countries.

Relationships Between Professional Autonomy and Occupational Roles

The second phase of the study was to identify the occupational roles that are associated with particular types of development represented in the countries surveyed. Results on 94 items from the questionnaire relating to knowledge and skill areas often associated with school psychology were subjected to cluster analysis in an effort to develop a meaningful conceptualization of the occupational roles that are central to school psychology internationally. The Statistical Analysis System program for Cluster Analysis (Statistical Analysis System Institute, 1988) was used for this analysis. Specifically, minimum variance clustering (i.e., Ward's method) was used to obtain internally connected clusters that would likely result in few homogeneous

hierarchies (Hair, Anderson, Tatham, & Grablowsky, 1979). This type of clustering was used in anticipation of organizing these items into their fewest groups and thereby determining the occupational domains that are most central to the profession on an international basis.

A total of seven occupational role clusters were identified. The strongest values were obtained for clusters identified as Psychological Assessment (C), Tests and Measurement (E), and Special Education Interventions (D). Vocational Guidance (F) was identified as less important and obtained an intermediate cluster value. Systems Interventions (A), Socialization (teaching values; G), and Biologically Based Interventions (interventions directed at students with severe physical handicaps; H) emerged as weakly salient and were assigned weak cluster values. Measures on the seven occupational domains and a composite measure (Central Roles; B) were obtained for the 54 countries and projected onto the multidimensional scaling space as vectors by means of multiple regression. Figure 46.2 presents the configuration of professional autonomy showing eight optimally regressed vectors relating to occupational roles.

The vectors indicate which countries are associated most strongly with each occupational domain. Regression coefficients for all occupational domains, except Biologically Based Interventions, were significantly correlated with the two-dimensional representation of professional autonomy, thus furnishing support for the validity of the two-dimensional model.

The vectors for Tests and Measurement, Special Education Interventions, and Psychological Assessment were closer to the higher regulation and the intraprofessional dimensions than they were to the low regulation and the extraprofessional dimensions. Countries that have school psychological services largely characterized by interventions in special education and psychological assessment are likely to be similar in that they have well-defined regulations that govern services and power bases that stem

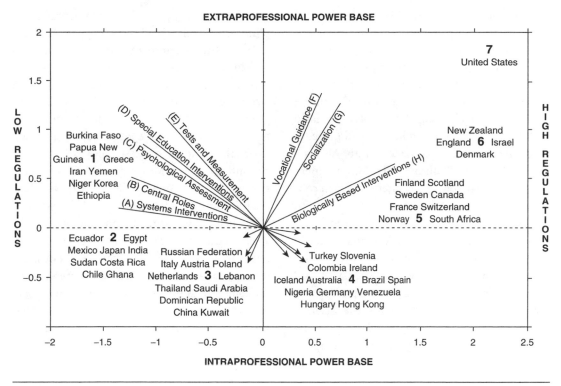

Figure 46.2   Configuration of professional autonomy with eight optimally regressed vectors relating to occupational roles

from within the profession of school psychology itself.

The vectors for Vocational Guidance and Socialization indicate that, in the countries closely associated with them, the roles are predominantly a function of the power bases sanctioning practice being within, rather than outside, school psychology. Power bases of school psychology in these countries appear to be relatively weak; they principally relate to the profession's ability to provide training for school-related psychological services. The fact that the vector for Systems Interventions is located nearly directly on the extraprofessional/intraprofessional dimension indicates that the ability of school psychology to provide interventions aimed at environmental modifications is a function of intraprofessional as well as extraprofessional power bases. Thus, the importance of interdisciplinary collaboration

emerges as an important factor that distinguishes school psychological practice at stronger levels of professional autonomy.

The Central Roles measure also is associated with high regulation. As a composite measure, its vector represents the dominant trends in school psychology. Thus, the vector's closest distance to the vector for Psychological Assessment reflects the importance of the latter within school psychology's international contexts.

Relationships Between Professional Autonomy and Threats to Professionalism

The third phase of the study was to determine whether there are differences in the threats to professionalism associated with differing levels of professional autonomy. The model depicted in Figure 46.2 proposes that relationships between extraprofessional and intraprofessional sources of influence have an impact on professional autonomy and that this impact determines the more or less central (centripetal versus centrifugal) occupational roles associated with school psychology in its international contexts. The model is consistent with Altman's explanation that disciplinary development occurs in a dynamic open system that is in continual exchange with its environment. The third phase of the investigation was critical to determining the heuristic value of Altman's model. In contrast with stage orientations, which view growth as movement toward a predetermined goal, growth in this model is conceptualized as the potential for change that exists in association with the threats toward divisiveness and stagnation created by centrifugal and centripetal trends. Accordingly, threats to professionalism were expected to exist in both high and low autonomy countries and to differ with regard to respective countries' identification with either central or more peripheral occupational roles.

There were two approaches to this inquiry. One consisted of obtaining ratings on the particular external and internal threats to professionalism existing within low versus high autonomy countries. The other consisted of obtaining ratings on sources of occupational stress differentiating the countries. The comparison data in the first case were based on endorsements on 15 questionnaire items relating to specified internal and external threats. Data in the second case were based on responses to a 3-point rating scale comprising 17 questionnaire items addressing specified sources of occupational stress.

External threats. One external threat stood out as differentiating the seven groups of countries most highly: low status of psychology in low autonomy countries. The compelling importance of the establishment of psychology to the development of school psychology points to the fact that psychology is the fundamental discipline with which school psychology is affiliated. Another strong external threat to professionalism in low autonomy countries is low public support for education. For all countries in Group 4, in comparison with neighboring groups, competition with other professional groups for jobs was reported to be a strong external threat to professionalism. Given the pressure to protect jobs, a direct route to maintaining the status quo is to emphasize roles that are traditionally associated with school psychology, such as assessment and intervention in special education. These may not be strongly relevant in low autonomy countries. Thus, the lack of financial resources and pressure to implement mainstream models of service create threats to professionalism in many countries throughout the world.

Internal threats. Ratings on internal threats to professionalism indicated that the inadequacy of professional standards was significantly associated with the countries' standing in professional autonomy. In particular, Groups 5 and 6 differed in their ratings on the lack of standards as a threat. Since the former was determined to have weaker extraprofessional power bases than the latter, the ability to detect differences on internal threats based on respondents' ratings in two neighboring groups in the multidimensional scaling configuration provided support for the two-dimensional conceptualization derived from multidimensional scaling.

Occupational stress. When data on the 17 variables relating to occupational stress were treated to a stepwise discriminant function analysis (Hair et al., 1979), a specific pattern of occupational stressors discriminated low versus high autonomy groups. This pattern related to professional isolation as associated with low autonomy, whereas low personal accomplishment, due to feelings of incompetence and need to compromise professional standards, was associated with high autonomy. The model yielded by discriminant function analysis correctly classified 20 out of 26 countries in the high autonomy group and 21 out of 28 countries in the low autonomy group. The model was considered to be a valid predictor of associations between low versus high professional autonomy and sources of occupational stress.

Results of the discriminant analysis implicated that a sense of professional isolation coexists with conditions that are prevalent in low autonomy countries. The lack of professional affiliations compounds threats to professionalism as low standards contribute to divisiveness. Conversely, a sense of low personal accomplishment, resulting from failure to meet high professional ideals, is a strong source of occupational stress in high autonomy countries. Many of these countries have the strong intraprofessional power bases that provide standards for professional preparation in school psychology but not the extraprofessional power bases for protecting practitioners' right to a professional title. These discrepancies tend to be associated with central (centripetal) models of practice that support the status quo but may not substantively fit the ecological niches in which they are implemented. Correlates are exceedingly high self-expectations and the frustration resulting from needing to make compromises between professional standards and organizational mandates.

Understanding the relationships among professional autonomy, occupational roles, and occupational stress is dependent on investigations conducted at a molar level of analysis to identify their systemic interrelatedness. Accordingly, the following summary analyses attempt to offer some explanations of the systemic conflict that is created when the intraprofessional and extraprofessional power bases sanctioning the practice of school psychology weakly support practitioners' perceptions of the meaningfulness of their occupational roles.

Relationships Between Professional Autonomy and Sources of Occupational Stress

Figure 46.3 presents the vectors on three occupational stress variables projected over the two-dimensional representation of professional autonomy. The occupational stress variables are those that were identified by the discriminant analysis as being significantly associated with levels of high versus low professional autonomy, when the variables were considered together as a group. Their respective relationships within the multidimensional scaling space provide information on the types of power bases that are associated with the practices most strongly associated with each source of occupational stress.

The positions of the vectors relative to each other provide information about these interrelationships. Two vectors representing Too High Self-Expectations and Need to Make Compromises are placed close together and run in similar directions. In contrast, the lack of close interrelations between the latter variable and No Opportunities to Confer With Colleagues is reflected in the wide angle between both their vectors. The near 90° angle (orthogonal) between Too High Self-Expectations and No Opportunities to Confer With Colleagues also implies strong differences between these two separate sources of stress.

The three vectors are most strongly associated with two groups of countries (i.e., Groups 3 and 4) that differ in the extent to which they are affiliated with institutionalized school psychology. These differences make the placement of the vectors conceptually meaningful. As alluded to previously, No Opportunities to Confer With Colleagues appears to relate to problems associated with having no strong affiliation with organizations that are devoted to advancing and promoting school psychology. The other two occupational stress variables point to problems in countries that are affiliated with school psychology organizations but

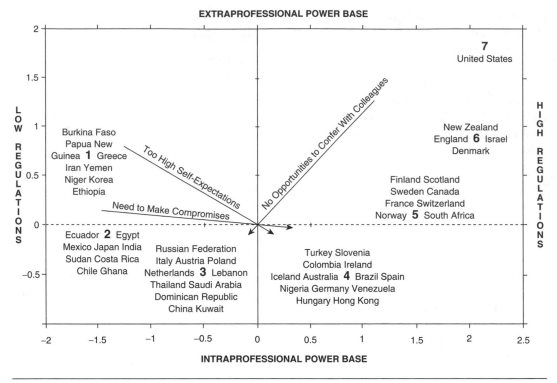

Figure 46.3 Configuration of professional autonomy with three optimally regressed vectors relating to occupational stress

have insufficiently strong external societal support to enforce professional standards. This situation is represented by the placement of the Compromises vector at the midpoint of the intraprofessional/extraprofessional dimension and toward the right on the low/high regulation dimension.

The other two occupational stress variables are similarly associated with mixed extraprofessional and intraprofessional power bases, as represented by their placement at the midpoint of Dimension 2 (i.e., power bases). However, they differ with regard to their establishment of standards as is represented by No Opportunities being placed to the left of Too High Expectations on Dimension 1 (i.e., regulation).

Although the placement of the vectors over the multidimensional scaling space has face validity, only the regression coefficient for the Need to Make Compromises variable was significantly associated with the two-dimensional

model of professional autonomy. Moreover, it was significantly associated only with the vertical dimension (i.e., regulation), implying that differences in the regulation of professional standards determine the extent to which this source of occupational stress is likely to be evidenced in diverse international contexts.

The Need to Make Compromises variable appears to be related to one identified as depersonalization in other studies of occupational stress among school psychologists (Huebner, 1992; Wise, 1985). In those studies, conducted in the United States, depersonalization was associated with interpersonal conflict within school settings, as the result of supervision by incompetent or inflexible supervisors, pressure from being caught between children's needs and administrative constraints, lack of consensus in staffing, and/or working with uncooperative administrators. Thus, depersonalization was defined by organizational variables rather than by individual differences.

Another variable, High Self-Expectations, bears some relationship to Compromises but was not significantly associated with the two-dimensional configuration. Self-expectations relate to feelings of personal competence; therefore, this variable is likely to be associated with individual differences that confound any systematic associations between the variable and the multidimensional scaling model of professional autonomy. No Opportunities to Confer With Colleagues was not associated significantly with the two-dimensional configuration. However, the variable's vector in Group 3 is consistent with the interpretation that countries in this quadrant of the multidimensional scaling space do not have a strong affiliation with institutionalized school psychology.

It may seem somewhat disturbing that the clearest source of occupational stress reflected in the above findings was related to the need to make compromises and was a source of stress associated with higher levels of professional autonomy. Moreover, relating Figure 46.3 (occupational stress) to Figure 46.2 (occupational roles), the placement of the vector for Compromise is seen to fall in the same multidimensional scaling vicinity as occupational roles that are central to school psychology. The implication is that differences exist in occupational stress as a function of professional autonomy and centrality of occupational roles. To better understand these findings, a concluding analysis focused on the centrality of occupational roles as a condition contributing to occupational stress in countries with differing levels of professional autonomy. For this analysis, a planned comparison (Hays, 1991) was used to test the hypothesis that certain forms of occupational stress are associated with a high level of professional autonomy and the centrality of occupational roles.

To conduct the planned comparison, two levels of professional autonomy (Weak and Strong) were formed by assigning countries in Groups 1 through 3 to the Weak category and countries in Groups 4 through 7 to the Strong category. Additionally, two levels of role centrality (High and Low) were constructed by using scores that had produced the Central Roles measure. The dependent variable was composed from scores obtained on two occupational stressors: Need to Make Compromises and Too High Self-Expectations. Scores on both these variables were summed to constitute a measure of burnout. This measure of burnout was believed to specifically refer to threats to professionalism created by a sense of depersonalization (from needing to make compromises) and of low competence (from failing to meet professional ideals), rather than created by the lack of resources. As a measure of the type of occupational stress that was associated with high autonomy countries, interest resided in knowing to what extent burnout may be due to role restriction.

Results on the planned comparison were highly significant for associating burnout with High Autonomy and High Role Centrality in contrast with Low Autonomy and Low Role Centrality. The results revealed that burnout, as related to a sense of low personal competence and depersonalization, is primarily a function of high professional autonomy in combination with the need to perform occupational roles that are central to the profession. The finding militates against deterministic views of progress that relate autonomy with the advantageous movement toward a known goal. Thus, the finding serves as a concluding statement on the heuristic value of contextual theory, as a competing framework for explaining disciplinary growth and change.

Threats Created by Centripetal Trends

In accordance with Altman's model, the centrality of occupational roles represents the consolidation of school psychology (i.e., dialectic complementarity in the model) that is achieved when the specialty's intraprofessional power bases are sufficiently strong to establish professional standards, particularly with regard to professional preparation. However, the high occupational stress reported in countries that can strongly support dominant roles is a reflection of systemic conflict (i.e., dialectic opposition in Altman's model). Problems relate to the restrictions imposed in implementing roles (i.e., psychological assessment and special education interventions) that are traditional to school psychology but that narrow the scope of professional practice.

The viability of roles that broaden the traditional scope of school psychology practice (e.g., systems interventions) was endorsed by a critical number of survey participants only in high autonomy countries. It appears that the knowledge and skills with regard to such interventions generally appear to be too narrow at present to have an impact in low autonomy countries. Nonetheless, respondents' endorsement of nontraditional roles as viable reveals that international school psychology comprises a vigorous open system of development. The trend toward role expansion is definitive and could eventually lead to a more ecologically based profession. Therefore, the time is ripe for understanding the process of change.

The Need to Capitalize on Diversity in Promoting Systemic Change

This study, which viewed school psychology's development from international perspectives, offered an optimal vantage point for seeing how progress in the field arises from the transactions that emerge from competing sources of influence arising extraprofessionally and intraprofessionally. Thus, this study supports Altman's contextual/transactional model. Unlike stage orientations, this stance counters against seeing progress within the specialty as predetermined (i.e., as movement toward some fixed ideal). The value of this position resides in believing that human effort actually can shape the future course of the field (cf. Alpert, 1985).

To some, this position may appear to contradict the findings of this study. As others had earlier observed (Oakland & Saigh, 1989), the study found that school psychologists experience high levels of stress in their occupational roles. Such conditions can favor developing forms of learned helplessness more than feelings of ability to influence the actions of social institutions, especially those within international sectors.

However, the study focused on power, not helplessness, and found that strong power bases exist within the specialty internationally. A first step toward working for change is to better understand the open system of interrelated structures that compose international school psychology.

Open systems of development derive their potential for power from the transactions that ensue between opposing forces within the system. The extraprofessional and intraprofessional forces influencing the development of school psychology internationally were seen to be residing in competition with one another. In high autonomy countries, intraprofessional trajectories favor centrifugal trends. The goal is professional specialization and the diversity of roles. This contrasts with the extraprofessional trajectory that favors centripetal trends. These are trends toward regulating circumscribed standards of practice. It was seen that effects of conflict between these two competing trajectories are role rigidity, feelings of depersonalization, and feelings of low competence. An opposite situation was seen in low autonomy countries. Here, intraprofessional influences favor centripetal trends in the consolidation and the centrality of roles. Conversely, extraprofessional influences in low autonomy countries cater to centrifugal trends due to their lack of regulation in sanctioning professional practice.

Effects of conflict were seen in a sense of isolation stemming from a lack of resources, lack of information, and low standards.

The fact that many conditions in low versus high autonomy countries work in diametric opposition to one another attests to the interrelatedness of the structures composing international school psychology as a total system of development. School psychologists' identification with psychology, internationally, is an overarching aspect of the cohesiveness that characterizes the field. Evidence of such cohesiveness allowed the development of two documents designed to promote the further legitimization of school psychology within its world contexts. One of these documents is the International School Psychology Association Guidelines for the Preparation of School Psychologists (Cunningham & Oakland, 1998), which followed publication of the International School Psychology Association Definition of School Psychology (Oakland & Cunningham, 1997). These documents were written with the intention of serving the needs of the diverse constituencies representing international school psychology.

Capitalizing on cultural diversity is important when modifying nonproductive centripetal trends that contribute to stagnation in the development of international school psychology. Accordingly, international school psychology's diverse community needs to establish channels of communication for expressing mutual respect and support, sharing knowledge, and furnishing methods of peer evaluation. Formative evaluations that are guided by their own internal standards are important for determining what may be possible for the specialty. By capitalizing on diversity, such evaluations are unlikely to be constrained by preconceived notions of what can be achieved.

This view of progress may be disconcerting to many, for it lacks a clear definition of ultimate goals. However, the evolutionary path for international school psychology remains uncharted. Open-ended explorations are likely to yield better knowledge of its contours than are more circumscribed excursions. For those who want to venture outward, let them be inspired by the enduring wisdom of William James, who wrote, during psychology's foundational period: "The changing conditions of history touch only the surface of the show. The altered equilibriums and redistributions only diversify our opportunities and open chances to us for new ideals" (James, 1899/1983, p. 149).

References

Alpert, J. (1985). Change within a profession: Change, future, prevention, and school psychology. *American Psychologist, 40,* 1112–1121.

Altman, I. (1987). Centripetal and centrifugal trends in psychology. *American Psychologist, 42,* 1058–1069.

Catterall, C. (Ed.). (1976). *Psychology in the schools in international perspective,* Vol. 1. Columbus, OH: International School Psychology Steering Committee.

Catterall, C. (Ed.). (1977). *Psychology in the schools in international perspective,* Vol. 2. Columbus, OH: International School Psychology Steering Committee.

Catterall, C. (Ed.). (1979). *Psychology in the schools in international perspective,* Vol. 3. Columbus, OH: International School Psychology Steering Committee.

Cunningham, J. (1994). A contextual investigation of the international development of psychology in the schools. *Dissertation Abstracts International, 55* (06), 1505A. (UMI No. 9428494)

Cunningham, J., & Oakland, T. (1998). International School Psychology Association guidelines for the preparation of school psychologists. *School Psychology International, 19,* 19–30.

Danziger, K. (1990). *Constructing the subject: Historical origins of psychological research.* New York: Cambridge University Press.

Hair, J. F., Anderson, R. E., Tatham, R. L., & Grablowsky, B. J. (1979). *Multivariate data analysis.* Tulsa, OK: Petroleum.

Hays, W. L. (1991). *Statistics* (4th ed.). New York: Holt, Rinehart & Winston.

Huebner, E. S. (1992). Burnout among school psychologists: An exploratory investigation into its nature, extent, and correlates. *School Psychology Quarterly, 7,* 129–136.

James, W. (1983). *Talks to teachers on psychology: And to students on some of life's ideals.* Cambridge, MA: Harvard University Press. (Original work published 1899)

Kruskal, J. B., & Wish, M. (1978). *Multidimensional scaling.* Beverly Hills, CA: Sage.

Lincoln, Y. S., & Guba, E. G. (1985). *Naturalistic inquiry.* Beverly Hills, CA: Sage.

Oakland, T. (1989, November). Report from the Standards and Practices Committee. *World-Go-Round,* pp. 6–7.

Oakland, T. (Ed.). (1992). Survey papers on school psychology worldwide [Special issue]. *School Psychology International, 13*(2).

Oakland, T. (2003). International school psychology: Psychology's worldwide portal to children and youth. *American Psychologist, 58,* 985–992.

Oakland, T., & Cunningham, J. (1992). A survey of school psychology in developed and developing countries. *School Psychology International, 13,* 99–130.

Oakland, T., & Cunningham, J. (1997). International School Psychology Association definition of school psychology. *School Psychology International, 18,* 195–200.

Oakland, T., & Cunningham, J. (1999). The futures of school psychology: Conceptual models for its development and examples of their application. In C. R. Reynolds & T. B. Gutkin (Eds.), *Handbook of school psychology* (pp. 34–54). New York: Wiley.

Oakland, T., & Saigh, P. A. (1989). Psychology in the schools: An introduction to international psychology in the schools. In P. A. Saigh & T. Oakland (Eds.), *International perspectives on psychology in the schools* (pp. 1–23). Hillsdale, NJ: Lawrence Erlbaum.

Statistical Analysis System Institute. (1988). *SAS/STAT user's guide* (Release 6.03). Cary, NC: Author.

Statistical Analysis System Institute. (1992). *SAS technical report P-229: SAS/STAT software: Changes and enhancements* (Release 6.07). Cary, NC: Author.

United Nations Educational, Scientific and Cultural Organization, International Bureau of Education. (1948). *School psychologists* (Publication No. 105). Paris: Author.

Wall, W. D. (Ed.). (1956). *Psychological services for schools.* New York: New York University Press for UNESCO Institute for Education.

Wise, P. S. (1985). School psychologists' rankings of stressful events. *Journal of School Psychology, 23,* 32–41.

47

The International School Psychology Association: Its Formation, Accomplishments, and Future Missions

Thomas D. Oakland

The formation of a profession follows a long and arduous process. Key qualities often occur in the following order. A respected body of knowledge that, over time, forms the basis for research and professional practice is the first to emerge. This knowledge is disseminated and archived through journals, books, and other sources. Educational institutions begin to create programs for the dissemination of this knowledge and to promote it through research and other scholarly activities. Restrictions may be placed on who has access to this knowledge.

As employment opportunities increase for those who have acquired this knowledge, educational institutions develop professional preparation programs that prepare persons for lifelong service to the public. These programs first prepare generalists and later may prepare specialists. Those within a profession work to form an association that serves their needs and those of the public. The scope of the first professional association generally is broad and attempts to bring all professionals who practice this profession under its umbrella. Other professional associations may emerge later to serve more specific needs.

The formation of a professional association may be the single most important event that signifies a profession. Once formed, an association generally creates a code of ethics designed to promote high standards for the delivery of professional services, defines the professional services provided by its members, establishes guidelines or standards for their preparation, approves or accredits institutions that meet its standards, and credentials members who display entry as well as advanced levels of knowledge and skills.

The formation and development of the International School Psychology Association (ISPA) displays many of these attributes. The purpose of this chapter is to provide a historical overview of ISPA and to discuss some emerging needs. The formation and development of ISPA are best understood within the context of the history of school psychology (Table 47.1). This broader topic is beyond the scope of this chapter. Those interested in learning more about the history of school psychology are advised to consult the following references (Catterall, 1976, 1977, 1979; Culbertson, 1983; Fagan & Wise, 2000; French, 1990; Oakland, 1993; Saigh & Oakland, 1989).

The origin of what would become ISPA occurred in 1972, when the American Psychological Association's Division of School Psychology formed the International School Psychology Committee. It provided needed leadership during the next 10 years. In 1973, the National Association of School Psychologists became a joint partner on this committee. The formation of the International School Psychology Committee was spearheaded by Frances Mullen within the Division of School Psychology and by Cal Catterall within the National Association of School Psychologists. Frances Mullen (1981) was a visionary dedicated to establishing infrastructures that could promote an interchange among psychologists internationally. For example, she served as president and secretary-general of the International Council of Psychologists and traveled internationally, somewhat widely, from her home in Chicago. Catterall and Anders Poulsen have had the most important impact on the foundation of ISPA.

Catterall was a highly respected school psychologist in the United States; he received an award for outstanding services as a school psychologist in California and later was elected president of the National Association of School Psychologists. More importantly, Catterall became centrally involved in promoting international interest in school psychology. For example, between 1974 and 1981, he organized traveling seminars to various countries. In 1975, he organized the first International School Psychology Committee–sponsored colloquium in Munich and in 1977, with Poulsen, one in Helsingor, Denmark. By 1981, Catterall had led study groups of school psychologists to countries on all inhabited continents (Table 47.2).

As noted earlier in this section, a respected body of knowledge is needed, one that is disseminated and archived through journals, books, and other sources. Catterall's three-volume edited work, *Psychology in the Schools in International Perspective,* provided the first knowledge as to the nature of school psychology internationally. Volume 1 (Catterall, 1976) focused on school psychology services in 12 countries: Western Germany, Austria, Denmark, Norway, Sweden, Britain, Colombia, Canada, New Zealand, Australia, Taiwan, and Pakistan. Services in Latin America and the American Dependent Schools Overseas also were discussed. Volume 2 (Catterall, 1977) focused on 13 countries: Ireland, Belgium, the Czechoslovak Socialist Republic, Switzerland, Turkey, Iran, Israel, Egypt, South Africa, India, Mexico, Puerto Rico, and the United States. Volume 3 (Catterall, 1979) focused on 8 countries: the Soviet Union, Poland, Italy, Thailand, Japan, Peru, Iceland, and Finland. Catterall also discussed conditions that affect school psychology and difficulties associated with the formation of international associations to address international issues.

Catterall's passion for his work and persistence in performing it are evident in his efforts to acquire and publish literature on school psychology in 33 countries. This initial literature was invaluable in demonstrating the international dimensions of school psychology practices; it also served to warrant the development of a professional association to attend to issues important to school psychologists and those they serve. Catterall's correspondence with

Table 47.1 Milestones in International School Psychology

1879	First psychology laboratory established, in Germany by Wundt
1896	First university-based child clinic established at the University of Pennsylvania by Lightner Witmer
Before 1899	First school-based child study department established, Antwerp, Belgium
1905	A reliable measure of mental ability published by Binet
1910	First appearance of the term *school psychologist* in print by Stern
1918	First person to hold the title "school psychologist," Arnold Gesell
1930	First book on school psychology, by Hildreth
1948	UNESCO-sponsored international conference on school psychology
1952	UNESCO-sponsored European conference on school psychology
1955	Thayer conference on school psychology in the United States
1972	Formation of the International School Psychology Committee (ISPC)
1975	First ISPC-sponsored international colloquium on school psychology
1979	International Year of the Child
1982	International School Psychology Association (ISPA) adopts its constitution and bylaws
1989	ISPA is officially recognized by UNESCO ISPA adopts a code of ethics ISPA approves a definition of school psychology
1996	ISPA approves a model professional preparation program for school psychologists

Table 47.2 Colloquia Sponsored by the International School Psychology Committee (1975–1980) and the International School Psychology Association (1982–2005)

1975	Munich, Germany
1977	Helsingor, Denmark
1979	York, England
1980	Jerusalem, Israel
1982	Stockholm, Sweden
1983	Indianapolis, Indiana, United States
1984	Orléans, France
1985	Southampton, England
1986	Nyborg, Denmark
1987	Interlaken, Switzerland
1988	Bamberg, Germany
1989	Ljubljana, Slovenia, Yugoslavia
1990	Newport, Rhode Island, United States
1991	Braga, Portugal
1992	Istanbul, Turkey
1993	Banská Bystrica, Slovakia
1994	Campinas, Brazil
1995	Dundee, Scotland
1996	Eger, Hungary
1997	Melbourne, Australia
1998	Jurmala, Latvia
1999	Kreuzlingen, Switzerland/Germany
2000	New Hampshire, United States
2001	Dinan, France
2002	Nyborg, Denmark
2003	Cancelled
2004	Exeter, England
2005	Athens, Greece
2006	Hangzhou, China

various school psychologists internationally promoted personal relationships as well as international understanding and cooperation.

His correspondence led to his establishing strong and lasting ties with Anders Poulsen. In 1974, Poulsen responded to Catterall's letter by remarking, "I wonder how you found me." Catterall's ability to ferret out leaders in school psychology, including Poulsen, served to broaden the base of support for developing an international infrastructure that could serve school psychology.

Like Catterall, Poulsen was a highly respected school psychologist in his country, Denmark. He too was actively involved in school psychology services through work, travel, and correspondence. Poulsen was instrumental in developing and maintaining high quality school psychology services in Denmark. In addition, he served as honorary president of the Danish Psychological Association's Committee on School Psychologists. Due to the esteem with which he was regarded, he was appointed to be a member of several important governmental committees and commissions devoted to developing basic education, special needs education, and school psychological services. Poulsen also had considerable international experience. For example, he served as a member of the Danish Association for International Co-operation (Mellemfolkeligt Samvirke), in which capacity he completed brief missions to various African and Asian countries. During 1961–1962, Poulsen held a United Nations Educational, Scientific and Cultural Organization post at the International Institute for Child Study in Thailand, a country with which he still has close connections. His many international contacts made it possible for him to arrange study trips for Danish school psychologists to more than 10 countries, beginning with the United States in 1976.

During the next 10 years, and prior to Catterall's death in 1984 while attending the ISPA colloquium in Orléans, France, Catterall and Poulsen developed a strong collaborative relationship, and each contributed his special qualities to the formation of ISPA. In summarizing his relationship with Catterall, Poulsen remarked,

> Generally we had an uncomplicated, cooperative relationship, and I deeply respected his dynamic and visionary leadership. I also believe that he respected my help shaping and defining the direction of ISPC [the International School Psychology Committee] in those early years of 1975–1976 as well as keeping plans close to the world of realities. (Poulsen, 2004, p. 1)

Thus, Catterall and Poulsen have been instrumentally involved in the formation of ISPA. Poulsen has been ISPA's most active and instrumental leader and is the only ISPA member who has maintained active leadership in the association from its beginning.

Sometimes events have unexpected outcomes. The International Year of the Child represents one of those events for international school psychology. In 1979, the United Nations sponsored an international meeting to highlight important issues pertaining to children's psychological, social, and educational needs; the nature of existing services; and the need to develop new programs consistent with each country's conditions, needs, and priorities. Events associated with the International Year of the Child served as a magnet, drawing school psychologists and others together, both within and between countries, in an effort to review and address the issues highlighted above.

In 1979, the International School Psychology Committee spearheaded its third colloquium on the International Year of the Child in York, England. Perhaps more important for school psychology, those participating in organizing this and prior conferences in Munich, Germany, and Helsingor, Denmark, began to see the importance of international collaboration and thus the need to establish an infrastructure to facilitate it. Moreover, those who attended these conferences valued the social and educational opportunities they offered. Increased interest and membership warranted an international association. The International School Psychology Committee had accomplished its goals and needed to be replaced by a structure that was international in origin and scope, one that better met the current and future needs of school psychologists.

Thus, in 1981, Catterall drafted the constitution and bylaws for what was to become the ISPA. Members approved these documents by written mailed ballots. Thus, in 1982, ISPA was formally founded at the Fifth International Colloquium in Stockholm. Poulsen was elected

ISPA's first president. Subsequent presidents were Herbert Bischoff (1985–1986), Jean-Claude Guillemard (1987–1988), Anna-Lisa Mellden (1989–1990), Stuart Hart (1991–1992), Robert Burden (1993–1995), Thomas Oakland (1995–1997), Anton Furman (1997–1999), Bernie Stein (1999–2001), Peg Dawson (2001–2003), Peter Farrell (2003–2005), and Nora Katona (2005–2007).

After establishing ISPA, members attended to developing an infrastructure expected of a mature profession, including an ethics code in 1990 (Oakland, Goldman, & Bischoff, 1997), a definition of the specialty of school psychology (Oakland & Cunningham, 1997), and guidelines for their preparation (Cunningham & Oakland, 1998). The latter two documents were approved by ISPA membership in 1996 and were based on survey data compiled by Oakland and Cunningham (1992).

ISPA's membership includes 28 national professional associations of school psychologists and slightly more than 600 individual members from approximately 50 countries. Members meet yearly at colloquia (Table 47.2). Many of these colloquia are organized to help promote the growth of school psychology in the host country.

Various crises have occurred (e.g., school shootings, earthquakes) that warrant interventions by school psychologists. Thus, to better serve its members, ISPA has developed a crisis intervention team that provides training as well as technical and, at times, personal support during times of crises. Recent examples include the earthquakes in Turkey and Greece.

ISPA's commitment to communication is seen on its Web site and in its quarterly newsletter, *World-Go-Round,* published since January 1973. ISPA's commitment to scholarship is seen in its supports for *School Psychology International,* a quarterly peer-reviewed journal. Efforts have not been made to develop a scholarly journal owned and managed by ISPA. ISPA also endeavors to promote scholarship through convention-related workshops and other sessions. An attempt by Oakland and

Phillips in 1999 to assist selected ISPA members to advance their scholarly abilities seemingly was unsuccessful.

Until recently, ISPA did little to commission scholarship on academic issues or on the status of school psychology. Recent work by Jimerson and other members of ISPA's research committee may signal a new commitment within ISPA for initiating and supporting research (e.g., Farrell, Jimerson, Kalambouka, & Benoit, 2005; Jimerson et al., 2004; Jimerson et al., 2006). The Association's small annual budget limits its ability to support scholarship.

Various persons associated with ISPA have engaged in scholarship beyond that published in *School Psychology International.* Catterall's three volumes and scholarship by Culbertson (1983), French (1990), Oakland (1993), and Saigh and Oakland (1989) all discuss international school psychology. These efforts were independent of ISPA.

Future Missions for the International School Psychology Association

ISPA is facing a number of challenges. Poulsen served as ISPA's executive secretary from 1983 to 2003, at first informally and, after 1987, formally. He was administrator of ISPA's central office in Copenhagen. Elisabeth Jacobsen, Lone Bjarkow, and Lissi Stocklund have ably assisted Poulsen in this office. All four are retiring. Thus, the Association's most immediate need is to appoint its next executive secretary, to move and to staff its office.

Maintaining a sufficiently large membership remains a challenge. Efforts to increase membership while not losing the personal relationships established among the members has been a long-standing issue. As noted earlier in this chapter, an association generally creates an ethics code, defines the professional qualities that constitute the specialty, establishes guidelines or standards for member preparation, approves or accredits institutions that meet its standards, and credentials members who display entry as well as advanced levels of knowledge and skills. The International School Psychology Association has achieved the first three, has been reluctant to develop a process that approves or accredits institutions that meet its standards, and has not considered the need to credential members who display entry as well as advanced levels of knowledge and skills.

References

Catterall, C. (Ed.). (1976). *Psychology in the schools in international perspective,* Vol. 1. Columbus, OH: International School Psychology Steering Committee.

Catterall, C. (Ed.). (1977). *Psychology in the schools in international perspective,* Vol. 2. Columbus, OH: International School Psychology Steering Committee.

Catterall, C. (Ed.). (1979). *Psychology in the schools in international perspective,* Vol. 3. Columbus, OH: International School Psychology Steering Committee.

Culbertson, F. (1983). International school psychology: Cross-cultural perspectives. In T. R. Kratochwill (Ed.), *Advances in school psychology* (Vol. 3, pp. 45–82). Hillsdale, NJ: Lawrence Erlbaum.

Cunningham, J., & Oakland, T. (1998). International School Psychology Association guidelines for the preparation of school psychologists. *School Psychology International, 19,* 19–30.

Fagan, T., & Wise, P. (2000). *School psychology: Past, present, and future.* Bethesda, MD: National Association of School Psychologists.

Farrell, P., Jimerson, S., Kalambouka, A., & Benoit, J. (2005). Teachers' perceptions of school psychologists in different countries. *School Psychology International, 26*(5), 525–544.

French, J. (1990). History of school psychology. In T. B. Gutkin & C. R. Reynolds (Eds.), *The handbook of school psychology* (2nd ed., pp. 3–20). New York: Wiley.

Jimerson, S. R., Graydon, K., Farrell, P., Kikas, E., Hatzichristou, C., Boce, E., Bashi, G., & International School Psychology Association Research Committee. (2004). The International School Psychology Survey: Development and data from Albania, Cyprus, Estonia, Greece and Northern England. *School Psychology International, 25*(3), 259–286.

Jimerson, S. R., Graydon, K., Yuen, M., Lam, S.-F., Thurm, J.-M., Klueva, N., Coyne, J., Loprete, L. J., Phillips, L., & International School Psychology Association Research Committee. (2006). The International School Psychology Survey: Data from Australia, China, Germany, Italy and Russia. *School Psychology International, 27*(1), 5–32.

Mullen, F. A. (1981). School psychology in the U.S.: Reminiscences of its origin. *Journal of School Psychology, 19,* 103–119.

Oakland, T. (1993). A brief history of international school psychology. *Journal of School Psychology, 31,* 109–122.

Oakland, T., & Cunningham, J. (1992). A survey of school psychology in developed and developing countries. *School Psychology International, 13,* 99–130.

Oakland, T., & Cunningham, J. (1997). International School Psychology Association definition of school psychology *School Psychology International, 18,* 195–200.

Oakland, T., Goldman, S., & Bischoff, H. (1997). Code of ethics of the International School Psychology Association. *School Psychology International, 18,* 291–298.

Oakland, T., & Saigh, P. (1989). Psychology in the schools: An introduction to international perspectives. In P. Saigh & T. Oakland (Eds.), *International perspectives on psychology in the schools* (pp. 1–22). Hillsdale, NJ: Lawrence Erlbaum.

Poulsen, A. (2004, June). Bringing the past forward: Part two. *World-Go-Round,* p. 1.

Saigh, P., & Oakland, T. (Eds.). (1989). *International perspectives on psychology in the schools.* Hillsdale, NJ: Lawrence Erlbaum.

48

The International School Psychology Survey: Insights From School Psychologists Around the World

Shane R. Jimerson

Kelly Graydon

Michael J. Curtis

Rene Staskal

U nderstanding the characteristics, training, roles, responsibilities, challenges, and research interests of school psychologists around the world is increasingly important as the field of school psychology continues to develop in many countries. During the past five decades, few systematic efforts have been made to gather information regarding school

AUTHORS' NOTES: This research emerged from the efforts of the International School Psychology Association Research Committee. Members of the 2001–2002 International School Psychology Association Research Committee contributed to the development of the International School Psychology Survey.

Portions of the tables are reprinted by permission of Sage Publications Ltd. (© SAGE Publications) from Jimerson, S. R., Graydon, K., Farrell, P., Kikas, E., Hatzichristou, C., Boce, E., Bashi, G., & International School Psychology Association Research Committee (2004) and from Jimerson, S. R., Graydon, K., Yuen, M., Lam, S.-F., Thurm, J.-M., Klueva, N., Coyne, J., Loprete, L. J., Phillips, J., & International School Psychology Association Research Committee (2006).

psychology practices around the globe (Catterall, 1976, 1977, 1979; Jimerson et al., 2004; Jimerson et al., 2006; Oakland & Cunningham, 1992; United Nations Educational, Scientific and Cultural Organization, 1948; Wall, 1956). A review of previous research examining school psychology around the globe is provided by Jimerson and colleagues (2004). Recent international efforts to systematically gather data from colleagues in countries around the world led to the development of the International School Psychology Survey (Jimerson et al., 2000, 2004). These scholarly efforts were inspired by pioneers of international school psychology, such as Tom Oakland and Cal Catterall, as well as by systematic data-based efforts to define school psychology at a national level by the National Association of School Psychologists (e.g., Curtis, Chesno Grier, Walker Abshier, Sutton, & Hunley, 2002) and prior efforts of the United Nations Educational, Scientific and Cultural Organization. This chapter reports valuable information regarding the profession of school psychology using data gathered in Albania, Cyprus, Estonia, Greece, Northern England, Australia, China (Hong Kong), Germany, Italy, Russia, and the United States.

Jimerson and the International School Psychology Association Research Committee developed the International School Psychology Survey through a careful process of modification and revision of the survey instrument previously used by the National Association of School Psychologists (2000; Curtis et al., 2002). This revision was then redistributed to international colleagues serving on the International School Psychology Association Research Committee (a complete description of the process is described in Jimerson et al., 2004). The International School Psychology Survey (Jimerson & International School Psychology Association Research Committee, 2002) contains 46 items that address five domains: (1) characteristics of school psychologists, (2) training and regulation of the profession, (3) roles and responsibilities, (4) challenges to the profession, and (5) research. Additionally, the

survey solicits feedback regarding the potential role of the International School Psychology Association in each country. The first 20 items on the survey represent general questions asked of all participants, whereas the remaining 26 items are to be completed only by those professionals employed in school settings. The survey items are predominantly multiple-choice questions, supplemented by several open-ended questions. The survey measures *characteristics* of the sample through the first 20 items, which ask participants for information ranging from gender and age to opinions regarding most and least favorite aspects of the profession. Six items addressing educational preparation, requirements for practice, and sources of funds for employment are used to collect information about *professional training and regulations.* Fifteen items—requesting estimates of the average number of hours respondents spent in various settings and engaged in specified tasks, and their opinions about the ideal roles of a school psychologist—assess the *roles and responsibilities* of school psychologists. The survey measures *challenges to the profession* through 2 items asking for the identification of internal and external factors that jeopardize the delivery of school psychological services in each country. To address the topic of *research*, 3 items ask for the perceived relevance of research to professional practice, the availability of research journals, and the most important research topics.

For a description of the distribution of the International School Psychology Survey in Albania, Cyprus, Estonia, Greece, Northern England, Australia, Hong Kong, Germany, Italy, and Russia, see previous publications (Jimerson et al., 2004; Jimerson et al., 2006). Researchers at the University of California at Santa Barbara distributed the International School Psychology Survey in the United States with assistance from collaborators at the University of South Florida. The sample was drawn from members of the National Association of School Psychologists. Reschly (2000) estimated that there are approximately 30,000 school psychologists in the

United States. Researchers mailed the survey to 1,235 members of the National Association of School Psychologists, representing a 10% random selection by state of all those who were identified as regular members within the membership database. Individuals were provided with a postage-paid response envelope to return the survey. A code number was assigned to the response envelope for each recipient to identify those who did and did not respond. When a completed survey was received, it was immediately separated from the return envelope to protect the identity of the respondent. Those who did not respond to the first mailing were sent another copy of the survey with an additional postage-paid response envelope. A total of 671 completed surveys were received, resulting in a 54% response rate. Among respondents, the reported primary positions included practicing school psychologists (80%), university faculty (7%), administrators (4%), psychologists (4%), counselors (1%), and other (4%; e.g., teachers, behavioral intervention specialists). The results reported for the United States represent the 531 surveys completed by practicing school psychologists.

Results of the International School Psychology Survey to Date

Descriptive analyses of the responses from school psychologists in the 11 countries participating in this project to date were completed and summarized (see Tables 48.1–48.10). The data and discussion presented in this section provide information regarding demographic characteristics, training and regulations, roles and responsibilities, challenges, and research interests for school psychologists in each of the 11 countries. Researchers recorded and synthesized answers to open-response items by content for summary purposes. Considering the diverse contexts of school psychological services in various countries, caution and careful consideration are warranted in the interpretation of the results. The handbook provides qualitative and contextual information that is essential for interpreting the results of the International School Psychology Survey.

Demographic Characteristics of School Psychologists

Similarities in the demographic characteristics of this sample suggest a relatively consistent profile for school psychologists around the world. Table 48.1 presents the characteristics of the school psychologists who completed the survey. The results of this study indicate that the majority of practicing school psychologists in most countries are female, which is consistent with previous research exploring the characteristics of school psychologists in the United States and other nations (Curtis, Hunley, Walker, & Baker, 1999; Jimerson et al., 2004; Oakland & Cunningham, 1992). The exception is Germany, which had an equal gender ratio.

The age range of school psychologists in the participating countries appears to be related to the length of time that the profession has existed in each country. Data from Albania yielded the youngest mean age of 24 years; data from Germany, Australia, Northern England, and the United States yielded mean ages greater than 46 years. Consistent with these findings, the average number of *years of school psychology experience* ranged from 2 to 24, with participants from Albania and Estonia reporting few years of experience and participants from Germany reporting the most years of experience. The older average ages of practitioners who also have more years of experience in some countries may be a particularly important consideration, depending on the number of professionals being prepared in school psychology and the relative demand. Trends in the United States may lead to a projected severe shortage of school psychologists in the next decade (Curtis, Chesno Grier, & Hunley, 2004; Curtis, Hunley, & Chesno Grier, 2004). Repeated administration of the survey in these countries

Table 48.1 Demographic Characteristics of School Psychologists*

Characteristic	Albania	Australia	China (Hong Kong)	Cyprus	Estonia	Germany	Greece	Italy	Northern England	Russia	United States
Participants	n = 11	n = 212	n = 24	n = 11	n = 24	n = 40	n = 50	n = 22	n = 73	n = 42	n = 531
Gender (%)	F = 100	F = 80	F = 78	F = 73	F = 92	F = 50	F = 84	F = 64	F = 63	F = 77	F = 77
	M = 0	M = 20	M = 22	M = 27	M = 8	M = 50	M = 16	M = 36	M = 37	M = 23	M = 23
Age range	23–25	23–71	28–53	25–59	22–61	33–64	20–59	28–57	28–65	19–57	25–79
Mean age	24	47	31	42	39	53	35	36	47	32	47
Average Years of Experience											
School psychology	2	10	7	8	4	24	8	7	12	5	14
Range	1–2	0.5–35	1–20	1–32	0.5–28	2–32	0.5–30	2–29	0.5–41	0–32	0–52
Teaching	2	6	3	<1	13	2	3	10	7	4	<1
Range	2–2	0–32	0–10	0–5	0.5–42	0–33	0–20	0–37	1–23	0–29	0–30
Highest Degree Held (%)											
Ph.D.	0	2	3	18	0	13	8	5	4	0	31
M.A.	0	75	97	82	12	87	70	40	93	98	69
B.A.	100	23	0	0	88	0	22	55	1	2	0
Fluent Languages											
Languages spoken fluently	Albanian English Italian French	English French	Cantonese Mandarin English	Greek English French German	Estonian English Russian	German English French	Greek English French	Italian English German French	English French	Russian English French German	English Spanish German French
% Speaking two or more languages	100	8	100	100	96	77	100	68	2	17	40
Languages of professional literature	Albanian English Italian French	English	English Chinese	Greek English French	English Estonian Russian	German English	Greek English French German	Italian English French	English French	Russian English French German	English
% Reading in two or more languages	100	0	100	100	96	54	100	73	1	12	23

*Includes results from Q. 11 (Years of experience working as a school psychologist), Q. 10 (Years of classroom teaching experience), Q. 15 (Highest degree earned), Q. 17 (Membership in professional organizations), Q. 4 (What languages do you speak fluently/communicate in?), and Q. 5 (What languages do you read professional literature in?).

during the upcoming years will help to facilitate an understanding of longitudinal trends in the profession of school psychology.

Years of teaching experience varied from less than 1 to 13. Whereas the 1956 United Nations Educational, Scientific and Cultural Organization report (Wall, 1956) recommended teaching experience as a requirement for school psychology practice, Oakland and Cunningham (1992) reported a trend of decreasing importance attached to prior teaching experience. Results from the current study are consistent with this trend, with the majority of school psychologists in the United States reporting no prior experience in teaching. Of the 11 countries completing the survey to date, only 2 require teaching experience prior to entry into the field (Australia and Northern England).

Data for the *highest degree held* (see Table 48.1) reflected the range of training options available in each country and the existing opportunities to study abroad. Across countries, the majority of respondents reported holding a master's degree. However, most participants in Albania, Estonia, and Italy practiced with a bachelor's degree. In Italy, where the profession is not yet recognized, training levels were the most diverse of any country sampled, with a nearly even split between bachelor's and master's/specialist-level training.

Data regarding *languages spoken fluently* varied greatly across countries. One hundred percent of school psychologists in Albania, Hong Kong, Cyprus, and Greece reported fluency in two or more languages, whereas less than 50% of school psychologists in Australia, Northern England, Russia, and the United States reported fluency in two or more languages. Participants across countries indicated English as the most common *language of professional literature,* whereas participants in six countries indicated French. The relative diversity of languages used in the other countries represents opportunities for sharing knowledge and resources across countries. Due to the fact that the most common second language in all countries was either English or French, international communication and publications in these languages may be valuable to international colleagues in many countries. However, it is important to note that only in Australia and Northern England did all of the respondents report fluency in English or French, suggesting that although these languages may be helpful for the sharing of information and resources, translation into other languages is also important.

Professional Characteristics of School Psychologists

Table 48.2 reports professional characteristics of participating school psychologists. The reported *ratio of school psychologists to school-age children* varied greatly across and within countries. Participants from Italy reported the smallest average ratio at 1 to 47. Data from Germany and Hong Kong yielded the largest average ratios at 1 to 16,549 and 1 to 19,065, respectively. Several possible explanations for the large range of ratios exist. For example, the very small ratios reported by the sample from Italy could represent the fact that school psychology is not yet a recognized profession in that country, and psychological practitioners were estimating the exact number of students with whom they had worked as clients; whether this contact was through private practice or on a contractual basis in the schools was not specified. (Thus, most children in the schools do not have direct and regular access to psychological services.) Follow-up with respondents from different countries may clarify whether this survey item is being interpreted differently. Another possible explanation that has been offered for the range of ratios reported is differences in gross national product between participating countries (Ezeilo, 1992; Oakland & Cunningham, 1992). Those countries with lower gross national products have previously been reported to have poorer school psychologist to student ratios. However, results from the International School Psychology Survey administrations thus far indicate that the ratios reported do not appear to be related to the

Table 48.2 Professional Characteristics of School Psychologists*

	Country										
Characteristic	Albania	Australia	China (Hong Kong)	Cyprus	Estonia	Germany	Greece	Italy	Northern England	Russia	United States
Ratio of school psychologists to schoolchildren	1:580	1:1,560	1:19,065	1:9,050	1:690	1:16,549	1:2,578	1:47	1:5,000	1:594	1:1,300
Range of ratios	200–1,500	10–11,000	300–40,000	1,000–12,000	200–1,400	1,000–100,000	30–4,000	6–105	60–13,000	100–1,350	15–9,000
National requirement of prior teaching experience	no	yes	no	no	no	no	no	no	yes	no	no
% Receiving supervision as a school psychologist	80	61	63	55	14	28	37	10	66	70	46
Number of hours in a full-time position	40	36	40	38	35	40	30	36	37	36	39
Range	16–40	40–40	35–40	35–39	35–40	38–42	2–30	18–40	35–50	18–38	25–52
Organization Membership											
International School Psychology Association (%)	0	3	0	0	4	0	4	0	1	—	3
National School Psychology Association (%)	100	84	34	0	66	48	14	23	44	— (40% in state/provincial school psychology organization)	97
National Psychology Association (%)	0	43	47	91	4	38	64	50	99	—	23

*Includes results from Q. 23 (Ratio of school psychologists to school-age children in your district/local authority), Q. 9 (Are you required to be a qualified teacher with teaching experience before becoming a school psychologist in your country?), Q. 32 (Do you receive supervision as a school psychologist?), Q. 19 (Please indicate how many hours a week constitutes a full-time position in your country), and Q. 17 (Membership in professional organizations).

gross national products of the participating countries. Further investigation is necessary to clarify the range of ratios revealed in this study.

In the United States, the National Association of School Psychologists recommends that 1 school psychologist be available to approximately every 1,000 students in order to provide appropriate professional services (National Association of School Psychologists, 2000). Practitioners responding to the current survey in the United States reported an average ratio of 1 school psychologist to every 1,300 students, which is a slight decline in the ratio reported for the 1999–2000 school year by Curtis and colleagues (2002; 1:1,631).

Data regarding the percentage of school psychologists who *receive supervision as school psychologists* vary among the countries; participants from Italy reported the smallest percentage (10%). In comparison, 80% of school psychologists from Albania reported receiving supervision. These results are reflective of diversity among professional training and regulations. Trends suggest that in the countries where school psychology is a recognized profession, the percentage of school psychologists receiving supervision tend to be higher; however, results from Germany and the United States are inconsistent with this finding. One possible explanation for this inconsistency may be related to the age and experience of school psychologists in the samples from these two countries; because these respondents were among the oldest and had the most years of experience of the countries sampled, they may be less likely to need professional supervision. However, practitioners from Northern England were of a similar age and experience level, yet reported receiving a much higher rate of supervision (66%). Additional research is necessary to better understand the significance of the variability in professional supervision in various countries.

With regard to *professional membership,* more than 50% of participants from the United States, Albania, Australia, Cyprus, Estonia, Greece, Italy, and Northern England reported belonging to either a national school psychology association or a national psychology association. Membership in professional organizations, similar to the highest degree earned, is related to the differences in options available in each country. Similar to the results found previously in all 10 countries completing the survey, very few school psychologists in the United States reported being members of the International School Psychology Association. The sampling procedure utilized in the United States (membership list of the National Association of School Psychologists) makes comparison regarding the percentage of school psychologists with membership in the national school psychology associations impossible. The relatively small percentage of practitioners reporting membership in the American Psychological Association suggests that school psychologists in the United States are much less likely than their international colleagues to be members of a national psychological association. However, it is possible that organizational options available in each country (e.g., an autonomous national school psychology association versus school psychology being primarily represented with a national psychological association) could be a factor in the differences among countries. Additional information regarding the size and scope of these organizations and the benefits of membership would also assist in understanding these differential membership rates.

Most and Least Liked Aspects of School Psychology

Table 48.3 reports open-ended responses to questions about *what participants like most and least about the field of school psychology.* Respondents from all countries surveyed reported working with students, teachers, and families as one of their favorite aspects of the profession. Other common responses across countries were related to producing positive changes and professional autonomy or flexibility. As for the least liked aspects of school psychology, administrative responsibilities, overwhelming workload or demands, and lack of organization or standards for the role of a school psychologist were common responses across countries. The commonality of responses across countries is notable considering the diverse composition of the multiple countries responding to the survey.

Table 48.4 reports results regarding the *percentage of time spent in different school psychology tasks*. It should be noted that the numbers included in this table represent the average endorsement for each item across participants and, therefore, do not necessarily add up to 100%. The exact percentage of respondents endorsing each activity (at any percentage) is represented in brackets for each activity. In almost all countries, the activity reported to consume the greatest percentage of respondents' time was *psychoeducational evaluations*. The next greatest percentages of time were spent on *consultation with teachers/staff, administrative responsibilities,* and *counseling students*. In comparison to other countries, school psychologists from Italy reported a very high percentage of time spent on *psychoeducational evaluations* and *counseling students*.

Participation in Activities on a Monthly Basis

Table 48.5 presents the average number of *specific school psychology tasks* performed monthly by respondents. School psychologists in most countries reported completing approximately 15 *psychoeducational assessments* monthly. Interestingly, school psychologists in other countries, such as Germany and Russia, reported completing a greater number of assessments (39 monthly assessments and 33 monthly assessments, respectively), yet reported that this activity composed a smaller percentage of their time (28% and 32%, respectively; see Table 48.4). On the other hand, the greater amount of time per case reported in the United States is consistent with the finding by Curtis and colleagues

(2002) that despite decreasing numbers of evaluations, the amount of time invested in related activities had increased markedly from that reported in earlier studies. In contrast, the average number of *students counseled individually* per month ranged from 5 (Italy) to 35 (Cyprus), with most data falling between 10 and 30 students.

With regard to the average number of *consultation cases* reported, the average number in the United States (16), Cyprus (20), Northern England (15), and Australia (18) represent the higher end of data points. In contrast, data from Albania and Germany yielded an average of 4 *consultation cases* per month. Responses for the number of *counseling groups* conducted across countries ranged from 0.6 (Hong Kong) to 6 (United States). With regard to *in-service programs/presentations*, participants reported conducting from 1 (Australia, Hong Kong, and Greece) to 7 (Estonia) per month. Responses for *primary prevention programs* conducted per month ranged from 1 to 6 across countries.

Perceptions and Participation in Ideal Roles, Responsibilities, and Activities

Perceptions of the *ideal school psychology role* and *extent of participation in this ideal role* are reported in Table 48.6. Responses varied across countries, making comparisons difficult. However, data for all countries regarding the most preferred role fell into one of four areas: psychoeducational evaluations, counseling students, providing primary prevention programs, and consultation with teachers/staff. Additionally, respondents unanimously rated *administrative responsibilities* as the least optimal role.

Regarding the reported *participation in the ideal role*, participants from Cyprus and Greece reported spending the largest percentage of time in ideal tasks, 45% and 38%, respectively. Compared with other countries, participants from the United States and Northern England

(Text continues on page 494)

Table 48.3   Most and Least Liked Aspects of School Psychology*

Most Liked Aspects of School Psychology

Albania	Australia	China (Hong Kong)	Cyprus	Estonia	Germany	Greece	Italy	Northern England	Russia	United States
Working with children	Working with children, families, and teachers	Ability to apply knowledge to help others/make changes	Communication	Ability to help	Variety of work	Counseling students	Working with students and families	Effecting change/making a difference	Working with children	Working with children, families, and teachers
Seeing successes	Effecting positive changes/making a difference	Working within a system	Counseling students	Seeing positive results	Professional independence/autonomy	Cooperation between child, family, school staff, and school psychologist	Effecting positive changes/making a difference	Working with people	Creative freedom	Effecting positive changes/making a difference
	Variety of tasks/flexibility of role	Autonomy/flexibility of role	Prevention programs	Direct contact with students	Working with people	Consultations with family	Contributing to growth of teachers	Variety/flexibility of work	Counseling	Autonomy/flexibility of role/variety of tasks

(Continued)

Table 48.3 (Continued)

Least Liked Aspects of School Psychology

Albania	Australia	China (Hong Kong)	Cyprus	Estonia	Germany	Greece	Italy	Northern England	Russia	United States
Feeling that advice is not taken seriously by parents and teachers	Administrative burden/ paperwork	Administrative burden/paperwork	Ratio of school psychologists to children	Lack of legislative organization/ regulation	Administrative responsibilities	Lack of acceptance of the role of the school psychologist by staff	Hard work/fatigue	Too much work for time available	Low salary	Administrative burden/ paperwork
Pressure/ demands	Overwhelming workload or caseload	Acting as a gatekeeper of special education	Administrative responsibilities	Difficulties working with teachers	High workload	Administrative responsibilities	Lack of acceptance/ understanding of the role of the school psychologist by staff	Pressure/ demands	Working with diagnostic materials without computers	Overloaded with work/spread too thin to complete work
Not having the power to intervene in all needed areas	Low salary and status	Unrealistically high expectations of administration or teachers	Lack of organization in school psychological services	Misconceptions of the school psychology role	Unrealistically high expectations of administration or teachers	Lack of organization in school psychological services	Having role/job determined by availability of money within a school	Administrative burden/ paperwork	No set requirements or professional standards	Litigation/liability/ fair hearings
Limited time for prevention and interventions	Limited time for prevention and interventions	Low salary and status		Low salary and status	Lack of support/ acceptance by other professionals					Report writing

*Includes results from Q. 45 (Please describe what you most like about being a school psychologist) and Q. 44 (Please describe what you least like about being a school psychologist).

Table 48.4   Average Percentage of Work Time Spent in Common School Psychology Activities*

Country

Work Activity	Albania Mean (Med.) {**}	Australia Mean (Med.) {**}	China (Hong Kong) Mean (Med.) {**}	Cyprus Mean (Med.) {**}	Estonia Mean (Med.) {**}	Germany Mean (Med.) {**}	Greece Mean (Med.) {**}	Italy Mean (Med.) {**}	Northern England Mean (Med.) {**}	Russia Mean (Med.) {**}	United States Mean (Med.) {**}
Psychoeducational evaluations	8 (8) {40}	22 (20) {85}	23 (20) {89}	23 (20) {82}	16 (12) {91}	28 (25) {87}	23 (20) {94}	70 (50) {40}	30 (23) {80}	32 (30) {74}	45 (43) {79}
Counseling students	51 (60) {80}	29 (25) {89}	17 (15) {78}	14 (10) {82}	34 (30) {91}	14 (10) {82}	30 (25) {84}	80 (80) {20}	14 (5) {49}	17 (15) {79}	15 (10) {49}
Providing direct interventions	9 (10) {60}	11 (10) {64}	*** (***) {***}	8 (8) {91}	8 (5) {74}	7 (5) {40}	16 (10) {63}	55 (30) {20}	18 (10) {61}	22 (15) {67}	10 (10) {53}
Providing primary prevention programs	6 (5) {40}	7 (5) {53}	11 (5) {59}	6 (5) {64}	6 (5) {78}	8 (5) {59}	13 (10) {55}	50 (20) {20}	16 (5) {46}	13 (10) {35}	9 (5) {28}
Consultation with teachers/staff	20 (20) {60}	14 (11) {94}	21 (20) {94}	14 (15) {82}	11 (10) {91}	13 (10) {75}	14 (11) {73}	35 (20) {50}	20 (10) {84}	11 (10) {79}	17 (15) {79}
Consultation with parents/families	12 (10) {60}	11 (10) {93}	11 (10) {91}	15 (15) {82}	9 (10) {91}	15 (15) {72}	19 (20) {94}	15 (10) {30}	15 (10) {79}	11 (10) {79}	9 (10) {71}
Conducting staff training and in-service programs	15 (8) {80}	6 (5) {64}	7 (5) {94}	8 (5) {91}	4 (3) {68}	15 (7.5) {70}	7 (5) {45}	60 (20) {20}	20 (5) {73}	9 (10) {73}	5 (5) {35}
Administrative responsibilities	10 (10) {20}	15 (10) {90}	13 (10) {87}	34 (28) {54}	4 (2) {65}	11 (10) {75}	9 (10) {40}	0 (0) {0}	27 (20) {84}	10 (5) {84}	16 (10) {52}

*Includes Q. 31 (% of your total work time).

**Numbers in the brackets indicate the % of respondents indicating that they spend a portion of their time engaged in the particular activity.

***Country coordinators did not include this item.

Table 48.5 Monthly Tasks of School Psychologists*

Number of Times Tasks Were Completed per Month	Country										
	Albania Mean (Med.) [Range]	Australia Mean (Med.) [Range]	China (Hong Kong) Mean (Med.) [Range]	Cyprus Mean (Med.) [Range]	Estonia Mean (Med.) [Range]	Germany Mean (Med.) [Range]	Greece Mean (Med.) [Range]	Italy Mean (Med.) [Range]	Northern England Mean (Med.) [Range]	Russia Mean (Med.) [Range]	United States Mean (Med.) [Range]
Psychoed. assessments completed (# of students)	4 (0) [0–15]	7 (5) [0–45]	6 (5) [0–23]	19 (20) [0–50]	19 (18) [0–60]	39 (5) [0–1,235]	8 (6) [0–50]	10 (4) [0–50]	13 (10) [0–60]	33 (20) [0–200]	10 (10) [1–50]
Students counseled individually	18 (10) [5–40]	29 (20) [0–130]	10 (5) [0–60]	35 (30) [0–100]	22 (15) [0–57]	13 (10) [0–45]	21 (15) [0–150]	5 (0) [0–15]	20 (20) [0–60]	14 (10) [0–120]	11 (6) [1–90]
Counseling groups	2 (1) [0–5]	2 (1) [0–25]	0.6 (0) [0–5]	1 (0) [0–10]	3 (2) [0–20]	3 (0) [0–36]	2 (0) [0–24]	2 (1) [0–6]	3 (0) [0–20]	5 (3) [0–50]	6 (4) [1–56]
Consultation cases	4 (5) [0–7.5]	18 (12) [0–120]	11 (8) [0–50]	20 (20) [0–60]	11 (10) [0–30]	4 (4) [0–10]	7 (5) [0–25]	5 (0) [0–18]	15 (12) [0–86]	7 (5) [0–30]	16 (10) [1–99]
In-service programs/ presentations	3 (2) [0–8]	1 (1) [0–4]	1 (1) [0–4]	4 (4) [0–10]	7 (1) [0–105]	2 (1) [0–120]	1 (1) [0–6]	5 (0) [0–32]	4 (1) [0–30]	3 (2.5) [0–15]	2 (1) [1–30]
Primary prevention programs	6 (5) [0–12]	1 (0.5) [0–20]	1 (0.1) [0–15]	5 (1) [0–21]	2 (1) [0–6.5]	2 (0) [0–40]	2 (1) [0–20]	0.3 (0) [0–2]	3 (0) [0–10]	3 (1.5) [0–50]	4 (2) [1–56]

*Includes results from Q. 24 (Average number of students per month counseled individually), Q. 25 (Average number of student counseling groups conducted per month), Q. 27 (Average number of students per month you have completed psychoeducational assessments with), Q. 28 (Average number of consultation cases per month in which you provided consultation to other educational professionals, e.g., consultations for interventions), Q. 29 (Average number of in-service programs/presentations you conducted for teachers, parents, and/or other personnel per month, e.g., special topic presentations, professional development presentations), and Q. 30 (Average number of primary prevention programs, e.g., working with the whole class to prevent future problems, per month).

Table 48.6 Ideal Roles/Responsibilities/Activities and Extent of Participation in the Ideal School Psychology Role*

	Country										
Ideal Roles for Rank Order	Albania	Australia	China (Hong Kong)	Cyprus	Estonia	Germany	Greece	Italy	Northern England	Russia	United States
Psychoed. evaluations	1	2	2	6	5	1	4	***	3	5	2
Counseling students	2	1	6	5	1	4	1	***	6	3	5
Providing direct interventions	3	5	**	7	4	6	6	***	7	**	4
Providing primary prevention programs	4	7	4	1	6	**	3	***	5	1	6
Consultation with teachers/staff	5	4	1	2	2	2	5	***	1	4	1
Consultation with parents/families	6	3	5	4	3	3	2	***	2	2	3
Conducting staff training and in-service/ education programs	7	6	3	3	7	5	7	***	4	6	7
Administrative responsibilities	8	8	7	8	8	7	8	***	8	7	8
% Participation in Ideal Role											
All the time	0	4	3	45	8	3	38	10	2	3	4
Great extent	60	39	22	45	46	27	54	40	19	44	27
Average amount	40	34	50	10	42	52	2	30	29	48	32
Limited extent	0	22	25	0	0	18	2	20	34	5	32
Not at all	0	1	0	0	4	0	4	0	1	0	5

*Includes Q. 42 (What would you include as the ideal roles/responsibilities/activities of school psychologists? RANK ORDER, 1 = *most ideal*, etc.), and Q. 43 (To what extent are you able to work in that ideal roles/responsibilities/activities?)

**Country coordinators did not include this item.

***Sample size (*n* = 8 for this item) too small to present results

reported spending the least amount of time in their ideal role.

External Challenges to School Psychology

Data relating to *external challenges to the delivery of school psychological services* are presented in Table 48.7. Comparison is difficult because data varied markedly across countries. However, two items demonstrated internal consistency. More than 40% of participants in Albania (46%), Australia (48%), Hong Kong (41%), Cyprus (46%), Estonia (67%), Germany (65%), and Italy (46%) identified *low status of school psychology* as an external challenge. Additionally, more than 40% of participants in all nations, except Russia and Italy, listed *lack of money to properly fund services* as an external challenge.

Internal Challenges to School Psychology

Perceived *internal challenges to the delivery of school psychological services* are reported in Table 48.8. Variation across countries makes general comparisons difficult. However, it can be noted that *lowering standards for selecting or preparing professionals* and *lack of peer support from other school psychologists* were generally endorsed at a lower rate than other internal challenges, indicating that these two areas are not perceived to be particularly problematic.

Research Importance and Interests

The International School Psychology Survey asked participants to rate the *importance of research to the profession of school psychology* in their country, as well as to list important topics in which research may be needed. Results for these survey items are presented in Table 48.9. The majority of respondents across countries reported believing that research is very relevant

to professional practice. Open-ended responses about important research topics by country reflect the diversity of the countries. Learning styles or difficulties or teaching strategies for particular populations were common responses across nations. Motivation was a commonly listed response in Hong Kong and Russia, and responses specific to teachers were common in Germany and Russia. Responses in Australia and Germany often listed particular disabilities or disorders (e.g., depression, attention-deficit/hyperactivity disorder).

Compared with previously gathered survey information from other countries, respondents in the United States highly valued research. However, consistent with the prior studies (Jimerson et al., 2004; Oakland & Cunningham, 1992), no respondents to this survey noted spending a significant portion of time on research-related activities, suggesting that school psychologists working in schools in general may want to be consumers but not producers of research. The consistency of responses across countries and the differences between the topics listed in other studies may be a result of changing priorities of practitioners and researchers or of the different sampling procedures utilized across studies.

Potential Contributions of the International School Psychology Association

Suggestions for potential International School Psychology Association contributions are listed in Table 48.10. Common responses across countries indicated that the International School Psychology Association could be helpful in distributing the results of research, in promoting collaboration among international colleagues, and in providing affordable training and workshops for practitioners. The annual International School Psychology Association Colloquium includes many presentations that highlight important research.

(Text continues on page 499)

Table 48.7 External Challenges Jeopardizing Service Delivery*

							Country						
External Challenges	Albania (%)	Australia (%)	China (Hong Kong) (%)	Cyprus (%)	Estonia (%)	Germany (%)	Greece (%)	Italy (%)	Northern England (%)	Russia (%)	United States (%)
Low status of school psychology	46	48	41	46	67	65	34	46	33	9	10
Low status of education in my country	27	18	3	18	25	43	24	18	12	2	13
Conflicts with competing professional groups	0	17	28	55	17	23	36	14	47	0	14
Other professional groups taking school psychology jobs	36	30	47	46	13	45	38	32	16	57	13
Lack of money to properly fund services	46	73	59	64	67	88	62	27	64	12	68
Lack of political stability	36	1	0	0	46	18	0	9	1	26	2
Lack of economic stability	36	1	22	9	46	33	14	9	1	21	6
Lack of public support for education	46	16	6	18	67	43	24	14	5	88	29
Low salaries for school psychologists	27	53	31	9	83	5	44	0	45	5	33

*Includes Q. 40 (Please indicate which of the following external challenges may jeopardize the delivery of psychological services within schools in your country)

495

Table 48.8   Internal Challenges Jeopardizing Service Delivery*

Internal Challenge	Country										
	Albania (%)	Australia (%)	China (Hong Kong) (%)	Cyprus (%)	Estonia (%)	Germany (%)	Greece (%)	Italy (%)	Northern England (%)	Russia (%)	United States (%)
Lack of leadership within the profession	36	34	75	27	50	40	32	23	39	10	10
Conflicts of leadership within the profession	0	1	19	64	8	15	30	9	18	2	8
Professional burnout	18	81	50	82	54	18	26	9	59	57	53
Lack of research and evaluation	36	29	84	73	42	48	46	23	46	12	10
Lowering standards for selecting or preparing professionals	18	38	31	27	25	3	26	18	21	26	12
Lack of professional standards governing professional services	36	18	47	27	50	38	42	23	10	19	5
More able professionals leaving the profession	46	34	41	0	33	3	12	14	22	55	20
Lack of peer support from other school psychologists	9	27	38	18	29	8	16	14	10	12	17
Lack of adequate supervision	36	49	53	64	63	38	40	18	18	19	22

*Includes Q. 41 (Please indicate which of the following internal challenges may jeopardize the delivery of psychological services within schools in your country)

Table 48.9 Importance of Psychological Research*

	Country										
Relevance Rating	*Albania (%)*	*Australia (%)*	*China (Hong Kong) (%)*	*Cyprus (%)*	*Estonia (%)*	*Germany (%)*	*Greece (%)*	*Italy (%)*	*Northern England (%)*	*Russia (%)*	*United States (%)*
Very relevant	0	58	50	100	76	13	88	33	67	62	71
Somewhat relevant	75	40	50	0	24	66	10	45	33	33	28
Not relevant	25	2	0	0	0	21	0	22	0	5	1
Commonly cited research topics needed											
	Institutionalization of school psychologists	Resilience	Motivation	Learning difficulties	School dropout	Reading and writing problems	Learning difficulties	Evaluations	Evaluations	Motivation	Efficacy of interventions/ evidence-based interventions
	Professional development	Mental health (e.g., depression, suicide)	Inclusion/ mainstreaming	School failure	Family factors	Teacher health (burnout prevention)	School failure	Prevention	Prevention	Social and psychological adaptations of teachers	Diagnosing/ interventions for learning disabilities
		Best practices in diagnosing and working with learning disabilities	Effective teaching/ learning strategies	Bullying-prevention programs	Intervention strategies for special needs population	Attention problems	Primary prevention programs	Teaching and learning	Teaching and learning	Influence of health, environment, and social aspects on education	Behavioral management
		Behavior management				Math difficulties	Differences in learning				Autism

*Includes Q. 37 (To what degree is psychological research important to professional practice in your country?) and Q. 38 (In your judgment, what are the major research topics needed for school psychology in your country?).

Table 48.10 Potential International School Psychology Association Contributions*

Country

Albania	Australia	China (Hong Kong)	Cyprus	Estonia	Germany	Greece	Italy	Northern England	Russia	United States
Provide training/ workshops	Provide affordable training/ workshops	Provide training/ workshops	Training workshops	Facilitate international contacts	Strengthening of the role of school psychologists worldwide	Training workshops	Provide training/ workshops	Distribute accurate research information	Provide training/ workshops/ professional growth opportunities	Provide opportunities abroad/ "exchange" programs
Provide (translate) professional literature	Provide professional literature/ resources	Share research information	Conduct and distribute research	Provide training/ workshops	Promoting international exchange of information/ resources	Clarify role of school psychologists	Help Italy define the role of a school psychologist/ legitimize the profession	Clarify role of school psychologists	Promoting international exchange of information/ resources	Distribute research-based information
Facilitate exchange of experience and expertise	Promoting collaboration among professionals	Promoting collaboration among professionals		Share research information	Public relations work	Conduct and distribute research	Help to create/ supervise a national association in Italy	Raise profile of school psychology	Development of professional standards	Gather/provide information regarding best practices worldwide
				Spread information about school psychology						

*Includes Q. 46 (Please provide information about how you believe the International School Psychology Association may contribute to the profession of school psychology around the world and in your country, and also indicate what you would most like the International School Psychology Association to address).

Conclusions

This chapter shares the results of the International School Psychology Survey data from Albania, Cyprus, Estonia, Greece, Northern England, Australia, Hong Kong, Germany, Italy, Russia, and the United States. These results reveal both similarities and differences in the characteristics, training, roles and responsibilities, challenges, and research interests of school psychologists in these countries. Through repeated administrations of the survey in participating countries (e.g., every 3 to 5 years), it would be possible to examine changes related to the preparation and practice of school psychologists. As additional countries complete the International School Psychology Survey, further information will be generated regarding the diversity and similarities of school psychologists and the evolution of school psychology around the world. Additional information such as that collected from the International School Psychology Survey should help new, as well as established, school psychological service delivery units plan future developments. Recognizing common ground and variations in the field of school psychology in countries around the world provides valuable information regarding the preparation and practices of school psychologists.

References

Catterall, C. (Ed.). (1976). *Psychology in the schools in international perspective*, Vol. 1. Columbus, OH: International School Psychology Steering Committee.

Catterall, C. (Ed.). (1977). *Psychology in the schools in international perspective*, Vol. 2. Columbus, OH: International School Psychology Steering Committee.

Catterall, C. (Ed.). (1979). *Psychology in the schools in international perspective*, Vol. 3. Columbus, OH: International School Psychology Steering Committee.

Curtis, M. J., Chesno Grier, J. E., & Hunley, S. A. (2004). The changing face of school psychology: Trends in data and projections for the future. *School Psychology Quarterly/ School Psychology Review, 18*(4), 49–66.

Curtis, M. J., Chesno Grier, J. E., Walker Abshier, D. W., Sutton, N. T., & Hunley, S. A. (2002). School psychology: Turning the corner into the twenty-first century. *Communiqué, 30*(8), 1, 5–6.

Curtis, M. J., Hunley, S. A., & Chesno Grier, J. E. (2004). The status of school psychology: Implications of a major personnel shortage. *Psychology in the Schools, 41*(4), 441–442.

Curtis, M. J., Hunley, S. A., Walker, K. J., & Baker, A. C. (1999). Demographic characteristics and professional practices in school psychology. *School Psychology Review, 28*(1), 104–116.

Ezeilo, B. N. (1992). The international school psychology survey, implications for Africa. *School Psychology International, 13,* 155–161.

Jimerson, S. R., Graydon, K., Farrell, P., Kikas, E., Hatzichristou, C., Boce, E., Bashi, G., & International School Psychology Association Research Committee. (2004). The International School Psychology Survey: Development and Data from Albania, Cyprus, Estonia, Greece and Northern England. *School Psychology International, 25*(3), 259–286.

Jimerson, S. R., Graydon, K., Yuen, M., Lam, S.-F., Thurm, J.-M., Klueva, N., Coyne, J., Loprete, L. J., Phillips, J., & International School Psychology Association Research Committee (2006). The International School Psychology Survey: data from Australia, China, Germany, Italy and Russia. *School Psychology International, 27*(1), 5–32.

Jimerson, S. R., & International School Psychology Association Research Committee. (2002). *The international school psychology survey.* (Available from the author at the University of California, Santa Barbara, Jimerson@education.ucsb.edu)

Lindsay, G. (1992). Educational psychologists and Europe. In S. Wolfendale, T. Bryans, M. Fox, A. Labram, & A. Sigston (Eds.), *The profession and practice of educational psychology.* London: Cassell.

National Association of School Psychologists. (2000). Guidelines for the provision of school psychological services. *Professional conduct manual.* Bethesda, MD: Author.

Oakland, T. D., & Cunningham, J. L. (1992). A survey of school psychology in developed and developing countries. *School Psychology International, 13,* 99–129.

Reschly, D. J. (2000). The present and future status of school psychology in the United States. *School Psychology Review, 29,* 507–522.

United Nations Educational, Scientific and Cultural Organization, International Bureau of Education. (1948). *School psychologists* (Publication No. 105). Paris: Author.

Wall, W. D. (Ed.). (1956). *Psychological services for schools.* New York: New York University Press for UNESCO Institute for Education.

49

School Psychology Internationally: A Synthesis of Findings

Peter T. Farrell

Shane R. Jimerson

Thomas D. Oakland

The contents of chapters within this handbook reflect the considerable achievement of school psychologists internationally. This concluding chapter provides a brief synthesis, highlighting some of the prominent similarities and differences among the 43 countries and drawing attention to certain challenges facing the speciality of school psychology in the coming years. The chapter begins with an overview of some educational, demographic, economic, and geographic characteristics within countries; these provide a context for the work of school psychologists. This is followed by a summary of the history and current status of school psychology and its infrastructure, the preparation of school psychologists, their roles and functions, and finally some current issues impacting school psychology.

Context of School Psychology Internationally

Given the diverse nature of the countries in which school psychological services are delivered, the contexts within which school psychologists work vary considerably. The impact of a country's educational system, demographic characteristics, economy, and geography are reviewed in this section.

Education Systems and School Psychology Services

School psychology services typically are better established and embedded within countries characterised by highly developed and legally mandated education systems that provide universal education for all children, including special education services for students with chronic, severe, and complex learning and behavioural disorders. School psychology services also are stronger in those countries with a well-established discipline of psychology, especially in its commitment to human services. These conditions are present in Australia, Canada, Israel, New Zealand, and the United States and in most Western European countries. However, there are exceptions to this general pattern. For example, although Japan has a highly developed general and special education system, school psychology services, as with other psychological services in Japan, are in the beginning stages of development.

Differences in school psychology services also are related to whether education services are managed by governments at the national, regional, or local level. Countries with highly centralised national systems of education tend to have a national curriculum managed and regulated by the national government, with decisions about the size, composition, and location of schools made nationally. In addition, within such systems, school principals often have little or no authority when appointing their staff or admitting students. In contrast, within less centrally managed systems, school principals have greater control over their budget, the hiring and termination of staff, student selection, and the development and implementation of curriculum. In some countries (e.g., Australia, Canada), education is managed at the state or provincial level, so services for children can vary between states. This, however, is not the case in the Russian Federation, where education is managed at the federal level, and hence individual states or regions have less flexibility with regard to policy making in education.

Demographic Characteristics and School Psychology Services

Not surprisingly, given the different sizes and diverse locations of the countries represented in this volume, their demographic characteristics vary enormously. Some countries are extremely small. For example, Malta is the most densely populated country in the European Union, with more than 1,265 persons per square kilometre. The Netherlands and Hong Kong also are small and densely populated. Although the landmasses of Australia and the contiguous 48 states in the United States are similar, Australia's population (20.3 million) is considerably smaller than that of the United States (295.7 million). The Russian Federation, with the largest landmass of any country in the world, has a population of 144.5 million, about half that of the United States.

In most countries, the population is largely urban. However, in other countries (e.g., India, Pakistan), the population is largely rural and lives in remote and difficult-to-access areas. School psychology services are less developed in rural areas, with many communities having no access to basic education and health services, let alone to school psychologists.

Economic Issues and School Psychology Services

The economic characteristics of the countries are also extremely varied. This is not surprising given the broadly reported differences in the economic conditions facing the so-called richer and poorer nations. This is reflected in the average per capita gross domestic product. It is US$1,900 in Zimbabwe, US$2,200 in Pakistan, and US$3,100 in India. In contrast, it is US$32,200 in Denmark, US$34,200 in Hong

Kong, and US$40,100 in the United States. Those living in rural areas typically earn far less than those living in urban areas.

Geography and School Psychology Services

A country's geographic size also can affect the management of its education services. This is particularly notable in large and sparsely populated countries such as Canada and Australia, where distances between schools can be vast, where recruitment and retention of teachers and other support staff are difficult, and where support services, including those offered by school psychologists, can be sparse.

Origins, History, and Current Status of School Psychology Internationally

The origins of school psychology can be traced to the beginning of the 20th century when, in some Western European countries and the United States, school officials and parents expressed concern that some children seemed less able to learn in general education classes. Therefore, some means of distinguishing those who could and could not succeed in these classes were needed. These distinctions were made possible, in part, through measures of intelligence that were being developed at this time and used by psychologists. Hence, in many countries, the speciality of school psychology became associated with testing students and, if needed, recommending alternative educational provision.

Countries with a high gross national product and a highly developed education system, including higher education, were better able to educate and employ school psychologists to fulfil these tasks. In other countries (e.g., Albania, Hungary, Italy), especially those that had few testing resources, the origins of school

psychology were associated less with assessment and more with services aimed at promoting the social, emotional, behavioural, and mental health of students.

Ratios Between School Psychologists and Students

Although all chapters provide some data on the ratio of school psychologists to students, an attempt to draw meaningful comparisons between these ratios is difficult. This is due, in part, to the fact that the ratios between urban and rural areas within countries vary tremendously. For example, in Moscow and the Krasnoyarsk Territory within the Russian Federation, the ratios are 1 to 700 and 1 to 500, respectively. However, these ratios are considerably larger throughout most of the Russian Federation. Similarly, in Estonia, the average ratio is 1 to 700 or 1 to 800 in those schools that employ school psychologists, almost all of which are in urban areas. However, there are no school psychologists in many rural areas.

Other authors estimate ratios of school psychologists to all students living in a country. For example, for school psychologists working in government schools, the ratios are 1 to 3,000 in England and Wales, 1 to 5,000 in Cyprus, and 1 to 13,100 in Hong Kong. However, in some countries, the figures are rough estimates, as they do not keep statistics on the number of school psychologists they employ.

Gender Ratios and Titles Among School Psychologists

The vast majority of school psychologists are women, typically around 80% and, in some countries, 100%. Although most countries use the term *school psychologist*, other terms (e.g., *educational psychologist, psychological counsellor, school counsellor,* and *guidance officer*) also are used. However, the professional titles used in various countries do not materially reflect differences in their roles and functions. The services provided by school psychologists internationally are remarkably similar despite their different titles.

Infrastructure of School Psychology Internationally

National Associations of School Psychology

The strength of school psychology within a country often is directly linked to the presence of a strong national association representing its members. The presence of strong national associations varies greatly between countries. Countries with a more highly developed discipline of psychology, a longer tradition of providing school psychology services, and larger numbers of school psychologists often have stronger professional associations than those that lack these three qualities.

Some countries have national professional associations devoted to school psychology, but most do not. Thus, school psychologists in many countries, especially developing countries, lack a strong professional advocate. The fact that school psychologists in many countries do not hold a credential or licence reflects this lack of a strong professional association. Thus, lacking opportunities to acquire these credentials, persons with various backgrounds may claim to be school psychologists.

School psychologists in countries with few colleagues generally do not have a professional association that focuses exclusively on school psychology. Thus, school psychologists often are members of the more general national professional association of psychologists. This national association may have a division designed to serve the interests of school psychology. School psychologists' affiliations with a national professional association may serve their interests until their ranks grow, and the numbers of school psychologists are sufficient to warrant the formation of a national association specific to their interests. The formation of strong links between a country's national psychological association and the school psychology association is valuable in advocating for the profession.

Certification and Licencing Issues

School psychology is stronger when provisions exist for certifying and licencing school psychologists and legally mandating their services. Almost all authors refer to the crucial importance of being credentialed or licenced in order to help the profession become established and respected and to ensure high standards for professional practice. One key consequence of a strong national professional association is its leadership in proposing and promulgating a system leading to the credentialing and licencing of school psychologists as well as statutory provisions for their services.

Variations in licencing arrangements between countries are to be expected. Licencing may be controlled at the national (e.g., Russian Federation, England and Wales) or regional (e.g., Australia, Canada, the United States) levels. Both national and state licensure laws may be influenced by policies established and promulgated by the national association. Thus, licencing requirements may be similar between states in some countries and differ considerably in others. For example, in Canada, some provinces grant credentials to schoolteachers who take a few courses in school psychology, whereas others require a degree in school psychology.

Preparation of School Psychologists Internationally

Considerable variation exists within and between countries in the entry criteria for preparing school psychologists, the length of preparation, the nature and duration of practicums and internships, and the final degree required (e.g., bachelor's, master's, specialist, or doctoral). The following offers a brief overview of key considerations related to the preparation of school psychologists internationally.

Program Entrance Criteria and Duration

All countries first require applicants to obtain a high school education as a prerequisite to enter a university undergraduate program. As is true for other professionals (e.g., dentistry, law, medicine), models used to prepare psychologists, including school psychologists, differ between and sometimes within countries. Some gain their professional qualification in a 4- to 5-year undergraduate program. The first and second years often focus on general psychology, and the third and fourth years often focus on acquiring applied and generic knowledge and skills important to the practice of psychology. A fifth year may be used for an internship.

Countries with more advanced standards for professional psychology practice typically require students to have an undergraduate degree, usually in psychology or one in which psychology is a significant component, prior to entrance into a graduate-level school psychology program. Most school psychology programs are at a master's level (typically 1 to 2 years of full-time study). In the United States, one also can obtain a specialist degree (often 2 years of full-time study plus a 1-year internship). Doctoral degrees (often 5 to 6 years of full-time study) are offered in Brazil, England and Wales, and the United States. Doctoral degrees require a 1-year internship in the United States.

Countries within the European Union are being urged to adapt all applied psychology programs to require a 3-year undergraduate degree in psychology followed by a 3-year professional training program that includes a 1-year internship. This follows the recommendations of a European Union Task force on training in applied psychology (Lunt, 2002).

Some locations require school psychologists to have a background in teaching. For example, the German state of Bavaria requires school psychologists to receive their training as part of their professional preparation to become teachers. Thus, students become qualified as teachers and as school psychologists and can fulfil both roles. Other countries (e.g., Australia, England and Wales, New Zealand, South Africa) have required school psychologists to have prior training and experience as teachers. However, this requirement is being dropped in England and Wales and may be dropped in Australia. Most countries do not require training and experience in teaching. Other countries prefer entrants to have some professional experience working with children.

Program Courses and Content

Despite these variations in professional preparation, the academic content of professional preparation in school psychology is similar. Although some differences in emphasis appear, all programs feature courses on child development, individual differences, disabilities, treatment methods, assessment, research, and statistics. Hence, despite differences in the length and patterns of preparation and the title of the degree, school psychologists internationally generally have taken similar courses and have had one or more practicums (typically supervised experiences during coursework) or internships (typically a half- to full-year supervised experience following the completion of coursework). However, school psychology programs differ in the courses they offer and in the depth of their coverage. These differences are due, in part, to their length, their degree of specialisation, and whether they are at the undergraduate, master's, specialist, or doctoral level. Undergraduate degrees tend to offer more foundation courses in the academic discipline of psychology, as these courses are considered relevant to students seeking any of the applied psychology specialisations (e.g., clinical, community, school, industrial/organisational). Undergraduate students may specialise in their clinical area of interest (e.g., school psychology) during their fourth or fifth year. Programs designed to link academic and professional preparation with applied practice are more likely to be offered at the master's and specialist levels. Longer programs typically provide greater depth and more research training.

Roles, Functions, and Responsibilities of School Psychologists Internationally

Similarities in the content of professional preparation programs become translated into similarities in services provided by school psychologists. Core services generally include direct (e.g., counselling, assessment, and assistance with academic work) and indirect (assessment) services to children, indirect (e.g., consultation) services to teachers and parents, and program enhancement services at the school or school system level (e.g., implementing intervention, including prevention, programs) to foster system change. The relative amount of time invested in their various services varies considerably between countries. The fact that few authors report school psychologists' involvement in research is troubling and warrants further consideration as to its negative impact on the development of school psychology nationally and internationally. The specialty of school psychology must assume leadership in developing a tradition of scholarship that contributes empirical knowledge regarding assessment and intervention services to promote the cognitive, emotional, and social development of students.

Current Issues Impacting School Psychology Internationally

Chapter authors were asked to comment on the current status and possible future of school psychology in their country, including their current hopes and concerns for the specialty. This section summarises these comments and their implications.

Economic Influences on School Psychology Services

The future strength of school psychology is closely associated with a country's economic wealth and its commitment to use this wealth to promote the education of all children. Money from taxes and other forms of economic support constitute resources that have a major impact on the amount of support governments can devote to public education, including school psychology services. Education must be seen as the critical primary service. Special education and school psychology services also must be seen as important secondary services.

Financial resources are directed first to general education and, if sufficient funds exist, then to special education and school psychology. For example, the governments of India, Pakistan, and Zimbabwe lack sufficient economic resources to adequately fund general education. Thus, governmental resources needed to support special education and school psychology are meagre. School psychologists working in countries that provide little to no financial support for public school services may find employment in private schools that obtain financial support from middle-class families.

Education Systems and School Psychology Services

The country's commitment to serve children with special needs through its public school system provides a barometer of the need and support for school psychological services. School psychology generally is strong in countries with well-established special education programs for children and with laws that require school psychologists to conduct psychoeducational evaluations and to engage in designing intervention services. School psychology generally is weak in countries that lack federal statutes that mandate their services and whose special education programs are inadequate.

Education policy impacts employment practices and thus school psychology. The impact of educational policy may be strongest when local education authorities determine employment practices, including those for school psychologists. This practice, together with the use of a seniority system that rewards long-term employees, typically has contributed to job security.

However, some school psychology services are being outsourced and school administrators are given more responsibility to purchase services from various specialties (e.g., school psychologists, counsellors, speech pathologists). This can lead to job insecurity and school psychologists being supervised by nonpsychologists. Thus, relationships between school psychologists and educational administrators are crucial at three levels: at the school level where daily practice occurs; at the local education level where employment and service policy decisions may occur; and at the national level where legislation and policy formation may occur. Chapter authors agree that school psychologists should be more active at all three levels in highlighting and promoting their services.

In some countries, people are uninformed about how school psychologists can contribute to important administrative decisions about psychological services at the local, regional, or national level. In some countries, professional associations that claim to represent school psychologists need to improve their effectiveness in promoting school psychology. In countries with more than one professional association, all need to speak with a common voice. In some countries, associations representing school and other specialty areas of psychology have been unable to resolve their vested interests, resulting in professional associations fighting amongst themselves and thus weakening their position in relation to their regional and national advocacy.

Employment Conditions of School Psychologists

School psychologists typically enter this speciality with the goal of serving children who have chronic behavioural, educational, and mental health needs. Various conditions prevent school psychologists from achieving this goal, including a high workload, meagre financial compensation, too few school psychologists, and limited opportunities to work directly with children, teachers, and parents. As a result, morale often is low amongst school psychologists and has an adverse impact on their job performance.

Employment conditions for school psychologists working in rural areas require considerable improvement. This requirement is somewhat universal and impacts all professions. Schools in rural areas often are less able to employ school psychologists, and the nature of their services often is more restricted than that provided in urban areas.

As noted previously, school psychology is held in higher regard when certification and licencing provisions exist. Obtaining licencing provisions is essential for the development of school psychology. However, in many countries, achieving this goal in the foreseeable future is uncertain. A number of countries are working to establish or to improve standards for preparation and continued professional development.

Roles and Responsibilities of School Psychologists

Traditional roles for school psychology (e.g., assessing students referred for behavioural, educational, or mental health problems) are broadening to include more consultative and preventive services. This change may be most apparent in countries that have a longer history of providing school psychology services. This change is likely to enable school psychologists to work more closely with teachers, parents, and others who work directly with children and may allow school psychologists to engage more with principals and others in positions of responsibility for planning and implementing systemwide interventions. School psychologists generally welcome this change and see it as a way for them to broaden their roles and discard the potentially stigmatising stereotype that all they do is test children. Some authors expressed a more cautionary tone, noting that professional preparation is inadequate for this new role and that maintaining the correct balance between traditional and emerging roles is important.

Standardised Tests and School Psychology Services

The establishment and growth of school psychology often is due to the use of standardised tests. School psychology generally is weak in countries that have few locally developed standardised tests. However, the long-term development of school psychology services is restricted when their practices emphasise only assessment services and provide few opportunities to serve their clients through consultative and intervention services.

The lack of affordable and suitable standardised tests constitutes the main concern of school psychologists in developing countries. In many countries with well-established services, school psychologists gained a foothold in education through their use of tests, especially intelligence tests. Their use of tests is seen as contributing to important school decisions and does not pose a threat to other specialists in education.

However, costs associated with test development often are prohibitive, especially in smaller countries and those in which a local language and dialects commonly are used. Costs associated with translating tests developed in other countries are less, yet still may be prohibitive. Translated tests may be culturally inappropriate and lack suitable norms and validity evidence. Furthermore, even if tests were available, suitable personnel to train school psychologists in their

use may not be widely available. Some also express concern that tests are being used by nonpsychologists who have no experience in this area. Thus, school psychologists in many countries desire more standardised tests normed on their population and for exclusive use of them.

Diversity and School Psychology Services

Attempts to meet the needs of diverse groups of students pose important challenges, especially for school psychologists who are unfamiliar with different cultures and languages (e.g., students from racial or ethnic backgrounds that differ from theirs as well as students who are recent immigrants and may not speak the country's native language). The increased mobility of people and resultant increase in the multicultural composition of the citizens in many countries warrant the preparation of school psychologists with awareness of and ability to work with children from diverse racial, cultural, and linguistic backgrounds. Some school psychology students are specialising in multicultural and bilingual school psychology.

Research and School Psychology Services

Many authors are concerned that few school psychologists are engaged in research and in publishing their work. This is due, in part, to their job descriptions that do not include time for research as well as a lack of preparation and desire to engage in research. The need for more research and other forms of scholarship designed to contribute to knowledge and skills needed by school psychologists is obvious. In many countries, universities have led the way in promoting and disseminating research to practitioners, professors, policymakers, and others. Persons contributing to this research typically hold doctoral degrees. Despite these needs, few countries are preparing doctoral-level school psychologists. Thus, school psychology has limited internal resources to engage in research and thus, unfortunately, is dependent on others for the further promotion of knowledge and skills.

Conclusions

The chapters in this volume present a comprehensive picture of school psychology internationally at the beginning of the 21st century. School psychologists are employed to enhance the mental health and educational well-being of children and youth and their schools, families, and communities. Their work is underpinned by core elements of academic psychology that are relevant to understanding learning and development, child psychopathology, and methods that can encourage change. Despite some of the concerns about the development of the profession that are reflected in many of the chapters, all the authors comment on the importance of school psychology services in the promotion of the mental health and education of all children. Furthermore, almost all countries report an increase in the numbers of people becoming school psychologists. This increase presumably reflects some confidence by school districts and other employers that school psychologists can offer valuable services. Studies of consumer views toward school psychologists (Farrell, Jimerson, Kalambouka, & Benoit, 2005; Gavrilidou, de Mesquita, & Mason, 1994; Gilman & Gabriel, 2004; Kikas, 1999; McKeever, 1996) report the value and esteem in which the specialty is held. Hence, school psychologists are making an important contribution to the lives of children and young people and the parents, teachers, and other professionals who work with them.

However, much still needs to be done. In many countries, school psychology is in its infancy and lacks an employment structure, including role definition or professional preparation programs. In countries with more established traditions of providing school psychology services, some ambiguity may exist as to the roles of school psychologists and limited opportunities for them to engage in research and evaluation. Further scholarship that advances the knowledge and skills of school psychologists and evaluative studies that address the impact of school psychologists are important for the future vitality of school psychology internationally.

References

Farrell, P., Jimerson, S., Kalambouka, A., & Benoit, J. (2005). Teachers' perceptions of school psychologists in different countries. *School Psychology International, 26*(5), 525–544.

Gavrilidou, M., de Mesquita, P. B., & Mason, E. J. (1994). Greek teachers' perceptions of school psychologists in solving classroom problems. *Journal of School Psychology, 32*, 293–304.

Gilman, R., & Gabriel, S. (2004). Perceptions of school psychological services by education professionals: Results from a multi-state survey pilot study. *School Psychology Review, 33*, 271–287.

Kikas, E. (1999). School psychology in Estonia: Expectations of teachers and school psychologists. *School Psychology International, 20*, 352–365.

Lunt, I. (2002). A common framework for the training of psychologists in Europe. *European Psychologist, 7*(3), 180–191.

McKeever, P. (1996). Consumer opinion of educational psychology services: A pilot survey. *Educational Psychology in Practice, 12*, 45–50.

Author Index

Subject Index

About the Editors

Shane R. Jimerson, Ph.D., is an Associate Professor in the Counseling, Clinical, and School Psychology Program and Associate Professor of Child and Adolescent Development at the University of California, Santa Barbara (UCSB). Among over 100 professional publications, he is coauthor of a five-book grief support group curriculum series *(The Mourning Child Grief Support Group Curriculum)*, coeditor of *Best Practices in School Crisis Prevention and Intervention,* coauthor of *Identifying, Assessing, and Treating Autism at School,* and the lead editor of *The Handbook of School Violence and School Safety.* He serves as the editor of *The California School Psychologist* journal, associate editor of the *School Psychology Review,* and is on the editorial boards of the *Journal of School Psychology* and *School Psychology Quarterly.* Dr. Jimerson has chaired and served on numerous boards and advisory committees at the state, national, and international levels. Dr. Jimerson received the Best Research Article of the Year Award from the Society for the Study of School Psychology in both 1998 and 2000. He also received the 2001 Outstanding Article of the Year Award from the National Association of School Psychologists' *School Psychology Review.* Dr. Jimerson's scholarly efforts were also recognized by the American Educational Research Association with the 2002 Early Career Award in Human Development. He and his UCSB research team received the 2003 and 2004 Outstanding Research Award from the California Association of School Psychologists. Also during 2003, Dr. Jimerson received the Lightner Witmer Early Career Contributions Award from Division 16 (School Psychology) of the American Psychological Association. His scholarship continues to highlight the importance of early experiences on subsequent development and emphasize the importance of research informing professional practice to promote the social and cognitive competence of children. Dr. Jimerson's e-mail address is jimerson@education.ucsb.edu.

Thomas D. Oakland, Ph.D., is University of Florida Research Foundation Professor. He is President of the International Foundation for Children's Education and past President of both the International School Psychology Association and the International Test Commission. He has worked in more than 40 countries. Dr. Oakland has authored more than 180 chapters and articles and five psychological tests. His authored, coauthored, and edited books include *Auditory Perception: Diagnosis and Development for Language and Reading Abilities, Assessing Minority Group Children, Nonbiased Assessment of Minority Group Children, Psychological and Educational Assessment of Minority Children, Divorced Fathers, International Perspectives on Psychology in the Schools, Identification of Gifted and Talented Students in Texas, International Perspectives on Assessment of Academic Achievement, Student Styles Questionnaire: Classroom Applications Booklet,* and *Standards* *for Educational and Psychological Testing.* Dr. Oakland is a licensed psychologist and board certified in school psychology, in neuropsychology, and as a forensic examiner. He has an active clinical practice and testifies frequently. His interests center on psychological and educational characteristics of children and youth, test development and use, international issues, legal and professional issues, and professionalism. He is the recipient of Distinguished Service Awards from the American Psychological Association's Division 16 (School Psychology) and the International School Psychology Association and received the 2002 National Association of School Psychology's Legend Award. Dr. Oakland also received the American Psychological Association's 2003 Award for Distinguished Contributions to the Advancement of Psychology Internationally. Dr. Oakland's e-mail address is oakland@coe.uf.edu.

Peter T. Farrell, Ph.D., is the Sarah Fielden Professor of Special Needs and Educational Psychology in the School of Education, University of Manchester, England, and past President of the International School Psychology Association. He is also a Fellow of the British Psychological Society. He has extensive experience as a trainer of school psychologists in the United Kingdom and has worked with psychologists in seven countries giving advice on the development of psychological services. In addition, he has been the invited keynote speaker at 17 international conferences on issues related to international school psychology. Dr. Farrell is the author (or coauthor) of seven books and has edited three others, including *Teaching Pupils With Learning Difficulties: Strategies and Solutions; Teaching Assistants: Practical Strategies for Effective Classroom Support;* and *Making Special Education Inclusive: From Research to Practice.* He has published more than 40 articles in academic peer-reviewed journals and has written 15 book chapters. In addition, he has directed or codirected 22 externally funded research projects. Throughout his career, Dr. Farrell has worked closely with the British Psychological Society on issues related to the development of psychological services in the United Kingdom and, thorough his links with the International School Psychology Association and the European Federation of Professional Psychologists' Association, he has been influential in helping to shape the development of psychological services in several countries. His e-mail address is peter .farrell@man.ac.uk.

About the Contributors

Mohammad Adnan Alghorani, Ph.D., is Assistant Professor of Educational Psychology, Thinking Skills, Psychology of the Gifted and Talented, Development of Elementary School Children, and Applied Research at UAE University, Al Ain, United Arab Emirates.

Svetlana V. Alyokhina, Ph.D., is a senior researcher in the Psychological Monitoring Section of the Research Department at the Moscow City University of Psychology and Education, Russian Federation.

Jean Annan, Ph.D., is a senior lecturer in Educational Psychology and coordinator of the Post-Graduate Diploma in Educational Psychology/Internship program at Massey University, New Zealand.

Roald Anthun, Ph.D., is a specialist in Clinical Psychology at the Clinic of Habilitation and Rehabilitation, Haukeland University Hospital, Norway.

Helen E. Bakker, Ph.D., child and youth psychologist specialist NIP and healthcare psychologist, is the program coordinator of the master's program in Child and Adolescent Psychology and an Assistant Professor in Developmental Psychology at Utrecht University, The Netherlands.

Wilma Barrow, M.Sc., is a tutor in the Educational Psychology professional training program in the Faculty of Education and Social Work at the University of Dundee, Scotland.

Paul A. Bartolo, Ph.D., is a senior lecturer in Educational Psychology and Coordinator of the M.Psy course for professional training in educational psychology at the University of Malta, and former President of the Malta Union of Professional Psychologists.

Luis Benites Morales, M.A. (Psychology), is Head of the Postgraduate Department and Professor at San Martín de Porres University, Peru.

Heinz Bosch, Lic.Phil., is Head of School Psychology Services in Wallisellen, Switzerland.

Frances Boulon-Díaz, Ph.D., is Adjunct Professor of School Psychology at the University of Puerto Rico, Río Piedras Campus, and at Interamerican University of Puerto Rico, Metro Campus, and is also president of the Puerto Rico Board of Psychologist Examiners.

Orlean Brown-Earle, Ph.D., is an Assistant Professor of Psychology at Northern Caribbean University, Jamaica, and a private practitioner throughout the island of Jamaica, West Indies.

Silvana Campagnaro, M.A., is a Professor of School Psychology at the Andrés Bello Catholic University, Caracas, Venezuela.

Herculano Ricardo Campos, Ph.D. (Education), is Professor of School Psychology at the Federal University of Rio Grande do Norte, Brazil.

Regis Chireshe, M.Sc., is a senior lecturer in Educational Psychology at the Masvingo State University, Masvingo, Zimbabwe.

Hyunhee Chung, Psy.D., is an Assistant Professor of Education at Keimyung University, Daegu, South Korea.

Lynette Collair, M.Ed.Psych., is a lecturer in Educational Psychology at the University of Stellenbosch, South Africa.

Julia Coyne, M.Ed., is a doctoral student in School Psychology at Loyola University-Chicago, United States.

Peadar P. Crowley, M.A., Reg. Psych. AFPSI, is a Regional Director of the National Educational Psychological Service, Department of Education and Science, Ireland.

Jacqueline L. Cunningham, Ph.D., is a child psychologist in the Department of Psychology at The Children's Hospital of Philadelphia, Pennsylvania, United States.

Michael Curtis, Ph.D., is Professor at the University of South Florida, United States.

Berenice Daniels, M.Sc. (Ed. Psych.), is the Chief Education Specialist for Specialized Learner and Educator Support in Metropole South Education District, South Africa.

Maritza Díaz Casapía, B.A.(Psychology), Lic.Psych., is Head of the Service of Psychology of the Municipal Defensory (Chorrillos, Lima) and Head of the Civil Association Sembrar, Peru.

Margareta Dinca, Ph.D., is a Professor of Developmental Psychology, Counselling Psychology, and Research Methods in Psychology in the Department of Psychology at the Titu Maiorescu University, Bucharest, Romania.

Nevin Dölek, Ph.D., is a psychologist at BAKIS Training and Psychological Counseling Center and is a part-time instructor in the Department of Educational Sciences at Bogaziçi University, Istanbul, Turkey.

Frida van Doorn, Ph.D., child and youth psychologist specialist NIP and healthcare psychologist, is a research associate with the Behavioral Problems in School Practice Research Group at Utrecht Professional University, The Netherlands.

Lothar Dunkel, D.Psych., M.S. Ed.Psych., is Director of School Psychology for the City of Münster, Germany.

Vijaya Dutt, M.Phil. (Special Education)., M.A. (Psychology), was Principal of the Centre for Special Education, Indian Institute of Cerebral Palsy, Kolkata, and is presently working as a psychologist at Applied Research International, Delhi, India.

Terence Edwards, M.Ed.Psych., PGD.Ed.Psych., is a lecturer in Educational Psychology and coordinator of the Master of Educational Psychology program at Massey University, New Zealand.

Michael Faulkner, Ph.D., a school psychologist of 20 years' experience, is now an academic faculty member in the School of Education at La Trobe University, Victoria, Australia.

Aurora Frunza, M.A., is a clinical psychologist and research assistant in the Department of Medical Psychology, Carol Davilla University of Medicine and Pharmacy, Bucharest, Romania.

Eva Gajdosová, Ph.D., is Senior Lecturer of School Psychology in the Department of Psychology, Comenius University, Bratislava, Slovakia.

Georgios Georgouleas, M.Sc., is a school psychologist at the School Psychological Service of Filekpaideftiki Etaireia and a Ph.D. candidate in the Department of Psychology, University of Athens, Greece.

Gražina Gintilienė, Ph.D., is an Associate Professor in the Department of General Psychology at Vilnius University, Lithuania.

Julio Antonio González-Pienda, Ph.D., is a Professor of Learning Disabilities and Educational and Instructional Psychology at the University of Oviedo, Spain.

Kelly Graydon, M.A., is a doctoral student in Counseling, Clinical, and School Psychology at the University of California, Santa Barbara, United States.

Jean-Claude Guillemard, Ph.D., is a school psychologist in Dourdan, France, and former president of the International School Psychology Association.

Raquel S. L. Guzzo, Ph.D., is a psychologist and Professor of School Psychology and Social and Emotional Development at the Pontifical Catholic University of Campinas, Brazil.

Elizabeth Hannah, M.Sc., is a tutor in the educational (school) psychology professional training program in the Faculty of Education and Social Work at the University of Dundee, Scotland.

Gina L. Harrison, Ph.D., is an Assistant Professor in the Department of Educational Psychology and Leadership Studies at the University of Victoria, British Columbia, Canada.

Chryse Hatzichristou, Ph.D., is a Professor of School Psychology and Director of the Center for Research and Practice of School Psychology, Department of Psychology, University of Athens, Greece.

Gabriela Herényiová, Ph.D., is a lecturer in School Psychology in the Department of Psychology, Comenius University, Bratislava, Slovakia.

Irina Holdevici, Ph.D., is a Professor of Clinical Psychology and Psychotherapy in the Department of Psychology at the Titu Maiorescu University, , Bucharest, Romania.

Toshinori Ishikuma, Ph.D., is a Professor of Psychology at the University of Tsukuba, Japan.

Joseph M. Kasayira, M.Sc., is a lecturer in Educational Psychology at Midlands State University, Gweru, Zimbabwe.

Nora Katona, Ph.D., is an Assistant Professor at the Psychology Institute at Eötvös Loránd University, Budapest, Hungary, and President of the International School Psychology Association.

Claire Kerr, M.Sc., is a tutor in the educational (school) psychology professional training program in the Faculty of Education and Social Work at the University of Dundee, Scotland.

Eve Kikas, Ph.D., is a Professor of Pre-Primary and Primary School Education at the University of Tartu, Estonia.

Daria A. Kutuzova, Ph.D., is a senior researcher in the Psychological Monitoring Section of the Research Department of the Moscow City University of Psychology and Education, Russian Federation.

Pirjo Laaksonen, Ps.L., is a psychologist in the Social and Health Department, in the Helsinki Regional Unit of the State Provincial Office of Southern Finland.

Kristiina Laitinen, Ps.M., is a senior advisor in Student Welfare in the Finnish National Board of Education, in Helsinki, Finland.

Shui-fong Lam, Ph.D., is an Associate Professor in the Department of Psychology at the University of Hong Kong.

Sandy Lazarus, Ph.D., is a Professor in the Faculty of Education at the University of the Western Cape, South Africa.

Carmen León, Ph.D., is a Professor of School Psychology and Developmental Psychology at Andrés Bello Catholic University, Caracas, Venezuela.

Sergei B. Malykh, Ph.D., D.Sc, is a Deputy Head of the Psychological Institute of the Russian Academy of Education, Vice Rector of the Moscow City University of Psychology and Education, and Vice President of the Russian Federation of Psychologists in Education, Russian Federation.

Terje Manger, Ph.D., is a Professor of Educational Psychology in the Department of Psychosocial Science at the University of Bergen, Norway.

Victor Martinelli, Ph.D., is a senior lecturer in Educational Psychology at the University of Malta, Secretary of the Malta Union of Professional Psychologists, and a member of the Malta Psychology Profession Board.

Milena Matos, M.Sc., is a Professor of School Psychology and Child Clinical Psychopathology at Andrés Bello Catholic University, Caracas, Venezuela.

César Merino Soto, B.A. in Psychology, Lic. Psych., is Professor at the Private University San Juan Bautista, Peruvian University Cayetano Heredia, and San Martin de Porres University; researcher at the Psychological Service of the Municipal Defensory (Chorrillos, Lima); and member of the Civil Association Sembrar, Peru.

Albertina Mitjáns Martínez, Ph.D, is a psychologist and Professor of Education at University of Brasília, Brazil.

Andrew A. Mogaji, Ph.D., is a Professor of Personnel and Organizational Psychology at the University of Lagos, Nigeria, and African Representative to the International Association for Cross Cultural Psychology.

Nadeen Moolla, M.Ed. (Ed.Psych.), is a lecturer in the Faculty of Education at the University of the Western Cape, South Africa.

Elias Mpofu, Ph.D., is a Professor of Rehabilitation Services at the The Pennsylvania State University, University Park, United States.

Juanita Mureika, M.A., is a school psychologist with the New Brunswick Department of Family and Community Services, Support Services to Education program in Fredericton, New Brunswick, Canada.

Gladiola Musabelliu, B.S., is a school psychologist and also teaches courses in introductory psychology in the Department of Psychology at the University of Tirana, Albania.

Magen M. Mutepfa, M.Ed., is an educational psychologist at the School Psychological Services and Special Education, Harare, Zimbabwe.

Taketo Nakao, M.S., is a graduate student of school psychology at the University of Florida, United States.

José Carlos Núñez, Ph.D., is a Professor of Learning Disabilities and Educational Psychology at the University of Oviedo, Spain.

Ernestina A. Papacosta, M.S.Ed., is an educational psychologist in the Educational Psychology Services, Ministry of Education and Culture, Nicosia, Cyprus.

Fotini Polychroni, Ph.D., is a psychologist at the Counseling Center of the Municipality of Athens and holds a teaching position in the Department of Psychology, University of Athens, Greece.

Anders Poulsen, Cand.Psych., dr.h.c., is a retired school psychologist, past Chair of the Danish Association of School Psychologists, and also a former President of the International School Psychology Association.

Shahid Waheed Qamar, M.Sc. (Psychology), M.Sc. (Applied Environmental Sciences), is a school psychologist and student counselor at the Counseling and Assessment Center, Lahore, and aspecial education instructor at the Centre of Mentally and Physically Affected Special Students (COMPASS), Lahore, Pakistan.

Irma Roca de Torres, Ph.D., is a retired professor of School, Developmental and General Psychology at the University of Puerto Rico, Río Piedras Campus; President of Puerto Rico's Mental Health Planning and Advisory Council; and member of the American Psychological Association's Council of Representatives.

Ken Ryba, Ph.D., is an Associate Professor in Educational Psychology and coordinator of the Educational Psychology Ph.D. programme at Massey University, New Zealand.

Donald H. Saklofske, Ph.D., is a Professor in the Division of Applied Psychology at the University of Calgary, Alberta, Canada.

Minna Salmi, Ps.M., is a leading school psychologist in the City of Vantaa in the metropolitan region of Finland.

Z. Hande Sart, Ph.D., is a full-time instructor in the Department of Educational Sciences at Bogazici University, Istanbul, Turkey.

Lukas Scherer, Ph.D., is a school psychologist and psychotherapist in private practice, Zurich, Switzerland.

Vicki L. Schwean, Ph.D., is a Professor and Associate Dean in the Division of Applied Psychology at the University of Calgary, Alberta, Canada.

Hyeonsook Shin, Ph.D., is an Assistant Professor of Education at the Chonnam National University, Gwangju, South Korea.

Yoshinori Shinohara, M.Ed., is a Professor of Special Support Education at the University of Tsukuba, Japan.

Elaine Smith, M.Sc., is director of the educational (school) psychology professional training program in the Faculty of Education & Social Work at the University of Dundee, Scotland.

Garry Squires, D Ed.Psy., is a tutor for Continuing Professional Doctorate in Educational Psychology, School of Education, University of Manchester and Senior Practitioner Educational Psychologist, Staffordshire, England.

Rene Staskal is a doctoral student in Counseling, Clinical Psychology, and School Psychology at the University of California, Santa Barbara, United States.

Bernie Stein, Ph.D., is a senior school and clinical psychologist and was Chief Psychologist in the Israeli Ministry of Education, 1994–2001, and President of the International School Psychology Association, 1999–2001.

Keith Topping, Ph.D., is Professor of Educational and Social Research and Dean of Research in the Faculty of Education and Social Work at the University of Dundee, Scotland.

Carlo Trombetta, Ph.D., is a Professor at the Università di Roma "La Sapienza" and past President of Società Italiana di Psicologia dell'Educazione e della Formazione (SIPEF), Italy.

Luminita Monica Vlad, M.A., is a school psychologist/counsellor at the Cezar Nicolau High School of Agricultural Studies, Branesti village, County Ilfov, Romania.

Luis Zapata Ponce, M.A. (Psychology), is Professor at San Ignacio de Loyola University and San Martín de Porres University and is Past Dean of Association of Psychologists of Peru.

Paul Zeberli, Lic.Phil., is Head of School Psychology Services in Regensdorf, Switzerland.

Hongwu Zhou is a Professor of Psychology at Zhejiang Research Institute of Education Science and Vice Secretary of the Chinese School Psychology Association.